Liberalism, Fascism, or Social Democracy

Liberalism, Fascism, or Social Democracy

Social Classes and the Political Origins of Regimes in Interwar Europe

GREGORY M. LUEBBERT

Preface by David Collier and Seymour Martin Lipset

New York   Oxford
OXFORD UNIVERSITY PRESS
1991

Oxford University Press

Oxford New York Toronto
Delhi Bombay Calcutta Madras Karachi
Petaling Jaya Singapore Hong Kong Tokyo
Nairobi Dar es Salaam Cape Town
Melbourne Auckland
and associated companies in
Berlin Ibadan

Library of Congress Cataloging-in-Publication Data
Luebbert, Gregory M.
Liberalism, fascism, or social democracy :
social classes and the political origins of regimes in interwar Europe
Gregory M. Luebbert.
p. cm. Includes bibliographical references and index.
ISBN 0-19-506610-3
ISBN 0-19-506611-1 (pbk.)
1. Europe—Politics and government—1871–1918.
2. Europe—Politics and government—20th century.
3. Labor movement—Europe—History.
4. Social structure—Europe—History.
5. Liberalism—Europe—History.
6. Socialism—Europe–History.
7. Democracy—History.
8. Fascism—Europe—History.
I. Title. JN94.A2L84 1991
306.2'094—dc20 90-38754

9 8 7 6 5 4 3 2 1

Printed in the United States of America
on acid-free paper

Preface

In the interwar period, a wide spectrum of national political regimes emerged in Europe, posing an abiding explanatory challenge to the social sciences. Gregory Luebbert offers a new account of the advent of these regimes. His study, which employs a remarkable combination of broad comparison and nuanced treatment of individual cases, will stand alongside the most sophisticated works of comparative-historical analysis.

Drawing on sources in a dozen languages, Luebbert analyzes the evolution of regimes throughout Western Europe. He explores liberal democracy in Britain, France, and Switzerland—with Belgium and the Netherlands corresponding to a subtype of this category; social democracy in Denmark, Norway, and Sweden, as well as in Czechoslovakia; and fascism in Germany, Italy, and Spain. The dynamics of fascism are placed in sharp relief through comparison with traditional dictatorships prevalent between the wars in Eastern Europe.

Luebbert's immediate focus, and his principal explanation for the appearance of different regimes, is the evolution of national political coalitions in the late nineteenth century and in the first decades of the twentieth. A central concern is how these coalitions were reshaped by a fundamental historical transition: the emergence of the organized working class as a major contender in national politics. The impact of the working class is not understood in isolation, however. Its influence was mediated by liberal parties, with their varied success in achieving dominance, and by rural politics, above all the political position of the middle peasantry.

Luebbert thus shows how the transformation of the workers' political role during a historically delimited period reset the parameters of politics. In this sense, his work is part of the larger tradition of research on cleavages, coalitions, and critical junctures in European development. Within that tradition, one of

Luebbert's many innovations is to place greater emphasis on explanatory factors located in the twentieth century.

A major strength of this study is the juxtaposition of a large number of cases and close historical analysis, yielding great analytic leverage in assessing rival explanations of regimes. For example, Luebbert offers a new perspective on the impact of rural elites, explored previously by Alexander Gerschenkron and Barrington Moore, Jr.; and on the consequences of leadership failure, a central concern of Juan J. Linz. Luebbert argues that although single-country studies and comparisons using fewer cases may support such explanations, his full set of cases does not.

The analysis thus provides an important reminder: findings are shaped by the frame of comparison. Like lenses that screen out different colors, alternative comparisons provide distinct optics on the cases. Each comparison reveals some elements of the underlying structure, and the use of multiple comparisons contributes to building a better understanding of that structure. Luebbert's book challenges us to continue this process of building.

Gregory Luebbert wrote this book while on the faculty of the Department of Political Science at the University of California, Berkeley, between 1982 and 1988. At the time of his tragic death in a white-water boating accident in 1988, at the age of 32, he had nearly completed the project. Fortunately for all of us, his close friend and colleague Giuseppe Di Palma had followed the work on the book so intently that he was able to pull the manuscript together, based on his knowledge of Luebbert's analytic goals. The arduous task of checking the citations was skillfully carried out by Soo Jin Kim. Luebbert's wife, Kathryn Hopps, devoted countless hours to rechecking references and to going over the edited version with great care. In this last task she received able assistance from Dennis Galvan.

We cannot identify all the colleagues whose help Greg Luebbert would have acknowledged, but we know he was grateful for the comments of Vinod Aggarwal, Gabriel Almond, Paul Buchanan, Giuseppe Di Palma, Joseph Fizman, Sharon Greene, Ernst Haas, Andrew Janos, Joseph LaPalombara, Daniel Verdier, and John Zysman. Soo Jin Kim and Daniel Verdier provided Luebbert with outstanding research assistance. Support from the National Fellows Program of the Hoover Institution facilitated the final year of writing. The Institute of International Studies at Berkeley gave substantial assistance throughout the project, including special support for the last phase of manuscript preparation.

In conjunction with the many efforts by friends and family to refine the manuscript, it is tempting to ask what final changes Greg Luebbert would have made, given the opportunity. We are aware of two. First, the treatment of rival explanations, which is now highly suggestive yet preliminary, was to have been expanded to capture more fully the interplay among alternative perspectives. Second, a fuller explication of subtypes within the classification of regimes was to have been an important addition.

Luebbert wished to stimulate new comparative discussion of these regime transformations, not to preempt it. As Luebbert's readers carry this debate forward, they should do so with the same energy that Luebbert brought to his own scholarship. At the same time, they will certainly want to remember that Lueb-

bert's work on the manuscript was not quite finished, and that we are fortunate indeed to have as nearly complete a book as we do.

It is a tragedy that Gregory Luebbert did not live to participate in the academic debate this study will surely produce. Given the speed with which he completed two ambitious books, one also laments the loss of an enormous future contribution to comparative social science.* The greatest tragedy, of course, is the loss of a close friend and colleague. Yet we can be grateful for what remains: a model of extraordinary scholarship and of human commitment to learning, to comparing, and to tackling the most ambitious questions with imagination and rigor.

David Collier and Seymour Martin Lipset

*His first book was *Comparative Democracy: Policymaking and Governing Coalitions in Europe and Israel* (New York: Columbia University Press, 1986). This book developed a model of how governing coalitions form in democratic countries and tested the model in a complex comparison of 67 cases of government formation drawn from seven countries.

Contents

II THE OUTCOMES

Contents

Liberalism, Fascism, or Social Democracy

1

Introduction

Three political–economic regimes emanated from the transition to rule by popular mandate in Western Europe—liberal democracy, social democracy, and fascism. This book is about their origins. The three regimes came into existence and stood as clear alternatives during the years between the two world wars. They were, above all, responses in politics and in the labor market to the demands of the working classes. Before 1914, workers' quest for political and economic rights remained circumscribed and the working-class challenge remained manageable. In much of Western Europe, it became unmanageable with the collapse of traditional barriers to working-class power in 1919. The years that followed were characterized by a search for political–economic formulas that would stabilize the balance of political power, provide effective means by which to govern the economy, and at the same time dissipate, accommodate, or crush the claims of organized workers. It was from those searches that liberal democracy, social democracy, and fascism emerged.

After 1945, the legitimacy of workers' rights was no longer questioned and fascism was no longer an option. The social effects of fascism itself, the defeat and occupation of the Axis powers, the appearance of a Keynesian welfare state consensus, and a new international economic and military order all served to reduce the range of regime possibilities. That range was collapsed to a continuum embracing social democracy and liberal democracy. New requirements of production in a more open international economy, inexorable demographic and democratic demands on the welfare state, and the Keynesian consensus of the 1950s and 1960s all blurred societies' locations on the continuum and generated at least a partial convergence of political and economic institutions and policies.

In the years between the wars, liberal democracy, social democracy, and fascism were alternatives in ways so fundamental as to be defining characteristics of the three regimes. Interwar liberal democracy rested on a coalition of the center-right. This was a coalition of middle-class consolidation, or so I argue. It was a coalition that broke with an historic tradition of liberal–labor cooperation in these societies and was aimed against the socialist working classes. Liberal democracy was also stabilized by the political isolation of the working classes and by the ineffectiveness of trade union organizations in liberal societies. That ineffectiveness derived from the organizational incoherence or pluralism of the unions, and when combined with the isolation of labor parties, crippled working-class movements, militated against a challenge to the established order, sustained a continued reliance on market rather than politically driven wage settlements, and discouraged a break when the depression came, with orthodox or neo-orthodox economic policies. A correlate was that, by comparison, little threat existed to competitive democratic politics in these societies. Britain, Switzerland, and France were liberal democracies between the world wars. Belgium and the Netherlands, led by hegemonic confessional movements, became variants of liberal democracies.

Social democratic political economies, by contrast, rested during the interwar years on alliances of the urban working classes and the family or middle peasantry. They preserved the democratic competitiveness of liberalism, but broke fundamentally with its economics. In these societies, the working classes, and in particular, the socialist trade union movements, were much more comprehensively and coherently organized. They had, as we shall see, the capacity to make these societies ungovernable by the traditional, market-oriented policies of liberalism. Social democracy broke with liberal democracy in assigning political power to working-class parties; in substituting political bargains for market-determined wage (and other price) settlements; in securing labor market peace and discipline through a social compact rather than trade union weakness; in jettisoning conventional deflationary liberal policies, in the face of the depression, in favor of stimulatory economic and social policies. In contrast to the residual political role granted to atomized trade unions in liberal societies, the peak associations of trade unions in social democracies were to acquire a kind of semisovereign status in the making of a range of state policies. This was a democratic version of corporatism. Norway, Sweden, Denmark, and Czechoslovakia became social democracies between the wars.

Corporatism of a different variety was to play a conspicuous role in fascist political economies. This corporatism also organized workers in centrally directed, comprehensive worker organizations. Unlike social democracy, fascist political economies did so not to integrate workers into the larger society, although to some degree that was the effect, but to subordinate and harness them to the ambitions of the party and state. Like social democracy, it broke with market–driven wage settlements and substituted politics for markets. Like social democracy, fascist political economies were inclined to break with economic orthodoxy to experiment with stimulatory policies. Fascism repudiated both the politics and the economics of liberalism; it substituted totalarianism, or some approximation of it, for democratic competition. Fascism, too, rested on a social coalition of the town and country, but it was one that combined the family peasantry with the urban middle classes rather than the urban working classes. The institutions and policies of fascism, like the institutions and policies of social democracy, followed from the logic of the subtending coalition, albeit, once in power, fascist movements were by their authoritarian nature less constrained by their supporting interests. Germany, Italy, and Spain became fascist dictatorships during the years between the wars.

A fourth outcome—one that was not an alternative for the advanced societies of Western Europe—was found in every Eastern European country except Czechoslovakia. That outcome was traditional dictatorship, and although the etiology of such regimes is not a cardinal focus of this book, I have used the preconditions and institutions of these dictatorships to make more distinctive the characteristics of fascist dictatorships. Without specifying the etiological and institutional differences between fascism and traditional dictatorship, we cannot understand why the interwar societies of the West could not have been governed as traditional dictatorships—why those societies, if governed as dictatorships, had to be governed as fascist dictatorships. Fascism was distinguished from traditional dictatorship in fundamental ways: in its complete suppression of representative institutions and autonomous working-class parties and trade unions; in its closer approximation of totalitarianism and greater intolerance of dissent and opposition; in its total control of the press; in its monopolistic ideology and comprehensive vision of the social order; in its commitment to popular mobilization in the service of the state and its rejection of the negative legitimacy of mass apathy; and in its total extirpation of socialism and reorganization and subordination of the working classes. This more totalitarian model reflected the higher level of mobilization that fascist, in contrast to traditional, dictators confronted. Fascism was quintessentially the dictatorship of modern, class-oriented societies.

The four regime outcomes are more fully specified in Chapters 6, 7, and 8. So, too, are the rationales for the locations of societies among them. For the present, let me make two points about these regimes emphatic. First, the regimes are ideal types. It is seldom difficult to locate interwar European societies among them, but the extent to which the societies corresponded to the idealized model of the regime varied. In this book, I am interested in explaining not only why societies developed into one of the four regimes, but why societies of the same basic regime varied in the degree to which they approximated the ideal.

The second point I want to emphasize is that the ideal types are not merely nominal or taxonomical categories. The regime types are derivative of and inseparable from a larger causal theory. They gain their meaning from that theory. Strictly speaking, a concept like social democracy or fascism can denote, not to say connote, anything we want it to. The practical constraint is, first, one of communication. I have tried to define the four regimes in a way that is not idiosyncratic; that makes them useful in scholarly discourse. The second constraint is theoretical, or metatheoretical. The value of concepts is in the way they aggregate and disaggregate similar and dissimilar objects, thereby generating new insights. In the end, whatever merit is attached to this book and its classificatory scheme is a function not of nominalistic debates, but of the extent to which the theory and the categories generate new insights and new research puzzles.

This implies that I am not much interested in debates about the "true" definition of fascism or anything else. The attributes of the four regimes denote what I take to be the theoretically decisive aspects of these regimes. In fact, the regimes can easily be seen to *connote* much more. One of the purposes of theoretical study is to separate attributes that are etiological necessities of the regime type from simple correlates of the type. There were correlates of liberalism, of social democracy, and of fascism and traditional dictatorship whose investigation remains intellectually intriguing and morally compelling. The essence of a social democratic political economy, it seems to me, is the subordination of market decisions to political bargains, especially in the determination of wages. A social democratic political economy, however, implies, among other things, a panoply of social welfare programs, active labor market policies, and, in collaboration with the state, peak associations directing activity in many spheres of the economy. I merely touch on some of these correlates, many of which emerged after 1945. It is an empirical question of some import whether these correlates were necessary consequences of social democratic hegemony, of changes in the international economy, or of changes in the international economy in conjunction with a particular domestic balance of political power. We cannot begin to address such questions in the absence of a reasonably compact definition that concentrates on the etiological attributes of the regime. Any other definition would simply define research questions out of existence. One of the functions of theory is to distinguish between those fundamental attributes of a regime (or anything else) that are inseparable from its etiology and those attributes that may be derivable in only a second-order fashion or may not be derivative of the etiology at all.

There were correlates of the particular species of each type of regime as well. Another purpose of theoretical study is to separate attributes that are etiological necessities of the type from attributes that are correlates of a particular species. The racism of German fascism is but one example. I have not included racism as a defining attribute of the fascist regime because I do not see it as essential to the etiology of that type of regime. I understand it to be, rather, an attribute of the German species of fascism. I should hope it self-evident that this is a theoretical rather than moral judgment. I have treated the distinctive developmental features of Italian fascism in the same way.

These remarks suggest what I should now make explicit. This book is an exercise in social science, at least as I understand social science. It is a search for a handful of "master variables" whose importance can be tested by explicit, empirically verifiable propositions. The search is necessarily constrained by the manifold problems of working with a small number of non-replicable experiences and with historical data that are often less comparable than we would like them to be. These methodological obstacles are sobering but by no means insurmountable. The rewards of comparative historical research, especially when guided by the theorizing proclivities of political scientists, seem to me to more than offset the obstacles. As I develop my own argument, I also attempt to evaluate the logic and empirics of some, although by no means all, of the more common interpretations of European political development, including accounts couched in terms of modernization theory, the timing and speed of industrialization, the role of landed elites, the speed of the democratic transition, political party polarization, working-class radicalism and reformism, and leadership. Most such interpretations, I believe, will be found wanting when put to the comparative test.

I am looking for a single set of variables and logically consistent causal connections that make sense of a broad range of national experiences rather than a collection of nation-specific explanations. Political science and history abound with sui generis accounts of individual nations or groups of nations that shared a common fate. We have no shortage of theories, for example, of why England became a liberal democracy, Germany and Italy became fascist, or Scandinavia became social democratic. Many of these theories appear quite compelling when examined through the lens of a single national experience or type of outcome, but lose much of their force when put to a broader comparative test. According to my understanding of social science, a theory that purports to explain why some societies became, for example, social democracies, should also provide an equally compelling explanation for why other societies did not become social democracies. That requires a similarly coherent explanation for each of the other types of outcomes. Those explanations, moreover, must be integrated: they must proceed from the same assumptions, employ the same variables, and so forth. I have tried to do this within the context of a comparative, historical narrative.

All of the interpretations I examine, and the one I advance, rest on causes located within individual societies rather than within the international economy or balance of power. This orientation reflects my conviction that the causal origins of the four regime outcomes were to be found in the ways in which millions of ordinary people sought to improve the quotidian material conditions of their lives through political activity. Politics, to be sure, is about much more than material interests and mass participation. But, the inescapable facts all theories of these regimes must confront are that no stable interwar regime could ever be formed if it lacked mass support; each type of regime was based on a distinctive social or class coalition; each regime was formed against or at the neglect of an excluded class; and, once formed, the regimes did not give primacy to the material interests of those who were not part of the founding coalition. These simple observations suggest to me that any theory must account for the regimes with reference to the material interests of millions of ordinary people.

Because mass material interests are the motor force of my argument, social classes and their political party representatives are its principal vehicles. But, as I hope to demonstrate, in important respects class interests did not dominate political alliances. We can account for neither the alliances that were formed nor those that were not without recourse to the role of regional, linguistic, and religious loyalties. Where liberal movements were successful before 1914, their appeal was reinforced by a religious cleavage. In the societies that were to become social democracies and fascist dictatorships— societies I refer to collectively as *aliberal*—it was of determining importance that liberal movements failed to establish their political hegemony before 1914. That failure was a consequence of divisions within the middle classes—about language, religion, and regional interests. These same divisions debilitated interwar liberal movements in aliberal societies and militated against any stabilizing coalition under liberal leadership.

Since I make regular references to classes, I want to make clear at the outset that I do not assume social classes possessed distinctive and coherent views of the world, class interests were the dominant interests of those who nominally belonged to a class, or classes acted as unitary actors. Rather the reader must accept only the more modest assumption that socialist parties mainly aspired to act as agents of the working classes and that liberal parties mainly aspired to act as agents of the middle classes. The empirical question examined at some length here is the comparative extent to which socialist parties and liberal parties were interclass coalitions or were homogeneous in their class bases. By focusing on the behavior and electoral bases of parties—their willingness to form cross-class electoral alliances, the level of popular support they received, the proportion of that support that appears to have come from a particular class—we can draw some conclusions about the comparative extent to which classes actually did behave in politics as unitary actors. Seen in a comparative perspective, the differences on this score are stunning.

In a book as long as this one, the reader deserves a preview of the essentials of the argument. In this preview, I sketch the core etiological differences among the three regimes of Western Europe and leave for the following chapters the supporting evidence and the more nuanced discussion of the differences among fundamentally similar transitional experiences and regimes.

I argue first that the essential feature that distinguished Britain, France, and Switzerland from other European societies before the Great War was the Lib-Labism[1] that emerged from the hegemony of liberal movements. From that Lib-Labism emerged a certain kind of working-class movement, one that would be politically, organizationally and even psychologically incapable of challenging a liberal order between the world wars.

In Britain the Liberal party and the reformed Conservative party alternated in power from the passage of the Second Reform Act in 1867 until the war. In Switzerland the Liberals and then the Radicals controlled every government between 1848 and 1919. In France, Republicans were dominant after 1877 and Radicals after 1898. In these societies, workers were able to make their influence felt first through an interclass coalition within the liberal parties and then through an alliance between their own parties and liberal parties. The latter proved more significant than the former, for unlike liberal parties elsewhere, those in Britain, France, and Switzerland were able to adjust to the appearance of independent working-class parties. When that independent mobilization took place, liberal parties were able to harness it in an alliance.

Liberals could make the concessions necessary to harness independent working-class movements to their cause because they had little to fear from a working-class movement, even a socialist one. They had little to fear because their most natural potential constituency, the middle classes, were not politically divided by antagonisms within them rooted in religious, regional, linguistic, and urban–rural differences. Indeed, these preindustrial cleavages, to the extent that they had any importance, served to reinforce the liberal appeal to the middle classes and helped to rally a majority, or effective majority, of the middle classes to liberalism.

For their part, working-class movements received a variety of benefits from Lib-Labism. In Switzerland, for example, Radicals were able to enact through the legislature measures of social reform for which workers could not secure majorities in national referenda. It was, as another example, because French Republicans needed the support of workers in their struggle against Conservatives that they met the three most important demands of French worker movements after 1877: the establishment of universal, free secular public education; the pardoning of the Communards; and the legislation of trade unions, collective bargaining, and the right to strike. These concrete gains were the currency that working-class leaders could exploit to justify their collaboration with liberals. Those leaders, and workers generally, received something still more potent, however ineffable it might be. That was acceptance and a measure of dignity. Given that, as we shall see, the material benefits that workers received in liberal societies were often less than they received in aliberal societies, that sense of acceptance, of legitimacy, looms very large in accounting for the behavior of working-class leaders in prewar liberal societies.

The establishment of representative government, not to be confused with democracy, was always a correlate of liberal hegemony, but it was not caused exclusively by it. In Norway, for example, it was the peasantry that was responsible for the adoption of a broad suffrage in the 1815 constitution and the establishment of parliamentary sovereignty in 1884. Yet neither of these events heralded the arrival of a hegemonic liberal movement. Indeed, the establishment of parliamentary sovereignty was followed almost immediately by liberal decline. It was the relationship between liberalism and working-class organizations that was crucial. The heart of this relationship was in its establishment of an interclass electoral coalition that politically empowered working-class leaders. Indeed, this combination of liberal hegemony and class collaboration could compensate to some degree for incomplete democratic development. This was the case in Britain, where a franchise much narrower than that found in many aliberal societies had no marked impact on the attitudes of workers' organizations. The key was liberal hegemony, for in all societies in which liberals were hegemonic an interclass coalition followed.

The stability of interwar liberal orders in Britain, France, and Switzerland was due in some measure to the fairly broad acceptance among workers of the political and economic institutions and policies that liberalism implied. Even more, however, the stability of liberal democracy was due to the formation of center-right coalitions of middle-class consolidation that left socialist parties isolated and ineffective and to the organizational incoherence of the trade unions. The rather broad working-class acceptance of the liberal order was rooted in prewar Lib-Labism, which had both validated the liberal order and working-class participation in it. The formation of center-right coalitions of middle-class consolidation, coalitions that now aggregated a broad expanse of the middle classes against the socialist working classes were made possible by the same comparative absence of internal cleavages that had once facilitated liberal hegemony. Under the interwar conditions of much heightened class conflict, and in the absence of those cleavages, political struggle was largely reduced to class struggle and working-class parties were deprived of middle-class allies.

The comparatively benign attitude of prewar liberal governments toward trade unions was, in turn, critical to the creation of organizationally incoherent trade union movements. It was that incoherence that, in its own turn, crippled British, French, and Swiss labor movements and limited the effectiveness of the challenges they could mount during the interwar years. In effect, those movements would not be able to hold liberal governments and employers hostage with their ability to subvert market mechanisms. Because they lacked such an ability, political peace and labor discipline could be enforced through the wage market.

In organizing themselves in the labor market, as in politics, worker activists confronted a choice. They could pursue their ambitions through alliances with liberals or through the comprehensive, coherent organization of the working classes. In practice, because comprehensive, coherent organization was a slow, arduous, and tedious strategy, it was never preferred if hegemonic allies were available. Where such allies were available, workers had been allowed to organize in the labor market before the war without undue opposition from the state and indeed, to call on the state as an ally in labor market disputes. In consequence, a network of balkanized trade union organizations was created with particularism as its foundation and reformism as its soul. Precisely because workers were not, contrary to Marx, an inherently revolutionary class, this pluralist pattern would be the "natural" outcome of a situation in which allies, especially in the state, could be substituted for coherent organization.

This was an organizational weakness that, to be sure, reflected the comparatively low level of class consciousness that had existed among these workers when the trade unions were being created, one appropriate for workers whose identities were grounded in local or regional, craft, or industrial interests rather than in their class. Yet the incoherence survived long after consciousness of class had been raised by the experience of the First World War. One can plausibly argue that by 1919 the level of working-class consciousness was as high in Britain, France, and perhaps even Switzerland as it was elsewhere in Western Europe. It probably was; but by then it was too late to create trade union organizations whose coherence was commensurate with that consciousness. For by then the organizational space had been filled. As we shall see, those in Britain, France, and Switzerland who favored a more comprehensive organization of workers, whether in political parties or in trade unions, always lost these battles in both the prewar and interwar periods. The intermediate result was that workers in the interwar years found themselves with neither their historic middle-class allies, who now regrouped against labor as class conflict became more salient, nor effective organizations of their own. The ultimate result was that there were few obstacles to a liberal democratic stabilization. Neither liberal economics nor democratic politics were seriously challenged.

Where liberals failed to establish their prewar hegemony, they failed because they could not straddle preindustrial cleavages within the middle classes. Having failed to establish their hegemony, liberal parties found the mobilization of a socialist working class enormously threatening—so threatening, in fact, that they consistently refused to ally themselves with socialist movements. Normally left without allies, and always without useful allies, socialist parties and trade unions concentrated on the comprehensive and coherent organization of the working classes. The result, by the final years of the peace, was that liberal parties, incapable of rallying politically divided middle classes, found themselves confronted by seemingly monolithic and rapidly expanding socialist parties and trade unions.

The crises of the war years and thereafter did nothing to heal the divisions within the middle classes. Indeed, liberal parties continued to dwindle as the middle classes became still more fractionalized politically. The discredit of liberalism was accelerated between the wars as coherent labor movements proved capable of subverting traditional market mechanisms. Trade unions in these societies proved strikingly successful in driving up real wages and labor's share of national income even in the face of what were already nearly depression levels of unemployment. This was in contrast to the failure of trade unions in the 1920s in liberal societies, where real wages stagnated or fell even at markedly lower levels of unemployment. In all aliberal societies, labor peace and discipline, and by correlate the stability of the political order, would require the subordination of markets to politics, whether democratic or authoritarian. In effect, political stabilization would require a fundamental break with the liberal model, for neither the labor-disciplining effects of a functioning wage market nor a durable center-right coalition would be available to underpin a liberal stabilization.

In almost all of the aliberal societies, the initial impulse at the time of the democratic breakthroughs of 1919 was to replicate the prewar British experience by forming coalitions of labor and reforming liberals. Yet in all cases such coalitions could either not be formed or soon fell apart. The failure of this Lib-Lab formula was accompanied or followed quickly by the failure of liberals to consolidate a coalition of the middle classes. Liberals proved incapable of overcoming divisions within the urban middle classes and between the urban and rural middle classes, incapable of addressing the grievances of the peasantry and incapable of disciplining organized labor. From then on, interwar politics and its associated instability must be seen as a search for an alternative coalition formula. If a coalition of the two urban classes could not be formed, and if liberals could not consolidate a coalition of the middle classes, the only coalition that could provide an adequate political majority would be one that joined an urban class with a rural class under either social democratic or fascist leadership. In the countryside, the alignment of the family peasantry was decisive.

Peasants in aliberal societies became truly free agents for the first time as a result of the war. Whereas before the war they had remained wedded to liberal or at least status quo parties, after the war they were willing to and capable of changing their alliances as they calculated and recalculated the material consequences of different alliance options. Urban liberals, who were less and less useful to peasants as allies and remained loath to aid them as they struggled with the effects of the war and then the commodity crisis of the late 1920s, were the first to feel the effects of the free agency of the family peasantry. In contrast to family peasants in liberal societies, who in the interwar years spread their support across a range of parties but remained generally supportive of the dominant center–right coalitions, family peasants in aliberal societies now began to act with considerable class coherence and demonstrated a willingness to break with their old political camps—so much so that they were now willing to align with urban workers, according to circumstances, and, under the new leadership of fascists, with the urban middle classes. How the family peasantry aligned itself was determined by whether or not socialist movements had become engaged in class conflicts within the countryside. Whenever socialists sought to organize the agrarian proletariat in politics and in the labor market, the family peasantry was pushed into the arms of fascists. Whether or not socialists sought to organize agrarian workers was in turn determined by whether those workers were politically available or had been previously organized by another movement. Where they had not been previously organized, the logic of democratic competition, the short-term imperative of maximizing popular support, drove socialists into the void.

When the family peasantry sided with urban workers, the outcome was a social democratic regime. When it sided with the urban middle classes, the outcome was fascism. In both instances, the distinctive features of the regimes were logical consequences of the interests of the subtending classes and the challenge posed by the classes initially excluded. The distinctive coherence of socialist working-class movements in aliberal societies was central to the form that both social democracy and fascism assumed. Social democracy reflected this through democratic corporatism. Fascism, too, had to respond to this legacy with a variant of corporatism and with a totalitarian variant of dictatorship. Both regimes, because they displaced liberal leadership and required the legitimation of immediate success, were more inclined to break with liberal economic orthodoxy and experiment with stimulatory policies.

I

THE ORIGINS

Ties That Would Divide: Liberal–Labor Alliances in Britain, France, and Switzerland before the War

Britain

The British experience of an alliance between workers and reforming liberals dates in a limited way from at least the 1830s, but for our purposes the most critical years were those after 1867 and the passage of the Second Reform Act. This act enfranchised about two-thirds of the urban working class. It was followed in 1874 by legislation that secured, or until the end of the century was thought to have secured, the legal rights of trade unions to picket peacefully, bargain collectively, and stand immune from suits for damages. The extension of the franchise and the reform of the trade union statutes, coupled with the establishment of the legal equality of employers and workers, fixed the basic context of working-class politics for the remainder of the prewar years.[1]

The reform years, 1867 to 1875, had been marked by energetic Conservative and Liberal efforts to gain working-class votes. Workers made their electoral participation felt for the first time in the campaign of 1874 and were probably instrumental in securing the victory of the Conservatives, who appeared more responsive to trade union demands.[2] The years between 1871 and 1875, however, were probably the only years in which a majority of workers supported the Tories. Thereafter, the bulk of the working-class electorate cast its ballot for the Liberals. Workers were, in effect, returning to an already established alliance with Radicalism, an alliance that had been based on temperance, nonconformity, secular education, and Gladstone's early advocacy of franchise reform.[3]

In the twenty years that followed the enlargement of the franchise, the Tory party succeeded in recasting itself. In 1885, aided by a revision of the constituency boundaries that increased the electoral weight of the suburbs, the Conservatives won a majority of the English boroughs. Satisfied with the reforms of Gladstone's first ministry (1868–1874), alarmed by the growing challenge to Britain's imperial position, and worried by the increased assertiveness of the trade unions, much of the urban (and now suburban) middle class abandoned the campaign against privilege and plumbed for the Tories as the party of order, stability, and imperial greatness. The Home Rule Crisis of 1885–86, which split the Liberal party and brought Whigs and Liberal Unionists into the Tory fold, completed the process of Tory transformation.[4]

Even after the transformation of the Conservative party, there would always be a substantial minority of workers who would vote for it.[5] Some voted Conservative (as many others voted Liberal) in deference to the political views of their employers.[6] Others recalled the Conservative championing of factory reform before 1850 or resented the Liberals' conciliatory attitude toward Roman Catholic Ireland. The Third Reform Act (1884) enfranchised many rural workers, and brought more competition for working-class support, with the Conservatives offering protection to counter the Liberals' guarantees of cheap food. Working-class conservatism remained a powerful force among workers who were neither abstainers nor Nonconformists, who worked in garrison and shipbuilding towns, or who were engaged in industries that sought protection from foreign competition.[7]

In 1880, the Conservative government sponsored a limited employers' liability act. In subsequent years, under both Liberal and Tory governments, several piecemeal acts were passed enhancing worker safety and employers' liability, and the number of mine and factory inspectors was increased. Also, workers began to appear on the magistrates' benches and on local school boards. These concessions were readily made because, through the 1880s, the demands of workers were not distinctive enough to impede their easy accommodation. Both parties courted the working-class vote and allowed workers some influence in selecting candidates and writing platforms. The effort by the Tories to solicit workers' votes was not duplicated by nonclerical Conservative parties anywhere else in Europe, and it is necessary to keep this in mind as one of several reasons working-class integration was more advanced in Britain than in any other European society, including other liberal societies.

Even so, the heart of the story is to be found in the alliance of workers and the Liberal party. The allegiance of workers, and more particularly the trade unions, to the Liberals was such that until the end of the century advocates of a separate working-class party fought an almost futile battle. The guidance provided by the trade unions was such that few workers were disposed to support a working-class candidate who was not a Liberal or a Conservative, or even to prefer a working-class Liberal or Conservative over candidates from the middle classes. "What do you say to the elections in the factory districts?" Engels asked Marx in 1868. "Everywhere the working class is the rag, tag and bobtail of the official parties . . . Not a single working-class candidate had the ghost of a chance, but my Lord Tom Noddy or any *parvenu* snob could have the workers' votes with pleasure."[8]

In the decades before the war, the electoral coalitions of Liberals and labor were made entirely at the local level, and in making these the trade union branches and trades councils, local umbrella organizations of trade unions, played a decisive role. They agreed to endorse and campaign for Liberal candidates who took friendly positions on issues of importance to the unions. In some instances, where workers were a particularly large share of the electorate, the local Liberal party agreed to sponsor a union-nominated candidate on the Liberal ticket. The number of workers who ran for Parliament on the Liberal ticket grew very slowly, however. In 1874, only two such candidates won seats. Not until 1880 were they joined by other successful candidates, and in 1890 there were still just eight working-class MPs.[9]

This low level of representation was less a result of Liberal rejection of working-class candidates than a lack of demand for such candidates from the trade unions. The unions were generally content to have labor interests represented by sympathetic Liberal (or in some instances Tory) MPs and were especially loathe to sponsor independent working-class candidates. Such candidates invariably ran a distant third behind the candidates of the two official parties, even in working-class districts.[10] That they did so suggests that union leaders knew what they were doing, that they were pursuing a course widely embraced by their constituents. "Most workers," in fact, "remained either apolitical or reformist . . . because they respected the classes above them, because they were not seriously dissatisfied with the pace of material and political advance, and because their grievances could usually be remedied by constitutional means."[11] It was an electorate, especially before the penultimate years of the century, that simply did not define the political world much in terms of class. Rather it saw its local and sectional interests and the religious and other differences between the Tories and Liberals as more important than those between the working and other classes. Throughout the prewar years, religious identity and the sectional interests of a trade union or industry were probably better indicators of how a worker would vote than was a worker's class standing.[12] Indeed, it would not be surprising if the best predictor of how a worker voted was how his employer voted.[13] A. L. Rowse, a Labor politician between the wars, recalled how, before he developed an interest in Labor politics, his father had always voted Liberal, "as all the china-clay workers voted Liberal, because the china-clay captains were Liberal."[14]

The level of accommodation offered by the established parties was always sufficient to ensure that until Home Rule, and especially the war, a great majority of the working-class electorate always supported either the Liberals or Conservatives.[15] This fact, combined with the reluctance of workers to vote for independent labor candidates even in overwhelmingly working-class districts, indicates about as clearly as any historical evidence can, the comparatively very high level of legitimacy that workers granted to the political and economic order of Victorian Britain.

The durability of the alliance between Liberals and workers and the consequently peculiar form the British labor movement assumed resulted from a succession of Liberal strategies that had the effect of containing and subordinating working-class politics. The strategic conundrum weighed heavily on the Liberal party as it sought to preserve its interclass alliance in the face of a more assertive working class and the competing Tory appeal to the middle classes. Until the Home Rule Crisis of 1885–86, two visions coexisted within the party about how best to preserve the alliance. The major question was whether it would be better preserved by directing attention toward or away from the material needs of workers. Before the Home Rule Crisis, Joseph Chamberlain, the leader of Birmingham Radicalism, proposed the former course. But the social demands of the Radical program proved too vague to mobilize the enthusiasm of working-class voters and too alarmist to do other than propel middle-class voters into the Conservative camp.[16]

Gladstone provided the alternative solution to the problem. Adamant in his opposition to "construction," to state interventionist social reform, which he believed would sap the foundations of self-help and manly independence, Gladstone sought to direct politics away from socially divisive domestic questions, appealing instead to the traditions of democratic internationalism that were common to both middle-class and working-class liberalism. From 1886, when Home Rule was soundly defeated in a new election, until his retirement in 1894, Gladstone's "Lost Cause" provided a unifying force for Liberals which enabled them to evade any resolution of the problems of domestic policy. The price of this evasion, however, was impotence and a noticeable alienation of labor.[17]

Democratic internationalism had an appeal but was not enough by itself to bind labor to the Liberals for long. Gladstone's final attempt to hold labor for the Liberals came in the Newcastle Program of 1892. The attempt was too late and too weak but not devoid of consequence. The program included the introduction of graduated death duties, abolition of plural voting, and disestablishment of the Church in Scotland and Wales. The most important demand of the unions—the eight-hour day—was only vaguely mentioned. With the departure of Gladstone in 1894, a third effort, ultimately also unsuccessful but nonetheless critical, was made to bind workers to the Liberal party. The "New Liberals" set out to produce a positive alternative to socialism that would be more acceptable to the growing number of working-class activists who could see no future in Gladstonian self-help.[18] Most of the central figures of New Liberalism were professional men, journalists, writers, and civil servants. If the old Liberal nexus of paternalist employer, responsible trade unionist, and nonconformist conscience was breaking down, the professional middle class, which was rapidly expanding in this period, could offer an alternative collectivist route to social harmony. Many of the New Liberals had been involved as young men in the settlement movement of the 1880s—middle-class observers of the East End of London or the poorer districts of provincial cities who had studied poverty on the spot and searched out its remedies. The New Liberals grounded their solutions to the problems of poverty in exhaustive attempts to establish the facts independently of the demands or assertions of organized workers and employers. In and around the great social surveys of Charles Booth in London and Seebohm Rowntree in York, New Liberals wove an ideology of "social science." They believed they had discovered a scientific diagnosis of poverty and scientific remedies for it. The confidence this belief gave them, as advocates of policy and, eventually, as the administrative architects of new state agencies, was no less important historically for being ill-founded.

After the Liberal landslide of 1906, piecemeal reforms derived from the New Liberalism's collectivist vision addressed particular ills affecting workers. Thus school meals for children, medical inspection in schools, noncontributory old age pensions, and industrial accident insurance schemes were introduced. The Trades Boards Act made it possible to fix legal minimum wages in sweated trades, putting a floor under the competitive driving down of wages. Before 1914, all this legislation probably had relatively little impact on the conditions of workers and the poor.[19] The importance of New Liberalism for working-class politics lay not in its success, but in its ability to generate social reforms that held out the promise of state action against poverty. From the 1890s onward, the New Liberalism had a profound impact on working-class politics, helping to persuade working-class activists that their interests continued to lie in cooperation with Liberals.

These reforms and the interclass alliance that subtended them were a reflection of the vested position the trade unions had acquired in Victorian Britain. Although the Lib–Lab alliance had been mainly the creation of the more elitist, craft-based unions of an earlier generation, it was only very slowly altered by the appearance of the New Unionism of 1889 through 1893. The New Unionism involved organizing into more general unions the less skilled workers in industries such as transport, in the gasworks, and on the docks.[20] An explosion of strike activity, commencing with the famous 1889 London dock strike, initiated a burst of labor organization that initially portended a much more cohesive and radical working-class movement. Most of the new unions withered, however, in the early 1890s and survived with only 10 to 25 percent of their peak membership. Their impact was of some import—they doubled the membership of the Trades Union Congress (TUC) from about 500,000 to 1 million in the mid-1890s—and they provided an organizational base for those in the working-class movement who advocated independent working-class representation.[21]

Yet, advocates of independent representation did not always repudiate collaboration with the Liberals; even fewer advocated the creation of a socialist party. The unions, old and new, were the main organizers of working-class politics and the main advocates of the Lib–Lab alliance, and to understand the weight of that alliance, we must consider the obstacles its supporters in the unions were able to erect in the prewar decades to a more independent labor course.

By the 1890s, a half dozen working-class movements were of some importance in organizing workers in politics: the older craft unions, the Trades Union Congress (TUC), the newer general unions, the Labor Electoral Association, the Social Democratic Federation (SDF), and the Independent Labor party (ILP). In general, the unions and the TUC opposed independent representation until the end of the century. Within the union movement, it was mainly in some of the newer general unions that support for independent representation was to be found. The Labor Electoral Association, the political arm of the TUC, also opposed independent representation. The SDF and the ILP, much less influential than the unions, endorsed independent candidates, but not necessarily socialist candidates.

The chief challenges to the trade unions' political hegemony among the workers came from the Social Democratic Federation and the Independent Labor Party, and neither of these challenges was of much effect. Both are worth looking at more closely, because they offered a fundamentally different vision of labor politics from that offered by the unions and that which eventually came to dominate Labor party politics. This alternative vision, especially in the case of the SDF, was one based explicitly on the centrality of class conflict, a rejection of Lib–Labism, a centralized, coherent, and comprehensive working-class movement in politics and in the labor market, and a radical reorganization of the economy. This vision paralleled the ambitions of socialist parties on the continent, especially parties in aliberal societies. While the vision emanated from the Independent Labor Party (ILP), too, the ILP's socialism was more cautious and lukewarm, couched more in terms of notions of justice and the ethical society, and more influenced by Fabian reformism.[22]

The SDF had less impact on British labor than had the ILP. Until the 1880s, socialism was essentially nonexistent in Britain, being largely the preserve of a handful of eccentric middle-class intellectuals. Marx's works were so little known in England in these years, notwithstanding his many years of residence there, that his death would have passed entirely without notice had not the *Times'* Paris correspondent written a piece on his stature on the continent.[23] Socialism, of course, had its greatest progress where Lib–Labism was least firmly entrenched, but even there that progress was never more than marginal. The SDF's membership (mainly middle class) never amounted to more than 1,000 in the 1880s, and it never succeeded in electing a single MP. The federation was always torn in its attitudes toward trade unionism, with its majority contemptuous of the unions as bastions of liberal capitalism and Gladstonian reformism.[24] With a few exceptions, trade unionists returned the contempt. Indeed, for much, probably most, of the working classes, the label "socialist" was one of derision. Alfred Williams, an SDF activist, complained of his workmates that "if you should take the pains of pointing out anything for their benefit they will tell you that you are mad, or curse you for a socialist. Anyone at the works who holds a view different from that of the crowd is called a socialist."[25] Robert Roberts found similar attitudes in prewar Salford, where Hyndman Hall—the home of the SDF—was said to have "about as much political impact on the neighbourhood as the nearby gasworks."[26]

The Independent Labor party, the most important prewar socialist movement in Britain, presented Lib–Labism with a more formidable challenge than the SDF precisely because it was better anchored in the trade unions, or at least in some of the new general unions. The ILP represented a political response to the severe setbacks the new unions had experienced after their initial prosperity. For years, its strongest area of support, the West Riding of Yorkshire, was an area where trade unions were conspicuously weak. Estimates of the ILP's membership vary, but even the most generous one I have encountered—35,000 members at its peak in 1895—points to its modest success.[27] It was never able to get one of its own elected to Parliament, but had some success on the local level. By 1906, it claimed 106 local councillors, 66 members of school boards, and 51 Poor Law Guardians.[28] Along with members of the SDF (which claimed about 10,000 members in the last years of the century), the ILP was vigorously involved through the force of its arguments in persuading local authorities to implement progressive legislation on housing, sanitation, relief work for the unemployed, and so on.

It is of some significance that at the ILP's founding conference in 1893, the groups that came together created a federation in the hope that the unions could be persuaded to join.[29] Although the national trade unions were invited to the founding conference, none sent delegates and there were only a handful of delegates from local trades councils and from trade union branches. The great majority of the delegates came from local independent labor parties (local working-class parties) or similar bodies. As it happened, no national unions were later inclined to affiliate. Indeed, just two years later, the ILP found that its most immediate concern was not to induce the participation of national unions but to deter its own colonization by local Lib–Lab unions and trades councils and to prevent the expulsion from the TUC of those trades councils that supported it and opposed Lib–Labism. As a result, in its second year, the ILP was compelled to reorganize itself as a unitary organization with local branches and individual memberships. In effect, the ILP reorganized itself to avoid the fate of earlier movements that had sought independent representation: colonization by the Lib–Lab unions.[30]

The SDF found no market for its vision of class politics, and the ILP was always stymied by the near monopoly of Lib–Labs in the main trade union organizations. The growth of the new unions representing unskilled and less-skilled workers in the early 1890s did create a balance in the TUC more favorable to independent labor representation. But to win broad trade union support for such a project, it was always necessary to define the undertakings in such a way that Lib–Labs would support them. The battles that were fought in the TUC in the early 1890s and that led to the creation of the Labor Representation Committee (LRC) are typical of both this and the organizational weapons that Lib–Labs could deploy against their opponents.

For years socialists and independents had fought an almost hopeless battle at the annual Trades Union Congresses to win support for a political levy, a concrete program, and independent representation. Finally, in 1893 the advocates of independent representation appeared to have won their battle. The TUC for the first time approved a separate fund for assisting independent labor candidates at both local and parliamentary elections. Each trade union was to be asked to subscribe 5s. for every hundred members, and the congress was to elect a special committee annually to represent the contributing societies to administer the fund. Candidates were to be chosen locally, but were to pledge themselves to the full labor program drawn up by the congress. Independents and socialists were keen to support such a body as a way to supersede the TUC-sponsored Labor Electoral Associations, which had "degenerated into a wing of the Liberal party."[31] Immediately after approving the levy, the congress for the first time approved the use of a test question that required sponsored candidates to endorse nationalization. At last, it appeared that a real victory had been achieved for independent representation and even socialism.[32]

The victory, however, was short-lived. When the Parliamentary Committee was asked to report the following year on the implementation of these resolutions, it informed the congress that only two unions had responded positively to the circular soliciting support for the levy and its administration. This was no doubt true, but the plain fact was that Lib–Labs controlled the TUC's Parliamentary Committee, the agency charged with implementing the resolutions. Although the Lib–Labs had been able to support the levy, they were repulsed by the socialist test question and proceeded to bury the whole project. In this, they "had the support of most of the secretaries of the big unions."[33] Having killed the resolutions of 1893, the supporters of Lib–Labism in 1895 went further and successfully expelled from the TUC many of the local trades councils that had sponsored the creation of the Independent Labor party.[34]

By the end of the century, the ILP had concluded that it could either very slowly build up its base of individual membership and preserve its socialism or join a federation with the trade unions and quickly acquire a much larger base, but at the cost of greatly diluting its socialism and accepting some degree of alliance with the Liberals.[35] Most of the trade unions had no interest in a separate working-class party until after the turn of the century. When they did finally commit themselves to such a party, it was not by encouraging their members to join the ILP or the SDF, but by creating a new organization based on federation. Such an organizational structure would ensure the hegemony of the unions in the new party. When the TUC sponsored such an organization—the Labor Representation Committee—in 1899, the ILP confronted its dilemma and, along with the SDF, opted for affiliation. When it did so, it implicitly accepted a vision of working-class politics premised mainly on sectionalism and unionism rather than class. It also confirmed its own insignificance.

The decision to create the LRC at the 1899 Trades Union Congress was hardly an enthusiastic one and was passed by a vote of just 546,000 to 434,000. The resolution was crafted in a way that allowed Lib–Labs to support it: it merely endorsed the creation of an organization whose purpose would be an increase in the number of labor MPs and a separate parliamentary caucus. Collaboration with liberals was not excluded and the LRC was in no way committed to socialism. In fact, the LRC had very little power. No political fund was created, and the financing of candidates remained in the hands of their local sponsoring organizations. In a move that measured the importance many trade unionists attached to the LRC, Ramsay MacDonald was elected its secretary because he was willing to take the job without pay. Most Lib–Lab trade unionists ignored it. Those who did not, joined it, like the railwaymen's leader Richard Bell, to undermine the influence of the ILP activists who wanted Labor to pursue a more independent line.[36]

The LRC fought the 1900 election with no definite program and with no clear attitude toward the Liberal party. It contested only ten seats and returned just two candidates. It then spent the next six years, in MacDonald's memorable phrase, "grow[ing] in obscurity."[37] Ultimately, it was the Taff Dale judgment that saved the LRC from the fate of the Labor Electoral Association. That it took a legal threat to their previously assumed position in society to persuade the unions to support the LRC speaks volumes about the essentially vested position that the unions had acquired, or thought they had acquired, in late Victorian Britain.

In the Taff Vale judgment, the High Court for the first time held a union liable for economic damages caused to an employer by a strike action.[38] Although they were initially divided in their response to the judgment, the unions—as they reflected on the size of the damages awarded—realized that the judgment portended a profound challenge to their position.[39] When it became apparent that the Conservative government was not going to provide an adequate remedy—full restoration of immunities—in Parliament, the LRC used the issue to induce unions to support independent representation. The result was a flurry of union affiliation with the LRC in 1902 and 1903. By 1905 the miners were the only significant section of labor that remained outside the LRC. It cannot be emphasized too strongly, however, that what most unions sought from the LRC was not a long-term alternative to the Liberal party but "a sufficiently strong bargaining position to force the

Liberal government to repeal the effects of the Taff Vale judgment. What they had in mind was bargaining strength vis-a-vis the Liberals rather than strict independence from both parties."[40]

Victories in several by-elections in 1902 and 1903 persuaded the Liberals that the LRC would have to be accommodated. Consequently, Herbert Gladstone (for the Liberals) and Ramsay MacDonald reached agreement on a list of thirty constituencies in which the LRC would be allowed a free run against Conservatives. Both sides had an interest in avoiding three-cornered contests that would split the traditional coalition and hand victory to the Conservatives. MacDonald also saw the agreement as a means to avoid testing Labor's dubious "independence." "By 1906 the essence of the LRC's independence lay in the fact that it had substituted a centralized accommodation with the Liberal Party for the local arrangements traditionally pursued. . . . The new Labor Party (formally constituted as such after the election [of 1906]) had arrived on the political scene not as the grave-digger of Liberalism, but as an integral part of a great Liberal revival."[41]

The alliance between Labor and the Liberals continued after the formation of the Labor party. Labor had to accommodate its tactics and its policies to the requirements of the interclass coalition on which it was so dependent. The extent of the dependence is made evident by the record of Labor's electoral successes and defeats in the years between 1906 and 1914. The key measure of dependence is provided by the number of seats Labor could win when it did not ally with the Liberals.

The new Labor party fought its first parliamentary election in 1906 and returned thirty members. Of the thirty, only five were elected in three-cornered contests that included both a Liberal and a Conservative opponent. Twenty-four had only Conservative or Unionist opponents; one had two Liberals against him in a two-seat constituency. Against this, out of twenty-six unsuccessful Labor party candidates, eighteen had to fight both Liberals and Tories, and only seven were beaten in straight fights against Conservatives or Unionists. In addition to the Labor party's nominees, thirteen candidates were put forward either by the Social Democratic Federation or under other socialist auspices. These all had to face three-cornered fights; they were all beaten. In addition to these thirty Labor party candidates, twenty-four Lib–Labs were elected in 1906. These twenty-four were trade unionists running directly on the Liberal party ticket.[42] It is plain, then, that the success of Labor party and other worker candidates was due to an alliance with the Liberals.

This pattern of dependent alliance was replicated in the two 1910 elections. In the first election Labor returned forty MPs, an increase of ten from 1906. This increase was due entirely to the accession of ten miners who had previously carried their constituencies on the Liberal ticket. Again, Labor owed almost all its seats to a combination of Labor and Liberal votes. Of the forty seats, thirty-nine were won without Liberal opposition. The thirty-four

Labor candidates who had Liberal and Tory opposition were all beaten. Another ten socialist candidates ran on a separate ticket and they were all defeated. The parliamentary party was not only critically dependent on the coalition with the Liberals, "but now even included a considerable number of men who were really Liberals, and had changed their party allegiance at the behest of the Miners' Federation without therewith altering their political attitudes."[43] In the second election of 1910, the Labor party put up sixty-two candidates and won forty-two seats, the miners again contributing seventeen. Again, Labor fought in alliance with the Liberals. Of the forty-two successful candidates, three were unopposed, and the other thirty-nine had only Conservative opponents. Of the twenty defeated candidates, nine fought only Conservatives and eleven had three-cornered fights.[44]

From 1911, the Liberals were no longer willing to stand down so that Labor might have straight fights against Tory candidates. From 1913, the Liberals, preoccupied with Home Rule and Welsh Disestablishment and increasingly offended by the upsurge of Labor unrest, practically ceased to make further concessions to the Labor party's demands. Yet, in the Commons, Labor was still voting for the government, even as in the constituencies collaboration between the Liberal and Labor parties had virtually ceased except in a few double constituencies. The Liberals were no longer willing to allow even former Liberals now running under the Labor banner an open field against the Tories. If there had been a general election in 1914, the Labor party would have been hard pressed to hold many of the seats it had won on the basis of the old relationship. In return, of course, many Liberal seats won on this basis would have been endangered.[45]

An understanding of the weakness of an independent labor movement must be found in the behavior of the unions and, ultimately, in the attitudes of the millions of workers who apparently endorsed the union behavior. The unions, as the ILP quickly discovered, consistently sought before the turn of the century to coopt, obstruct, isolate, and delegitimate independent movements that attempted to define politics mainly in terms of class rather than sectional and union interests. In this, the unions were successful—so much so, as it turned out, that the legacy of their success defined the character of British working-class politics and thereby of the larger political and economic order for decades to come. The message to be drawn from the historical material is unambiguous: very few British workers had much use for class politics precisely because Lib–Labism gave them a measure of confidence, however small, that was sufficient to undermine a more comprehensive vision. Lib–Labism taught them to see the political world more in terms of sectional rather than class interests and created a kind of working–class particularism. It is possible to adduce innumerable anecdotes that mirror this attitude, but the most compelling evidence for it is simply in the voting behavior of workers, the conduct of the unions, and the organizational sectionalism of the unions. Union organization and behavior are matters to which we shall return in due course. It is certainly the case that working-class consciousness rose after 1890. It rose much more dramatically after 1914, but never enough to force a fundamental restructuring of trade union organizations in a way that, through greater centralization, comprehensiveness and cohesion, would have given greater operational meaning to a higher level of consciousness.

Liberals, after all, had much to offer. So much, in fact, that the great majority of workers did not vote for the Labor party until after the war had destroyed the Liberal party. Above all, at least as far as the trade unions were concerned, the Liberals were acceptable allies because they supported the vested position the unions had acquired in the social order. Legislatively, as well, the Liberals endorsed a range of reforms. These reforms, although generally piecemeal, ad hoc, and falling short of Labor's expectations, were sufficient to convince labor activists that the political institutions of Britain could be used, at least by an autonomous labor party, to bring about effective social change. That conviction, as we shall see when we examine the French experience, was vastly more determining than the palliatives that were actually legislated.

In the electoral arena, Liberals could offer the trade unionist Lib–Labs the same thing the unions offered the men and women of the ILP: a mass constituency for their political agenda. Just as the ILP found the appeal of the unions' mass base irresistible, the unions found the appeal of the interclass coalition with the Liberals to be irresistible. This interclass strategy was a conditioning one in that it constrained the platform of Labor: not alienating Liberals was critical, and Labor normally had to subordinate its own agenda to that of the Liberal party. It is particularly telling that as they prepared for the 1906 campaign, local LRCs, many of them led by the ILP activists, were induced by MacDonald to nominate Liberal trade unionists rather than socialists, "or to disguise socialist candidates as pure-and-simple Labor men." Their dependence on trade union financing and on the electoral coalition inherited from traditional Lib–Labism made it impossible for ILP activists to act as they were wont to either in campaigns or in the House of Commons.[46] The alliance was also a conditioning one in that it bound the working class to the established institutions of British society. The Liberal party thus served as a critical bridge between the working class and the modern liberal order.

For a brief moment in 1889–90, it had seemed possible that an alliance between socialist politics and the poorer sections of the workers, who were then rushing in to the new unions, could remake the whole working-class movement. In fact, the promises of the ILP and the New Unionism were never fulfilled. The formation of the Labor party at the turn of the century represented not a victory for the advocates of a more cohesive, class-oriented workers' movement, but the effective containment of that impulse in the old Labor traditions. To the extent that Liberals and even the Conservatives accommodated workers' demands, the need for a more unified, cohesive class-based movement such as the SDF and ILP proposed became less evident. This had consequences—we shall take a much closer look at them in Chapters 5 and 6—both for the way workers were organized in the labor market and the way a substantial part of the working class accepted as legitimate a liberal political economy. In doing so it secured the continuity of institutions and even policies in the interwar period.

France

Electoral cooperation, again arrived at by scattered local understandings rather than national pacts, was equally critical to the success of the French Socialist party and its several predecessors. When Theodore Zeldin records that "alliances with the Radicals made possible most of the Socialist victories at the polls, which they could never have achieved if they had remained an isolated, antirepublican party," he is merely summarizing the conventional wisdom of historians of the period.[47] Without such arrangements many safe Socialist seats would have been endangered, among them even the seat of the Socialist leader Jean Jaurès.[48] Alliances for the second ballot were made locally by committees representing the different parties, with little guidance provided or control exercised by the national parties. These alliances sometimes resulted in a Radical standing down in favor of a Socialist, but more often in a Socialist standing down for a Radical.

If the value of such alliances is understood narrowly in terms of social legislation, then their results were modest at best, but probably not for the reason commonly supposed. "One of the common misconceptions about the Third Republic, before the 1914 War, is that it passed very little social legislation. On the contrary, there was a great deal of it."[49] The Republic did so in the same ad hoc, piecemeal fashion that characterized social legislation in prewar Britain. In 1893 legislation was approved by which all citizens without financial resources were provided with medical care in the home or, if necessary, in a hospital. Every commune was required to establish a bureau d'assistance, to make lists of those entitled to such assistance. The state paid a subsidy of 80 percent. By 1897, those entitled to such assistance number 1.9 million persons, but the benefits paid were very modest and the incurably ill were excluded. A scheme of public assistance to the aged, infirm, and incurably ill was carried in 1905. It provided for the relief of the sick over seventy years of age. By 1914, the state's subsidy of the program had risen to more than 100 million francs a year (from 49 million in 1907) and more than half a million individuals received it. "But the poor still received on average only 34.9 francs each annually, compared to 180 francs distributed to almost twice as many in England."[50] The first obligatory pension scheme was introduced in 1910, having been delayed in the Assembly and Senate for almost a decade by the opposition of both unions and employers. The state contributed half of the payment for each worker, while the employer and worker each contributed 25 percent. In 1912, the pensionable age was reduced from sixty-five to sixty. In 1913, assistance was provided to large families with small incomes.[51]

There was only one factory act on the statute book in 1870, an 1841 child labor law. The Catholics of the National Assembly actually showed more interest in this question than the Republicans, and a stricter law was passed in 1874. An 1892 law covered both women and children, but the machinery of enforcement was lax. Trade unions, collective bargaining, and the right to strike were given legal affirmation in 1884, and in 1890 the *livret* was abolished, effectively giving workers and employers legal equality. When Alexander Millerand accepted office as Minister of Labor in the government of Réné Waldeck-Rousseau, he hoped to carry through a major program of labor legislation, but many of his plans, including a scheme for the compulsory arbitration of strikes, came to nothing. He did, however, get through a law establishing a voluntary arbitration scheme and this was gradually resorted to with considerable frequency by workers. Millerand also moved legislation on hours of work which, by 1904, led to the ten-hour day for all workers, including men, in establishments employing women or children. Other legislation of this kind included the law of 1898 establishing a generous industrial accident insurance fund that compensated workers regardless of liability and a law of 1906 mandating a compulsory weekly rest day. Further progress was made only by privileged groups of workers such as miners and railwaymen, who enjoyed special protection because their industries operated under concessions from the state and, in the case of the miners, because they were numerous enough to elect deputies who fought for their interests in the Assembly. The miners got a pension scheme in 1894 and the railwaymen in 1909, and the eight-hour day was enforced in the mines in 1905.[52]

This mixed record is often invoked to illustrate the marginal position of workers in the Republic and to explain their alleged alienation from it.[53] Yet, judging by a variety of indicators, the working classes, or a determining fraction of them, did accept the Republic. There can hardly be any doubt that French workers were less well compensated politically and materially and less well integrated than workers in Britain. Yet, the appeal of the Republic was more complex than this conventional viewpoint, a spurious by-product of noncomparative studies, suggests. When we view the relationship between the growth of welfare state institutions and the attitudes of working-class movements more comparatively, as we do in Chapter 4, we can see that the attitudes of working-class movements before 1914 had little to do with the material benefits of social reform. The determinants of integration were to be found elsewhere. Most important was whether the dominant political strata acknowledged the legitimacy of workers' aspirations. That legitimacy was recognized by the acceptance of working-class leaders in the governing circle, and especially by the willingness of the middle classes to form coalitions with workers. In practice, the coalition was the key; working-class leaders never had entree to a governing circle in the absence of an interclass coalition. The ineffable correlate of this, insofar as the implied values of national leaders shaped the popular culture, was probably a measure of dignity for workers on a day-to-day basis.

The appeal of the Republic to workers and especially to their leaders was along these lines. It had more to do with the legitimacy it gave to workers' aspirations and to the promise of what could be gained through class collaboration than with the material benefits actually delivered. This was an appeal that could not be duplicated in aliberal societies, where class collaboration was not an option and workers' aspirations were consequently delegitimated. To be sure, considerable evidence suggests this appeal was losing its force in the last years of peace. In all three liberal societies, the patience of workers and their leaders seemed to be wearing thin, and Lib–Lab alliances were unwinding. From the earlier experience of collaboration, however, followed a distinctive set of values and a pattern of trade union organization and vested interests that would endure long after the collaboration had come to an end.

If the ultimate results of collaboration always fell short of socialist hopes for social reform, the alliances nonetheless provided the Socialists with a greater voice than they otherwise would have had and served to enmesh the worker movement, or an important fraction of its leaders, in the Republican order. Indeed, the French Socialists were just about as successful in acquiring legislative power as British Labor was before the war. Neither party, as it happened, had much of a legislative record to boast of before the War.

Labor's principal accomplishment between its formation in 1901 and the war was the repeal of the Taff Vale decision, an accomplishment that merely restored previously established privileges. This was an outcome to which Liberal candidates had to commit themselves to gain local Labor support in the 1906 election. The new Parliament quickly revised Taff Vale in a manner that was satisfactory to Labor. Indeed the Liberal government found that it had to withdraw its own bill and accept Labor's because so many of the Liberal MPs had given Labor's position a complete endorsement during their campaigns. Despite this considerable victory, the Labor party was, as we have seen, of only residual importance in the remaining years before the Great War because of its position of subservience to the Liberal government. It found itself in this position, above all, because of its acute dependence on a coalition of Liberal and Labor voters. The party was aware of this and consequently shaped its electoral policy so as to minimize conflict with Liberals, especially in the two-member constituencies.[54] This relationship of dependence was compounded by the dominance during most of these years of issues tied to the Liberal agenda: free trade, the budget conflict with the House of Lords, and Irish Home Rule. Each of these issues overshadowed Labor's own agenda and simultaneously obliged Labor to sustain the Liberal government. After 1906, Labor could no longer vote against the government without risking its defeat, and therewith the triumph of the House of Lords and the defeat of the budget and Irish Home Rule. The Liberals were aware that Labor would not attempt to turn the government out and argued that all controversial issues had to be postponed until the constitutional crises were resolved.[55]

In principle, Labor had a choice: it could opt to break with the Liberals, pursue a more aggressively socialist line, and consequently accept a much lower level of electoral success. The price of this, beyond the loss of most parliamentary seats, would be the breakup of Labor itself. For it was deeply divided between its reformist trade union majority, committed to collaboration with the Liberals, and its more socialist minority. In its inception, Labor had been a coalition of socialists and trade unionists, and the former had hoped that the creation of the party would serve to wean the unionists from the Liberals. This ultimately occurred, but on terms that were dictated by the trade unionists rather than the socialists. This outcome was predetermined, so to speak, by the availability of Liberal allies. For such allies were irresistible, on the one hand, and able to redefine the constituency on which Labor depended, and therefore its behavior, on the other.

The position of the French Socialists was analogous in certain respects. Socialists provided essential support for the ministries of Léon Bourgeois and Réné Waldeck-Rousseau and then, more important, for the *Bloc de Gauche* that sustained the ministry of Emile Combes between 1902 and 1905. French Radicals, like British Liberals, could argue that the socialist agenda had to be deferred until after the resolution of a great crisis and the accomplishment of an historic task. The great crisis was the Dreyfus Affair, brought to an end by the election of 1902, which provided a great victory for the center-left coalition of moderate Republicans, Radicals, Independents, and Socialists. These four groups, while keeping their individual identities, had formed a *Comité d' Action* in 1901 to fight the election. Together they won thirty-five more seats. With the great crisis defused, the historic mission could be accomplished: the disestablishment of the Church, completed legislatively in 1905 by the Combes ministry.

Combes' ministry was the only one in the prewar Republic to have a firm legislative majority, and this majority was substantially dependent on socialist participation. In 1902 it was, in fact, the *Delegation des Gauches* that took power. This majority was held together by a directorate of party managers. The directorate's origins went back to 1893, when it had begun as a loose combination of groups, but now it took over the leadership of Parliament and organized the majority for Combes. Each member of the directorate represented about ten deputies: seven were Moderates, eight Radicals, six Radical Socialists, and five Socialists. The real leadership came from Jean Jaurès, who repeatedly saved the majority from disintegration. The Socialist leader was elected one of the vice-presidents of the Chamber and, in fact, became the secret "leader of the house."[56] Anticlericalism was, as historians of the Republic remind us, the only policy a group as diverse as the Bloc could agree on, and as soon as disestablishment was legislated, the Bloc fell apart.

The formation of the unified Socialist Party (the SFIO) in 1905 might be construed as the opposite of the British experience, for antiministerialists of the Socialist Party of France (PSdF), consisting of the Guesdists and Blanquists, made withdrawal of support for governments the condition of the merging with the ministerialists of the French Socialist Party (PSF), mainly the Independent Socialists led by Jaurès. It was as if the British socialists had induced the trade unionists to accept their vision of the Labor party. It is true that after 1905, the SFIO remained in opposition to Radical governments. Yet that is not the full story and is somewhat misleading. The similarities between the experiences of the two parties are more significant for our story than the differences. The difference is that British Labor supported a Liberal government after 1905 and accomplished little, while French socialists ceased supporting liberal governments and accomplished little.

The more telling similarity is that interclass electoral coalitions remained vital to the prosperity of both parties. In France collaboration continued apace in electoral coalitions at the constituency level. It is a mistake to dismiss this as an artifact of the two-ballot system. For what ultimately was decisive was not the rules of the game, but the voters' behavior—in particular their willingness to form interclass coalitions. Similar electoral rules existed in Norway and Germany, but it was not possible in those countries to make such interclass coalitions.[57] In France, these coalitions were vital to the growth of the Socialist electorate, and the growth of the electorate was, in turn, vital to the Socialist attitude toward the Republic. The electoral strength of the SFIO increased steadily: in 1906 it had 877,000 votes and fifty-four seats; in 1914 it had 1.4 million votes, nearly 17 percent of the total, and 103 seats, making it the second largest party. Its appeal and base extended far beyond the working class, and its 1914 manifesto appealed to workers, peasants, shopkeepers, artisans, and "all men of sincere conscience who suffer from the moral disorder and economic anarchy of the present society."[58]

Unlike the German SPD, but like British Labor, the SFIO thus neither could have become nor sought to become a countersociety that offered a whole way of life to its members and kept the working class apart from the values of middle-class society. It is highly significant that the usual auxiliary activities, such as women's sections and youth movements, were hardly developed. Such a strategy would have been comparable to the one advocated by British socialists in the Labor party. And just as it would have isolated and undercut a substantially vested party in Britain, it would have done the same in France. The great impact of the liberal allies, and therefore the great success of Republican institutions, was precisely in allowing the tension within the SFIO between the Jaurèsians and the Guesdists to be reconciled—implicitly in favor of the Republic—by the belief that in the near future the growing socialist electorate would give the Socialists real political power peacefully and through Republican institutions.

That this belief created no more than a truce between the two wings of the party, and that a section of the party broke with the Republic and created a communist party after the war, definitely draws a line between the British and French experiences. Yet, again, the difference is less important than the similarity: the emergence of a working class sufficiently accommodated to prewar institutions—and in its trade union organizations sufficiently divided—that the institutions' essential continuity after the war was not threatened. The single most important fact to be explained about interwar France is that, unlike almost all other European societies, it remained a liberal democracy. The radicalization of a part of the working class that the creation of the Communist party represented acquired its greatest importance not in the threat that an isolated party posed to the interwar Republic, but in the further division and weakness it introduced into an already weakly organized and divided working class. Indeed, a cohesively and comprehensively organized but reformist working-class movement would have been a much greater threat to interwar liberalism than the divided and partly radicalized movement that actually emerged.

The Radicals provided an important bridge between workers and the Republic, which merits further scrutiny. The Radicals of the 1880s had actually been divided into two groups, the *Gauche Radicale*, who kept open the links to the conservative Republicans, and the Radical Socialists under Georges Clemenceau. Here socialism implied little more than an interest in the social question, but this in itself was significant. Conservative Republicans had defined liberty and equality in narrowly political terms and "were at a loss when confronted with problems unimagined in 1789."[59] Radicals, in contrast, retained a commitment to state intervention in the economy: they called for a revision of the railway contracts and a progressive income tax. They opposed protectionism because it would raise food prices; they encouraged the formation of trade unions, supported workers in strike actions, condemned the use of the military in strikes, and supported legislation establishing pensions, disability insurance, and health care for indigents and governing hours of work.[60]

There was much in the Radical program that appealed to workers. Indeed, in the 1870s and 1880s, Radicals had won most of their electoral support from urban areas and workers. As Boulangerism detached some workers from Radicalism, the Radical base moved to the countryside and the traditional left-wing areas of the south. As Radicalism's base shifted, its reformist impulses dissipated somewhat, but it was not prepared to write off its working-class constituency without a struggle. It was Léon Bourgeois who provided the Radicals with a new doctrine in his book, *La Solidarité* (1896). Solidarism sought to reconcile liberalism with the need for new social institutions by showing that a just society depended on mutual obligations and on cooperation rather than individualism, and it allowed Radicals to accept social legislation more readily. The crux of the theory was *solidarité,* the mutual dependence that existed among individuals and social classes. *Solidarité* sought to demonstrate that each member of society was indebted to all others. Self-interest and self-preservation required that individuals fulfill "social duties" for one another. "Man living in society and being unable to live without it, is at all times a *debtor* toward society."[61] Thus, as a philosophical doctrine, *solidarité* sought to establish the rationale for a more equitable distribution of the benefits and responsibilities of membership in the national community. As a program of political action, it sought to advance the specific set of social reforms associated with Radicalism.[62]

It was underpinned empirically by interventionism. Interventionism, a research school led by members of the faculties of law at Parisian and provincial universities, was analogous in many respects to the social science that sustained the New Liberalism in Britain.[63] Many of these investigators subsequently became the administrators of the state programs they advocated, and they maintained a close advisory relationship with the more reform-minded radicals in the years between 1900 and 1914. They endorsed the solidarist insurance programs and emphasized that only obligatory legislation could create meaningful security for workers.[64]

Interventionism emphasized the investigation of the problems of workers and the poor and the development of state-sponsored solutions to these problems. Paul Pic, one of the leading interventionists, succinctly summarized both their method and their central focus:

> The problem of the working class is a wage which is sufficient to both support a family and save for the future. This causes the precarious condition of the worker. The remedy is social economy, a science of observation applied to practical realities and possible ameliorations, rather than metaphysical speculations.[65]

Interventionists rejected classical liberal notions of the *liberté de travail,* because they saw an unequal relationship between employers and workers. Strong trade unions, they argued, were the key to equalizing this relationship. They advocated a variety of legislation to strengthen reformist trade unions, regulate labor relations and improve workplace conditions.[66]

Solidarism was the Radical attempt to accommodate workers to the Republic and the Republic to the workers without alienating the middle classes. Like the British Liberal party's New Liberalism, it ultimately failed to hold workers for liberalism. Even so, it demonstrated an awareness of the plight of workers, if not the solutions to that plight. It thereby indicated that the gulf between liberalism and the workers was not nearly as great as it was in, say, Germany. One searches in vain for an equivalent doctrine among German liberals. From solidarism, reformist Socialists, who were most of the Socialists in politics after 1890, inferred that political conflict could not be reduced simply to class conflict. Most important, solidarism sought to emphasize that the Republic was, should be, or could be a set of institutions that stood above narrow class interests. Combined with a steadily increasing Socialist electorate, it made plausible the notion that workers, too, could use the Republican institutions for their own ends. Thus, the Jaurèsian view that the institutions of the Republic could be used to complete the French Revolution in the social sphere.[67]

That the availability of radical allies exercised a powerful influence on the attitudes of workers, trade unions, and Socialist leaders can hardly be doubted. The best indicators of workers' attitudes are to be found in the way they voted and conducted strikes, and we shall turn to these matters presently. More than in most movements, the attitudes of prewar reformist socialism in France can be understood through the attitudes of a leader. For Jaurés, who dominated parliamentary Socialism in these years, the Radical party always "remained an important political ally."[68] Indeed, for Jaurés, cooperation became virtually synonymous with Socialist practice.[69] It was Jaurés' calculation that, once the clerical question was resolved, the Radicals would be forced to give way to a growing Socialist party or accept a great part of the socialist program. As it happened, Radicalism neither gave way nor embraced the Socialist program. Hemmed in by the individualist mentality of its middle-class constituency, repeatedly deflected by the intractable conservatism of the Senate, and frightened by the upsurge of worker protest after the separation of the Church, the Radical party could never provide an effective vanguard of reform, especially of reform along the collectivist lines envisioned by socialism. Instead, it continued to embrace solidarism, a doctrine that cast the state as an ameliorator of inequalities to an extent that would allow the workers to gain the economic independence so dear to the hearts of the middle classes. And even solidarism lived and died at a purely rhetorical level, for Radicals were never able to implement its prerequisite, the graduated income tax, until the exigencies of the war demanded it.[70]

The constituencies of radicalism and socialism partly overlapped, with each drawing support from peasants, the lower middle classes, and workers, albeit not in equal parts. As a result, much of socialism's electoral growth over time came from displacing radicalism in the old Radical strongholds of the center and south. As often as not—and this is instructive of the overlapping constituencies—these socialist successes did not come about because a Socialist candidate defeated an incumbent Radical, but because a Socialist succeeded a retiring Radical. The retirement of the Radical and the absence of a claimant to his local organization provided a Socialist candidate with an opportunity to assume leadership of the constituency.[71]

The consequences of the collaboration cut both ways, shaping the Radical party and its lower middle class and peasant constituency as well. Until the Boulanger Crisis of the eighties, most workers had voted for the Radicals.

And even after Boulangerism had served as the midwife of working-class socialism, the Radicals continued to solicit and receive worker support. This is made clear by voting trends in the heavily working-class *banlieue* ringing Paris, the developing "Red Belt." The demise of Boulangerism left the way open for socialism to supplant radicalism as the leading political force in these peripheral factory towns in Assembly elections. Saint-Denis, Saint-Ouen, Aubervilliers, Puteaux, Suresnes, Ivry Villejuif, Choisy-le-Roi, and Gentilly all sent Socialists to the Chamber of Deputies in the election of 1893. Socialists were able to maintain their hold on most of these seats through the war and gradually extend their successes to other suburban districts. But even in this core of Socialist success, the Socialist position remained tenuous, and Radicals continued to compete with considerable success for workers' votes. Socialist victories were fragile, subject to frequent setbacks, and never based on the overwhelming majorities that Radicals had been able to muster in the first two decades after the Commune. The most evident failure was the Socialists' inability to win municipal elections or to maintain their control over local administrations after scoring temporary victories. The most common theme running through these elections was the workers' predilection to reward pragmatism and reformism, even when that meant turning out Socialist administrations in favor of Radical administrations, something workers did regularly. It was not until 1912 that the SFIO really consolidated its hold on these districts.[72]

> These new Socialist councils of the second decade of the twentieth century were infused with a spirit of sober responsibility and with an eagerness to improve the lives of their constituents. The first Socialist mayor of Puteaux, Lucien Voilin, set the tone by stating that the goal of his administration was to "demonstrate that the proletariat is capable of managing public affairs." Here and in other industrial towns Socialist councilmen addressed the pressing problem of workers' housing with ambitious but financially viable projects. Beyond this, they strove to offer the possibility of more healthful lives to their electors by building public bath houses, sending poor children on vacations in the country, funding anti-tubercular dispensaries, and other such measures. Acts of symbolic defiance were limited to naming streets after Socialist heroes. Thus, socialism consummated its success in the suburbs as an energetic but tame force.[73]

Even as late as the 1910 election, the SFIO faced stiff first-ballot competition in these core areas of the industrial proletariat. Lenard Berlanstein has shown that even under the most optimistic assumptions, outside of Belleville the SFIO received the support of no more than half of the voting workers in these districts. In Belleville, he calculates, it might have received as much as three-quarters of the worker vote. These calculations, however, are based on the improbable assumption that all Socialist votes came from workers and that the rate of abstention among workers was no higher than among the general population. We already know that a large share of the

Socialist vote—at least one-third and possibly one-half nationwide—came from outside the working class. If we relax either or both of Berlanstein's assumptions to say, more realistically but still generously, that three-quarters of the Socialist vote in these districts came from workers, then we can infer that not more than 30 to 40 percent of voting workers in them cast their ballots for Socialists.[74] This low level of worker support, even in such hard-core working–class districts, is revealing of both the ability of Radicals to gain a substantial share of the working-class vote and of the Socialists' ability to reach outside the working class for electoral support.

The distinctiveness of interclass coalitions in France and the other liberal societies will be more apparent when we examine the absence of such coalitions in aliberal societies in Chapter 3. For the moment, a brief comparison with the experience of the German Social Democratic Party (SPD) will help put matters in perspective. The first contrast is provided by the simple fact that the Social Democrats were winning the support of 35 percent of the national electorate just before the war; the SFIO was winning just 17 percent. Given the much larger size of the German industrial proletariat, however, this aggregate figure becomes significant only when we disaggregate the sources of the SPD's support. The more compelling contrast is therefore provided first by the ability of the Social Democrats to mobilize the working-class vote in a run-of-the-mill industrial city—Dortmund—and second by the comparative inability of the Social Democrats to broaden their electoral base on the second ballot. The comparison of voting in Dortmund and the *banlieue* is especially revealing because, unlike the *banlieue* districts, socialist organization came late to Dortmund, and the city never had the importance for German Social Democrats that the *banlieue* had for French Socialists. In effect, while the *banlieue* offered French Socialists one of their most natural areas of success, Dortmund was simply one of many cities with a large number of workers and, for the Social Democrats, was more typical than exceptional. There is no reason to suppose that the SPD did less well among workers in other industrial centers. If anything, they probably did better. Even so, as early as 1903, according to Stanley Suval's investigation, the Social Democrats were gaining 89 percent of the Protestant blue-collar vote and the National Liberals were obtaining 91 percent of the Protestant white-collar vote.[75] The contrast with the French (and British) experiences could hardly be stronger. And as Suval concludes of German voters, "Those loyal to other groupings, particularly to the bourgeois parties, would simply refuse to cross over the line and vote SPD in runoff elections. It was for this reason that the SPD had to win the overwhelming number of its seats in the first election or not win them at all."[76]

Given the basic comparability of the electoral systems in use in the Third Republic and in Wilhelmine elections, the percentage of second ballot victories is especially instructive. It provides us with a crude index of the degree to which socialist parties were able to reach beyond their core constituency and form interclass coalitions. In the last four Reichstag elections before the war, the SPD gained 35 percent of its seats on the second ballot. In the last five elections before the war, the French Socialists won 54 percent of their seats on the second ballot. The figures for the individual years are even more revealing. The two elections in which the French Socialists emphasized their autonomy from the Radicals, 1902 and 1906, resulted in a below-average second ballot performance: 47 and 40 percent, respectively. In the previous and succeeding elections, the figures were 63 (1898), 61 (1910), and 59 (1914) percent, respectively. In contrast, SPD performance was virtually unchanged by shifts in strategy or appeals to liberal voters. When the SPD emphasized its socialism and antimilitarism in 1907, it won 33 percent of its seats on the second ballot. When it tried (unsuccessfully) to make an electoral coalition with the Progressives on the second 1912 ballot, it still won only 36 percent of its seats in the second round.[77]

Weakness of the Labor Movement in Britain and France

In Britain, the coalition with the Liberals was led by the trade unions, who then created a party that reflected their own historical experience. In France, the coalition with the Radicals was pursued by socialist parties, which neither succeeded in creating a union movement nor collaborated closely with the one that did exist, at least not with that part of it that the General Labor Union (CGT) organized after 1895. There was a juncture at which it seemed possible that a close relationship would develop between a working-class party and a trade union movement in France. The first trade union congress, held in 1876, revealed no inclination toward aparliamentarism. The congress doubted the prospects for reforms from the middle classes, but its remedy was that the workers should elect their own representatives to parliament. Slowly, socialist views and notions of class conflict penetrated the unions. This occurred mainly under the influence of Jules Guesde, who sought to build a close relationship between his Party of Socialist Workers (actually established at an 1879 Marseilles trade union congress) and the unions (or at least those in Guesde's Federation of Unions). Had this relationship endured, the result might have been a party whose backbone was, as in Britain, to be found in the unions. As it happened, the wedding was brief, for as Guesde accommodated himself to the Republic and emphasized a curious mix of personal authoritarianism, electoral politics, reformism, and orthodox Marxism, the unions—which had never been much penetrated by Guesde's organization—moved to positions that emphasized, variously, antiparliamentarism, aparliamentarism, syndicalism, and reformism. The final break came in 1892, when the congress of unions approved the doctrine of the general strike and Guesde and his followers walked out.[78] The idiosyncrasies of Guesde aside, the aborted relationship must be understood mainly in terms of the gap between the success of the socialist parties and of the trade unions.

The parties progressed more quickly in politics than the unions did in the labor market, because the parties encountered less tenacious opposition, had a larger potential constituency, and were less affected by the divisions within the working class. If we are to understand the divergent paths of the parties and unions, and thereby the more limited impact of Lib–Labism in France, we must examine the extent of trade union success and the obstacles that the socioeconomic structure of France and the composition of the working class posed for the unions. The point is not simply to decipher the extent to which the French experience approximated our model of the liberal transition, but to understand the extent to which the more marginal Lib–Labism position in the labor market was a product of state repression producing labor alienation or was inherent in the social structure itself.

Let us start by examining the organizational success of union movements in Britain and France. In Britain, notwithstanding the much longer and more thoroughgoing tradition of industrialism, only a minority of the labor force— about 22 percent—belonged to a trade union just before the war.[79] In France, a much less and more unevenly industrialized country, the figure was about 5 percent in the same year.[80] Historians, Marxists and non-Marxists alike, have been inclined to point to the relative weakness of French trade unions as an indicator of the repressiveness of the state and have, in turn, interpreted syndicalism as a measure of labor's alienation from the Republic.[81]

There can be no doubt that trade unions in France were weaker, whether weakness is defined in terms of the population enrolled, organizational coherence, or success in collective bargaining. In only a very small percentage of French strikes did anything resembling face-to-face collective bargaining occur. Instead, an employer would keep posting a new bill of wages and conditions until workers either returned or he could replace them. The common estimate is that, although unions participated in about three-quarters of the strikes between 1898 and 1914, in only about 6 percent of them did unions formally negotiate with employers. Collective agreements were even less frequent. Given the intensity of employer resistance and the consequent existence of unions mainly on the municipal rather than plant level, the role of unions was to "mobilize and direct, not to settle and negotiate."[82] There is no doubt, then, that French unions were weaker. The issues that must be resolved are, first, just how much weaker they were; second, the extent to which syndicalism can be interpreted as a sign of alienation from the Republic; and third, whether this weakness and syndicalism were the result of state policies.

To address the first of these questions, we must start by asking what percentage of the most relevant part of the labor force—industrial workers— was enrolled in trade unions. As a first approximation, because in neither Britain nor France were agricultural trade unions of any significance, we can begin by asking what part of the nonagricultural labor force was in trade unions.[83] In Britain, just before the war, about 92 percent of the labor force was employed outside of the agricultural sector; in France, the equivalent figure was about 57 percent.[84] In effect, then, trade unions in Britain enrolled just over one in four nonagricultural workers; in France, just about one in ten members of the nonagricultural labor force were in trade unions.

These percentages overstate the difference, however, because the industrial structures of the two countries were very dissimilar. France had not only a much smaller industrial and transport sector, but a much larger population of self-employed artisans and tradesmen and a larger tertiary sector. In France, the 1906 census revealed that more than one-third of wage earners were still self-employed.[85] The result was a much smaller industrial proletariat. The importance of disaggregating the figures becomes especially clear if we focus on the social core of the trade union movement: the male industrial proletariat. In France, this population amounted to about 3.6 million people in a total labor force of about 20 million; in Britain to about 9.5 million in a total labor force of just over 18 million.[86] These figures make clear just how different the socioeconomic structures of the two countries were.

In Britain, of the 4 million trade unionists, about 10 percent were women, leaving a residual of about 3.6 million male trade unionists. This amounted to 38 percent of the male industrial labor force. We cannot be as confident of the percentage of female trade unionists in France, except that it was extremely small.[87] If we assume it was comparable to the British share, 10 percent, we have 900,000 male trade unionists in France, or 25 percent of the male industrial labor force. In sum, when we disaggregate the numbers and examine the extent of union membership among the prewar union movement's core constituency, male industrial workers, we find the difference in rate of union membership is still marked—38 percent versus 25 percent—but is much less than that implied by the aggregate labor force figures. The aggregate data suggested that the ratio of trade union enrollment was on the order of 4.3 to 1; disaggregation reduces the ratio to about 1.5 to 1.

This difference appears less marked still when we take into account the comparatively small size of French firms. In 1906, the average French workplace employed fewer than 10 workers; indeed, 60 percent of French workers were employed by firms with fewer than 10 workers. Just 20 percent were employed by firms with more than 500 workers; only 12 percent were employed in firms with more than 1,000 workers.[88] No comparable data exist for Britain, but among economic historians there seems to be little doubt that the level of concentration was substantially higher in Britain and of a less recent vintage.[89] Large-scale factory employment did not begin to overshadow small-scale production in France until about 1890. This point had already been reached in Britain about a half-century earlier. The scale of employment was important because, as a general rule, in the prewar period unionization advanced more rapidly in large units of production than in smaller ones.[90] All other things being equal (especially skill level), the organization of small firms was more difficult because the relationship between the employer and worker was a more personalized and informal one and control of the labor supply was more difficult in an atomized labor market.[91]

Another way to approach the matter is to focus on the concentration of labor geographically rather than by firm. All other things again being equal, we should expect that a higher level of urbanization and concentration of population would be more supportive of organization. In the decades before the war, France became not so much an industrial country as a rural country with major industrial areas. Up to the war, most Frenchmen continued to live in a village or small town rather than an industrial conurbation. By 1911, France had only sixteen towns with over 100,000 inhabitants; Britain had thirty-five.[92] While 62 percent of the population of England lived in towns of over 10,000 by about 1890, only about 26 percent of the French population did so.[93] In effect, then, higher concentrations of labor within firms and cities over a more extended period of time should have created a more congenial climate for labor organization in Britain.

A further fundamental difference in the two national experiences must be taken into account if we are to comprehend the level of unionization in France. In Britain the industrial proletariat of the half-century before the war was recruited from an already existing proletariat and from the artisan community. In France, although no precise data are available to us, historians seem to agree that it came in large measure from the peasantry. Theodore Zeldin, for instance, stresses the agrarian origins of "a large proportion" of the workers in mining and manufacturing in the 1890s.[94] The origins of the workers varied from industry to industry. Metal workers, textile workers, and glass makers were almost always the sons and daughters of industrial workers. Tony Judt has pointed out that the mine workers at Carmaux, at La Machine in the Niévre, and in Commentry, for example, were drawn overwhelmingly from the local peasant community.[95] So were many of the workers in such old industrial regions as the area around Thiers, "where in 1894 the workers preferred 'their liberty' [to work the fields] to higher wages, and the bosses had to resign themselves to this attitude."[96] At the beginning of the Republic, half of the workers in the Parisian building trades were migratory peasants.[97] Much small industry—especially brick making, tanning, porcelain factories, quarries, and tile works—was scattered in rural areas, and workers moved back and forth from industry to the fields. The peasant origin of these workers was important in several ways. Most broadly, it created a much more heterogeneous working class, one that was correspondingly more difficult to organize.

As late as the First World War, . . . particularism was still exhibited by such migrant workers as the glaziers from the Val Soana in Savoy, who lived all together in "tight and homogeneous" communities, speaking a special jargon that not even Savoyards could understand. Such "tight homogeneous" communities resulted in Parisian ghettos of immigrants from certain regions: Auvergnats clustered around the Rue de la Roquette in the eleventh arrondissement, Bretons around the west-country railway terminal at Montparnasse in the fourteenth and fifteenth arrondissements, Alsatians around La Villette to the northeast, in the nineteenth arrondissement.[98]

Above all, peasants were more likely than workers from industrial or artisan backgrounds to see work in the mines or factory as temporary and as an improvement over their previous situation. For, "though people such as these came to the city for months or even years, their eyes remained fixed on the home society. . . . Their work did not insert them into the urban realm . . . but screwed them more firmly into the limited world of the parish, family and culture of their birth."[99] As a result, they were less inclined than workers with industrial or artisan origins to be attracted to trade unions. According to one investigation conducted by a doctor in the Tarn, what these workers sought by migrating to urban industry were higher wages, more regular work throughout the year, insurance against illness, and a pension.[100]

These were advantages more readily available in industry than agriculture. The newly arrived peasant was less worldly, less well educated, less likely to see the world in terms of class conflict, and more optimistic—his own progress confirmed the value of hard work and frugality—and he had a smaller family to support.[101] Factory or mine work was a temporary stop, a way to increase one's income and savings before returning to the countryside. For such workers, leaving the country did not mean leaving the old values and way of life. Miners in Carmaux—heavily recruited from the countryside—for instance, were likely to keep working a small piece of land. Forty-four percent still owned a piece of land at the end of the century. When their hours of labor in the mines were reduced by law, they increased the time they devoted to their land, working half of a peasant's day. They viewed their wages from the mines as a means to buy the things they could not produce for themselves. The amounts they could save from their wages were enough to buy a piece of land or a house. This was often combined with a small inheritance or dowry. These peasant workers were loathe to borrow money from their employers, and preferred to take mortgages from private lenders at higher rates. This same independence was reflected in their distrust of unions and detestation of union subscriptions. The sums they could dispose of were miniscule but sufficient to differentiate them from workers from artisanal and industrial backgrounds, and sufficient, when reinforced by their distinct values, to drive a wedge between themselves and such workers. These peasant workers, seeing industrial labor as a temporary improvement in their situation, were much less likely to embrace unionization or see any common interests with those from other backgrounds. This situation gradually changed as workers with peasant origins concluded that they were not going to be able to leave the industrial work force. Industrial life was eventually the great homogenizer. But until this occurred, the outlook of these workers and the heterogeneity they introduced into the working class inhibited unionization.[102]

The continued ties to a rural way of life, the consequently greater heterogeneity of the working class, the smaller size of the proletariat and of the typical workplace, and the smaller number of great industrial cities go some distance—although it is difficult to know exactly how far—in accounting for the lower level of unionization in France. The minimum conclusion we can safely reach is that it would be surprising indeed, in light of these differences, if the level of unionization in France had been close to that in Britain. These differences also compel us to view with a critical eye explanations for the low level of unionization couched in terms of a repressive Republic.

The received wisdom in the historiography of French labor, much of which is found in even the recent revisionist studies of syndicalism, runs like this: The experience of the Commune weakened the position of the French labor aristocracy—the more skilled craft workers—thus removing them as a conserving force within the working class. French employers, for various reasons—economic, political, cultural, according to the author at hand— were much less accepting of unionization than their British counterparts; the French state was more likely to intervene, sometimes violently, on behalf of employers. Contracts were simply implicit or oral agreements and no more than a truce, to be broken by either workers or employers as the opportunity arose. French unions, because of employer resistance, were small, decentralized, weak on the shop floor, impoverished, and unable to sustain extended strikes. In frustration, workers turned to syndicalism and its revolutionary utopianism, a doctrine that provided hope where organizational efforts could not. Marxist scholars, especially, have portrayed the Republican state as the tool of employers, ever ready to put down worker movements that threatened profitability.[103]

There are certainly elements of reality in this traditional portrait, but without serious qualification, it becomes merely a caricature. Several points need to be emphasized. First, the success of unions in Britain, although comparatively greater than elsewhere in these years, was, as we have seen, far from complete. Further, given the longer and more uniform experience of industrialization in Britain, we would expect a higher level of union organization there. Also, this level did not come without a measure of violence. If it appears to have, it is only because we have begun our story after the repression of the years from 1789 to 1830 and the violence of the Chartist period. Second, an undue focus on the CGT exaggerates the impact of syndicalism;

an exaggerated concern with syndicalism results in an overstatement of the degree to which workers rejected the Republic. Many unions did not belong to the CGT, and most of those that did were not revolutionary.[104] Third, there is indeed compelling evidence that most workers not only did not reject the Republic, but saw it as their main ally in the battles with employers. Let us take up these latter points in turn.

It is difficult to know with confidence what workers meant when they declared themselves syndicalists. We do know from the testimonies collected by Felicien Challaye that for many workers, to be a syndicalist implied little that was revolutionary. Instead, the notion harkened back to the traditional artisanal ideals of independence and dignity and production associations as a means of achieving this.[105] For an important number of other workers, however, syndicalism did have a revolutionary meaning. The essence of revolutionary syndicalism was a joining of socialist notions of class conflict and rejection of capitalism with an anarchistic commitment to direct action, the strike, and the destruction of state authority. After the revolution, capitalism would be superseded by worker control. Syndicalists were less sanguine than socialists about either the propensity of capitalism to collapse from its own contradictions or the prospects for reforming it through parliamentary means. Syndicalists also differed from socialists in their conviction that there was no point in waiting for the support of the majority of the working class. Syndicalism was, rather, a doctrine that justified the revolutionary claims of minorities.[106]

The CGT embraced syndicalism vigorously. Its constituent trade unions, however, did not necessarily do so. This paradox was an artifact of the CGT's voting system. Every union in the Confederation had a single vote, regardless of its size. The small unions, which tended to be revolutionary precisely because their small size deprived them of any opportunity to improve their members' conditions, thus controlled the CGT. This point cannot be stated too emphatically, for the six smallest unions, with a total membership of only twenty-seven, had the same voting rights as the six largest, which had about 90,000 members.[107] According to Challaye, unions representing as few as 45,000 members (23 percent of the 1906 membership) were sufficient to produce majorities on all CGT questions because of the large number of small unions to which these members belonged.[108] As it was, the executive committee controlled about one-third of the votes, which were yielded to it by unions so small they could not afford to send a delegate to national congresses. It is difficult to escape the conclusion that the behavior and especially the rhetoric of the CGT are a poor guide to the actual preferences of the unions.

A majority of the unions in the CGT were either *revolutionary reformists* or *reformist syndicalists* or they were not syndicalists at all. Revolutionary reformists saw social reforms as the means to bring about the revolution. They called themselves revolutionaries, but explained that this meant simply that "every reform which snatches a piece of capital or a piece of authority from the employer, to give it to the worker, is a revolutionary reform . . . we are revolutionaries because we have proved that historically the Revolution is destined to take place."[109] The reformist syndicalists, too, embraced the ultimate aims of syndicalism—an economy based on workers' cooperatives—but rejected the use of strikes or revolutionary means to obtain this end. These unions concentrated on immediate practical reforms and the building of coherent, comprehensive organizations for the purposes of collective bargaining. They were not antiparliamentary, but aparliamentary. They disdained a close relationship with a political party because they thought the way to recruit new members was first to respect their varying political beliefs, whether syndicalist, socialist, radical, or apolitical. There was, after all, little alternative, given the political and cultural heterogeneity of the working class. Reformists, revolutionary or otherwise, insisted that strikes should be used only as a last resort, should be aimed at the immediate material needs of workers, and should be used only after affected workers had been polled. The general rule was that smaller unions in the CGT, because they were less effective, were more likely to be revolutionary. This was not an ironclad rule, however. Some of the larger federations were normally reformist but periodically adopted revolutionary language. Among these were the miners and railwaymen. Other workers, in printing and textiles, for instance, were consistently reformist, while still others, in the building trades and metal works, were consistently revolutionary.

Undue attention to the larger national confederations or even the unions in the CGT, however, is quite misleading. This is in the first place because most unions were part of neither a confederation nor the CGT. In 1912, there were more than 5,000 local and provincial trade unions in France, with average membership of only about 100. Outside of Paris and the Nord, their character was hardly that of trade unions at all; it was more one of fraternal clubs or even traditional guilds. In backward provinces like Ardéche, not a single union belonged to the CGT. In such areas, the purpose of unions was not to fight employers, but to limit competition among them and restrict the supply of apprentices.[110] Their attitude toward the CGT was likely to be one of indifference or revulsion. Indeed, historians have long observed that one of the most potent obstacles to prewar unionization was syndicalism itself, a doctrine much of the working class viewed with disdain.[111]

Undue attention to the national federations is misleading in the second place because the federations, whatever their political orientation, were dominated by a handful of activists. It is typical that the reformist secretary of the federation of miners in the Nord and Pas-de-Calais, Emile Basly, repeatedly ignored referenda in 1901 and 1902 that endorsed a strike because only a minority of the unionized miners even bothered to vote. Rarely did a ballot or meeting of any union attract the participation of a majority of members. This, of course, was not a uniquely French situation. We have numerous reports of the low level of interest in union activities among British workers.[112] But if French workers shared with British workers all the usual reasons for inactivity in the unions, they had an additional and more compelling one: the unions, as we shall see, contributed almost nothing to the probability that a strike would be successful. The safest generalization that can be made is that most union members did not care most of the time what the handful of activists who ran the union did until it adversely impinged on their lives. It is typical that in 1909, when the Senate finally passed a law establishing pensions for railwaymen, the reformist leader of the union, Guérard, was forced to resign because of provisions in the new law that the members found unacceptable. Leadership passed to radicals who promptly called a strike. The strike was a disaster, and so the members responded by deposing the radicals and restoring Guérard.[113]

That most union members cared so little what their unions did most of the time is instructive, for it suggests that even among organized workers, the unions were not seen to be very important organizations. This is indeed borne out by the inability of unions to lead strikes more effectively than workers who called their own strikes. We know from data collected by Peter Stearns that in the decade before the war, unions negotiated only a very small percentage of strikes, at most 12.4 percent in 1905 and as few as 2.1 percent in 1912. Furthermore, the rate of strike failure for strikes involving unions was virtually identical to the rate for strikes that did not involve unions.[114] In other words, workers were discovering that unionization was not improving their ability to strike successfully. In this context, it is hardly surprising that the membership rate was low and that workers had only a very limited willingness to pay union subscriptions. Of course, a vicious circle was at work here: unwillingness to pay resulted in the unions' inability to increase strike effectiveness. As we shall see, however, there was a rational solution to this dilemma—one that both obviated the need for a higher level of organization and increased the probability of strike success in the face of tenacious employer resistance: to induce state intervention.

However unions identified themselves ideologically, we know that revolutionary syndicalism had nothing to do with their strike demands. Stearns has demonstrated that both syndicalist and nonsyndicalist unions expressed the same overwhelmingly material strike demands.[115] It is pushing the data too far to conclude, as Stearns has, that the consistent absence of political demands demonstrates the syndicalist vision had no meaning for the rank and file. Workers might well have taken seriously that vision of an ideal world. But even if they did, it makes little sense, in the absence of political aims, to suppose that workers either rejected the Republic or were striking against it. Given the growth of the Socialist vote, it makes at least as much sense to suppose that workers saw the democratic institutions of the Republic as the means to that ideal world. In any event, the absence of articulated political aims clearly cannot be attributed to a repressive state, because workers challenging states vastly more repressive than the Third Republic were able to articulate political demands when they cared to. The general strikes in Belgium, Spain, and Russia come readily to mind.

This is not to say that workers' attitudes toward the Republic played no role in strikes. Charles Tilly and Edward Shorter have stressed the relationship between strike waves and political change. It is plausible to infer that political change was associated with increased strike activity because change raised workers' expectations of state assistance. The periods of political change that were associated with increased strikes were periods in which governments emerged that workers expected to be *more* sympathetic to their causes. The years of upsurge of strike activity were years in which Socialists either supported governments (1900, 1902, 1904, 1905, 1906), or a government appeared that workers mistakenly expected to be especially sympathetic (Clemenceau's in 1906; Clemenceau had previously had a reputation as the workers' friend), or in which tight labor markets favored strike activity (1910).[116]

These two findings—that political demands were absent and that strikes were correlated with favorable political change—seem to suggest precisely such a conclusion. Certainly nothing in these years suggested a more vulnerable or provocative state, a condition that should have obtained if political change was inducing workers on these occasions to strike *against* the state. The only partial exception to this is the hard line on disruptions of public order taken by Clemenceau's government in 1906 and 1907, and that provocation *followed* the upsurge of strikes. The only conclusion consistent with the absence of political demands, the association with political change and the absence of a vulnerable or provocative state, seems to be that politics did indeed matter, but in the sense that workers were more likely to strike when they thought the state would come to their aid.

Indeed, the evidence that workers perceived the Republic as an important ally in their battles with employers and that it actually played this role is compelling. Along with Peter Stearns, the most important empirical research that sheds light on this is again that of Shorter and Tilly. They stress that their "strike data suggest that the government's main preoccupation in labor relations was the preservation of public order, rather than the strangulation of working-class political movements. And the maintenance of order, like a two-edged sword, could work against the interests of those demanding repression just as against those creating disorder."[117] They have concluded that French strikes were short, dramatic, and demonstrative precisely because strikers wanted state intervention, and that strikers had a "fundamentally favorable attitude to the state."[118]

That strikers had such an attitude should hardly be a surprise, given that state intervention was their most powerful weapon against employers. This intervention could occur either through the mediation service provided by justices of the peace (JPs) or through the intervention of regular functionaries from the town mayor up to a minister. Between 1900 and 1914, JPs mediated about 25 percent of strikes; higher officials mediated an additional percentage. A JP's intervention could occur on his own initiative or at the request of workers or employers. In almost half of these cases (48.3 percent) the mediation was requested by the workers. In another 46 percent of the cases, it was initiated by the JP himself. It is instructive that employers almost never requested this mediation and that 85 percent of the rejections of a JP's services came from employers. That workers would welcome the intervention of the JP or a higher functionary is clear enough: he decided about three-quarters of the cases in favor of the workers. The intervention of higher officials was about equally favorable to workers. In the period 1895 to 1898, only 49 percent of strikes succeeded or ended in a compromise when the state did not intervene. With state intervention, the rate of success or compromise rose dramatically to 87 percent. In the period between 1910 and 1914, success or compromise occurred in 91 percent of the cases of intervention and in only 48 percent of the cases without it.[119] As we noted earlier, the participation of a union in a strike made no difference in the rate of success or compromise. But the state's intervention made an enormous difference. Workers were, in effect, learning that it made little sense to expend much time and money on elaborate organization; it was more effective to strike in a fashion that was highly visible and dramatic and thereby induced state intervention.

Shorter and Tilly make the following conclusion:

> The chief implication of these findings is to explode a myth in the historiography of the French labor movement. The myth is that the government invariably repressed strikes, bringing wherever possible the power of the state against worker militants on behalf of employers. Our data show that the government stepped into a strike reluctantly, but that when it did so, it acted to moderate employer repressiveness and to restore industrial peace to a region by pressuring both sides for compromise. The strikers, conscious of how meager their strength was in the face of employer power, were eager to compromise so as to gain at least some of their demands. The employers were reluctant to give in at all, and so from the government's viewpoint, the nut to crack in a strike was the employer, not the union.[120]

We cannot say with any precision how much of the lower level of unionization in France must be attributed to the greater rate of recruitment of industrial workers from the peasantry, the greater heterogeneity of the proletariat, its smaller size, the lower level of urbanization, and the smaller size of French workplaces. The only safe conclusion is that it would have been surprising if the level of unionization had been close to the British level. In many of these socioeconomic aspects, the French experience was actually more comparable to much of the continental experience than to the British. Holding the political situation constant, we would certainly expect that, in view of the socioeconomic conditions, the rate of unionization would be lower in France than in Britain. All of the socioeconomic variables point to this. The much higher unionization rates in aliberal societies with similar socioeconomic conditions to France, and France's lower level of unionization compared with Britain, which is politically similar and socioeconomically distinct, suggests that the differences between France and its aliberal neighbors must be accounted for politically while those between France and Britain were substantially, although not entirely, due to socioeconomic differences.

Switzerland

The weakness of the trade union movement in prewar Switzerland, in a political context that was, by the standards of those years, remarkably open to working-class influence, further confirms the importance of socioeconomic rather than political differences in accounting for levels of union density among liberal societies, for Switzerland had a level of trade union enrollment even lower than France's. Only 15 percent of Switzerland's male industrial workers were enrolled in the Schweizerisches Gewerkschaftsbund (SGB) around 1910.[121] Even this figure is an exaggeration, because fully half of the SGB members in the years before the war were foreign workers. Such workers constituted about 26 percent of the industrial labor force.[122] In effect, among Swiss citizens, the fraction of the male industrial proletariat in the SGB was only about 10 percent. That is less than half of the comparable figure for France.[123]

Industry's ties to agricultural employment were even more intimate in Switzerland, where rural property ownership was especially widespread and most industry was found adjacent to hydroelectric power in rural valleys. Switzerland was more industrialized than France—just 26 percent of the labor force was engaged solely in agriculture by 1910—but not more urbanized. As in France, only 26 percent of the population lived in towns of more than 10,000 inhabitants.[124] No major industrial centers were comparable to those found in England or northern France. A large fraction of the industrial labor force combined agricultural and industrial employment or supplemented the latter with a family plot. An additional large fraction of the labor force was tied to industry only by home work, especially in textiles.[125]

Trade unions enjoyed a less secure position in Switzerland than in Britain, and in some ways they were probably even worse off than their French counterparts. They enrolled a much smaller share of the industrial labor force than unions in either of the other two liberal societies. They were better organized, at least among skilled workers, than the French unions, but less well organized than the British. If part of their weakness must be attributed to Switzerland's socioeconomic circumstances, another fraction is probably accounted for (although little research is available to help us) by the cleavage between national and foreign workers. Foreign workers probably constituted close to half of the unskilled industrial labor force, made up about half of the trade union membership, and were entirely disenfranchised politically. Among the foreign attributes they brought with them were the ideologies of French and Italian syndicalism and German bureaucracy. None of these appear to have been much appreciated by skilled Swiss workers.[126]

Among the better organized skilled workers—especially in typography, clock and watch making, and later the metal trades—Swiss workers predominated. Along with construction, in which foreign workers predominated, these were almost the only industries in which trade unions were important before the war. In 1896, when the SGB had only about 9,200 workers, 4,700 of these were watch makers.[127] In other industries, textiles for example, trade union enrollment was miniscule.[128]

Among skilled Swiss workers, traditions of collective bargaining stretched back to the 1850s and, although strikes were well known, the unions functioned as much as professional interest groups as agents of class conflict.[129] It was typical of the petit bourgeois attitudes of these workers that in 1899, when a compulsory accident and sickness insurance law was put to a referendum, it was vigorously opposed by the workers' cooperative insurance funds. Only when health insurance was made optional and cooperatives were made eligible for subsidies could the law overcome the opposition of the workers' own organizations.[130] Until the final years of the century, the main political and economic organization of Swiss workers was the Grütliverein, actually a component of the Radicals' *Volksverein*. The main tenet of the Grütli was that workers must be improved through education and other forms of self-help. The Grütliverein long envisioned a society with harmony and cooperation among the classes. These ideas died hard, and as late as the turn of the century, the Grütli served as an important organizational bridge between the middle and working classes.[131] For a long time, until at least the turn of the century, the unions in which the Swiss workers predominated were sympathetic to the liberals and received their political support.[132] They were probably in less need of political support than French workers precisely because their concentration in skilled positions in small shops gave them more leverage.

The unions of these workers were overwhelmingly local in their orientation, and such impetus as there was to broader collaboration came more often from a need to work together in referenda campaigns than from a desire to create a united front against employers.[133] It was typical of this localist orientation that the national confederation, the SGB, which was established as a highly centralized organization with practically no members, lost all of its authority as it gained members.[134]

Nowhere in Europe was the hegemony of liberals more complete than in Switzerland. The victory of anticlerical liberals over conservative Catholics in the Sonderbund War of 1848 was overwhelming and allowed them to establish a new, more centralized, and substantially secularized political order. The new constitution provided for nearly complete manhood suffrage as well as the right to bargain collectively, to strike, and to wage economic boycotts. Between 1848 and 1919, just three nonliberals were permitted to sit on the Federal Council, the national executive body.[135] After 1878, dominance passed decisively from the old liberals to their more anticlerical, reformist, and centralizing successors, the Radicals. The Radicals completed the process of secularization by legalizing civil marriage, confirming the supremacy of civil authority, excluding the churches from public education, and abolishing ecclesiastical jurisdictions.[136]

During the decades before the world war, the Radicals and their various offspring, principally the Radical Democrats and Democrats, never received less than 50 percent of the popular vote. The plurality electoral system translated this support into almost total control of the state. It was first within the Radical fold and then in alliance with it that workers were organized in politics. The Radicals were probably Europe's first genuine *volkspartei*, drawing their support broadly from all language communities, urban and rural areas, the middle classes, and workers. Even a fraction of the Catholic minority came to support the Radicals.[137] The plasticity of the Radicals was aided by the fact that it was not a truly centralized national party; rather it was more an alliance of cantonal parties that came together in the national legislature. It was at the cantonal level that electoral alliances were made. They were made, according to local circumstances, with workers, with Conservative Liberals, and even with Catholics.[138]

Given the limited competence of the federal government in social and economic matters, much of the cooperation between Radicals and workers and many of the social reforms to which workers aspired were implemented at the cantonal level. This was especially the case in such industrialized cantons as Glarus. It was typical that the 1864 factory laws in Glarus became the model for similar laws in other cantons and for the 1877 federal laws.[139] Social insurance legislation followed the same pattern, with the first laws being enacted in Zurich in the 1850s and then in Basel-Stadt and Lucerne in the 1870s.[140]

The cantonal definition of the parties helped ensure that linguistic differences would not be projected onto the national political stage. Throughout the prewar years, the Radicals always allotted two of the seven seats on the Federal Council to members of the minority French or Italian language communities. It is worth emphasizing, however, that the more fundamental solution to linguistic heterogeneity had already been arrived at long before the transition to mass politics and inhered in the centuries-old federalism of Switzerland. In practice, language differences did not generate significant political conflicts in the nineteenth century, and certainly did not generate lines of conflict along which mass politics were organized. Rather the central divide was between the forces of clericalism and anticlericalism, and these sentiments transcended linguistic differences.

While the binding force of the Radical coalition was anticlericalism, the Radicals contributed to the coalition's durability by their masterful ability to mediate the conflicting interests of their constituents, especially those between workers and industrialists. In an ad hoc fashion reminiscent of British Liberals, although less extensive, Swiss Radicals sustained not only a legal code and political climate comparatively favorable to trade unions, but also enacted legislation providing for factory inspections, restrictions on child labor, voluntary sickness insurance and compulsory industrial accident insurance, established strike arbitration facilities, and made collectively negotiated contracts legally enforceable.[141]

Until 1900 Switzerland had no independent working-class movement worth mentioning. The largest workers' movement remained the liberal-oriented Grütliverein. In 1890, the Grütliverein had about 16,000 members to the young Social Democratic party's 2,000. Over the next decade, cooperation between the Grütlianer and the Social Democrats grew. In 1892, the Grütliverein adopted an electoral platform with social democracy as its goal, although its members rejected a move to merge the two organizations. That merger came a decade later, at a time when membership in the two was about equal.

It was indicative of the political heterogeneity of the Swiss working class that the SGB was unwilling to cooperate formally with the Social Democratic party until 1908.[142] The most compelling evidence of the weakness of class-consciousness among Swiss workers in the prewar years is provided by the low level of electoral support that the Social Democratic party received among them. This was in spite of the fact that the prewar socialism of Swiss Social Democracy was of a diluted sort; the emphasis of the party was always more on democracy than on socialism. As Peter Bieler, the biographer of party founder Albert Streck, aptly characterized it, the party was "the extension of the Radicals to the fourth estate."[143] Until 1904, its program was essentially identical to that of the Radical Democrats, with whom it cooperated electorally and in the National Council in a reformist alliance known as the *Social Political Group*. It was only in 1904 that the party formally adopted Marxism and assumed a more explicitly class-oriented attitude. This move to the left was driven principally by the underrepresentation of the Social Democrats in the National Council, a consequence of the plurality system, and by the acceptance for the first time of the disenfranchised and more radicalized foreign workers into the party.[144]

In the final decade of peace, the Social Democratic party acquired impressive popular support, receiving 20 percent of the popular vote in the 1911 election.[145] It is important to note, however, that this success was vitally dependent on electoral alliances with liberals. Without those alliances, its

share of the vote fell to just 10 percent in 1914.[146] Most of the Social
Democratic vote probably did not even come from workers, the majority of
whom probably continued to vote for some variety of a liberal—Radical,
Radical Democrat, or Democrat—until the war. Little direct data are available on the composition of the social democratic electorate of the prewar
years, but a few elementary inferences that point to its mixed-class composition are possible. In 1911, the Social Democrats received just over 80,000
votes.[147] According to the 1910 census, there were just over 400,000 male
adult Swiss industrial workers. Voter turnout, as a percentage of the adult
male Swiss population, was 48 percent. Erich Gruner has found that the
turnout was only slightly above average in both cities of more than 10,000
inhabitants and in industrial areas, regions in which the Social Democrats did
their best.[148] We can thus infer that the Social Democrats could not have
been receiving much more than 40 percent of the working-class vote even if
only workers voted for Socialists.

In fact, most of the votes Socialists received were probably not even cast
by workers. One way to infer this is to look at the dependence of Social
Democratic candidates on alliances with liberal groups. Before 1919, legislators were elected from multimember districts by absolute majorities, with
runoff elections when necessary. Political parties presented lists of candidates
in each district. Joint lists were especially common in runoff elections, but
alliances on the first ballot also occurred. Between 1899 and 1911, the Social
Democrats advanced 146 first ballot candidates not endorsed by a liberal
group. Just nine of these candidates, or 6 percent, were victorious. Another
thirty-two first-ballot candidates received liberal endorsements. Of these,
twelve, or 31 percent, were successful. On runoff ballots, only 13 percent of
the Socialist candidates were successful without a Liberal endorsement. With
such an endorsement, 73 percent of the candidates were successful. Combining first- and second-ballot candidacies, we find that Socialists were successful just 7 percent of the time without endorsements, but 49 percent of the
time with them. In sum, 70 percent of the Socialist seats in the National
Council were won with the endorsement of another party. Put another way,
the Socialist candidate was five times more likely to win if endorsed by a
Liberal electoral group.[149] It was typical of this dependence that, in 1905,
when the language of class conflict had a central place in the election and
alliances were suspended, the Social Democrats won just two seats, compared to their previous and subsequent seven, even as their share of the vote
rose from 12 to 14 percent.[150]

Epilogue

In Switzerland, the coalition with the Radicals was led by a social democratic
party, one that collaborated closely with the principal trade union confedera-

tion, the Schweizerisches Gewerkschaftsbund, after 1908. In Britain, the coalition with the Liberals was led by the trade unions, which then created a party that reflected their own historical experience and maintained the coalition up to the outbreak of the war. In France, the coalition with the Radicals was of a shorter duration and was pursued by socialist parties, who neither succeeded in creating a union movement nor collaborated closely with the one that did exist, at least not with that part of it organized by the CGT. Moreover, the unions, although generally supported by the Radicals, never developed a close relationship with them in the manner that the British unions did with the Liberals. The briefer coalition between Socialism and Liberalism, the less constraining relationship between Socialists and trade unions, and the withdrawal of the unions from partisan politics all point to a mixture of socioeconomic differences and the weaker influence of the interclass coalition on the formation of the French working-class movement than occurred in Britain or even Switzerland. To this extent, there was indeed a political difference between Britain and France and there is no doubt that the French working class was less fully integrated than those of Britain or Switzerland before 1914. This lower level of citizenship, especially economic, was in turn responsible for the more radical orientation of a fraction of the working-class movement that emerged in France before 1914. We must keep this radicalism in perspective, however. It was a radicalism of a minority of the labor movement; revolutionary syndicalism, after all, was quintessentially the ideology of ineffective minorities. Judging by the behavior of working-class voters, the Socialist party, and the trade unions, most workers apparently did accept the Republic. And in winning this acceptance, the collaboration with liberalism and the successes it generated for both the Socialist party and, indirectly, the trade unions were critical. In this respect the political differences among Britain, Switzerland, and France were differences in degree rather than kind, whereas those between these three societies and aliberal societies were, as we shall see, differences in kind.

The working-class movements that emerged before the war in the liberal societies were inextricably entwined in interclass coalitions with politically hegemonic liberal movements. These coalitions, which had no parallel in aliberal societies, were apparent in the behavior of parties, voters, and trade unions. In all three countries, again without parallel in aliberal societies, this coalition induced the growth of a powerful liberal reform current among politically powerful liberals. Liberals who held the keys to national political power acknowledged the legitimacy of workers' aspirations and brought working-class leaders into the national governing circle. Materially satisfying those aspirations was another matter, one that obviously became more pressing in the final years of peace. Nonetheless, in all three countries, workers were sufficiently accommodated by liberals that their movements were characterized by substantial acceptance of the political and economic order and a level of class consciousness before the war that was strikingly low by the standards of aliberal societies. Working-class movements in each case, although more completely in Britain and Switzerland, concluded from their experiences that the established political institutions were sufficiently flexible that growing worker parties could use them to their own ends. Moreover, as we shall now begin to see, in all three countries the prewar trade unions encountered climates sufficiently benign that they had little incentive to create coherent organizations with centralized leadership. In this, they embarked on a trajectory profoundly different from that followed by trade unions in aliberal societies. In the end, after the class awakening that Swiss, French, and British workers experienced as a result of the deprivations of war, it would be this absence of class coherence and leadership that would be decisive in crippling these movements during the interwar years.

3

Cleavage Structures and the Failure of Liberal Movements in Late Nineteenth-Century Europe

Societies that became social democracies or fascist dictatorships between the world wars were distinguished from Britain, France, and Switzerland by the failure of their prewar experiments with Lib–Labism. The failure of Lib–Labism was rooted in the failure of liberalism itself. Liberalism's failure derived from its inability to rally sufficient middle-class support. The critical question is why the middle classes were less supportive of liberal parties in most European countries than they were in Britain, France, and Switzerland. To put the question in a more tractable form, we will ask why liberal parties in most of Europe were less effective in establishing their dominance—that is, in surmounting the obstacles to an extended run of society-shaping political power in the years before 1914.

For such parties, gaining dominance required the establishment of parliamentary sovereignty, where it was not inherited, and the creation of an adequate mass base within the middle classes. The latter was, of course, often the key to the former. Indeed, if a liberal movement could not establish such a base, it would, as in Denmark in the 1860s and in Germany in the 1870s, lose its interest in advancing the authority of the legislature. By examining the specific historical moments at which liberal parties failed to establish parliamentary sovereignty or an adequate electoral base among the middle classes, we will develop a better understanding of the forces that handicapped them.

Moreover, since we are interested in a liberal dominance that was led by the urban wing of the party—as it always was where liberals established their dominance—we focus particularly on the fate of this part of the liberal movement.

The lack of liberal dominance was crucial to the pattern of working-class mobilization and organization that followed, that is, for class formation. Workers could pursue their political and economic interests in only two ways: through an alliance with reforming liberals or through self-organization. The balance between the two routes workers followed was contingent on the availability of a politically effective liberal ally. The pattern of class formation in turn had essential consequences for the later course of interwar politics. It opened certain historical regime options and closed others. In this chapter, I attempt to identify the conditions that handicapped liberal parties. In Chapters 4 and 5 I try to sort out the ways in which this less effective liberalism altered the course of the formation of the working class before 1914.

Liberal Weakness: A Survey

Let us first briefly survey the level of success that liberal parties attained, using as our initial reference point their governing power during the years of mass mobilization, from roughly 1870 to 1914. We will take up the individual national experiences in more detail later. Two societies, Belgium and the Netherlands, most closely approximated the British–French–Swiss pattern of liberal hegemony. In Belgium, parliamentary sovereignty was established by 1847. In the years immediately after the 1830 separation, Belgian Liberals and Catholics governed together in a coalition of national unity. This coalition, as parliamentary sovereignty itself, reflected the desire of the national bourgeoisie to circumscribe the authority of an externally imposed monarch. As the need for this unity receded in the following decade, it was replaced by loose coalitions of Liberals and Catholics that alternated in power, in a society in which politics was still very much an elite avocation. In the critical years of mass mobilization, the Catholic party, by then a well-formed national organization, was the dominant governing force. It controlled an absolute majority in every parliament from 1884 to 1914.[1]

As in Belgium, parliamentary sovereignty, having been secured in 1847, was an established fact in the Netherlands well before the mass mobilization of the late nineteenth century. Also as in Belgium, political activity remained narrowly circumscribed until the religious and school disputes of the 1880s stimulated mass interest in the state's activities and demands for suffrage reform. The first identifiably party-based government was a coalition of religious parties that governed from 1888 to 1891. Thereafter the Liberal party and the religious parties alternated in power until the outbreak of the war. The Liberal party governed in the periods 1891–1901, 1905–08, and 1913–18. In 1894 the Liberals were torn asunder by their differences over franchise reform, so that for the remainder of the prewar years, no unified liberal party existed. Rather, the party broke into radical, moderate, and conservative factions. The governments that the moderate and conservative liberals provided between 1894 and 1901 were consequently minority governments regularly dependent on Catholic and Protestant party votes. The governments formed in 1905 and 1913 likewise depended on the support of the religious parties and the Labor party. The religious parties governed during the intervening years, 1901–05 and 1908–13.[2] In both Belgium and the Netherlands, the main lines of political conflict during these years remained between clerical and anticlerical interests, supplemented by partially subtending regional conflicts. Class conflict became salient in politics only in the final decade of the nineteenth century.

In Scandinavia, liberalism made its best showing in Denmark and its weakest in Sweden. In the former, parliamentary sovereignty was effectively established in 1901; in the latter, parliament became semisovereign in 1906 and effectively sovereign only in 1917. The sovereignty of the Norwegian parliament was recognized by the King of Sweden–Norway in 1884 under pressure of a constantly growing proparliament political movement in Norway. For twenty years a political movement that came to be known as the *Venstre* (the Left, sometimes translated as the Liberals) had fomented popular, mainly rural, support for the parliamentary cause. At every step in the slowly developing crisis, the Venstre turned to the country for a larger antimonarchical majority. In 1884, when the parliament impeached some of the King's ministers amidst a background of growing popular militias and the specter of civil war, the King relented and appointed a government that reflected the majority in the Storting. Thereafter, the Left alternated government majorities with the Right (*Höyre*) until the war.

In Denmark, a somewhat comparable process occurred, but did not compel the King to accept the sovereignty of parliament until 1901. For several decades before that, the Danish Venstre had succeeded in increasing its majority in the Folketing, only to find that the King's ministers could govern on the basis of a majority in the much more conservative and narrowly elected upper house, the Landsting. By 1901, the conservative minority in the Folketing had been so reduced that the King could not govern without a government that corresponded to the Folketing majority. From 1901 until the outbreak of World War I, the country was governed by minority liberal governments of various types, as the Venstre began to break up immediately following the victory of 1901.

In Sweden, the King avoided yielding parliamentary sovereignty even longer, not recognizing it until 1917 and then only in the crisis atmosphere of the Russian Revolution and fear of revolution in Sweden. From the abolition of the Estates in 1866, a reform that actually consolidated conservative power, until 1905 the country was governed by conservative bureaucrats answerable to the King. Their base of power was in the plutocratic First

Chamber of the Riksdag, in which only 6,100 Swedes were even eligible to serve.[3] Practically no parties existed outside the informal groupings in the Riksdag until lines were drawn for and against free trade in the penultimate decade of the nineteenth century. Indeed, there was no liberal party of significance until that time. As it was, a cohesive Liberal Parliamentary party took shape only in 1900, and the National Liberal Federation, a nationwide electoral organization, came into being only in 1902. A short-lived minority Liberal government existed from November 1905 to May 1906. It sought but failed to pass a suffrage reform. The appearance of this government marked the acquisition by the Riksdag of at least semisovereign status; the King was, for the first time, compelled to take explicit account of the sentiments of the Riksdag. A second minority government was in power from October 1911 to February 1914.

In Italy, liberals sponsored national unification and the authority of the parliament was established early on. But mass mobilization then occurred *against* the liberal order, and Liberals, although nominally governing, never established a comfortable dominance of Italian politics.

Parliamentary sovereignty was not obtained in Germany, Austria, and the rest of central and eastern Europe until 1919. German liberals, of course, lost their battles with Bismarck in the 1860s and 1870s, and found themselves first outmaneuvered and then overwhelmed by the universal suffrage Bismarck introduced in Reichstag elections. The balance between crown and parliament in Germany was essentially similar to Sweden's: a nominally autonomous government that was not obliged to work with a parliamentary majority, but nonetheless found it convenient in varying degrees to listen to that majority and seek to convert or divide it.

In summary, liberal parties were never able to establish their dominance in any of these societies. They were most effective in the Netherlands and Belgium, less so in Denmark, and still less so in Italy, Norway, Sweden, and Germany. In the Netherlands, liberals were able to share power on an alternating basis with the religious parties after 1888; in Belgium they were excluded from power continuously after 1884 but had had a substantial run of government power before that and were one of the two major parties in a society in which parliamentary power mattered greatly.

In Norway and Denmark, liberal parties had periods of government power, too, after the supremacy of parliament was established. But in Norway these were liberals of a very different type from those found in the Netherlands and Belgium, not to mention Britain, France, and Switzerland. To translate the original term, *Venstre*, into the English "liberal" rather than the literal "left" obscures at least as much as it reveals about this movement. These were not liberals whose agenda was defined mainly by the ambitions of the urban middle classes, but rather movements of independent peasants who sought, above all, to curtail the spending authority and reject the territorial, cultural, linguistic, and religious dominance of cosmopolitan, latitudinarian urban oligarchs. In their economic and cultural ambitions, these urban oligarchs had much more in common with continental liberals than did the peasant "liberals" who challenged them. In Sweden, too, liberalism was shaped by movements of cultural and religious defense, although less decisively than in Norway. But Swedish liberalism was even less successful than the Norwegian variant in establishing its political authority. Indeed, its failure to realize its political agenda before the war was virtually complete, and by the time the agenda was realized, Liberals were surpassed and marginalized by Social Democrats. This and the distinctive characteristics of Scandinavian liberalism are matters to which we shall return in due course.

Some Explanations of Liberal Weakness

Late Industrialization

How can we account for this pattern of liberal weakness? One answer is that liberal parties, and democratization more generally, were impeded in most of Europe before the war because late industrialization delayed the growth of the middle classes. That is to say, the social structure was "immature." This line of thought can be found in most political development literature, both liberal and Marxist. The theme of late and rapid industrialization, with a plethora of side effects that need not detain us here, has long been advanced since Marx as one explanation for the political enfeeblement of, in particular, the German middle classes.[4] It is certainly the case that at some outer limit, the social structure defines the range of political possibilities. The problem is to know where that outer limit is. It is true enough that most of these societies began to industrialize at a later date—Belgium aside, only after 1840 and in some cases not until the 1880s (Sweden) or even 1890s (Italy). Thus, the amount of time that the urban middle classes had to assert themselves through liberal (or any other) parties before the Great War, the ensuing disruptions, and the example of the Bolshevik Revolution was briefer than it had been in Britain and France. Also, later industrialization often meant a greater role for the state in industrial development.[5] This, in turn, meant a correspondingly greater dependence of the middle classes on the state, a less plausible case for the liberal ideology and a weaker claim to be the natural governing classes.

Yet, a quick glance at the data on industrialization makes it clear that a more efficient explanation than this must be found.[6] Three groups of societies are apparent: the industrial societies of Western Europe with liberal hegemony, the industrial societies of Western Europe without liberal hegemony, and the less industrial societies of the European periphery. Within Western Europe, industrialization is far from sufficient to explain the political power of liberal parties. The level of industrialization—the lack of a sociological base—can efficiently account for the vulnerability of liberal parties outside this group: in Eastern Europe, Finland and, more marginally, Spain. Even in the last-mentioned, as we shall see, the debility of the liberal movement had as much to do with the specific nature of political conflict as with an inadequate social base.

Among the cases of liberal hegemony, Britain, because it was the first industrial society, is more misleading than informative. Early industrialization in Britain had brought about such a radical reduction in the agricultural population and created such an ample urban middle strata by the late nineteenth century that focusing on Britain can distort our understanding of the level of social transformation necessary to sustain a flourishing liberal movement.

Switzerland and France had dominant liberal movements with about one-third and more than two-fifths of their active populations, respectively, still on the land. In this they were not distinct from many of the countries that lacked liberal hegemony. France had a primary sector similar in size or actually larger than Belgium, the Netherlands, Denmark, Germany, and Norway. It is true, of course, that these data do not take account of the timing and speed of industrialization. Nor do they tell us much about the variety of social structures that subtended even comparable levels of industrialization. Industrialization began earlier and occurred more gradually in France and especially Switzerland than in some of the other societies. The timing, pace, and turn-of-the-century social result of French industrialization were not, however, very different from the experiences of a number of other countries.

If industrial development per se were important, we would expect Belgium to provide more favorable conditions than France, for industrialization commenced earlier, resulted in greater affluence at mid-century, and had proceeded further by the end of the nineteenth century in Belgium.[7] Denmark began to industrialize later but at a still comparatively early date, in the 1850s and 1860s—about twenty years after the starting point of sustained industrialization in France. Both societies were at similar levels of development at the end of the century. In both Belgium and Denmark the rate of industrialization was, as in France, very gradual. In the Netherlands, where a large manufacturing sector did not appear until the twentieth century, but a thoroughly commercialized economy based on shipping and commerce existed throughout the second half of the nineteenth century, the primary sector was markedly smaller than France's. Development in Denmark, too, was based heavily on trade and shipping, and, lacking any significant natural resource endowment, large-scale manufacturing never had a major presence in Denmark before the war. As in France, in both the Netherlands and Denmark the family peasantry constituted the backbone of the social structure. Indeed, the residual aristocracy in the Netherlands and Denmark was a much less important social and political force than it was in France. The result in France, the Netherlands, and Denmark, despite the variations in their patterns of industrialization, was a social structure that was heavily oriented toward small firms, the petite bourgeoisie, and family farms. Although the available data are not strictly comparable, they are adequate to make this point. In the Netherlands, in 1899, 24 percent of the nonagricultural labor force consisted of employers and the self-employed.[8] One-third of French wage-earners were self-employed in 1906.[9] In Denmark, 50 percent of urban wage-earners were self-employed in 1914. In 1906, 60 percent of French workers were employed by firms with between one and ten employees. In Denmark 41 percent of urban workers were in firms with between one and five employees; 47 percent were in firms with between one and twenty employees.[10] Another source reports that the average number of Danish workers per enterprise in 1914 was just thirty-four.[11] In Belgium, where heavy industry was a central feature of industrialization, the petite bourgeoisie was a weaker force in the cities. In 1900, 20 percent of the nonagricultural labor force consisted of employers and the self-employed.[12]

Again, although the data are neither strictly comparable nor completely reliable, a similar picture of petit-bourgeois dominance emerges in agriculture. In 1908, 38 percent of French holdings were less than one hectare; 46 percent were between one and ten; 14 percent were between ten and forty.[13] The situation in Belgium was similar, although the higher density of population meant that the average farm was considerably smaller than in France. Seventy-six percent of holdings were less than two hectares; 18 percent were between two and ten hectares.[14] In Denmark, just before the war, the number of dwarf holdings was much larger (a point that will be of great significance later on), but there were still an impressive number of middle-size units and very few large ones. There were about 2,000 owners of estates of twelve *hartkorn* (a Danish unit of land valuation) or more; about 70,000 owners of units of one to twelve *hartkorn;* and about 100,000 owners of units of less than one *hartkorn.*[15]

The similarities between France and Germany are especially worth considering, because they are so regularly portrayed as social opposites. This contrast, however, rests more securely on the social structures that existed just before the First World War—that is, at the *end* of the liberal era—than it does on the conditions that obtained at the historically decisive juncture for liberalism in each country. In the late 1870s and early 1880s, when a liberal movement was on the verge of political hegemony in France and on the verge of political irrelevance in Germany, the social circumstances were similar in several respects. In France, 39 percent of the labor force remained in the agricultural sector; in Germany 43 percent did.[16] The petit-bourgeois character for which France became known was still apparent in urban Germany: in 1875, firms employing up to five workers accounted for 64 percent of the total 18.6 million employed. It was only over the next three decades that the powerful concentration of employment for which Germany became known occurred. By 1907 only 32 percent of workers were in small firms (i.e., firms employing up to five workers) and an extraordinary 42 percent were in firms with over fifty employees.[17] Germany, too, notwithstanding its substantial landed elite, did have a large middle strata in the countryside. The traditional distinction between landholding patterns east and west of the Elbe and undue attention to the Junkers have tended to obscure this. In Germany as a whole, just over 20 percent of holdings, mostly east of the Elbe, were large estates.[18] To be sure, this was not fertile soil for liberalism. But the remaining 80 percent of holdings ran the spectrum from dwarf plots to large family farms. Most of these occupied an intermediate position and were located in the west, where the patterns of landholding were very similar to those found in Belgium and France. In this region, 22 percent of holdings were less than five hectares, 40 percent were between five and twenty hectares, and 30 percent were between twenty and one hundred.[19] The problem for German liberalism, as we shall see, was not so much sociological as political, for this social structure also turned out to be inhospitable to liberalism.

In Norway, although industrialization began several decades later (1870s through 1880s) and then occurred with great rapidity, the outcome by the end of the century was a level of industrialization and a social structure of small firms and small farms that was very similar to that of Denmark. The political outcome was again a weak liberal movement. In contrast, industrialization in Sweden began still later (1890s), was very rapid, and produced a heavily concentrated pattern of ownership and employment. But it also had a weak liberal outcome not far removed from that found in Norway and Denmark.[20] The contrasts within Scandinavia alone are enough to make doubtful any adequate connection between industrialization, the social structure, and liberalism. None of these variations either within Scandinavia or within the larger group of countries can be easily correlated with the success of liberalism. On balance, then, it is difficult to see that among these societies and between them and Switzerland and France, the experiences of industrialization or the resulting social structures efficiently explain the variety of liberal outcomes. In none of them were liberal parties hegemonic.

Suffrage and Sovereignty

We should note as well that the breadth of the suffrage was unrelated to either liberal hegemony or, independent of hegemony, to the liberal ability to collaborate with working-class movements. The suffrage requirements varied widely among these societies and within them according to the body being elected, but in none of them was an equal and comprehensive suffrage established until after the war.[21] The vote was severely restricted in the Netherlands until 1919. In Belgium it was restricted until 1894, when the franchise was widened but plural voting was introduced; only in 1919 was comprehensive and equal manhood suffrage introduced. In Sweden, the franchise remained among the most reactionary in Europe—second only to the Prussian Landtag's—until manhood suffrage limited by tax qualifications was established for lower house elections in 1909.[22] For municipal and county elections and thereby the indirectly elected upper house, a system of plurality voting remained in effect until 1918, ensuring conservative control of that chamber. In Norway, the first election with manhood suffrage was fought in 1900, but plurality electoral districts that disproportionately rewarded the largest parties (and rural areas) drastically undercut working-class representation and were not reformed until after the war. In Germany, universal suffrage was introduced in Reichstag elections in 1871, but the Reichstag itself was not sovereign and voting rights remained very unequal in Prussia and some of the other states until establishment of the Weimar Republic. In effect, in all of these societies the rights of mass participation remained severely circumscribed, although in different ways—in some cases through narrow or unequal voting rights, in others through unsovereign legislatures, in still others through both.

Where liberals were dominant, legislatures were sovereign. But legislative sovereignty in the absence of liberal dominance tells us little about the course of working-class inclusion. Legislatures, as we noted earlier, could gain sovereignty through other than liberal efforts. Likewise, the extension of the franchise is not informative. As the data indicate, a number of societies had voting rights that extended to a larger part of the adult population than Britain.[23] Whether more or less broadly based than in Britain, whether the legislature was sovereign or not (in the absence of liberal hegemony), does not seem to determine whether liberal hegemony or the kind of liberal–labor collaboration we saw in Britain and France occurred.

Cleavage Structures and the Failure of Liberal Movements

If neither the level of industrialization, its timing, rate, or type, the occurrence of a bourgeois revolution, nor the extent of the franchise can adequately account for the ineffectiveness of these liberal movements, what can? It seems that the distinctive nature of nation-state formation provides the most efficient explanation for the ineffectiveness of these liberal movements. As we shall see in more detail subsequently, liberal movements in these societies were crippled by divisions within the middle classes that originated in the preindustrial epoch. Conflicts of national territory, religion, the center versus the periphery, the city versus the country, and national communities remained divisive at the time of mass mobilization. These preindustrial cleavages were sufficiently potent to prevent an adequate fraction of the middle classes from being rallied by liberal movements.[24] This can be seen quite clearly if we examine the specific historic moments at which liberals sought to establish parliamentary sovereignty where it was not inherited or sought to build an electoral base during the years of mass mobilization.

Belgium and the Netherlands

Belgium provides virtually a paradigmatic case of the obstacles liberal parties encountered in establishing a mass electoral base. The regime that emerged from the Liberal Revolution of 1830 obscured the inherent isolation of Belgian liberals for four decades until growing electoral participation in the countryside and among the urban lower middle classes overwhelmed the Liberals. The improbable Union of Opposition that came together against Dutch overlordship in 1828 to 1830 joined Catholics, who sought liberation from the Protestant House of Orange, with Liberals, who sought to free industry from the stultifying policies of the Hague. Catholics rebelled against northern efforts to create a system of secular secondary and university education in the south and sought to liberate the hierarchy from the Orangist supervision attached to life under the Concordat. Both Catholics and Liberals rejected the Orangist attempt to impose the Dutch language on the south and to discriminate against southerners in state appointments. Combining forces against the official candidates in 1828, the Union won a resounding victory that led to Belgian independence two years later. The constitutional settlement of 1830 reflected the competing interests that had been brought together in the Union. Liberals accepted state subsidies for the independent Catholic Church; Catholics accepted the primacy of civil marriage and a secular, liberal state.[25]

The 1840s were a period of growing tension between the two camps as a pattern of clear-cut competition and alternation between them began to develop. Liberals won a decisive electoral victory in 1847 and prevailed on a reluctant King Leopold to invite them to form a government, thus establishing the principle of parliamentary rule. In 1848, the Chambers agreed to lower the property qualifications for the electorate to the constitutional minimum. This measure doubled the urban electorate and added one-third to the rural. With this the national electorate included about 5 percent of the adult male population. It doubled again over the next forty years without any changes in the property qualifications. The requirements for voting in municipal elections were lower, and in these about twice as many men—still, only about 25 percent of adult males—were enfranchised.[26]

This circumscribed participation had the virtue of permitting Liberals, whose constituency was limited almost exclusively to the urban, francophone, increasingly anticlerical middle class, to alternate in power for several decades with Catholics in a society in which Catholics were an overwhelming majority and Dutch speakers were a substantial majority (57 percent in the first linguistic census, which undoubtedly understated the reality).[27] Liberal cabinets governed about half of the time between 1848 and 1884. The limits of the power that could be derived from such a narrow constituency were reached in the early 1880s, however. These limits reflected the rapidly growing participation of the lower urban orders and of the peasantry, among whom the authority of the Catholic Church, and therefore the leadership of the Catholic party, were beyond question. As a result, the Liberal party was almost completely shut out of the countryside.[28]

It is especially significant that the turning point came in the wake of a Liberal attempt to establish a system of secular secondary schools in areas already served by free Catholic schools. This challenge to the Church provoked the mobilization of the theretofore semidormant Catholic masses and sealed the decline of the Liberal party.[29] The Catholic party built a winning coalition of the urban lower middle classes, the peasantry, and a substantial share of the working class, and on this basis won an absolute majority of seats at every election from 1884 to the 1920s. This hegemony was not altered by the introduction in 1894 of manhood suffrage, plurality voting (which favored the Liberals), and proportional representation. The Catholic party insisted on compulsory voting to bring out the rural vote.

This hegemony was reinforced by a growing alliance between the Catholics and the Flamingants, the Christian Democratic movement of Flemish nationalists who coexisted uneasily with the Catholic party after 1880. The Flamingant contribution to Catholic victories in Antwerp and a few other key cities brought about a rapprochement between them and the Catholics more generally. Although in the following decade the bilingual character of the north was acknowledged through a series of laws, by then the more militant were demanding a redefinition of the linguistic status of Brussels as well. Adamant opposition from the Liberals, overwhelmingly francophone, further reinforced the Catholic–Flamingant alliance.[30] In the most critical years, then, the Liberal party was marginalized because, given its francophone and especially its anticlerical, baggage, it could not penetrate the countryside to make an alliance with the agrarian middle class.

A similar if less complete process of liberal advance and then decline occurred during the same years in the Netherlands. Liberal elites dominated in the preparty era from 1848 until the late 1870s, but they were then increasingly threatened by the mobilization of Calvinists and Catholics. As in Belgium, competing secular and religious claims on the schools provoked the formation of modern parties. It was not mere coincidence that the suffrage reform of 1888 provided the religious parties with a clear-cut victory and allowed them to form their first government.[31] In both Belgium and the Netherlands growing participation favored liberalism's opponents because liberals could not overcome their urban or religious isolation and concentrate on the common interests of the middle classes as they had done in France and Switzerland.

In the long run, this isolation of liberals would be rather less consequential in Belgium and the Netherlands than in most other societies. For in these countries the character of working-class formation was decisively shaped by the availability of allies in the religious trade unions and parties.

Scandinavia

The lines of conflict that debilitated liberal movements varied, but the most common were, in fact, between the town and country and between religious communities. In Scandinavia, the sociological axis on which much of liberalism's vulnerability turned was to be found in the tenuous bridge between the urban and rural middle classes. France, rather than England, provides the most instructive counterpoint here because, unlike England, it had not become so overwhelmingly urban and industrial that rural interests were compelled in the late nineteenth century to seek allies among these sectors. As we saw in Chapter 2, French liberalism in both its Republican and then Radical manifestations was premised on a mass base that combined urban and rural support. In the absence of either part of this coalition, French liberalism, especially Radicalism, would have been crippled. It could never have aggregated sufficient mass support to gain the dominance it did in the final decades before the war.

Analogous coalitions were virtually impossible to construct in Scandinavia. Whereas in France, Britain, and Switzerland the decisive struggles between urban and rural interests preceded the entrance of workers into politics, in Scandinavia they accompanied it.[32] The countryside was divided within itself and from the city by religious, territorial, and cultural conflicts. This was most true of Norway, where centuries of foreign domination exercised through urban oligarchs provided the historical backdrop to the struggles of the nineteenth century. As the leading student of Norwegian development, Stein Rokkan, has written: "Mobilization did not lead to cultural integration; instead it produced a widespread breakdown in human communication and generated a number of 'countercultures' essentially hostile to the established standards and models of the original elite."[33] A process that was fundamentally the same but less intense occurred in Sweden. A still more muted version of this occurred in Denmark. In neither Sweden nor Denmark did urban–rural conflict receive the same level of reinforcement from cultural struggle that it did in Norway.

In all three countries, urban–rural coalitions under liberal leadership had an ad hoc character and began to disintegrate as soon as parliamentary sovereignty was obtained. In Norway, where parliamentarism came earliest, secular, cosmopolitan urban radicals provided the leadership and rural districts provided the mass base for the campaign that wrested parliamentarism from the King of Sweden–Norway in 1884. Notwithstanding its leadership, the campaign was above all an antiurban, antioligarchical, and anti-Swedish movement. It was the antioligarchical and anti-Swedish elements that temporarily bound the prevailing coalition together.[34] More revealing than the victory in 1884 is the unraveling of the coalition that soon followed when these binding elements were removed. Almost immediately on the heels of the 1884 victory, the coalition began to come apart. The first split came only four years after the victory in 1884: the fundamentalist wing of the party could not cooperate with the more latitudinarian and mainly urban radicals. The fundamentalists established a new party, the Moderate Liberals, which gained enough support to deprive the Venstre of a majority in the 1889 poll. A Conservative government thus followed for two years. In practice, the Venstre had ceased to govern in the spring of 1885.

By that time, the party's Storting delegation had already become so fractionalized between urban and rural and religious and secular interests that Prime Minister Johan Sverdrup was forced to abandon even the pretense of party government. Incapable of containing the conflicts in his own party, Sverdrup governed for the next three years by cobbling together shifting majorities that routinely depended on Conservative votes.[35] These were years of paralysis for the Venstre. It suffered from such dissention that it had to be refounded (in the literal sense) in 1889.

It is especially important that the issue which finally destroyed Sverdrup's government, and with it the original party, was church reform. Sverdrup's ministry, deriving most of its support from the fundamentalist wing of the party, sought Storting approval of a law that would have provided fundamentalists with greater control of local churches. Latitudinarian Liberals first abandoned the government on the key vote and later demanded its resignation.[36]

For the next two decades the Venstre, even during periods when it had a governing majority, was repeatedly torn asunder by conflicts over the national language, church governance, prohibition, and the economic conflicts between farming and industry. The conflicts within the Venstre, a congeries of local electoral associations of very different orientations, were frequently as intense as the conflicts between the Venstre and the Right. Broadly speaking, at least four different and only partly overlapping political communities were active under the Venstre label. The first and second of these were the communities of intellectual and professional radicals who had provided the leadership of the parliamentary movement.

In Oslo, among whose middle classes the party never fared well, these men were mainly speakers of Riksmal, the Dano–Norwegian language that for centuries had been the lingua franca of the urban elite. In Bergen and the towns of the southwest, the Venstre community was generally committed to the establishment of Landsmal, the traditional vernacular of the isolated regions.

The third community within the Venstre was the pietistic Christian community of the southwest. The fourth distinct community consisted of that part of the agrarian population—whatever its regional, linguistic, and religious orientations—that defined its interests mainly in terms of conflicts between the economic interests of agriculture and industry.

The linguistic divisions accentuated the regional divisions, as Landsmal became entrenched in some of the inner valleys of the east and along the fjords and coast of the south and the west, but remained in the minority in the central rural areas and the cities of the east, the Trondelag, and the north.[37]

In effect, the Venstre did not come to power until the final decade of the nineteenth century. It then remained a party dominated by conservative western farmers whose main ambition was to reduce their tax burden. Their dominance in the party—about 70 percent of the members of the Stortingvenstre were farmers or in occupations connected with farming—and their commitment to a parsimonious state meant the subordination of urban liberals committed to social reforms.[38]

These economic differences were reinforced by the concentration among farmers of the countercultural movements of Landsmal, the lay church, and prohibition. Support for the party consequently remained weak in the populous Oslo area. The party did not do poorly in urban areas because there were few middle class votes to be had in them; it did poorly because the middle classes were voting for the Right in Oslo, the surrounding region, and Trondheim. Among the three major urban areas, the Liberals fared well only in the countercultural capital of Bergen. In Oslo, in the four elections of 1882, 1888, 1897, and 1903, the Right averaged 62.4 percent of the vote. In the same elections, the Liberals averaged just 29.8 percent of the vote. This Right dominance was replicated in the Oslofjord and the Tröndelag regions. It was reversed in Bergen.[39] Because the Venstre could never overcome this regional isolation, it was precluded from making a dominant coalition that combined the urban and rural middle classes.

In fact, the party could agree on little, save its desire to keep the Conservatives out and its demand for equality in the union with Sweden, a demand that remained moot until 1905. It was indicative of its divisions that although it had a Storting majority throughout the 1890s, it could govern for only about half of these years. Between 1893 and 1895 a Conservative government was in power; between 1895 and 1898 a coalition of the center–left and Right was in power. Taking the twenty-four-year period from 1889 to 1913, the Left governed for ten years, coalitions governed for seven, and the Right governed for seven.[40]

The experiences of Swedish liberalism echoed the urban–rural cleavage found in Norway, albeit in a more muted way. Liberals in Sweden did not have the advantage, however, of challenging a foreign monarch whose local authority had never been well established. The central state had once made Sweden a great power and had centuries of accrued legitimacy behind it. Swedish society was much more stratified, containing a powerful bureaucratic state and a landed elite wedded to the authority and status of the bureaucracy and monarchy. In these respects, Swedish society bore a closer resemblance to Prussia than to Norway. In Norway, there was no great power legacy, the central bureaucracy had been the agent of a foreign power for 300 years, and the indigenous nobility, never a major force, was disestablished in 1815.[41]

This legacy of the bureaucratic state, along with Sweden's comparatively late industrialization, no doubt goes some way to account for the enfeeblement of Swedish liberalism. But before we call in such diffuse explanations, we should recall that Sweden had an equally long legacy of successful challenges to the authority of the monarchy. For several hundred years, the rhythm of Swedish politics had mainly been counted by a shifting balance of power between the monarchy and the estates. A coup d'etat brought autocratic rule to an end in 1718. For the next half century, in the time that came to be known as the Age of Freedom, the estates successfully hobbled the monarchy. A pattern of lively political competition between contending protoparties (the "Caps" and the "Hats") characterized estate politics during this era. A royal coup against the estates restored the autocracy in 1772; another coup ended it in 1809. For the remainder of the nineteenth century a balance of power existed between the Riksdag (which succeeded the estates in 1866) and the monarchy.[42]

This mixed legacy and the contrast with Norway suggest that the failure of Swedish liberalism was due less to amorphous historical traditions than to the greater ability of the monarch to deploy practical political power in Sweden in the face of an ineffective liberal challenge. The institutional manifestation of this power was to be found in the entrenched position of the aristocrat and civil servant-dominated First Chamber of the Riksdag. In effect, a divided liberal movement in Norway could succeed in establishing parliamentary sovereignty in 1884 because it faced a locally weak opponent. In Sweden, a divided liberal movement was slower to gain parliamentarism, succeeding only between 1906 and 1917, because it encountered a locally powerful opponent. The question that must concern us now, however, is why Swedish liberals were divided.

The principal line of struggle from the abolition of the estates in 1866 to the tariff debates of the 1880s was between the peasants, who dominated the Second Chamber of the Riksdag, and the aristocrats, large landowners and civil servants who controlled the First Chamber. This was not fundamentally altered by the tariff debates. In these, the First Chamber had a protectionist majority and the Second Chamber normally had a free-trade majority. The question of protection was less important for its outcome (the protectionists prevailed in 1888) than for the upsurge of political interest and the demands for participation that the debate sparked. Only in the final decade of the nineteenth century did a modern liberal movement committed to parliamentarism and suffrage reform appear. This movement had its center of gravity in the Second Chamber and among the peasantry that provided the backbone of that chamber. In 1905, 109 of 230 members of the Second Chamber were farmers; an unknown but undoubtedly substantial additional number were in occupations tied to farming. The share would have been higher still if the electoral laws had not heavily favored the representation of urban areas.[43] With this electoral distortion providing the explanation, until 1911 the Liberals about evenly divided the number of seats they won in rural and urban districts. Once the distortion was eliminated, they were transformed into a party that was three-quarters rural.[44]

The failure of Swedish liberalism and the centrality of the urban–rural divide to this failure is most apparent in the liberals' flawed attempts to establish Second Chamber parliamentarism and to reform the franchise. Only in Prussia was there a franchise that was this restrictive for so long. As late as 1896, only 6 percent of the population—about 20 percent of the adult males—had the right to vote in Sweden.[45] The reactionary quality of this situation was compounded by the use of multiple voting in communal elections.

Franchise reform was the motor force of Swedish liberalism for almost two decades. Year after year, liberals in the Riksdag introduced motions, without success, to extend and reform the ballot. Mass support for this had been growing since the early 1890s, when a broadly based popular movement first appeared in favor of it. As early as 1893, a "People's Parliament" had been elected parallel to the regular Riksdag to express the popular demand for reform. In this campaign, organized by Liberals and Social Democrats (and repeated in 1896), more votes were cast for the popular parliament than for candidates for the Riksdag. In 1903, the Social Democrats and the trade unions organized a three-day, nationwide general strike for manhood suffrage. By one estimate, 85 percent of the industrial workers in Sweden participated in this strike.[46] Against this backdrop of broad popular support and the lateness of reform in comparison with Sweden's neighbors (even Finland introduced universal suffrage in 1905) most historians of the reform movement have concentrated on understanding why it was so slow to succeed in Sweden.[47]

When reform finally won Riksdag approval in 1907, it was carried by a conservative government that succeeded where a liberal government had failed the year before. To be sure, this would never have occurred, had the Liberals not articulated the demand for it. But the defeat of Karl Staaff's Liberal ministry was a double blow to liberalism. For the government, with a left majority in the Second Chamber, was not only unable to hold together its own troops for franchise reform; it was unable to make parliamentary government work. The Liberal ministry had been forced on the King and was the first ministry based on definite party support in the more popular lower house. Its defeat was a double one for the liberal movement and showed it to be incapable of realizing even its most vital ambitions. In Swedish historiography, much of the blame for this has been ascribed to Staaff's personality: he was, to be sure, inept, mercurial, and bull-headed.[48] Staaff, however, was a man of the radical, urban wing of Swedish liberalism. He seems to have had little understanding of and even less sympathy for the political plight of the moderate liberal peasantry, especially that key part of it threatened by the growing political influence of industry in northern company towns. Staaff failed because he could not overcome, perhaps even in his own mind, the gulf between his rural and urban supporters. The conservative government of Arvid Lindman prevailed precisely because it could play on the urban–rural divisions within the liberal movement.[49]

Staaff proposed a reform that included manhood suffrage for Second Chamber elections and a preservation of the established procedure for the election of the First Chamber. He assumed that if the Second Chamber were given a broad popular base, the First Chamber would wither in importance in a fashion analogous to the British House of Lords. This strategy was countered in the Upper House by a conservative farmer of broad influence, Alfred Petersson i Påboda. The "Påboda line," as it came to be known, demanded as a conservative guarantee the use of proportional representation in First Chamber and communal elections and manhood suffrage in lower house elections. The Påboda line preserved the influence of the upper house and diluted the impact of the newly enfranchised working-class voters. For a critical part of the moderate liberal peasantry the Påboda line exercised an important appeal as that sector calculated a loss of political influence following on the inclusion of new urban strata.[50] The peasantry, in fact, had for some time been ambivalent about an extension of voting rights. In the 1870s and 1880s, the Lantmannaparti, the party of middle peasants that dominated the lower house until the 1890s, had been favorably disposed to an extension of the franchise—at least in rural areas—as a means to increase its leverage vis-à-vis the large landowners and state officials who dominated the upper chamber.[51] This attitude evolved as the political implications of franchise reform in a rapidly industrializing society became more transparent. Staaff's ministry, caught between the fears of the Liberal party's rural wing, the demands of its urban radicals, and the egging on of the already ascendant Social Democrats, failed to take account of this. The upshot was that the First Chamber approved a bill that followed closely the Påboda line, while a bare majority of the lower chamber passed Staaff's bill. Unable to resolve the standoff or persuade the King to dissolve the lower chamber (Staaff expected an enlarged majority there to break the impasse), Staaff was compelled to resign in defeat. The King detested both Staaff and parliamentary government, but he had a sense of humor. He refused Staaff's request for a dissolution and sacked him on the pretext that it was "unparliamentary" to dissolve a chamber that had just approved a government bill.

Staaff was succeeded by the conservative Arvid Lindman, who proceeded to do what Staaff could not: build a coalition for electoral reform in both houses that included the support of the critical moderate liberal agrarians. Lindman prevailed with a modified version of the Påboda line. The modifications allowed him to split the liberals in the lower house and win sufficient support among agrarian liberals to carry the measure. The essential modification was in the revision of plurality voting in a fashion that bolstered the position of farmers threatened by the growing political clout of northern timber companies.[52] In effect, Lindman struck a bargain in which farmers were persuaded to yield a substantial measure of electoral power in exchange for increased leverage in communal voting and in elections to the First Chamber, and for restraints on the new working-class vote.[53] Their position in communal voting (and indirectly, the First Chamber) was improved by a reduction in plurality voting, the establishment of salaries for legislators, and a lowering of the income and property requirements for First Chamber membership. At the same time, an increase in the voting age from twenty-one to twenty-four and other residual restrictions slowed the effect of working-class enfranchisement.

The entire episode was a major debacle for parliamentary government, for the Liberal party, and above all for the reformist urban wing of the party. It was on the ability of that wing to establish its leadership of a dominant liberal movement that the success of the liberal–labor alliance and the character of working-class formation depended. As it happened, Lindman remained in power until 1911, when Staaff again formed another ministry. This, too, proved a fiasco because it was again torn largely along urban–rural lines. This time the issue was military spending, which urban reformers sought to curtail in favor of social reform. The issue provoked a constitutional crisis and tormented the party until the outbreak of the war, which perforce compelled the capitulation of the urban radicals. The two 1914 elections, which reflected these contretemps, were further setbacks for the urban wing of the party. The party lost seats across the country. This was especially the case in the cities, where workers opted for the surging Social Democratic party and a fraction of the urban middle class shifted its support to the Conservatives.[54]

These last blows to Swedish liberalism were almost beside the point. Its time, having never actually arrived, was placed ineluctably in the past because of the fast-growing Social Democrats, who already controlled 64 Second Chamber seats to the Liberals 102 after the 1911 election. At the end of their era, Swedish Liberals had less to show for their efforts than their sister parties in either Norway or Denmark. Even the principle of Second Chamber parliamentary government was not irrevocably established until 1917.

To be sure, industrialization came later to Sweden than to the other Scandinavian countries.[55] But before the electoral reform, the Liberal party had actually been well balanced between its urban and rural wings; the exaggerated representation of the cities actually compensated in substantial measure for the later industrialization, that is, for the comparatively late appearance of the urban middle classes. The party suffered less from an imbalance between the town and country than from the difficulty it encountered in reconciling their competing interests.

Moreover, and this is the point that must be hammered home, when the Liberals' era came to an end, it was not mainly because of late industrialization and even less the radicalizing effects of the war. Just as late industrialization meant a late start for political liberalism because it meant the comparatively late appearance of the urban middle classes, it also meant the late appearance of industrial workers. In principle, at least in the absence of the war and the Bolshevik Revolution, the formation of these workers into a class could have happened much more slowly than it actually did—for example, as slowly as it did in Britain and France. It was precisely because this autonomous formation of the working class occurred so quickly that Swedish liberalism's time, sociologically and chronologically speaking, passed so quickly. This process spelled the end of the opportunity for an effective liberal–labor coalition. And this autonomous formation, as we shall see, was irrevocably in train long before the radicalizing experiences of either the war or the Bolshevik Revolution.

If we accept the assumption that workers had only two routes to political power, in an alliance with a dominant liberal movement or through self-organization, then it can be seen that the process of class formation occurred quickly in Sweden precisely because Swedish liberalism was very ineffective. The self-organization occurred rapidly in Sweden (as in Norway) precisely because there was no dominant liberal movement through which workers could pursue their political agenda. Indeed, in the Swedish case, the liberal movement did not just lack dominance, given the contretemps of Staaff's ministries, it was almost an abject failure. To square the circle, this failure was not due to the separate mobilization of the workers; it was the cause of the separate mobilization. The failure of liberalism was due to the divisions within liberalism itself.

Danish liberalism was plagued for more than half a century by a similar conflict between the town and country. The successive advances and retreats of Danish liberalism were mainly marked by the making and unmaking of the urban-rural coalitions that subtended it. Three epochs neatly define the course of liberal politics in Denmark. The first of these was between 1848 and 1864, the years when the National Liberal party was dominant. The second epoch lasted until 1901, when the Venstre finally succeeded in establishing the sovereignty of the Folketing. The final period lasted until 1913, during which the Venstre dominated Danish politics but then began to be eclipsed by the Social Democrats.

Absolutism came to an end only in 1848, when Frederick VII was forced by popular unrest in the spring of that year to declare himself a constitutional monarch. This unrest, which fit the larger pattern of revolution and attempted revolution that swept the continent in those months, was more effective in Denmark than in almost any other European society, for there it brought about a genuine change in the political order. The new order lasted until 1866, and in the absence of a growing split between the urban and rural wings of the liberal movement, would have endured indefinitely beyond that year. Had it done so, liberalism in Denmark would have had a long run of political dominance and the course of politics in the twentieth century would have undoubtedly been very different.

The constitution that ended Danish absolutism was at the time the most democratic in Europe. The June Constitution, as it came to be known, established a two-chamber legislative body, the Rigsdag, that was elected on an equal and general suffrage for most men over thirty years of age not receiving poor relief. The franchise extended even to landless agriculture workers. The constitution, moreover, gave the Rigsdag the implicit authority to remove a government. It also provided for freedom of speech, the press, and religion. This remarkable change was brought about by a coalition of family peasants and urban liberals.

The three groups that were decisive in the struggles of later decades became organized just before and after the revolution of 1848: the Venstre, the Center or National Liberals and the landed aristocrats, and bureaucratic elites who formed the Right.[56] Of these, only the first was organized before 1848. Its core was created with the formation of the Friends of the Farmers Society (Bondevennernes Selskab) in 1846. The Society had a political program that included reform of the peasants' military obligations, commutation of leaseholds into freeholds, the end of villeinage, and so forth. Its program could be summarized in a single demand: the social and political equality of the peasantry. When the tensions of 1848 began to boil over, the Society was ready, and the farmers in effect preempted the political field because of their superior organization. In alliance with the National Liberals, they had a great influence on the institutions that followed the end of absolutism. Their foremost demand was general manhood suffrage, which they prevailed on Frederick VII to use in the election of a constituent assembly and subsequently won inclusion of in the June Constitution. It was a measure of the Society's influence that it placed candidates in forty-three of the fifty-four electoral districts on the islands and managed to have thirty of these candidates elected to the constituent assembly. In the first Folketing of 1849, thirty-three of its forty-six candidates were successful. Together with its allies in Jutland, the Society, whose political arm became the Venstre, commanded a majority or near majority in every Folketing until the revision of the constitution in 1866.[57]

The Venstre did not exist as a national organization, but rather as a Folketing group and an appellation that candidates sought. Even so, the key to the peasants success was in their extraordinary organizational network. This network rested on district activists well-known to local peasants and able to recruit them to serve on Society committees and in electoral associations. The local Society foremen were responsible for thousands of political meetings that at times brought together only a local handful and other times 10,000 or even 20,000 individuals. In every district an electoral committee existed, and in many districts these committees remained active even between elections. This organizational network was reinforced by the political capture of many peasant associations, in particular savings and fire insurance associations. These associations were created in the 1840s and 1850s to liberate peasants from the financial hold of the great landowners and urban financial interests. Election to their leading positions immediately became politicized and contingent on views compatible with Venstre's.[58]

This agitation produced extraordinary success for the peasants, but it also isolated them.[59] The campaign for equal and general manhood suffrage, especially, planted the seeds of a split between them and their urban allies, the National Liberals. The National Liberals had been among the first supporters of a free constitution in Denmark at a time in the late 1830s and early 1840s when the peasants remained loyal to the absolutist state. From 1841, there was growing cooperation between the peasants and the Liberals, and the Liberals played a central role in the establishment of the peasant's Society. They were never enthusiastic about the general suffrage, but stood by the peasants in 1848 and 1849 and together introduced the June Constitution, a move that was aimed against their common enemies: the aristocratic landowners and the elite civil servants who dominated the state apparatus. Together the urban Liberals and the rural Venstre implemented most of the Society's political program by 1851.

The eventual revision of the June Constitution and the failure of liberalism during this period are ultimately the story of the growing gulf between the Venstre and the National Liberals. In 1866, this gulf finally provided the great landed interests with the opening they needed to assert themselves and jettison the constitution. Three decades of rule by landed and bureaucratic elites and the remnants of the increasingly conservative National Liberals followed.

As in Norway and Sweden, popular mobilization led to the politicization of historical animosities rather than integration. The conflict between the peasants and the urban liberals was one between two social worlds whose experiences, environment, education, and economic conditions were entirely different. It was compounded by the composition of the upper strata of the National Liberals, who were not merely urban dwellers but cosmopolitan academics—sometimes referred to as the "Professors' Party"—who assumed their right to rule on the basis of their superior education and culture, their broader intellectual horizons, and their association with the leading ideas of the times. In a fashion that mimicked the gulf between the educated German Liberals and the *Volk*, the breakdown in communication between the *dannede* National Liberals and the *almue* was almost total. This good breeding, which the Nationalists assumed was their main qualification for power, was in reality the main barrier to their leading the people they wanted to lead. No matter how hard they tried to overcome it, they always generated mistrust and suspicion among rural inhabitants.

In the negotiations leading to the June Constitution, the peasants and the National Liberals had agreed that it would be a mistake to establish separate representation for the towns and countryside. They did not want to create an artificial divide between each other. The result was that most of the electoral districts consisted of a provincial town and a surrounding rural area. It soon became apparent, however, that the system did not serve to advance an understanding between the town and country. In fact, it brought them into direct confrontation with each other and institutionalized the historical animosity in the modern political arrangements. The Liberals, given their view that they should be elected on personal merits, saw little need for electoral organizations. In view of the well-developed organizations of the peasants, Liberals and the urban interests they represented soon came to feel seriously threatened. There are many accounts of elections during this period leading to unrest, even riots, between farmers and town dwellers, when farmers came to town to cast their ballots. Even if this was not caused by the parties, town inhabitants were soon voting overwhelmingly for the National Liberals, because they were the party of urban interests, and peasants were voting overwhelmingly for Venstre candidates. It is to this divide more than anything else that the failure of Danish liberalism in the 1860s must be attributed.

As a result of this identification—town dwellers with the National Liberals or occasionally with the Conservatives, and rural residents with the Venstre—a Radical Venstre movement, which had appeared in Copenhagen and Aarhus in 1848, was crushed. These radicals had had enormous importance as allies of the peasants in 1848 and had collaborated closely with them. With their disappearance, the main bridge between the National Liberals and the peasants also disappeared.[60]

The damage this cleavage did to liberalism was compounded by another cleavage. What a modern social scientist would call a center–periphery cleavage dominated Danish politics from 1852 to 1864. The cleavage was induced by the uncertain status of the duchies of Sleswig, Holstein, and Lauenburg. In the Three Years War (1848–50), as it came to be known in Danish historiography, the Danes succeeded in suppressing a separatist movement and repulsing an invasion of troops from the North German Confederation. National Liberals wanted to annex Sleswig to the Eider River and jettison Holstein and Lauenburg, but were opposed in this by both the monarch and the landed aristocracy.

The entire issue further divided the Venstre and the Liberals, because the state was under pressure from the Great Powers to find a conservative constitutional formula for the inclusion of the duchies. This first led to a supplemental constitution to govern joint affairs in 1855. The franchise for this constitution's elected body was extremely narrow and reflected the growing Liberal belief that franchise reform was an imperative if the Liberals were to avoid being swamped by the Venstre. In 1863, a National Liberal ministry sought to solve both of its problems with one quick move. After twelve years of fruitless negotiations with the Great Powers, it broke them off and dissolved the ties to Holstein and Lauenburg, at the same time establishing a common constitution for Denmark and Sleswig. This constitution included a Folketing that had the same franchise as provided in the June Constitution, and a Landsting (upper chamber) that was partly appointed by the monarch and partly elected by the narrow franchise of the 1855 constitution. This move was expected to resolve the status of the duchies and simultaneously secure National Liberal dominance of the state through control of the Landsting.

Instead, it provoked the Dano–Prussian War of 1864 and the ensuing catastrophic defeat, for which the Liberals were held responsible. Christian IX immediately sacked the government and negotiations were opened for a new constitution that would supersede both the June Constitution and the common constitution of 1864. It was at this point that the landed aristocracy and the bureaucratic elites reasserted themselves. The landed elites (*godsejerne*) were the ultimate victors, because they could manipulate the animosities between the Venstre and the National Liberals and the latter's desire for a revised franchise. The bottom line was that the Venstre could not save the June Constitution without the support of the Liberals, and the Liberals wanted a franchise law that provided them with control of the upper chamber. The constitution that emerged in 1866 provided this through a narrowly elected upper chamber, the Landsting.

The second epoch in the life of Danish liberalism followed from this, as the Venstre, after a few years of disorientation, spent the final three decades of the century trying to restore the Folketing sovereignty that had been implied in 1848. The National Liberals moved to the right and formed a coalition with the godsejerne. Together they controlled the Landsting and thus the state apparatus. The *kamp for demokrati* turned on Venstre's efforts, through the majority it always had in the Folketing after 1872, to obstruct budgetary appropriations. More fundamentally, this struggle can be seen as a long march to rebuild the urban–rural coalition that had been shattered in the 1850s.

The right governments survived for so long because they could manipulate divisions within the Venstre.[61] The most fundamental of these harkened back to the territorial crisis of the 1860s. For some years, the National wing of Venstre was committed to reoccupation of the duchies, to a nationalist foreign policy and to comparatively high military expenditures.[62] Even after the revanchism lost its plausibility, the nationalism endured. And, indeed, as Germany's military power grew in the 1880s, a popular movement in favor of the military and especially the fortification of Copenhagen developed a substantial following across much of the country.[63] The accommodationists, or Moderate Venstre as they came to be known, were consequently inclined to negotiate with the government. The popular Venstre, as it was then referred to, rejected revanchism and military expenditures. Its basic tactic was to hold the authority to raise taxes and appropriations hostage to its demand that the government accept the sovereignty of the Folketing. Between 1884 and 1893, the country had no regular budget. A succession of conservative governments, who themselves represented interests favorable to the army, were able to manipulate this division with great dexterity. In a manner that emulated Bismarck's behavior in the 1860s, the governments of J. B. S. Estrup enacted provisional budgets when the Folketing refused to approve the regular appropriations. Given a steadily growing source of income from tolls, it could then confront the Venstre with a fait accompli and induce the more accommodative wing of the party to negotiate on the government's terms. Only after 1894, when a compromise was reached on military policy, fortifications around Copenhagen, and a policy of strict neutrality, was the Venstre able to overcome this divide and act more coherently. The compromise was supported by the accommodationists and opposed by the more intransigent wing of the Venstre.

The Venstre was then able to act more coherently not because the accommodationist wing of the party, the Moderate Venstre, was then won over by the more radical wing, but because it was made superfluous by a growing urban base for the radicals who in the early 1890s came to be known as the Reform Venstre. By 1895, the Reform Venstre and its Social Democratic allies were able to win a majority of the Folketing's seats even in an election in which the Moderates and the Right collaborated. In effect, this process of realignment allowed the Reform Venstre to bridge the old division between the town and country.[64]

It was only in the penultimate decade of the century that the Venstre broke through the urban barrier. Until then, the Right completely controlled the cities. This domination was so thorough that it amounted to a comprehensive urban-rural divide—even urban workers formed their initial political identification as town dwellers and voted overwhelmingly for the Right. In Copenhagen, 40 percent of the Right vote came from the working class.[65] This did not change until the appearance of the Social Democratic party in the 1880s, at which time workers shifted their allegiance from the Right to the Social Democrats, never having paused to support Liberals unless they were endorsed by the worker's party. The Venstre did not win a single seat in Copenhagen until it began to make inroads into the community of middle-class radicals and made electoral pacts with the Social Democrats in the 1880s. In 1884, a new coalition of the Venstre, Social Democrats, and middle-class radicals led by Viggo Horup finally won four Folketing seats in Copenhagen. Two seats were won by Social Democrats. This new urban presence was joined in the Reform party to a faction of the rural Venstre led by I. C. Christensen.[66]

In effect, the Venstre was being reorganized to include a growing strata of antimilitarist social reformers heavily leavened with journalists and academics. Horup, a flame-tongued journalist who had become the leader of this new wing of the party in the 1880s, was conscious that the old Venstre's main weakness had been its lack of appeal to opinion-shaping urban intellectuals and its consequent inability to gain a mass base in the cities.[67] This more radical element infused new life into the party and pushed it to take a more coherent line toward the government. It also rekindled the old urban-rural tensions within the liberal coalition, tensions that would ultimately lead to a new split. For the time being, however, this renewed coalition of urban and rural interests finally provided the margin necessary to crush the Right in Folketing elections—in 1901 the Right won just 8 of 102 Folketing seats—and compel the acceptance of Folketing sovereignty.

The change of 1901, which came to be known as the system shift, inaugurated the third stage of Danish liberalism. The Venstre and its offshoot the Radical Venstre governed until 1920, almost always with the support of the Social Democrats. The appearance of the Radical Venstre in 1905 was symptomatic of the life that remained in the old urban–rural cleavage and the problem of the military. The Radicals broke with the parent party because, having made its constitutional point, the Venstre was no longer opposed to a professional standing army. Moreover, the first Venstre government, between 1901 and 1905, showed less enthusiasm for social reform and devoted itself, at the expense of smallholders, to the interests of the middle-class farmers who were the backbone of its constituency. The new party sought to represent middle-class urban radicals and rural smallholders.[68]

The appearance of this party was critical on both counts. It provided an essential reformist bridge between the middle classes and the Social Democrats; with Social Democratic support it was able to govern in 1909 to 1910 and from 1913 to 1920. By 1906 the Radicals and the Social Democrats controlled 40 percent of the Folketing vote. In organizing smallholders, the Radicals largely preempted the Social Democrats among this strata, and this, too, proved crucial to the later course of Danish politics. Until the introduction of proportional representation in 1915, the two parties maintained an electoral truce, with the Social Democrats agreeing not to compete against the Radicals in rural Jutland, where the Venstre was especially strong.

The Venstre and Radical Venstre governments, although sometimes formally minority administrations, normally had ample Folketing support from the left and were reasonably effective. The first government, between 1901 and 1905, carried important legislation that established a progressive income tax; reformed the education system; extended the franchise; established new labor laws that provided, with trade union approval, for mediation and binding arbitration services; and introduced a system of unemployment insurance that encouraged trade union enrollment by fixing a lower tax on union members.

In sum, although liberalism came late to Denmark and was made unstable by the division of the Venstre in 1905, it was more successful here than in either Norway or Sweden. There was a period of brief but effective liberal rule before the war, and Social Democrats did have comparatively successful urban middle-class allies both in the left wing of the Venstre and subsequently in the Radical Venstre.

In the struggle to bind urban and rural interests, liberalism in Denmark ran a course similar to the one we traced in Norway and Sweden. This urban-rural divide received less reinforcement, however, from religious, cultural, linguistic, and regional differences. The liberal coalition, in fact, succeeded much earlier in Denmark, and in the absence of the crises provoked by the duchies, the parliamentary institutions that coalition built would probably have endured, albeit in modified form. It is clear that even before their defeat in 1864, the National Liberals had lost much of their enthusiasm for the broad suffrage and some of their enthusiasm for the alliance with the Venstre. The former strained the latter, but did not make it impossible. The loss of the duchies devastated the National Liberals, however, and compounded the urgency of Landsting reform. In the wake of the war, such reform became the sine qua non of their political survival and in the extreme form the National Liberals now required provoked a complete rupture with the Venstre. In the aftermath of that rupture, the polarization between the town and country was virtually complete and several decades had to pass before it was again possible to bridge it. That occurred only when class conflict began to erode the solidarity of the city, especially the Copenhagen, electorate and provide the Venstre with new middle- and working-class allies. In this sense, the level of industrial development mattered a great deal; for the growth of the working class created a new set of issues that dissolved the old urban solidarity. Denmark was hardly alone in acquiring a working class, however. The same processes did not lead to the reinvigoration of liberal coalitions in Norway or Sweden. On the contrary, they strained them further, suggesting that the most fundamental difference between them and Denmark was that in Denmark the historical animosities were less intense, and therefore less debilitating, to begin with.

Germany

The alliance that was made temporarily in the 1840s and 1850s between the National Liberals and the peasantry in Denmark could not be made at all in Germany. It was this inability of German liberals to reach out to the peasants and their causally prior inability to overcome their own regional and religious divisions that undermined German liberalism in 1848. Whereas in Denmark the liberal alliance ran aground over urban–rural conflicts, in Germany divisions within the liberal community were so intense and debilitating that by the time liberals were able to overcome them, the programs necessary to cement an alliance with the peasantry had already been implemented by conservative governments.

The alienation of the peasantry cannot be explained by the unwillingness of liberals to fulfill an adequate portion of the peasants' demands. The material demands of German peasants were remarkably similar to those of their brethren north of the Eider. As in Denmark, peasants demanded the commutation of leaseholds into freeholds, the end of villeinage, debt relief, and more generally the abrogation of the hereditary privileges of the landed aristocracy. And as in Denmark, liberals were generally willing to satisfy peasant demands up to, but not including, compulsory transfers of land titles. In effect, in both countries, liberals were willing to complete the introduction of capitalist property relations in the countryside. In neither country were they willing to go beyond this. It is correct to say that in both Denmark and Germany the ambitions of land-hungry peasants went well beyond agrarian capitalism. But it is equally correct to say that in both cases they were willing to accept this as the best available outcome. It at least meant the end of feudal obligations.[69]

We know for a fact that these were the terms on which the National Liberals and Venstre settled, and we must assume that German peasants were equally available to the Frankfurt liberals on these terms. We must assume this because these were the terms on which peasants ultimately made a tacit alliance with supporters of the conservative monarchy in Germany. Conservatives allied with peasants not by offering them more than liberals were willing to offer, but by vigorously implementing the liberals' own limited program of agrarian capitalism.[70] Thus, the measures for commuting manorial dues, annulling feudal privileges, eliminating tax exemptions, terminating servile obligations without compensation, and abolishing private jurisdiction were promptly and effectively enacted by conservative governments in the various German states.[71] The liberals' ties to the peasants thus came apart not because of the promises liberals made or failed to make, but because for some reason conservatives were able to implement the liberal program more quickly than were liberals themselves.

A sweeping victory throughout Germany in the elections in the spring of 1848 gave liberals overwhelming control of the Frankfurt Assembly. Notwithstanding the opportunity this victory provided, Liberals were incapable of implementing their own agrarian program because their disagreements over the unification formula delayed agreement on a new constitutional order at Frankfurt for so long. The unification formula had three dimensions. The first of these concerned the relationship between the Parliament and the monarch and the Parliament and the nation. These ideological issues, if we may call them that, focused on the balance of sovereignty between the two institutions, the question of whether a monarch should be provided for, whether unification should come through federalist or unitary institutions, and the size of the franchise. These ideological concerns dominated debate during the first period of the Frankfurt Parliament, from May to October 1848. During this period, the Frankfurt fractions could be fairly neatly arrayed on the simple left–right dimension and there was no correlation between the delegates' positions on this dimension and their confessional orientation or regional commitments.[72] Whether they supported a *grossdeutsch* or *kleindeutsch* solution, much or little regional autonomy, Protestant hegemony, or a Catholic–Protestant balance did not correlate with their ideological orientation. Catholic delegates were scattered widely over all of the political groupings.[73] The delegates from Austria also spread widely through the whole spectrum of ideological positions.[74] These ideological disputes were inherently more tractable than the differences that arose after October, and if the debate had remained on this level the Assembly would have been much more likely to come to an early conclusion.

From October 1848, the debate shifted to the alternative *kleindeutsch* and *grossdeutsch* solutions. The former, of course, would result in a unified Germany that excluded Austria. It would therefore be predominantly Protestant and under Prussian hegemony. The *grossdeutsch* solution envisioned the inclusion of Catholic Austria in the new German nation. Only Austria was capable of balancing Prussia in a unified Germany, and a decision to include it would be one of the first magnitude. The outcome would be a Germany more agrarian, more liberal, more Catholic, and with a counterweight to Prussia available to the smaller more liberal, agrarian, and Catholic states of the south and west.

The problem of these two competing formulas came to center stage in October 1848. It was this problem more than any other that defeated the liberals at Frankfurt by prolonging their deliberations until long after the revolutionary moment had passed in the country at large and after the conservatives had had an opportunity to regroup and implement their agrarian reform program. The importance of the two competing formulas was in their forcing to the forefront lines of cleavage on which liberals could not agree: they pitted Prussians against Austrians, Prussians against southwest particularists, Catholics against Protestants. The more tractable and negotiable issues of the balance between the crown and parliament were now subordinated or, worse, recast in terms of the regional conflicts.

In October, the Assembly passed a resolution prohibiting the inclusion of non-German territories into the new nation. This practically compelled the Austrians to choose between the division of the Habsburg Empire and the exclusion of Austria from the new Germany.[75] With the restoration later in the month of conservative governments in Berlin and Vienna, the Austrian Minister-President of the provisional government proposed negotiations with Vienna over the status of the non-German Habsburg lands. Until this time the predominant view of the Assembly had been that it alone was the sovereign authority in Germany and that there should be no negotiations with Vienna or Berlin. The Minister-President's proposal of negotiation was unacceptable to most of the Assembly and provoked it to depose him. This provoked a breakdown of the old alignment on left–right lines and forced a reorganization of the delegates according to their regional and religious identities.[76] The most fundamental divide came to be between those who wished to exclude Austria and those who wished to include it, with Prussians and Protestants on one side and Austrians, particularists, and Catholics on the other. It was indicative of the extent to which these cleavages now debilitated the Assembly that the Assembly's own conduct came increasingly to depend on external events. The restoration of conservative administrations in Berlin and Vienna were merely the first of these.

When the first vote was taken in January 1849 to make the Prussian King the hereditary emperor of united Germany, the *grossdeutsch* faction (favoring inclusion of Austria, being more sympathetic to the southwest particularists and Catholics) could prevail in rejecting this by aligning with what remained of the original left and with the particularists.[77] However, in March 1849 the Austrian Emperor dissolved the Reichstag and unilaterally imposed a constitution on the whole Empire, thus making Austrian inclusion even more unattractive, and making still more difficult the residual left and the particularists' use of Austrian inclusion as a counterweight to Prussian hegemony. With this, what remained of the old left struck a deal with the Prussians exchanging their support for a *kleindeutsch* solution for concessions on the suffrage. This opened the way for a bare majority (267 versus 263) in favor of a Prussian emperor and by corollary the *kleindeutsch* solution.[78] With this resolved, it was possible to dispatch the remaining issues with alacrity. By this late date, however, the liberals found that when the Prussian King rejected their proffered crown, they had no means to impose the constitution. The political atmosphere in the country was now quite different from that of the previous spring, when mass uprisings had compelled the retreat of humiliated conservatives.

By the time the liberals reached agreement on the shape of their new order, conservatives, unhindered by unification because they had little interest in it, had preempted the liberals by gaining the support of the peasantry. In this circumstance, the King of Prussia could freely reject the "crown from the gutter," confident that without the support of the peasants the liberals had nowhere to go but home. Home indeed they did go, convinced that they had been sold out by *das Volk*.

This conveniently self-serving myth became the basis for the German liberals' historic and enduring distrust of mass action, and to that extent at least assumed an important reality of its own. But like all great political myths, it obscured more than it revealed by ignoring the original sources of the peasants' alienation. Those sources were in the inability of liberals to deliver on their own program. In that context, peasants demonstrated a clear understanding of how they could most rationally pursue their interests. They were neither duped by conservatives nor inherently authoritarian. This is a point of some consequence, because the liberal (and even conservative) interpretation of the events of 1848 laid the basis for a long running notion in German historiography of the inherent conservatism of the peasantry. It was a notion that reappeared subsequently in liberal (and socialist) interpretations of the peasants' support for the Junkers later in the century and for fascism between the wars. It was a notion that, by assuming the conservatism, naivete, or irrationality of the peasantry, militated against an enquiry into the defects in German liberalism (and later socialism) that repeatedly made rational a peasant alliance with the Right.

German peasants were in fact quite vigorously involved in the early activities of the liberal movement. They expected that a new constitutional order would satisfy their material interests. As soon as the Frankfurt Assembly was convened, peasants sought to plead their cause to it in the form of countless petitions from even the most remote villages. There is no reason to suppose, then, that they were less interested than their Danish cousins in an opening of the political system to their influence or that they failed to connect such an opening to the advancement of their material interests. Much evidence suggests that they understood the early liberal movement in just these terms. German peasants were, in fact, making themselves available to both liberals and conservatives, for they were simultaneously petitioning the state governments in Baden, Saxony, Mecklenburg, Bavaria, and Prussia. Danish peasants had, in the 1830s and early 1840s, first sought the assistance of the conservative state and, having found the state unresponsive, allied with the National Liberals. German peasants simply pursued both routes simultaneously.[79] Unlike Danish peasants, however, German peasants had ultimately to choose between the immediate gratification of their material claims by efficient conservatives and their more remote and hypothetical gratification by fractious liberals.

In 1848–49, again in the 1860s, and still again in the 1870s, religious and regional differences were at the heart of the liberals' inability to establish their own constitutional order. Few liberals in 1848 sought parliamentary sovereignty. The Frankfurt constitution was, in fact, ambiguous about the balance of sovereignty, a point that has been emphasized by historians.[80] The ambivalence this reflected seems, in comparative perspective, less important than is often thought. None of the constitutions that emerged from the revolutions of 1848, including the extremely liberal Danish constitution, provided unambiguously for the sovereignty of a legislature. At this early date liberals throughout Europe were still inclined to believe that the establishment of a constitutional order that provided them with a secure base of parliamentary power would be sufficient to ensure cooperation between them and a monarch. The long struggles between legislatures and monarchs were still in the future and not generally foreseen by most liberals. What was at stake was the constitutional order in which this subsequent battle would be waged. In Germany, unlike Denmark, liberals lost even this preliminary skirmish. It would haunt them for the remainder of the century.

The decade that followed was one of repression and disillusionment for German liberals. The political ambitions of the Prussian monarch continued to dilate on the preservation of his traditional authority within the confines of Prussia.[81] In both this institutional conservatism and the "little Prussia" mentality that accompanied it, the monarch found himself at odds with the liberals, who were more committed than ever to German unification (ex

Austria) under Prussian hegemony. The monarch was especially loath to adopt a policy that challenged Austrian interests, as the liberal strategy necessarily did. Unification responded to both the nationalist and material ambitions of the liberals, which could never be achieved in the cramped confines of the Zollverein, the Custom Union. Given the state's lack of interest with regard to unification, strengthening the Prussian Diet's influence on state policy became the means by which liberals could induce the pursuit of their material and nationalist interests in unification.

In this, the liberals were greatly helped by the joint effects of rapid economic growth in the 1850s and the three-class franchise. The prospering economy pushed a growing share of the liberals' constituency into the first and second franchise categories, with their accompanying multiple votes.[82] In the election of 1858, the liberals gained a clear majority of 210 Landtag seats compared with the conservatives whose seats were dramatically reduced from 236 to 59. With this great victory, liberals assumed that they had secured an effective source of pressure on the government. They were soon disabused of this notion, however, by the conservative Upper House's repeated rejection of even small reforms and by the monarch's continued resistance to an anti-Austrian policy. Liberal discontent was expressed by the rejection of the government's Army Reform Bill in 1860. The ensuing constitutional conflicts between the King and the liberals were essentially a struggle between the opposing claims of royal and legislative authority,[83] establishment of the latter being the prerequisite to liberal hegemony. When moderate liberals and conservatives in the Diet combined in May 1861 to pass a provisional army bill, those who wanted to hold such measures hostage created the first organized liberal party in Germany, the Progressive Party (*Fortschrittpartei*).

In the wake of this, three liberal groups now existed in the Diet: the Progressives, the Bockum-Dolffes group (left-center), and the Grabow group (old liberals).[84] In the election of December 1861, the Progressives gained more than 100 seats, while the old liberals gained 95, and the left-center gained 50. In March 1862, the Progressives, in alliances with the left-center, refused to pass another provisional army bill, whereupon the King immediately dissolved the chamber. The Progressives and the left-center returned from the new election stronger still. The Progressives now controlled 135 seats and the Bockum-Dolffes group controlled 96. The old liberals lost 4 seats and the conservatives were reduced to a humiliating 10 seats.[85] In September, the Progressives and the left-center once again refused to fund William's army. Into this constitutional crisis William called as his Chancellor Otto von Bismarck.

Bismarck's brilliance was in the dual nature of his strategy of defense of the crown's prerogatives. On the one hand, he essentially ignored the Diet's authority to approve expenditures, thus forcing the liberals from a position of increasing their leverage over the state to one of defending established con-

stitutional prerogatives. On the other hand, he implemented the liberal agenda in virtually all spheres, thus eventually depriving the liberals of the
ultimate rationale for enhanced parliamentary authority. The most important
change Bismarck brought about was in jettisoning the state's pro-Austrian
policy. By turning on Austria (first in the Dano–Prussian War of 1864),
Bismarck adopted the *kleindeutsch* unification formula dear to Prussian liberals' hearts.

The successful wars against Denmark, Austria, and France compelled
liberals to make the same hard choice that peasants had faced in 1848:
between what was desirable and what was possible.[86] The 1866 election,
which took place on the same day as the great victory against the Austrians at
Königgrätz and *after* Bismarck had made known his intention to use universal suffrage in elections to the revamped North German Confederation Reichstag, provided the answer of the liberals' Mittelstand constituency. Conservatives leapt from 38 to 142 seats and the Progressives and left-center fell
from 253 to 148.[87] Sensing the changing mood of much of the Mittelstand,
many of the liberals who retained their seats now opted to subordinate their
democratic ambitions to their aspirations for national unity and material
progress. The liberal denouement came in the form of the approval of the
1866 Indemnity Bill, which acknowledged the budgetary rights of the Diet
but retrospectively authorized the state's unapproved expenditures. When the
bill was finally passed by 230 to 75, half of the Progressives and two-thirds
of the left-center voted for it.[88] Many of the now pro-government liberals
who voted for the bill broke with the Progressives the next year and formed
the National Liberal Party. Thus, at the beginning of the Empire the liberal
movement found itself divided and demoralized.

For the German liberal movement, the defeat was a seminal one. It failed
to establish its dominance even when united on its national goals. In 1848,
the liberals had failed because the playing field was all of Germany, and on
such a field the regional and religious cleavages were necessarily decisive. In
the 1860s, however, the playing field was limited to Prussia, where liberals
shared a common ambition to see a Protestant-dominated Germany unified
by a hegemonic Prussia. Even during this period, however, Bismarck could
succeed only because he could implicitly play off the divisions with the
German (as opposed to the strictly Prussian) liberal community. Had German
liberals not continued to be divided by regional and religious identities in the
1860s, the entire issue of unification and the *kleindeutsch* strategy would
have been less available for Bismarck's manipulation simply because the
success of the *kleindeutsch* strategy would have meant less to Prussian liberals. Indeed, even in 1867 and 1871 in the writing of the constitutions of the
North German Confederation and then the Empire, the ability to manipulate
these intra-German cleavages among the liberals was critical to Bismarck's
success. To induce the support of Prussian liberals in containing decentraliz-
ing particularists from the southwestern states, Bismarck had to concede very

little. Bismarck simply conceded the "nominal" responsibility of the Chancellor to the parliament and recognized its right to approve budgets. In effect, the rather authoritarian constitutional formulations of the North German Confederation and the Empire were possible in large measure because Prussian liberals were so anxious to limit the institutional influence accorded their Catholic and particularist liberal opponents. After 1871, the playing field overtly shifted back to all of Germany, and the old regional and religious cleavages again became explicitly determining sources of division and failure among the liberals.

In a Faustian bargain to gain recognition of the parliament's budgetary rights, the liberals of the North German Confederation Reichstag had approved an exceptional military budget that remained in effect until the end of 1871. At that time, the Imperial Reichstag agreed to extend this "temporary" arrangement for another three years. This extension, of course, occurred in the immediate wake of Bismarck's great victory over the French. When the issue returned in 1874, it provided another occasion for liberals to assert the rights of the parliament. In fact, this issue nearly brought German liberalism to its knees. This liberal failure was, for reasons we will take up subsequently, the last great opportunity for liberals to assert their leadership in Germany. The outcome is well-known to students of German history: in the end, the Reichstag approved Bismarck's Septennial Bill, which provided the military budget for seven years and practically abrogated the Reichstag's budgetary authority (80 percent of state expenditures were for the army) until 1881. On the final vote all of the National Liberals and fourteen of the Progressives supported the government's bill.[89]

The question is, why did the liberals commit this act of political suicide? That is, why were parliamentary prerogatives now of so little importance to the liberals? The answer can no longer be that the liberals were simply overwhelmed by the glory of Bismarck's military triumphs. Indeed, tension between the liberals and Bismarck had been growing anew ever since 1871. Rather, the liberals confronted another hard choice between what was attainable and what was desirable. Their understanding of this was decisively conditioned by the new political conjuncture in which they found themselves. Germany was now unified, universal suffrage was in place, and mass political mobilization was proceeding apace. In this context, the old regional and religious divisions of the Mittelstand returned yet again to defeat the liberals. The most fundamental of facts is that these divisions made a unified Germany a dangerous place to be a liberal.

There was a great deal less to recommend parliamentary authority in a society in which liberals could no longer be confident of their own control of parliament. Liberals understood well that universal suffrage would be a disaster for them. As one Prussian democrat put it in 1866: "We men of the Progressive Party fear nothing as much as the equal, general and direct suffrage, because it would reduce our numbers frightfully. . . . Everyone trembles for this seat."[90] Notwithstanding the liberals' historic fear of *das Volk*, universal suffrage was not a threat because the class cleavage had become decisive at this early stage. If liberals felt threatened by the votes of the lower orders, it was not so much because the lower orders were voting for Socialists as they were for Catholics and particularists. The Socialist share of the vote remained modest for years to come, and if incipient socialism had been the only threat to the liberals, parliamentary sovereignty would not have been incompatible with antisocialist laws.[91] Rather, universal suffrage, especially in a unified Germany, was incompatible with liberal hegemony because religious and regional cleavages, most important among the Mittelstand (which after all continued to provide most parts of the lower orders, especially among Catholics, with their political guidance), prevented liberals from establishing an adequate mass base.

Liberals were threatened by neither universal suffrage per se nor by the abruptness of its introduction. France, too, it is well to recall, introduced universal suffrage in the same year and with equal suddenness, and in the wake of a military *defeat* that hardly provided much to recommend middle-class leadership. Yet neither the scope nor the abruptness of the suffrage debilitated French liberalism. Indeed, it was precisely in this context of an alliance between a substantial fraction of the middle class and the lower urban and rural orders that French liberalism went on to its heyday. Rather than the timing or the scope of the suffrage, what counted was the way in which traditional cleavages structured the use of that suffrage. The most important handicap for liberals, and the real threat of universal suffrage in these years, derived from the old conflicts between nationalists and particularists and especially Catholics and anticlerical Protestants.

Particularist opposition to the Prussian-led centralization of the new nation could mobilize substantial support in some of the newly annexed Prussian territories, in some of the southern states, which had joined the Empire only reluctantly, and especially among the populations of national minorities. Since the liberals were stout supporters of national unity and the national economy, they were invariably regarded as the major enemy by the particularists.

In Hanover, there immediately emerged a strong particularist party, the Guelphs, which pursued a policy of constant confrontation with the National Liberals even after unification. The electoral data demonstrate vividly the Guelph's erosion of the National Liberal base even in this heavily Protestant territory.[92] In the southern states of Bavaria, Württemberg, Baden, and Hesse-Darmstadt, the liberals suffered substantial defeats from the first election to the newly established Zollparlament in 1868. Fifty-seven of the eighty-three delegates elected by the voters in these states were opposed to unification. In Württemberg, all seventeen delegates were particularists. In Bavaria, twenty-six particularists were elected; liberals had to be satisfied with securing twelve seats. Even in the traditional liberal stronghold of

Baden, where the liberals managed to secure a majority, clerical–particu-larists mounted a strong challenge. Only in Hesse-Darmstadt could liberals claim a clear victory.[93] After unification, particularists continued to under-mine the liberals in these states. This was especially the case in Württem-berg, where even among a population that was 65 percent Protestant, the par-ticularist German People's Party made inroads into the liberal electorate. In 1871, the People's Party was unable to elect a single deputy to the Reichstag, whereas the National Liberals elected twelve deputies. By 1881, however, the People's Party was able to elect six and the National Liberals none.[94]

The liberals did even more poorly among the national minorities. In Posen, the Poles elected seven, eight, eight, eight, and nine of their own delegates at the elections of 1871, 1874, 1877, 1878 and 1881. The National Liberals elected two, one, one, one, and none.[95] In Alsace-Lorraine, the Alsace-Lorraine Regional Party monopolized all of the fifteen districts throughout the elections between 1874 and 1887.[96] The strength of the particularists in the Reichstag increased steadily throughout the 1870s.[97]

Until the 1860s a distinctive political consciousness had not emerged among the mass of German Catholics, and a large part of the Catholic Mittelstand supported the liberal movement.[98] Indeed, considering the heav-ily Catholic states of the south and west were also the most tolerant and in many ways the most progressive, the potential for an alliance of the two Mittelstände around the liberal cause was obvious.

In principle, it might seem possible that a liberating alliance of liberals and Catholics of the sort that made Belgium independent and endured there until the 1870s could have been formed. That this alliance fell apart in Belgium just as the Catholic–Protestant cleavage was intensifying in Ger-many certainly points to part of the problem: the general growth of clerical–anticlerical tension in Europe in this decade following not only from German but from Italian unification and the ensuing confrontation between the Pa-pacy and liberalism. Pius IX's Syllabus of Errors in 1864 and the declaration of Papal infallibility in 1870 were virtually declarations of war on liberalism. The *Kulturkampf*, the Imperial campaign of discrimination against German Catholics, enthusiastically advocated by liberals as a means both to consoli-date unification and to weaken their main organized antagonist, was a part of this larger escalation of animosity. The most fundamental difference between Belgium and Germany, however, reaches back to the conflicts of 1848: the *kleindeutsch* formula was one that presupposed unification under *Prussian* hegemony and for that reason constituted a loss rather than a gain of freedom for Catholics. It was not merely coincidental that while Belgian Catholics and liberals could collaborate peacefully, German unification occurred only because of Prussia's overwhelming military force.

Whatever chance there might have been of a liberal–Catholic coalition dissipated quickly after unification. Catholics, who had initially received the Declaration of Papal Infallibility with acute embarrassment—felt even by the bishops who had attended the Vatican Council—soon accepted it less from religious conviction than from an emotional reaction to the exaggerated rhetoric that came from the government and the liberals.[99]

The Catholic Center party was established only in 1870, but immediately gained fifty-seven seats in the 1871 Reichstag elections. This represented the considerable sum of 18.6 percent of the electorate—a stunning success for such a new party and one that no doubt explains the frightened reaction of the liberals to it. Yet it was considerably less than the 32 percent share of Catholics in the population.[100] At this time, many Catholics continued to support liberal candidates. For example, in Bavaria, where Catholics accounted for 71 percent of the population, liberals could still gain thirty seats and 58 percent of the vote.[101] In Aachen, where Catholics were 95 percent of the population, liberals still managed 20 percent of the vote and one seat in 1871.[102]

The great burst of polarization occurred between the elections of 1871 and 1874. The total rate of participation in the latter year was up sharply—from 51 to 61 percent.[103] In that year, the National Liberals gained 40.6 percent of the vote in districts that were more than three-quarters Protestant and 35.1 percent in districts where Protestants were one-half to three-quarters of the population. The Center Party, on the other hand, won 63 percent of the vote (compared with 44.7 in 1871) in districts that were more than three-quarters Catholic and 37 percent (28 percent in 1871) in districts with populations 50 to 75 percent Catholic.[104] The rapidity of Catholic mobilization was, to say the least, impressive. In some areas, the Center Party came to virtually monopolize the electorate. In Aachen, the Catholic share of the vote rose from 58 percent in 1871 to 93 percent in 1874.[105] In Bavaria, the number of liberal delegates to the Reichstag was reduced from thirty in 1871 to sixteen in 1874 and to just ten in 1881. The Catholic delegation rose from eighteen in 1871 to thirty-two in 1874.[106] Participation rates were distinctly higher in heavily Catholic districts than they were in heavily Protestant districts.[107] The efficiency of the Catholic mobilization is also indicated by the constant increase in the number of Catholic party candidates at Reichstag elections: 145 (1871), 189 (1874), 197 (1877), 213 (1878), and 218 (1881).[108]

Taken together with the growing vote for particularists and ethnic minorities, this Catholic vote had devastating implications for the liberals. Together the two cleavages decisively blocked the possibility of the liberals extending their mass base at just that critical historical juncture at which German politics entered the period of mass mobilization. Unlike Belgium, where it was possible for a time to make a coalition among clerical and anticlerical fractions of the middle classes, and unlike France and Switzerland, where anticlericalism tended to cement a large fraction of the middle classes to liberalism, in Germany these conflicts critically divided the middle classes. It was thus inevitable that the National Liberals and the Progressives, once the largest parties in the Reichstag, were of only marginal importance after 1881. Whereas the National Liberals received 30.1 percent of the vote in 1871, ten years later their share had fallen to just 14.7 percent. The Progressives, once the great liberal party of Germany, received only 8.8 percent of the popular vote in 1871 and averaged between 7 and 13 percent at elections over the next decade.[109]

It is possible, of course, that German liberals would have failed to establish their dominance even if they had been able to avoid the pitfalls of nationalist and religious conflict. It is quite possible to adduce other explanations—the powerful role of the Junkers, the skill of Bismarck, the prestige of the monarchy, for instance—to account for liberalism's failure. All such approaches have undoubtedly greatly added to our understanding of the course of German history. The experiences of other European societies, however, suggest that the balance of probabilities would have been very much more in the liberals' favor if they had been able to bind the Catholic and Protestant Mittelstände. The bottom line, if we may employ such language, is that the essential currency of liberal political power throughout Europe in the late nineteenth century was mass support. The essence of the period was the shift from oligarchic and elite politics to mass politics. Without mass support, liberals never succeeded. With it, many other obstacles, as we have seen, could sooner or later be overcome.

For the longer term, I argue that it made little difference whether liberals did not overcome these obstacles at all as in Germany, overcame them only very late in the mobilizational game, as in Sweden, or only temporarily as in Norway and Italy. In the absence of liberal hegemony throughout the mobilizational race of the last thirty years before the Great War, the range of choice among political and economic institutions would be fundamentally the same between the two world wars. Such a conclusion (which, of course, remains to be demonstrated) in any case depends fundamentally on the terms of reference employed to define the range of choice. In other respects, certainly—and not least for the political experience before 1914—it mattered a great deal whether liberals succeeded early and then faltered, succeeded only partially and at a late date, or did not succeed at all.

Italy

While powerful feudal elites have often been pointed to as the main obstacle to the success of German liberalism, it is precisely the absence of these elites that has been adduced to account for the premature success and ultimate failure of Italian liberalism. Antonio Gramsci has drawn our attention to what he has described as the premature victory of the liberal bourgeoisie in Italy. As feudalism had been destroyed before capitalist development took an industrial turn in Italy (a point that could be made with equal force but, tellingly, without the same consequences in Norway and the Netherlands), the narrow ruling strata that directed the extension of Piedmont's institutions to the rest of the peninsula found themselves initially without a challenge from the right (there were no advocates of a return to an ancien regime) or from the left (there was equally no industrial proletariat). Gramsci saw the Risorgimento as a limited bourgeois revolution that could be undertaken without broad class alliances, but which consequently produced a weak state devoid of legitimacy.[110]

The narrow middle-class strata found at the apex of this state were never able to establish a mass following in *le pays réel* and were besieged almost from the outset by challenges emanating from Catholics and the peasantry and later from socialists. It was in large measure the challenge of practicing Catholics and the liberals' inability to respond to it that determined the subsequent liberal inability to meet the socialist challenge. The liberal order became a fortress behind which a besieged fraction of the upper middle classes took refuge against the clerical challenge. Only as long as the peasants remained illiterate, the pope obdurate, and the small proletariat quiescent were liberals secure.

It cannot be stated too emphatically that unification had been the work of a small minority of the northern propertied anticlerical middle class, mainly its agrarian elements. Moreover, its success had been contingent much more on favorable international circumstances than on popular support among Italians. The vast majority of the public remained indifferent or hostile to unification, a point that was driven home to the liberals by the wave of peasant rebellions that swept the south in the 1870s. The suppression of this *brigantaggio*, as liberals came to call it, amounted virtually to a civil war and cost more lives than all the wars of unification put together. The isolation of the liberal elite was apparent, as well, in the waging of a war with Austria in alliance with France rather than the calling forth of a popular uprising; in the annexation of the rest of Italy to Piedmont and the use of plebiscites rather than a constituent assembly to provide a common constitutional framework; in the narrowness of the suffrage (1.9 percent of the population); in the strict extension of Piedmont's institutions and administrative practices to the rest of the peninsula; in the widespread reliance on northern carpetbaggers to administer and police the south; and in resort to a version of the centralized model of prefectoral control borrowed from France to maintain public order.

Unification occurred in the face of unqualified opposition from the Catholic Church. Rome itself was forcibly occupied. The Church, unwilling to surrender its temporal authority, refused to recognize the legitimacy of the new state. Indeed, it declared a veritable war on the state and demanded that the faithful choose between liberalism and Catholicism. Pius IX, branding the King a "sacrilegious usurper" and excommunicating all those associated with unification, forbade Catholics from participation in the affairs of the state, as either voters or officeholders. The Church rejected liberalism in toto by such pronouncements as the Syllabus of Errors in 1864 and by the Proclamation of Papal Infallibility in 1870.

The Syllabus rejected reconciliation or compromise "with progress, with liberalism and with modern civilization." It condemned freedom of conscience and worship, the sovereignty of the secular state and the new state's claims to a monopoly in matters of education and matrimony. The Syllabus confronted every Catholic with a clear choice: "either liberal or Catholic, either Catholic or liberal." To profess liberal Catholicism was, in Pius IX's words, "to embrace simultaneously God and the devil."[111] It was not in the Vatican's power to undertake the forcible overthrow of the state, but it refused to cooperate with or even acknowledge the legitimate existence of the state. In 1874, Pius pronounced the Encyclical *Non Expedit,* which prohibited the faithful from participating in the politics of the new state. If it is not possible to measure with precision the effect this had, it is nonetheless clear from the low rate of electoral participation (seldom did more than half of those eligible vote, often only a third) even under the extremely narrow franchise, that a large part of the population did indeed reject the liberal state.[112]

The story of liberalism in the years before 1914 is in fact mainly the story of the narrow elites' declining ability to preserve its political authority in the absence of mass support. On the whole, the early years were a period of consolidation, and popular demands were limited. The traditional center-right governed until it was undone by its own fiscal probity in 1876, ushering in the rule of the center-left under Agostino Depretis. The right did not so much go into opposition as it melted away. There was, in fact, little to distinguish the right and left. The left was somewhat more progressive, somewhat more representative of the south, slightly more anticlerical, less respectful of civil liberties, predisposed to a slight enlargement of the franchise and the abolition of the most hated indirect tax, the grist tax.

Agostino Depretis is blamed for having introduced the practice of *trasformismo,* "of assuring the government of an adequate majority in Parliament either by a preliminary deal with the more prominent members of the opposition, and by eventually absorbing them into the government, or by means of favoritism, and by corrupting those deputies who had previously been less marked by the stains of parliamentary life; or by a combination of these methods."[113] *Trasformismo* was simply a more crass version of the *connubio* of left and right by which Camillo Benso di Cavour had consolidated his position in Piedmont in 1852. It was a logical method of balancing competing claims in the Parliament when the franchise was so restrictive and participation even narrower, and when the main line of conflict was not in the Parliament but between the country and the increasingly besieged liberal interests in the Parliament. Under Depretis the left extended the vote to the lower limit of the middle class (7 percent of the population) by easing property and literacy requirements. It was in fact immediately in the wake of this and symptomatic of the unease it engendered even on the left that Depretis made his famous appeal for a *trasformismo.*[114]

This practice had much to recommend it among an elite more united than divided. This unity stemmed from its extreme narrowness and its class-specific base. Given the availability of prefects to make and unmake local majorities and the small electorate, there was little need for political parties. The electoral rules, and especially the attention to literacy requirements, were intended to ensure the exclusion of the presumably Catholic peasantry. Even among those with the right to vote, one-half to two-thirds did not. How much of this was due to ignorance, to apathy, or to the papal rejection of the regime is not known. But between the efficiency of the prefects, the literacy requirements (more than two-thirds of the adult population remained illiterate in the 1880s) and the proscriptions of Pius IX, liberals could take comfort in the fact that the untutored masses remained unthreatening throughout the years of Depretis' "parliamentary dictatorship."

In 1887 leadership passed to Francesco Crispi, who dominated Parliament until 1896. During Crispi's years, the liberal order came under an increasing threat from the country and Crispi responded with a policy of repression at home and imperialism abroad. "It was, one may say, a colonialism for domestic use, created for the purpose of internal policy, to convince the Italians that Italy too was a great power, and so to surround with a halo of prestige a state that would otherwise have had little."[115] His years in office and the repressive governments from 1896 to 1900 marked a major crisis in the liberal order that emerged from the Risorgimento, one that nearly brought the constitutional system to an end. The 1890s were a decade of growing popular challenge to the regime by both socialists and practicing Catholics. There was no direct reduction of the suffrage. The return to single-member constituencies and enforcement of stricter residency requirements in 1894 did, however, reduce the number of eligible voters by almost 29 percent, from 9.4 to 6.7 percent of the population. This disenfranchised more than 800,000 men.[116] In the absence of the defeat at Adowa, which brought about Crispi's fall in 1896, the authoritarianism very likely would have become fully formed. As it was, the conservative governments of di Rudini and General Pelloux that followed in the period 1896 to 1900 tried but failed to make repression work.

> Amid strikes and riots, the crisis of distribution brought repression that sparked a crisis of legitimacy, and underscored the weak penetration of a regime poorly informed and ill-equipped to handle such crises or to ease the resentment of citizens excluded from effective participation in politics. Violence in Sicily and workers' risings in Milan in 1898 were met by troops, mass arrests, and the closing of "subversive" newspapers and organizations, socialist and Catholic.[117]

At its core, the problems were those of an order that was without its own organizational presence in society—lacking any effective liberal parties—and was without legitimate institutional means by which its opponents could articulate their grievances.

[The] growing isolation of the liberals was . . . rooted in the static, non--representative nature of the institutional framework. Despite new problems posed by industrialization and the politicization of previously inactive social strata, the liberals failed to develop mechanisms and structures with which they might have both mobilized the bourgeoisie and integrated the under-classes. This widening gap between a dynamic society and a static institutional framework was apparent in the insularity of parliamentary life, where the rise and fall of governments had less to do with crisis situations or fundamental differences over public policy, than with success or failure in forming and maintaining amorphous *combinazioni* among deputies who, as an autonomous group, had themselves elected quite independent of outside forces and interests.[118]

Having found repression wanting, a majority of the liberal elite rallied around Giovanni Giolitti's policy of broadened participation. The final period, that of Giolitti (1900–14), was marked by a recognition that repression had failed but also by an inability to make accommodation work. The keys to this accommodation were two extensions of the franchise, the first in 1903 and the second in 1911. Giolitti's aim was to stabilize the liberal order by establishing a liberal–labor alliance. To extend the suffrage in a society in which workers and peasants were increasingly hardened against the regime, however, was to court disaster. The measure of this was the repression and coercion with which Giolitti sought to manage the elections of 1904, 1909, and 1913.[119] He could now create his own liberal majority in the Parliament of 500 deputies only by coercing victories in the 200 or so southern constituencies while allowing (there was little alternative) open fights in the north. With his southern core and 100 or so northern deputies susceptible to the appeals of *trasformismo,* Giolitti could count on a stable parliamentary majority. To this he sought to add the support of the growing Italian Socialist Party. The Socialists, or at least the plurality of them led by Filippo Turati, were initially inclined to an alliance, but always contemptuous of liberalism. The party was decisively radicalized by the shift to manhood suffrage in 1911 and the Libyan War in 1912.

It is not plausible to suppose that it would have been possible, in the absence of this colonial war, to cement the liberal–labor alliance. The war was an effort by Giolitti to accommodate the nationalist fraction of the middle classes. Its main significance, however, was in indicating that polarization in Italy had reached such a level that imperialism—which in Britain, America, and France actually had the positive integrative effect of giving workers and the middle classes something in common to cheer about—was sufficient to break the alliance. It was a mark of socialism's already great alienation (neither the Boer War, the Spanish-American War, nor Indochina could have the same effect in Britain, America, or France) that a colonial war was itself sufficient to complete the collapse of the liberal–labor alliance. It was a peculiar feature of societies in which liberalism was besieged—Italy, Belgium, the Netherlands, Germany—that imperialism and nationalism became class divisive rather than integrative. The irony is that it was in just these societies, where imperial ambitions were launched mainly for the purposes of domestic integration, that such ambitions were most disintegrative. In contrast, imperialism turned out to be most integrative in those societies in which its ambitions were least well thought out in terms of domestic integration—Britain, France, and America; that is, where integration was less an issue to begin with.

Between the extension of the suffrage in 1911 and its implementation in the 1913 election, the Libyan War intervened to destroy Giolitti's hopes of a liberal–labor alliance. The upshot was that Giolitti turned to the incipient Catholic movement, which was now freed from the radical isolationism of earlier years and frightened into an alliance with Giolitti by the fear of socialism. The liberal–Catholic alliance still represented only a very partial Catholic accommodation to liberalism: a Catholic could support a liberal only where the likely alternative was a radical anticlerical victory. The alliance was cemented just before the 1913 elections by the Gentiloni Pact between Giolitti and Count Gentiloni, head of the Unione Cattolica Italiana. It speaks volumes about the continued isolation of Catholics and liberals and the suspicion among large sections of each community that both Giolitti and Gentiloni thought it essential to keep the formal existence of the pact a secret. This pact, like the aborted attempt to make a deal with the socialists, was necessitated by manhood suffrage, which was itself required by the illegitimacy of the liberal order and the previous failure of repression.

> Doing all that he could to "make" the 1913 election, Giolitti emerged with a majority, but one which was clearly smaller, more heterogeneous and fragile than those of the past when liberals had complete parliamentary hegemony. Liberals now had 318 seats out of 508, 52 fewer than their previous tally of 370 seats; of this 318 seats, 288 had been dependent upon external support from catholics.[120]

Just as the attempt at legitimation through accommodation failed with the socialists, it also failed with the Catholics when the Radicals (Left Liberals) learned of the Gentiloni Pact and induced Giolitti to resign. This necessarily represented the last installment of Giolitti's accommodationist line before the outbreak of the Great War.

Italian liberalism never established its political hegemony insofar as it never penetrated society and it remained isolated behind a fortress of restrictive institutions until the opening up of those institutions destroyed it. The key to this isolation was in its inability to bridge the clerical–anticlerical cleavage. That cleavage left liberals isolated and poorly positioned to build alliances later with socialists.

Here we must paraphrase our earlier remarks about the passing of Swedish liberalism's heyday. When the liberals' era passed without ever having been firmly established, it was not mainly due to late industrialization, although industrialization was surely the proximate cause of the turn-of-the century mobilization of Catholics and workers. Even less was it due to the radicalizing effects of the Great War, which remained to be fought. As late industrialization meant the comparatively late appearance of an urban industrial middle class, it also meant the late appearance of an industrial proletariat and mass mobilization generally. In principle, the autonomous formation of these workers into a class could have occurred much more gradually than it actually did. It occurred so quickly because it occurred in opposition to the liberal order. It was precisely because this autonomous formation occurred so quickly that liberalism's time passed as soon as it did. This process spelled the end of the opportunity for an effective liberal–labor coalition. This autonomous formation, as we shall see in more detail in the next chapter, was irrevocably in train well before the collapse of Giolitti's liberal–labor coalition in 1912.

Modernization, Cleavages, and Political Struggles

There is a paradox in the relationship between industrialization and liberalism. On the one hand, we can agree with Gramsci that the absence of capitalist industrialization and the extreme social backwardness more generally limited the social base for liberalism at the end of the Risorgimento.[121] Yet it was precisely in those early years—during the era of Depretis, when Italy was most backward—that liberals were most secure. An enlargement of the middle classes did not make liberalism more secure. It was industrialization, heightened mobility, and the spread of literacy that provoked the mass mobilization besieging liberalism in the final decades before the war. The implication of the Gramscian analysis, and on this score much liberal thinking, is that liberalism would have encountered a more congenial environment in Italy (and in other comparably situated societies) if it had appeared at a time when a higher level of affluence and literacy had been obtained. A greater level of modernization would presumably have produced a large middle strata and a more integrated society.[122] As we saw at the beginning of this chapter, that was precisely the argument Ralf Dahrendorf made about Germany.[123] Presumably, this conclusion derives from a comparison, at least implicit, with the flourishing of liberalism in Britain and France. It was not, however, a higher level of modernization that produced more favorable conditions for liberalism in Britain and France.

The experiences of Italy and the several other societies we have considered suggest that the causality this notion implies—that greater affluence and education would have eroded the traditional lines of conflict that left liberalism isolated—had very little relevance to the final decades of the nineteenth century. Modernization leading to the erosion of traditional lines of conflict may explain a great deal in interepochal terms. That is, it may explain much if we are contrasting, say, the late nineteenth century with the period between the two world wars or the interwar period with the present.[124] But what counted at the turn of the century was less the absolute level of modernization, its timing, or its pace than the inherited lines of conflict on which this modernization was superimposed. The further modernization proceeded, the more vulnerable liberalism became.

Liberalism did not become vulnerable, however, because modernization provoked acute class conflict. In Britain, France, and Switzerland, liberalism was weakened between the wars by intense class conflict, but this class conflict was caused by modernization in only the most remote and uninformative way. In all of the other societies we have examined, liberalism was already in retreat *before* class conflict became a central feature of politics. In all of these cases, liberalism was impaled on conflicts that were accentuated by modernization, but preceded worker mobilization. Indeed, in two cases, Denmark and Sweden, the limited success liberalism did have at the end of the century was not in spite of rising class conflict, but because growing class conflict gave liberals new allies, for a brief historical moment. Those new allies were useful precisely because they helped compensate for the liberals' inability to bridge more traditional divisions.

Let us put a finer point on the relationship between modernization, inherited cleavages, and political struggle in this epoch: French peasants were not more likely than their Italian counterparts to make alliances with urban liberals because greater literacy had taught them the foolishness of clerical ways. Rather, whatever their level of literacy, the anticlerical identity that they inherited from the Revolution already gave them something in common with anticlerical liberals. Literacy encouraged their participation in politics, but along inherited lines. All of the experiences we have considered, in fact, have suggested just that: industrialization, increased mobility, and literacy actually brought into political life social divisions whose political implications had previously been latent. Modernization, after some minimal level, was politically neutral. What were not neutral were the historical animosities that modernization awoke.

Where Backwardness Mattered

At some outer point, the nature of the social structure and the level of modernization did indeed matter. There was undoubtedly a level of backwardness below which no liberal movement could expect to anchor itself in society. The question is at what level was backwardness so substantial that cleavages within the middle classes no longer determined liberalism's failure? When did a lack of modernization cease to be neutral?

It was surely not neutral when it was so pervasive that politics was a largely oligarchic affair. There had to be a middle class, and a politically attentive, economically independent middle class at that. If such a class hardly existed, the cleavages within it cannot be held to have caused liberalism's failure. This is certainly one of the most fundamental distinctions to be drawn between the experiences of prewar Western and Eastern Europe. In the most extreme cases, throughout many parts of Eastern Europe, levels of industrialization were much lower and the middle classes (both urban and rural) much smaller than in the West—so much so that, in such territories (Lithuania, Latvia, Estonia, Poland, and the Balkans) the class structure was so inappropriate that liberal movements could never be more than alienated voices in swamps of backwardness.[125] Elsewhere in Eastern Europe, the level of modernization was greater, but still a handicap for liberals. In the cities, in the place of an economically independent middle class a kind of ersatz middle class appeared, dependent on state employment and foreign capital. In the countryside, a landed elite often continued to lord over an impoverished and illiterate peasantry. Under these circumstances, such liberal institutions as appeared—written constitutions, manhood suffrage, and parliaments, for example—were merely epigonic. "The Portuguese constitution of 1822, the Bulgarian constitution of 1879, the Serbian constitution of 1889. . . are cases in point, with their provisions for universal suffrage and vast powers vested in the elective branch of government."[126] The main function of such liberal institutions, as Andrew Janos has compellingly and perceptively argued, was to serve as the emblems—for foreign and domestic consumption—of modernity in premodern societies.[127]

Spain: A Borderline Case

The dividing line between the Western and Eastern experiences appears to have run through Spain. Spanish liberals were beset by the Eastern burden of backwardness and the Western burden of infelicitous cleavages. Many of the attributes of Eastern backwardness—widespread illiteracy and apathy, a state-dependent middle class, regions of latifundia agriculture, highly centralized but inefficient state structures—were characteristic of Restoration Spain. Indeed, parts of Eastern Europe, including Finland, Bohemia, Hungary, and Austria, were as industrialized as or more industrialized than Spain.[128] At the same time, Spanish liberals were crippled by many of the ethnic, regional, and religious conflicts that were characteristic of the West. I hasten to add that these conflicts abounded in the East, too. Throughout the East, for example, the entrepreneurial fraction of the middle classes was becoming increasingly dominated by immigrants and ethnic minorities. The political potential of what Fred Riggs has called this "pariah entrepreneurship" was, naturally, severely limited by its ethnopolitical inferiority.[129] As Andrew Janos has observed,

> In Poland, Hungary and Romania, these entrepreneurs were largely drawn
> from Jewish immigrant communities, whose members replaced classes of
> "native" German entrepreneurs. In the Balkans, the modern entrepreneurs of
> the *carsija* were mostly Armenians and Greeks. . . . In Bulgaria, by the end
> of the nineteenth century only a small minority of merchants and artisans
> were natives, the majority were Armenians, Turks and Sepharidic Jews. In
> Serbia, more than two-fifths of the urban bourgeoisie was of Albano-Greek,
> or Tsintsar, origin. In Portugal, English, Hanseatic and French traders were
> replacing native entrepreneurs.[130]

This disjunction between economic power and political power was characteristic of early capitalism in backward societies, and it was paralleled in
Spain by the alienation of the more industrially advanced Catalonia, Valen-
cia, and the Basque country from the politically hegemonic but backward
Castile.

Such cleavages had less political importance in the East, however, because the industrial sectors in these societies were miniscule or because the
societies themselves were not independent. Where independence was lacking, the implications of the cleavages were somewhat muted because ultimate
authority was not in local hands. This was a fundamental difference; for
Spain, while sharing the backwardness of the East, also shared the national
independence of the West. Spanish politics were consequently not subordinated to the kinds of intraimperial struggles that characterized politics in the
dependent territories of the Russian, German, and Habsburg empires. Spanish liberals did not, for instance, have the "good fortune" of their Finnish
counterparts in being able to unite the urban and rural middle classes against
a Russification campaign during the critical turn-of-the-century years of mobilization. It is more than a little informative that, notwithstanding the bitter
urban–rural, class, and ethnolinguistic divisions that festered within Finland
and would soon burst forth, the Finnish middle classes during these years
were divided almost solely by the tactical question of how truculently to
resist the Russians.

In effect, the cleavages and backwardness of Spain were allowed to play
themselves out in all their political consequences because liberals could
neither subsume their differences in a national struggle nor avoid responsibility as lesser actors on a larger imperial stage.[131] What united Spanish liberals
with other Western liberals was the fact that, acting in an independent nation,
their success or failure was their own. In common with many Western liberal
movements, they could consequently be just successful enough before the
war to be judged a failure, but not successful enough to establish their
hegemony. Unlike other western liberals, however, their failure was guaranteed not simply by their own divisions, but by the backwardness of the
society in which they struggled. In combining national independence with
divisions within the middle classes *and* backwardness, Spain thus brought
together two distinctive experiences. An adequate account of Spanish liber-

alism's failure must include the effects of both inherited cleavages and the lack of modernity.

The pivotal conflict of nineteenth-century Spain was between the forces of clericalism and anticlericalism. The Restoration settlement of 1875 marked no more than a truce—arrived at by mutual exhaustion—between these two forces. The Liberals, the heirs of the old anticlerical Progressives, accepted the Restoration because it provided them with a partial victory— civil marriage, universal suffrage, trials by jury, and so forth—and at the same time, through the *turno pacífico,* guaranteed them access to the booty of state office. For both the Liberals and the Conservatives, the Restoration had the considerable benefit of eliding from the political equation, at least for a time, the spasmodic interventions of the officers' corps and the lower orders.[132]

The key to this tranquility was the *turno,* which guaranteed that the Conservatives and Liberals would alternate in power and made the Cortes the arena through which conflicts could be negotiated unhampered by unruly officers and mobs. The system worked because Liberals and Conservatives were willing to concede power whenever they found their "situation" exhausted. In practice, this meant that the Conservatives would stand aside whenever it appeared that a period of Liberal rule would deflect criticism from the Bourbon monarchy. The incoming government could then "make" its Cortes majority through the cacique system, a network of patronage that ran from the minister of the interior to a Liberal or Conservative wirepuller (sometimes one and the same) in every village in Spain.[133]

The massive electoral fraud on which this system was predicated became problematic only after the Disaster of 1898. That disaster was the loss of the Cuban, Puerto Rican, and Philippine residues of empire in the Spanish– American War. The loss of the colonies and destruction of the navy (it had just one day of target practice a year and could never afford enough coal to run at full speed) were an indictment the political order could never live down.[134]

The disaster, because it so vividly displayed the inadequacies of the Madrid regime and meant the loss of important foreign markets, reawakened the historical animosities between backward Castile and the more industrially advanced Basque and Catalan territories.[135] These animosities reached back centuries to the earlier independent and semi-independent status of the territories and to their cultural and linguistic distinctiveness. For hundreds of years this distinctiveness had been acknowledged in the *fueros,* or historic liberties, of these regions. In part as a defense of the *fueros,* rural Catalonia and the Basque provinces had been the heartland of the ultra-Catholic Carlist challenge to Madrid throughout the century. The centralizing Bourbons managed to retrieve the last of the regional prerogatives only in the 1820s and 1830s in the case of Catalonia and after the third Carlist War (1875) in the Basque lands. Almost as soon as the regional prerogatives were squelched, cultural–nationalist movements began to flourish in each area. It was only after 1898, however, that the political dimension again became decisive. For it was then that the cultural nationalism merged with the clerical sentiments of rural Carlist traditions and the economic interests of urban manufacturers to make Catalan nationalism a powerful and disintegrating force in Spanish politics. The principal agent of Catalan nationalism was the Lliga Catalana, which monopolized the Catalan right after 1901. The clerical, regionalist Lliga could reach an enduring accommodation with neither the clerical, centralizing Conservatives nor the anticlerical, centralizing Liberals.[136]

If regionalism and clericalism prevented the Lliga middle classes from reaching an accommodation with Madrid, conflicts within Catalonia equally prevented the possibility of them providing leadership of the more industrialized peripheries *against* Madrid. Within Catalonia, the more affluent sectors of the middle classes were nationalist and clerical; the lower middle classes were not. The former were thus united by the nationalist and clericalist Lliga, the latter were united by the antinationalist and anticlerical Republican party. It was possible for these two parties to bridge their differences—as they did in 1907 in the Solidaridad Catalana alliance—only when Catalan interests were seen to be under extraordinary attack by Madrid.[137]

The Restoration order came under growing pressure, as well, from a revivification of the clerical–anticlerical struggle. After 1898, Liberal and Conservative governments respectively competed in enacting and rescinding restraints on the Church. Liberal anticlericalism was no doubt motivated in part by a desire to integrate workers without addressing class issues. But it was also spurred by the pressing problems of educational reform—43 percent of the adult population remained illiterate in 1900 in a society in which the Church dominated education—and the economic threat, real or perceived, that the regular orders posed for both workers and the lower middle classes in urban areas. As well as dominating education, the Church was an important force in the urban economy. Joaquín Aguilera, the secretary of the Catalan manufacturers' association (Fomento del Trabajo Nacional) estimated in 1912 that the church "controlled, without exaggeration, one-third of the capital wealth in Spain." Whether this was the case, smaller producers especially felt keenly threatened by the Church's ability to employ low-wage labor and to escape most taxation.[138]

Regionalism, the Church, and to a lesser extent class conflict were the essential axes on which Spanish politics rotated between 1898 and the military seizure of power in 1923. These conflicts did not simply prevent a hegemonic liberal coalition; in practice, they prevented the appearance of any effective governing coalition, thus creating the conditions that invited a military takeover in 1923. It is obvious that backwardness made more difficult the accommodation of these cleavages. The backwardness of Spanish society was both indexed by and mediated through the role of the army, the weakness of civil agencies and political parties, the massiveness of electoral fraud, and the disjunction of political and economic power. These manifestations of backwardness are worth examining, because they draw a line between Italy and Spain. Backwardness was much more determining in Spain than it was in Italy. This was so in part simply because Spain was a less modern society, with a smaller industrial sector and a larger population of illiterates.[139] But the lesser modernity of Spain was more determining, as well, because of how the balance of political forces accentuated the authority of the less modern sectors of society.

The electoral fraud that underpinned the Restoration was itself contingent on widespread illiteracy and apathy. As modernization proceeded, because mobilization occurred against the established order, that fraud became more difficult and soon had to be supplemented by heavy doses of coercion. In this, Spain was not unlike Italy. But there was a fundamental difference, for in the north of Italy coercion and fraud receded after 1898 under Giolitti, even as it reached "perfection," as William Salomone put it, in the south.[140] In the north Giolitti sought an accommodation with the workers and Catholics excluded from the liberal order. In Spain coercion and fraud intensified in the more developed regions.[141] This distinctive Spanish response was, in effect, a resort to the practices of a backward society. In this, it surely reflected the *mentalité* of the sectors whence the ruling Liberals and Conservatives came. More to the point, the political importance of the coercion was mainly in its application to the more advanced peripheries rather than to the still torpid hinterland, and in seeking to squelch the nationalism and working-class radicalism of the peripheries, it definitely reflected the *mentalité* of Castile and Andalusia.

In short, a different balance of political power, one that gave greater weight to Catalonia in particular, would likely have yielded a different response to the crises after 1898. The political balance that existed, however, was rooted in the peculiar manner in which the cleavage structure divorced the modern sectors of the economy from political power. It was a cleavage structure that, by impeding both the accommodation of the periphery and its hegemony, reinforced the political authority of the more backward regions of the country, and thereby allowed backwardness to be more determining in Spain than it was in Italy.

In Italy, too, there existed the potential for a regional conflict between the more affluent, literate, and industrial north versus the impoverished, illiterate, and rural south. The regional contrasts could hardly have been more pronounced. Per capita income in the north was about double what it was in the south. Illiteracy rates were about two and a half to three times higher in the south than in the north.[142] But in Italy, unification under a liberal order was a northern project that from the earliest days served the interests of northern manufacturing at the expense of the much more backward south. Unification meant the creation of a national market for northern manufactures that came at the expense of such infant industry as existed in the south. Industrial tariffs, first raised in 1887, also worked mainly to the benefit of the north by raising the prices of manufactured goods, of which the south was a net consumer. Even agricultural protection worked disproportionately to the benefit of the farmers of the north and the center, where yields-per-acre were much higher, for southern agriculture was in large measure simply subsistence production.[143] As Christopher Seton-Watson has put it, "In 1887 the south was overruled by the north and became its economic tributary."[144] The distribution of taxation was a further indicator of the state's northern orientation. In 1910, the economist Maffeo Pantaleoni calculated that northern Italy, with 48 percent of the national wealth, paid 40 percent of the nation's taxes; the center with 25 percent, paid 28 percent; and the south, with 27 percent of the national wealth, paid 32 percent of the nation's taxes.[145] This distortion was compounded by the distribution of the national debt, which grew rapidly after unification. In effect, because the debt was purchased overwhelmingly by the northern middle classes and because the state was not using the debt for southern investment, southern taxpayers were subsidizing the investment income of the north.[146] This was in keeping with the recruitment patterns of national Liberal leadership: most Liberal leaders were northerners. Indeed, they were notorious for their ignorance of conditions in the south, many of them never having ventured below Rome in their entire lives. It was also in keeping with the larger pattern of political competition: elections in the south were noncompetitive and provided the Liberals, through patronage and fraud, with an ironclad quota of parliamentary seats. The north provided the main arena of mobilization and competition, and it was to northern interests that Liberals had to attend if they were to preserve their power. All of this amounts to saying that throughout the liberal era, Italian state power was largely geared to the interests of the north, the more modern sector of society.

This conjunction of the modern economy and political power did not exist in Spain. National political power resided in Madrid with the Conservative and Liberal parties, who mainly reflected the economic interests of landed elites of rural Castile and Andalusia. The modern economy, however, was in the peripheral regions. After 1908, the Basque territories alone accounted for 30 percent of industrial investment.[147] It was indicative of the disjunction that Catalonia, with one-eighth of the total population, provided the state with one-quarter of its revenue but received back just one-tenth of the state's expenditures.[148] In effect, the modern sectors were subsidizing the backward sectors. To be sure, peripheral industry benefited from high tariff protection, but it suffered at the same time from the high taxes on industry and commerce to the benefit of agriculture, the inability of the bloated state to make itself more efficient, and its consequent inability to make the infrastructural and social investments that would stimulate industry. These inherent obstacles to modernization were compounded by the loss of the colonies and the stabilization program that followed 1898. Although exports to the colonies accounted for only a miniscule fraction of peripheral production, they were a vital source of the foreign exchange required for industrial modernization. Catalan textiles were especially hurt by this loss. Between 1899 and 1905, the government carried out a program of severe economic policies that relieved the treasury of its heavy debts; but it imposed higher excise and business taxes, still keeping taxes on agriculture minimal, thus further favoring the agrarian interests with which the Conservatives and Liberals were associated.[149]

Spanish backwardness, then, was a kind of original sin: it could be overcome only by redistributing political power to the more modern sectors, but that redistribution could not occur because the inherited cleavages prevented those sectors from either combining under the leadership of Catalonia or reaching an accommodation with Madrid. In effect, the peculiar cleavage structure reinforced the political hegemony of the less modern parts of Spain.

The growing involvement of the army was a clear signal of the weakness of state agencies and the low level of political mobilization outside of the peripheries.[150] The distinctive feature was not the role of the army as a domestic instrument of state power—common enough throughout Western Europe—but its growing encroachment in previously civil matters and ultimately its attack on the state. The role of the military was also distinctive because—and again backwardness combines with inherited cleavages—it was in Spain alone in Western Europe that the most modern sectors of the middle classes saw the military as an enemy. After 1898, antipathy to the army was rife among all sectors of Catalan society. The officers' corps, for its part, despised Catalan nationalism as a threat to its vision of a great Spain. This polarization reached its critical moment in 1905, with the enactment of the Law of Jurisdictions, which allowed the military to prosecute its civilian critics in military courts.[151] From this point, Liberal and Conservative governments became progressively more dependent on the armed forces while the armed forces became progressively more autonomous. The military was provoked to demand the law by the ridicule it received from a Catalan humor magazine. In Catalonia the response to the Law of Jurisdictions—seen to be aimed specifically at Catalonia—was the temporary alliance of all Catalan parties in Solidaridad Catalana, a kind of regional popular front.[152] Thus, we have the otherwise unprecedented phenomenon of Liberal and Conservative governments menacing even the most advanced sectors of the middle classes with the armed forces.

Nowhere else in Western Europe could armies act as such autonomous agents. The return to praetorianism after 1898 was possible because civilian institutions—state agencies and political parties—were very weak. The military became a decisive political force because it was one of the few cohesive institutions in a society in which there were no institutions that could legitimately claim to speak for the nation. Neither state agencies—essentially bloated dispersers of patronage for a dependent middle class—nor political parties disposed of such legitimacy. Parties were by no means weak simply because of fraudulent elections. Elsewhere, at higher levels of modernization and mobilization, it was the norm for the excluded to create coherent parties—with regular dues, membership lists, a party press, and a network of organization—to demand reform. Rather, Spanish parties were weak above all because of the apathy that inhered in backwardness and the alienation that inhered in the more advanced sectors.

The praetorianism of the Spanish military was all the more striking because the military was itself as delegitimated as the state it eventually seized. After the humiliation of 1898 (and more ignominious defeats were soon to come in Morocco), the officers' corps itself entered the twentieth century with "the conviction that they would never be useful for anything."[153]

The appropriate counterpoints are provided by Germany and Italy, for Germany had a military with an illustrious past in an institutionally strong society while Italy had a military of no particular distinction in a more backward but still comparatively modern society. Also, in both Germany and Italy, the level of political mobilization was markedly higher. To be sure, in the crises of the early 1860s, a court faction around the Chief of the Military Cabinet, Edwin von Manteuffel, had urged a coup on Bismarck and the Prussian King. But the King and his minister had been able to hold the Prussian army in check then and later. Likewise, although Bismarck contemplated a *Staatsstreich* in 1890 as his troubles mounted, and William II did the same a few years later, there was no question of the army intervening without direction from the government. And even so obtuse and militaristic a figure as William II soon came to understand that the military could not provide the answer in a society such as Germany. In December 1913, he wrote: "In Latin and Central America *Staatsstreiche* may belong to the instruments of the art of government. In Germany, thank God, they are not customary and must not become so, whether they come from above or below. People who dare to recommend such action are dangerous people, more dangerous for the maintenance of the monarchy than the wildest Social Democrat."[154]

Notwithstanding the activism of the officers' corps in bureaucratic politics, and its constant attempts to liberate itself from Reichstag supervision, the German army remained firmly under civilian control before 1914. Admittedly, the German military had little incentive to intervene between the establishment of the empire and the outbreak of the war. The nearest analogy to the Law of Jurisdictions was provided by the Zabern Incident in 1913. In November of that year a garrison commander in Alsace (a quasi-occupied territory), ignoring the proper civilian authorities, declared a local state of siege in response to disorders touched off by a junior officer's insulting remarks about the local population. The matter was complicated by the poor relations between William II (who initially came to the officer's defense) and the Reichstag (which roundly condemned him). But the essential point is that the Chancellor, Bethmann Hollweg, intervened to end the siege and relieve the officer.[155] Still more instructive, the Italian army, even in the crises of the

1890s, did not attempt to intervene *against* the established order. The Italian state was liberal property, liberals having prevailed both politically and militarily in the unification. In the process of their victory they had created important mass loyalties within a substantial fraction of the middle classes. No military claque could expect to govern in the face of those loyalties, not to mention the mass mobilization against them that followed. Even amidst the traumas of the postwar years, the German and Italian militaries remained secondary actors. As both Hitler and Mussolini would demonstrate, the key to seizing power in such organized and mobilized societies was in recombining mass loyalties rather than seizing the Cortes.

There was, then, a level of modernity in Western Europe below which the failure of the liberal movement cannot adequately be accounted for solely by the inherited cleavage structure. That level was found in Spain. Spain's peculiar combination of backwardness and inherited cleavages within an independent society had important implications not only for the failure of liberalism, but through that failure for the nature of liberal–labor relationships, the organization of the working class, and the political orders that emerged and collapsed in the interwar period. These are themes to which we shall return.

Epilogue

In the specific case of Italy, the rapid formation of sectors opposed to the liberal order might have been modified if liberals had been able to bridge the clerical–anticlerical cleavage sooner and more completely, perhaps in a manner analogous to Danish liberalism's eventual conquest of the urban–rural cleavage in the late 1890s. Overcoming that division—by opening up new reservoirs of support—stabilized at least for a brief time the leadership of Denmark's liberals.

Given the sociological realities, however, a more plausible alternative to a broadened base for liberal leadership was provided by the experience of Belgium. Rather than reaching a modus vivendi with liberals, Catholics in Italy might have asserted themselves earlier, as they did in Belgium, and beaten liberals at their own game. From this point of view, the turning point was not in the failure of liberals to reach an earlier accommodation with Catholics or socialists, outcomes that were never within reach, but in the refusal of Catholics to enter the liberal order and compete politically at an earlier date. Given the breadth of the Catholic base, the outcome might have been several decades of Catholic hegemony, as it was in Belgium—with its distinctive implications for working-class inclusion—rather than a long run of besieged liberalism.

In an obvious sense, the essential problem in all of these societies was one of an inadequate level of nation-state development. The late formation of nation-states in Germany and Italy and throughout Eastern Europe resulted in heterogeneous societies with only minimally developed senses of national community. One reading of this might be that if national unification had come earlier, a more fully developed sense of national community—common identity—would have taken shape.

An inadequate level of nation-state development was, in the most literal sense, the first obstacle that liberals in Finland, the Baltic states, and the Habsburg territories faced. Liberals in Britain and France found themselves mainly unthreatened by preindustrial conflicts before the war, and then mainly threatened by class conflict after it. Liberals elsewhere in Western Europe found themselves threatened mainly by preindustrial conflicts until just before the war, and then mainly by class conflict after it. Liberals in Eastern Europe, when they finally came to power immediately after World War I, found themselves simultaneously assaulted by both preindustrial conflicts *and* class conflict.

In some areas, an absence of national unification would have produced more homogeneous societies. Sometimes, unification produced heterogeneity. For example, the Prussian middle classes and the Prussian liberal community were distinctly more coherent than the *German* middle classes and liberal community. If Germany had remained divided, liberals in Prussia would have been much more likely to impose their hegemony on Prussia. The same can be said of liberals in the other German states.

Yet more was at work here than the timing or scope of national unification. Sweden and Denmark, after all, had longer national histories and higher levels of political integration than did Belgium, the Netherlands, or Switzerland. Yet liberals in Sweden and Denmark suffered from the same sorts of debilitating inherited divisions that crippled liberals in the Low Countries. Moreover, in Switzerland, which had a briefer history of unity and a lower level of political integration, and sufficient anti–integrationist impulses to provoke a civil war in 1848, liberals were not, as we saw in Chapter 2, debilitated by these divisions.

Ultimately, what distinguished societies in which liberalism was weak was not the sociological presence of the cleavages. It is by no means apparent that Britain and especially France and Switzerland had fewer such inherited cleavages. Nor were they distinguished by the simple politicization of the cleavages. More important was the manner in which the cleavages became politically important. That is to say, whether they mainly divided the middle classes from within or mainly divided them from conservatives. When the latter was the case, the cleavage actually served to reinforce the relationship between the middle classes (or, more accurately, a decisive fraction of them) and the liberal movement and aided liberal hegemony. In France and Switzerland religious conflict united anticlerical liberals against the Catholic right; in Britain, Methodism and Dissent united Liberals against Anglican Tories.

Moreover, the appearance of a divisive cleavage within the liberal community was not determining if that cleavage became politically important only after liberalism had established its hegemony and effectively incorporated the working class. This was the case with Irish Home Rule (a center–periphery dispute) within the British Liberals in the 1890s. By that time liberalism had already established its undisputed dominance in Britain both through the narrow vehicle of the Liberal party and more generally through liberalism's penetration of the reformed Conservative party. More than anything else, this reformation of the Tories was the most distinctive consequence of the radical reduction in the size of the agricultural sector in Britain. No other conservative party in Europe experienced such a change before the war.[156] In any case, Home Rule did not come to divide Liberals until after the liberal–labor coalition had been firmly cemented.

Elsewhere, these preindustrial cleavages divided liberal communities and the middle classes and handicapped liberals in their pursuit of parliamentary sovereignty and an adequate mass base. They thereby undermined the liberal quest for dominance. Just how much of a mass base constituted an "adequate" base is impossible to say. It was a function of the electoral system and the cleavage structure. The minimum statement to be made, however, is that to be adequate the mass base had to provide liberals with a compelling legislative majority for an extended period of time. Where liberals were denied this, the implications for the formation of the working class were enormous. It is to those implications that we must now turn.

The Break with Liberalism
and the Formation of Working-Class
Movements

Abortive Lib–Labism and the Rise of Working-Class Movements

The failure of liberal parties to establish their dominance in the years before
the war meant that liberals soon found themselves simultaneously attacked
by traditional oligarchs, parts of the urban and rural middle classes, and
workers. Paradoxically, the same divisions that prevented liberal parties from
establishing their dominance also prevented liberals from making the kind of
liberal–labor alliances that were so characteristic of politics in prewar Britain, France, and Switzerland. Most liberal leaders rejected such alliances,
and those who were inclined toward them quickly found that the anxieties of
the voters and activists they represented made it difficult and often impossible
to persuade the latter to accept such alliances. For these alliances soon
required concessions that increased the economic or political leverage of
autonomously organized workers. Even when liberal parties were able to ally
with working-class movements, the latter found that in view of the feebleness
of the liberal cause, success required an emphasis on autonomous class
organization rather than an interclass alliance.

We saw in Chapter 3 that liberalism in these societies generally reached
the limits of its political potential even before workers began to organize
themselves independently. In their earliest stages, these liberal coalitions
normally embraced that fraction of the working class that had the right to
vote. Liberals often sponsored benefit societies and cooperatives for workers,
sometimes even trade unions, and accepted the existence within the liberal
party of workers' sections. They were often willing, as well, to sponsor or at
least contemplate a range of social reforms. The essence of this liberal
accommodation, however, was the desire to acquaint workers with such
middle-class virtues as sobriety, thrift, and diligence, thereby providing them

with the means to acquire property and to accede to the middle class. A German liberal, Friedrich Harkort, pithily captured the hopes of early liberal reformers when he opined that, "If the proletarian is given property of some kind, he will join the existing order, the Bürgertum."[1] As Harkort's musing suggests, this sort of liberal accommodation would not be easily reconciled with the organization of workers as a separate class.

It is certainly true that in Britain, France, and Switzerland liberals were confronted with independent working-class movements in the two decades before the Great War. It is equally true that liberals first responded by collaboration within the liberal movement aimed at accommodating workers to the world of the middle classes. The critical difference was that these were successful liberal movements. They were consequently both more capable of accommodating demands as time passed for alliances more nearly among equals and of defining the political agenda. They were also in possession of an ideology more marketable within the working classes precisely because it had been legitimated by its success. Lib–Labism thus provided a plausible alternative to a focus on coherent organization of the working-class.

Politically conscious workers suffered no shortage of alternative models of organization in the quarter-century before the war. It is instructive that they rarely were impressed by the Lib–Labism practiced in Britain (or in an even more extreme form in the United States) or by its more diluted variant in France. Rather, the more coherent class organization implied in Marxism and quickly engineered in Germany became the point of departure for most working-class movements. In the literature from Scandinavia, the Low Countries, Italy, and Spain one rarely encounters activists enamoured of the British model and its variants.

Rather, insofar as these models exercised many working-class imaginations, it was ironically through the inspiration provided by French and American syndicalism. French syndicalism exerted considerable influence in Italy and Spain and was echoed as well in a more remote way in Sweden.[2] It came to Norway, too, where it had a much greater impact than it had had in Sweden, through the immigration of Swedish workers alienated by the failure of the 1909 general strike.[3]

It is doubly ironic that among the many currents of the American labor movement, it was mainly on the rivulets of socialism and the syndicalism of the International Workers of the World (IWW) that European activists dilated. The classic example of this was provided by Martin Tranmael, a Norwegian labor leader of nearly legendary stature in his homeland. Tranmael was the author of the famous 1911 "Trondheim Resolution" that launched Norwegian syndicalism. Under his leadership it became the most potent syndicalism in the West, one from which the French could have learned much. Tranmael spent several years observing socialist activities and IWW syndicalism in America at the turn of the century. The main, albeit somewhat contradictory, lessons he drew from this experience were about the importance of comprehensive class organization and the viability of syndicalism.[4]

If activists concentrated on these peripheral aspects of the labor movements in America, Britain, and France, it was mainly because unlike the more mainstream aspects of these movements, these peripheral elements seemed to ring most true in the social and political environments of their homelands. It was for the same reason that the German trade unions and Social Democratic party, rather than the flaccid and particularistic British and French parties and unions, became the leading models of working class organization in Europe. In a number of societies, including those of Denmark, Norway, and Sweden, the local socialist parties adopted verbatim the German Social Democrats' Gotha Program as their own. Trade unions likewise mimicked many features of German union organization. It would be difficult to imagine, and more difficult to find, examples of successful socialist parties that turned to the SFIO or the ILP for guidance.

The most proximate cause of this was the distinctly less hospitable environment in which labor movements had to work in most European countries. This less hospitable environment was a product of the failure of liberalism. The environment was less hospitable in several ways. In the first place, the ideologies of liberal social reform that we examined in Chapter 2 were echoed in only a muted way in these societies and never gained the influence they acquired in Britain and France. More fundamentally, because the reformist ideology was largely the ideological superstructure of a subtending alliance, it was an environment that put a premium on coherent working-class organization rather than interclass alliances. Such alliances were of little value if they were rejected almost in toto by liberals, as they were in Norway, Spain, Italy, and Germany; if they accentuated inherited divisions within the liberal community, as they did in Sweden; or if they were with liberals who failed to establish their own hegemony until late in the day and then did so only weakly, as in Denmark.

The Low Countries, where liberalism was defeated and superseded by hegemonic clerical movements, represent distinctive variants of this experience. To a significant degree hegemonic clericalism provided a substitute ally for the working-class movement, with important consequences for the pattern of class organization.

This chapter presents the story of how the failure of interclass alliances led to the creation of comparatively more coherent working-class movements before 1914. In examining the breakdown of alliances, we focus on the limited and ineffective nature of liberal–labor electoral cooperation, the struggle between liberals and socialists for the loyalty of trade unions and working-class voters, and the residual role of social policy in this struggle. We focus on liberal–labor electoral alliances and the absence thereof, because such alliances went to the heart of, and mirrored the larger climate of, class collaboration and conflict in society and the economy.

Class collaboration in politics could reflect a comparatively benign employer attitude in the labor market, as it did in the exceptional case of Britain, or it could be used to offset employer intransigence, as in France and some of the American states. If, however, state power could not be called into play on behalf of workers, whether the state remained nominally neutral or was overtly hostile, workers were compelled to organize themselves more coherently in both politics and the labor market. They were, so to speak, left to their own devices. And their most important device was not their growing numbers, as Marxist, anarchists, and syndicalists have all long dreamed, but their collective power.

In the next chapter, we take up the consequences of aborted interclass alliances for the organization of that collective power, paying particular attention to the more coherent nature of trade union movements, the distinctive relationship between socialist parties and trade unions, and the indicators of a higher level of working-class consciousness before the war. For the longer run—that is, for the interwar period—it was the legacy of organization rather than class consciousness that mattered. Circumstantial evidence makes it plausible to suppose that class consciousness in Britain and France "caught up" with this higher level. What did not catch up, but would prove a determining factor, was the inherited organizational legacy that harnessed and directed or dissipated and diffused that class consciousness.

When Johan Sverdrup, the leader of the Norwegian Liberals, formed his first government in 1884, he established a labor commission that was dominated by the social radical wing of his party. The commission's brief was to review labor laws and social policies and to keep the incipient "labor movement on a healthy and reasonable track."[5] Social radicals were willing to go some distance to accommodate workers. The commission, which mirrored a conscious effort by Liberal leaders to keep workers in the Liberal fold, proposed as early as 1885 to limit the working day to just ten hours. In a comparative historical perspective, and especially in view of Norway's modest industrialization, this was a bold proposal indeed. The ten-hour day would not be realized generally in Western Europe for another two decades. Of course, when the labor commission's recommendation was submitted to the Storting, where the Liberals possessed a nominal majority, the party delegation was divided and the work day remained largely unregulated.[6]

In Norwegian historiography, this failure of Liberal social reforms has sometimes been cited as a turning point in the young labor movement's alienation from the Liberals.[7] In fact, however, Norway's record of social reform was not conspicuously worse than a number of European countries before 1914, not the least France's. Before that time, neither the level of socioeconomic modernization nor the percentage of the popular vote received by working-class parties can account for national differences in social reform.[8] There was, rather, a powerful inverse relationship between the strength of liberalism and social reform. This conclusion is supported by

Peter Flora and Jens Alber's pathbreaking project on the origins of the welfare state. Flora and Alber have examined the timing of legislation in four areas of social insurance (accident, sickness, retirement, and unemployment). Their categories differ from those employed here, as they distinguish not between societies with hegemonic and weak liberal movements, but between dualist–constitutional monarchies and parliamentary democracies. Within the former category they place Sweden, Germany, Austria and, before 1901, Denmark. Within the latter category are Britain, France, Switzerland, the Netherlands, Belgium, Norway, Italy, and, after 1901, Denmark. Using their categories, they find a greater propensity for reform in the dualist–constitutional monarchies. Although I find extremely problematic their classification of Belgium, Norway, and Italy as parliamentary democracies, this dichotomy does provide a crude index of the strength of liberalism. If, in keeping with the argument of this book, the countries are reorganized to distinguish Britain, France, and Switzerland from all of the rest, the relationship between liberalism and the late realization of social reform becomes even more powerful. This is true whether one examines the entire period of their data, 1883 to 1914, or the subsets before and after 1901. It is especially the case insofar as the great bulk of reform in liberal societies is concentrated in the post-1901 period and in Britain, where the maximum number of reform measures was introduced before 1914. The relationship between weak liberalism and reformism can be seen by recomputing Flora and Alber's data. If the countries are regrouped according to weak and strong liberalism, even with Denmark problematically placed in the latter category after 1901, the ratio of realized social insurance laws to potential social insurance laws for the period from 1883 to 1914 is twenty-four of thirty-six for the weak liberal countries and ten of twenty-eight for the strong liberal countries.[9]

This contrast no doubt derives from the attempts by both liberals and conservatives to gain working-class support without actually extending a measure of political legitimacy to the autonomous representatives of the working class. When, for instance, Norway enacted its first health insurance measure in 1909, it was, tellingly, supported in the Storting by most Liberals and most Conservatives, but opposed by the Labor party. The Labor party opposed the measure because it was based on a tax on workers' incomes.[10] This particular instance illustrates that the costs of such a reformist strategy could easily be displaced onto the objects of the strategy. Whatever costs such policies carried, they were much less, or appeared to be less, for both liberals and conservatives, than actually sharing political power. Bismarck's primitive welfare state was merely the first and most dramatic example of this strategy.[11]

Given that it was the societies in which liberalism was weak and social reform most advanced where workers became most alienated, we can only assume that the presence or absence of social reforms per se was not a determining factor. This apparent indeterminacy might have been rooted in the limited positive impact any of these policies had on the day-to-day lives of workers at this early stage. In the case of the vaunted German pensions, for instance, few German workers actually lived long enough to enjoy their miserly benefits.[12] It seems just as likely that social reforms were indeterminate because the decisive strata of the working class, the politically active strata, wanted not diluted social reform but social and political acceptance, the sine qua non of which was a share of political and economic power.[13] Members of those strata, after all, were quickly settling into life-long *careers* in the political and labor-market organizations of the working class. The essential currency of those careers was more likely to be society's acknowledgement of one's authoritative role than accident insurance. The latter probably counted only if it enhanced the activists' authority, which is to say, if they won it.

It was in this context that liberal–labor alliances were determining. Such alliances provided a mark of acceptance and a share of power, or at least a plausible prospect of it in the not-to-distant future. That was the principal lesson drawn from the discussion of liberal–labor alliances in Britain, France, and Switzerland in Chapter 2. Social reforms mainly entered the picture tangentially: alliances required a leading role for a reforming wing of the liberal movement, and such a wing necessarily advertised itself by its commitment to reform. Such a reformist wing could not prevail in politics if liberal supporters were already divided by an incomplete national revolution and felt correspondingly besieged. But what counted in the small number of years before the Great War changed the world was more the alliance than its social policy product.

Germany

Liberal–labor cooperation miscarried earlier in Germany—by 1871—than in any other European country. It did so because at that early date Germany uniquely combined a comparatively large working class with the first unambiguous failure of a liberal movement. In the other comparably or more industrialized societies of Western Europe—Britain, France, Belgium, and even Denmark—liberalism was either hegemonic or ascendant during these years. Indeed, even in the less industrialized societies of Norway, Italy, and the Netherlands, liberalism was either still ascendant or hegemonic during these years. Only in much less industrialized Spain and Sweden, with their much smaller working classes, was this not the case. The failure of German liberalism was, of course, inextricably tied to the process of national unification in the 1860s. In this, the seminal moment came with the capitulation of most liberals following the Prussian victory over Austria in 1866. This defeat of liberalism provoked the collapse of liberal–labor cooperation.

The first political opportunities for German workers grew out of the originally nonpolitical workers' educational associations that were sponsored by middle-class reformers. These associations expressed the liberal conviction that education and self-help would be the main means of working-class improvement.[14] At this time, there was still no clear organizational distinction between liberal and working-class movements in Germany.[15] In the 1860s, as the constitutional struggles in Prussia intensified, liberals sought to enlist the support of these workers' associations on behalf of unification and constitutional reform.

In Prussia, the first distinctively working-class movement that was not directly subordinated to the liberals appeared with the formation of the ADAV (Allgemeine Deutsche Arbeiterverein) in 1863. The ADAV ultimately became the leading north German force in the making of the Social Democratic party, so its origins are worth our attention. The ADAV was initially a non-Marxist workers' party whose main aim was universal suffrage.[16] It came into being because of the break between the Leipzig Workers' Educational Association and the Liberals' Nationalverein. This break was provoked when the Leipzig Educational Association sought full membership within the Nationalverein for manual workers. This appeal for equal status was rebuffed by the Liberals.[17] In doing so, the Liberals revealed their reluctance to accede to the Leipzig Association's principal aim, universal suffrage. This was a turning point because, in substance, the Liberals were acknowledging their unwillingness to collaborate on equal terms with workers even *within* a liberal association. It was only in consequence of this that the Leipzig Association was willing to participate in the founding of the autonomous, but still non-Marxist, ADAV.[18] The Leipzig Association's importance here is more than merely illustrative: it provided the leadership of the newly created ADAV.[19] After its establishment, ADAV found itself in constant conflicts with the Liberals over universal suffrage and the place of state-supported workers' cooperatives in the new Germany. It is important to stress, however, that it remained open to cooperation with anyone willing to accommodate these ambitions. It was even willing to work with the conservative Prussian government, so at this point it was certainly not a radical working-class movement rejecting cooperation with its social "betters."[20]

Rather, the rejection came mainly from the Liberals and the conservative government. The turning point was the Prussian victory over Austria in 1866. In the aftermath of that victory, the Liberals began to disintegrate, as a large fraction abandoned the demands for constitutional reform and moved to support the government. Here it is important to recall that Bismarck was able to manipulate Prussian Liberals in this fashion because he could play on their obsession with unification by means of the *kleindeutsch* strategy. In the absence of the regional and religious cleavages in the larger German liberal community that gave meaning to it, Bismarck's ability to make good the *kleindeutsch* dream would have had little pull among the northern liberals.

The Liberal's retreat was accelerated in 1867 when Bismarck introduced a general suffrage in the elections to the North German Confederation, for a general suffrage in such a heterogeneous society made the Liberals even more vulnerable and correspondingly more dependent on the state for the enactment of their own program.[21] With the Liberals' enthusiasm for democratic reform thus waning, the ADAV could expect neither governmental concessions in return for support against the Liberals nor a reformist alliance with the Liberals. Instead, ADAV now found itself faced with a united front of the conservative Prussian government and most Liberals. Thus, the settlement of the Prussian constitutional conflicts and the resulting collaboration between Bismarck and the National Liberals forced ADAV to pursue an independent political course. It was only at this conjuncture that ADAV adopted an explicitly socialist program.[22]

Even as the ADAV was forming an autonomous workers' organization, most workers remained politically wedded to the Liberals. In this, their main vehicle was the VDAV (Verband Deutscher Arbeitervereine), created in 1863. In 1865, VDAV included about 100 local associations with more than 20,000 members, mostly from Saxony and south of the Main.[23] In time, VDAV became the principal organization of workers in the non-Prussian territories brought into the North German Confederation in 1866. VDAV, too, was not a socialist movement at its inception, but rather a radical–liberal movement of workers in close cooperation with the liberal German People's Party. Liberal leaders of the VDAV sought to make it a part of the larger liberal movement and bind it to their ambition of reform through parliamentary government. At the same time, these leaders sought to discourage those tendencies within VDAV, then in a minority, that wanted an independent, not to mention socialist, workers' organization.[24]

Like its northern counterpart, the VDAV moved toward a break with liberalism and then to socialism only after the Prussian victory in 1866. Before the war, a sound basis for cooperation had been provided by the preoccupation of southern workers with national rather than social issues. The war resolved the national question, however. Moreover, Bismarck's provision of a general suffrage satisfied one of the VDAV's main constitutional aspirations. In consequence, the attention of the workers in VDAV turned to social issues. Whereas in the north Lib–Labism came to an end because liberals rejected it, in the territories brought into the Confederation in 1866, it came to an end because the only liberals willing to align with VDAV, the People's party, were incapable of offering the VDAV an effective ally on the social issues. This conclusion was driven home to the VDAV by the People's party's inability to protect the interests of workers in the Reichstag of the North German Confederation, which legislated a series of economic reforms largely at the expense of workers in 1867.[25] VDAV's adoption of a socialist program at its Nürnberg Congress in 1868 was a consequence of the weakness of the democratic liberals.[26] The liberals' desperate efforts to stem the tide and even Karl Liebknecht's reluctance to sever the relationship with them could not prevent the evolution of the VDAV into an independent socialist party, the SDAP (Sozialdemokratische Arbeiterpartei) at Eisenach in 1869.

The unification of the nation, the alliance of the Liberals and Bismarck, and the growing estrangement of VDAV and ADAV from the Liberals made most of the differences between the two working-class movements inconsequential and laid the foundations for a unified, and now socialist, working-class movement. In 1875, the VDAV and ADAV merged to create the Socialist Workers' Party of Germany. This unification took place at a Congress in Gotha, and the famed Gotha Program became the platform on which the unification occurred.[27]

Working-class consciousness certainly remained inchoate in the mid-1870s. The new socialist party had no more than 30,000 or 40,000 members and it polled just 7 percent of the vote. The great majority of wage-earners remained loyal to the other parties, or did not bother to vote. This was true even if we limit our attention solely to urban, Protestant workers.[28]

The period of Social Democratic growth was framed by the antisocialist laws. In the year when the Antisocialist Law was enacted, 1878, the Social Democratic party was still receiving just 7.6 percent of the vote. It had perhaps 35,000 members. By 1890, when the law was allowed to lapse, the party had 19.7 percent of the vote and 100,000 members. It was by then, in terms of electoral strength, the largest party in the Reich. By the autumn of 1890, as Vernon Lidtke has shown, the party had developed a refined sense of parliamentary tactics, a more coherent Marxian ideology, a close relationship with the trade unions, and a greatly broadened electoral base.[29]

The break with the Liberals was made definitive by the enactment of the Antisocialist Law, which all of the National Liberals endorsed.[30] The law allowed the police to arrest hundreds of socialist leaders, suppress the party press, close down socialist trade unions, and prevent public meetings. It did not prevent party candidates from running for office. That the Liberals embraced the Antisocialist Law was itself a direct consequence of their own desperate position after unification. Unalterably subordinated by the conservative state and apparently under siege by the mobilization of workers, Catholics, particularists, and minorities, the Antisocialist Law (like the failed Kulturkampf before it) seemed to provide a mechanism by which liberals could secure themselves and their middle-class interests.

It was because German Social Democracy became the first working-class movement in a society of failed liberalism that it exerted such an influence on working-class movements in other comparatively situated societies. Socialist movements did not "arrive," that is, achieve enduring electoral breakthroughs, elsewhere until about 1900. In retrospect, the timing of these breakthroughs can be pinpointed with some precision: 1894 in Belgium, 1895 in Denmark, 1900 in Italy, 1903 in Norway, 1905 in Sweden, 1906 in the Netherlands, 1917 in Spain.[31] By the middle of the 1890s, at a time when other socialist parties were still in their infancy, the Social Democrats were the largest party in Germany, so it is no surprise that they exerted such an influence on the thinking of socialists elsewhere.

Just as the party became a model for other socialists, the response of the German liberals and the Bismarckian state to social democracy also became a model of sorts for governments and liberals elsewhere. The Bismarckian strategy, supported by German liberals, of attempting to wean the working class from socialism through welfare-state measures and antisocialist legislation, became a negative model because the antisocialist laws so patently backfired. The growth of social democracy between 1878 and 1890 made it clear that such a blunt instrument as the antisocialist laws was counterproductive. That it was inadequate to stem the growth of a socialist working-class movement was apparent, after all, even to the Kaiser and the National Liberals, who refused to renew the legislation without modifications in 1890 and consequently caused its expiration.[32] That such laws were not adopted elsewhere does not tell us, ipso facto, that liberals in other societies were more tolerant of socialism. It merely tells us that liberal parties and government offices elsewhere in Europe were not tenanted by men incapable of learning from two decades of experience in Germany. In fact, as we shall see, liberals in other European societies were often even *more* hostile to social democracy than German liberals. But because they had the benefit of the prior German experience, they could articulate that hostility in more subtle, and often more effective, ways. Moreover, as we shall see, whether that hostility was articulated bluntly or subtly, would ultimately be of no enduring consequence. The labor movements that took shape in either case were remarkably similar.

To return to the German experience: through the lives of the Antisocialist Law, Bismarck's cartel, Miquel's *Sammlungspolitik,* and the Bülow Bloc, all of which had at their root the containment of Social Democracy,[33] cooperation with liberals could hardly have been on the Social Democrat's national agenda.[34] The possibility of such cooperation began to receive renewed attention within the party only as the Bülow Bloc, the electoral cartel of the Conservatives, Liberals, and Progressives, began to disintegrate after the elections of 1907. The bloc came to an end in 1909, when the Conservatives and their partners could not reach an agreement on reform of the tax system.[35] The Progressives, although not the National Liberals, then entered an electoral alliance with the Social Democrats.

From the outset, it was an alliance of only limited value to the Social Democrats, for it was with a party whose main motive in entering into it was simply to survive. With the end of the bloc, the Progressives, the smallest national party in the Reichstag, were compelled to find an ally or risk the loss of nearly all of their seats in the Reichstag elections of 1912. For the Socialists, the rationale for the alliance lay in the prospect that it would eventuate in a reform majority in the Reichstag.[36]

On the first ballot of the 1912 election, the Social Democrats won sixty-four seats while the Progressives failed to win even a single seat. The Progressives agreed to support second-ballot Socialist candidates in thirty-one districts in which the opponent would be a candidate supported by the government's Blue–Black (Conservative and Catholic) coalition. In return, the Social Democrats agreed to suspend their campaign in fourteen districts in which they faced Progressives. Additionally, the Social Democrats supported Progressive candidates in another twenty-one districts in which they faced a Blue–Black candidate. The Progressives won all thirty-five of these alliance seats. They won another seven seats on their own. In effect, thirty-five of the forty-two seats they gained were owed to Social Democratic support.[37]

The Progressive leadership, however, found it virtually impossible to induce its supporters to cast their votes for Social Democratic candidates. In fact, the Progressive leadership advised its voters to opt for a National Liberal if the alternative were a Social Democrat. The most striking breach of the alliance, however, was at the mass level. In twenty-five of the thirty-one districts in which the Progressives pledged their support of Socialist candidates, the behavior of their middle-class supporters crucially affected the outcome. In twenty-one of these twenty-five districts, a majority of Progressive votes actually went to Conservative candidates. So the net real gain to the Social Democrats from the alliance was just four seats. In substance, even where Progressive leaders were willing to make the interclass alliance, middle-class voters were not.

What is striking about this alliance is not simply that middle-class voters, even those on the left, were unwilling to support it, but that Social Democratic voters *were* willing to support it. Their years of political isolation notwithstanding, Social Democratic voters remained receptive to class collaboration. Indeed, revisionist Social Democratic leaders were even willing to contemplate an alliance that would have included their old persecutor, the National Liberals. That such an alliance—"from Bebel to Bassermann"—remained unformed was due to the opposition of the Social Democratic left and to the National Liberal leaders' understanding that their electorate would not tolerate it, even if the party's leaders wanted it.[38] In this pattern of middle-class parties and voters rejecting class collaboration, Germany, as the first society of debilitated liberalism, set a pattern of aborted class collaboration that appeared again and again as vulnerable liberal movements elsewhere in Western Europe were confronted by independent working-class movements. The essence of an effective alliance was not simply that it accepted workers in the liberal movement, but that it accepted electoral cooperation with autonomous worker movements. The experience of Norway, where the labor movement became among the most isolated in Europe, makes this apparent.

Norway

Workers remained loyal to the reorganized Norwegian Liberal party in 1891. The socialist Labor party had been established only in 1887, and remained no more than a cipher in Norwegian politics through the last decade of the century. Well-established workers' sections existed within the Liberal party in Oslo, Bergen, and Trondheim and the party had actually sponsored many of the extant trade unions. It had a close relationship to them and could count on their support at election time.[39]

As the decade passed, the worker sections within the party became increasingly dissatisfied with their subordinate position and advanced demands for a greater say in the selection of Storting candidates. Liberals were willing to devise arrangements that allowed liberal workers to sponsor a liberal working-class candidate in each of the major cities. The essence of these arrangements was that they guaranteed that middle-class liberals would remain in control of the actual nomination process and that the outcome would be the selection of a safe candidate. This worked best in Bergen, where it was used in 1894, 1897, and 1900. In the first election, liberal workers were represented by a museum director and in the next two by a long-time leader of a local craft association.[40] The arrangements failed completely in Oslo and Trondheim, where the local liberal associations placed so many restrictions on the process that in the end liberal workers were never able to abide by the arrangements and middle-class liberals were left free to select the "workers' " candidates.[41] That liberals were unwilling to cooperate even with their own workers' sections did not augur well for the future of class alliances in Norway.

As the decade proceeded, the demands for more worker autonomy mounted. They were partly constrained by the common commitment to the enactment of manhood suffrage, for which Liberals finally mustered an adequate majority and sufficient coherence to carry through in 1898. Liberals assumed that manhood suffrage would rebound mainly in their favor.[42] But by 1900, the growing disenchantment of liberal workers with their own party was already approaching the point of no return.

Both liberal and socialist worker associations now demanded from the Liberal party electoral alliances between equals—that is, an equal say about who the candidates would be in the districts in which they collaborated. They also demanded a role in formulating an election program, although this appears to have been much less of an obstacle, at least from the workers' point of view. Both liberal and socialist working-class organizations were willing to campaign on the official Liberal election program, which was committed to several social reforms. In the end, the Liberal Party was unwilling to make an alliance with any independent working-class party, *even on the basis of the Liberal program.*

In 1899, the national meeting of the liberal workers' association, De Forenede norske Arbeidersamfund (DfnA) invited the "democratic" parties to form an electoral alliance. The Socialist Labor party, a hitherto isolated and ineffective fraction of the movement, immediately embraced the proposal. It seemed a real chance to press the Liberals into three-cornered cooperation, or at least provide workers with a real alternative to the Liberals.[43]

Once before, in 1894, the Labor party had offered the Liberals an alliance, but the Liberals had said no.[44] At the time this was an unproblematic position, because the party controlled the liberal workers and their organizations. By 1899, there was a danger that the grip would be broken. The Liberals' tactical response was to attempt to retain control of the liberal workers while excluding the socialists from an alliance.

They failed to do this. The two labor groups continued to negotiate after the Liberal party withdrew. The national Liberal Party organization was willing to cooperate with liberal workers on the traditional basis, but refused to align with either independently organized liberal workers or the socialists. Behind this decision was a pervasive fear within the party that such an alliance would alienate a decisive fraction of the party's agrarian supporters, whose leading ambition was to reduce public expenditures.[45] The upshot was that the decision making shifted to the local level.

By this time in Oslo, the socialists had already won over most of the unionized workers. If they now managed to win a large part of the working-class electorate, it would be a disaster for the Liberals, whose prospects in the city were critically dependent on workers' votes. It would be an even greater disaster for the traditional organizer of those votes, the liberal workers' associations. There were two types of these in the city: the general Labor Society (Arbeidersamfunn) and the liberal trade unions. The unions, under the umbrella of the Norsk Fagforbund, a union organization which the Liberals had created in 1893, sought to rally workers in a revolt against the patron. Most of the unions were ready for such a revolt, but most of the Labor Societies were not. The latter created a new organization (Kristiania demokratiska Arbeiderorganisasjonen) for the purpose of collaborating with the Liberals at the election. Negotiators were able to bridge the programmatic differences with the Liberals but were unable to come to terms on the nomination procedures. The Liberals demanded control of the nomination process.[46] It was a critical juncture: the Liberals in the most important city in the country would not work even with *liberal* workers if they were independently organized.

The result was that the Conservatives swept the city. The Liberals received only about as many votes as they had before the introduction of manhood suffrage; the Labor party received about 4,000 votes and the liberal worker associations, unable to deliver the votes of those workers who were newly enfranchised, were shown to be irrelevant.[47]

This pattern was repeated in other cities. In Bergen the Liberals rejected a coalition with the Labor party. They also rejected cooperation with independent nonsocialist workers, on whose behalf the dockworkers' union sought to negotiate with the Liberals. The dockworkers demanded that workers be allowed to nominate two candidates and two alternates for the Storting. A minority of the local Liberal Party steering committee was willing to accept this, but the majority insisted on the old arrangements. The result was that, although the Liberals carried the city, they did so by a much reduced margin. This pattern was duplicated in Trondheim and Drammen, the other two towns with large numbers of workers.[48]

If the election of 1900 was a setback for the Liberals, the election of 1903 was a disaster. As the 1903 election approached, the Liberal party formally broke apart in a number of cities. In Bergen, the Moderates (the Liberal right) provoked a split and effectively took over the local organization when the left proved too accommodating of labor. The same thing happened in Trondheim. There the formal split was provoked when it became known that the local association had reached an agreement to cooperate at the next election with the Labor party. This appears to have been one of the few occasions on which a local Liberal party actually agreed to an alliance with the Labor party. Fifty of 70 leaders in the Trondheim Liberal party rejected the alliance. Similar divisions occurred elsewhere. In Skien and Hammerfest, among others, Moderates aligned with Conservatives to defeat candidates nominated by left Liberals.[49]

The deepest divisions occurred in the two northern counties, where a complete realignment of the party system occurred. Most traditional Liberals formed electoral alliances with Conservatives against labor candidates, both socialist and liberal. In this polarization, "there was no room for an independent Liberal policy." In about half of the Hedemark districts, alliances were made between the local Liberal and Conservative parties against worker lists. In others, regular Liberal lists appeared, or mixed lists of Liberals and Conservatives, or Liberals and workers, but never Liberals and socialists. The result was that the Conservatives won two seats and the Labor Party won three.[50]

In the other northern county, Kristians Amt, the Liberals had managed to win the election in 1900 by cooperating with Liberal labor. In only a few districts was there a tendency to align with the Conservatives. By 1903, the division was complete. On one side stood an alliance of the Liberals and Liberal Labor (Johan Castberg's Labor Democrats); on the other, an alliance (the Coalition party) of Liberals and Conservatives. There was nothing in between. Again in 1903, the Liberals won the seats, but by a much reduced margin.[51]

This breakup of the Liberals was repeated in other parts of the country. In Tromso, the Liberals and Conservatives formed an alliance, but three socialists were elected. Only in Trondhjeim and Drammen did the Liberals and the Labor party form an alliance. In Larvik one was attempted but failed. In Oslo, liberal–labor cooperation ran aground again on control of the nominations. This time Liberal Labor, now mainly organized in Castberg's Labor Democrats, made an alliance with the Labor party. By this time, the Labor party had gained the dominant position of leadership within the Oslo working class.[52]

Taking the nation as a whole, the general rule appears to have been that a local Liberal party association remained intact only if its left did not attempt an alliance with Labor. Where it did, the bulk of the party rejected it, either breaking away or recapturing the local organization.

The defeat the Liberals suffered in 1903 was not unexpected, but its dimensions were. It lost about one-fifth of the vote it had received in 1900. Compared to that election, more than 10 percent of the voters had abandoned the party. It lost more than one-third of its Storting seats. Together with their new-found liberal allies, the Conservatives won 67 of 117 seats. The Labor party received about 10 percent of the vote.[53]

In a statistical analysis, Gabriel Oidne has shown that the Liberal losses were much greater in districts in which the Labor party also competed. In most of these, he finds a clear relationship between Labor's advance and liberal decline. The Conservative totals, however, appear to be unperturbed by Labor participation in a contest.[54] In effect, the Liberals were losing their working-class base while keeping—or we might say in order to keep—their middle-class base.

It might be more accurate to say that the Liberals were jettisoning their working-class base, for in these years, it is important to emphasize, alliances were rejected by the Liberals themselves rather than by Liberal Labor or the socialist Labor party. The working-class parties regularly sought such alliances in 1894, 1897, 1900, and 1903. It was only in 1906 that the Labor party took the formal decision not to enter into any kind of alliance with another party.[55] By that time, Liberal Labor was little more than a shadow of its previous self. Castberg's Labor Democrats gained just 4.8 percent of the vote in 1906. In the same year, the Labor party received 16 percent of the vote. By 1912 the Labor vote had risen to 26 percent, and the Labor Democrats had become no more than a minor appendage of the Liberal party.[56]

After 1903, and especially after the 1906 election, the question of alliances was a moot one. The socialist working-class movement was irreversibly launched. More important, as we shall see later, it was launched down a road that would emphasize its isolation in Norwegian society. As early as 1900, the Liberal party had adopted a vehemently antisocialist line.[57] Its opposition to the Labor party was driven home by the electoral reform of 1906, which was supported by both Liberals and Conservatives and aimed squarely at the Labor party. The reform abolished the old district-by-district system of electoral colleges and multiple seats and substituted a plurality system of direct elections that redounded to the benefit of the two larger parties. Thus, for example, in 1912, the Liberals received 37 percent of the vote and 62 percent of the Storting seats. In 1915, they received 33 percent of the vote and 65 percent of the seats.[58] The revision of the electoral law provided the Liberals with an alternative to a coalition with either the Conservatives or Labor.

With the loss of its working-class support and the dissolution of the union with Sweden completed, the Liberal party underwent something of a "third founding" in 1906–07. Three trends were apparent in the party. The first, led by Christian Michelsen, advocated an accommodation with the Conservatives that would be aimed at the socialists. Much of the impetus within Norway for a definitive solution to the union problem in 1903 to 1905 had, in fact, derived from a desire to clear the table for a unified front against socialist labor.[59] The second trend in the party consisted of its reformist left, which remained sympathetic to an alliance with labor, even socialist labor. The foremost proponent of this line was Johan Castberg, whose Labor Democrats floated between being a fraction of the Liberal party and an independent party. Most liberals, however, remained committed to an independent Liberal party aligned with neither the Conservatives nor Labor. In the reshuffling of the party that occurred with the end of the union, it was this majority with the reformers as a junior appendage who remained in control. The result was that the party remained committed to social reforms, but intensely antisocialist and opposed to an alliance with Labor.[60]

Just as it had in 1900 (although not in 1903), the Liberal party again campaigned in 1906 on a program of broad social reform. It was committed to health insurance, accident insurance, and pensions. Judging by the continuous growth of the Labor party, however, this commitment to social reform had little appeal to working-class voters in the absence of a commitment to the sharing of power.

Sweden

During the same years that the divorce between liberalism and the socialist working-class movement was becoming unbridgeable in Norway, a limited amount of collaboration occurred between urban Liberals and Socialists in Sweden. This collaboration appears at first glance to undermine the contention that Lib–Labism was a product only of societies that had hegemonic liberal movements. After all, we saw in Chapter 3 that the liberal movement failed more completely in Sweden than in almost any other Western European society.

Sweden was not an exception to the proposition that liberal movements would not make alliances with autonomous working-class movements. Although urban radicals were willing to make such alliances, the alliances were rejected by the larger liberal movement, which broke with the radicals and refused to accept their agenda regarding both suffrage reform and, later, defense policy, the two leading questions of the day. In effect, it proved impossible to combine in one movement both agrarians and urban radicals as long as the latter were aligned with Social Democrats. The dilemma for the radicals was that the alliance with the Social Democrats quickly became a requisite of their own local power, but simultaneously made it impossible for them to lead an effective liberal movement. Within a short time, this untenable position cost the radicals both their influence in the liberal movement and their local political base.

The Social Democrats' plunge into electoral politics did not begin auspiciously. The first Riksdag election in which the party ran candidates occurred in 1890, when it offered three candidates in Stockholm and others in Malmö, Hälsingborg, Ystad, Lund, Göteborg, and Norrköpping. The party's strongest vote getter in Stockholm was its leader, Hjalmar Branting, who drew the support of just 186 voters. Branting and the other Social Democratic candidates ran in alliances with a newly established group of radical Liberals known as the "Democrats." The Democrats were such a fragile group that their electoral organization apparently did not survive the voting. The Social Democrats' principal opponents were referred to by the contemporary press as the "Official Liberals." Of the 10,400 votes cast in Stockholm, the Official Liberals received 5,800 and swept thereby all of the city's mandates.[61]

The Social Democrats tried again in 1893, challenging the Official Liberals in Stockholm and elsewhere. This time the Social Democrats placed their candidates on the list sponsored by the Universal Suffrage Association. The association consisted of radical Liberals and Socialists and stood in opposition to the city's Liberal establishment, which again won all of the city's mandates handily. Branting received 432 votes. In Malmö, too, the Socialists ran on a combined list with radical Liberals, but the Conservatives won there as they had in the past. In Göteborg and Norrköpping, the Socialists did not bother to advance any of their own candidates this time around. Instead they endorsed radicals. Whatever the value of the endorsement, the radicals lost the election.[62]

The Socialists' essential problem was, of course, the franchise law, which restricted the vote to adult men whose annual income was at least 800-kroner and who could prove that they had paid the communal tax. These two requirements disenfranchised the great majority of the working class until the turn of the century. Even as workers' incomes surpassed the 800-kroner threshold with increasing frequency, they remained excluded from the electorate in large numbers by the latter requirement. Between 1896 and 1908, those who qualified by income but were excluded by the tax qualification varied in Stockholm from 48 to 63 percent of the nominal electorate.[63]

Even so, the Social Democrats had their first electoral success in 1896, when Hjalmar Branting was elected to the Riksdag from Stockholm's fifth district. Branting received 822 votes, sufficient to give him the fourth and final seat on the Liberal party's list.[64] This was the first instance of successful liberal–labor cooperation. Branting was even endorsed by *Dagens Nyheter,* the city's leading journal of liberal opinion, as "the spokesman of organized labor and the thousands of the unrepresented, whose hopes and illusions he embodies." The paper left unstated the relative weight it assigned those "hopes and illusions." In any event, the liberal party on whose list Branting was elected, the Folkparti, was formed as the agent of the urban liberal establishment in 1895. As the *Dagens Nyheter* endorsement reveals, Branting and the reformist brand of social democracy for which he stood had been accepted by that establishment. Three years earlier, the newspaper had raged against the socialist menace.[65]

The circumstances leading to the formation of the Folkparti and the inclusion of Branting on its Stockholm list go to the heart of Swedish liberalism's problem. The party was formed to unite liberals, and the Social Democrats were brought into the fold, because during the previous year the old Rural Party, frightened by modern liberalism and especially socialism, and increasingly conservative on suffrage reform, had been reorganized—overcoming the old division between free traders and protectionists—and moved toward an alliance with the Conservatives of the First Chamber. In effect, the growing divide between urban liberals and their potential rural allies had provoked the formation of the Folkparti and the inclusion of the Social Democrats as a counter to the threat of a more unified Rural party.[66]

For the first time in five years, the Rural party had rejected all proposals for reform during the 1895 Riksdag session. This growing conservatism was a response to the events surrounding the calling of the People's Parliaments in 1893 and 1896. These were unofficial bodies elected by universal suffrage with the intention of pressuring the government and Riksdag to accept reform. The Parliaments had been among the young Social Democratic party's first consequential initiatives. The socialists' intention was to confront the Riksdag with its demands for reform. If these demands were ignored, a general strike would be called, followed by the assembly of another People's Parliament, "so all-inclusive and imposing that there could be no thought of further resistance. . ." To lend substance to these vague threats, the party urged all workers to enlist in voluntary rifle associations.[67] The national Universal Suffrage Association, reluctant to compromise its cause by close association with the Social Democrats but also unwilling to be preempted by the Social Democrats, reluctantly agreed to endorse the call for a People's Parliament.[68]

The large turnout for the unofficial vote was impressive, and the parliament met in Stockholm in the spring of 1893. But when it adjourned a few months later, it could not point to any concrete accomplishments. Party leaders in the Second Chamber would not go beyond a modest reduction in the tax qualification. The socialists had urged the parliament to consider ways of applying further pressure, such as a general strike, a concerted refusal to serve in the army and to pay taxes, or the formation of large-scale rifle associations. The parliaments' overwhelming liberal majority, however, refused to do more than agree to call another parliament for 1896.[69] As Branting himself later acknowledged, the liberals' fear that socialist agitation would alienate moderate reformers proved to be justified. The Rural party would not go below a 500 kroner income requirement in its 1893 election program and soon moved away even from that.[70]

All of this was not without consequences for the Folkparti, which quickly moderated its own reform ambitions in an attempt to gain rural support, campaigning in 1896 merely for a reduction of the income qualification to 500 kroner and in 1899 for a compromise that would have enfranchised all local voters over twenty-five years old. (The local electorate was only about twice the size of the small Second Chamber electorate.) Like its liberal successors, the Folkparti lived a schizophrenic life in 1896 and 1899. It allowed Social Democrats a very limited presence on its Stockholm lists because the conservatism of the Rural party compelled it to maximize its urban base and because, in any case, it had little control over what its own local associations did. At the same time, it ignored the Social Democrats' reform program and diluted its own to win agrarian support.[71]

Not much happened in the way of the liberal–labor alliance over the next few years. In 1898, at a by-election in Ystad, a socialist, F. V. Thorsson, was put up as the candidate of the unified left. But he was deserted, in the view of the Social Democrats, by moderate Liberals, with the result that the Conservative candidate won the seat.[72] After the anticlimax of the second People's Parliament in 1896, the socialists devoted themselves increasingly to the idea of a general strike to enforce suffrage reform. Liberals, to the socialists' disdain, pursued a petition to the King. In 1899, Branting was again elected on the Folkparti ticket in Stockholm. In 1902, the Social Democrats and the trade unions staged their long-discussed national strike on behalf of universal suffrage. It was a remarkable success: by one estimate, 85 percent of the industrial workers in Stockholm participated. Moreover, the response of the Stockholm police was so harsh that the strike probably actually won the workers a modicum of middle-class sympathy.[73]

The most important events around this time, however, were the formation of the Liberal Coalition party in the Riksdag in 1900 and the national Liberal Electoral Association in 1902. The Coalition party joined together the old Folkparti, urban reformers, some liberal farmers, nonconformist teetotallers, and intellectuals. As its name implied, the party was a compromise, and it was agreed that stressing the radical element would only alarm farmers, whose support was crucial if the party was to become a force in the Second Chamber. This was borne in mind in 1900 when its steering committee was formed. Sixten von Friesen was made chairman not only because he was a leading Liberal, but because he was among the few urban Liberals who possessed the confidence of the farmers. With the hope of persuading more Second Chamber farmers to join, four of the six positions of the steering committee went to farmers. As ever trying to walk a fine line, the newest liberal movement also pledged itself to social reform, with a program that included demands for factory inspection, state insurance for accidents, legalized collective agreements, arbitration, sick pay, and home mortgage assistance.[74] The new party was supplemented in 1902 by the National Liberal Association, whose aim was the election of candidates committed to suffrage reform.[75]

In 1902 Hjalmar Branting was again elected in Stockholm in an alliance with the Liberals, and this time he was joined in the Riksdag by three socialists similarly elected in Malmö, Ystad, and Västerås. The Social Democrats still, however, advanced candidates in just 12 of 230 constituencies. The party's total vote, nationwide, was 8,751, or about 5 percent of the votes cast.[76] A growing number of workers were now surmounting the 800 kroner income requirement. The Social Democrats estimated that about 10,000 workers nationwide probably cast ballots in this election. If this estimate is correct, given that a total of 181,000 votes were cast, workers still constituted only about 6 percent of the voting electorate. Just over one in four members (27.5 percent) of the adult male population was eligible to vote.[77]

In 1905, the first election at which the Social Democrats had any real impact, the party placed candidates in 27 of 230 constituencies and won thirteen seats. In the thirteen in which it elected a candidate, it received a total of 26,083 votes. In the twenty-seven districts as a whole, it received a total of about 45,000 votes.[78] As in 1902, the party ran as an informal ally of the Liberal party, ensuring that in marginal districts the two would not cost each other seats. In both years, because the Social Democrats competed in such a small fraction of the constituencies and because these were overwhelmingly working-class districts, it was an alliance that cost neither party greatly.

In 1908, all thirty-three of the Social Democrats' candidates were elected. Only these thirty-three were on the ballot, as the Liberals and Social Democrats arranged not to run candidates against each other in districts in which such competition would cost one of the parties a seat. The Social Democratic candidates received a total of 54,000 votes. The party also claimed that it was responsible for transferring to Liberal candidates another 21,000 votes. If this was so, its total electorate now amounted to about 75,000 voters, or one-quarter of those who cast ballots.[79]

The elections of 1905 and 1908 were the high point of Social Democratic–Liberal cooperation in Sweden. Before 1905 the Socialist party was such a marginal actor that the cooperation was necessarily severely limited. After 1908, the franchise was reformed and extended to a much larger part of the adult male population. At the same time, proportional representation was introduced, eliminating any incentive to cooperate. Moreover, the Liberal party began to suffer a series of devastating electoral defeats in the urban areas in which it might otherwise have offered the Social Democrats a valuable alliance.

Throughout this first decade of the century, the central problem of the urban Liberals remained as it had been in earlier years: to hold together the Liberal party and collaborate with the Social Democrats in the cities. In this the party failed. As we saw in Chapter 3, the movement broke apart on urban–rural lines because the agrarians would not support Karl Staaff's franchise reform. The key event, in this context, was not the King's refusal to dissolve the First Chamber and his dismissal of Staaff's ministry in 1906. It was, rather, the refusal of the agrarian wing of the party to stand by Staaff after this. The Conservative ministry of Arvid Lindman succeeded the following year in enacting a suffrage reform to its own liking because it broke the Liberal party. Agrarian Liberals broke with Staaff precisely because Lindman offered them a suffrage formula that was aimed *against* the Social Democrats. It was a suffrage reform that would enlarge the electorate, but at the same time provide conservative guarantees, as they were called, through proportional representation, the influence of the First Chamber, and residual tax qualifications (several hundred thousand male workers remained disenfranchised) that would all serve to constrain the power of the Social Democrats. It was for just this reason that the agrarians found it an attractive formula and the Social Democrats voted against it.[80] Lindman understood better than Staaff the antipathy of the Liberal farmers for the Social Democrats and their radical urban allies.

The Conservatives remained in office until 1911. It was then that Karl Staaff had his second taste of ministerial power. As franchise reform had overwhelmed politics earlier, the Defense Struggle now did so. The Liberal party once again broke apart because the agrarian wing would not embrace the antidefense policies of the urban wing and the Social Democrats. The struggle was much more than a dispute about how much to spend on the military. It was in fact a conflict about the fundamental nature of Swedish society and the merit of the democratic state. On one side stood those forces who rejected a class-based model of society and were captivated by Swedish nationalism, and the authority of the military and the King against the political parties and the Riksdag. On the other side were urban radicals and socialists who sought to establish the primacy of the Riksdag (still far from assured) and wanted a state committed to the attenuation of class conflict.[81] It was in these respects analogous to the almost simultaneous Dreyfus Affair in France, and it is most telling that while *L'Affair* brought liberals and socialists together on behalf of the Republic, *Den Striden* broke the liberal movement.

In the end, the war and the growing conservatism of his own party forced Staaff's capitulation on the issue. In retrospect, this is no surprise, because the Liberal party's center of gravity had been shifted decisively by the 1911 election, the first under the reformed suffrage. The party was devastated in the cities, as the middle classes shifted decisively to the Conservatives and the newly enfranchised workers voted for the Social Democrats. The Liberals emerged with an electorate that was now three-quarters rural.[82] The movement of a large fraction of the urban middle classes away from liberalism was accelerated by the General Strike and Lockout of the summer and autumn of 1909, which severely polarized urban opinion and placed the Liberal party in the ineffective position of criticizing both the workers and the Conservative government, which stood solidly behind the employers. One indication of the conflict's impact on middle-class opinion was the shift to the Conservative party of two previously liberal influential journals, *Svenska Dagbladet* and *Aftonbladet*.[83]

The demise of the urban reformers had already been forecast by the break between the Liberal party and the "Lindhagen group" in 1907. Karl Lindhagen, the premier leader of Stockholm radicals, had left the party in that year because of its rightward shift on the franchise, its resistance to agrarian reform, and more generally the declining influence of the party's radicals. It was indicative of radicalism's decline that Lindhagen contemplated and then rejected a plan to launch a new party of urban radicals because he saw too little support for it.[84]

Liberalism in Sweden, then, foundered on a preindustrial cleavage which prevented the movement from establishing its political dominance. Moreover, it proved to be impossible to create a liberal movement that could, as in France, combine mass support in the countryside and the towns in alliance with a socialist working-class movement. The roots of the conflicts between the urban and rural wings of Swedish liberalism long predated the appearance of the socialist working class, and it would reverse the essential causality at work to suppose that it was the attempt to include the separately organized working class in the alliance that broke the movement. Rather, the appearance of the socialist movement simply reinforced inherited tensions. The additional mass support that workers could provide was essential to the Liberal movement's prospects of success, and especially to its urban wing's prospects. But if urban Liberals found that those workers were a key ingredient of their local power base, they also quickly discovered that the inclusion of those workers enormously complicated the relationship with the countryside.

In that the problem of an alliance with socialists accelerated the breach within liberalism along the lines of the inherited cleavage, Sweden actually provides a kind of paradigmatic case of a liberal movement crippled by a preindustrial cleavage and therefore unable to make an alliance, not to mention an effective one, with an independent working-class party. In Norway, Germany, and Italy, liberalism was made ineffective by inherited cleavages within the middle classes, but the question of an alliance with independently organized workers did not provoke a split along the traditional cleavage lines, because such an alliance was essentially rejected by the entire liberal movement, including by, for the most part, what passed for its urban radical wing.

In Norway, as far as we can discern from the available evidence, there were no more than two or three instances in which a local liberal association, not to mention the national party, was willing to make a tactical alliance with a Labor candidate. None of these was successful, and they always appear to have been repudiated by the majority of the local association, whether it was urban or rural. How can we account for this difference between Norway and Sweden?

It is certain that the difference did not lie in the social democratic parties. Although each always had a radical wing, both were preponderantly reformist during these years.[85] The radical syndicalism that became a major feature of Norwegian labor was not an organized force until 1911 and did not assert its leadership of the movement until after the war. In both Norway and Sweden, the social democratic parties openly courted alliances with liberals in their formative years.

Rather, the difference appears to be found in the timing of the two liberal movements. Liberalism and socialism were politically organized at the same time in Sweden, and at a time when the enfranchised population, especially the enfranchised working-class population, was comparatively very small—so small, in fact, that until 1902 the tiny Social Democratic vote could not possibly threaten the Liberal party. Moreover, in urban areas the game was a more felicitous one for both parties until the franchise reform. This was especially true for the Liberal party, whose Riksdag contingent grew steadily between 1891 and 1906.[86]

In contrast, in Norway, the electoral appearance of the Labor party coincided much more closely with the introduction of manhood suffrage. Given the larger electorate, the Labor party could pose a markedly more immediate threat to the Norwegian Liberals. Moreover, a larger proportion of the Norwegian working class was enfranchised *before* the 1898 franchise reform. In Norway, in 1897, at the last election before the reform, 43 percent of the adult male population already had the vote. In Sweden, at the same time, only 24 percent of the adult male population had the right to vote, and this figure had still risen to only 34 percent at the last prereform election in 1908.[87] Because the prereform Norwegian working-class electorate had been both larger and solidly in the Liberal camp, as it had never been in Sweden, where it was more fully excluded from participation, the appearance of the Labor party represented a much greater threat to the established Liberal party. Norwegian Liberals had, so to speak, already colonized the prereform working-class electorate and trade unions. In the absence of such colonization, there was really no parallel experience of struggle between socialists and liberals for a part of the liberal movement in Sweden. Finally, the Liberal party in Norway had a longer history as an institutionalized alliance, however flaccid, of urban and rural interests. In Norway as in Sweden, opposition to an alliance with workers derived above all from the antagonism it aroused among farmers. This antagonism, and the desire that it not lead to a breach in the party, were themes that appeared constantly in Liberal surveys of the risks of an alliance with workers. The difference, of course, was that in Norway the alliance with the countryside was an organized fact with organized mechanisms of defense. In Sweden, it was merely an hypothesis, and one that the national party organization largely lacked the capacity to enforce at the local level.[88]

Denmark

Liberals had more success in Denmark than in any of the other countries we discussed in Chapter 3. To an extent paralleled only in Belgium and the Netherlands, the Danish liberal movement succeeded in transforming the constitutional order as early as 1848. Liberals maintained their dominance through the 1850s, faltering at that time because of the fissure between the Venstre and the National Liberals. Whereas Belgian and Dutch liberalism were eclipsed in the 1880s, Danish liberalism reasserted itself. A reorganized liberal movement, originating in the countryside and slowly reestablishing itself in the cities, began to take form. As early as 1872, it acquired an enduring majority in the Folketing.

Handicapped by its own divisions and the slow growth of its urban beachhead, two decades were required before a decisive liberal breakthrough issued from this majority. Yet the existence of that majority ushered in a period, from the end of the 1870s, of "parallel government," in which sovereignty was, in practice, divided between the king's ministers aligned with the conservative Landsting and the liberal majority in the Folketing. That majority gained its influence in large measure through its control of Folketing committees and its capacity to obstruct budgetary measures. The obstruction of the finance bill in the 1870s and the later refusal to approve new sources of revenues were merely the most dramatic examples of this. It was indicative of that divided sovereignty that even the bête noire of the liberals, J. B. S. Estrup's two-decade long Conservative ministry, never sought to implement measures that could not muster majorities in both chambers.[89]

The constitutional shift of the 1860s had narrowed the franchise and implicitly enlarged the role of the upper house. There had never been any question, however, that the king's ministers could simply govern against the will of the Riksdag. Even the king's most conservative supporters acknowledged that the government needed at least a Landsting majority. In practice, the Conservative governments repeatedly found that they had to have the cooperation of the Folketing majority as well. For some years, the divisions within the Venstre allowed the ministers to gain that majority. In effect, the balance of sovereignty shifted from one that was ambiguous and favored the Folketing to one that was ambiguous and divided sovereignty between the ministers and the Folketing. In this situation, liberals were by no means without influence.

During these years, the liberal alliance between the town and country was gradually recemented, and in the process, the conservative presence in the Folketing and Landsting was chipped away. This Conservative decline reached its denouement in 1901, when divisions within the Landsting and its further decline in the Folketing exhausted the Conservative capacity, and even more the Conservative will, to govern. The appointment of a Liberal ministry in that year marked the system shift that formally established the sovereignty of the Riksdag. Thenceforth, Liberals governed through the war years.

Yet this was a liberal movement whose definitive success came comparatively late—no "breakthrough" occurred until 1901. Liberalism's position was even thereafter a rather fragile one. The liberal governments that followed after 1901 were often minority governments, and the first, provided by the old Venstre, proved that the urban–rural conflict within liberalism had been subordinated rather than eliminated. The government's fixation with the concerns of the rural middle class provoked an almost immediate rupture in the party, with urban radicals quickly departing to form their own party, the Radical Venstre. That fixation also alienated the Social Democrats, who terminated their long-standing alliance with the Venstre in 1903. These divisions, which might have been of enduring importance, proved otherwise because the Social Democrats immediately acquired a new liberal ally, the Radicals, who alternated in power with the Venstre and proved the key to the Social Democrats' own breakthrough.

Danish liberalism, then, might best be described as having attained a position of "quasi-hegemony," for its course was distinct from both the enfeebled liberal movements of most of the continent and from the hegemonic liberalism of Britain and France. On balance, it was rather closer to the former than to the latter.

This more favorable course for liberalism had important consequences for the formation of the labor movement. In the first place, the Liberal victory at midcentury had created a very generous franchise, at the time aimed at incorporating the broad agrarian mass on which the Venstre depended. The Folketing franchise remained comparatively generous even after the contraction of 1866. In consequence of this Liberal legacy, the Danish working class was born largely enfranchised. By the late 1880s, when the labor movement was being institutionalized, three-quarters of the male working class already had the right to vote in Folketing elections.[90]

The Social Democratic party provided Liberals with a critical ally during almost all of the years between 1884 and the outbreak of the war. They had a common cause in their demand that the sovereignty of the Folketing be acknowledged and that the communal (and therefore Landsting) franchise be restored. In Liberal lore, these became a demand for the restoration of the 1848 constitution. Because of this alliance and because the Liberal majority could exercise considerable influence on the government through its control of the Folketing, Danish workers encountered a state more favorably disposed than did workers in other societies in which liberalism failed to gain outright dominance. The state's attitude toward the workers, in both politics and the labor market, was comparatively benign both before and after the system shift.

Unlike the labor movements in Norway and Sweden, then, the Danish movement never experienced the isolation imposed by liberal rejection and ineffectiveness. The availability and comparative effectiveness of this alliance, in turn, critically affected the labor movement's conception of its own road to power. But just as the relationship was distinct from Norway, Sweden, and the other countries discussed in this and the previous chapter, it was also distinct from the liberal–labor relationship we found in Britain and France. Later in this chapter we examine the way in which this relationship and the quasi-hegemony that sustained it yielded a diluted version of a labor movement under weak liberalism. For the moment the task at hand is to consider the alliance itself.

Although the first Lib–Lab electoral alliance was made in 1877—the Venstre supported a Social Democratic candidate in one district in exchange for the socialists' endorsement in the remaining 101 districts—the alliance began to assume significance only in 1884. Until that time, Conservative candidates had had a virtual monopoly on seats elected by urban voters. In 1879 Conservatives received more than 88 percent of the urban vote.[91] The first liberal electoral association was not even established in Copenhagen until 1883.[92] The Conservative monopoly was broken for the first time in 1884 by a Social Democrat–Liberal alliance, which managed to win two Copenhagen seats for the Venstre and two for the Social Democrats. The Venstre also won seats in Aarhus, Frederiskberg, and Randers.[93] From this time onward, the parties worked together in the Folketing and made electoral pacts at every election until 1903.

The urban gains of 1884 were all but wiped out in 1887, when the Conservatives retook all of the lost seats save one held by Social Democrats in Copenhagen.[94] In 1890, Social Democrats ran candidates in ten districts, all but one of which was in an urban area. The party won two seats in Copenhagen while the Venstre won two there and one in Aarhus.[95] In 1892, the Social Democrats retained the Copenhagen seats, and their total vote rose to 20,000.[96]

The Social Democrats' first real impact was felt in 1895, when the party won seven of the sixteen available Copenhagen seats and picked up another in Aarhus, with a total of 24,500 votes. Its share of the national vote had risen from 3.5 percent in 1887 to a much more consequential 11.1 percent in 1895. It now offered candidates in 18 of 114 districts, again virtually all in purely urban districts.[97] These districts were chosen in negotiations with the Venstre, and the essence of the bargain the parties made now as in other elections was that the Social Democrats would provide the candidate of the Left mainly in heavily working-class urban districts, while the Venstre would carry the Left's banner in virtually all rural districts in which the Left had a plausible chance and in most middle-class urban districts.[98]

The alliance continued in the 1898 election and reached its pinnacle and conclusion in the 1901 election, which ushered in the system shift. The Social Democrats now won 14 seats (out of 114) and 19 percent of the vote by competing in thirty districts.[99]

Several aspects of this collaboration are worth emphasizing. In the first place, Social Democratic candidates, and especially Social Democratic victories, were limited almost exclusively to urban areas. Of the forty-two seats the party won in all of the elections between 1884 and 1901, thirty-nine were in purely urban districts, two were in mixed districts, and just one was in a completely rural district.[100] The rural victory, however, was a fluke: in 1890, the local liberal association in Skjoldelev (north of Aarhus) divided between two liberal candidates. Under the circumstances, the Social Democrats ran their own man and won the seat in a four-way race. The party lost the seat at the next election.[101] The second characteristic of importance pertains to the timing of the Social Democrats' contribution: before 1894, the party had only a marginal impact. The third point to note is that they thenceforth played a critical role in realigning urban workers from the right to the left, electing not only their own candidates but urban liberals who were dependent on working-class votes. Before the Social Democrats became a force to be reckoned with, urban workers had been a linchpin of the Conservative electorate, providing between 16 and 40 percent, varying by district, of the urban vote for Conservative candidates. As a group, they were the second largest component of the Conservative electorate.[102]

The dependence of urban liberals on Social Democratic endorsements was demonstrated vividly by the 1903 election, by which time the alliance had fallen apart. Without that alliance, the Liberals lost five of the seven seats they had previously held in Copenhagen, retaining only two in districts in which the Social Democrats did not present candidates. Among the lost Liberal seats, four went to Conservatives and one went to a Social Democrat. Overall, the Social Democratic share of the vote rose from 19 percent to 22 percent, while the Liberal share rose from 39 to 46 percent.[103] Notwithstanding its setback in Copenhagen, gains elsewhere limited the overall Liberal loss to just two seats. The pattern of seat changes and the overall result tell us that, during the alliance, the transfer of votes had been mainly in one direction—from Social Democrats to Liberals—and that urban Liberal success, especially in Copenhagen, had become critically dependent on the alliance.

But the result also tells us that the contribution of the Social Democrats to the Venstre's success was limited. That is, it was limited to the working-class and mixed districts of Copenhagen, for the Venstre did not really suffer outside these districts when the alliance was terminated. Elsewhere, it was winning on its own.[104]

These inferences were certainly not lost on defeated middle-class radicals. As in Stockholm, Copenhagen liberals came to understand quickly that they could not be influential within their own party—could not even get elected—if they were not aligned with social democracy, but likewise they could not prevent a breach between Social Democrats and agrarian liberals.

The Liberal government that came to power in 1901 was supported in the Folketing by the Social Democrats and was carefully balanced to reflect the mixture of urban and rural interests that had refounded the party in 1895. The new government faced several pressing issues, including tax and land reform, tariffs, and defense policy. On all of these the agrarians showed themselves to be increasingly conservative, inclined to align with the independent landed elites in the Landsting, and concerned mainly with the interests of their core agrarian middle class constituency.[105] This tendency had been apparent even before the system shift. State efforts to help smallholders to buy land for themselves, for example, had always been carefully controlled by the representatives of the rural middle class. The Smallholdings Act of 1899, for instance, which introduced the principle of state loans to smallholders, restricted the plots that could be purchased to a size insufficient to provide the new owners with an adequate income. They were, however, too large for the owner to take a full-time job in addition to running his smallholding. In this way, farmers in need of inexpensive labor were still assured of a plentiful supply. Likewise, when in 1903 the farmers finally achieved their long-standing goal of tax reform, they devised a new system that placed a disproportionate burden on smallholders.[106] The government's conservatism was a profound disappointment to the Social Democrats, so much so that the party voted at its 1903 congress to terminate all cooperation with the Venstre. Urban radicals and representatives of smallholders and agrarian workers proved equally alienated, and by 1905 they had formed their own party, the Radical Venstre, with fifteen Folketing members.[107]

This party, which was led by middle-class progressives but had a rural social base as well in the smallholders and agrarian workers, made an electoral alliance with the Social Democrats in 1906 that was maintained until proportional representation was introduced in 1920. The essence of the bargain was as it had been with the old Venstre: Social Democrats conceded almost all purely rural districts to the Liberals, especially in Jutland, where the number of smallholders and landless workers was large, while dividing the urban districts according to their class composition.[108] The Radicals governed with Social Democratic support in 1909–10 and from 1911 through the war years.

The essential question is this: Why were Danish farmers, the backbone of the Venstre, not driven earlier to a more conservative posture by the mobilization of urban workers? That, after all, had been at the root of the failure of Lib–Labism in Norway and Sweden. In the longer run, as we have seen, this did happen in Denmark. Once the system shift had taken place, agrarian Liberals drew away from urban radicals and Social Democrats. Yet, before then, the relationship with the labor movement was a relatively harmonious one.

The key to understanding the relative equanimity with which liberal farmers greeted the Social Democrats is to be found in several features that distinguished liberalism in Denmark from liberalism in Norway, Sweden, and elsewhere. The first and most central of these is that it was historically more cohesive and successful. Danish liberalism suffered only one fundamental division: the break with the cities. Once this break had occurred, what remained of the movement was in fact comparatively homogeneous and based heavily on the support of the single largest class in Danish society, the rural middle class. This middle class was not, as it was in Norway, fractured by regional, linguistic, and religious differences. At the same time that the movement was more cohesive than it was in Norway, it was more successful than it was in Sweden. Danish liberalism had a history of dominance from which it could draw confidence. It had, in fact, transformed the constitutional order and asserted its hegemony for two decades. During that time, its agrarian constituency had discovered that it could, indeed, implement its program in alliance with urban interests through parliamentary institutions.[109] Moreover, even during the 1880s and 1890s, when liberals were seeking to reestablish their hegemony, they were comparatively successful. We have already seen that through their Folketing majority they exerted much influence on the government. More important, the obstacle to their reasserted hegemony was found less in the need to enlarge their social base than in the simple need to grind down the conservative opposition in constitutional terms. This was especially the case after the 1894 agreement on defense policy was reached between Moderate Liberals and Conservatives. That agreement, by defusing the defense issue, removed the main impediment to a more cohesive and reorganized Liberal party that transcended the old urban–rural divide. At the same time it deprived Conservatives of their most powerful trump card—Danish nationalism—and compelled the resignation of the long-running government of J. B. S. Estrup. The government's resignation, a quid pro quo of Moderate Liberal cooperation, was itself a partial recognition of the Folketing's sovereignty: the lower house could compel a government's resignation.[110]

This situation was distinctly less dangerous than that in which liberals in Norway and Sweden found themselves. In those countries during the years of worker mobilization, it did not, given the divisions within liberalism, take an astute observer to realize that the social foundations of the movements were precarious. Liberals in those societies had to struggle to gain majorities (in

Norway and Sweden) and hold them together (in Norway), even before worker mobilization became a threat. They found themselves in this situation because of the divisions within their own core constituencies. In this context, the prospect of a socialist mobilization of workers, especially in conjunction with a reformed franchise, was an acute menace. In Denmark, however, liberals already had a majority of mass support without the workers and with the most progressive franchise in Scandinavia. There could be less doubt, then, that they were the movement with the broadest support in Danish society. Consequently, they could be more confident that if Folketing parliamentarism was established they would be the principal beneficiaries.

This brings us to the second reason for the more relaxed response of Danish farmers to social democratic mobilization. Much of the Venstre's progress, certainly until 1895, was entirely independent of, indeed we can say occurred in spite of, the behavior of working-class voters. For before that time its ally, the Social Democratic party, was receiving only a small fraction of the vote: 3.5, 5.5, and 6.5 percent, respectively, in 1887, 1890, and 1893. Even if we generously assume that it was transferring half as many votes as it was receiving, it was still a residual force in the Venstre advance. This was doubly true, because the Social Democrats' appeal was heavily concentrated in a handful of Copenhagen districts. The consistently weak showing of Social Democratic candidates outside of Copenhagen[111] and the results of the 1903 election, fought without the alliance, demonstrated that.[112] The Venstre, then, was not only advancing toward its goal of overwhelming its opponents in mass support, it was doing so, through the early 1890s, without yet relying extensively on workers' votes.

The correlate of this, and the third reason for the comparative calm with which agrarians greeted social democratic advances, is that the central importance of social democracy was not to be found simply in mobilizing working-class voters, a concept as misleading as informative at this conjuncture, but in *realigning* working-class votes. Whereas in Norway Social Democratic mobilization represented a direct assault on liberalism because it sought to plunder a liberal constituency, in Denmark it was an assault on conservatism, liberalism's archenemy. Danish workers were already voting in large numbers when Social Democracy became an important movement, and, as stated before, they were voting for the Conservatives.[113] Social Democratic mobilization, then, represented a coup for the agrarians: it not only pilfered the constituency of the Venstre's archenemy, it delivered those votes to the Venstre. That was something the Venstre, given its exclusion from the cities, could never have done on its own.

Belgium and the Netherlands

As we saw in Chapter 3, the election of 1884 was a seminal one in Belgium. Of the great Catholic victory, the Liberal leader Walther Frère-Orban remarked "This is not a defeat, this is a disaster."[114] Indeed it was. The Catholic party that came to power in that year thenceforth controlled an absolute majority in the Second Chamber and formed every government until the end of the World War. The essence of this victory was the ability of the Catholics to join the mobilization of peasants with growing support in urban areas. In 1884, for the first time, Catholics swept Brussels, long a Liberal stronghold.[115]

For the past decade, Liberals had focused on their conflict with the clerical party, which had raised issues around which Liberals could unite, and had ignored pleas for social and electoral reform, which had divided them. Having been so soundly beaten by the Catholic party, Liberals now turned to the issues that divided them. From these divisions emerged the Progressives, who for a time set themselves up as a separate party favoring franchise and social reform. The Liberal party as a whole, however, was no closer to an understanding on reform in 1894, when the issue was forced, than it had been a decade earlier. The reform, which introduced manhood suffrage with plural voting, did not come about because of the exertions of Liberals. Franchise reform divided Liberals and Catholics, and the Constituante that met to debate it in 1892 and 1893 was hopelessly deadlocked and ready to go home when the Socialist party and trade unions called a general strike. The strike led 200,000 industrial workers to put down their tools and provoked extensive rioting and thirteen deaths. Reform was the price that Socialist leaders demanded for the termination of the strike. Genuinely harrowed by the prospect of revolution, Liberals and Catholics conceded manhood suffrage, but qualified it with a system of plural voting.[116] This worked moderately to the advantage of both of the nonsocialist parties, but advantaged the Liberals more than the Catholics.[117]

Yet, in the long run, the reform did nothing to help the Liberals. Between 1894 and 1900, the party's share of the vote fell from 29 to 22 percent. By 1912, it was just 11.2 percent. In 1894, the Liberal party lost 41 seats and in 1896 a further 8 seats. In 1896 and 1898, the party was reduced to just 13 seats (out of 152) in the Second Chamber. The Socialists hovered around 28 seats throughout the decade, while the Catholics piled up massive majorities, with 104 seats in 1894, 111 in 1896, and 112 in 1898.[118] The issue was no longer what the Liberals might do to regain power, it was rather what they might do to survive as a party in the Second Chamber. For the Socialists had become the main party of opposition.[119]

The essential problem for the Liberals was that the political participation of the countryside and of the lower middle classes in the cities had worked to the benefit of the Catholics, while workers who abandoned the political guidance of the Church voted for Socialists. In effect, the Liberals found themselves imprisoned behind the walls of their own fortress of upper-class urban secularism. The Liberal dilemma was made worse in the late 1890s as parts of the secular middle class, fearful of the growing Socialist movement and recognizing the Liberal party as a lost cause, opted for Catholic candidates.[120]

The political consequences of this isolation were compounded by the electoral system itself. After the loss of Brussels, the Liberals found themselves competing without a regional stronghold in a plurality system that rewarded concentrated support. Their mean share of the vote between 1894 and 1912 was 23 percent in Flanders, 26.5 percent in Wallonia, and 28.8 percent in Brussels. Whereas Liberal voters were spread rather evenly across the country, Catholic and Socialist voters were concentrated. The Catholics' average share of the vote during the same period was 65 percent in Flanders, 42 percent in Brussels, and 38 percent in Wallonia. For the Socialists, the figures were 6.8 percent in Flanders, 34.5 percent in Wallonia, and 22.7 percent in Brussels. Within Wallonia, the Socialist vote was heavily concentrated in Liége, Mons, and Charleroi.[121]

The grimness of the Liberal situation and the dangers inherent in Socialists providing the main opposition impressed even Catholic leaders—so much so, that to prop up the Liberals, the Catholics in 1899 sponsored the introduction of qualified proportional representation with district lists.[122]

Proportional representation saved the Liberal party. But it was not a pure variety of proportional representation; it relied on multimember district lists, and Liberals found themselves critically dependent before and after its introduction on alliances with the Socialists. These alliances were made in 1896, 1898, 1906, 1908, 1910, and 1912. There was no mystery to them. The Socialists were the party with the larger mass base, the dominant party in the alliance, and the Liberals were simply trying to survive.[123] The Socialists became the main party of opposition (twenty-eight seats versus twenty) as early as 1894, the first occasion on which the Socialists seriously entered the electoral arena. Although proportional representation gave the Liberals a slight advantage in seats after 1900, the Socialists remained the party with the larger mass base. In the eleven elections fought between 1894 and 1914, the Liberals led the Socialists in the popular vote only twice; in 1894 they received 537,000 votes versus the Socialists' 311,000, and in 1900 they received 502,000 versus 461,000. In six of the eleven elections the Socialists drew more support; in the other three the relative balance was obscured by the alliance arrangements.[124]

It is instructive that the sole occasion on which the Liberal–Socialist cartel thought it might actually be able to wrest power from the Catholics resulted instead in a devastating defeat. By June 1912, the Catholics had been in power for twenty-eight years and, judging by the returns of the several previous elections, were slowly suffering a loss of support. This loss appeared to be accelerated by new school legislation that would equalize support for church and state institutions. When the measure was presented to the Chamber, it provoked widespread demonstrations and riots.[125] Moreover, the census of 1910 had resulted in an enlargement of the Second

Chamber and redistricting that created nineteen new seats in urban areas that could be expected to plumb for Liberal and Socialist candidates.[126]

It seemed, then, the ideal occasion for Liberals and Socialists to force the Catholics from power. The anticipation of power led the two parties to make the most comprehensive cartel of the prewar years and to stand on a common program that included an array of franchise and social reforms.[127] In the past, cartels had been merely an expedient, had involved no common program and had not been expected actually to bring down the Catholic government. If the cartel was victorious, the Liberals would provide the government and the Socialists would support it in the Chamber.

As it happened, the voting produced a stunning victory for the Catholics, who actually increased their Second Chamber fraction from 86 to 101 seats. Of the nineteen new seats, fifteen went to the Catholics and four to the Socialists. The Liberals retained only the seats they had previously held. Because most of the new seats were in traditional Liberal strongholds, we do not have to look far to find the explanation for this defeat: middle-class voters were punishing the Liberal party for its unprecedented fraternization with the Socialists.[128] For the Liberals, the principal lesson was that they could win power neither with the Socialists nor without them.

An alliance with a despairing and debilitated liberal movement, one whose voters abandoned it when it took the Socialists seriously, competing against an unshakeable Catholic hegemony, was hardly the sort of alliance likely to convince Socialists that Lib–Labism offered a plausible road to power. In consequence, Socialists in Belgium as elsewhere were forced to concentrate on the coherent organization of workers, or at least of the secular workers available to them. This was a task they accomplished with distinction, creating one of the most united working-class movements in prewar Europe. Although the Belgian Workers' party, which brought together various socialist movements, was not even created until 1885, the Socialists entered parliament in 1894 in numbers unequalled at the time anywhere in Europe. As a contemporary observer of the party remarked, the party tried "to fight the workers' battles all round—as consumer, producer, and citizen; its methods are not unique, but their coordination is. . . ."[129]

Yet the Socialists, after their spectacular successes during the first ten years of the reformed franchise, found they had reached the limits of their prewar potential. Their share of the vote stagnated at around 20 percent during the last decade of peace. This stagnation was only marginally due to the plurality voting system.[130] It was more fundamentally due to the success of the Catholic party in mobilizing a large fraction, probably half, of the working class. Indicative of this was the fact that just before the war, Catholic trade unions, with 110,000 members, enrolled almost as many workers as Socialist unions did, with 125,000 members.[131] The root of the anticlerical Socialists' problem was their inability to penetrate the Flemish working class, whose devotion to the faith raised an insuperable barrier.

Flanders, although less industrialized than Wallonia at this time, nonetheless had acquired a large industrial sector by 1890, and in the next three decades it grew to encompass half of the region's work force. Yet, between 1894 and 1912, the Socialists averaged just 6.8 percent of the Flemish vote compared to 34.5 percent of the Walloon vote. Although historical data are not available, historians are in broad agreement that it was the density of the Catholic social complex in Flanders—churches and church schools, trade unions, friendly societies, and other associations—that blocked the Socialist penetration of the region.[132]

It is clear that the Catholic party was a genuinely interclass party. Its Christian Democratic workers association, the Ligue démocratique chrétienne de Belgique, had 200,000 members by 1911.[133] Catholic mutual aid societies had 500,000 members by 1909.[134] Although its Christian Democratic wing, the agent of Catholic workers' political interests, never established supremacy within the party, it did play a decisive role in leading the party to accommodate workers. And the party, while anathema to the Socialists because of its clericalism, was much more receptive to workers' demands for a living wage than were the Socialists' Liberal allies. It was a Catholic government that removed the ban on trade unions owning property, a ban that had long been the principal legal obstacle to labor market organization. It was likewise a Catholic government that placed severe restrictions on Sunday labor, established subsidized unemployment insurance, enforced worker safety legislation, and in a variety of other ways interceded on behalf of workers. If these intercessions were often less than Socialists would have liked, it was nonetheless significant that almost all social legislation was passed by Catholic and Socialist votes in opposition to the Liberals.[135] The Catholic party, in practice, became the main vehicle through which workers' anxieties and ambitions were articulated in governing circles, both before the war and in the interwar period.

The interwar result, as we shall see, was a socialist working-class movement that was, on the one hand, following from the enfeeblement of liberalism, exceptionally cohesive, and on the other hand, as a result of the continued Catholic hegemony and the strength of the Catholic appeal among workers, crippled both by its virtual exclusion from power and by its inability to unite secular and Catholic workers.

The experience of the Netherlands, which need not long detain us here, was little more than a variant of this. Dutch Liberals, although undermined by the mobilization of workers and the faithful, never experienced the cataclysmic defeat that their brothers to the south suffered. Liberal hegemony came to an end with the coming to power of the Catholic–Protestant coalition in 1888. That government lasted until 1891, when it was replaced by a liberal one. Liberals remained nominally in power until 1901. In reality, however, the Liberal party came apart in 1894 over the extension of the suffrage. Broken into Radical, Moderate, and Conservative parties, subsequent liberal governments were dependent on Moderate, Conservative, and religious party support. Within the context of the story we are telling, it is, of course, highly significant that a vulnerable Liberal party was nearly destroyed by a debate over the political capacity of the working class, a question dramatically distilled in the issue of franchise extension.[136] Even the Radical remnants of this party showed little inclination to cooperate with the Socialists, and in practice liberal–labor electoral coalitions were never a feature of prewar politics.[137] It was only in 1913 that the Liberals managed to regroup and campaign for the first time in two decades on a common program.

Dutch socialism remained a minor force until the last decade of peace: before 1901 it never had more than 2 members in Parliament, and as late as 1909 the party had no more than 9,000 members. It suffered the same fundamental handicap that plagued the Belgian movement: before and after the war, a large fraction of the working class was organized in politics and in the labor market by clerical parties and trade unions. In 1914, the Socialist unions had 84,000 members; the religious unions had about 40,000 members. More interestingly, and as befits a society with a long history of liberal hegemony and a still powerful liberal movement, 142,000 workers were in trade unions not affiliated with *any* federation.[138] The final parallel with Belgium is that the clerical parties dominated interwar politics: no government in those two decades was ever formed without them and, indeed, given their parliamentary base and ideological centrality, no government could have been formed without them.

Italy

The narrowness of the franchise—and more fundamentally the subtending Liberal insecurity it reflected—militated against meaningful liberal–labor collaboration in Italy before the turn of the century. Until the franchise was reformed in 1882, no more than 7 percent of the male population could vote. Even after the reform, which extended the vote to the lower edges of the northern urban middle classes, working-class participation remained restricted to a small number of skilled northern artisans. Rising incomes and increased literacy among northern urban workers began to push markedly more of them above the threshold of the franchise law only in the late 1880s. It was indicative of the insecurity of Liberals that when workers did begin to vote with greater frequency, the Liberal response was to purge the electoral registers, thus returning the rate of enfranchisement to its 1882 level.[139]

In this situation, the few instances of liberal–labor alliances that obtained before the end of the century were necessarily sporadic, isolated, and divorced from the main impulses of liberal politics. The main occasion came in the alliance between the Radicals, themselves a marginal force, and the Workers' party in Lombardy in 1886. Even this proved bootless when Liberal

Prime Minister Agostino Depretis intervened to break it.[140] The Workers' Party thereafter gravitated toward socialism. To concentrate on alliances among such marginal forces, however, is to miss the root of the early divorce between workers and liberalism in Italy. That root was found in the almost complete rejection by the Liberal establishment of any cooperation with any workers movement. It was that rejection that underlay the narrow franchise and, more important, the broad and enduring Liberal opposition to its reform. Lib–labism could be no more than an hypothesis until Liberals discovered in the 1890s that worker mobilization could no longer be adequately met simply by repression.

It would be a mistake, however, to suppose that the narrow franchise and the antipathy of Liberals were in their origins aimed principally at the working class as such. Rather, through the 1880s, Italian workers were in the main the inadvertent victims of a larger struggle. Not the least of the reasons for thinking this is simply that virtually no working class yet existed to be victimized. For even in 1882, when the franchise was reformed for the first time, the working class hardly existed in the modern sense of a class aware of a set of common interests that set it apart from, and in conflict with, the rest of society. Even in the most modern of northern cities at this early time, workers were overwhelmingly independent artisans.[141] They seem to have had no clear political alignment: a few were anarchists, a few were socialists, some were sympathetic to Liberals, Radicals, or Republicans. Most were probably inclined toward confessionalism or were apolitical. If they posed any threat to the liberal order, it was not as an independently and antagonistically organized anarchist or socialist class. Neither anarchism, which flourished briefly in the late 1870s "but was never again after 1880 of more than peripheral importance," nor socialism, which "at no time constituted a serious threat to law and order" before the 1890s, appealed to more than a miniscule fraction of workers.[142]

Rather, to the extent that workers posed a threat to the liberal order in the 1870s and 1880s, it was not because many of them thought of themselves as belonging to a distinct class, but because whatever political consciousness most of them possessed was confessional. In this, workers in these early years, aside from the few that adhered to Republicanism, Radicalism, and Socialism, were simply a part of the larger society that was hostile to the Liberals. That, in any event, would seem to be the inescapable inference to be drawn from the weakness of socialism and anarchism in the 1880s and the subsequent pattern of worker mobilization.

Decades later, when workers had full freedom to organize themselves and when confessionalism came out of its self-imposed exile, it was to confessionalism that a large fraction of the working class turned. It was only just after the war that the Church dropped all inhibitions on political participation and manhood suffrage was obtained. The best indicator of the working-class orientation is provided by the comparative strength of Socialist and Catholic trade unions just after the war. In 1920, before attacks on socialist unions commenced, the socialist Confederazione Generale del Lavoro (CGL) enrolled 2.2 million workers and the two-year-old Catholic unions (CIL) enrolled about 1.2 million workers.[143] That this substantial fraction of the working class opted for confessionalism is made all the more striking because it came after several decades of rapid industrialization, after the traumas of the war, after the inspiration of the Russian Revolution, and after two decades of open Socialist agitation. In view of their subsequent alignment, it seems impossible not to infer that if workers could have voted in the 1880s or even 1890s, the great majority of them, especially in the countryside, would have opted for a confessional party, had such a party existed.[144]

In Italy even more than in Belgium, the bias of the electoral law reflected the vulnerability of liberals in a predominantly confessional society. The 1882 law, which relied on a literacy requirement, and more subtly on districts that often gave anticlerical urban areas dominance over confessional rural areas, is the case in point.[145] The law granted the vote to males over twenty-one who could read and write and meet residual tax qualifications. The tax qualification could be residual because at that time, 63 percent of the population, including almost all of the peasantry and a large fraction of the artisans and workers even in Lombardy and Piedmont, were still illiterate. Only in the most progressive cities of the north—Milan, Turin, Genoa—had workers begun to send their children to school. Those parts of the lower middle class and upper working class who could read and write and who were given the vote were concentrated in the cities, and more particularly in the northern cities that were already the backbone of anticlericalism. Since the electoral districts in the north were defined in a manner that ensured—especially in view of the high rate of Catholic abstention—that the urban areas had more electors than the rural areas, the electoral system could be counted on to reinforce the dominance of the liberals in the north. And this electoral arrangement, by combining the hegemony of the anticlerical urban areas in the north with a high northern rate of Catholic abstention and fraud in the south, could be relied on to preserve the liberals' position of leadership nationally.[146] It was, in fact, a brilliant, albeit Machiavellian, response to an otherwise untenable situation.

Unfortunately, because it was an arrangement that was inadvertently contingent on the exclusion of workers from the franchise and militated against the potential integration that Lib–Labism offered, its longer-term consequence was that workers—and the ones that count here were the northern urban workers and the agrarian workers of the Po Valley, as the remainder were still politically torpid—were virtually from the dawn of their self-consciousness forced to organize themselves outside of and against the liberal community. If the only challenge Liberals had confronted had been from secular workers, they might well have been able to accommodate the challenge. But because this was not the only challenge, and the political order could not be opened to secular workers without simultaneously opening it to confessional workers and perhaps, worst of all, the peasantry, Liberals could not accommodate the fraction of the working class that might initially have been amenable to them. As it was, of course, Liberals had good reason to fear the confessional orientation of workers and peasants.

It was because Liberals could not, as they could in France, prevail over confessional forces in a universal and fraud-free suffrage that workers had to be excluded. The exclusion of workers *as a class* was thus not so much a direct intention of the Liberals as it was an unintended by-product of the liberals' struggle against a predominantly confessional society. To be sure, because this exclusion had the result of provoking, as workers became aware of themselves as a class, an alienated and antagonistic working class movement, compelling reasons soon appeared for treating the working class as a threat in its own right.

That was the central theme of the 1890s. With some differences among them, the governments of Francesco Crispi, Antonio di Rudinì, and Luigi Pelloux each sought to employ repression to stifle the growth of a socialist working class. Crispi's campaign commenced at the end of 1893, nominally prompted by the agitation of the Sicilian Fasci (organizations of mainly agrarian workers). His efforts, however, were directed largely against northern socialism. The unified Socialist party, not even founded until 1892, reported a membership, no doubt exaggerated, just one year later of 299 affiliated organizations and 108,000 members.[147] Crispi's response included a purging of the electoral registers that reduced the share enfranchised by about one-third.[148] He also revised the public security law to make liable to prosecution advocates of class struggle. In October 1894 he dissolved the Socialist party and 248 other "subversive" organizations. The party headquarters, newspapers, trade unions, and other worker organizations were indiscriminately shut down. Even Socialist deputies were arrested.[149]

For understanding the longer course of class relations in Italy, it is vital to observe that this strategy of authoritarianism at home was coupled with Crispi's foreign policy of prestige and imperialism abroad. The essential ambition of the policy of prestige and imperialism—which mainly served to bring Italy into mindless and futile conflicts with the French—was to gain recognition for Italy as one of the great powers of Europe. This was a policy whose logic was grounded in domestic political struggles rather than in the balance of power.[150] Indeed, in the latter terms the imperatives were for accommodation with the French and British reinsurance in the Mediterranean. For the Liberal right, however, imperialism and the search for great power status became the domestic equivalent of Bismarck's welfare state. Success abroad might substitute for participatory rights at home to induce mass loyalty.[151] If the assumption that imperialism would generate loyalty was dubious, it was nonetheless certain that failed imperialism would provoke disloyalty. And when 100,000 dervishes annihilated Italy's Ethiopian Army on the road to Adowa, Crispi's fate was sealed. It was a national humiliation of historic importance and for a time (but only for a time) discredited the imperialist strategy. Henceforth, however, there would always be a constituency on the Liberal right, one that grew more broadly based and vocal over time, for a strategy of imperialism and authoritarianism.[152]

Di Rudinì followed Crispi with an unstable coalition that could satisfy neither the left nor right Liberals. To secure his position on the right, Di Rudinì launched a new campaign against the Socialists. Again, trade unions, cooperatives, and chambers of labor were dissolved and deputies from the left, not only Socialists, were arrested. To secure his position among left Liberals Di Rudinì simultaneously launched a new campaign of anti-clericalism, closing or dissolving thousands of parochial committees and hundreds of other Catholic institutions.[153] As it happened, Di Rudinì's two-front strategy alienated both the right, which now wanted an entente with the Catholics aimed against the Socialists, and the left, which wanted an entente with the nonliberal left (the Estrema Sinistra) against the right. For the longer term, Di Rudinì's government is important mainly because its indiscriminate campaign against the left Radicals, Republicans, and Socialists emphasized the common interest of these groups in preserving the civil liberties of the constitution—so much so, that in 1899, when Di Rudinì's successor, Pelloux, introduced his reactionary public safety bill, the Socialists officially abandoned their policy of parliamentary abstention and isolation and adopted Turati's "prudent tactics of alliances."[154]

The decade-long strategy of repression reached both its peak and its denouement under Pelloux (1898–1900). Pelloux's attempts to abort the constitution sealed a parliamentary alliance of the left Liberals and the Estrema Sinistra, an alliance that, through its filibustering, forced Pelloux to go to the voters in June 1900 in an attempt to gain a majority adequate to force through his public safety bill. The components of the Estrema Sinistra campaigned in alliance and nearly doubled the number of their deputies. At the same time the left Liberals under Giolitti and Giuseppe Zanardelli were able to win 116 seats. It was the alliance of the Estrema and the left Liberals, together with some dissident right Liberals, that forced Pelloux's resignation by defeating the public safety bill for the last time in June 1900.

Socialists never again entered an electoral coalition with nonsocialist parties in a national election. But the success of the 1900 alliance and the alliance within the parliament of the left Liberals and Socialists did profoundly affect Socialist thinking. For a majority of Socialists had discovered that their own interests could best be served by an alliance with the left Liberals.[155]

That alliance provided the underpinnings of Giolitti's ambitious, indeed one might say heroic, but ultimately futile attempt to extend the limits of *trasformismo* to include the socialist working class of the north. Giolittismo was a logical consequence of repression's failure. At its heart, it was a strategy aimed at stabilizing liberal power by opening the regime to workers and accepting a detente with Catholics. It was a response to the failure of repression in the 1890s, and the conclusion that issued from it that "No one could any longer delude himself with the idea that it was possible to prevent the working classes from attaining their share of influence."[156]

Giovanni Giolitti was the undisputed master of the era (1900–1914) that came to bear his name.[157] Whether he was the prime minister, the minister of the interior, or out of government, he dominated the parliamentary majority on which all governments depended. This majority combined his own left Liberals with the Socialists and the few explicitly Catholic deputies in the Chamber. The northern members of the majority, who came to the Chamber of Deputies by their success in now fairly legitimate elections, were supplemented by a couple hundred southern placemen, or *askaris* as they were called, who owed their election to Giolitti's mastery of southern fraud and patronage. "They were politically neutral, dumb and unambitious, their reason for being there was to give the government their votes."[158] The *askaris,* and by corollary the massive fraud in the south, were an indispensable ingredient of Giolitti's strategy of accommodating the workers in the north. In this, they are indicative of acute isolation that Liberals, whether of the left or the right, continued to feel.

Giolitti's policy in the north can be described as "the policy of liberty for all within the limits of the law." After 1900, Socialists were free to organize, and workers outside the public sector were almost entirely unrestricted in forming trade unions. The state ceased to intervene in strikes on behalf of employers. Indeed, Giolitti's prefects now occasionally intervened on behalf of the workers. The essence of the policy, however, was one of studied neutrality, as the state implicitly encouraged workers and employers to organize themselves and to find the rhythm of their relationship. Workers were quite free to picket and strike; employers were free to employ strike breakers. If Giolitti's prefects came down hard on public sector strikes and violence, they otherwise accepted with remarkable equanimity the explosion of strikes that accompanied this opening to the left in the first years of the century.[159]

The liberal–labor coalition that dominated the Chamber was able to enact an impressive array of social reforms intended to improve the conditions of workers during these years. Legislation that created night schools and public libraries (to reduce illiteracy), and enforced a weekly day of rest and business closings on holidays, a strengthened workmen's compensation fund, a program of low-cost workmen's homes, a maternity insurance scheme, more generous public relief, and restrictions on female and child labor all were products of this coalition.[160]

Giolittismo was not without its effects on the Socialist trade unions and party. Reformism predominated in the unions and party between 1903 and 1911. In the election of 1909, the party made impressive gains, rising from

29 to 41 deputies. By the party congress of 1910, the dominance of reformism gave every appearance of being final and irreversible, and Giolitti could, as he did in April 1911, survey his apparent accomplishments with some satisfaction.[161] "Eight years have gone by, the country has gone ahead, the Socialist party has greatly moderated its program, and Karl Marx has been relegated to the attic."[162]

Giolitti's genius was to comprehend what must be done. Italy's tragedy was that its inheritance prevented this comprehension, like the Heglian owl of Minerva rising at dusk, until it was too late, and then ensured that it would be stillborn in its application.[163] For no sooner had Giolitti proclaimed the success of Giolittismo than it began to collapse. The capstone of Giolitti's strategy had been his plan in 1911 to create a program of old-age pensions and disability insurance and to introduce universal manhood suffrage. Giolitti's left Liberals would preserve themselves in the brave new world of universal suffrage by an electoral coalition with the Socialists in the north and a reinforcement of the *askaris* in the south.[164]

Manhood suffrage, however, could not come without a price attached to it. And that price, to win the sufferance of Liberals, was the Libyan War. The Libyan War was Giolitti's way of compensating them for manhood suffrage.[165] It was not an adventure he saw any merit in otherwise. It was, rather, forced on him, and he resisted it to the end, invoking as his explanation to the Chamber "historical fatality," and declaring "I did not undertake the Libyan War out of enthusiasm—quite the contrary!"[166] This imperialist essay intervened between the presentation of the manhood suffrage bill and the election of 1913, and aborted the liberal–labor alliance on which Giolitti had premised electoral reform.

A trasformismo that embraced manhood suffrage in a sense *required* imperialism. Libya was not simply a caesura in the evolution of Giolitti's otherwise keen analytical powers. Giolitti's decision was a gamble, to be sure, in the sense that it was derivative of a larger strategy. It was not a gamble, however, in the sense that he probably could have enacted universal suffrage and a Lib–Lab coalition without it. But imperialism, because it legitimated the agenda of those Liberals who wanted integration not through Lib–Labism but through imperialism abroad and authoritarianism at home, was a betrayal of the Socialists and incompatible with a Lib–Lab coalition. In the minds of Socialists it harkened back to the repression and imperialism of the Crispini in the 1890s, and consequently it immediately destroyed the credibility of reformist leaders within the Socialist party.[167] When those leaders were purged forthwith, Lib–Labism went with them. This was the real "historical fatality"—to turn Giolitti's own phrase—of the Libyan War.

It is enough to say that the balance of probabilities strongly favored such an adventure, or a comparable attempt to pacify nationalist sentiment; without such pacification, Lib–Labism would not have been tolerated by right Liberals. This was made clear when Sidney Sonnino, the leader of the right

Liberals, explained that his support for Giolitti's government derived not from his enthusiasm for the government but from his enthusiasm for the Libyan War.[168] And, indeed, there was an integrative logic to the war, for the support of the war did not come only from nationalists and right Liberals. In fact, during and after the war (it no doubt mattered greatly that Italy was victorious), almost all sectors of the political elite, presumably responding to popular sentiment, vied with one another in demonstrating their support for the adventure. Even such right-wing Socialists as Angelo Cabrini, Ivanhoe Bonomi, and Leonida Bissolati indicated a reluctant acceptance of it.[169]

If we wish to comprehend why Lib–Labism and universal suffrage would otherwise have been intolerable to the right, we must look to the earlier isolation of Italian liberalism. Given the inherited isolation of the Liberals, left and right, from a large fraction of the Italian confessional middle class, and given the illegitimacy of the liberal order that issued from that isolation, Liberals—especially but not only those on the right—could not countenance universal suffrage in the absence of some essay aimed at shoring up their legitimacy. The analytical essence of the matter is in the origin of the illegitimacy that in turn necessitated such drastic measures. The origin of the illegitimacy was in the divorce between the Liberals and confessional Italy. In the end, then, we find ourselves having come full circle: Liberals, isolated from the confessional majority, could accommodate workers only if they could simultaneously legitimate their rule, and in practice the most effective available means they could identify to do so came at the expense of Lib–Labism.

Spain

The problems of a Lib–Lab alliance in Spain were those of an alliance between an infant socialist movement with a residual middle-class cause in pursuit of electoral victories in a country where elections counted for little. Socialism's limit was that in a backward country it had few working-class auditors until the First World War. Outside of Madrid and the Asturian mines, where socialism had some appeal, and Barcelona, where workers dilated on the anarchist vision, there were few industrial workers. There were even fewer who voted. Before the alliance with Republicanism, Socialists could not win even 7,000 votes in Madrid and never secured a Cortes seat. The alliance with the Republicans between 1909 and 1919 provided the Socialists with their first victory in a Cortes election and also allowed them to gain seats on municipal councils. In 1909, the Socialists accepted a "Conjunction" with the Reformist Republicans to fight the reactionary ministry of Antonio Maura. The importance of the Conjunction to even such minimal success as the Socialists enjoyed was apparent in Pablo Iglesias's Cortes victory. In 1907 he had polled only 6,000 votes—fewer even than he had won in 1901.

With the Republicans' support he polled 40,589 in 1910. When the Conjunction ended in 1919, his total sank back to just 17,000.[170] The problem for the Socialists, of course, was that the corruption of the returns and the backwardness of the society profoundly limited their own political potential.

The other problem for the Socialists was that the only middle-class tendency that deigned to align with them—and not without fueling its own fissiparous tendencies—was Republicanism. Republicans had been the losers in the restoration settlement of 1878, and they were the great residual of middle-class politics. Republicans spoke for those fractions of the middle classes that were neither politically indifferent, wedded to the dynastic Conservatives or Liberals, clerically inclined, nor attached to one of the peripheral nationalisms. Republicanism was what was left, and it never amounted to much until the fall of the monarchy in 1930. It stood, above all, for fair elections and competent administration. In the years before De Rivera's dictatorship, some Republicans were federalists; some would settle for responsible government in a constitutional monarchy. Some were social radicals; others reformists.[171]

Republicanism was kept a peripheral strand of middle-class alienation for all the same reasons that a liberal movement as such was always crippled: by Spain's backwardness and the conflicts between clericalism and anticlericalism, regional nationalism, and Castilian hideboundness. Republicanism, as a voice "against that which exists," could not accommodate the dynastic Liberals, whose liberalism was in any event strictly nominal. Republicanism was anticlerical and could consequently not align, except under the most exceptional circumstances, with the clerical, middle-class nationalism of Catalonia and the Basque provinces. By the same token it could not act as a bridge between Socialists and what might then have been an effective liberal movement.

On only two occasions before the 1923 dictatorship was the Socialist–Republican Conjunction extended to the Catalan middle classes. The first occurred in 1909, when the Republicans joined the Solidaridad Catalana in protest of the repressive Maura government's Moroccan policy, its rigging of elections, and its imposition of quasi-military rule in Catalonia. This alliance brought together the Socialists, the Republicans, the clerical, conservative middle-class nationalism of the Lliga, and the anticlericalism of Alejandro Lerroux's lower-middle-class Catalan Radicals. It disintegrated soon enough. After a setback in Morocco, the government called up Barcelonese reservists. There followed the Tragic Week riots in which workers looted churches, burned convents, killed monks, and "liberated" nuns. More than a hundred workers were shot in the streets and more executions followed. In the wake of this, the conflicts between the clericals and anticlericals in Solidaridad could not be contained and brought the alliance to an end. Additionally, the clerical Lliga was appeased by a new tariff schedule and a modest measure of devolution (the Law of Mancomunidades), which was enacted by decree in 1913.[172]

The second occasion was provided by the 1917 Assembly Movement, which marked Lib–Labism's last chance in Restoration Spain and the final opportunity to reform the Restoration order. The Assembly Movement was an alliance of disaffected junior military officers, Catalan nationalists, Re‑ publicans, and Socialists. It sought a constituent Cortes that would reform the political order and grant Home Rule to Catalonia. It came to an end when a Socialist-led General Strike and a confrontation between striking workers and the army frightened the Catalan middle classes and pushed the Lliga into the waiting arms of the government in Madrid. The Madrid government offered the Lliga a substantial measure of autonomy to govern Catalonia, and especially its economic policies. That and its fear of working-class unruliness were enough to induce the Lliga to bail out of the Assembly Movement.[173]

Imperialism, Nationalism, and Class Integration

To be sure, Spain's Moroccan ambitions as Italy's in Libya derived from multiple motivations, including prospective material gains, the psychological gratifications of great power status, and so forth. Such a complex phe‑ nomenon cannot, and need not, be reduced to a single cause. Yet the cen‑ trality of the integrative appeal for aliberal, and especially Italian, advocates of imperialism was unmistakable.[174] In this, Italy was not apart from Ger‑ many, where such motivations were also unmistakable in the pursuit of *Weltpolitik*. Nor was the integrative ambition absent from the imperial ambi‑ tions of Belgium and the Netherlands, although in those countries hegemonic clericalism made integration a less pressing concern.

National integration was also an apparent motive of British and French imperialism, but it seems to have been a less urgent one. If one might say that French and especially British imperialism grew more naturally from geopolit‑ ical interests, it is even more to the point that the imperialism of these countries gained much impetus from a kind of cultural imperative or "civiliz‑ ing mission," as it was called in the nineteenth century. Although this was a central theme of British and French imperialists and evangelical Dutch Prot‑ estants, it was not a theme that meant much to advocates of imperialism in Italy, Spain, Belgium, and Germany. It might be that the British and French were simply more sophistic in cloaking their imperial ambitions in legitimat‑ ing myths intended for domestic consumption, but it seems more probable that national power and prestige—psychological unity—were more funda‑ mental urges of German imperialism.

The centrality of the integrative impulse in German imperialism has been emphasized, albeit with distinctive interpretations, by such different histo‑

rians as Hans-Ulrich Wehler and Geoff Eley. Wehler sought to explain most of German foreign policy from Bismarck to World War I as a conservative response to internal tensions and class conflicts and to interpret what he called social imperialism in these terms.[175] For Wehler, social imperialism was the unifying thread in German foreign policy from Bismarck's combination of cartel politics and overseas expansion in the 1880s to Johannes von Miquel's *Sammlungspolitik,* Alfred von Tirpitz' naval expansion, Bülow's merging of *Sammlungspolitik* and *Weltpolitik,* and then finally Germany's entry into the First World War. To reduce all of these stages of German foreign policy solely to a conservative demand for domestic order may be excessive, but even Geoff Eley, Wehler's most trenchant critic, has not quarreled with Wehler's interpretation of German foreign policy as mainly derivative of integrative ambitions. Eley, rather than rejecting the integrative impulse, has rejected the conservative bent that Wehler gave to it. Instead, he has stressed the role of social imperialism as part of a larger package of domestic social reforms that were together intended as a coherent strategy of domestic integration. In this sense, the integrationist impulse is given an even more central place in Eley's revisionist interpretation.[176] Eley's emphasis on the connection between integrative imperialism and domestic social reforms conforms with the connection we have suggested between the early growth of the welfare state and imperialism and nationalism in aliberal societies.

The integrationist impulse that Wehler and Eley have stressed in German foreign policy has been given similar saliency by students of Italy and Spain.[177] In effect, the domestic consumption that had to be satisfied in Germany, Spain, and Italy was the need for a more binding national identity rather than a moral mission.

If we step back from the narrower question of imperialism, which was partly a function of military potential, and consider the broader category of nationalism, these imperialist drives to integration appear simply as part of a larger pattern. Among the militarily weak, too, nationalism played or sought to play a central integrative function in the late nineteenth and early twentieth centuries. Because the Norwegian experience is so little known outside of Scandinavia, it is worth emphasizing that for Norwegian Liberals, nationalism played an absolutely indispensable role in first cementing the Liberal coalition in the 1880s and then holding it together as the strains within the middle classes and between them and the working classes became more acute at the end of the century. It was exactly because the Liberals around Johan Sverdrup understood the potency of the nationalist appeal that they were able to succeed where previous liberals had failed in melding diverse interests in a single coalition.[178] There was, in subsequent years, a causally direct and immediate relationship between the appearance of strains in the coalition and the Liberals' manipulation of nationalist sentiments: every time those strains threatened the coalition, Liberal leaders sought to up the nationalist ante by escalating their demands on Stockholm.[179] Thus, although imperialism was not an integrative option for Norwegian Liberals, a campaign for national independence was. And let us not forget that even many of the Conservatives, who had previously been sympathetic to Stockholm, concluded by 1903 that the growing Socialist menace made it wise to endorse the Liberals' demands so that a united front might be formed against the Socialists.[180]

Even in Denmark, where the disintegrative strains were markedly less, nationalism was not without its political value, with both Liberals and Conservatives resorting to it in turn to hold their coalitions together. The obsession of the National Liberals with retention of the duchies and the long-running antipathy toward Germany, and especially the explicit manipulation of the issue of fortifications around Copenhagen by J. B. S. Estrup's semi-authoritarian Conservative government of the 1880s, were both aimed at welding together coalitions capable of stabilizing political orders.[181] If retention of the duchies and fortifications around Copenhagen seem rather less grandiose than *Weltpolitik* or Libya, that is no more than a reflection of the "politics of scale" and should be allowed to obscure neither the centrality nor the potency these appeals exercised in Danish politics. Let us not, as so many American social scientists have been wont to do, confuse the problems of small nations with small problems.

The problems of integration raised by divided middle classes and alienated working classes had a different slant according to the time, country, and groups involved. In some instances, the question was one of integration among pre-working-class sectors; in others, it was integration of workers themselves; in still others, it was integration of other sectors against the working class. Sometimes, as in Italy, all of these were on the same agenda simultaneously. The agenda was a function of the cleavage—inherited preindustrial or class—that needed to be bridged. Whatever the agenda, but especially when it included class conflict, a distinctive brand of imperialism and nationalism constituted one and the welfare state constituted another alternative to an extension of political participation. And just as early welfare state measures were clustered in those societies in which liberalism was weak and Lib–Labism ineffective, so too were imperialist and nationalist agendas that had as a core ambition working-class integration and containment.

In the absence of a null case, it is not easy to say how effective imperialism and nationalism were as integrative devices. The evidence that they had a considerable appeal even among workers is more than circumstantial. For example, both the Norwegian and Swedish socialist parties wanted the union issue off the agenda because they saw it as an obstacle to the development of a working-class consciousness.[182] And the German Social Democrats suffered a major electoral setback when they made opposition to *Weltpolitik* the centerpiece of their campaign in 1907.[183] Also, there appears to have been at least modest support for the successful Libyan conquest among Italian work-

ers, although they showed less than gracious enthusiasm for the earlier
Ethiopian catastrophe.[184] On the other hand, it was not patriotism that pullu-
lated among the Barcelonese workers as they rioted against the call-up for
Moroccan duty in 1909. But given the manifest incompetence of the officers'
corps, the call-up could hardly have evoked prodromes of national glory.
Moreover, their antimilitarism might actually be read as a sign of their
integration into Catalan society.[185]

Beyond the obvious point that aspiring integrators normally found victory
more efficacious than defeat, we can conclude that whatever integrative
appeal imperialism and nationalism exerted among workers in these societies, it was, like the early welfare state, not enough to compensate for the
absence of Lib–Labism. Not enough, because it was precisely in these
societies that working-class movements became most coherently organized
before the war and therefore most threatening to the established order between the wars.

A Note on Leadership and Choice

Among the liberal leaders who struggled to make Lib–Labism succeed, the
Swede Karl Staaff and the Italian Giovanni Giolitti were easily the leading
figures of the period. These two contemporaries dominated national politics
in their homelands, and the leadership they exercised within their respective
movements was markedly greater than that exercised by liberal leaders elsewhere. It is not really possible to discuss Swedish and Italian liberalism
without referring to them, because the weight of their personalities was so
great.

Yet, as we have seen, even Staaff and Giolitti ultimately failed in their
larger ambition of labor inclusion, and in the end their similar strategies and
distinctive styles mattered little. Their failures are instructive, for we would
be hard pressed to find two leaders more different in their styles, tempera-
ment, and skills. Whereas Giolitti was dispassionate and calculating, never
given to verbosity or flights of emotion, Staaff was mercurial, unpredictable
and silver-tonged. Giolitti once told the Chamber: "When I have said what I
have to say, I find it impossible to continue to speak."[186] Staaff could
continue forever. Whereas Giolitti was the master wirepuller, always moving
events behind the scenes, Staaff sought to lead personally and by the force of
his vision and the righteousness of his cause. Whereas Giolitti delighted in
manipulating his minions, Staaff was personally inept. Whereas Giolitti responded to temporary defeats by calculating three moves ahead, Staaff was
more likely to become cataleptic. Whereas Giolitti showed appropriate deference for the upper house and the monarchy, Staaff intimated disdain border-
ing on contempt for such institutions. Whereas Giolitti was happy to make
use of the inherited southern miasma, with its fraud, bribery, and coercion,

Staaff neither could nor, more important at the moment, would have done so. To his critics, Giolitti was the energumen of Italian politics, the prime minister of the *malavita,* as Gaetano Salvemini put it. Staaff might have been accused of being too good for this world or, still worse, of thinking of himself as such.[187]

Both men were political masters, albeit for very different reasons. That they failed to implement their common vision, as did less distinguished Lib–Lab leaders elsewhere, was rooted in the structure of their social–political situations. The structure was provided by the inherited cleavages within the middle classes, and it was those cleavages that defined, sometimes directly and sometimes more remotely, the range of choices and room for maneuver each had. Imprisoned by those limited choices, even the most consummate leaders could not make Lib–Labism work, for in the end, it was not one of the available choices.

Epilogue

These structures were, to be sure, socially rooted. But it is worth stressing once again that what mattered in the failure of Lib–Labism was neither social heterogeneity as such nor the sociology of class, but the *political*–sociology of religion, language, ethnicity, and region. It was the political playing out of these divisions within the middle classes that made all of these otherwise diverse national experiences fundamentally similar and, in militating against Lib–Labism, pushed them down a separate road from the one taken by Britain, France, and Switzerland.

Neither the cleavages themselves nor their immediate effects were identical from one country to the next. Sometimes, as in Belgium and the Netherlands, the cleavages broke a previously long-hegemonic liberal movement when mass politics came to the fore. In Norway, they crippled a liberal movement as soon as it gained power. In other instances, Germany and Spain, they prevented a liberal movement from ever coming to power or so delayed and weakened it, as in Sweden and more marginally in Denmark, that it gained power only late and shakily. In one case, Italy, they ensured that once in power, Liberals would govern isolated from and in opposition to a predominantly hostile society.

Just as the cleavages varied in the ways they caused liberals to fail, they variably affected the way in which Lib–Labism failed. In some cases— Denmark and Sweden—essays in Lib–Labism broke an enfeebled liberal movement along the cleavage line itself. In other cases—Norway, Germany, Spain—the liberal vulnerability that issued from the cleavages provoked essentially the entire movement to repudiate Lib–Labism. In Italy, at the end of the Giolittian era as at its beginning, Lib–Labism proved incompatible with the agenda liberal preservation required. In other cases—Belgium and to a lesser extent, the Netherlands—the cleavage meant that liberalism was replaced by hegemonic clericalism.

As these societies were first pushed down the same road by their debile liberalism, they were subsequently pushed further down that same road by their enfeebled Lib–Labism. The central feature of this was that such Lib–Lab coalitions as appeared were not sufficient—in contrast to those in Britain, France, Switzerland, and the intermediate case of Denmark—to make compelling the belief that interclass coalitions offered a plausible road to working-class power. In the absence of that plausibility the only option that remained for working-class leaders was to make exceptionally coherent class organizations. As that coherence materialized, it further consolidated the distinctive trajectory of these societies, for in the crises of the interwar period, it would create some options for political–economic stabilization and close others. To revert to our earlier language, that coherence would become one of the structures limiting the range of choice.

The Organization
of Workers: Liberal and Aliberal
Societies Compared

The greater coherence of labor in aliberal societies was rooted in its prewar formation. This higher level of class organization was apparent before the war in both political competition and trade union organization. It followed from the lack of allies in government, in parliament and in electoral competition and, more indirectly, from the divisions within the middle classes whence the atmosphere of hostility and absence of allies eventuated. Compared with what appeared in liberal societies, the result was a decidedly higher level of party and trade union organization and penetration of working-class life. There also appears to have been a greater consciousness among both workers and the middle classes of themselves as classes. This more comprehensive mobilization of workers in turn decisively shaped the possibilities for political and economic regime stabilization between the wars.

Parties

The contrast between liberal and aliberal societies in the levels of prewar party organization and penetration of working-class life was a fundamental one. It was, we might say, the difference between parties organized as militias and parties organized as professional armies. Comparatively speaking, the labor parties in liberal societies were satisfied to function as parties of representation, as sporadically active electoral machines. In aliberal societies, labor parties became parties of mobilization and sought to bind together a class as a commander binds together an army. The distinctiveness of the two varieties of working-class entry into politics is apparent in the more local orientation of parties in liberal societies, in their weaker party organizations, the small circulations of their labor newspapers, in the comparatively meager share of the working-class vote that went to labor parties in Britain, France, and Switzerland, and in the larger fraction of the middle-class vote that these labor parties received.

In France, and even more in Britain, the militias of the working class were little more than loosely knit agglomerations of local worker interests. As in a militia, the essential decisions were almost always taken locally. It was not merely the candidates, but also the criteria by which they were selected that were determined locally. It would be impossible to assert, especially about the Labor Representation Committee and prewar Labor party, that the national organization exercised ultimate authority or stood for a concrete body of thought the subscription to which was a prerequisite of local nomination.[1] This contrasts with the insistence of labor parties in aliberal societies that they would, as the Norwegian Labor party put it in 1906, "acknowledge. . . only candidates who endorse all of the principles of the party's program."[2] Rather, in both France and Britain, the national organizations largely followed and reflected rather than led and shaped local candidates and attitudes. This was doubly true in Britain, where candidates were likely to be representatives of particularistic trade union interests. The difference was not so much that labor politicians in Britain rejected the notion that they were representatives of the working class as a whole. They certainly saw themselves in those terms. Rather, the difference was to be found in the understanding attached to working-class interests. In Britain, labor politicians to a much greater degree than elsewhere understood class interests to be synonymous with the interests of the trade unions.[3]

The ductility of labor parties in liberal societies was a product of the national political climates in which they matured and perhaps even a functional requisite of locally created interclass coalitions. Because such coalitions were rooted in local circumstances and those circumstances varied enormously, making them in itself required labor parties whose centers of gravity were local. In this, labor parties to a substantial degree became the mirror images of their middle-class allies, whose own parties had little corporate substance. It is a measure of the local orientation of labor in liberal societies that in the many elections in which liberals and labor allied in prewar Britain, France, and Switzerland, on only one occasion was an alliance negotiated between national party leaders. That occasion was the agreement struck between Ramsay MacDonald and Herbert Gladstone in 1906. Apropos that alliance, James Hinton's summary is worth recalling:

> By 1906, the essence of the LRC's independence lay in the fact that it had substituted a centralized accommodation with the Liberal party for the local arrangements traditionally pursued. The new Labor party (formally constituted as such after the election [of 1906]) had arrived on the political scene not as the grave-digger of Liberalism, but as an integral part of a great Liberal revival.[4]

Even this central agreement reflected the half-baked character of the LRC organization: MacDonald's essay was simply an exercise in personal diplomacy. He neither sought, felt the need for, nor was rebuked for not attaining the prior approval of the LRC.[5]

One sure sign of the greater clout of central party machinery elsewhere is that the Lib–Lab electoral alliances that were made were negotiated at the national level and with the approval of the central governing body of the party. They were then imposed on the local party organizations, which only rarely sought to defy the central agreement. This was the case in Germany in 1912; in all of the alliances struck in Denmark between the Venstre and the Social Democrats and the Radicals and the Social Democrats; in all of the deals made between Liberals and Socialists in Belgium; and in the understandings reached between Swedish Liberals and Social Democrats.[6] In all of these countries and all of these national elections, I have not found a local labor party that made an alliance without the consent of the national party.[7] To be sure, had a local party in Britain, France, or Switzerland sought such an authorization, it would have known whom to ask. But it is revealing in itself of the national organizations' weakness that local parties never felt the need for such dispensations.

Socialist parties elsewhere acquired a more decidedly corporate identity, based on well-articulated, hierarchical organizations. In contrast to the experiences in the liberal societies, building the national party organization itself became a major activity. This meant creating permanent associations on a local, district, and regional level that were in regular communication with the national office.[8] The essence of this organizational network was rooted not in reaching local understandings with middle-class interests, but in organizing (one might even say, colonizing) the entire working class and thereby creating an effective movement. Adequate measures of the greater seriousness that these parties attached to mobilizing the entire working class as a class rather than as a collection of discrete interests are difficult to come by. It would be simple enough to muster statements from the standard party histories that emphasize comprehensive class organization and the cultivation of class identity as the basic goal of these parties. It was typical of the greater concern with class organization that trade union and party leaders outside liberal societies saw the socialist parties and unions as inseparable halves of a single movement, whereas British trade unionists for long disdained any independent labor party and French trade union leaders wished to stand aloof from the SFIO. Thus, in 1898 Hjalmar Branting, the leader of Swedish socialism, could greet the delegates to the constitutional convention of the national trade union confederation by observing that "the labor movement is a single entity, working in a trade-union direction and in a political direction, neither stifling the other, but supporting each other and working hand in hand for social emancipation."[9]

Ultimately, however, we must infer the greater commitment of party leaders to class mobilization and the receptiveness of workers to this, not from anecdotal evidence, but from the outcome, a much higher level of worker support. We will turn to the electoral data presently, but it is worthwhile to specify as best we can the underlying infrastructural differences between the two kinds of parties, because they reflected alternative patterns of working-class entry into politics. Two indicators, admittedly crude, are of some help. The first of these concerns the availability of a party apparatus; the second measures the volume of communication between parties and workers.

Figures on party membership are not very informative, because in some cases trade union membership conferred automatic party membership. Likewise, by themselves, data on the size of the paid party bureaucracy are not revealing, because the need for such professional activists varied enormously according to national circumstances. Obstacles to rapid travel and communication could make such cadres less useful if they were either very low, as in Belgium, the Netherlands, and Denmark, or sometimes nearly insuperable, as in Norway and Sweden. Moreover, where a highly efficient and centralized trade union movement was in close collaboration with a party, and union members were almost always party members, such a separate party structure was superfluous.

Party Organization

Whatever the national circumstances, a minimum claim can be made: an effective party required an organizational apparatus. On this count we can draw a line between labor parties in liberal societies and parties elsewhere, for the British and French parties manifestly lacked such structures. In Britain, the prewar Labor party's paid staff consisted of exactly one person, a full-time clerk assigned to Ramsay MacDonald, who had himself been made secretary of the LRC largely because he was willing to devote all of his energies to it without compensation.[10] In France, the entire paid staff of the SFIO consisted of six officials. There would not have been even this many had parliamentary deputies not surrendered a fraction of their salaries to the party. One half of the party's income came from the deputies' contributions.[11] The German party stood as the extreme alternative to this. By 1912, in addition to its large central office staff, it employed forty regional secretaries and eighty-four local secretaries, "with the number," according to Otto Braun, "happily growing almost weekly."[12] Other continental parties—with typically a dozen or so paid officials—never reached the level of bureaucracy that made the SPD famous.

They did not, however, lack for well-developed organizational structures. Unlike the German party, they did not need a large bureaucracy, for they had at hand the parallel organizations of the trade unions. It is well to recall that the German party bureaucracy did not take shape until after 1900, that is, after the rapid growth of the Free Trade unions and their consequent fixation with short-term advantages fueled the breach between them and the party.[13] It will not do, of course, to imply that after 1906 the relationship between the Free Trade Unions and the SPD was anything but fundamentally cooperative and sympathetic. The unions even provided the party with an important organizational arm. In Scandinavia, Italy, Belgium, and the Netherlands, where both the parties and unions were at an earlier stage of development, a large party bureaucracy was superfluous and the relationship between the unions and parties was still more supportive than it was in Germany. Trade unions were, for instance, more willing to strike to dramatize a political point. Thus, May Day demonstrations and general strikes for suffrage reform (there were four such strikes in Belgium and two in Sweden) were less contentious. In such countries, the progenitors of the unions and the parties were often the same individuals, and the local union associations became effectively local party offices. In Sweden in the 1890s, the Social Democratic party and national unions jointly funded agitators and organizers who worked to arouse interest in trade unionism and socialism and to establish locals in various trades and industries.[14] The party itself took the initiative in organizing groups of workers outside the jurisdictions of the existing trade union nationals. At its 1891 convention, the party coordinated efforts to organize seamen and iron miners. These efforts led to the establishment in 1895 of the national Iron Mine Workers Union. Again in 1894, it coordinated the organization of sawmill workers. In 1897 the party directed the organization of workers in communications and transportation, railwaymen in particular.[15]

In Norway, the first conquests of the socialist movement were the trade unions, which had previously been in the liberal camp. By 1903, socialists had won virtually complete control of the Oslo, Trondheim, and Bergen unions, and by 1906 they had largely done the same in the remainder of the country. It was because liberals were unwilling to accommodate the expectations of local union associations for independent working-class representation that socialists could prevail in these struggles and make use of the organizational network that the growing union movement provided.[16]

In Denmark, too, the distinction between socialist political activity and trade union organization was blurred. After the repression of the Free Trade Union Central Committee in 1879, the newly formed Social Democratic party functioned for the next seven years as the coordinating body for socialist trade unions. In 1886, fifty-four socialist locals formed the Copenhagen Federation of Trade Unions, the predecessors of the LO, under party auspices. From the start the affiliated unions were committed to support socialism and the Social Democratic party, so that the growth of these unions amounted to the growth of the party's own organization.[17]

Much the same relationship developed in Italy, the vicissitudes of Italian socialist politics notwithstanding. Such prominent union leaders as Angelo Cabrini, Pietro Chiesa, and Rinaldo Rigola were among the PSI leadership in the parliament. Rigola was the leader of the CGL from its establishment until

1919. Within a year of the CGL's founding in 1906, party and union leaders had developed principles to govern the relationship that included political general strikes. Collaboration between the PSI and CGL was close during the years of peak reformist authority within the PSI (1908–12), with union policy being determined largely by men who were also party leaders. The collaboration continued even after the maximalists assumed control of the party in 1912, with the unions supporting the party's policies by the general strike called to protest the Libyan War and by the "Red Week" in 1914.[18]

In Britain and France the parties were underpinned by neither an effective bureaucracy of the sort that the SPD enjoyed nor the organizational network that trade unions offered parties elsewhere. The result in both cases was that the parties were organizationally enfeebled. The diffident attitude of the French unions toward the Socialist party is a subject that numerous scholars of French labor have discussed. They were aparliamentary—not antiparliamentary—because, revealingly, union leaders saw such neutrality as the key to attracting support in the heterogeneous French working class.[19] Here it is more important to recall the peculiar nature of the union–party relationship in Britain.

To be sure, the trade unions provided the organizational backbone of the LRC and the Labor party. The unions were the organizations of the British workers and, as we saw in Chapter 2, no political movement could hope to be successful without their support. It was precisely because union support was indispensable and they could not get it on their own that the Social Democratic Federation and the Independent Labor party both opted for participation in the LRC. Yet we must also recall the circumstances that led the unions to ignore, first, the Social Democratic Federation and then the Independent Labor party, and then to embrace the LRC. The unions disdained the SDF and the ILP precisely because the latter wanted to create coherent class-oriented movements that would terminate Lib–Labism. In effect, the SDF and ILP wanted the kind of movement that was being created out of necessity in so many other European countries, and it was for that reason that the unions rejected them.[20]

When the unions finally did rush to support the LRC in 1903, it was not because they had had a change of heart about the desirability of a class-oriented movement and Lib–Labism. Indeed, the TUC had already shorn the LRC of its anti-Lib–Labism and much of its class orientation at its inception. Rather, when the unions finally did take the LRC seriously, it was because the Taff-Vale ruling, which was an assault on vested union privileges, made a political defense of those privileges imperative. In sum, when the unions finally took seriously an independent political movement, it was not because they were markedly interested in the political organization of a class—in which case they would have been attracted instead to the models the SDF and ILP had to offer—but because they wanted a political defense of the sectional interests of their members within the context of continued Lib–Labism.[21]

In rejecting the SDF and ILP the unions rejected the normal continental pattern of class organization. This was not, it bears emphasizing, simply a lapse in the analytical facilities of union leaders. It was a conscious choice, one based precisely on the fact that the anti-Lib–Labism, the explicit socialism, and the class consciousness of the SDF and ILP were repugnant to many of the union leaders. These decisions resulted, of course, in a prewar political movement that was conservative, particularistic, and organizationally incapable of an appeal to workers as a class. In sum, then, in both Britain and France labor parties lacked the class-oriented *apparati* that were provided elsewhere by either party bureaucracies or trade unions.

It has been a standard practice for students of French labor to account for the organizational enfeeblement of the SFIO (and the CGT) according to its late formation and ideological-cum-factional divisions.[22] As empirical descriptions these are correct, but as causal explanations they are entirely inadequate. For they imply that labor parties formed earlier and more coherently elsewhere were simply historical accidents or cultural idiosyncrasies that somehow managed in their formative years not to be encumbered by such divisiveness. In fact, nothing in the early history of labor movements elsewhere distinguishes them as more consensual. Like the French movement, they were preoccupied by internal struggles before (and after) the war. Under the leadership of Martin Tranmael, the best organized syndicalist movement in Europe took shape within the larger reformist Norwegian labor movement in the years before the war. In 1911 syndicalists gained control of the Trondheim Central Trades Council and passed the famous Trondheim Resolution, which called for, among other things, resorting to violence and sabotage and an end to all collective bargaining.[23] Before Primo de Rivera's dictatorship crushed the anarchists, Spanish labor was deeply divided between syndicalists and socialists.[24] In Sweden, there appeared a constant battle between the reformist leaders of the Social Democratic party and the radicals of the Young Socialists.[25] In Italy, the tensions between the maximalists and minimalists came to a head in 1911, when the former managed to have the latter expelled from the PSI.[26] Similar tensions were apparent between revisionists and leftists in prewar German Social Democracy.[27] In the Netherlands, the same conflicts led to the creation of the first communist party in Western Europe even before the First World War.[28]

If there was any difference between the experiences of these movements and the French movement, it is not that these were less divided by ideological conflicts, but that in these movements the organizational imperative was more apparent to all contenders. It is striking, for example, that the struggle between reformists and syndicalists in Norway was less about the importance of organization than whether that organization should be used for revolutionary ends. When the Norwegian syndicalists clamored for more spontaneity and local control, it was not because they disdained organizations as such, as

French syndicalists did. Rather, syndicalism in Norway was in many respects a demand for better organization. At a time when the national trade unions were still partly organized along craft lines, syndicalists fought to have them reorganized nationally along strictly industrial lines. For "it was part of the syndicalist theory that craft division weakened the labor movement, and rendered difficult the employment of the general strike."[29]

What distinguished labor in aliberal societies was not a lack of ideological heterogeneity, but the more frequent conviction among all ideological tendencies that comprehensive class organization was imperative. To make this point empirically would require another book; it must suffice to refer the reader to the vast and excellent body of literature now available on national labor movements. The consensus of that literature, it seems to me, is that ideological heterogeneity was a constant rather than a variable among early labor movements. The question that was decided over time was which ideology best fit national circumstances. This question, reflecting national realities, was decided in Britain emphatically in favor of liberalism and trade union particularism, in France and Switzerland in favor of a distinctive mixture of liberalism and socialism, and elsewhere emphatically in favor of socialism and comprehensive class organization.

French labor was similarly undistinguished by either an oft-cited obsessive individualism or a bizarre national predilection for penurious organizations.[30] If we take as an indicator of individualism the turnover of union membership, then individualism was at least as characteristic of prewar German as it was of French labor. Likewise, the German unions were not born with flush treasuries. In the late 1890s, union dues in Germany were not much higher than in France.[31] Rather, over time they became much higher because a more compelling case could be made for them in an aliberal society. The impoverishment of the SFIO and unions and their organizational enfeeblement reflected the ambivalent position of workers in French society.

The SFIO and the CGT were indifferently organized because for a long time making a unified and coherent labor movement was simply less urgent in France. To be sure, after a point, this incoherence itself became institutionalized and came to reflect a certain distribution of power within the labor movement. As we shall see in Chapter 6, it could not be overcome once it was firmly entrenched, even as an awareness of its limitations grew. But with respect to the prewar period, our argument has amounted to the proposition that French labor was less isolated socially and politically and existed in a less hostile world. This is not to say that antebellum France was benevolent to workers or socialists—indeed, it might be read above all as a statement of the remarkably low expectations of workers everywhere before the war; it is only to say that it was less menacing than Italy, Norway, or Germany in the same period.

Party Press

Just as party infrastructure was a prerequisite to effective mobilization of workers, so it was essential that party leaders have under their own control a medium by which they could regularly communicate with workers. In the prewar years, the essential medium of communication was provided by party-owned newspapers. To be sure, party leaders could count to some degree on nonparty newspapers and other media—public meetings, handbills, and so forth—to communicate their attitudes and mold worker opinion, but only through newspaper ownership could leaders do this consistently and without distortion. Moreover, a party press could reach that large fraction of the working class that remained outside the trade union nexus everywhere before the war. In these respects, then, the size of the party press tells us something about not only the receptiveness of workers to the party's message but the seriousness party leaders attached to class mobilization.

Although little importance can be attached to the absolute numbers, and they are best viewed as measures of gross differences, the circulation figures we have assembled for the prewar labor party newspapers are striking in their variation. This is especially the case when we control for the size of the industrial labor force. The number of male workers in the secondary and tertiary sectors for each copy of a daily or weekly newspaper printed ranges from 214 workers in Britain to 3.5 workers in Denmark. Between these extremes, the numbers of workers per newspaper are 67.8 in Italy, 53.3 in France, 39.0 in the Netherlands, 13.0 in Switzerland, 9.0 in Belgium, 9.0 in Germany, 4.9 in Sweden, and 4.2 in Norway.[32] Strictly speaking, the figure of 214 workers per newspaper printed overstates the size of the party press in Britain. This figure is based on a problematic classification of the *Daily Herald,* first established as a printers' strike sheet in 1911, as a labor newspaper. In fact, neither the LRC nor the Labor party ever published a newspaper in prewar Britain. In this, they were alone in Europe. We might also have included the *Daily Citizen,* which appeared for the first time in 1913, had a circulation comparable to the *Herald*'s, and supported the Labor party.[33] But in either case, the figure for Britain is such an outlier that we need not be much concerned. The figure for France is likewise something of an exaggeration, because it is based not only on the press run of the official *Humanité,* but on the press run of Gustave Hervé's *Guerre Sociale,* which was neither a party newspaper nor generally supportive of the party. If Herve's newspaper is not counted, the figure for France rises to nearly 100. The comparatively high figure for Italy must be weighed against the exceptionally low disposable incomes of Italian workers and the fact that more than one-third of the adult population remained illiterate before the war. Finally, the figure for Belgium is for the year 1923, and it surely overstates the size of the prewar press. Even if the prewar press run was only half of the 1923 figure, however, it would still generate a ratio of eighteen workers per newspaper printed. With these qualifications in mind, the figures accord rather well with what we should expect: Britain and France are at the high end, followed by the Netherlands, where a still potent liberalism and powerful confessional parties circumscribed labor activity. In Belgium, where political competition became much more distinctly bipolar than in the Netherlands as socialism replaced liberalism as the Catholic party's main antagonist, and elsewhere, a distinct category appears. Within that category, there seems to be little to be gained by attaching any significance to the rank order, for at some point differences in population density, affluence, literacy, and so forth no doubt became important.

Votes

The labor parties in Britain and France lacked both the infrastructure and the means of communication that were the mark of mobilizational parties. Not surprisingly, they also lacked the mass support of a mobilized class. Nothing makes this clearer than the comparative levels of electoral support that prewar parties received. In the final balloting before the war, the share of the vote that went to labor parties ranged from 6.4 percent in Britain to 36 percent in Sweden. In Switzerland it was 10.1 percent; in France it was 17 percent; in the Netherlands 19 percent; in Italy 23 percent; in Belgium and Denmark 30 percent; and in Norway 32 percent.[34] To put these figures in still sharper relief, we must recall that the secondary and tertiary male labor forces (electorates were normally limited to men) were, in descending rank order, largest as a fraction of the total labor force in Britain, followed by Switzerland, Belgium, Germany, the Netherlands, France, Denmark, Norway, Sweden, and Italy.[35] In all cases labor parties in aliberal societies, then, were doing better than British Labor, the Swiss Social Democrats, and the SFIO, and in most cases they were doing so at lower levels of industrialization.

Moreover, we must recall from Chapter 2 that a large fraction of the labor vote in Britain, France, and Switzerland came from the middle classes. In France and Switzerland, this share might have been as much as half.[36] In Switzerland, the Socialists owed 70 percent of the National Council seats they won before 1912 to endorsements from other parties.[37] Although in Chapter 2 we made some headway in factoring out the middle-class share of the labor vote in Germany, for other countries the historical data are less adequate.[38] We do know from the research of Olle Johansson that the Social Democrats were having a great deal more success among Swedish workers than the SFIO was among French workers. From his study of the class composition of electoral districts in the 1911 election—the first fought under the reformed franchise—Johansson has calculated that in the nation as a whole, 68 percent of urban workers cast their votes for the Social Democrats.

Only 25 percent voted for the Liberals. Among workers in the countryside (much industry was rural), the share going to the Social Democrats rose to 80 percent.[39] This stands in rather sharp contrast to the experience of the French Socialists who, as we saw, could not win a majority among workers even in the most heavily working-class districts surrounding Paris and the Swiss Social Democrats, who could not have been receiving more than about 40 percent of the working-class vote. It is also in stark contrast to the experience of the British Labor party, which could not win a majority of the working-class vote. "Given a choice between Liberal and other candidates, the majority of all working men still voted Liberal."[40]

Moreover, it follows from all that has been said about the break between liberalism and socialism that the share of the middle-class vote that socialists were receiving was much smaller in aliberal societies than it was in Britain, France, and Switzerland. This almost necessarily was the case, if only because there were so few electoral alliances among socialists and liberals in the aliberal countries. In fact, the small share of the middle-class vote going to labor parties in these societies had much deeper roots. The most straightforward interpretation that can be attached to the normal refusal of liberal parties to ally with labor parties was simply that they understood their voters would not tolerate them. The absence of cross-class voting was not caused by the paucity of electoral alliances. Rather, it is more plausible to suppose that the absence of alliances followed from the unwillingness of middle-class voters to vote across class lines.

In effect, the labor vote in Britain, France, and Switzerland, modest as it was, overstated the working-class support for these parties. Typically, when the Swiss Social Democrats declined alliances with liberals in 1914, their share of the popular vote fell from 20 to 10 percent.[41] By corollary, we can infer that a distinctly larger share of the middle-class vote went to nonsocialist parties in aliberal societies. This amounts to saying that politics in aliberal societies was markedly more polarized along class lines on the eve of the war.

To sum the matter up, we must conclude that just before the war socialist parties in aliberal societies were receiving a much smaller share of the middle-class vote and a markedly larger share of the working-class vote. The pattern of greater socialist success within the working class occurred frequently, moreover, at a much earlier level of industrialization. Also, labor parties in these societies had more effective national machinery, were engaged in a higher level of communication with workers, and in sum, were more committed to the comprehensive mobilization of workers as a class.

Trade Unions: Membership and Organizational Coherence

This distinctive political mobilization of workers in aliberal societies was paralleled before the war by their more comprehensive and coherent organization in the labor market. This is evident in the greater prewar density of trade union membership, especially in unions affiliated with a national socialist confederation, and in the more centralized organization of trade unions.

We calculated in Chapter 2 that 38 and 25 percent of the male industrial labor forces were enrolled in trade unions in Britain and France just before the war.[42] If we ask what share of the male industrial labor force in each country was enrolled in a union that belonged to a national socialist confederation, and classify the TUC and CGT as such confederations, we find that about 20 and 13 percent, respectively, of the labor forces were so enrolled. For Switzerland, the equivalent figure for SGB membership was 15 percent; indeed, among Swiss citizens it was only about 7.5 percent.[43] These figures are strikingly low compared to the figures for aliberal societies. In Belgium and the Netherlands, where confessionalism powerfully retarded the growth of the labor movement, the figures are 19 and 18 percent, respectively, of the male labor force in a trade union and 10 and 12 percent in a union belonging to a national socialist confederation. Elsewhere, the figures rise dramatically. In Norway, where virtually all trade unions belonged to the national confederation, the Landsorganisasjon, 35 percent of male industrial workers belonged to a union within the confederation by 1914. The equivalent share for Denmark was 61 percent in 1914. For Sweden, it was 43 percent in 1908, before the unsuccessful general strike of 1909 decimated the LO, and 31 percent in 1914. In Germany, 30 percent of the male industrial labor force belonged to a trade union that was affiliated with the General Commission of the Free Trade Unions. Even in backward Italy, where confessionalism before the war and repression before 1900 remained powerful brakes on socialist trade union activity, as much as 16 percent of the male industrial labor force may have been enrolled in CGL federations by 1914.[44] In Spain, 19 percent of the male industrial labor force belonged to the UGT.[45]

These figures for confederal membership, striking as they are, are still more impressive when we recall the less favorable circumstances under which membership growth occurred. In all of these societies, industrialization commenced much later than in Britain, and in Norway, Sweden, Denmark, Italy, and Spain it commenced later than in France and Switzerland. Moreover, in Spain almost continuously, in Germany until 1890, and in Italy until 1900, state repression severely limited trade union growth. Yet trade union membership generally and membership in confederal unions in particular were growing at a rate without parallel in Britain, France, and Switzerland. An examination of the aggregate numbers alone does not allow us to fully appreciate the distinctiveness of trade unionism in aliberal societies, however. We must also consider the nature of the confederations and their constituent unions.

It takes virtually an act of faith to describe the CGT, the SGB, and especially the TUC as national confederations. As national bodies, these entities had, as we have seen, almost no corporate substance after the war and still less before it.[46] Edward Shorter and Charles Tilly have described the prewar CGT as "much more like someone standing on a table shouting exhortations during a bar-room brawl than a general directing his armies across the field of battle."[47] In their prewar manifestations, the TUC and the CGT are better viewed as annual and biannual gatherings in which the constituent unions debated theoretical, political, and labor market issues than as the directors general of national labor movements. The SGB's role was also no more than to serve as "a center for information."[48] The impoverishment of the CGT was legendary: its annual income was one-tenth the income of the national printers' federation.[49] The TUC and the CGT could exert no control over their constituents. Neither organization could intervene in strikes as the representatives of labor; neither could authorize or terminate a strike; neither controlled access to strike funds; neither could coordinate work stoppages among the constituent unions. Indeed, only with difficulty could either even claim to speak for the majority of unionized workers. Only a slight majority of prewar British trade unionists even belonged to TUC-affiliated trade unions, and the voting procedures of the CGT, whose affiliated unions enrolled about one-half of organized French workers by 1914, allowed a handful of unions representing a minuscule fraction of CGT workers to control its decisions.[50] In Switzerland, the SGB began its life as a highly centralized confederation with practically no members. As its membership grew, its central authority disappeared. By 1906, the constituent unions had deprived the SGB of all authority over strikes and strike funds. At the 1908 SGB Congress, the confederation was stripped of its last vestiges of authority and officially declared to be no more than a gatherer of such statistics as the constituent unions chose to provide.[51] By contrast, in Germany 68 percent of organized workers were in Free Trade Union federations in 1913; this reflected a decline from 76 percent in 1907 and a growth in employer-sponsored yellow unions.[52] In Belgium and the Netherlands most organized workers belonged to unions in the socialist confederations, and in Denmark, Norway, and Sweden, virtually all organized workers belonged to confederal unions.

Even in Spain, the UGT could claim to speak for 148,000 of the 253,000 organized workers in 1913.[53] Spain, to be sure, was a special case. Its special nature did not derive from anything exceptional about the UGT, however. For the UGT was a highly centralized apparatus with all the attributes of other socialist trade unions in aliberal societies. Spain was, rather, a special case because the UGT was neither the leading representative of the working class nor even a force, given the backwardness of the Spanish economy, of any real consequence on the prewar political scene. Even during the final crisis of the old regime, between 1917 and 1923, it was never more than a second-rate movement. It was displaced in the final years of the restoration order by the anarcho-syndicalist CNT, which remained the main agent of Spanish workers until it was crushed by the Primo de Rivera dictatorship in the 1920s.[54] At its peak in 1920, the CNT probably had the loyalty of about a million workers; the UGT could never claim more than about 200,000 members.[55] Moreover, the CNT monopolized labor precisely in those parts of Spain that were most modern. Ultimately, the destruction of the CNT and the growth of the UGT during the 1920s would create a labor movement in Spain more analogous to those found elsewhere in Western Europe. It was during those years that Spain for the first time acquired a powerful and modern socialist labor movement—a story we take up at greater length in Chapters 7 and 8. For the moment, we need only observe that as marginal a force as the UGT was in prewar Spain, it was already laying the organizational groundwork for a highly centralized labor movement, one that grouped workers in a small number of national federations and concentrated authority at its apex.[56] At the heart of the UGT's inferiority was its inability to penetrate the Barcelonese working class.[57] With its centralized bureaucracy and high dues, it remained overwhelmingly an organization of the comparatively privileged socialist labor aristocracy of Madrid transport workers and Asturian miners in the years before the dictatorship.[58] This division among Spanish workers itself reflected the unique combination of failed Western liberalism and Eastern backwardness, of the disjunction of political power and economic power between Castile and the periphery of which we spoke in Chapter 3, and to which we shall return subsequently when we take up the De Rivera dictatorship.

In crucial respects, the confederations in aliberal societies and their constituent unions stand in sharp contrast to the confederations and unions that were taking form in liberal societies. In aliberal societies, trade union membership was concentrated in fewer unions and decision-making authority was more centralized. In Britain just before the war, the 100 largest unions enrolled about two-thirds of all organized workers. The exact shares were 71 percent in 1911, 61 percent in 1912, and 73 percent in 1914. These 100 principal unions included no fewer than 11 in the building trades, 16 in mining and quarrying, 16 in metal, engineering, and shipbuilding, 21 in textiles, and 11 in transport.[59]

In France, the CGT was composed of the 144 *bourses du travail* and about 52 national federations in 1914. The bourses were urban labor centrals, umbrella organizations that combined workers in many different crafts and industries. They divided the labor movement by region and gave it much of its localist orientation. The federations, with the exception of the Printers', were strictly chimerical. Strike funds hardly existed at any level, and decisions to strike were almost always local or, at best, regional. They were normally made not by union leaders but by rank-and-file workers.[60] These were the central facts of French unions—small size, decentralized structure, and localist orientation; in 1905 the average union had just 170 members.[61]

Let us put these organizational weaknesses in bas-relief. In Germany, 76 percent of Free Trade Union–organized workers were enrolled in just ten national federations, the largest four of which enrolled 52 percent of organized workers in 1914.[62] Consolidation of craft unions reduced the number of national federations affiliated with the General Commission from sixty-six in 1906 to forty-six in 1914.[63] In Sweden, the four largest unions enrolled 64 percent of the organized workers in 1916. The thirteen largest enrolled 74 percent.[64] In Denmark, the single largest national federation—the Laborers' Federation—organized 33 percent of trade unionists, the three largest national federations organized 50 percent of trade unionists, and the ten largest organized 76 percent.[65] In Norway, the Laborers' Federation included one-quarter of all organized workers, the three largest federations included 55 percent of organized workers, and the ten largest included 81 percent.[66] In Belgium, 65 percent of the workers in socialist-affiliated unions belonged to national federations in 1914, and this share rose to 96 percent by 1919.[67] In 1922, the five largest Belgian federations enrolled 76 percent of the workers organized by socialist unions.[68] In Italy in 1920, the four largest federations organized 56 percent of industrial workers enrolled in the CGL.[69] More than half of the members of the Spanish UGT were enrolled in just two unions, in mining and transportation, in 1918.[70] In the Spanish case this concentration is partly a reflection of the underorganization of many sectors of the economy and of the almost total failure of the UGT to penetrate the anarchist stronghold of Barcelona. The norm in all of these countries was, nonetheless, that fewer than ten national federations included three-quarters of the trade union population. In Britain, about ten times as many unions were required to aggregate the same share.

There were, to be sure, national federations in prewar Britain, but these were of an altogether different sort than those found in aliberal societies. British federations often existed only on paper, the classic example being the General Federation of Trade Unions, which nominally enrolled over 900,000 workers but completely lacked authority over its constituent unions.[71] The flaw in British federations was that, with few exceptions, they had neither strike funds nor the authority to call strikes or bargain collectively. For this reason we must speak of the 100 principal unions, for it was within these unions that control of strike funds, strikes, and collective bargaining resided. In aliberal societies, these levers of power were in the hands of the national confederations or the national federations.

The pluralism of British trade unionism was gradually reduced during the interwar years. In 1920 there were 1,384 independent unions; by 1942 this had fallen to 976. By that time the 16 largest enrolled almost 60 percent of trade unionists.[72] In effect, British labor reached a level of concentration by the middle of World War II that had been surpassed in aliberal societies by about 1905. In France, too, pluralism was at least nominally reduced. Already in 1912 Leon Jouhaux had been able to introduce reforms that eliminated the bourses as a separate section of the CGT. That did not diminish their reality for workers. Over the longer haul, the role of the bourses relative to the federations in coordinating strike action actually increased from one that was about comparable to one that was actually greater. "In no case may one argue that over the years [1895 to 1929] the industrial federation became a more powerful synchronizer of collective action, nor that territorial-based organization (be it *bourse du travail,* PCF cellule or whatever) waned as a result."[73] In 1919, Jouhaux sought to bolster central leadership by creating an executive committee of leaders of major federations. Alas, we shall see in Chapter 6 that just as the CGT could not control the federations because it had no resources at its disposal, so too the federations could not control the local associations.[74] In the meantime, concentration and to a greater degree, centralization had continued to advance elsewhere. In Germany, the number of independent national federations that made up the interwar national confederation, the ADGB, declined from fifty-two in 1919 to thirty in 1931.[75]

Centralization reached its peak in the prewar years in Norway, where the confederation, the LO, controlled most strike funds and insisted on its right to approve all collective agreements and even negotiating positions not limited to purely local questions.[76] In Sweden, the LO had at its disposal funds that could be used only in support of workers made unemployed by lockouts. Moreover, it had no statutory authority to intervene in contract negotiations. Its de facto authority and its ability to elicit worker solidarity were considerable, however, deriving largely from the small number of federations that dominated the LO. In practice, the LO regularly intervened in negotiations in the years before the 1909 general strike and lockout, and for the strike and lockout itself it provided undisputed leadership.[77]

A comparison of this strike with the 1926 general strike in Britain illustrates the fundamentally different levels of coherence among labor movements in liberal and aliberal societies. The British strike fell apart in a few days, because the TUC executive could neither negotiate on behalf of the miners nor induce them to make concessions on their own. The Swedish strike lasted five weeks, during which the leadership of the LO was never disputed. For those five weeks, virtually every organized worker in Sweden stayed out and the national economy was brought to a standstill.[78] That was a level of class discipline of which British and French trade unionists, the latter with their almost pathetic one-day "general" strikes, could not even dream.

In Denmark, which had nominally the least centralized of the Scandinavian LO's, control of strike funds resided with the national federations. The reality, however, was that, because membership was concentrated in so few federations, the LO was able to play a decisive role. The lockout and general strike of 1899 was concluded by the *Septemberforliget,* a master agreement between the LO and the national employers association that governed labor relations for decades to come. Thereafter, national bargaining became increasingly centralized under the leadership of the national federations and the guidance of the LO.[79]

Even in Italy, where national trade unionism could hardly take root before 1900 and CGL authority was constantly challenged by the regionalism of the chambers of labor and the unaffiliated syndicalist unions, the final prewar decade saw a marked tendency toward a more centralized movement. Although the CGL, founded only in 1906, could not completely shift the loyalty of organized workers from the regional chambers to the national confederation, efforts toward greater centralization were made repeatedly. These efforts were mainly directed toward strengthening the national federations and toward strictly controlling strikes and strike funds by the confederation. The 1908 congress required that the regional chambers and the national federations consult with the confederation before calling strikes that involved a majority of workers in an industry or province. Strikes called in the absence of such consultation would be denied funds. After 1911, local unions could gain confederal affiliation only through a chamber or national federation. A running, albeit inconclusive, battle was fought during these years between the chambers and the federations for representation in and control of the national confederation. In 1911, the congress decided that at future congresses chambers should be allowed to represent only those workers not in national federations. In 1914, half of the congress delegates were allotted to the chambers and half to the federations.[80]

As the Italian example indicates, this higher level of centralization that characterized trade union authority in aliberal societies came about incrementally, for these movements were not born more centralized than their British and French analogs. Proposals to provide the Danish LO with a centralized strike fund and the authority to intervene in wage disputes were overwhelmingly rejected in the constitutional debates from which the LO issued.[81] The Swedish LO was at its creation intended to serve as nothing more than a clearinghouse for statistical data and a forum for debate. Its paid staff consisted of one person.[82] In Germany, the Halberstadt Congress that established the General Commission of the Free Trade Unions in 1892 rejected a proposal to grant the commission control of strike funds. Indeed, the commission's statutory authority was simultaneously vague and limited: it was authorized to publish a newspaper, gather statistics, correspond with foreign labor movements, and encourage unionization in unorganized industries. A majority of delegates were unwilling to do more than recommend the centralization of related craft associations. For six years a battle was fought between "localists," who wanted authority concentrated at the urban level and a weak national organization, and "centralists" who wanted a powerful General Commission and consolidated authority in a small number of national unions.[83] In this, the turning point came at the 1896 congress, when the Zentralverbände were able to deprive the local intercraft associations of their control of strike funds and their right of representation at the national congress. In the following years the General Commission "was to extend its influence far beyond the . . . imagination of its founders."[84] During those same years the more than 3,000 craft associations that had existed in 1891 were consolidated by cartel agreements into the 46 Zentralverbände that underpinned the General Commission by 1914.[85]

The Norwegian LO, which became the most authoritative confederation in prewar Europe, initially did not control a regular strike fund. It had the authority only to make special assessments. In its first years it looked much like the French CGT, consisting of a congeries of urban centrals and national federations. Two of the most powerful national federations, the Metalworkers and the Typographers, at first refused to affiliate because the urban centrals were given membership in the LO. The LO thus found that only by inducing the urban centrals to withdraw from wage disputes was it able to gain the adherence of the Typographers and Metalworkers. In the competition between the local associations and the national federations, the latter prevailed, and it was their success that was the first step to the consolidation of the LO.[86]

In the Netherlands centralization took a major step forward when the Nederlands Verbond van Vakverenigingen was created by fifteen industrial federations in 1906. Membership in the NVV was limited to these industrial unions, which were highly centralized and based on a common model. "The components were to be highly centralized . . . [and] pledged themselves to maintain high compulsory dues, their own strike funds, salaried administrators, and, where possible, to publish their own newspaper."[87] The establishment of the NVV marked a break with the much more decentralized, free-wheeling organizational style of the older Nederlands Arbeids Secretariaat, the theretofore main national trade union organization. The NAS was an anarcho-syndicalist movement that, armed with a one-man national secretariat, emphasized strong local organizations that bridged industrial sectors and emphasized psychological preparation for revolution.[88] By 1914, the NVV had almost entirely displaced it.[89]

The central agency of the Belgian trade unions, the Trade Union Commission, created only in 1898, was intended only as a research bureau. "Up to that time, the trade unions . . . had been, so to speak, strangers to one another, and, even within the limits of each individual craft, had not had the least connection with one another."[90] Yet, by 1914, the Belgian unions were among the most centralized in Europe, in large measure due to the growth of the commission's own authority. By the beginning of the war, the commission had gained the right to decide all jurisdictional disputes among unions, succeeded in imposing the principle of centralized national federation on the unions, and gained the authority to tap the various federations' strike funds to subsidize the strikes of other federations.

In 1908 [the commission] began an energetic propaganda in favor of centralization. Rejected at first by the workers in the building trades, this form of organization, then quite new in Belgium, was subsequently adopted, and put into operation in 1909. Factory workers, tobacco workers, and coach makers soon afterwards followed suit. . . . the unions one after the other accepted this centralized organization; its adoption was indeed so general that the Trade Union Congress in 1914 decided that henceforth only national [federations] should be allowed to affiliate to the Commission, a measure that did not fail to exercise a strong influence on the groups which had not already centralized.[91]

In 1911, just 11.5 percent of Belgian trade unionists belonged to national federations; by 1914, 65 percent belonged to such federations, and 96 percent belonged in 1919.[92]

The trade unions in aliberal societies, then, acquired a more centralized leadership and were willing to accept it because, to a much greater extent than in Britain and France, they found a common enemy in the political and economic authority structures of aliberal societies. The political context in which trade unions acted is a subject to which we shall return presently. For the moment let us simply draw the most fundamental line: in none of these societies did the state frequently intervene on behalf of labor, as it did in France, or provide a legal framework that gave trade unions a juridically privileged, supralegal position, as it did in Britain.

At the same time trade unions acted in an essentially inhospitable political environment, they also struggled against a more determined foe in the employer class. Employers were themselves far better organized in aliberal societies and more likely to act in a united front against trade unions. This greater coherence among employers was the most immediate and proximate cause impelling trade unions toward greater centralization of authority. The process of labor and employer centralization was a reciprocal one, with the increment of authority on one side impelling an additional increment on the other. When Hamburg workers sought to implement the Second International's call for May Day strikes in 1890, the Hamburg-Altona Employers' Association responded with a general lockout. That lockout provoked a meeting of all trade union organizations for the purpose of establishing an effective defense "against the attacks of arrogant entrepreneurs," whence emerged the General Commission of the Free Trade Unions.[93] Likewise, faced with the growing membership of the new Norwegian Employers' Association, the national unions in Norway ceded to the LO the right to call sympathy strikes and to assume direct leadership over disputes involving more than one national union.[94] As a conscious strategy of labor market relations, centralization was much more a product of employer efforts, however. In retrospect, labor centralization appears to have been more reactive than proactive. Gunnar Ousland has written that what served most to secure unification of all the trade unions in Norway was the solidarity displayed by employers. . . . The Federation of Labor and the Metalworkers' Union received an expression of that during the metal trades lockout in Bergen in 1903, and still more sharply in the molders' controversy of 1904, where the employers threatened to lock out the other workers, and the Metalworkers' Union sought to mediate. The strike that occurred among the unions convinced the majority that practical and effective leadership of the important disputes could be secured only after all unions were within the Federation.[95]

In Denmark, Norway, and Sweden, employers sought first to break labor with a united front and then, when that failed, to impose centralized national agreements on the unions. Employer organization reached such a level of refinement that strikebreakers were regularly imported from as far away as England. Both the 1899 lockout in Denmark and the 1909 lockout in Sweden were preventive wars launched by national employers' associations frightened by the growth of the trade unions. Centralized negotiations were one of two principal demands (the other being the complete freedom to hire and terminate workers) employers sought to impose on Danish and Swedish labor in these lockouts. Such agreements were expected to prevent unions from generalizing settlements reached with the most vulnerable or profitable employers.[96]

It was a mark of the greater coherence of the employer class that they were able to resort to lockouts with regularity in aliberal societies. Indeed, they became a standard tool of labor relations. The Danish lockout of 1899, which the Employers' Association itself termed a "declaration of war," lasted more than three months and affected about 20 percent on the non-agricultural labor force.[97] The 1909 Swedish lockout lasted five weeks. One indicator of the extent of employer organization, the quality of the antagonist trade unions encountered, is to be found in the number of workers who were locked out for each worker who went on strike. In Denmark, on average in the twelve years before the war, one worker was locked out each year for every 1.2 that went on strike. In Germany, one was locked out for every 2.5 that went on strike. In Sweden during the same period, the ratio was 1 to 3.14. Revealingly, in France, just one worker was locked out for every sixty-two that went on strike.[98]

The decisive impetus for an umbrella labor market organization of German employers came from a five-month-long strike by textile workers in Crimmitschau in 1903–04. In December the Centralverband deutscher Industrieller summoned its members to provide the Crimmitschau owners with financial support, and in April 1904 it provided the leadership for establishing the Hauptstelle deutscher Arbeitergeberverbände, which united major employers to combat the trade unions. At the same time the Verein deutscher Arbeitgeberverbände was created to organize employers in the metal industries and smaller craft workshops. Although the interests of the small and large employers often conflicted on issues of the national economy, they demonstrated remarkable unanimity in their antipathy toward the Free Trade Unions and the Social Democratic party. In December 1904 the two employer associations were able to make a cartel agreement, and in 1913 they merged into the Vereinigung deutscher Arbeitergeberverbände. To combat the trade unions and the Social Democratic party, the employers developed a system of strike insurance and an effective blacklist. This blacklist prevented workers who participated in party or trade union activity from finding employment at another factory. It was arranged among the employment agents that only those workers who could provide the certificate of good conduct would be reemployed.[99]

Even in Italy rapid organizational progress was made by employer organizations in the decade before the war. Throughout the 1890s Italian employers, bolstered by the repressive state, seemed confident that trade union expansion was no more than a transient pathology. But as union growth continued in the new century, Italian employers, too, were compelled to centralize their responses. Before the war, concerted employer action was frustrated less by the individualism of Italian employers than by Giolitti's interventions. Giolitti sought to protect the reformist CGL unions while mercilessly subjugating the more politically oriented syndicalist unions. Giolitti consequently encouraged concerted employer responses against the syndicalists while discouraging employer concertation against CGL federations. Thus, for example, Giolitti's intervention blocked a lockout against the reformist metalworkers' strike in the spring of 1913. Between 1907 and 1910, the Turin industrialists were repeatedly able to break syndicalist-led strikes with organized lockouts. Milanese industrialists likewise broke syndicalist-led strikes in July and August 1913 by responding with a lockout.[100]

The first organization of employers intended to bargain collectively in more than one industry was created in Turin in 1906, when seventy-five major employers established the Piedmont Industrial League. Industrialists in other parts of Italy soon followed this example and, in 1910, the Italian Confederation of Industrialists was founded. In 1920 this was renamed the General Confederation of Italian Industry (Confindustria). By 1920, Confindustria claimed to represent not only virtually all of the major Italian employers, but three-quarters of medium-sized firms as well.[101]

In Britain and France lookouts were comparatively rare, not the least because British and French employers were so poorly organized. As late as 1936, when Swedish, Danish, Norwegian, and Belgian employers were effectively organized in one or two national associations for collective bargaining purposes British employers remained grouped in 270 national associations and 1,550 local and regional associations.[102] Before 1914, French employers were effectively organized only in glass manufacturing and metallurgy. As Peter Stearns has argued, the weakness of employer unions reflected the weakness of French trade unions and the acute conflicts between large and small firms that was characteristic of prewar industrial politics. Most employers were not organized and most of those who were, were in organizations that were socially oriented and quite loose. Even the better organized employer unions often broke down when put to the test by a strike, for rarely was more than a minority of relevant employers enrolled. Prewar France did not experience a concentration of employer organization. Rather, as employers became organized, they did so in a proliferating number of groups. The number of employer associations tripled between 1897 and 1913, reaching a total of more than 5,000 just before the War.[103] After the war, French employers continued to resist more effective organization, and the main national agency, the Confédération Générale de la Production Française, was formed mainly in response to government-offered incentives rather than to a perceived need for protection against trade unions.[104] The CGPF was a loosely organized confederation whose activities and interests were largely confined to lobbying the bureaucracy. It left questions of wages and labor conditions to a plethora of industrial and regional groups, to which most firms did not belong.[105]

A Note on Industrial Concentration

The greater coherence of trade union movements in aliberal societies has sometimes been seen as a product of more concentrated employment—that is, of the larger factory size that was sometimes an attribute of late industrialization.[106] There are two reasons to doubt such an interpretation. First, as we saw in Chapter 3, Denmark and Norway shared with France a predominance of petit bourgeois production. In all three countries, manufacturing was characterized by small firms. In France, one-third of wage earners were self-employed in 1906 and 60 percent of workers were employed by firms with ten or fewer employees. In Denmark, 50 percent of urban wage-earners were self-employed in 1914 and 41 percent were in firms of one to five employees; 47 percent were in firms of fewer than twenty employees. In Norway, too, employment in small firms predominated.[107] Yet Norway and Denmark both developed exceptionally coherent labor movements while France did not. In Norway, this coherence derived from the extraordinary authority of the LO. In Denmark, it derived less from the authority of the LO than from the concentration of trade union membership in a handful of unions. Similar employment patterns produced different trade union movements. Per contra, Swedish and German manufacturing were much more characterized by the large factor often associated with late industrialization.[108] Yet in both countries the same sorts of coherent trade union movements appeared that emerged under very different employment conditions in Norway and Denmark.

There is another reason to doubt that the type of trade union movement that emerged before the war was much influenced by economies of scale in manufacturing. In all of these societies, whatever the industrial structure, mainly skilled workers from smaller firms constituted the great majority of trade union and socialist party members and activists.[109] In Germany, which was not atypical in this respect, "Free Union strength remained concentrated in smaller firms where conditions remained similar to those of a workshop in a handicraft. . . . Before the war the Free Unions had made hardly any inroads in heavy industry, iron and steel, or chemicals. In other words, the Marxists had yet to gain a foothold in the core of the modern industrial proletariat."[110] Larger firms in aliberal societies were likely to be the most difficult of all to organize because the owners of such firms were best positioned to resist trade unions and because their workers were disproportionately unskilled. These workers were probably disproportionately unskilled even in comparison with workers in large British and French factories, where craft traditions long continued even in many large firms. In aliberal societies, in contrast, late industrialization generally meant an early introduction of craft-diminishing technologies. The archetype of the unskilled prewar proletarian was the female textile operative. Her work day did not end after a dozen or more grueling hours, for she was normally a married woman with a husband and children and domestic duties that beckoned as soon as she left the factory gate. The obstacles to organizing such workers were almost insuperable, for they labored for more hours for lower pay and were more prone to exhaustion, less attached to a particular firm or locale, more easily replaced, and more likely to be poorly educated.[111]

Variations in the industrial structure may be of some residual value in understanding differences in the levels and forms of organization among fundamentally similar societies. The differences in union density in Britain and France probably have to be accounted for to some degree in these terms, for British firms were markedly larger than French firms and the New Unions of the 1890s made the unskilled workers who tenanted those British workplaces the first in Europe to be organized.[112] But in accounting for the differences in labor coherence among liberal and aliberal societies, industrial structure will not take us far. That fundamental difference was derived not from the timing of industrialization or manufacturing technologies but from politics.

A Note on the Role of the State

In aliberal societies, comprehensive class organization and centralized leadership of trade unions were acceptable because they were an obviously necessary response in societies, in contrast to Britain, France, and Switzerland, in which state power was decisive and the middle classes were repelled by the prospect of political alliances with workers. The same liberal alienation that precluded Lib–Labism also reflected a less favorable middle-class and employer attitude toward trade unions. For liberals to attempt to isolate socialist parties was inevitably to attack the trade unions, because the parties were the political defenders of the trade unions in a world in which politics critically determined the unions' prospects for success. In every aliberal society, the intermediate case of Denmark being the exception, steps were taken or institutions preserved in the decades before the war with the expressed aim of crippling the political power of socialist parties. In Norway, the electoral law was revised to ensure the underrepresentation of the Labor party in the Storting. In Sweden, the Netherlands, and Italy (until 1912) the franchise remained restricted. In Belgium plural voting was inaugurated. In Germany plural voting in Prussian elections and the inferiority of the Reichstag served the same end. In Spain fraud and coercion were always at hand.

In the absence of the influence working-class parties and voters could exert in Lib–Lab alliances, the state's attitude oscillated between malignant indifference and outright repression. For the longer run, the differences eventuating from states that sought largely to stand aloof from the labor market (as in Scandinavia) and states that for a time actively repressed unions (as in Italy and Germany) were nugatory. As long as the state did not intervene affirmatively on behalf of trade unions, workers would always be at a disadvantage in the labor market, for the capitalist deck was stacked heavily in favor of the employers. Workers would always have to rely mainly on their own devices, the main one of which was comprehensive organization.

There were, to be sure, differences among states in their policies toward trade unions. In Scandinavia, trade unions were never made illegal, as the socialist unions were in Germany between 1878 and 1890. Even so, in the first years of the century Swedish governments were pleased to send trade union leaders to prison for six to eighteen months, and socialist demonstrations and strikes were frequently broken with police and military intervention.[113] In Norway, Liberals and Conservatives regularly threatened to legislate compulsory arbitration, a turn of events that, given the balance of political power, would have been a disaster for the unions. Indeed, a Liberal government prepared such legislation in the spring of 1914, and only the coming of the war a few months later prevented its passage.[114] In the Netherlands, the Kuyper government's response to the 1903 strike of Amsterdam dockworkers and railwaymen was to outlaw all strikes by railway workers.[115] In 1906 it enacted legislation that restricted the conditions under which any strike was permitted and allowed employers to collect civil damages for illegal strikes.[116] In Belgium, policemen and troops were regularly deployed to break strikes rather than merely to maintain public order. Notwithstanding the repression before 1890 and the continued refusal of large employers to negotiate collectively, about 2,000,000 German workers were covered by collective agreements by 1914.[117] Moreover, the influence of German trade unions extended far beyond the workers covered by collective agreements, because major employers were increasingly forced to take account of the union threat in the final decade of peace. Thus, the explosion of "preemptive" organization of yellow unions so common among large employers in the Rhineland.[118] The Spanish liberals' 1889 Law of Association affirmed the right to organize trade unions, bargain collectively, and strike.[119] Nowhere were de jure rights more unrelated to reality: the physical repression of Spanish trade unions before the war was without parallel in Western Europe. Trade unions and collective bargaining were not illegal in pre-Giolittian Italy, but that absence of illegality was hardly an adequate defense against repeated repression. Even under Giolitti, Italian employers were rarely willing to bargain in good faith—thus the dearth of written agreements. Most bargaining was implicit: strikes came to an end not with a written agreement, but with a tacit understanding about the new wage and conditions of work.[120] Prewar legal codes, then, tell us little about the actual conditions under which unions labored.

After 1900 the aliberal norm was for governments to adopt a position of crippling indifference. The calculated detachment of the Swedish government during the 1909 general strike and lockout is a case in point. Throughout the strike/lockout's five weeks, the government studiously avoided intervention. It was, of course, precisely such intervention that the LO secretariat had counted on to save the day, so that the government's refusal to engage itself was tantamount to support for the employers.[121] It is impossible to imagine a contemporary British or French government passively sitting out a five-day general strike, not to mention one that lasted five weeks. Indeed, the British and French governments routinely mediated much smaller disputes in the years before the war, and in so doing regularly served as a critical ally of the unions. After about 1900 governments, at least outside of Spain, where conditions were more variable, understood that unions could not be crassly repressed. Governments were increasingly inclined to leave matters mainly in the hands of employers, making only sporadic incursions into the field with, from the unions' view, kibitzing legislation.

Governments in aliberal societies commonly left matters in the hands of employers, refusing to weigh in with any regularity on behalf of workers. It was this common response that generated the remarkably similar pattern of working-class mobilization in these societies. The essence of that mobilization was the striking coherence of these labor movements. It no doubt mattered a great deal to the working-class victims of these governments whether the government's response before 1900 was a violent one, as it often was in Spain, Italy, and even Belgium, merely repressive as in Germany, or just harassing as in Norway, Sweden, and the Netherlands. But for the longer haul, these initial state responses seem to have had little consequence. There is no correlation between them and the type of organization, or the radicalism and reformism, or the ideologies that characterized labor movements in the interwar years. For the longer haul, what counted about the prewar period was whether or not the state could be counted on to act with some frequency as an ally. Where it could not be, a legacy of class coherence emerged and endured into the interwar period.

Epilogue: Toward the Great War

The common properties of labor movements in aliberal societies, then, were an extraordinary breadth of worker loyalty to socialist parties and unions; the parties' penetration and mobilization of workers through the party and trade union bureaucracies and the party press; the growth of highly centralized and comparatively comprehensive trade unions; and the close relationships between the parties and unions. Taken together, these constituted a level of class coherence that was totally alien to liberal societies. Even before the war, worker movements constituted the strongest organized body of opinion that existed in aliberal societies, save those societies dominated by hegemonic clericalism.

It was this organizational network that would harness the explosive postwar mobilization of workers. This mobilization would take place against politically divided and insecure middle classes. For the same divisions that had prevented the middle classes from establishing their political dominance before the war would remain embedded in the party systems and prevent middle-class unity in the face of the working-class juggernaut after the war. This crisis of class relations, moreover, occurred in societies in which the legitimacy of working-class power, especially the power to govern, remained bitterly contested and a third force, the family peasantry, quickly established itself as an indispensable player. What to do with the working class, in fact, became the existential question of interwar politics. Ultimately, the regime crises of those years can be read as attempts to find a solution to the problem of integrating comprehensively organized working-class movements. The several regime alternatives that in principle constitute solutions to this problem—liberal democracy, social democracy, and fascism—each assumed a different pattern of class alliances among the three players.

In light of the story as it has developed thus far, little appears to be gained by extended debates about whether working-class movements had suffered from *embourgeoisement* or revisionism in the last decade of the peace.[122] They were all revisionist insofar as the leading movements in every Western European country, leaving aside the special case of Spain, accepted that political power was the sine qua non of success and that, in industrial societies where workers were a minority and the levers of economic power were largely beyond their reach, political power could only be gained through careful organization and electoral victories. Countless monographs on everyday worker life and endless debates of purely antiquarian interest are possible about whether the revisionism of party and trade union leaders reflected the "true" values of the workers. Such debates are of strictly antiquarian interest because, in the fast-unfolding epoch of mass politics, the only values of enduring consequence, of more than spasmodic importance, were those that were organized.

The onrush of mass politics was radically accelerated by the war and the Bolshevik revolution that issued from it. The war and revolution probably did as much to foster class consciousness and polarization as all the years of industrialization that preceded it. Not the least of the war's effects was in the way it uprooted, alienated, disoriented, and therefore made more susceptible to socialist appeals on their return home (from factories or the front) millions of young men who had previously been beyond the reach of socialist organizers. The impact of the war was hardly milder in adjacent neutralist countries traumatized by the economic boom and bust cycle of the war and peace. In a sense, the war was the great homogenizer: it markedly reduced the prior differences in the levels of political mobilization among Western European societies. Ironically, it did more for socialist parties in liberal societies than in aliberal societies. The former now "caught up" with the latter in the size of the vote they received. The war was a great homogenizer as well in the sense that, throughout Western Europe, the political mobilization of the countryside now caught up with the city. Peasants in one society after another became much more autonomous of liberalism than they had been in the prewar period. They became political agents in their own right and insisted that they be courted on their own terms. It will not be possible to comprehend interwar politics without attention to the conflicts between peasants and urban dwellers.

These are all themes to which we return in due course. For the moment, let us consider how the war aborted certain tendencies related to revisionism that were apparent in aliberal societies in the last years of peace. It is tempting to think that in some societies, foremost among them Italy, Germany, and Sweden, another generation of peace might have resulted in stable political and economic orders very different from those that eventually emerged in the interwar years. If the organizational parameters into which mass politics would unfold had already been defined in these societies, a number of other parameters that decisively shaped the interwar outcomes remained incipient. Surely the level of mobilization—of participation and demands on the state—was lower. Unskilled workers had not yet flooded labor movements. Peasants remained comparatively quiescent and aligned with, if not liberal parties, at least establishment parties. The radicalizing effect of the war on urban class relations did not occur. However polarized urban class relations obviously were in aliberal societies in 1914, they had obviously not experienced the qualitative transformation that the war and revolution induced. Moreover, the profound delegitimation that liberalism suffered as a result of the war remained in the future. Finally, the train of economic crises the war unleashed, which tormented interwar regimes, remained in the future.

In Italy the Giolittian coalition was not necessarily dead, the Libyan War notwithstanding. Certainly the Giolittian epoch had marked the first tentative steps toward an accommodation between Liberals and workers. Giolitti had even extended to the Socialists an invitation to join his governments in 1903 and 1908. His plan for suffrage reform had obviously been premised on an enduring Lib–Lab alliance. In Sweden, too, an invitation was extended to Socialists by Karl Staaf just before the war. In Germany, the electoral alliance with the Progressives was made with the hope that it would yield a reformist Reichstag majority that could break the constitutional deadlock. In Belgium and the Netherlands, where the political hegemony of religious parties made the whole issue less urgent, similar steps were taken just before the war. In the Netherlands, Liberals invited Socialists to support their government in 1913. In Belgium, the alliance between the Socialists and Liberals in 1912 was made with the clear intention of forming a government if the voters allowed it. All of these overtures failed, it is true. Where socialists received invitations to join governments, they came from enfeebled Liberal parties who extended them largely because they knew in advance that they would be declined. Where alliances depended on voters, as in Belgium and Germany, middle-class voters rejected them. Only in the intermediate case of Denmark did a Socialist party join a Liberal government just before the war. And in Denmark, as we saw, a late version of Lib–Labism had already existed for some years.

In the absence of the war, a more stable accommodation between workers and liberals might well have unfolded in these societies. At the least, socialists and liberals would have had more time to reach a modus vivendi unharried by the interwar distributional crisis between the cities and countryside. That crisis and the rural mobilization it unleashed, as we shall see, profoundly altered the balance of political power. Given the distinctive organization of the working class, the accommodation that might have been would not have borne much resemblance to the accommodation that had already been reached in Britain and France. Late prewar Denmark, where cooperation between liberals and labor had developed late and a master agreement defining the basic rules of collective bargaining had been reached between the LO and Employers' Association in 1899, probably provides as good an indication as any of how other societies might have evolved, at least under the most optimistic assumptions, had the war not intervened.

But of course the war did intervene before these optimistic assumptions could come into play. And until the end of the epoch the war so ruthlessly defined, in the face of hostile liberal movements, indifferent or hostile states, and disciplined employers, neither the particularism of British labor nor the organizational flaccidity of French labor were viable options. Class organization was the only choice. Ole Lian, for many years the secretary of the

Norwegian LO, allegorically captured the essential ambition of these organizations when he wrote in 1912 that,

> Just as a great river must be diverted through canals and turbines so that its power can become effective, so shall the labor movement gather the working masses and direct their combined flow down through its organizations to the wheels that drive the economy. From everywhere we draw the workers, regulating every little stream, gathering the streams in great rivers until it is all gathered in a vast flood aimed at the main wheels of the economy.[123]

Much of what has been seen as revisionism or conservatism has been inferred from the commitment of working-class leaders to the preservation of their organizations. Because organization was the main weapon of workers and because creating class organizations was such an arduous task, we should not be surprised in retrospect that these men and women sometimes conflated the interests of the class with those of the organizations and seemed obsessed with preserving them. At times this required caution and accommodation in politics and the labor market, as in Germany in the last years of the Empire, in Sweden after the defeat of the general strike, and in Spain during the years of De Rivera's dictatorship. At other times, preserving the organizational infrastructure required radicalism, as in Sweden during the year leading up to the general strike and in Norway after the explosion of syndicalism in 1911. If the central theme was the preservation of organizations, that was above all because it remained true that those organizations were all workers in aliberal societies had. For this reason the leader of the German unions, Carl Legien, could earnestly enjoin his party comrades, as no British or French trade unionist could, that "Die Organisation ist alles!"[124]

THE OUTCOMES

6

War, Crisis, and the Stabilization of the Liberal Order

The net effect of the pattern of labor inclusion described in Chapter 2 was the continuation between the wars in Britain, France, and Switzerland of liberal political economies capable of enduring the interwar crises. James Joll's observation about interwar France might, pari passu, have been made about Britain or Switzerland:

> The power of the French middle classes, for all the economic and social changes and the psychological damage caused by the war, remained at least until the 1930s politically little different in structure from what it had been before the war. The rulers of the Third Republic, faced with the threat of revolution, had succeeded to a large extent in a conservative reconstruction of the old state and had found that the old constitutional methods had been adequate for their purposes.[1]

The most important fact to be explained about these interwar societies is their essential continuity as liberal political economies at a time when the rest of Europe was in a state of upheaval. These liberal orders had five interrelated, fundamental features that distinguished them from those societies that became social democratic or fascist. The essence of these features was that they remained market-oriented, middle-class dominated democracies. In the first place, in contrast to societies that became fascist dictatorships, competitive democratic politics survived the interwar crises. Moreover, and this is the second element of continuity, it did so with no appreciable shift in the balance of class power. This contrasted with societies that became social democracies. Working-class movements and interests in all three liberal societies, in fact, were politically marginalized. As James Joll observed, and as we shall see in more detail, political power remained overwhelmingly in the hands of the middle classes. The third element of continuity was the continued dependence of the trade unions on the tightness of labor markets and the ability of liberal states to rely on markets to discipline trade unions. This contrasted with the experiences of both societies that became social democracies and those that became fascist dictatorships. The fourth element of continuity, which followed from the third, was the still junior political status of the trade unions. There was no need for liberal states to grant the trade unions a senior consultative political role, as they gained in social democracies, no need for the state to gain the collaboration of the unions to implement its own economic policies and preserve labor market peace. By the same token, there was no incentive to crush labor and remake it under mechanisms of state control, as fascism would. The fifth element of continuity was the tenacious reliance of liberal states on orthodox, or neo-orthodox, market-oriented economic policies even in the face of the Great Depression.

I think we are justified in speaking of these five elements of continuity in their totality as a political and economic order. Likewise, because the inauguration of social democratic and fascist regimes marked such a break in these respects, it seems sensible to speak of fundamentally new political economies with their appearance. It is about some of the continuities that we must concern ourselves in this chapter.

Insofar as the political upheaval in the interwar years was, above all, an expression of acute class conflict and a search for institutions to contain that conflict, the explanation for the comparative continuity of British, French, and Swiss institutions must be found in how this class conflict was mitigated, contained, and dissipated by the legacies of prewar liberal hegemony and Lib–Labism. The answer to the puzzle of why competitive democratic politics continued under middle-class hegemony rests in the absence of a working-class challenge to that order. In the absence of a threat from the working classes, there was little incentive to break with the old democratic, market-oriented, middle-class dominant ways. In this chapter I discuss why that challenge could not be mounted.

At the outset, let me simply declare, as a matter of temporary expedience, that trade unions in liberal societies remained subject to market discipline. I will substantiate this claim in the next chapter, and will also attempt to show that in interwar aliberal societies markets failed to discipline labor. In this chapter, I discuss *why* trade unions in liberal societies could not escape market discipline, *why* trade unions and labor parties could not bring about a change in the balance of class power—why, in sum, there was no threat to middle-class hegemony or competitive politics, and no impetus to break with economic orthodoxy in the 1930s.

The keys to this continuity were rooted in the several effects of prewar liberal hegemony. First, because acceptance of these regimes was so widespread among working class leaders, they were for the most part not even inclined to challenge the interwar political and economic orders. Second, the accommodation of working-class movements that liberal hegemony permitted had, as a by-product, generated profoundly incoherent trade union organizations. That incoherence made trade union leaders incapable of acting as agents of the working class as a whole. The incoherence of the unions prevented them from subverting the discipline of the markets and from forming a united front against employers and the state. In short, it denied them the opportunity to substitute for market outcomes a political bargain with employers and the state. At several critical junctures in interwar Britain, France, and Switzerland it seemed that such a bargain might be struck. At each juncture, labor's potential was undercut by the divisions within the trade unions. I discuss those critical moments at some length in the pages that follow because their story indicates so much more clearly than aggregate data alone possibly can the limits that incoherence imposed. In the next chapter, we turn to the aggregate data on wages, prices, and unemployment for a comparative perspective on the longer-term price labor paid for that incoherence.

The story will not be complete, however, until we comprehend the third enduring effect of prewar liberal hegemony. As we have seen, that hegemony had rested on the comparative unimportance of preindustrial cleavages—language, region, religion—among the middle-class parties. It was precisely the absence of these cleavages that had permitted the ascendance of liberal parties before the war. And it was this same absence that, in the new context of more polarized class politics, now permitted the appearance of a comparatively united antisocialist right in the party system. Party competition came increasingly to turn on a clear-cut choice between a working-class party and an antisocialist party or coalition. This straightforward pattern of left–right competition crippled working-class parties and left the trade unions without an effective ally.

In the first place, this meant that, since workers were nowhere a majority of the electorate, labor parties were condemned to minority status in the interwar years. It also meant that, because class issues were almost the only issues, these labor parties could not attempt, as their counterparts elsewhere sometimes could, to manipulate the divisions within the nonsocialist camp in search of reliable allies. The result was that even when they did come to power, as in Britain in 1924 and 1931 and France in 1936, they were keenly dependent on the reformist goodwill, transient squabbles, or class fear of the nonsocialists who tolerated or supported them. The power of working-class parties was consequently inherently ephemeral even when exercised.

It was these several features of interwar working-class politics—the incoherence of the trade unions, the capacity of the middle classes to realign in an antisocialist coalition, and the consequent isolation of the labor parties—that accounted for the inability of these labor movements to mount a serious challenge to the liberal orders. And because there was no challenge, there

was no need to resort to innovative economic policies and no need to substitute politics for markets or dictatorship for democracy.

Postwar Crises and Liberal Responses

Britain, France, and Switzerland were not immune to the crises and upheaval
that raged across Europe in the two years after the Armistice. For France,
especially, the war had been a traumatic experience. More than any other
combatant in the west, France suffered from the slow-motion laying to waste
of its population and northeastern territory. Eight million Frenchmen had
been mobilized—one-fifth of the total population. Of these, almost three out
of every four were casualties: 4.5 million were wounded and over 1.3 million
killed.

The statistics, grim as they are, hardly reveal the full scope of the social
and psychological damage of the four years of carnage. Gradually the horri-
ble losses in what seemed a hopelessly inconclusive struggle, the reports of
scandalous profiteering, the increased regimentation of labor, the intolerable
housing conditions in munitions-making towns, the mounting cost of living,
and increasing war–weariness created a deep discontent with the war and the
political orders held responsible for it. Throughout Europe, but especially in
the East, where it had never been well-established, liberalism was one of the
war's principal victims. The war was the antithesis of all that liberalism, with
its faith in reason, progress, and science, had promised. Already under strain
from the Great Depression and commodity crises of the 1880s, the brutality
of industrial life, and the surge of class conflict in the years immediately
before the war, liberalism was now indicted for the war and for the economic
dislocations that followed.[2] This strain was reinforced, generally beyond the
breaking point, by the economic crises of the 1930s. From the right liberalism was confronted by various strands of fascism, along with the more
traditional right, while from the left it was assaulted by an often radicalized
socialism and especially Bolshevism. The upshot was the decline, in varying
measure, of reformist liberal parties and the polarization of class relations.

The impact of the Bolshevik Revolution can hardly be overstated. Much
of the prewar legitimacy of reformist liberalism and social democracy had
derived from the conviction among workers that there were no other credible
alternatives. Coming on the heels of the war strains, the revolution recast the
range of choice that both reformist and radical workers, and consequently the
middle classes, perceived. As the British reformist Seebohm Rowntree put it
in 1920, "We have come to regard many conditions as intolerable which
before had only seemed inevitable. . . . We have completely revised our
notions as to what is possible or impossible."[3]

By making plausible for the first time the idea of a workers' revolution,
the Russian Revolution raised the stakes of class politics and accentuated

class conflicts throughout Europe. The polarization that issued from these heightened hopes and fears led middle-class leaders to conflate Bolshevism, anarchism, syndicalism, and working-class reformism. In their panic, they attacked these various strands of the working class movement as if they were an undifferentiated mass. That the perceived danger of revolution was more than merely hypothetical seemed to be confirmed as attempted revolutions, street fighting, rumors of coups d'etat, and class-based civil wars swept across a European axis running from Leningrad to Madrid between 1917 and 1923. It is clear that, in 1919 and 1920 and in 1926 in Britain and 1934 and 1936 in France, some politicians even in these two countries thought that revolution was just around the corner. Confusing the prospective rebirth of the Triple Alliance with Bolshevism, Bonar Law cataclysmically prophesied to the Commons in March 1919 that: "If such a struggle comes, it can have only one end—or there is an end of government in this country."[4] A month later, Lloyd George told Law that "failure to win [against the threatened coal strike] would inevitably lead to a Soviet Republic—so that we ought to have our plans thoroughly worked out."[5]

In retrospect it seems certain that the revolutionary potential of British and French workers was extremely limited between the wars, and these limits were immanent in the prewar pattern of labor inclusion. Leaders of labor, industry, and government resorted to cataclysmic language partly in genuine fear and partly for political effect. Much of the fear of upheaval in Britain and France was induced by government ignorance of workers' attitudes and was colored by generalizations drawn from worker uprisings elsewhere in Europe.

That this was the case for France is especially significant, because the established order in France had been more vulnerable before 1914, and France had suffered much more in the war than the other democratic combatants. The constitutional order of the Third Republic never gained the measure of legitimacy acquired across the Channel or even across the Alps. For we have already seen that some parts of the French working class rejected the Republic even before the experience of the war and that for some other parts allegiance to the Republic was contingent. Also, an important fraction of the French Right had always disdained the Republic. In the interwar years, these two strands of anti-Republicanism appeared as communism and fascism. France, unlike most other continental societies, was able to endure the political storms of the interwar years without resorting to either a reorganization of liberal economic institutions, the abandonment of liberal economic policies, or the abandonment of democracy. The fascist threat was turned back, as previous threats to the Republic had been, by another coalition of parts of the middle classes and the workers. Communism, ironically, received its greatest popular support when it reversed itself and rallied to the Republic.[6]

At the outbreak of the First World War and during its first two and a half years, labor in Britain and France rallied almost without qualification to the defense of the liberal order. Socialist and Labor politicians entered national coalitions, and trade unionists were invited to participate in a plethora of industrial councils intended to manage war production. In exchange, governing coalitions promised a more equitable distribution of the national bounty after the war. Working-class dissent and strikes, rare during the first two years of the war and then limited to narrowly cast economic issues, became a growing problem in 1917 and exploded after the armistice.[7] In addition to demands for wage increases, union recognition, the eight-hour day and so forth, the strikes were accompanied by proposals from the trade unions and parties for reorganizations of the national economy premised on an authoritative union role in governing the economy, limited nationalization, greater worker participation in management, and major improvements in the range of social insurance programs. During and immediately after the war, trade unions in both countries, as elsewhere, experienced an explosion of membership. In France, CGT enrollment rose from about 700,000 in 1914 to 2 million in 1920; in Britain TUC membership rose from about 2.6 million in 1914 to 6.5 million in 1920. These new members came to the unions with vague but intensely held expectations of change that reflected the rising tide of unrest throughout society. They came into labor organizations lacking previous union experience and found no apparatus readily able to absorb and direct them. A great number represented a new type of member: unskilled and semiskilled machine operators. These new workers, especially in France, were products of a "second industrial revolution, violently carried through in the worst conditions."[8]

The middle-class governing coalitions in Britain and France responded in 1919 and 1920 to this labor unrest in a way that echoed the prewar experience, with a mixture of accommodation, assimilation, and control.[9] By 1921, in both countries the postwar boom had come to an end, unemployment was rising, protesters were exhausted and demoralized, union membership was declining, and the unions were receding in importance. In Britain, the deflation occurring in the second half of 1919 raised unemployment from 2 percent in 1919–20 to 12 percent by the middle of 1921.[10] Thereafter, it never dropped below 10 percent in the interwar years. TUC membership, having peaked at 6.5 million in 1919, began a steady decline that ran the course of the decade until it reached 3.6 million in 1929. The density of TUC membership fell from 55 percent of the male labor force in 1920 to 29 percent in 1931.[11] In France, unemployment was a less pressing constraint, never rising over 8 percent even in the depths of the 1930s depression.[12] Trade union membership fell from about 2 million in 1920 to 1.1 million in the CGT and CGTU seven years later.[13]

On the whole, the unions had very little to show for their efforts in the first two postwar years. On both sides of the Channel, governments and employers largely succeeded in rapidly restoring prewar industrial practices. The trade unions opposed this but were organizationally incapable of significantly modifying it, not to mention preventing it. These immediate postwar years were one of several critical periods in which labor had its best opportunity to improve substantially its position in the political and economic order. In Britain the next, and last, great surge of interwar labor protest would not occur until the General Strike of 1926. In France, labor would not assert itself again until the victory of the Popular Front and the General Strike in 1936. In all of these instances—1919–20, 1926, and 1936, which constituted the critical junctures at which an insurgent labor movement had, or parts of it thought it had, an historic opportunity to fundamentally change its political and economic position—the labor movement was defeated.

Setting aside for the moment the balance of party power, these defeats can be traced most immediately to the organizational incoherence and decentralization of the trade unions. In the French case, these obstacles to a more effective labor movement were reinforced by the split between communism and socialism, a split which itself was rooted in the prewar French experience. Except for the socialist–communist split, these were products of the movements' early success. In this sense, it was their very success before 1914 that came back to haunt and limit them after 1918. Before the war a decentralized and ill-coordinated union movement had been adequate because, on the one hand, a much smaller part of the labor force was enrolled and union demands were more limited, and, on the other hand, union activity seldom posed such a direct challenge to the state. In Britain, unions found a comparatively tolerant employer class and a reasonably accommodating state. In France, unions, although often pitted against intransigent employers, still had a measure of success because they found they could frequently induce the intervention of the state on their behalf. Indeed, this peculiar combination of a state ally and an intolerant employer class had the effect of making French unions doubly weak, because they were not only decentralized and poorly coordinated, but unlike their British counterparts, feebly established on the shop-floor as well. In either case, the obstacles to union success before the war were insufficient to make a more centralized and cohesive movement a rational response. The comparison between the two cases suggests that the key to centralization before the war was in the state's attitude. An intransigent employer class would not induce centralization unless it was reinforced by an antagonistic or indifferent state. If state assistance could be substituted to a degree for shop-floor organization, employer intransigence would merely produce a shop-floor vacuum and shift local associations to the more difficult-to-organize municipal level. Paradoxically, if both the state and employers were intransigent, as in Germany and other aliberal prewar societies, the outcome was a highly centralized and coordinated movement as well as a powerful shop-floor presence. In that situation, there was no alternative to powerful organizations. In Chapter 7 we examine the prewar organizational incoherence of British and French trade unions in light of the much more centralized and authoritative unions that appeared before the war in aliberal societies. Here we need mainly be concerned with the interwar consequences of that incoherence.

The war had the effect, through the explosion of union membership and the escalation of union demands, of making the unions more threatening not only to employers but to the state. Due to the nature of the union's demands, for the first time the state became a principal target of union activity. Moving beyond the relatively narrow confines of hours and wages and onto the broader plain of nationalization, regulation of whole industries, and national economic policy, the new claims of the unions had a quality that was inherently more menacing to the state. Moreover, the much larger number of workers that unions now sought to represent made their actions more disruptive of the economy. In consequence, once the wartime emergency had passed, the state was less likely to assist unions. It was more likely to play for time, as it did in 1919 and 1920, when it felt acutely threatened, or to sponsor the privatization of industrial relations as it did subsequently.

If the unions were to realize their loftier ambitions, or even to be effective on the narrower range of hour and wage claims for the much larger number of workers they now enrolled, a more effective set of organizations would be necessary. Within the unions, some certainly saw that a reorganization of labor itself, especially the creation of a more centralized and coherent trade union movement, was a prerequisite to an effective pursuit of either broader ambitions or the interests of more members. They sought to create more authoritative confederations and to reorganize unions on an industrial basis. Again, however, the relative success of labor before 1914 conditioned what was possible in the interwar years. As we shall see, attempts to create a more centralized and coherent trade union movement were repeatedly turned back because they threatened not simply the established political and economic order, but the political empires that union officials had created for themselves before and during the war.

It must be emphasized that these defeats were less the result of a hostile state than they were the result of fratricide in the labor movement itself. A reorganization of labor would have required a redistribution of power within the unions, and labor leaders had on their side an adequate mixture of organizational weapons, tradition, past success, and social acceptance to resist moves that threatened their status. It is of enormous importance, as we shall note, that it made little difference whether the insurgents were radicals or reformists, whether the dominant union leaders were radicals or reformists, or whether they were allied with a labor party that was radical or reformist. It was not ideology but the prewar inheritance that was determining here. And in limiting the reform of the labor movement, that prewar inheritance also limited the challenge to the liberal order and ensured its essential continuity. The double irony here is that it was the success of working-class movements before 1914 that decreased their likelihood of success after 1918 and thereby increased the likelihood that these societies would survive the interwar crises. To understand this, we must now examine in more detail the causes of labor's defeats in 1919–20, 1926, and 1936 and the failure of those who sought a more coherent trade union movement.

The Defeat of the Working-Class Movement
Britain

Before 1914, the Trades Union Congress amounted to little more than an annual gathering of union leaders. The Parliamentary Committee, which sought to maintain continuity between the annual congresses, was composed of individuals who devoted most of their time to concerns other than those of the TUC. The entire permanent staff of the TUC consisted of the Parliamentary Committee Secretary and a single clerk. The stepped-up relationship with the state and industry during the war encouraged the creation of a modest TUC staff to coordinate the activities of separate unions. Such coordination was especially encouraged by the introduction of industry-wide arbitration in 1915, which forced the multiple unions that typically organized a single industry to coordinate their pay claims. Improved coordination was also encouraged by the concentration of industry that war production fostered. For many socialists in the union movement, this concentration in industry foreshadowed the coming of the socialist state, with the giant private monopolies ultimately being converted to public ownership. During the war, the government had in fact temporarily taken over such industries as coal and the railroads and directly intervened in the management of many others. Until the arrival of public ownership, it was clear to many trade unionists that the increasing concentration and centralization of the capitalist economy required a similar reorganization of labor. Only by concentrating its power in a more authoritative national confederation and by moving from craft and general unions to industry-wide unions could the trade union movement act as a countervailing force to large-scale capitalist industry.

This need had long been stressed by socialists in the unions, but before the war only limited headway had been made. During the war, some advances occurred in achieving closer working relations between the various unions: a number of federations were formed, and after the Armistice a number of important union mergers resulted in the creation of very large organizations such as the Amalgamated Engineering Union and the Transport and General Workers Union. As far as improved coordination of union activity was concerned, however, the enlargement of the general unions was a problematic gain, for the number of unions operating in many industries increased. This progress in consolidating the forces of labor was offset to some extent by the vast increase in union membership that took place in the years up to 1920, for many of the new recruits formed their own unions rather than joining those already in existence, thus multiplying the number of separate organizations and intensifying the problem of coordinating union activity.

Industrial unionism was one of the great causes of the British trade union left in the 1920s, but one that made only marginal progress. It drew its support from left-wing elements and from unions, irrespective of ideology, already constituted on an industrial basis. The reorganization that had been implemented in 1921 to govern elections to the TUC General Council was an expressed aspiration to move to industrial unionism from a hodge-podge of industrial, craft, and general unions. Since 1923, the General Council had made several efforts to promote amalgamation among unions in individual industries, sponsoring conferences in the metal trades, textiles, printing, the post office, insurance, dyeing and bleaching, distribution, leather, and building. By the Edinburgh TUC in 1927, the single success was in the unimportant case of the amalgamation of the dyeing and bleaching unions in January 1927.

As the General Council observed, "however desirous it may be to achieve amalgamations amongst its constituent unions, the real driving force must come from the unions themselves, and no efforts which the council may make can accomplish their object if they are met in a reluctant spirit."[14] It was, of course, the vested interests of the established unions, especially the general unions, that made for this "reluctant spirit." The successful amalgamation of several craft unions in the most important general union, the Transport and General Workers Union, evidenced the obstacles that had to be overcome. Immediately after the war, various schemes were discussed for amalgamating the general and transport workers. Mergers required the approval of the rank-and-file, and in this the attitudes of union leaders were critical. The first attempt was a merger of the London Dockworkers and the General Workers. The rank-and-file of the former rejected the merger, and the general conclusion was that the Dockers' leader, Ernest Bevin, was unenthusiastic because he would not have been the chief officer of the amalgamated union. Bevin subsequently pursued a different amalgamation scheme including the Transport Workers Federation and the General Workers, a combination of unions in which Bevin was more likely to win a position of leadership. Bevin pursued this tenaciously, and had no trouble persuading his own Dockers to endorse it. As expected, he was elected general secretary of the new union.

The creation of the new union was revealing as well because it required a system of dual administration. This involved creating both a national executive and "trade group secretaryships and national trade group committees, which could be used to persuade the secretaries and executives of interested unions that, if they joined, they would continue to hold positions of wide-ranging authority within the new organization."[15] The making of such trade groups was inherent to the logic of general unionism and the basis for its appeal against industrial unionism.

The principal argument used to defend the established order was that technological change made for constantly shifting boundaries that prevented the drawing of clear-cut lines between industries. "The real point, however, was that in practical terms industrial unionism was ruled out because it would mean the dismembering of the General Unions, which the latter would never agree to."[16] The General Council's conclusion on amalgamation, which derived from a realistic assessment of its own lack of authority, was that any amalgamation would have to be on the initiative of the individual unions. This conclusion was affirmed by a vote of 2 million to 1.8 million at the 1927 TUC. In this, the attitudes of the two largest general unions, the National Union of General and Municipal Workers and the Transport and General Workers Union—whose general workers section gave it a stake in "half the industries and services in the country"[17]—were decisive in defeating the efforts of the left and the industrial unions. The 1927 vote came to be accepted as authoritative, and little more was heard of amalgamation until after 1945.[18]

Beyond the failure of industrial unionism, the labor movement was further handicapped by the absence of a single directing agency for the movement as a whole. The TUC was a powerless vacuum at the head of the movement. Ernest Bevin properly described the movement in 1919 as "a great shapeless mass, all the time struggling to coordinate its efforts, but finding itself without a head to direct."[19] The lack of an effective center had two consequences in 1919 and 1920. First, it meant that the substantial gains in wages and shorter hours of the immediate postwar boom were somewhat transient; when the trade cycle turned downward wage declines outpaced price declines, so that the unions were only partially successful in preserving the earlier wage gains.[20] Labor's postwar offensive took the form of a series of uncoordinated strikes that were capable of gaining these short-term concessions but not of preserving them or gaining a fundamental change in the position of workers in industry. This missed opportunity for fundamental change was the second consequence of the absence of an effective center in 1919 and 1920.

There was no shortage of strategies for the reform of British society at the end of the war; such strategies were advanced under the rubric of "reconstruction." Throughout the war years and during the 1918 election—in which Lloyd George campaigned on a reform platform of "homes fit for heroes"—the government repeatedly pledged reconstruction. A Ministry for Reconstruction was established and countless conferences and studies commissioned to plan an enlarged state role in the economy and social reform. Lloyd George himself set the tone when he responded in March 1917 to the Labor party demand for nationalization with the much-publicized promise: "I believe the settlement after the war will succeed in proportion to its audacity."[21] Although the meaning of reconstruction varied, in addition to an extension of the suffrage, it minimally connoted an enlargement of the welfare state, especially in the areas of housing and education, an enlarged role for trade unions in governing circles, and some measure of compensation through improved wages and working conditions for the sacrifices labor had made during the war.

Labor assumed, and the government implied, that these improved wages and conditions would be obtained by continuing some measure of the wartime collectivism after the war. The trade unions had very concrete and optimistic expectations of what reconstruction would entail. Beyond the extension of the suffrage, which was expected to make the Labor Party a major player for the first time (a notion quickly disabused by the 1918 poll), the unions anticipated the legal establishment of the forty-eight-hour work week; legislated wage minimums; the restoration of the prewar restrictive practices that had been diluted; a much enlarged housing and education program; a return to free collective bargaining based on national (as against district or local) agreements; an extensive continued government role in the management of industry and trade union participation in management; stepped-up government consultation with the unions; and nationalization of at least the railroads and mines.

As late as July 1919 Lloyd George was willing to contemplate "such radical proposals as abandoning support of the exchange rate, fostering new industries, protection against foreign dumping, state investment in weak but essential industries like iron and steel, and control over electricity generation, standardization and industrial research."[22] By the second half of 1919, however, reconstruction was obviously in jeopardy, under growing pressure from business for decontrol, reduced wages, and longer hours, from the Treasury for spending cuts, and from Tory MPs for a government withdrawal from industrial relations. Between 1919 and 1921, the government found itself uncomfortably compelled to act as a mediator between business, pressing for decontrol and wage reductions, and unions, threatening direct action to prevent these. The government's central dilemma was that whenever it pressed management to concede workers' demands it further politicized industrial relations. Failing to apply such pressure, however, risked an immediate explosion of industrial unrest. The essence of the government's strategy was to play for time, making concessions as necessary to workers, propping up more moderate union leaders, and splitting the Triple Alliance from the TUC. By the time Lloyd George's government fell in 1922, wartime controls had largely been dropped, reconstruction abandoned, and social spending scaled back. The unions were divided and in retreat in the face of an employer campaign for wage reductions. It was "possibly the most significant defeat ever suffered by the British labor movement."[23]

In large measure, this defeat was a result of the lack of coherent strategy such as an authoritative trade union center might have provided. This was especially apparent in the labor movement's response to the National Industrial Conference (NIC) and to the Whitely Committee. In February 1919, the government called a National Industrial Conference, with the claimed objective of promoting a better climate of industrial relations. The attitude of the union movement was divided, as it had been earlier to the proposals of the government's Whitely Committee in 1917. The latter had sought to improve the status of workers by giving unions more say in general matters affecting industry, aside from wages and hours. It had proposed the creation of Joint Councils for each industry, with subsidiary bodies at the level of the district and the individual firm. The report had been endorsed by the government, but the unions' reactions to it were divided, and the TUC took no definite position on it. For the trade union left, the Whitely Committee report appeared to be an attempt to divert the unions from claims to real authority in industry. The left now saw the call for a National Industrial Conference in much the same terms. Some unions agreed to participate, but the three most powerful unions who formed the Triple Alliance—the Miners, Railwaymen, and Transport workers—declined. They saw the conference, no doubt correctly, as a government ploy to divert union militancy. The unions that participated, too, reached the same conclusion and withdrew in 1921. Before they did so they made a number of thoughtful proposals urging the government to maintain full employment by introducing public works schemes and minimum wages. Given the critical dependence of the union movement on tightness in the labor markets for its success and the subsequent downturn that erased most of its immediate postwar gains, these proposals were of obvious importance. But they suffered severely in 1919 because they did not have the weight of much of the union movement behind them. One must wonder to what extent the government and employers were able to succeed in their strategy of playing for time precisely because they were not confronted by a united and determined union movement. A more coherent movement might have compelled the government to bargain more forthrightly. Even if we assume that the moderate union strategy that participation in the NIC implied was futile, we cannot suppose the more uncompromising strategy of those who rejected the NIC would be any more effective. For as it turned out, just as the movement refused to unite behind a common position in the NIC, it also refused to unite behind the more uncompromising strategy endorsed by the Triple Alliance and especially by the Miners' Federation. Either way, it was the absence of subtending coherence that was responsible for the failures of these years.

Early in 1919 the Miners' Federation of Great Britain (MFGB) had demanded nationalization of the mining industry and a substantial increment of worker control in management. In response, and to buy time, the government appointed the Sankey Commission to study nationalization. By August 1919, the government felt it could openly reject the Miners' demand, although the commission narrowly endorsed nationalization. The announcement rejecting nationalization was accompanied by a refusal to introduce legislation limiting hours or minimum wages, and movement to a more orthodox, deflationary economic policy that included reductions in housing expenditures and other social programs. The Miners, after discussions with their Triple Alliance partners, agreed to defer a strike until after the annual TUC met in Glasgow. At the Congress, the Miners sought movement support for their demands for joint control and nationalization, with the implication that a general strike would be resorted to if necessary to force the government's hand. Understanding this implication, the Congress agreed to review the issue only if the government remained obdurate, and in the meantime to support a campaign of education on behalf of nationalization. This compromise was forced on the Miners by their own allies in the Triple Alliance, the Railwaymen. The National Union of Railwaymen, in principle committed to the nationalization of its own industry, was unwilling to endorse the Miners because it had just completed its own strike on behalf of higher wages. The strike, which paralyzed the country for nine days (Lloyd George called it a "civil war"[24]), forced the personal intervention of Lloyd George when it began to spread to the dockworkers. The upshot was a major wage victory for the railwaymen and, subsequently, for the dockers. It is particularly instructive that an ad hoc "Mediation Committee" of leaders of unions affected by the strike persuaded the government that if "they persisted with their attack on railway wages, widely seen as the beginning of a general counter-offensive against wartime wage gains, widespread sympathetic action could not be avoided."[25] The Railwaymen's leadership was not willing to force a confrontation with the government over nationalization or to coordinate its own strike activity with that of the Miners. When the government's position was unyielding on the railways, the Railwaymen's leadership called a strike without consulting the MFGB. Having just struck alone against the government, albeit with the support of the Mediation Committee, the railway workers' leaders could not now credibly threaten to strike again on behalf of nationalization of the mines, even if they had been inclined to do so.

Not surprisingly, the propaganda campaign on behalf of nationalization was a failure, and when a special TUC met again in the spring of 1920 to reconsider supporting the Miners, the Miners were again told no support would be forthcoming for industrial action for nationalization. Thenceforth, the Miners dropped the demand for nationalization, but by the autumn of 1920 Miners' wages were back on the agenda, since the government was now set to decontrol the industry. War control had involved the creation of a national profits pool, a system that made it possible for the MFGB to negotiate wages nationally. Decontrol would end the pool and force a return to district negotiations, which would allow the owners to play off one district against another and destroy the federation. In October 1920, the Miners struck for a wage increase and against decontrol. As in the case of the railway strike a year earlier, it was the threat of sympathetic action that forced the government to compromise, offering an immediate wage increase and negotiations with the owners to establish a national wage board.

Shortly after this, the price of coal began to fall and the government, caught paying a growing subsidy to the industry, announced it would bring forward the date of decontrol to the end of March. There was now no possibility that the owners would agree to a national wages board. The outcome would be the end of the profits pool, a shift to district settlements, and sharp wage reductions. On April 1, the Miners struck. After some hesitation, the leaders of the Railwaymen and the Transport Workers agreed to strike from April 15, but then reversed themselves at the last moment. This reversal—known as "Black Friday"—marked the end of the Triple Alliance as an effective threat and the beginning of a major employer campaign against wages. After three months, the Miners went back at wages that, in many cases, left them worse off than they had been before the war.

The point is not whether nationalization was a sound or unsound objective, whether a general strike was a proper or improper strategy, whether the miners' expectations were realistic or unrealistic given the declining price of coal, but that the movement was incapable of formulating any coherent objectives or strategy in the absence of a powerful coordinating center. As it was, literally no one with any authority even thought about, much less acted on, coherent strategy for the trade union movement, as opposed to the constituent unions. The result was that choices tended to be framed in ways that were almost guaranteed to bring about the long-run failure of the unions. That is, the choices the unions faced were almost always cataclysmic; capitulation or a general strike. Neither the organizational capacity nor the planning facilities to devise and implement more subtle strategies was available. As it happened, the trade union movement was incapable of securing any fundamental changes in industry in 1919 or 1920. It could not secure continuation of collectivism, the moderate objectives of implementation of the Whitely Committee report, or the full-employment policies, 48-hour week, or wage minimums discussed at the Industrial Conference or the establishment of National Industrial Councils also discussed there. Nor had it achieved the nationalization and workers' control preferred by the Triple Alliance. Even Lloyd George's watered-down tripartism floundered. Such collaboration "was, at this stage of history, inconceivable, because the TUC could not become representative, even if the Cabinet had not pursued its vendetta against the Triple Alliance."[26] The reality was that the union movement had no program, strategy, or agency to direct its activity. The result was that it had achieved virtually nothing and stood ready to lose even the wage and hour gains it had obtained. When the boom broke in 1920, "the trade unions found themselves on the defensive in a world that was uncomfortably like that of pre-1914."[27] By 1924, money wages had fallen by up to a third.[28]

The problem was not that trade union leaders were unaware of the need for an effective central authority; it was that they were unwilling to cede authority to such an agency. The 1919 railway strike, in particular, prompted efforts to create such an agency in the form of a TUC General Council that would supersede the old Parliamentary Committee. Under a scheme devised by G. D. H. Cole, the unions were to be divided into seventeen industrial groups, each of which would nominate a number of candidates for its quota of seats on the council. They would be elected, however, by the TUC as a whole. The point was to strengthen the authority of the central body. This, however, represented the limit of the movement's willingness to accept centralization. The unions rejected proposals to give the council a permanent secretary elected by the TUC as a whole rather than the council, and rejected proposals that would have given the council the implicit authority to limit strike activity. The new council actually changed the TUC very little. It lacked any executive authority over unions, it had no authority to mediate, and there was no limitation on the autonomy of unions, no control over strike decisions, the timing or coordination of strikes, or the use of strike funds. Indeed, the individual unions were under no requirement even to consult with the council. This absence of authority reflected an understanding on the part of the council's sponsors that the individual unions would accept nothing more. The positive functions of the council were left largely undefined. In effect, the council could function as little more than an agency for collecting and sharing information, the TUC staff being particularly concerned on this point because it often learned of strikes only by reading about them in the newspapers.[29]

Between 1921 and 1924 various proposals were made to the TUC to strengthen the hand of the General Council. Until the 1924 TUC, the proposals were always rejected by unions unwilling to cede any of their authority. During these same years, unions fought a defensive action to preserve the wage gains and shorter hours they had won in 1919 and 1920. In general, the eight-hour day was preserved, but the record of success on wages was more mixed as employers took advantage of the weaker labor market to regain their profit margins. Employment rose some in 1924, signaling the end of the slump, but then leveled off with at least a million out of work for the remainder of the decade. Defensiveness thus was the main characteristic of trade union activity for the balance of the decade. Employer demands for wage reductions were reinforced when Britain returned to the Gold Standard in 1925 at prewar parity. With the pound so overvalued, export industries had a special incentive to demand wage reductions.

It was in this context that the mine owners demanded wage reductions and longer days of miners in 1925. The MFGB turned for assistance to the General Council in July 1925. With nationalization no longer an issue, the council agreed to intervene on behalf of the Miners and mobilize, if it came to it, a general strike to support the Miners' position. The miners, the best organized workers in the country, could plausibly argue that they were fighting on behalf of all trade unionists, for if the owners could force wage reductions on them, employers elsewhere would rush to follow suit in their own industries.[30]

The General Council offered its support because it had been successful in winning an increment of authority from the TUC in 1924. At the 1924 Congress, a resolution had been approved giving the council the authority to mediate disputes and, failing in that, to mobilize support for a union thus engaged in a strike. The council acquired this additional authority—minus the organizational apparati or sanctions required to make it effective—because a pronounced shift to the left had occurred on the council and in the TUC in 1924. This shift was provoked by dissatisfaction with the orthodox performance of the first Labor government and with continued high unemployment. Unions, especially the Miners, who had previously been loath to cede authority to the council when they expected its moderate majority would use new powers mainly to restrain unions, were more willing to grant the authority when they expected a left majority on the council would use the new powers mainly to rally support. However, there were definite limits to the authority the unions would cede, even when the council was controlled by a left majority. Neither in 1924 nor in 1925, when control of the council was still in the hands of the left, was the TUC willing to grant the council the authority to call unions out on strike, to stop a strike from occurring, or to terminate one. Opinion on such a grant of authority was divided, and a motion supporting it was thus set aside for further study.[31] The relationship of the constituent unions to the council thus remained a purely voluntary one—and one, as it would soon turn out, that was inadequate.

It was inadequate because, as the General Strike of 1926 demonstrated, the council had only a very limited and peculiar brand of authority. It had the authority to ask unions to strike in support of the miners when they were already inclined to do so, but it had the authority neither to reach a settlement on behalf of the miners nor to control the activities of strikers. The prelude to the strike, the 1925 crisis, is revealing. By threatening an embargo on coal deliveries, the council had been able to induce the Baldwin government to subsidize the industry until 1926 and thereby relieve pressure on wages. It was an important victory for the council, but it also foreshadowed the failure of 1926. For the council had emphasized organizing support for the miners while they were left free to define their own program. The miners' unqualified rejection of wage reductions, an increase in the seven-hour day, and an end to national agreements in favor of regional agreements had not been questioned. Under the circumstances, this was a brand of central authority that any union would welcome—unqualified support for unqualified demands—but that was inherently untenable. The Baldwin government's capitulation to the threat of an embargo was a defeat that the government would not be willing to suffer again but that diverted attention from the inherent inadequacy of General Council authority.

As the expiration of the subsidy in May 1926 approached and the government prepared for coal deliveries in the face of another embargo, it became obvious that, barring an unexpected last minute settlement, a general strike would ensue.[32] The council arranged to coordinate strike activity and to negotiate on behalf of the miners. Given the generalized threat of wage reductions and the high level of tension in the labor movement, the council encountered little opposition in mobilizing support for the miners. A nearly complete stoppage would occur in transport, printing, building, iron and steel, electricity and gas, and of course in mining. If necessary, further industries would subsequently be called out. The second aspect of the council's scheme turned out to be more difficult to implement. The miners were unwilling to accept any modification of their three-point position and insisted that the council, although it could represent them, could not accept a settlement for them. In effect, then, the dilemma for the council was that it had no negotiating authority.

This dilemma was compounded because once the strike was underway it quickly became apparent that the government's preparations were sufficient to defeat the strike in the long run unless the unions escalated the dispute. Caught between its lack of negotiating authority and the need to escalate in order to win, the council quickly backed down. It embraced the mere hope that the terms of a settlement suggested by a Royal Commission would be acceptable to both sides (they were acceptable to neither) and called off the strike. The miners were left to fight alone. The damage done to the reputation of the TUC was so profound, and the prospects for a more centralized union movement so irremediably damaged, that the conduct of the council has been the source of endless debates in the historiography of British trade unionism.

Whatever the wisdom, or lack of it, of the council's decisions, the strike and the council's decision to terminate it put certain inherent deficiencies in the authority structure of the union movement in bas-relief. First, the miners were absolutely opposed to ceding to the council the authority to decide a settlement for them. Even if the strike had been successful, the council would still have lacked the authority necessary, for it could hardly be expected that this pattern could be replicated in other industries. Applied to other industries, it was an arrangement that would have destroyed the union movement. Moreover, there is no reason to suppose that, after the heat of 1926 had subsided, the council could have continued to mobilize unions on each others' behalf for non-negotiable positions. Insofar as the miners and other unions were unwilling to cede authority, then, any victory would once again have been a purely singular affair. And the fact that even after the council called off the strike the miners continued for many months to strike alone and to insist on their three points suggests that things would not have been different even if the council had stuck by the miners. For the rest of the union movement could not have been expected to hold out indefinitely. It was, as the council perceived, only a matter of time until its defeat—unless it could escalate the dispute.

And this brings us to the second salient feature of the strike—the overwhelming fear (terror is a more apt description) on the part of the council that if it escalated the dispute, it would lose control of its troops. Escalating the dispute implied taking steps to disrupt the emergency arrangements the state had made, arrangements that were becoming more effective by the day. Such an open challenge to the authority of the state, by vigorous picketing, for instance, ran the risk of exploding into a physical confrontation that would involve rioting and bloodshed unless the council could keep a very tight reign on the escalation. And the council obviously lacked the organizational infrastructure that would have provided it with such a tight reign. Faced with the potential for violence, aware of its lack of control, and without the authority to actually negotiate for the miners, the council capitulated.

It can always be argued that if different individuals had been in control of the council, it might have made different decisions leading to a different outcome. This possibility cannot be denied, but it can be discounted. A different council, one controlled by the trade union left, would have faced the same institutional handicaps. It might have faced them later rather than sooner, and it might have faced them after more rather than less violence had occurred (the strike was remarkably free of violence), but it would certainly have faced them. To suppose otherwise is to deny the institutional handicaps under which the council operated, and the position is simply not tenable. A genuinely revolutionary council might even then have decided to press on. But to presume a genuinely revolutionary council is to posit an entirely different labor movement. Even on the left, there were virtually no genuine revolutionaries. It seems most plausible to suppose that a different leadership, as long as it was committed to constitutional limits, might have resulted in a denouement that was different on the margins and in its timing, but, given the institutional deficiencies of the labor movement, the strike was ultimately doomed to fail.

If this much can be granted, it can immediately be seen that the unfavorable balance of probabilities was substantially determined by the prewar experience. For it was that prewar experience that had generated a trade union movement whose leaders were overwhelmingly committed to the constitutional order and a trade union structure that, in large measure because of its early success, debilitated subsequent attempts to exercise authority from the center. If the absence of central authority and the incoherence of the union movement are necessary parts of an explanation of the trade union movement's defeats in these years, it cannot be inferred that greater centralization and coherence alone would have been sufficient to make the movement victorious. Even in the absence of a more favorable party political balance, a better organized movement could no doubt have been more effective, but a fundamentally different outcome in 1926 required a sympathetic government. Such a different outcome was at least outlined by the proposals of the Tory Labor Minister, Arthur Steel-Maitland, and by the proposals of the Samuel Commission, the commission that had been charged with the review of the coal industry in 1925–26. The commission had recommended against the lengthening of the work day or the end of national agreements. These were to be preserved but accompanied by wage cuts, stepped-up investment, and a reorganization of the industry that would close down inefficient pit heads. Labor would have to be persuaded to accept the lost jobs and wages in exchange for a larger share in future profits. Such an industrial pact required a government willing to impose the reorganization on the owners and willing to guarantee the level of investment required. Such a pact might have served as a model for a range of industries, especially if combined with such government concessions to labor as the ratification of the 1921 Washington Convention on the 48-hour week. This alternative vision of industrial relations was advanced, with little effect, by Steel-Maitland.[33]

It was not, however, one that a Tory government fundamentally in sympathy with the coal owners could be expected to pursue. It required a different balance of political power, and that balance was just as much precluded by the prewar experience of labor inclusion as the incoherence of the union movement was determined by it. The weakness of the Labor party provides the conditioning background to the behavior of the unions in these years. After the disappointing experience of the first minority Labor government, it was brought home to the unions that they were not going to have a reliable and effective political ally for a long time to come. If the absence of a coherent organization made it likely that the General Strike would fail, the absence of a sympathetic government made it likely that it would occur, for without a political ally the unions could defend themselves only by industrial action.

To complete the story, then, it is necessary to account for the weakness of the Labor party. This, too, was rooted in the prewar hegemony of liberals. It was no longer, however, simply a matter of a low level of working-class consciousness and a correspondingly low level of working-class support for the party. The connection was more subtle than that: the same lack of critical cleavages within the middle classes that had made possible liberal hegemony before 1914 now made possible a cohesive right. This cohesiveness, in turn, deprived the Labor party of the opportunity to manipulate enduring divisions among nonsocialist parties and thereby gain the kind of reliable ally that would have given it effective political power. We will return to this point through a comparative analysis after examining the incoherence of the French trade unions and its consequences between the wars.

France

The postwar defeat of the CGT was quick in coming, thoroughgoing, and unambiguous. Like the TUC, the CGT assumed that at least some measure of the cooperation between labor, the state and capital that had developed during the war would continue after the armistice. Through this collaboration, French workers had acquired important new potential rights. Government agencies had required collective bargaining procedures of their suppliers, and industries classified as essential to the war effort had been required to introduce compulsory arbitration and parity committees of workers and managers to resolve disputes. It was generally assumed on the left that these gains would be consolidated and extended after the war.[34]

The CGT's vision of the postwar order was proclaimed in its "Minimum Program," adopted immediately after the armistice in 1918. Despite the vagueness of many of its formulas and the radical intonation of its rhetoric, the program reflected the reformism the CGT had unambiguously embraced during the war and would pursue after the turmoil of 1919 and 1920 and the exit of the communists in 1921. The program proposed social reform within the existing society, nationalization of several key industries, and the creation of a National Economic Council in which labor would have vested representation. The most immediate ambitions of the CGT were to raise wages to offset the losses of wartime inflation and to gain the legal enactment of the eight-hour day and forty-eight-hour week. The program also demanded the determination of wages by collective bargaining, the extension of trade union rights to government employees, and the establishment or enlargement of old age, sickness, disability, and unemployment insurance. The CGT expected that at least industries such as the railways, which had been taken over by the state during the war, would be nationalized. Rather than state ownership, it proposed that nationalized industries be administered as mixed public corporations by representatives of workers, managers, and consumers.[35]

As in Britain, many trade union leaders in France saw little hope of achieving the goals of the labor movement if implementation of those goals was left to the hodge-podge of national and regional unions that made up the trade union movement and officially convened as the CGT just once every two years. In 1912, CGT Secretary General Léon Jouhaux established the CGT makeup as a collection of national federations and departmental (mixed trade) unions. Local unions (*syndicats*) could belong to the CGT only indirectly, through their membership in these two overlapping sets of organizations. In addition, Jouhaux promoted consolidation of rival federations and brought the parallel *bourses du travail* under the control of the departmental unions. The dual set of constituent organizations sent delegates to the CGT Congress every two years, but the CGT still had no real corporate or financial substance.[36]

Only the advent of the war and Clemenceau's policy of involving labor in the management of wartime production thrust the CGT leadership into the limelight. The CGT's wartime prominence, however, was contingent on Clemenceau's sufferance, the availability of resources quite outside of CGT control and for ends that were defined mainly by Clemenceau rather than the CGT. When the state's agenda changed, that sufferance and those resources could just as easily be withdrawn, taking with them much of the CGT's authority.[37]

In December 1918, Jouhaux asked for and obtained structural reforms that were intended to strengthen and institutionalize the central authority of the confederation. In an effort to bolster the organizational resources at his command, Jouhaux proposed the creation of a standing Comité Confédéral National (CCN) comprising the heads of all the national federations and departmental unions and intended to serve as a policymaking body in the interims between congresses. In between the CCN's three or four annual meetings, a smaller Comité Administratif, drawn from CCN members residing in the Paris region, would be available for consultation and direction.[38]

Still, the CGT lacked both the authority and the confidence to call unilaterally or terminate a strike. When the confederation began to consider industrial action on behalf of the Minimum Program, its first move was to establish a cartel of the main federations (construction, road transport, railroad, seamen, miners, dockers, and metalworkers) to support the project. It was, in fact, this body of selected federation representatives that would decide whether strikes would be sanctioned in the first year after the armistice. The reasons for this extra ad hoc body were simple: despite the prestige that had derived from having the ear of the government during and immediately after the war and despite the increased institutionalization of its decision-making apparatus, the CGT still lacked the independent legitimacy and means required to call or control strikes.[39] What became clear in the major strikes of 1919 and 1920 was that the federations, normally as organizationally undeveloped and financially enfeebled as the CGT itself, also lacked the capacity to control their constituents.

Employers and the state in France, as in Britain and elsewhere immediately after the war, responded to the labor unrest with a mixture of concessions and temporizing. The Clemenceau government appointed the CGT leader, Léon Jouhaux, to the Peace Conference delegation, committed itself to the labor clauses of the Versailles Treaty and, most important, put through legislation in April 1919 enacting a general eight-hour day. The legislation was only an enabling act, which left the specifics to be negotiated between employers and the unions. Legislation making collective agreements legally enforceable for the time was also approved. The number of collective agreements grew rapidly at first: in 1919 (the peak year until 1936) 557 new agreements were registered with the Ministry of Labor, compared to a prewar high of 252 in 1910 and a wartime low of virtually none in 1915 and 1916.[40] With a booming economy, a CGT membership that grew from under a million in 1914 to over 2 million in 1919, and a state and employer class on the defensive, the number of strikes for shorter hours and higher wages exploded, and many of these were temporarily successful.

As in Britain, several critical historical moments can be found in this labor unrest, and in these moments the debilitating effect of the inherited lack of coherence and central authority in the trade union movement can be seen. The first of these was the strike in 1919 by 200,000 metalworkers in the Paris region. The Federation of Metalworkers had just succeeded in negotiating the first national agreement ever reached between a national employers' association and a national federation. The agreement provided for the implementation of the eight-hour day and wage increases. The strike began as a repudiation of the terms of the agreement and of the national metalworkers leadership by a departmental consortium of local unions (Comité d'entente). Having seized authority from the national federation, the local unions quickly lost control of the strike to improvised communal "action committees," which were themselves incapable of either coordinating their actions or inducing workers to remain out. While the action committees professed social revolution in Saint-Denis and other communes around Paris, the employers responded with a lockout. The federation was forced, hat in hand so to speak, to reenter negotiations with the Paris employers. On June 21, the federation managed to obtain an agreement confirming the forty-eight-hour week without a wage cut, that is, without the previously negotiated increase in wages. This agreement did not persuade the strike leaders to call for an immediate return to work, but by the end of the month the strike collapsed as workers began to return to the shops on their own. In the end, the workers got neither the terms of the original agreement nor the revolutionary demands articulated by some of the action committees. It was, in fact, a catastrophic defeat, for it left the workers worse off—many were dismissed and employers took the offensive—than they were beforehand. Moreover, the strike was a turning point, because it led to an awareness on the part of the government and the employers that they had the upper hand.[41]

The definitive labor defeat occurred with the railway and general strike of 1920. An irregular but successful rail strike in February 1920 was settled by government intervention. The accord on which the settlement was based allowed for revocations and other sanctions that had been declared before the accord but halted any further sanctions. The imposition of those sanctions was nonetheless seen as an act of bad faith by many trade unionists since the strike had been a success; the success of a strike had traditionally been measured by the absence or withdrawal of employer sanctions.[42] Late in April, the federation called the workers out again, effective May 1, demanding the withdrawal of all sanctions and immediate nationalization of the lines. The federation's national council was divided between the left and the right, but this division seems not to have been decisive, because the left had a definite majority. More debilitating was the lack of a coherent strategy: the plans for nationalization had not been worked out and were hardly understood by the rank-and-file, much less the general public. Half of the members did not answer the strike call and instead worked double shifts. The government kept some traffic moving and provisioned Paris. So ill-planned was the strike, which was given an explicitly revolutionary color by the union's dominant left, that when the government arrested the executive committee on May 2, no substitute leadership was authorized to take over until May 5, when the CGT intervened to appoint interim officers.[43] The union had not consulted the CGT in calling the strike, which the CGT had in fact tried to discourage. But given the fast approaching May 1 deadline, the union persuaded the CGT leadership to back it with a call for a general strike.

> This was one of the best examples in French labor history of the absolute autonomy of the groups constituting the General Confederation of Labor. The Federation of Railwaymen made an independent declaration of strike upon a basis which would practically demand the support of other organizations. Although the strike order was issued independently by the railwaymen, before assurance of support was secured from the General Confederation of Labor, the central organization decided to uphold their action. The majority of the General Confederation was not enthusiastic, and that organization was forced into the strike by the revolutionary elements. It had long been a principal claim of the General Confederation that the essential industries of France should be nationalized. When, therefore, the railwaymen, one of the most powerful federations in the syndicalist movement, declared a general strike in favor of nationalization, the General Confederation was helpless to refuse to support the strike, and was forced to enter the struggle at the side of the radicals. . . . "The strike was voted . . . not with the enthusiasm of men who go to battle with the conviction of triumph; they went to battle because they were obliged to go."[44]

Three successive "waves of assault," a week apart, were to paralyze the national economy. After the first (miners, dockers, and seamen) and second waves (metalworkers, road transport, and building trades) were launched, it was clear that the strike was going to be another catastrophic failure. The third wave was never called out. A month after the strike had begun, the last of the railwaymen went back to work completely beaten. Twenty thousand railwaymen were dismissed and the government initiated court proceedings to dissolve the CGT.[45]

Much has been made of the ideological conflicts between the left and right in the interwar French labor movement, especially regarding the failure of the strikes immediately after the war.[46] In fact, these ideological differences had little to do with the failure of the strikes. Ideological competition became important as a flag for competition between different levels of authority and different principles of organization within the labor movement. The 1919 metalworkers strike and the 1920 railway workers strike were cases of burgeoning subunits of the union movement exercising their own authority—in fact, seeking to preserve historically confirmed prerogatives—in ways that the nominally superordinate entities were powerless to prevent.

The Federation of Metalworkers' paying membership was severely reduced at the outset of the war, from about 27,000 in 1913 to just 1,000 in 1915. Thanks to the introduction of production-line methods in the many new establishments opened to produce for the war, the pool of workers and dues-paying equivalents and estimated members (members paid their dues, on average, about half the time) rose to 100,000 and 200,000, respectively, by the end of 1918. In 1919 paid membership suddenly leaped to 150,000. In spite of the defeat of the 1919 strike, paid membership continued to climb to 200,000 in the first half of 1920.[47] The railroad workers' membership likewise exploded: from a wartime low of 11,000 to 352,000 in 1920.[48] The problem for the unions was that they lacked an organizational network capable of absorbing and directing even the small number of prewar members, much less the new ones. Much of the ideological conflict within the movement in 1919 and 1920 is most instructively seen as a contest over the kind of organization that should be created to harness the energy of the new members. As it was, although the metalworkers' and railroad workers' unions were sometimes capable of unleashing a strike, they proved as impotent as their superiors in the CGT in controlling their subordinates. In the absence of an effective organization, the energy released by the growth of membership was simply dissipated. It was more fundamentally this organizational weakness rather than ideological struggles as such that debilitated the movement.

The essential distinction between the right and left in this period was that the latter anticipated the escalation of labor conflicts into a social revolution while the right found this thinking, at the least, problematic and at worst extremely dangerous. Consequently, the *minoritaires* tended to favor most strikes while the *majoritaires* were more circumspect.[49]

It is insufficient to leave the distinction between the left and right at that, however. For as the very terms suggest, these two tendencies complemented each, with the right majority initially controlling most of the positions of trade union power. Nevertheless, both had significant influence and played off of each other, much as two political parties that are about to reverse roles in government and opposition. Thus, many of the statements and actions of the opposition minority were as much bids for power as genuine expressions of ideology. For example, when a strike did not escalate into social revolution, as the left putatively expected, this was blamed on the right. As the Bolshevik revolution and postwar mobilization began to shift the balance of power in favor of the left, this counterbalancing relationship became more unstable.[50] When a dissident faction gained control of local, departmental, or federal leadership, it often found itself without a vocal opposition to enforce moderation and a refinement of goals. More important, the strike plans were distinctly nonorganizational: once a strike was called, it was assumed that it would take care of itself.[51]

What underlay these differences in strike policy, then, was above all differences in experience. *Majoritaire* caution and insistence on meticulous planning were grounded in experiences of confrontation with hostile employers with a weakly organized labor force. *Minoritaire* radicalism and optimism were largely the result of a lack of this sobering experience. Only after a strike had been called did the new leaders begin to see the need to concretize their goals and maintain strict control over those involved.[52] By that time, it was usually too late.

It is doubtful that any ideology could have turned these strikes into labor victories. For the French labor movement was about as organizationally equipped to defeat management and the state as Czarist Russia was to defeat Germany. The fact that the Federation of Metalworkers and the CGT were unable to prevent the strikes of 1919 and 1920, respectively, is testimony to their frailty: these entities simply lacked the means to restrain, or mobilize, their subordinates.

This had little to do with ideological struggles. The 1919 strike represented a departmental revolt against a leftist leadership at the federation level. In fact, Merrheim, the leader of the Federation of Metalworkers was the leader of the most important *extrême-gauche* faction within the CGT.[53] Only his subsequent disputes with the Parisian local caused him to be labelled *majoritaire*. The fact that Alphonse Merrheim, then the Comité d'entente, and finally many members of the action committees successively behaved in restrained ways suggests that it was not the stated ideology that mattered as much as the position—and vulnerability—connected with organizational leadership.[54] Those in leadership positions were painfully aware of their weaknesses, sought all assistance possible, and wanted all actions carefully planned, whether they were on the left or the right. On the other hand, outside critics were much more optimistic about the movement's clout and believed it merely needed to be flexed.

More fundamental than ideology to the enfeeblement of the movement were conflicts over traditional rights of autonomy. Those lower in the hierarchy, whatever their ideology, jealously guarded their traditional independence and simply did whatever they wished, whether or not this coincided with the desires or plans of others in the union movement and whether or not it meant striking. This was true independently of the craft in question. The Paris railroad workers' decision not to support the metalworkers' strike was instigated and promoted by the leftist Gaston Monmousseau, who led a national rail strike the following year.[55] This refusal of support was decisive in isolating the metalworkers from the rest of the union movement. And while tens of thousands of chemical workers did walk off the job during the metalworkers strike, they did so to pursue their own goals and never joined the metalworkers in any real sense.[56]

The importance of union autonomy, as opposed to ideological differences, is even clearer in the case of the 1920 rail strike. At the Railroad Workers' Federation Congress at the end of April, the left won control of the Federation's Executive Bureau, including the critical secretaryship. Surprise protest resignations by the *majoritaire* leaders gave the left control of the quasi-legislative Executive Commission, making left dominance of the federation even more complete.[57]

As the more moderate leadership had discovered in 1919, leftist leadership would now find that the available organization was inadequate to control the workers, only this time the workers were reluctant where they had once been enthusiastic to strike. After the twenty-four-hour May Day general strike, most railworkers on the eastern line and all workers in Alsace-Lorraine returned to work. The story was the same on the strategically vital northern line, where the union leadership actually ordered the members back on the job. These lines were, to be sure, controlled by the right, but they were not alone in ignoring the federation. Some leftist strongholds, such as Bésançon and Dole, remained aloof and the line most critically affected by the February strike, the Paris-Lyon-Marseilles, actually had the highest back-to-work turnout.[58]

Meanwhile, the moderate CGT leadership, however reluctantly, backed the strike. The overwhelmingly *majoritaire* dockers and seamen turned out in support of the rail strike, but also had their own axes to grind, particularly regarding the length of the work day. On the other hand, the *minoritaire* Paris metalworkers critically undermined the damage potential of the entire rail strike by themselves calling a strike on May 5. This they did in spite of desperate pleas from the *minoritaire* leadership of the railroad workers. The *minoritaire* construction workers made similar rumblings. It was this uncontrollable restlessness on the part of some to join the fray as much as the railworkers need for help to make it "over the hump" that led the CGT leaders to call out the "second wave" on May 10.[59]

Finally, in the midst of this tragicomic farrago came the intervention of militant defenders of federation autonomy. At their May 16 meeting, the CGT-appointed interim leaders of the railroad union were on the verge of calling off the strike when the newly released Monmousseau suddenly appeared, like a bad dream no doubt, with his entourage of supporters. Monmousseau and his officials had been in prison and in hiding since May 2. Now, anxious to rid his union of CGT control at almost any price, he was able to win extension of the strike for an additional two weeks.[60] Given that the companies were imposing escalating sanctions, the price of this independence was a great increase in the number of dismissals, demotions, and delayed promotions.[61]

In all of these strikes, leaders, whatever their ideological predilections, sought to take advantage of what they saw as dramatically increased union strength, namely, swelled membership rolls. The lack of trade union movement coherence—the absence of central direction and organizational infrastructure capable of allocating sanctions and rewards—made it impossible for even the most savvy leaders to harness this mushrooming energy. While ideological competition and factionalism may be seen as a sort of proximate cause of the incoherence of French strikes in 1919 and 1920, these were rather markers for two different principles of organization, one that emphasized centralized control and careful planning, and another that emphasized autonomy, spontaneity, particularistic interests, and a traditional distribution of power within the movement. In this, the left sought to preserve the prewar organizational legacy. But it was precisely that legacy, rather than ideological disputes as such, that made it impossible for either the left or the right to lead a successful trade union movement.

Membership in the CGT fell from a peak of perhaps 2 million in 1920 to about half of that at the end of the year and to about 600,000 by the end of 1921. None of the demands of the Minimum Program, not even the eight-hour day, were realized. The strikes that occurred after May 1920 were no longer aimed at the conquest of new rights. Union efforts were now spent in an attempt to preserve previous gains and to resist the offensive launched by employers to reduce wages, extend working hours, and break the unions. The strikes in the textile industry and the fate of the eight-hour day in the maritime and railway industries were indicative of this. In March 1920, the textile workers of Tourcoing and Roubaix had gone on strike for increased wages, which they secured. In August and September 1921, they struck again, this time in protest against successive wage reductions. The strike was successful only in that a smaller reduction in wages was forced on the workers than had at first been proposed.[62]

In 1921 and 1922 various attempts were made to change the application of the eight-hour law in different industries. In July 1922, the Federation of Maritime Workers decided to call a strike if the Rio decree, changing the application of that law in the merchant marine, was made effective. A strike against the decree in September failed. At about the same time the application of the law was changed on the railroads. A distinction was made between "actual work" and "time on duty," and the hours of labor were figured on the basis of a year rather than a week. For workers who were engaged in actual work throughout their period of duty, the hours of duty might not exceed ten per day. But in cases in which work was intermittent, the hours of duty might be twelve or fifteen. This resulted in an increase of from 400 to 500 hours per year.[63] As Charles Maier has observed, "What the eight-hour controversy finally revealed was the strength, not the weakness of the French *patronat*."[64] Faced with genuinely revolutionary threats, Maier notes, employers in Italy and Germany readily conceded the eight-hour day as a small price to undermine the radical thrust. In France, revolution seemed remote, and the more fundamentally secure employer class could afford to resist even the eight-hour day.[65]

The final denouement was played out in the split between the CGT's reformist majority and the "revolutionary" minority that formed the communist CGTU in 1921. Thereafter both confederations were condemned to a decade and a half of impotence, with the former opting for collaboration with the state, mainly with the power-oriented Radical Socialists, while the latter wallowed in the rhetoric of revolution in a most unrevolutionary society.

With its collapsed membership and enfeebled organization, the CGT returned to its prewar practice of exerting itself mainly to gain the state's approbation and intervention rather than prevail against the employers in the labor market. Labor relations and strikes came to depend increasingly on the state and on the ineffable force of public opinion rather than on the attitudes of the rival parties. The CGT even supported legislation in 1925 that would have made government intervention compulsory in all labor disputes. It now rarely struck, and when it did, the purpose was to call the attention of the state to its troubles rather than to defeat the employers. This strategy was known as the *politique de présence*. It meant that while the CGT rejected actual participation in the government, it sought a role for itself in all government discussions of labor and sought to bolster its own credibility by calling into play the state's sympathy.[66] In other words, the unions increasingly saw their role as one of lobbying and bargaining with the state. The Ministry of Labor decreed the CGT to be the union normally most representative of labor and the one with which employers should thus bargain. But by 1933, only 7.5 percent of wage earners were affected by collective bargaining, mainly in mining and shipping; in the metal industry only 1.4 percent of workers were affected.[67] Although the CGT's membership skyrocketed in 1936 and millions of workers temporarily won collective contracts, little actually changed as a result of the Popular Front and the General Strike. The state's support remained indispensable to the CGT. Indeed, the state was not merely an ally in the political sphere, it was a substitute for coherent union organization. In both the Matignon Accord and the subsequent resolution of disputes, it was necessary to call in the state's authority to make good the CGT's own ineffectiveness: after 1936, all but 4 percent of labor market disputes were decided by the government.[68]

This point must be emphasized: the split between the CGT and CGTU *followed* the labor defeats and was as much a consequence as a cause of them. During the critical moments, communists in the CGT were, following Lenin's advice, committed not to breaking the CGT but to colonizing it. It was only in the summer of 1920, *after* the lost strikes and at the time of the Bolshevik offensive in Poland, that the Moscow Theses were proclaimed and the issue of rupture surfaced.[69] There is no doubt, to be sure, that the left–right tension in the CGT and the affiliates had a long history. It can be traced to the prewar period—and in that sense was well anchored in the prewar experience of partial labor inclusion—and to the wartime conflicts between supporters of the *union sacrée* and its critics. On balance, however, the left–right conflicts were of secondary importance: neither the left nor the right could control the CGT, a federation, or even a local, even when it had a clear majority, because it lacked the institutional means.

This is driven home by an examination of the 1936 General Strike, the last great opportunity of French labor between the wars, for then there was no question of conflict between communists and reformists. Indeed, as it turned out, in 1936 the CGT could not control its constituents even when there was no left–right struggle within itself *and* a pro-labor government was in power.[70]

The CGT and the CGTU merged as the Popular Front unfolded between 1934 and 1936. The Communist party, in the Popular Front but not in Léon Blum's cabinet, repeatedly endorsed Blum's reform strategy and worked frantically in the unions and outside of them to end the sitdown strikes of

June 1936. In this, the posture of the Communists was indistinguishable from that of its Popular Front allies, the Socialists, Radical Socialists, and the CGT. The Communists "in no way sought the strike wave of May–June 1936, and, though they capitalized on it very well . . . they did everything they could to convince the strikers to go back to work at the earliest possible moment."[71]

> Blum, the majority of his party, the CGT and even the Communists regarded the labor upheaval not as an opportunity but as an obstacle, a danger to the immediate task at hand—the experiment of the Popular Front government based on combined working-class and middle-class support and seeking the broadest possible unity. . . . There were different shades of emphasis in the thought of [Maurice] Thorez, Jouhaux and Blum at this moment, but all three saw in the labor upheaval an untimely challenge to their immediate objectives. Individually and together, they sought ways and means to end it.[72]

On this occasion, then, there was no question of ideological fratricide debilitating the labor movement. Rather, the causes of the Popular Front's failure can be pinpointed with great specificity and were to be found in the organizational enfeeblement of the trade unions and the dependent position of the Socialists in the party system. The organizational weakness of the unions prevented them from devising and pursuing a coherent strategy for the implementation and defense of the gains of the Matignon Agreement, both when the Blum government was in office and after. The dependent position of the Socialist party denied it the opportunity to break with liberal orthodoxy in its economic policies and thus doomed it to failure on the economic front. On both counts we can see the limits of labor's political potential in a liberal order.

The sitdown strikes that commenced first with the Parisian metalworkers on May 14 rapidly became a national strike involving about 1.5 million workers. The strikes began spontaneously as a response to the Popular Front victory two weeks earlier. The principal demands of workers included collective bargaining rights, guaranteed minimum wages, paid vacations, a forty-hour work week, the right to elect shop stewards, and wage increases. Everywhere the strikes took a common form. The workers remained in the plants day and night, posting security guards, solicitously caring for the machinery. The strikers anticipated a left government that on the one hand would enact a French "New Deal" and on the other hand never dare to use force against them. Perceiving the vulnerability of employers, workers took matters into their own hands. The CGT, it must be emphasized, was caught totally unaware by the strikes: it did not initiate them and was powerless to end them.

> The CGT leadership, non-Communist and Communist, sought to check what was rapidly becoming a runaway movement. Jouhaux made every effort to calm the workers and induce them to return to work. He feared that labor's

role in the political life of the country would be jeopardized if the middle classes were unduly antagonized. . . . Concern grew as the strikes went beyond control. A member of the CGT administrative committee later recalled the anxiety that prevailed in that national office. Despite the tone of the CGT newspaper, *Le Peuple,* and the communiques of the labor federations celebrating the irresistible advance of the movement and recommending calm and discipline, everywhere the trade union leaders were finding it impossible to lead the strikes, to stop them from spreading, or to foresee the consequences.[73]

It was, in the classic fashion, the intervention of the state that finally ended the strikes. This intervention came in the form of the famous Matignon Agreement and the associated legislative reforms. The Matignon Agreement was reached between the CGT and the CGPF (Confederation Générale de la Production Française) through the mediation of Léon Blum. It was, to be sure, a seemingly historic agreement. For it ensured the right of all workers to bargain collectively and belong to trade unions. Union membership rose from about one million to over 5 million by the end of 1937. The accord guaranteed to all workers two weeks of annual paid vacation, authorized the election of shop stewards, and provided wage increases averaging 12 percent. It was accompanied by legislation mandating a forty-hour work week, collective bargaining, and the annual holiday. In addition, measures would be introduced providing for a public works program, the nationalization of private munitions manufacture, a wheat office to raise and stabilize agricultural prices, extension of compulsory schooling, reform of the statutes governing the Bank of France, and repeal of retrenchment decrees affecting civil service workers and veterans. A second series of measures was to follow later, including a broad revamping of the tax system.

The most important feature of the Matignon Agreement and the state intervention that subtended it, however, was precisely its transience. The appearance of the socialist-led government and the formation of the Popular Front itself were a fluke that no one, least of all employers, could expect to last long. The alliance of Communists, Socialists, and middle-class reformers was contingent on an improbable coincidence of Moscow's momentary security needs, France's own security problems, and the already waning rightist threat that had first been manifested in February 1934. It was an alliance that was brought to office mainly on a negative program—defense against fascism—in a society in which it was already increasingly apparent that the domestic threat of fascism had always been remote. Since the fall of the conservative Doumergue government in late 1934 did not produce the fascist putsch that had been threatened, most people came to realize that the threat of French fascism had been much exaggerated.[74]

The Popular Front had only secondarily been formed to respond to the depression, and in this it was critically limited by the Socialist's need to propitiate the Radicals. An alliance so dependent on the international constellation of forces and on the appetite of the Radicals for economic and social reform was not likely to be an enduring one. Neither the Communist loyalty to the Republican order nor the Radical commitment to reform could be expected to last long. In this, as we shall see, it was the Radicals rather than the Communists who were decisive at the political level in bringing the Popular Front to an end.

By the middle of July, almost all strikers had returned to work, the critical legislation had been passed and workers looked forward to the speedy implementation of the particulars of the Matignon Agreement. By September, however, renewed strike activity was beginning as workers found their wage gains eroded by rapidly rising prices and employers resistant to the implementation of the forty-hour week and other specifics of the agreement.[75] As before, these strikes were spontaneous and uncoordinated.[76] At the end of the year, the government was forced to resort to legislation providing compulsory arbitration to contain another explosion of labor unrest. The point that must be emphasized about this resort to arbitration, as about the intervention of the state in labor relations more generally in these years, is that it was a conscious attempt by the state to compensate for the inability of the CGT to control the behavior of its members. Indeed, compulsory arbitration was first proposed in September by the Secretary-General of the CGT, Léon Jouhaux, precisely as a means to this end and in response to the renewed explosion of labor unrest.[77]

The government's own political capital was rapidly being run down with both workers and the middle classes by the continued deterioration of the economy, by an investors' strike that long outran the workers' strike, and by an arbitration system that did not fully compensate workers for price increases.[78] Having for months resisted it, Blum's government had finally been forced to devalue the franc in September 1936. In February of the following year, under growing pressure from the Radicals and the economy, Blum announced a "pause" in reform legislation and a program of retrenchment. In March, Blum finally gave in completely to economic orthodoxy, abandoning his government's public works program and handing control of the Exchange Stabilization Fund to financial conservatives. Shortly thereafter, in June 1937, the first Popular Front government fell because the Radicals would not support it in its confrontation with the Senate over its demand for emergency economic authority. Blum's ministry was succeeded by one that included Socialists but was now led by the Radicals. The reformist impulse was clearly spent, and employers, feeling more secure, accelerated their own offensive as they sought to undo the commitments they had entered into at the Matignon Palace.

When the Daladier government issued a decree revising the forty-hour week law in November 1938, the CGT promptly called a general strike. Just as the CGT had been unable to restrain workers from striking in 1936, it was now helpless to induce them to strike in 1938. Very few workers answered the call, and the strike proved an unmitigated calamity for the CGT. The aftermath was a great wave of dismissals of strikers and union activists.[79] By the end of 1938, 3,000 of the CGT's 18,000 local unions had disintegrated.[80] Employers systematically flouted the Matignon Agreements—now a dead letter—and millions of workers left the CGT. When the war came, the CGT yet again had perhaps as few as one million members.[81]

Switzerland

Like their counterparts in Britain and France, Swiss unions had a vision of a reformed postwar order. In their pursuit of it, they failed still more quickly and unambiguously. The vision was summarized in the nine-point program of the 1918 General Strike. The program included the eight-hour day and forty-eight-hour week, wage increases, the introduction of proportional representation, the enactment of compulsory old age and disability insurance, the right of women to vote, a reorganization of the army, a guarantee of a job for all, a state monopoly of foreign trade, and measures to stabilize food prices.[82] Implicit in this program was the demand that the unions be accepted as a major player in the governance of the economy. The strike lasted three days and was, by the admission of the union leaders themselves, largely a failure. At the end of it, workers had gained wage increases that would subsequently be eroded, the eight-hour day and forty-eight-hour week, that would soon come under attack, and proportional representation in National Council elections.[83] Proportional representation had, in fact, already been approved by a referendum, so that the only question was one of bringing forward the next election.[84] As it happened, Socialists did win more National council seats with proportional representation, but they could exercise no influence on the government in the face of an overwhelming antisocialist coalition.

SGB membership reached its peak in 1920 at 223,000, or 26.6 percent of the male labor force. It then fell by a third by 1922 and recovered only slowly, stabilizing at about 190,000 in the final years of the decade. This was the lowest level of union density in interwar Europe, and even it was misleading: only 65,000 SGB members were covered by collective contracts in 1929.[85] The weakness that derived from this limited penetration of the working classes was compounded by the incoherence of the unions. After 1908, as we saw in Chapter 5, the SGB functioned as no more than an information-gathering agency. In this, it was analogous to the TUC. Strike funds and the decision to strike were made by individual federations or even local units. Most collective bargaining was local or regional rather than industry-wide. The individual federations became entirely autonomous.[86] Also, separate federations were formed for state employees, postal workers, and railworkers, so that fewer than two-thirds of unionized workers were enrolled in SGB federations between the wars.[87] Within the SGB federations there were enormous variations in organizational strength. The largest and most important was the Federation of Metalworkers and Watchmakers (SMUV). The SMUV controlled its own funds for strikes, unemployment, sickness, accidents, and general relief. It was entirely beyond the control of the SGB. Even this leading union, however, enrolled only 61,000 of the 162,000 workers in the metal and watchmaking industries in the late 1920s.[88] In the textile industry, which was still the single largest employer in the late 1920s, only 8,000 of the 91,000 factory workers were organized in the Factory and Textile Workers' Federation.[89] Other federations existed which were even more weakly organized.[90]

The story of the trade unions in Switzerland lacks the drama of the British and French experiences. There were, in practice, no critical junctures at which the Swiss unions had the potential to substitute for the workings of the market a political bargain with employers and the state. Trade unions were simply too weak for that. Konrad Ilg, the leader of the SMUV, acknowledged as much in a moment of candor in 1937 when he remarked that "[There has been] no single strike in the history of our association that has been a major success in important trade union matters."[91] Moreover, the Social Democratic party, which never received a level of support comparable to that given to the socialist left in Britain and France, remained entirely isolated by an antisocialist middle-class coalition until 1943, when the party effectively wrote off its social democratic identity in exchange for a seat on the Federal Council.

The years between the wars were grim for the Social Democrats. Class tensions had been greatly heightened by the war and the General Strike. With linguistic differences having lost most of their political punch even before the era of mass politics, and with the secularization of the state now irreversibly secured, politics was reduced in large measure to class conflict. The introduction of proportional representation ended the majorities of the Radicals but, in circumstances in which political conflict was couched almost exclusively in terms of a battle between the working-class left and the middle-class right, this proved almost epiphenomenal. For the enactment of proportional representation was immediately followed by an alliance of Radicals and Conservative Catholics in which the Radicals controlled a majority of the Federal Council seats until 1943.[92] This coalition should not be confused with the consensual, permanent all-party coalitions that evolved in Switzerland after 1943. That style of governance belongs to an altogether different epoch and was itself premised on the transformation of the Social Democratic party. Rather, the coalition of the 1920s was one of middle-class consolidation whose raison d'être was the isolation of the Social Democratic party.[93] Although its share of the popular vote rose modestly, the party was systematically ignored by the governing coalition. It could not point to a single major legislative success during these years. Its most ambitious schemes, for a federal grain monopoly, for compulsory pensions, and, in response to the Great Depression, for a program of public works and economic expansion, were all decisively defeated in referenda.[94] When the nonsocialists finally accepted the Social Democrats as a major political player in 1943, it was because the Social Democrats had come to recognize the futility of their opposition. No doubt this shift was motivated on both sides to some degree by the wartime emergency, but it was premised on the Social Democrats' prior acknowledgment of the sterility of isolated opposition. The turning point was in the Social Democrats' revision of their party program in 1935. The new program abandoned the commitment to class struggle and socialization and endorsed the nonsocialists' program of national defense.[95] In 1936, the party supported the government's defense loans. In 1938, it voted for the government's financial policies. In 1939, it supported a broad grant of emergency power to the Federal Council.[96]

After the General Strike of 1918, the Swiss trade unions remained quiescent and ineffective for the remainder of the interwar years. They had the lowest strike rate in Europe; strikes virtually disappeared after the middle of the 1920s.[97] They were also, judging by the change in the real wages of Swiss workers, the least effective unions in Europe. Indeed, it is difficult to see that they made any contribution to workers' real wages, which seem to have remained governed entirely by market forces.[98] Swiss unions, after a burst of radicalism in 1918 and a subsequent collapse of membership, were returning to their prewar roots as interest group advocates of workers in various industries. It was indicative of the weakness of the class-orientation of the Swiss unions that the leading confederation, the SGB, expunged from its program in 1927 all references to socialism.[99] Indeed, in 1937, the constituent federations even renounced the right to strike and posted an indemnity bond to guarantee their compliance. In exchange, a very unequal exchange given the inherent balance of power in labor markets, employers pledged not to resort to lockouts.

It was this renunciation of the strike weapon rather than a failed challenge to the liberal order that constituted the dramatic event in the interwar history of Swiss labor. The accord renouncing strikes was a straightforward admission on the part of the unions of their ineffectiveness and an attempt to make the best of a desperate situation.[100] If the weakness of the unions guaranteed that they could not mount an effective challenge entirely apart from their incoherence, their incoherence did guarantee that the abandonment of the strike weapon would not occur as part of a larger strategic bargain struck with the state and employers.

Following a sharp devaluation of the Swiss franc in 1936, the government granted the Ministry of Economics the authority to resolve all wage disputes that could not be negotiated between employers and workers. Neither employers nor unions favored this, but for the unions compulsory arbitration was particularly menacing, given the composition of the Federal Council. The initial overture to the employers came, significantly, not from the SGB, but from the SMUV, which neither consulted the SGB nor sought its approval.[101] Indeed, the SGB played no role in the negotiations. Once the SMUV had completed negotiations renouncing strikes and lockouts with employers in the watch and metal industries, the other unions and the SGB had no choice but to accept this as a fait accompli.[102] For the confederation and the other unions could not possibly act effectively without the support of the SMUV. The accord institutionalized the decentralization and weakness of the union movement. It fixed the initial locus of collective bargaining at the enterprise level and restricted the objects of bargaining to wages, hours, and benefits.[103] In effect, this agreement laid the foundations for the evolution of Swiss trade unions that would occur after the war. In that evolution, they became the junior partners of employers in the management of Swiss industry.[104] This role paralleled the one assumed by the Social Democratic party in its relationship with the liberal state.

Stabilization of the Liberal Order

To point to the incoherence of the trade unions accounts only in part for the weak threat labor movements posed to liberal political economies between the wars. We have seen repeatedly that the behavior of the unions was conditioned by the balance of political power. Trade unions could not look to the state for an ally in their battles with employers. In Switzerland a center–right coalition was formed in 1919 explicitly to isolate the Social Democratic party. The coalition remained in power throughout the interwar years. Working-class parties in Britain and France gained power only briefly between the wars, and when they did, they were markedly ineffective. It is an understatement to say that the unions found these labor governments a disappointment. The governments of Ramsay MacDonald in 1924 and especially 1931 and of Léon Blum in 1936 and 1937 are remembered mainly for the orthodoxy of their economic policies and, in much historiography, the betrayal of their movements. Whether they betrayed their movements or not, they were incapable of posing a substantial threat to the traditional orders in Britain and France.

Let us first note what is *not* sufficient to account for the political weakness of labor in Britain and France between the wars. These parties were not ineffective simply because they received a smaller share of the popular vote than labor parties elsewhere, although their level of popular support did continue to lag behind somewhat.[105] Working-class parties in these societies were no longer as weak as they had been before 1914, because workers had a lower level of class consciousness. Judging by the admittedly crude index of share of the popular vote cast, we must conclude that the war and postwar crises encouraged a convergence, albeit a still incomplete one, of class-consciousness across Europe. Socialists in France, Social Democrats in Switzerland, and labor parties in clerically dominated Belgium and the

Netherlands still lagged behind somewhat. Yet no working class in Europe was so large that it could elect a majority government by itself, even if it voted in perfect unison.

The key to working-class power, then, had to be in the ability of the parties to find nonsocialist allies. The historical irony is that it was precisely those conditions that had facilitated interclass alliances in Britain, France, and Switzerland before the war that inhibited them after the war. In the comparatively depolarized class relations of prewar liberal societies, the absence of deep-running cleavages within the middle classes had allowed liberal parties to unite a large fraction of the middle classes with a fraction of the working class. This alliance had been the foundation of liberal hegemony. The same comparative absence of cleavages within the middle classes after the war, however, in the context of much heightened class tensions, now had the effect of allowing for the creation of a cohesive nonsocialist party, as with the British Conservatives, or alliance, as with the French Bloc Nationale and the Swiss antisocialist front. No inherited historical antagonism with the middle classes could prevent this regrouping. In all three countries, the political power of reforming liberals declined as voters shifted to a more clearly defined pattern of class voting. The result was the appearance of an essentially bilateral pattern of competition that pitted socialists against nonsocialists. In this, the socialists were bound to suffer, because given the minority position of the working classes, they could gain power only through an alliance with a part of the nonsocialist community. There would be no opportunity for such alliances, however.

An alliance that provided socialists with a durable governing majority, and thereby authentic political power, required divisions within the nonsocialist community that were as intense as those between it and the socialist community. Historically, these middle-class divisions had been provided by cleavages between the town and country, between regions, and between religious and linguistic communities. It was just these divisions that had prevented liberal hegemony in the aliberal societies, and it was these same divisions, still firmly embedded in their party systems, that returned to prevent the interwar political consolidation of the middle classes in them. These divisions prevented middle-class consolidation, as we shall see in Chapter 7, in the quite literal sense that it proved impossible in aliberal societies to create nonsocialist governing majorities. By preventing that consolidation, they provided socialist parties with an opportunity to detach a part of the middle class—in practice the agrarian middle class—and form an alliance with it.

In liberal societies, creating stable nonsocialist governing majorities was not a problem during the interwar years, the superficial turnover of the French governments notwithstanding. In fact, the center–right majorities that governed these societies were very stable. In Britain, this alliance was first between the Lloyd George Liberals and the Conservative party, from 1919 to

1922, and after the disintegration of the Liberals, within the Conservative party. The Conservatives continuously commanded a parliamentary majority after 1922, save during the brief and ill-fated interludes of Ramsay Mac-Donald's governments in 1924 and 1929 through 1931. Even during Mac-Donald's second government, the real balance of power rested with the Liberal and Conservative majority in the Commons, and MacDonald could survive only by bowing to this reality. In France, the center–right formula was found in the Bloc Nationale and the various permutations of it that governed, aside from Edouard Herriot's ten-month-long center–left administration in 1924–25 and the Popular Front of 1936 through 1938. In Switzerland, a stable center–right formula was provided by the Federal Council alliance between the Radicals and the Conservative Catholics. This alliance was supplemented after 1929 by the occupation of one of the seven Federal Council seats by the Farmers, Traders, and Citizens party.

Prewar liberal party hegemony had required not the absence of preindustrial cleavages, but that a politically effective majority of the middle classes was unified rather than divided by the cleavages. The experiences of Britain, Switzerland, and France indicate that the decisive point was not whether these cleavages existed in the party system, not to mention in society-at-large, but whether they served to consolidate or undermine a liberal movement. Swiss Liberals and then Radicals were constantly in conflict with Catholics over clerical issues and the related questions of central authority. Indeed, as late as 1848, the cleavage had been intense enough to provoke the Sonderbund War. Outnumbering Catholics about four-to-one in the legislature, however, the dominance of Liberals and Radicals was never challenged. Indeed, insofar as secularism was a part of the liberal identity in Switzerland, the cleavage actually served to reinforce the cohesiveness of the liberal community. And insofar as the majority of the Swiss middle-class electorate was Protestant, the cleavage reinforced the hegemony of the liberal parties. Anticlericalism served the same function in France. Indeed, anticlericalism in France and, in a more residual way, dissent in Britain both reinforced middle-class support for liberalism and provided an important bridge between middle-class liberalism and the working class.

The essential point at present is that because in the formative prewar years of the French and Swiss party systems these cleavages aggregated a majority of the middle classes behind liberalism for four or more decades, they allowed for an interlude in which the subtending issues were definitively resolved. In both cases, the victory of the secular state was irreversibly established by 1914; so much so that this was no longer challenged even by Catholics. The consequence was that in the interwar years, politics in these two countries and in Britain, where the Irish issue was definitively resolved immediately after the war, was reduced almost exclusively to class politics. This was in sharp contrast (we shall take a detailed look at this in the next chapter) to interwar politics in the old aliberal societies. In those societies, nothing was resolved in the prewar years, and cleavages other than class remained very much alive.

This reduction of conflict almost exclusively to class conflict had a number of consequences, all of which were detrimental to socialist parties. First, it meant that socialist parties in liberal societies had very few opportunities to manipulate inherited divisions within the middle classes and thereby gain reliable allies. What linguistic, religious, territorial, or agricultural conflicts could socialists in Britain, France, and Switzerland have manipulated to split the nonsocialist bloc? To whom could they have made the concessions? Where socialists successfully manipulated such divisions, they allied with the agrarian middle class. Britain no longer even had a politically potent agrarian middle class. In France and Switzerland, agrarian support was spread across the party spectrum, and farmers did not relate to the larger set of political conflicts mainly as farmers. Their orientation was first and foremost left versus right. It was from this reduction of political conflict to such polar terms that there emerged the long runs of nonsocialist political power in the interwar years.

The salience of class conflict and the absence of other cleavages meant, in the second place, that socialist parties could woo middle-class support only by making concessions on class-related issues. In practice, in the 1920s and 1930s this meant on macroeconomic and social policies—thus, the strikingly orthodox economic policies pursued by both the MacDonald and Blum ministries. Third, the exclusive focus on class conflict meant, in turn, that the key to working-class parties gaining political power was in their making concessions that largely compelled them to abandon their own agenda. Thus followed the profound alienation that the MacDonald and Blum ministries engendered among trade unionists. Fourth, it meant that even when working-class parties could come to office, they would have only a tenuous hold on power. They would have an opportunity only when the right was temporarily unavailable. This could occur when the right was in the process of consolidating itself, as in Britain after the 1924 and 1929 elections; or when a part of the right was temporarily frightened into an alliance by fascism or social unrest, as in France in 1936. The problem with these opportunities was that they were both temporary and unstable. They made left power contingent on events and conflicts not subject to the left's control. There was nothing the British Labor party could do to deter the middle class abandonment of the Liberals from 1924 and the subsequent consolidation of the modern Conservative party. And while this was taking place, it could have its brief periods in power only to the extent that it acted like the minority government it actually was. Likewise, the French Socialist party could do little to increase the appetite of the Radicals for social reform or economic innovation; nor could it do much to increase the Radicals' fear of fascism.

For the moment, to complete our story we need only recall two ways in which the dependent position of labor parties in Britain and France manifested itself, reinforced the enfeeblement of the labor movement as a whole, and thereby secured the institutional and policy continuity of these societies. The prison of dependence that these labor parties found themselves in was expressed by their inability to break with economic orthodoxy in the 1930s and by the correlate obsession of MacDonald, Blum, and their followers to demonstrate that labor parties could be trusted with government power. As James Hinton has recorded:

> The Labor leadership saw their first experience of office as an opportunity . . . to demonstrate their capacity to govern "responsibly." The Cabinet . . . was punctilious in its observation of established rituals—provoking one Clydeside shipyard worker to shout at an ILP meeting: "A worker's government, ye ca' it! Its a bloody lum [top] hat government like a' the rest."[106]

Both MacDonald and Blum wanted, above all, to demonstrate that labor could form a government like any other party, "without," as MacDonald had once put it to Blum, "the earth opening up or the sky falling." Both, as Joel Colton has written of Blum, were "determined to demonstrate that the Socialists could exercise power within the legal and constitutional framework. . . ."[107] "[Blum's] deepest pride was that the party had not violated the trust that had been placed in it. He told the 1937 congress: '[The country] has come to understand that it could place its destiny in our hands without fear. . . . It no longer fears us; it trusts us.' He had fulfilled his personal mission."[108] It is always possible to speculate that a different set of leaders would have produced different policies with different outcomes. But it must be borne in mind that their ascensions to party leadership were not simply random outcomes. These leaders came to the summits of their parties in an inherited political context. If the parties were handicapped by leaders obsessed with gaining middle-class approbation, the appearance of such leaders was made probable by the dependent position of the parties and the entire previous history of class collaboration that had been central to the development of these labor movements. Seen in this way, the leadership of MacDonald and Blum was by no means a deviation from past experience; it was rather the logical conclusion of that experience.

Reflecting more than simply the sum of their parties' pasts or their own predilections, the policies of these men were indicators of a genuine need to gain the tolerance of middle-class parties and their voters (and investors) on terms that were inherently unfavorable to labor. The attitudes of Blum and MacDonald reflected an acute (albeit not necessarily astute) understanding of the limits of labor's governmental power in an economy in which private investors were frightened, in which labor governments lacked the means either to assuage the fears or to control the behavior of investors and in which party alliances were tenuous. In this context, the goodwill of investors, and the middle classes more generally, was essential, and both scrupulous observation of constitutional and legal norms and economic orthodoxy were the only ways to pursue that goodwill.

It was in pursuit of these ends that the three governments embraced orthodox economic policies. In both 1924 and especially 1929 through 1931, MacDonald's governments remained committed to the Gold Standard, balanced budgets, and spending cuts. Throughout 1930 and 1931, the Labor government survived only by accepting its dependence on committees of inquiry on the economy in the Commons. MacDonald's behavior, at least before joining the Tory government, was neither treasonous nor exceptional in 1931. The majority of the Labor cabinet, in fact, was committed to reaching an agreement with the opposition parties on spending cuts.[109] The hypothetical alternative was an alliance with the Liberal party that Lloyd George was trying to revive. It might have been premised on expansionary policies. But this was in reality no alternative at all, even if some trade union leaders were keen to pursue it. That Labor party leaders uniformly rejected such policies while trade union leaders endorsed them reflected the fact that the latter did not have to govern. There could be no working parliamentary majority for stimulus unless Lloyd George could carry all fifty-eight Liberal MPs with him. He could not do this. Indeed, many of the Liberals were already in revolt against the support Lloyd George had been extending to the Labor government.[110]

MacDonald, Snowden, and the cabinet majority can surely be faulted for a lack of imagination. But it was a lack that was perfectly congruent with the narrow range of choice Labor encountered. Most fundamentally, that range of choice was narrow because the Labor party could neither break with its past experience of integration into British society and the ingrained ideological predispositions that accompanied that nor avail itself of intense, historically rooted divisions within the middle classes. Seen from this vantage point, it seems doubtful that in failing to make an alliance with Lloyd George's Liberals, Labor, as Peter Gourevitch has suggested, "missed the opportunity to establish a political hegemony like that of its Swedish counterpart." For, in the absence of deeply fractured middle classes, there never was such an opportunity.[111]

Blum's government was equally orthodox.[112] It repeatedly postponed a devaluation of the franc. Only in September 1936, when it was no longer avoidable, did the government accept devaluation. As Blum later admitted, he was aware that devaluation was "almost inevitable. . . . We knew it, [Vincent] Auriol and I. We [were] not children."[113] The government waited, however, because the Radicals opposed devaluation and because the government hoped that it could break the run on the franc by winning the confidence of investors. For the same reason, it refused, once devaluation was a fact, to institute exchange controls. It likewise refused to interfere with the traditional autonomy of the Bank of France and, indeed, appointed three conservatives to advise on the operation of the Exchange Stabilization Fund. "The presence of these men was intended to inspire confidence in financial circles, but Blum, with singular lack of foresight, seemed utterly unaware that if they were to desert him, his government would be lost."[114] The abrupt abandonment of limited deficit spending and public works projects after just a half year was likewise due to pressure from the Radicals and the investment community. The problem for the Socialists was that, in the end, their economic policies were both indistinguishable from those of the nonsocialist parties and doomed to fail. Their conservatism alienated workers and their failure alienated everyone.

Not surprisingly, the center–right governments that bracketed these labor experiments in Britain and France and that governed throughout the Depression in Switzerland adhered tenaciously to economic orthodoxy. When they shifted from it, they did so only to what Peter Gourevitch has called "neo-orthodoxy," a combination of competitive devaluation, cartelization, and protectionism rather than the more radical break embodied by Keynesian stimulation policies.[115] In France, stimulation policies came about unintentionally and only because the Popular Front government could not end the General Strike without conceding major wage increases. Even then the reduction in work hours largely offset the stimulatory effect of these gains. As it was, the life of this break with economic orthodoxy can be measured in months—about seven. It came to an end even before Leon Blum's ministry did. For in January 1937, Blum's ministry declared a pause in social reforms and a retrenchment. In the return to orthodoxy, the actual collapse of the first Popular Front government a few months later was anticlimactic.

Epilogue

Alliances of the center and right succeeded in restabilizing competitive democracies in Britain, France, and Switzerland after World War I, and the subtending balance of class power that the dominance of those parties implied remained unshaken through the Depression. Labor parties were marginalized in politics; trade unions were marginalized in the market. The opportunities for the left to govern were few and transient, and when they came they did so at the expense of labor's program. As minority parties in societies in which the essence of politics was class politics, labor could govern only by making alliances that deprived it of its own agenda. Trade unions were equally ineffective in the marketplace. They failed, partly because of their lack of political allies and partly because of their own incoherence, in substituting a political bargain with the state and employers for market-driven wage settlements. As we shall see in the next chapter, markets did work in determining wages in interwar liberal societies. Because they worked, because the center–right alliances that governed were unchallenged, because the disruptive capacity of the unions was limited, and because at least among labor leaders the political and economic institutions of liberal societies remained esteemed, the economic and political orders as a whole were little threatened even in the Depression years. They were not threatened enough, in any event, to induce institutional changes—indeed, not even enough to induce major economic policy changes. The MacDonald government remained committed to orthodoxy; the Popular Front broke with orthodoxy for only a few months. Center–right governments were no more inclined to innovate.

There is not much reason to believe that workers, at least in Britain and France, were any longer less class conscious than workers in other European societies. The size of the left vote suggests that the experiences of the war and postwar crises were converging experiences for workers throughout Western Europe. The sense of belonging to the same class seems to have been much less determining than the inherited institutions that harnessed or diffused that consciousness. In this sense, too, the historical experience and the institutional legacy were decisive. They were much more decisive, it would seem, than the balance of left and right power and ideological struggles in labor movements. We have found repeatedly that whether the unions were ideologically cohesive or divided, dominated by a left or a right, made little difference. Neither the left nor the right could make the inherited trade union organizations work.

This history of labor advance and defeat was superficially similar in some respects to what occurred elsewhere in Europe at the same time. In Britain, France, and Switzerland, however, the surges and defeats of labor were absorbed, and the story ended with the reequilibration of liberal political economies. Elsewhere, these surges and defeats were not the end of the story, but the beginning of it, for neither the reequilibration of the prewar orders nor the stabilization of liberal political economies proved possible. Elsewhere, stabilization required different class alliances, institutions, and policies.

Narrowing the Aliberal Outcomes: Liberalism's Final Failure and the Irrelevance of Traditional Dictatorship

In the end, it was possible to stabilize aliberal societies only with social democracy or fascism. It was not possible to stabilize them as liberal orders, because the requisite alliances could not be made and market-oriented policies could not be made to work at a tolerable cost. In principle, there were two liberal alliance possibilities: the Lib–Labism of prewar liberal orders and the middle-class consolidation of interwar liberal orders. Outside of Denmark, where a late but durable Lib–Lab alliance had been established at the turn of the century, and Belgium and the Netherlands, where the hegemony of the interclass clerical parties provided a substitute coalition, the search for an effective alliance of the urban working and middle classes or of the middle classes alone was futile. The alliances either could not be made at all or quickly fell apart, leaving in their wake ineffective minority governments dependent on constantly shifting, issue-specific coalitions.

Lib–Labism failed in the interwar years in all of the societies in which it had failed before the war, and it did so for the same reasons. To these was added the additional burden of the still more intense class conflict that the war had engendered. Middle-class consolidation, too, remained as unattainable as it had been before the war, and again for the same reasons. The old cleavages within the middle classes were revived and even hardened as they were reinforced by the new conflicts that issued from the war. The result was the continued fragmentation of the middle classes as support for old liberal parties dwindled and new parties emerged.

While in Britain, France, and Switzerland the crises of the immediate postwar months were ridden out by the representatives of traditional interests, who then carried on with no significant shift in the distribution of political and economic power, the contemporary crises in aliberal societies culminated in the removal of the representatives of the traditional ruling sectors and a profound shift in the balance of power. The forced opening of political power to working-class parties undermined constitutional orders that had been engineered to keep government power out of their hands. Those constitutional barriers were pushed aside in 1919 and 1920. The institutional changes and the changes in the balance of political and economic power in these societies were all incomplete, however, insofar as the broadening of participation undermined the old orders without providing the new orders with a stable social base.

This amounted to a partial regime shift that left these societies in political limbo until the shift later culminated in fascism or social democracy. This was a state of limbo in the sense that the new constitutional orders were formally established, but lacked dominant movements that brought together broad and stable social coalitions to underpin them. In contrast, in their formative stages the institutions of Victorian Britain, Republican France, and confederal Switzerland had all been identifiably the political projects of broadly based social coalitions. Even the political institutions of pre- and postwar Belgium and the Netherlands rested on the broad and stable coalitions formed by the religious parties.

The shock of the postwar crises was much less in the liberal societies because there was no question in them of extending political power to a new class. Liberalism and the interests for which it stood, if not the old liberal parties, remained hegemonic. Workers had already been included: the postwar extension of the franchise in Britain, the nominal reinforcement of trade union rights in France, and the adoption of proportional representation in Switzerland merely extended participatory rights along lines that had been firmly set before 1914. These reforms did not bring to the threshold of political power movements whose right to participate was disputed by any significant sector of society. More fundamental than even the attitude of the workers toward the political order—since workers in liberal societies were, in any case, organizationally incapable of posing much of a threat—was the attitude of the middle classes toward the legitimacy of worker participation in the exercise of political power. This legitimacy, which had already been broadly accepted before the war, remained unchallenged.

The new constitutional orders that appeared after the war in the aliberal societies belonged, after the early collapse of their founding coalitions, to no particular social groups. They instead divided political and economic power in a way that neither allowed the prewar elites to carry on effectively nor encouraged a new coalition to supplant them. The period between the end of the war and the establishment of fascist and social democratic regimes in these societies can be read, above all, as one of a search for a stabilizing coalition that would join some adequate combination of the middle classes, working classes, and peasantry in support of the constitutional order.

This was an interlude in which the state was, so to speak, up for grabs and incapable of exerting much autonomous influence on other actors. States were stymied by their inadequate social foundations and by the unworkability of their classical economic policies. Nowhere, as we shall see, was this impotence more glaring than in the states' inability to gain the submission of the trade unions to market discipline. While the divisions within the middle classes and conflicts between the middle and working classes impeded the formation of a stable coalition and thus contributed to a weak state, the failure of market-oriented policies in the face of coherent trade unions was at the root of these weak states' failures. These failures were apparent even before the economic crash of 1929 and 1930. The failure of liberal economic policies marked yet another respect in which a liberal solution proved unworkable.

The cumulative effect of the legacies of working-class coherence, middle-class divisiveness, and the continued failure of the strategies of Lib–Labism and middle-class consolidation was to make the democracies that appeared in these societies in 1919 no more than simulacra of the liberal orders that were restabilized in Britain, France, and Switzerland. For neither the liberal social coalitions, the liberal economic policies, nor the patterns of class organization that underpinned those policies were available in aliberal societies. Let us first examine the effects of middle-class divisiveness and the failure of Lib–Labism and middle–class consolidation. We will then turn to the inability of markets to discipline trade unions.

Neither Liberalism Nor Lib–Labism

Denmark

In Denmark, where Lib–Labism had been a late but determining feature of prewar politics, there also occurred no regime shift–cum–crisis comparable to those found in Norway, Sweden, Germany, Spain, and Italy. Danish Lib–Labism had already been successful in removing the institutional barriers to working-class power by its responsibility for the change of system in 1901 and franchise reform in 1915. The latter had made an already broad franchise nearly universal, and the subsequent revisions of the electoral law in 1918 and 1920 were comparatively minor. The Danish Social Democrats' prewar ally, the Radicals, governed throughout the years from 1913 to 1920, and did so with Social Democratic support. In November 1918, the Social Democratic leader Thorvald Stauning joined the government as Minister of Social Affairs to oversee the implementation of a range of reforms that were probably crucial in containing radical impulses within the working class.[1] Although the strike rate was very high by international standards in 1919 and

1920, strikes were directed at employers rather than the political order, and any threat to the latter was residual.[2]

There was consequently no abrupt collapse of an old governing coalition; nor was there a desperate search in the 1920s for a new stabilizing coalition. The closest approximation of a regime crisis in these years was provided by the Easter Crisis of 1920. A few days before Easter, the King, Christian X, deposed a Lib–Lab government with a Folketing majority and sought to appoint a conservative, nonparliamentary government in its place. This move was precipitated by conservative dissatisfaction with the coalition's Schleswig policy, reacquisition of parts of the territories lost to Germany in 1864 having been placed on the agenda by Germany's defeat. The removal of the coalition coincided with threats by Copenhagen employers of a lockout and provoked a Socialist threat of a general strike. The strike threat lead the King and employers to back down, so that the King's government was removed, the principle of Folketing sovereignty was reaffirmed, and the unions were successful in gaining most of the demands they had made of employers. The crisis has been a source of much debate among Danish historians.[3] From our point of view, however, it is mainly significant precisely because it changed nothing. The Social Democrats and the unions were not challenging the established order; they were defending it.

When the crisis was resolved and new elections held, the Lib–Lab alliance was replaced by an alliance of the Conservatives and the Liberals— that is, by a coalition of middle class consolidation. This middle-class coalition governed between 1920 and 1924 and again between 1926 and 1929. During the intervening two years the Social Democrats formed their first government with the support of their middle-class Radical allies. These were stable coalitions based on Folketing majorities; they were unhindered by the shifting of alliances from issue to issue that had such a catalytic effect in Norway, Sweden, Germany, Spain, and Italy. There was also little of the middle-class fragmentation that was important elsewhere. The four major parties of the prewar era persisted, with the Liberals continuing to dominate rural areas and especially the agrarian middle classes; the Conservatives were mainly a party of the urban middle classes, the Radicals were the party of the shrinking but still important progressive fraction of the urban middle classes, and the Social Democrats were the party of urban workers.[4]

If, as a result of its earlier experience of Lib–Labism, Denmark enjoyed a more stable and effective political order during these years, as we shall see, its governments still had to confront the problem of governing a society in which labor had become powerfully and coherently organized before Lib–Labism was effective. While its prewar Lib–Labism and more stable pattern of interwar alliances gave it something in common with liberal societies, its powerful working-class movement would give it something in common with aliberal societies.

Germany

The story was very different in the other old aliberal societies, where constitutional change was the main theme of 1919 and 1920. Germany provides the most dramatic example of this. The revolution of 1919 deposed the Kaiser, allowed the Social Democrats to help write a constitution that made the Reichstag sovereign, and equalized the Prussian franchise. It thus removed the constitutional barriers to Social Democratic political power. The revolution was a failure, however, in that removing these barriers was tantamount to neither the permanent withdrawal from politics of the traditional interests they had protected nor to the creation of a regime-stabilizing coalition that could make the new institutions work.

The *Interfraktioneller Ausschuss* of Social Democrats and middle-class parties that had been made in 1918 and 1919 was a transient one premised on the ending of the war, the establishment of a republic, and the Stinnes-Legien agreement between industry and labor. That agreement sought to stabilize the economy, preserve private property rights, and legitimize the role of the trade unions.[5] The coalition's effect was temporarily to exclude authoritarian and conservative forces in making the new order. The dissolution of the coalition was not long in coming, however. It started with the end of the industry–labor agreement in 1923 and the attempt by employers to reduce social benefits and limit the influence of the unions.[6]

As elsewhere, liberals and social democrats in Germany defined the alternative stabilization formulas as either a coalition of parts of the middle classes and labor or a coalition of the middle classes. Neither of these formulas worked. The former, which had inaugurated the Weimar Republic, was resorted to for five years, the latter for two years. For seven years neither was attainable and minority or presidential cabinets were in power.[7] The essential problem was that neither the gulf between the working and middle classes nor the historical fissures within the middle classes could be overcome. By 1923 Lib–Labism had largely exhausted itself, having run aground on the growing ambition of employers to repeal the gains of labor in 1919 and 1920 and the consequent pressure under which middle-class parties came. After 1923, the short-lived resurrection of Lib–Labism in 1928–29 aside, the burden shifted largely to efforts to patch together coalitions among elements of the middle classes. The inherited divisions—between classes, between regions, between religions—were overlaid and reinforced by new foreign and economic policy conflicts over revanchism, reparations, and currency stabilization.[8] Thus, the new political context did not mollify the inherited divisions but instead reinforced and compounded them. In effect, the historical patterns of mobilization that had undermined liberal hegemony and Lib–Labism before the war survived to define the range of political choice in the 1920s rather than to be dissolved by those new choices. Ultimately, fascism succeeded precisely where social democracy and liberalism failed: in overcoming historical animosities and recombining social classes in a coalition that had been beyond the reach of either of the older movements.

This was a system on the brink of collapse—propped up only by the lack of a clear alternative—as early as the end of 1928. Thereafter the government became increasingly and necessarily an agency independent of the parties in the Reichstag and dependent on the prerogatives of the president. The parties preferred reluctant toleration of such governments, which provided them with vetoes of symbolic value, to resolution of the conflicts that divided them.[9] As Gustav Stolper wrote at the time: "What we have today is a coalition of ministers, not a coalition of parties. There are no parties committed to the government any more, only opposition parties."[10] This was the situation of the Weimar system, it bears emphasizing, in 1929, at a time when neither the economic crisis nor the Nazis were yet major forces on the political scene.

Sweden

A similarly incomplete regime shift occurred in Sweden from 1917 to 1919. The conservative ministry of Hjalmar Hammarskjöld had governed through most of the war, resting firmly on the support of the royal house, big business, and the supporters of a strong defense policy. Its appointment in 1914 had constituted a frank repudiation by the King of the principle of parliamentary sovereignty, and this repudiation was hardly diminished by the appointment of a Conservative party ministry in March 1917. For the new government was determined to prevent the establishment of parliamentary democracy or the reform of the franchise. By the autumn, however, it had been forced from office by food riots and the unreliability of the army. In one garrison after another soldiers demonstrated their solidarity with the workers. "It would subsequently be impossible to use military units as security forces . . . and thus . . . the army, the ultimate support of the [Conservatives] was neutralized." Worker and soldier unrest was further inflamed in February and March 1918 by the inclination of the Conservatives to intervene in the Finnish Civil War on the side of the Whites.[11]

A coalition of Liberals and Social Democrats came to power in October 1918 and, as in Germany, oversaw what came to be known in Swedish history as "the democratic breakthrough."[12] The constitutional reform at the heart of this breakthrough consisted not only of the establishment of parliamentary sovereignty, which gained de facto acceptance with the appointment of the Liberal–Social Democratic coalition, but of the franchise reform that followed, eliminating tax qualifications, providing universal and equal suffrage in Second Chamber and township (and therefore upper house) elections, and establishing the political equality of women. As in Germany, this constituted a fundamental shift in the regime in that it extended participatory rights to a previously substantially excluded class that could not simply be absorbed within the confines of the historical patterns.

In compelling this regime shift, the fear of civil war was decisive.[13] For Conservatives well understood that if they brought down the Liberal–Social Democratic coalition by obstructing reform in the upper house, they could install their own government only by a civil war. This awareness, colored as it was by the events in Russia and Finland and the uselessness of the army, was sufficient to force the Conservatives' acceptance of suffrage reform in 1918. The transient fear of civil war did not, however, provide an enduring basis for the Liberal–Social Democratic coalition that oversaw the transition.

Having achieved its breakthrough, Lib–Labism came to an end in March 1920. The proximate causes were provided by disagreements over social policies and township taxation. The subtending reality was that a Lib–Labism that had failed to bridge class conflicts in the vastly less polarized years before the Great War could hardly be expected to do so now in conditions of much heightened tension. For once the immediate threat of civil war had been defused and the institutional shift had been achieved, there remained little on which Social Democrats and Liberals could agree. During the ensuing years the urban wing of the Liberal party split in half and the rural wing broke away to create the Farmers' party. A short-lived minority Social Democratic government followed the collapse of the coalition. When it came to an end after six months, a nonparty conservative ministry came to power. During the next dozen years, nine separate ministries tried to govern the country, the longest lasting just two years. None of these could command a Riksdag majority. Social Democrats tried to govern alone for about three of these twelve years. During the other nine years, governments were provided by various combinations of Liberals and Conservatives. Steven Koblik, using language that could have been taken from any study of Weimar Germany, has summarized the experience of these years:

> . . . the parliament mirrored the splintered social and political interests of Swedish society. The Liberals were extremely naive in their hope for continued cooperation among the left parties; indeed the Liberals themselves could not even stay together and split into two parties between 1924 and 1934. The Socialists . . . found their expectations unfulfilled. What existed instead . . . was a number of different interest groups whose size and strength tended to counterbalance one another. No one group could dominate the others and alliances of convenience developed whereby cooperation was achieved on a given issue; once that issue had been settled the alliance would disappear. . . . In these circumstances no broadly conceived political program could be initiated. Pressing needs . . . were not dealt with effectively because of the inability of the Riksdag to find a program acceptable to a stable majority.[14]

Norway

During the critical days in which members of the Swedish royal house weighed the prospects of civil war against the dangers of franchise reform, Prince Karl acidly remarked that reform would provide Sweden with "truly Norwegian conditions."[15] By that he seems to have meant enfranchised anarchy. For in Norway, where the prewar franchise had been much more encompassing than it was in Sweden, the labor unrest and the revolutionary impulse were still more dramatic. Whereas mainstream Social Democrats in Sweden were able to retain control of their party and manipulate mass discontent, in Norway left radicals were a majority in the party and displaced the Social Democrats.

References to revolutionary impulses must, of course, be immediately qualified, for neither in Norway nor anywhere else in Western Europe did Leninist working-class parties exist. Organizationally none of these parties was equipped to lead or harness a revolution, for they had all grown up as parties of competitive mass mobilization. Within the context of Western Europe, however, the Norwegian Labor party was as radical as any of the larger national movements. Only in Norway and Italy did the majority of the party join the Third International. It was the right-wing social democratic minority that broke away and existed in isolation for some years. If the Labor majority preached the radical message of class warfare, power to workers' and soldiers' councils, and socialism, it was still not communist so much as syndicalist. The syndicalist Labor Opposition movement that had originated in Trondheim in 1911 seized control of the trade union confederation and, through it, the Labor party in 1918 through 1920.[16]

Whereas the prewar containment of working-class power in Sweden had been constitutionally premised on a narrow franchise, in Norway it had been conditioned on a plurality representation and gerrymandering that crippled the Labor party in the Storting. The old law—which had been an antisocialist project of the Liberal party—had guaranteed that nonsocialists would always be able to form majority governments.[17] From 1920, a vote for Labor became roughly equal to a vote for the Liberals or Conservatives, and neither of the latter was any longer guaranteed a governing majority. As in Sweden, this transformation came about in response to working-class unrest. The reform of 1920 introduced proportional representation and completed the extension of the franchise. The latter, which enlarged the electorate by less than 10 percent, when combined with the reform of the representation formula, was enough to break the grip of the old ruling coalition without actually replacing it.[18]

The outcome was a decade and a half of debile governments.[19] Between 1919 and 1933, fourteen governments, all based on Storting minorities, were formed. Neither Lib–Labism nor middle class consolidation proved possible. Liberals and Labor were unwilling to govern together; Liberals, Conservatives, and Agrarians, an offshoot of the Liberal party, were unwilling to govern together. Only once did the Labor party form a government, and then for only eighteen days. As in most other aliberal societies, governments relied on shifting coalitions capable of agreements on single issues but incapable of agreement on a broader program.[20] The inherited conflicts within the middle classes were reinforced and magnified rather than attenuated by the crises of the 1920s. It was typical of this that the new Farmers' party, which could often support the Conservatives on cultural issues, could not accept the Conservatives' (and Liberals') insistence on a return to the gold standard at the prewar parity.[21] Indeed, the main feature of the period was the further political fragmentation of the middle classes, as a new Agrarian party came into existence in 1920, largely at the expense of the Liberals, and some liberal voters shifted to the Conservatives as the best defense against working-class radicalism. In 1933 the Liberals suffered a further loss with the appearance in the southwest of the Christian People's party.[22] Cultural conflicts continued to divide the Liberals from within as well as from the Conservatives. In the first half of the 1920s, four governments were brought down, three elections fought, and two referenda held on the issue of temperance, a matter that focused the inherited conflicts between regions, cultures, and religious temperaments. Disputes over agrarian and urban interests, church governance, education, and language reinforced the divisions.[23]

Italy

Nowhere did the attempt at liberal stabilization fail more swiftly and succinctly than in Italy, where fascists were in power by November 1922. The electoral reform of 1913, which in shifting the arena decisively to mass politics raised the Socialist share of the vote to about 24 percent, had already put the liberals under siege. The reform of 1919, which further enlarged the franchise and introduced proportional representation, and the birth of the Catholic Popolare party completed the transition. Between them, the Popolari and Socialists controlled a majority of the Chamber of Deputies after the 1919 election and no effective majority was possible without one of them.[24]

The Socialist and Catholic challenges did not lead to a Liberal consolidation. Rather, the secular middle-class community continued to fragment. The old struggle between imperialists and democrats, apparent as far back as 1887 and engaged by the Libyan War, was revived with the intervention in 1915, a decision whose logic again rested on a domestic rather than an international calculus. Neither intervention nor pyrrhic victory was sufficient to create a more stable base for the old order, however. When the Salandra government took Italy into the war, its decision did not serve to bridge the old divisions; rather it hardened them. The fragmentation of the secular middle class was made all the worse by the lack of an organized Liberal party before 1913; in the absence of a broader franchise and open southern elections, there had been no organizational imperative for such a party.[25]

The search for a Lib–Lab solution was exhausted even before Giolitti made his final effort on its behalf when he took office for the last time in June 1921. The fragmentation meant that Giolitti and his neutralist Liberals had no viable alliance to offer to reformist Socialists. Giolitti's principal bid for lib–lab power and an accommodation with the Catholics had been provided by his 1919 Dronero Program, which neither induced the return of his erstwhile allies nor provided a rallying point for Liberals. Instead it earned him the title of "Bolshevik of the Order of the Annunciation."[26] Liberals, existing as a half dozen factions in the Chamber and divided between the left and the right, interventionists and neutralists, could neither act together nor induce the Socialists to align with them.[27] The Socialists' maximalist leadership, brought to power by the Libyan adventure and confirmed by the 1915 intervention, would not have been available even if a coherent reformist Liberal movement had existed with which to collaborate. The reformist wing of the Socialist party, which broke away in 1922, and the CGL might have been available, however. Indeed, the CGL leadership worked desperately in 1922 to arrange an accommodation with Liberals and the Popolari. Neither of these historic divides could be bridged.[28] Like its Norwegian counterpart, the Socialist party was unwilling to contemplate shared power and talked of revolution while in practice it remained inactive. The extreme enfeeblement of Italian liberalism, however, meant that unlike Norwegian labor, Italian socialism would not have time to reappraise the nature of the crisis. Antonio Gramsci optimistically compared Francesco Nitti, Giolitti's predecessor, to Kerensky and implied that he would give way to an Italian Lenin.[29] Claudio Treves, a reformist Socialist, more accurately distilled the essence of the situation when he observed, in words addressed to the Liberals, that "the tragedy of the present crisis [is that] you can no longer impose your order on us, and we cannot yet impose ours on you."[30]

The one option that remained was stabilization through an alliance of Liberals and the Popolari. Neither Liberals nor Catholics could accept such a formula. Giolitti and his supporters could not stomach demands for a settlement with the Vatican.[31] Luigi Facta, who followed Giolitti after Bonomi in the premiership and sought a settlement with the Popolari, found his efforts in this direction undermined by renewed anticlericalism within the Liberal ranks and the Popolari's demand for compulsory religious instruction in state schools and a comprehensive program rather than ad hoc understandings.[32] With Facta's failure, the way was open for Mussolini, who succeeded in building a social coalition where Liberals, Socialists, and Catholics had failed.

Spain

In Spain, the two established parties of the Restoration order, the Liberals and Liberal Conservatives, continued to dominate the Madrid parliament during the war years through their support among the central and southern rural and small-town middle classes. The more advanced middle classes of the north and east turned increasingly against the Madrid parties, but "instead of finding allies to support their interests, they split along regional lines. . . ."[33] The year 1917 saw the appearance of the Assembly Movement, and with it the last opportunity to stabilize and reform the old order through the calling of a freely elected Constituent Cortes. The movement was an alliance of workers, the peripheral middle classes, and dissident junior army officers against the Madrid government. Gerald Brenan aptly captured the choice this movement embodied: "This was a critical moment in Spanish history. The large industrialists of Spain, in alliance with the Socialists and other left-wing parties, had come out in open revolution against the government. It was not any longer a mere question of Basque or Catalan regionalism. What was to be decided was whether the factory owners of the north or the large landowners of Castile and Andalusia should have the chief share in governing the country. . . ."[34] The decision was in favor of the landowners of Castile and Andalusia.

The alliance disintegrated within a few months, the proximate cause being a labor dispute on the Northern Railway, a bastion of the Socialist UGT. The subtending cause was the economic particularism of the Catalan industrialists and the Madrid government's ability to manipulate it. The railway dispute was on the verge of settlement when the Madrid government, searching for a crack in the alliance, rejected its terms. A strike that spread across the country soon followed, and with it military intervention: seventy were killed, hundreds wounded, and 2,000 imprisoned. Thereafter, an alliance that included officers and workers was out of the question. The Lliga Catalana, representing the frightened Barcelona middle classes and the fulcrum of the alliance, broke the Lib–Lab alliance by opting for an agreement with Madrid that put the Lliga leader, Francisco Cambó, in the Madrid government and in all matters of tariffs and the Catalan economy generally gave Cambó a free hand. This move to the right killed the alliance and, by provoking the formation of the Catalan Esquerra, further divided the Catalan middle classes.[35]

With the failure of the Assembly Movement, the old order disintegrated rapidly. After the 1918 election, which despite massive bribery and corruption failed to return an effective majority, governments could control neither the Cortes nor the streets. Violence became endemic: between 1919 and 1923, more than 700 people were assassinated in Catalonia alone, among them a prime minister.[36] The economic upheaval of the war provoked the explosive growth of the syndicalist CNT in 1917 and 1918 and almost continuous labor unrest, which the government had the authority neither to pacify nor to crush. The only organized authority in the country was the army, and in this situation it was a short step to General Miguel Primo de Rivera's *pronunciamiento* in 1923.

Primo de Rivera's regime was not a fascist dictatorship, but rather a traditional authoritarian order of the same sort found throughout Eastern Europe during most of the twenties and thirties. Its support, which was initially quite substantial, came mainly from the middle classes, including those of the periphery, which had grown tired of the constant crises of the old order but were not ready to write off representative government. It was intended as an interim dictatorship, one whose raison d'être was to break the unruliness of labor, pending a return to representative government.[37] In that respect, which draws a very fundamental distinction between it and fascism, it represented the crisis transformation of liberalism into authoritarianism rather than a wholesale abandonment of liberalism. Because it was not a thorough break with liberalism, it did not remake according to its own ideology the organizations that mediated between society and the state. Instead, it tolerated those that were not too disruptive and applied force to those it found unruly.

As the return to representative government became a more remote possibility, the point of the dictatorship became less apparent, for lacking its own ideology and institutional ambitions, it could neither offer Spain a regular alternative to representative government nor, in the end, resist the demands for its restoration. For "it had no ideology, no program, and no clear idea about how to institutionalize itself."[38] The absence of institutional ambitions, especially regarding labor, was the key. Like other traditional dictatorships, it did not seek to reconstruct labor. Instead, it crushed the movement that threatened it most, the CNT, and allowed a fairly domesticated UGT to exist within narrow confines.[39]

During the seven-year life of the dictatorship, Socialist labor matured into the best organized body of opinion in the country. When the dictatorship fell in 1930, the Socialist party emerged as the largest in the country and the Socialist trade unions had a virtual monopoly on the organization of Spanish workers. Membership during these years remained unchanged until 1927, after which it grew only modestly, from about 200,000 to 270,000 in 1930.[40] But the Socialist unions used the interlude of the dictatorship to establish an organizational infrastructure throughout the country even as Primo de Rivera was forcibly destroying anarcho-syndicalism.[41] With the end of the dictatorship in 1930, UGT and Socialist party membership skyrocketed, and they acquired an organizational density at least comparable to Italian socialism in the early postwar years.[42]

This modernization of Spanish socialism would not have been possible in the absence of the modernization of much of Spanish society itself by the dictatorship. The regime had powerful developmental commitments that markedly upgraded transport, power generation, education, and social services.[43] It was probably the first in Europe to use deficits on its capital accounts to stimulate infrastructural growth. Primo de Rivera, who was no economist but fancied himself a man of the people, was said to have celebrated the manipulation of the accounts to show a long-term balance on the capital side by ordering the state pawn shops to redeem all the mattresses of the poor.[44] Data on real wages for these years are notoriously unreliable, but it seems clear that whatever their course Spanish workers perceived themselves to be making real gains in their standards of living. This may have been as much due to the greater availability of employment, including public employment, as to changes in wages. Also, "a number of other elements combined to create the sensation of improvement in the welfare of the working class. . . . These factors included price controls, the gradual spread of social insurance, programs for low-cost housing, schools, hospitals, and public health. . . . Those were the intangibles behind 'los felices veinte.' "[45]

The relative prosperity of these years and the growth of the Socialist movement were important in setting the stage for the Republican order established in 1930, for that order was brought into existence by a Lib–Lab coalition and under conditions that were decidedly unpolarized.[46] Yet the cycle would begin again, with Spain now experiencing the same sort of political decay that had occurred elsewhere in Europe in the 1920s and for the same reasons. For the removal of the constitutional barriers to labor participation was by no means tantamount to the establishment of a stabilizing coalition. The first three years of the Republic revealed the same failure of both Lib–Labism and middle-class consolidation, the same political fragmentation of the middle classes, the same inability to form durable governing coalitions that was prevalent elsewhere.

If the dictatorship had been an attempt to stabilize the distribution of power that inhered in the institutions of the old Restoration Monarchy, the collapse of the dictatorship and then the Monarchy itself created a power vacuum into which the political interests previously excluded could now step. With Primo de Rivera's departure for the churches and brothels of Paris (he is said to have spent the rest of his days moving from one to the other), the Castilian and Andalusian interests that had once been the backbone of the old Restoration Liberal and Conservative parties found themselves in disarray. The August 1930 Pact of San Sebastian formalized a coalition of parts of the middle classes and the Socialist working classes. Representation of the middle classes was provided by the moderate Radicals and by the Republican left. The pact subscribers agreed with representatives of Catalonia on the establishment of a democratic republic that would prepare for the regional autonomy of Catalonia as well as full civil liberty and equality.[47]

Beyond this, however, there was not much they could agree on, and from this amorphous coalition emerged a constantly proliferating number of middle-class parties, as conflicts over the two historic issues of the Church and regional autonomy were compounded by divisions over agrarian and social reform.[48] By 1930, the nonsocialist Republicans, who had been organized in 1929 as the Radical Republican, Federal Republican, and Republican Action parties, divided further to include the Radical Socialists, the Progressives, the Catalan Left (Esquerra) and Catalan Action parties as well. To these were added the Basque Nationalist party and the left Galician party (ORGA) in 1931. In 1933, the Radical Socialists and Federal Republicans each divided into three parties.[49] Some of these divisions reflected only the instability of a newborn party system and conflicts among ambitious politicians. But the more substantial subtending conflicts over the enforcement of anticlerical legislation, of regional autonomy and social and agrarian reform were tearing the middle-class left apart internally and at the same time continuously diminishing the fraction of the middle-class left willing to align with the Socialists.

The most fundamental of the divisions within the middle classes concerned attitudes toward the Church. The nonsocialist left was anticlerical and willing to align with the Socialists, but it could not carry enough of the middle classes with it to create a stable coalition. It was, moreover, unenthusiastic about the Socialists' agrarian and social reforms, and consequently could align with the Socialists only with difficulty. The Socialists, for their part, were much less enthused by the anticlericalism that energized the left Republicans. By 1933 the Radicals, originally part of the Republican coalition, were no longer willing to underwrite the agrarian reform of the Socialists and the anticlericalism of the nonsocialist left. With their withdrawal from the coalition, a government based on a Lib–Lab alliance could no longer survive in the Cortes, and there was no choice but to dissolve the Cortes at least two years early.[50]

The middle-class right was sympathetic to the Church, and thus prevented from aligning with anticlerical middle classes. Middle-class consolidation, then, depended on a shaky alliance of the Catholic CEDA and the Radicals who had deserted the original Republican coalition. After the 1933 election, an unstable series of center–right governments based on this formula followed one after another for three years. This formula, too, failed. The proximate cause of its failure was financial scandals in which leading Radicals were implicated. The subtending cause was the turmoil within the Radical party itself that its ambivalent attitudes on land reform, restoration of Jesuit properties, and maintenance of Catholic schools engendered. Middle-class consolidation was further inhibited by disputes over regional autonomy. The Basque Nationalists, who were Catholic and conservative but insisted on an autonomy statute for Vizcaya, Alava, and Guipúzcoa, would have been natural allies of the CEDA and Radicals but were alienated by the latter's refusal to support an autonomy statute. The middle-class left, which by this time dominated Catalonia, was unavailable because of its insistence on regional autonomy—the center–right government had obstructed Catalonian

Generalitat's efforts to implement its own land reform—and its anti-clericalism.[51] With the collapse of the Radical–CEDA government, the strategies of both Lib–Labism and middle-class consolidation had unambiguously failed. Another premature dissolution of the Cortes followed.[52] The election that ensued pitted these two governing formulas against each other, with the Popular Front attempting to resuscitate Lib–Labism and the right struggling for an adequate consolidation of the middle classes. The popular vote was almost dead even: about 4 million for the left, 4 million for the right, and one-half million for the disintegrating center.[53] Although the electoral system provided the Popular Front with a parliamentary majority, it did not provide it with the coherence to govern, and the collapse of public order that followed between February and June 1936 set the stage for General Franco's *pronunciamiento* and the Civil War.

Belgium and the Netherlands

Among the societies in which prewar Lib–Labism had failed, it was only in Belgium and the Netherlands that the syndrome of constitutional breakthrough leading to political deadlock was avoided. The elimination of plurality voting in Belgium and the enlargement of the previously very narrow Dutch franchise proved a less profound shock to the established orders because in both societies the prewar hegemony of clericalism was sustained and provided a stabilizing interclass coalition even in the more democratic context. In both countries, the confessional parties and trade unions absorbed a large fraction of the working class. The combined membership of the Catholic and Protestant trade union confederations in the Netherlands reached 80 percent of the total social democratic trade union membership. The Catholic unions in Belgium enrolled about 35 percent of the organized labor force.[54] In Belgium the Catholic party dominated every government formed between 1919 and World War II. Every Dutch government formed was a coalition of the confessional parties; Liberals participated only infrequently. In Belgium, the Catholic party could play the Socialist party off against the Liberal party, and in practice the Catholics were unwilling to include the Socialists in any government that did not include the Liberals. The Dutch Labor party remained frozen in opposition for the entire interwar period.[55] The combination of hegemonic clericalism and labor movements divided between socialism and Catholicism in Belgium and socialism, Catholicism, and Protestantism in the Netherlands reproduced a continuity of political power and, as we shall see, even economic policies that were functionally similar to the continuities found in liberal societies.

Elsewhere, constitutional mechanisms by which traditional elites had preserved their power were broken in 1919, but supplanting those elites required removal of more than the old barriers. It required the making of a new regime–stabilizing coalition. In most societies the search for that coalition required more than a decade. In the years of that search, Norway, Sweden, Italy, Germany, and Republican Spain suffered a common syndrome of failed Lib–Labism, aborted middle class consolidation, ineffectual minority governments, shifting alliances, and political deadlock. At their best, these political arrangements provided for no more than a truce between contending interests, especially labor and capital but, as time passed, included agriculture as well. In times of crisis, politics tended to be reduced to a naked struggle among competing interests with few mechanisms available to regulate that struggle and no national myths or traditions available to obscure privilege or justify collective sacrifices. All of this provided the cumulative sense in which these societies suffered a perpetual regime crisis in the years before social democratic or fascist stabilization. It was within this context that states sought to grapple with the narrower but nonetheless existential question of trade union unruliness.

Politics Against Markets

The quintessence of a liberal order was the combination of competitively elected governments that rested on middle-class support with management of the economy principally through market rather than political mechanisms. This distinctiveness translated into an ability to manage the economy without undue concern for the collaboration of labor market organizations. Because trade unions remained incapable of a coherent defense of their earlier wage gains, it was entirely possible for the state, after the passing of the immediate postwar crises, to govern without regard to the attitudes of those organizations. In the context of the 1920s, this meant that it was possible for governments to impose normally deflationary policies as they sought to stabilize currencies and return to conditions of profitability without concern that trade unions would undermine those policies and thereby the government that sponsored them. A government, then, could succeed, at least by its own orthodox lights, without either the collaboration or the demolition and reconstitution of the trade unions. Even if there were occasions, Britain in 1926 being the principal one, when the trade unions could prove obstreperous, the unions' prospects for success remained critically dependent on the support of the state. If the state found the unions' conduct disagreeable, it could withhold its support and the unions would suffer a crushing defeat, as 1926 made patently clear. It was, then, a situation in which the balance of power—given the incoherence of the trade unions and the consolidation of middle-class support behind conservative majorities—profoundly favored a continuation of liberal, market-oriented policies and the political institutions that accompanied them. This, as we have seen, was no less true of the 1930s than of the 1920s. British and Swiss labor remained entirely passive and incapable of extracting policy changes after 1930 while the energy of the French Popular Front was deflected and dissipated in short order.

These were not, then, political and economic orders much threatened by the interwar crises of the 1920s and 1930s, and there was correspondingly little support for either a "sovereignization" of labor organizations within a democratic context of their destruction and reorganization by way of fascism. In aliberal societies, social democracy and fascism represented the basic alternatives to this liberal continuity. In both, the failure of market-oriented liberal policies would require a more self-consciously political solution to the disruptive capacity of trade unions. In social democracies this would entail a measure of sovereignty for trade unions, one that made the unions a critical actor in setting the national agenda. This involved centralized tripartite bargaining among the state, employers and trade unions, and the tying of trade union behavior to understandings on the economic and social policies the state would pursue. In liberal societies, governing coalitions had no need and less incentive to pursue such institutional innovation. Indeed, labor could not have been included in liberal societies in the democratic corporatist manner that would come to characterize social democracy even if those who governed had wanted this, for labor no more had the organizational requisites for such inclusion than it did for an effective defense of workers' interests in the marketplace. Aside from the enlargement of the franchise, then, these liberal societies remained much as they had been before 1914 in their political institutions and organization of the economy.

Indeed, even in their economic policies the 1930s brought forth little innovation. Britain, France, and Switzerland for long adhered tenaciously to economic orthodoxy and then shifted only to neo-orthodoxy—a combination of competitive devaluation, cartelization, and protectionism—rather than to the more radical break embodied by Keynesian stimulation policies.[56] There was likewise no break with orthodoxy in the two societies, Belgium and the Netherlands, in which confessional movements remained hegemonic. Governments in both countries responded to the Depression by moving toward austerity budgets, sharp cutbacks in public spending including pensions and unemployment compensation, education and social services, and a freezing and subsequent rollbacks of wage and salary compensation in the public sector. As the crisis deepened, so did the resolve the governments attached to the implementation of these policies.[57] As in liberal societies, policies evolved only toward neo-orthodoxy: a system of import quotas and licenses and cartels. This lack of innovation did not reflect an absence of awareness of the alternatives. The labor parties in both countries advanced a *Plan van der Arbeid* that included minimum wages, agricultural supports, fiscal deficits, rotation of employment, extension of the forty-hour week, and public works projects. Both plans failed for political reasons. In the Netherlands, the confessional parties refused to countenance such a break with orthodoxy and—given their own dominance and the socialists' inability to rise above 22 percent of the vote—came under little pressure to do so. In Belgium, the Socialists entered a Catholic–Liberal coalition in 1935 with Hendrik de Mann as Minister of Public Works and the hope that the coalition would adopt the *Plan van der Arbeid*. But "the bourgeois majority in the coalition simply refused to do so and thus began five years of coalition frustrations for the [Socialists]."[58]

In other societies in which liberalism had failed, the situation was very different. Failed liberalism resulted in powerfully organized actors in the labor market, and those trade unions had the coherence to undermine the state's policies if they found them unattractive. Ultimately in these societies the state could combine labor peace with a stable mass base only with the collaboration of either the trade unions or employers, or both. The balance of power between labor and employers in that collaboration itself became a function of the kind of urban–rural coalition that would eventually replace the faulted alternatives of Lib–Labism and middle-class consolidation. That coalition, along with the question of why it appeared so much more quickly in some societies than in others, takes us well ahead of ourselves, however. For the present we must attend to the antecedent incompatibility of the inherited labor movements and a liberal stabilization.

A liberal order assumed the workability of market-driven economic policies. Let us start by examining the ways in which markets fell short in disciplining the wage demands and strike activity of trade unions in aliberal societies. In Chapter 6, we examined in some detail the inability of British, French, and Swiss trade unions to challenge the established order and the ways that inability derived from their incoherence. We must now consider the reverse image of that incoherence by considering the ability of trade unions to protect their members in aliberal societies. That ability appears to have had less to do with the sheer number of troops that trade unions could deploy than with their ability to deploy them effectively. Trade union membership exploded everywhere in 1919 and 1920. After a decline in the early 1920s, it rose and stabilized in the second half of the decade. Trade union density in Britain, France, and Switzerland continued to lag behind in that of aliberal societies, but there is only a very weak relationship between trade union density and the course of real wages.[59] Let us keep in mind that during the decade in question, the 1920s, the greater success of trade unions in aliberal societies was not a function of having their allied labor parties in power. During almost all of the years we examine, governments were controlled by nonsocialist parties.

Nor was greater success a function of superior industrial growth in these societies. Indeed, little relationship existed between the course of economic growth and the course of real wages in Western Europe during the 1920s. The best improvements in industrial output appeared in France, Italy, Switzerland, Sweden, and Germany. Belgium, Britain, and the Netherlands did rather more poorly; Denmark and Norway lagged still further behind.[60]

Yet the best gains in real wages occurred in Germany, Sweden, Denmark, and Norway. Real wages followed a more mixed course in Italy and stagnated or actually declined in France, Belgium, the Netherlands, Switzerland, and Britain.[61]

During these years, attempted cuts in state spending, taxes, and wages were more often than not de rigueur as one state after another sought to return to the gold standard and then to preserve the value of its currency. There was an almost fanatical belief in the virtue of gold and the need to restore monetary and exchange stability at the earliest possible moment. The repegging of currencies to gold, or to gold-backed currencies, came to be regarded as a sign of national economic virility, and only Spain failed to do this before the system collapsed for good in 1931. But no coordinated plan of restoration was attempted, and governments fixed the value of their currencies on an ad hoc basis and almost without reference to relevant costs and prices. Stabilization was consequently a long, drawn-out affair that lasted almost the entire decade. Even after a government had restored the relationship between its currency and gold, the problem of preserving the fixed value of the currency remained everywhere, save in France and perhaps Germany where currencies were undervalued. And in every country after the immediate postwar crises of 1919–20 had been digested, entirely aside from the problem of returning to the gold standard, orthodoxy advised—and government's sought to embrace—a preference for investment over consumption. No government in power for any length of time, then—certainly not after the German Social Democrats withdrew from the Weimar coalition in 1923 and before the Spanish Socialists joined the Republican coalition in 1931—was committed to substantial gains in workers' incomes.

The primary purpose of the prewar gold standard had been to safeguard external stability even if this meant, as it sometimes did, sacrificing domestic stability. The old system, which had actually existed for only about a quarter of a century before the Great War, had worked reasonably well because business cycles were then in comparative harmony and lower levels of political mobilization made for lower levels of demands on states. The mass mobilization, shift to fairly universal franchises, and dyssynchronization of business cycles that followed from the war made the subordination of domestic economic activity to exchange stability vastly more difficult. For that subordination produced strong pressures on industrial wages.

Broadly speaking, there were three routes back to the gold standard in the 1920s. Societies that pursued the first route sought to return to prewar parity. That normally meant that a currency must take a forced march upward of 30 percent or more. In the extreme case of Denmark, it meant recouping a 70 percent drop in the value of the krona. Among the countries that returned to parity were Denmark, Britain, Norway, Sweden, Switzerland, and the Netherlands. In all of these, the restoration of parity produced overvalued currencies that could be sustained only by almost continuous deflationary pressures. To devalue was out of the question, since this would have involved a serious loss of prestige. The alternative, therefore, was to adjust the domestic economy to accord with the exchange rate, which involved compressing domestic cost and price levels and squeezing wages. Sweden, the Netherlands, and Switzerland returned to parity in 1923 and 1924, following severe bouts of deflation. In Sweden, production and income in percentage terms fell twice as far in 1920 through 1922 as they did in the 1929 collapse.[62]

Britain, whose international banks and shipping and insurance industries prevailed in their struggle against domestic manufacturers for an early return to convertibility at a high rate, followed in 1925. The subsequent sharp deflationary pressure led to the industrial demands for wage cuts that, in turn, provoked the 1926 General Strike and so polarized manufacturing and the unions. The governments and central banks in Norway and Denmark induced full-scale depressions for several years starting in 1924, to return to prewar parity. Indeed, in Norway these self-induced wounds cut deeper into economic activity than even the collapse of 1929–32.[63] The Italian government did not seek to restore the prewar parity, but it did sustain a decidedly overvalued currency. In August 1926, Mussolini promised to "defend the lira to the last breath, to the last drop of blood."[64] Whose breath and blood he did not say, but the sharp deflation that followed brought industrial expansion to a halt and unemployment grew precipitously. Mussolini's authoritarian state provided a prodrome of one type of solution when, in the face of the pressure on the lira, it enforced a wage reduction of 10 percent in 1927. Elsewhere competitive politics precluded such a dramatic response, at least for a few more years.

At the other extreme were countries that experienced bouts of hyperinflation leading to complete economic collapse and the introduction of new currencies before a return to gold. Among these were Hungary, Poland, Austria, and Germany. In Germany, recovery from the inflation and subsequent stabilization of the mark were not really completed until a minor crises, leading to the collapse of some of the cumbersome industrial empires that had been formed during the inflation, was surmounted in 1926. The inflation wiped out most fixed debts, it is true; but it also wiped out most working capital. Much of the investment made during the inflation had been in industries that were already antiquated and suffering excess capacity, so that much reorganization and renovation was required after stabilization. Extensive rationalization after 1925 eliminated jobs and plants and generated comparatively high unemployment rates notwithstanding the deficits the Weimar state ran on its accounts.

Between the extremes of the return to prewar parity and hyperinflation were the experiences of such societies as Belgium and France, which incurred minor bouts of inflation before deflating at mid-decade. In both cases reconstruction was financed by inflationary government borrowing against the assumption of future German reparations. In the end, the reparations were not forthcoming to the extent expected—in France they covered only about one-third of the costs of reconstruction—and orthodoxy prevailed. In France, in the wake of an exchange crisis Raymond Poincaré's conservative government stabilized the franc in 1926 through a sharp deflation. Belgium, whose own currency was tied closely to the French franc, followed a similar course.[65]

In a decade in which orthodoxy advised that real wages should at least remain stable, if not decline, trade unions in aliberal societies were having remarkable success in preserving the real value of workers' wages. They were, in fact, markedly increasing the value of wages. They were doing so, moreover, even under conditions of exceptionally high unemployment. Their success was so great, in fact, that at least some evidence suggests they were simultaneously increasing labor's share of national income. This stands in stark contrast to the experience of trade unions in liberal societies, where real wages stagnated or fell and labor's share of national income declined even in the context of comparatively low unemployment rates.

The data on wages, prices, unemployment and share of national income are seldom complete and almost never standardized for the years between the Great War and the Depression. In the case of Spain, where wages and the collective bargaining power of trade unions varied enormously according to the locale in the last years of the Restoration order, about all we can say is that the wages of skilled workers, especially trade unionists, probably out-paced prices while the wages of other workers often did not.[66] Historians are in general agreement that workers experienced an improvement in their standards of living during the *dictadura*.[67] Real wages in industry and es-pecially agriculture rose sharply from 1931, with agricultural wages then falling after early 1934 under the center–right government.[68] For other coun-tries, actual data are available, but it will not do to put too fine a point on the numbers. It is possible to discern fundamental differences in the directions and magnitudes of the changes. Let us start with the single most important conditioning variable for trade unions, the level of unemployment. Unem-ployment was decidedly lower during the 1920s in the liberal societies. In Switzerland, for which only partial data are available, the rate never rose above the 3.6 percent of 1922. By 1923, it had fallen back to 1.7 percent. During the years 1926 through 1929, it averaged just 2.5 percent.[69] Unem-ployment data are even less complete for France. Alfred Sauvy's incomplete figures for the labor force as a whole suggest that the rates were 2.5 percent in 1921, 1.2 percent in 1926, and 2.1 percent in 1931.[70] The estimates made by Walter Galenson and Arnold Zellner are higher, although still com-paratively low, but are limited to employment in mining, manufacturing, and construction. Their average for the years 1921 to 1930 is 3.4 percent.[71] Whatever the precise numbers, we can be sure that the French rate was comparatively low in the 1920s. For even in the worst year of the Depression, according to Galenson and Zellner, unemployment remained fairly low in France: unemployment in mining, manufacturing, and construction did not rise above 15.4 percent even in 1932.[72] Among the liberal societies, Britain had the highest rate of unemployment: for the years 1921 through 1929, it averaged 12.1 percent.[73] In the Netherlands and Belgium, where hegemonic clericalism and labor movements divided by clericalism and socialism reproduced a situation analogous in many respects to that in liberal societies, the average annual unemployment rates for the years 1921 to 1929 were 3.6 and 3.2 percent, respectively.[74] In Germany, the average annual rate for the same years was 9.2 percent. In Sweden it was 14.2 percent; in Norway it was 16.8; and in Denmark it was 17.1 percent.[75] Given these unemployment rates, we would expect, in the absence of other interventions, that real wages would change most favorably for labor in Switzerland, France, Belgium, and the Netherlands, followed by Germany, Britain, Sweden, Norway, and Denmark, in that order.

There were, of course, other interventions, not the least of which were provided by the trade unions. In liberal societies and in Belgium and the Netherlands, real wages either stagnated or fell during the decade. In France from 1921 through 1929, real hourly wages for industrial workers fell by 22 percent.[76] In Britain in the years 1920 through 1930, real hourly wages of industrial workers rose just 2 percent; for the years 1922 through 1930, they rose 3 percent.[77] In Switzerland, the years 1922 through 1929 saw workers receive an increase in real hourly wages of just 5 percent.[78] In Belgium, between 1920 and 1930, the hourly money wage for industrial workers declined 17 percent while the retail price index rose 92 percent.[79] In the Netherlands real wages rose by 4 percent during the period 1926 through 1930, the only years for which data are available.[80]

In Italy, as everywhere, real wages rose sharply in the boom years of 1918 through 1921. They then started an almost continuous descent with the beginning of the destruction of the unions in the middle of 1921.[81] In Germany, which had an unemployment rate of more than three times the rates in Switzerland, France, Belgium, and the Netherlands and three-quarters of the rate in Britain, real hourly wages in industry rose by 63 percent during the years 1924 through 1930, the only years for which data are available.[82]

K. G. Hildebrand has written of the Scandinavian experience that "the general situation certainly did not give labor a strong bargaining position. Nevertheless, wages seem to have risen somewhat more than might have been expected. In Norway real hourly industrial wages almost doubled during the years 1914–1939. In Sweden the increase was more than 80 percent; in Denmark it was a little less. Most of the increase occurred in the twenties."[83] Indeed, in Sweden, real hourly wages in industry rose 65 percent between 1919 and 1930. In Norway, workers received a gain of 43 percent between 1919 and 1930 and 17 percent between 1922 and 1930. Danish workers, who suffered the highest unemployment in Europe, nonetheless had a real gain in hourly industrial wages of 19 percent between 1919 and 1930 and 12 percent between 1922 and 1930.[84]

There is some evidence that workers' shares of national income were actually increasing in these societies even as they were decreasing in liberal societies. Paul Jostock has shown that in Germany the share of national income consumed by wages and salaries rose from 46.5 percent in 1913 to 60.3 percent in 1930; the share going to industrial entrepreneurs fell from 22.3 percent to 15.1 percent.[85] Peter Flora and his collaborators have concluded that the standardized (i.e., controlling for the size of the sector) share of national income going to labor rose from 61.2 percent to 81.9 percent between 1913 and 1929. Using the same measure and again controlling for the size of the sector, Flora has shown that the share of income going to British workers rose from 63.6 percent to 75.6 percent between 1914 and 1920 and then fell fairly continuously to 67.7 percent in 1930. Peter Hart's figures suggest a rise in the profits of British industry of nearly 14 percent between 1926 and 1929 at a time when wage earnings were static.[86] Again by the same measure, Flora's data indicate that in Switzerland labor's share of national income rose from 59.4 to 61.7 percent between 1910 and 1924; it then fell back to 58.0 percent by 1929.[87] Elsewhere, the evidence of the change of labor's share of national income is more inferential. In France, real wages advanced a mere 10 percent for the entire period 1914 through 1929, as against an increase of one-third or so in industrial production.[88] Between 1925 and 1929, as real wages stagnated, industrial production rose by one-quarter and real per capita income rose by 17 percent.[89] In Belgium and the Netherlands real wages declined even as industrial production and real per capita net domestic product was rising. In Norway and Sweden, real wages grew more quickly than real per capita net domestic product and industrial production.[90] In Denmark, real hourly wages in industry rose more quickly than real hourly product per worker employed in industry.[91]

We may marvel at the capacity of workers in aliberal societies to extract such wage gains against the backdrop of sometimes depression-level rates of unemployment. The debile middle-class minorities and coalitions that sought to govern for most of these years probably did not. For the problem remained that the trade unions that were responsible for the wage gains were making these societies ungovernable by conventional liberal means. Wages were not responding to deflationary policies; indeed their exceptional inelasticity must account in part for the extraordinary levels of unemployment. From the governments' point of view, this peculiar combination of high growth in real wages, depression-level unemployment (except in Germany), and economic stagnation (except in Sweden and more marginally Germany) was the worst of all possible worlds. Moreover, and entirely aside from the inability of governments to enforce their will through market mechanisms, trade unions were making these societies ungovernable by the extraordinary rate of strike activity that they perpetuated even after the great upheavals of 1919 and

1920, and even in the face of the subsequent spectacular and generally unfavorable gyrations in the business cycle. Once again, we encounter problems of data comparability. The sources on which students of long-term trends in strike activity have had to rely for their data are not equally reliable and prone to use somewhat different definitions.[92] Nonetheless, if we are content to make crude distinctions between high and low levels of strike activity and between directions of change—distinctions that are satisfactory for our purposes—the broad outlines of the differences among labor movements seem apparent from the works of Douglas Hibbs, Jr., of Walter Korpi and Michael Shalev, and of Peter Flora and his collaborators.

Hibbs' research has shown that for the interwar period as a whole (1919–1938) Norway, Sweden, Britain, and Denmark had, in that order, the highest volume of strike activity in Europe. France, Belgium, and the Netherlands followed at much lower levels. Italy, for the short period between the end of the war and the repression of the trade unions in 1921, also had an above-average volume of strike activity. Hibbs' data do not include Germany and Switzerland, but the research of Walter Korpi and Michael Shalev does. That research shows Germany with the highest and Switzerland the lowest number of man-days lost per 1,000 nonagricultural workers in Europe between 1919 and 1932.[93]

Labor movements in aliberal societies, then, appear to have been much more strike-prone. This is even more apparent when we take account of the direction of change in trends across time. Everywhere, of course, strike activity tended to diminish after the explosive years of 1919 and 1920. But given this decline from the immediate postwar peak, trends nonetheless remain within the trends. The scoring of Britain, the single liberal society with a high level of strike activity for the period as a whole, is actually an artifact of strikes in the first half of the 1920s and especially the catastrophic strike of 1926. Hibbs' data show that after 1926 the volume of strikes in Britain plummets to less than one-half of the 1921–25 level and remains low for the rest of the interwar period. In Norway, Sweden, and Germany, too, it declines after 1920, but the decline halts at a markedly higher level than in Britain after 1926, and especially higher than in France and Switzerland. In Norway and Sweden, even with markedly higher levels of unemployment, the rate remains at about three times the level found in Britain.[94] Only in Denmark after 1925, in large measure under the weight of an unemployment rate about double the British rate, did it fall to a stabilized level somewhat below the British rate.[95]

In sum, strikes, even under conditions of significantly higher unemployment, were being resorted to with markedly greater frequency in aliberal societies. Moreover, judging by the course of real wages, they were more successful than strikes in liberal societies. It was this combination of exceptional strike volume, high unemployment, rapidly growing real wages, and, for the most part, economic stagnation that characterized the challenge governments faced in aliberal societies in the 1920s and early 1930s. Those governments, of course, rested on deeply fractured coalitions and sought to lead states whose legitimacy was itself problematic.

It was in this cumulative sense that the years before social democratic and fascist stabilization were years of perpetual crisis and liberal failure. Liberal failure did not preclude democratic success, of course. It would still be possible for these societies to be governed as representative democracies. But it was not possible for them to be governed as stable, effective representative democracies without the acquiescence of labor. And given the coherence of labor, that acquiescence could not be obtained through reliance on market forces, for acquiescence would not be forthcoming from labor movements capable of resisting markets, especially when the solicitors of the acquiescence were so patently enfeebled. Ultimately, the acquiescence or actual support of labor—and thus stability, effectiveness, and even legitimacy—would require that politics be substituted in an important measure for markets. And that substitution would require another coalition with a distinctive ideology and different policies.

Irrelevance of Traditional Dictatorship

One of the effects of the war had been the collapse of the old empires of Eastern and Central Europe. The collapse of these empires and the establishment of independent nation-states removed the imperial context that had so heavily conditioned politics in these societies in the years before the war. In the interwar years, domestic conflicts assumed a much more decisive role than they had previously had in shaping the political economies of Eastern and Central Europe.

The balance of forces in these societies was distinctive because liberal parties in them had attained neither the hegemony they had once enjoyed in Britain, France, and Switzerland nor the discredit they had suffered in aliberal societies. The balance of forces was distinctive as well because the countryside remained at lower level of mobilization than in the West, and urban workers, who were a smaller fraction of society, remained less well organized than in the West. Thus, Eastern Europe provides an instructive contrast. Not the least of the insights we can gain from the Eastern experience is in understanding why it was that the old aliberal societies of the West could not acquire the traditional dictatorships that became so common in the East.

It was no more possible to induce labor acquiescence in the aliberal West by the imposition of such traditional dictatorships than it was by the creation of liberal regimes. Here I am interested only in adumbrating the essential characteristics of the traditional dictatorships. That should be enough to make clear why they were not even resorted to in the West, except in the

Primo de Rivera interlude in Spain, and why Western authoritarianism required fascism.

Traditional dictatorships were appropriate only for traditional societies. In all of the societies where such regimes appeared between the wars, more than half of the labor force remained employed in agriculture. In Hungary the share was 51 percent; in Latvia, 55 percent; in Estonia, 56 percent; in Finland, 57 percent; in Poland, 60 percent; in Lithuania, 70 percent; in Romania, 72 percent; in Bulgaria, 75 percent; in Yugoslavia, 76 percent; and in Albania, 80 percent.[96] In contrast, the percentage of the male labor force engaged in manufacturing was small. It was just 9 percent in Lithuania, 11 percent in Romania, 13 percent in Bulgaria, 14 percent in Yugoslavia, 18 percent in Finland and Greece, 19 percent in Latvia, 20 percent in Estonia, 22 percent in Poland, and 26 percent in Hungary.[97] Indicative of the backwardness of these societies, exports were overwhelmingly primary products and an exceptionally high share of industry was in foreign hands. Foreigners owned 33 percent of the outstanding shares in Polish joint-stock companies, including 52 percent of the shares in mining and 65 percent in metallurgy.[98] In Hungary, foreigners controlled 17 percent of the capital in stock companies. In Yugoslavia, the share of foreign ownership was 35 percent; in Bulgaria, 48 percent, and in Romania, 80 percent.[99]

The essential characteristic of these regimes was their defense of a fraction of the urban middle classes and traditional agrarian interests in societies in which the threat from the organized urban working classes remained comparatively low. Urban workers could become a destabilizing force only if they could unite with the much larger class of surplus agrarian labor. For this reason, these states made the existence of urban unions conditional on their agreement not to become engaged in the countryside. One of the main features of Eastern European agriculture was that far more people were on the land than were actually required to work it. There are various ways to measure the size of the superfluous agricultural population. One is to compare the level of agricultural production with the general European level. This certainly overstates the size of the redundant population, since the more capital-intensive technologies of Western agriculture were not available whatever the demographic conditions. By this measure, however, the surplus population ranged from 22 percent in Hungary to 77 percent in Albania.[100] By the less exacting standard of agricultural production in relation to land resources, the surplus populations of Yugoslavia, Bulgaria, and Romania, respectively, would have been 43, 31, and 15 percent.[101]

These were, to say the least, not revolutionary regimes. They were rather counterrevolutionary regimes that sought to preserve the interests of prewar elites. The urban middle classes in whose interests the regimes existed usually belonged to the ethnically dominant, state-dependent sector. Modern economic power was more often in the hands of, in addition to foreigners, pariah ethnic minorities whose opportunities to exercise political power were decidedly limited. In Poland and Hungary these were Germans and Jews; in the Balkans they were Greeks, Jews, and Armenians. The members of the ethnically dominant middle classes were more likely to make a living by finding a sinecure in the bloated state bureaucracies. Hugh Seton-Watson nicely captured the *mentalité* of this class in his description of Balkan bureaucrats:

> The Balkan official does not like to work. He considers himself so fine a fellow that the state should be proud to support him for life and should not ask him to make efforts that will tax his intellect or character. A visitor to a Balkan Ministry or Police Headquarters in the middle of the morning will find the rooms filled with good-natured fellows comfortably enjoying a cup of Turkish coffee and a chat with their friends. The papers lie on their desks. Outside stand, sit and squat patient queues of peasants awaiting their various permits and receipts. Foreigners and citizens with *protekcja* obtain swift and prompt attention, but the people can wait. They have waited many hundreds of years . . . and a few more hours will not make much difference.[102]

The almost complete unworkability of competitive politics in these societies, as in Restoration Spain, derived less from a working-class threat than from the profound backwardness of most of these societies and the hyperfractionalization of their middle classes. In Finland, about 12 percent of the population, disproportionately concentrated among urban elites and larger landowners, was Swedish-speaking. In Latvia, 25 percent of the population, mainly Russians, White Russians, Poles, and Slavs, was not Latvian.[103] The population was further divided between Protestants (55 percent) and Catholics.[104] In Poland, 30 percent of the population was not ethnically Polish.[105] Jews, heavily concentrated in the more modern sectors of the economy, were 25 percent of the population in towns of more than 20,000.[106] In Romania, 30 percent of the population was not ethnically Romanian; Romanians themselves were deeply divided between the more traditional sectors of the Old Kingdom (Regat) and the more modern population of recently acquired Transylvania.[107] In Yugoslavia, about 25 percent of the population was not Serbo-Croatian, a designation that itself meant little and included Montenegrins, Bosnian Moslems, Macedonians, and Bulgarians.[108] In Hungary, Germans and Jews dominated the modern economy. Jews were 23 percent of the population of Budapest, 45 percent of the work force in commerce and banking, and 89 percent of the plants in the iron and metal industries were owned by Jews.[109] Even in Bulgaria, reduced by its defeat in the war to its narrowest ethnic frontiers, minorities constituted 10 percent of the population. In Greece, dispossessed refugees from Turkey, where they had previously been disproportionately middle-class traders, made up 20 percent of the population by 1930. Albania was divided among Moslems, Catholics, and Orthodox. In the south, large landowners were mainly Moslems, peasants were mainly Orthodox Christians.[110]

These were traditional dictatorships in the sense that they almost always preserved limited representative institutions or promised their restoration at some point in the future. They all had had at least a brief experience with competitive politics after World War I. Most of their parliamentary orders were modeled on the constitution of the Third Republic in France. When the democratic orders collapsed, sometimes in a few months, sometimes not for a decade, at least some of the appurtenances of competitive politics were preserved. Constitutions were modified or suspended rather than abolished. In the quasi-constitutional dictatorships that emerged, legislatures continued to function, albeit with severely truncated powers, in Greece, Bulgaria, Yugoslavia, Romania, Poland, Hungary, and Finland. Poland was typical: the Sejm survived Pilsudski's coup, but it no longer had the power to remove a government from office. Legislatures were done away with altogether only in Lithuania, Latvia, and Estonia, but even these preserved some political pluralism.[111] In the others, limited electoral competition remained, with the state party confident that it could make an acceptable outcome in most, especially rural, districts and guarantee itself a majority. In Finland, the victorious Whites simply outlawed the Communist party—which had previously received a quarter of the vote—and perpetually threatened to do the same to the intimidated Socialist party.[112] In Romania the opposition National Peasant party was sometimes even allowed to win an election and form a government, although actual authority was highly centralized in the hands of the "first peasant," King Carol, after 1930.[113] In Poland, where the franchise was not reduced after Pilsudski came to power in a coup d'etat in 1926, the electoral performance of his "Non-Party Bloc for Cooperation with the Government" was bolstered by timely arrests of leading members of the opposition, coercion of voters by local administrators, and ample access to the state's treasury,. In 1935 a new electoral law was passed that impeded the campaigns of opposition parties and provoked them to boycott the elections of 1935 and 1938.[114] The Horthy regime in Hungary was almost a paradigm of the type. In 1922, it abolished the secret and universal suffrage that had been inaugurated in 1919. It reverted to open voting in rural districts and reduced the share of the population enfranchised from about 40 percent to 27 percent.[115] Dissent was not entirely squelched. István Bethlen, Regent Nikolaus Horthy's first prime minister, reached an agreement with the socialist leaders that let them out of jail and permitted the reappearance of their trade unions. The unions were given the right to bargain collectively in exchange for their pledge not to organize in the countryside or among civil servants, railway workers, and postal workers. Some measure of press freedom remained. The Hungarian Socialists were allowed to publish newspapers as long as those papers did not question the basic premises of the regime.[116]

This restrained authoritarianism was typical of the posture these regimes adopted toward labor. They were generally content to tolerate domesticated socialist parties and trade unions. Socialist parties were often granted limited rights to compete with the government party or parties. Trade unions had a limited right to organize certain workers—never agrarian and never in vital industries—and limited rights to bargain collectively and strike. The essential feature was that trade unions were sufficiently hobbled that they could never pose a danger to the state or key employers. This subordination and domestication of the unions was possible because the working class itself was small. There was consequently no need to crush socialist organizations and then replace them with state-sponsored unions and movements that sought, as fascism did, to stamp out all worker dissent and mobilize workers for the fascist state's purposes. They were, then, in both their political and labor market institutions, regimes distinguished by a lack of institutional innovation.

The constituencies of socialist parties and unions were, moreover, mainly limited to comparatively privileged skilled urban workers, who were less of a threat than the often radicalized peasant movements prevalent in these countries. These movements were a major force in Bulgaria and Romania, Lithuania, Latvia, and Estonia, and had been during the civil wars in Finland and Hungary. The security of the dictatorial regimes rested, above all, on the containment of this radical peasant threat. The failure of Bela Kun's short-lived Red republic in Hungary owed much to its alienation of the agrarian proletariat. In turn, the subsequent security of the Horthy regime rested heavily on its ability to disenfranchise this sector and to restore the coercive authority of the gentry.[117]

These regimes were distinguished as well by their lack of ideological content, save nationalism. That nationalism followed from their subordination to Western capitalism, their frequent revanchism, their conditional existence in the wake of the collapse of the traditional hegemons of Eastern Europe—Russia, Imperial Germany, the Habsburg and Ottoman empires—and the imperative of a veneer over the ethnic conflicts that roiled within them. Nationalism, however, was neither the exclusive property of these regimes nor a wellspring of the institutional arrangements. These regimes possessed no ideologies with institutional implications of the sorts that inhered in liberalism, social democracy, and fascism. Liberalism implied markets and interest group pluralism. Social democracy implied the centrality of class organizations and the subordination of markets to politics. Fascism implied the subordination of classes and harnessing them to the purposes of the party and nation. Traditional dictatorship and nationalism implied nothing about the political organization of society other than the suppression of dissent. The fascist accretions—paper corporatism and shirts, whether blue, green, or black—that sometimes appeared in these societies with the growing prestige of fascism and nazism in the 1930s were mere simulacra—forms without content, epochal emblems of modernity, as representative institutions had been in the heyday of liberalism. To be sure, nazism and fascism in Germany and especially Italy, the ideologies of putatively "proletarian" nations seeking their place in the world, had some resonance within the revanchist movements of Hungary, Finland, Bulgaria, and (significantly) nonrevanchist Romania. But the existence of such movements, which in any event never came to power and were often repressed by their governments, no more made these societies fascist than the existence of parliaments in them had earlier made them liberal.

Austria and Czechoslovakia were the only two eastern societies that did not fit this pattern of backwardness, and in both the collapse of the democratic orders was inextricably tied to the interventions of great powers. The extinguishing of democracy in Czechoslovakia was, in the end, a straightforward case of military conquest. Of more interest is the coalition that stabilized Czech democracy in the twenties and thirties, which is examined in Chapter 8. Austria, whose own leaders transformed it into a traditional dictatorship in response to external pressures, we consider here.

Austria, in fact, was almost a paradigmatic example of an aliberal Western society in its developmental experience. It had a level of industrialization that made it a part of the West rather than the East. It had a powerfully organized and coherent labor movement, with a socialist party that received more than 40 percent of the vote throughout the life of the Republic and an allied trade union movement that was among the most centralized and densely organized in Europe.[118]

Austrian liberalism failed under the Habsburgs as miserably as any liberal movement in the West.[119] This failure was inextricably linked to Austria's position in the Empire. A liberal movement could neither succeed in the Empire as a whole, because of the latter's multinational character, nor succeed in Austria alone, because of the dynasty's ability to govern against Austro-German liberalism by manipulating the anti-German sentiments of other national communities. The critical epoch occurred under the premiership of Count Taaffe (1879–93), who broke the ascent of the Austro-German liberals by making an alliance against them with Bohemian and Moravian conservatives and Polish and German landowners outside of Austria.[120] As one of Taaffe's ministers acknowledged, "it was possible to rule Austria without the [Austrian] Germans."[121] Surrounded by the "Iron Ring," German liberals were forced to choose between a conservative, centralized Empire under German hegemony and a federalist and more liberal solution. This dilemma was clarified in the language conflicts with the Czechs and especially in the struggle over the proposed Badeni ordinances of 1897. The ordinances would have ensured complete equality for the Czech and German languages in Bohemia. German street demonstrations were able to kill the ordinances and with them the possibility of a federalist solution to the national conflicts. At the same time, the liberals could defeat the ordinances only by implicitly abandoning their aspirations for power.[122] After 1897, Austria was governed by nonparliamentary ministers, mainly officials, until the collapse of the Empire.

Czech liberals faced the same dilemma. Just as Austro-German liberals could not align with liberals of other nationalities, the liberal Young Czech movement of the years after 1890 could not align with the German minorities of Bohemia, Moravia, and Silesia. Those German minorities were doubly important, because they were the economically dominant sector of the most industrialized region of the Empire. The threat that Czech nationalism posed to their local hegemony drove them into the arms of the conservative dynasty.[123]

The dilemma of the Austro-Germans accelerated the collapse of the liberal movement. It was the more nationalist Pan-Germans who "broke away first from the Liberal mother tree."[124] A more serious blow, however, was the creation of the Christian Social party, which became the strongest party in the Austrian parliament in 1907. The party assumed a position of dominance in the interwar Republic analogous to that of the Catholic party in Belgium, albeit one less secure. In the absence of intolerable pressures from first Mussolini and then Hitler, that hegemony might well have preserved the institutions of the Republic, albeit with more stress than was apparent in Belgium. As it was, the collapse into traditional dictatorship in 1934 cannot be understood apart from the external pressures. The growing polarization between the Catholics and Socialists was powerfully fueled first by the activities of the paramilitary Heimwehr, whose effectiveness depended on Mussolini's financial support and diplomatic protection. The existence of the Heimwehr was essential in inducing the Socialists to establish their own paramilitary force, in encouraging a reception for the revolutionary rhetoric of the Socialist left, and in leading conservative Catholics to toy with the idea that they could use the Heimwehr to crush the socialists militarily.[125]

With Hitler's rise to power, the pan-German element of the Heimwehr regrouped in the Nazi party. The Catholic prime minister, Dollfuss, who was no Nazi, was not opposed to the democratic order, and was committed to preserving Austria's independence, soon found his position untenable. He had either to make his government dependent on Nazi support, compromise with the Socialists, or make himself a dictator. The first choice implied the growth of Nazi power and ultimately the end of Austrian independence. The second was unacceptable to Mussolini, who could still exert pressure through the Heimwehr, and foundered on Socialist diffidence.[126] The third was the route Engelbert Dollfuss and his successor, Kurt Schuschnigg, ultimately chose after banning the National Socialists.

It is because the interventions of Hitler and Mussolini defined this range of choice that the dictatorship cannot be understood apart from Austria's international position. The least we can say is that in the absence of German and Italian pressure, Dollfuss and Schuschnigg would not have had to choose between a dictatorship and a government with the Socialists. Moreover, in the absence of that intervention there would have been fewer obstacles, both immediately, in the form of Mussolini's opposition, and historically, in the form of the growing gulf between the Catholics and Socialists, to a Catholic–Socialist coalition. In establishing the dictatorship, Dollfuss was clearly responding to Italian pressure exerted through the Heimwehr; the Socialists were correct when they referred to him as the Heimwehr's "prisoner."[127] The alliance between the Catholic Social party and the Heimwehr in the Vaterland Front was intended to create an effective response to the Nazi challenge.[128] The subsequent disarming of the Socialist's paramilitary organization, the outlawing of the Socialist party and trade unions, and the signing of the Rome Protocols by which, on paper, Austria became an Italian satellite were necessary consequences of Dollfuss's alliance decision.

As it was, Dollfuss's successor, Schuschnigg, almost succeeded in making the Catholic–Socialist alliance that would have restored Austrian democracy. When Mussolini's escapades in Ethiopia compelled an Italo-German rapprochement, the value of the Italian connection disappeared and the way was open for a growing Nazi penetration of the Austrian state under pressure from Hitler.[129] The crisis came to a head in March 1938, when Schuschnigg, desperately trying to stave off an impending *Anschluss*, proposed a referendum of Austrian independence and invited the Socialists, who responded favorably, to join him in a coalition.[130] Once again, foreign intervention was decisive: Hitler forced Schuschnigg to abandon the referendum and the coalition.[131] Three days later the German army marched in.

Austria's experiences, both under the Empire and during the life of the Republic, were so heavily shaped by its international position that they shed little light on the more normal experiences of aliberal societies. The appearance of traditional dictatorships almost everywhere else in Eastern Europe does, however, inform our understanding of the Western aliberal experience. The limited pluralism that continued in those societies under dictatorships and the absence of substantive ideologies and of fascist organizations of labor point to the comparative weakness of their labor parties and trade unions and more generally to the low level of political mobilization. In the face of such limited mobilization, a traditional dictatorship was entirely sufficient to protect the interests of those served by the regimes. The fascist organization of labor and a rationalizing fascist ideology were altogether unnecessary.

On the other hand, it is inconceivable that such a dictatorship could have remained in power for long in the highly mobilized and modern societies of the aliberal West, where neither weak labor movements nor sheer backwardness could be counted on to contain dissent. The authoritarian regimes that appeared in the aliberal West were revolutionary regimes: they sought to disenfranchise, in the fullest sense, the working classes, and to destroy political and labor market gains that had been generations in the making. Accomplishing this required something much closer to totalitarianism. Granted, fascism reached its "perfection" in Germany, where the society was most mobilized and the revolutionary break with labor's past the most profound. In Italy, the society was less mobilized and labor was weaker to begin with. That was still more true in Spain. Thus, in Italy and even more in Spain, fascist reconstruction could be less thoroughgoing. This was the case in Spain because Franco came to power having beaten his opponents militarily. Nonetheless, in each of these societies, authoritarian stabilization required much more than it did in the East: the closing of parliaments, the extinguishing of all political parties, the stifling of all press freedom, and especially the destruction of the working-class movements and their replacement by monopolistic organizations of state control. This was not a difference in degree; it amounted to a difference in the kind of regime. In practice, these steps were probably interdependent. For in the highly mobilized West, an authoritarian regime probably could not succeed at any of them for long unless it did all of them. In the West, dissent had become institutionalized and a way of life among all sectors and classes. A regime certainly could not close the parliament, silence the press, and destroy the parties for long without destroying the socialist movement. It is, to say the least, unimaginable that Hitler or Mussolini or even the militarily victorious Franco could have reached "Eastern" understandings with the socialists by which the latter restrained their criticisms and curtailed their organizing and strike activity. No, in the face of such broad mobilization and such powerful movements—with their centralized direction, long histories, and powerful working-class expectations and loyalties—durable authoritarianism had to be the real thing. It had to be fascism.

Social Democracy and Fascism

Social democracy and fascism were the political economies of societies in which middle-class divisiveness and working-class coherence subverted liberal stabilization and modernity and mass mobilization precluded traditional dictatorship. Social democratic political economies constituted a fundamental break with liberal political economies in several vital respects: the political hegemony of working-class parties; the participation of trade unions in governance as semisovereign entities; the subordination of markets to politics, especially in wage determination; and the more radical break with liberal economic orthodoxy in response to the depression.

Fascism was distinguished from traditional dictatorship in equally fundamental ways: the complete suppression of representative institutions; its closer approximation of totalitarianism and greater intolerance of dissent and opposition; its commitment to popular mobilization in the service of the state and its rejection of the negative legitimacy of mass apathy; its total extirpation of socialism and reorganization and subordination of the working classes; its rejection of liberal economic and political dogma; and the primacy of politics over markets. This more totalitarian model reflected the higher level of mobilization that fascist, in contrast to traditional, dictators confronted.

Social Democracy: The Scandinavian Solution

The foundation of Social Democratic hegemony was provided by the political alliances that were formed in the 1930s between urban workers and family peasants.[1] The Kanslergade Agreement reached between the Danish

Social Democrats, the Agrarian Liberals, and peasant organizations in 1933 was typical of the agreements that underpinned such alliances. Its main features were (i) expansion of public employment, (ii) a prohibition against strikes and lockouts and a wage freeze for one year, (iii) social welfare reforms, (iv) a 20 million kroner reduction in agricultural property taxes, (v) a reduction of agricultural interest rates and state assistance in the conversion of more costly loans, (vi) continuation of earlier debt relief arrangements for farmers, (vii) state subsidies for farmers who reduced their livestock inventories, and (viii) a devaluation of the krone from 18.16 to 22.50 per pound sterling.[2]

Industrial workers were the main beneficiaries of the first three parts of the agreement. The imposition of a wage freeze and a prohibition against lockouts was of particular importance, as employers were demanding a 20 percent reduction in wages and preparing for a lockout at this time. Existing wage agreements were similarly renewed by state intervention and compulsory arbitration in 1934, 1936, and 1937. The other parts of the agreement benefitted peasants. Similar agreements were reached in Sweden in 1933 and in Norway in 1935. They involved a combination of agricultural price supports, interest rate reductions and debt restructuring for farmers, protective tariffs, and rural tax relief in exchange for increased public works and expanded unemployment and other social benefits.[3]

We shall see that it was possible to make these agreements, and the compromises between urban and rural interests that they entailed, because the distribution of wealth within the countryside was not at issue. Socialists had no incentive to challenge that distribution, and the class standing of the family peasantry that formed the backbone of the agrarian wing of the alliance remained unthreatened. It is striking that the agreements offered little relief for smallholders and agrarian workers. Indeed, these crisis agreements actually reinforced the existing position of middle peasants in the rural class structure and came in part at the expense of the rural proletariat. It was for this reason that the Swedish Communists were "violently opposed to the crisis agreement, which they characterized as a fraud against the consumers and small-scale farmers."[4]

Behind all of these agreements lay the middle peasants' concern with the effects of state employment on the cost and availability of agricultural labor. Peasants had long been inclined to oppose public works employment because of its tendency to deplete the supply and increase the cost of rural labor. Thus, when the Swedish Social Democrats won Agrarian party endorsement of public works projects, they were forced to accept that wages on these projects would be calculated "with regard to the wage situation within agriculture and forestry."[5]

The alliances rested on a common farmer–worker interest in stimulation policies, but these policies took varied forms according to national circumstances. In Denmark, where agriculture was oriented toward exports, the focus was on the restoration of agricultural exports. A revived agricultural economy could then generate a renewed demand for industrial products. In Norway and Sweden, where agriculture produced for the home market, the stimulation was mainly effected through subventions to agriculture and expansionary monetary policies. In Norway, government subsidies to agriculture rose from 15 million kroner in 1930 to 59 million in 1938.[6] In effect, urban workers accepted higher food prices in exchange for the peasants' support for public works, social welfare programs, unemployment relief, and what was at least advertised as deficit spending. The net stimulus provided by the fiscal policies of Norwegian and Swedish Social Democrats was minimal. Indicators of public spending and taxing make clear that in their net effect, the rhetoric of stimulation notwithstanding, fiscal policies were probably neutral rather than stimulatory.[7] Rather than increasing the public debt, Social Democratic fiscal policies produced, by both higher spending *and* higher taxing of the urban middle classes, a transfer of income to poorer groups. In the break with orthodoxy, monetary policy was far more important than fiscal policy. In Norway, the stock of money in circulation was increased by 75 million kroner, from 250 million to 325 million, in 1936. In three years, the volume of notes in circulation increased by 60 percent.[8] In Sweden, the money stock increased by 50 percent between 1933 and 1936.[9] This is in striking contrast with the pre-rearmament monetary policies of societies in which orthodoxy prevailed. The volume of money in circulation remained essentially constant in Switzerland between 1933 and 1938, rose in France by less than 10 percent between 1932 and 1937, rose by less than 20 percent in the same period in Belgium, contracted in the Netherlands, and rose by just over 10 percent in Britain between 1930 and 1935. As rapid rearmament became a central determinant of British economic policy, the money supply expanded by about 25 percent between 1936 and 1939.[10]

In the end, what counted most was the political psychology rather than the economics—fiscal or monetary—of recovery. Social Democrats advertised their policies as a break with orthodoxy and created expectations of recovery. In retrospect it appears that recovery had more to do with a general upswing in international activity than with stimulatory policies. But whatever the economic value of those policies or the expectations they engendered, it was nonetheless the declared break with orthodoxy that allowed Social Democrats to reap the political rewards of recovery.[11]

By making a coalition that satisfied the interests of peasants, Social Democrats accomplished several things. Above all, they created a stable power base. They did this not just by giving the peasantry a vested interest in the continuity of Social Democratic power, but by binding to the state the trade unions with which they were aligned. The essential features of this corporatist inclusion of labor were to be found in the establishment of a legal and political context that accelerated the growth of union membership, reinforced the authority over workers of centralized and monopolistic trade unions, created almost insuperable obstacles to the growth of renegade associations, extended to trade unions semisovereign status in making social policies, and resorted to centralized wage settlements lubricated by a state commitment to full employment, income redistribution, and the socialization of part of the employers' wage bill. To be sure, this social democratic model did not emerge full blown with the making of the farm–labor coalition. Rather, like the institutions of fascism, these institutions took shape gradually. Unlike the institutions of fascism, they continued to evolve after World War II and reached their "mature" form only in the early 1950s, when economic recovery and incipient inflation made the coordination of economic claims all the more imperative.

The most explicit break with market mechanisms, especially in the determination of wages, occurred with the 1938 Saltsjöbaden Agreement in Sweden. The 1936 election confirmed the hegemony of the Social Democratic–Agrarian alliance and induced Swedish big business to accommodate itself to the new balance of power. In that political context, representatives of labor, business, agriculture, and the government negotiated a social compact. The terms of the agreement were business acceptance of Social Democratic government, high wages and social welfare benefits, full employment fiscal policies, and an activist state, in exchange for peace in the labor markets and continued private control of capital markets and ownership of property. In this arrangement, centrally negotiated wages became a function not simply of bargaining between unions and employers, but of growing welfare benefits, and the state's commitment to full employment and income redistribution. Agricultural prices, in turn, became tied to urban wages and industrial prices. The state's role was to lubricate negotiations among the peak associations by deploying its own taxing and spending policies in a manner that made concessions among peak associations easier. In effect, the state intervened to socialize part of the cost of settlements. A similar bargain was reached in Norway in 1935 and, in a less comprehensive form, as a part of the Kanslergade Agreement in Denmark in 1933.[12]

The coalitions in Norway and Sweden marked a more abrupt break with the past than did the coalition in Denmark. The break with economic orthodoxy was less pronounced in Denmark, where the policy emphasis was on neo-orthodox market reorganization rather than on fiscal or monetary stimulation. Any stimulation was inadvertent and came from increased consumption that income transfers generated. Even in the Social Democratic party, little credence was attached to the theories of economic stimulation that became the focus of Social Democratic economists in Norway and Sweden.[13] Liberalism had been more successful before the war in Denmark than in the northern countries, had provided workers with a more effective ally, and had suffered less discredit in the 1920s. Even after the alliance was struck between Danish Social Democracy and the Agrarian Liberals, the Radical Liberals representing the progressive fraction of the urban middle classes and some smallholders remained in the governing coalition with the Social Democrats. The Radicals were, however, an appendage rather than a principal and had nowhere else to go. The principals to the Kanslergade agreement were the Agrarian Liberals and the Social Democrats. Because the Danish labor movement had not suffered the dearth of effective allies the Norwegian and Swedish movements suffered, Danish trade unions, however centralized they were compared to British, French, and Swiss unions, never experienced the same centralizing imperative in their formative years that Norwegian and Swedish unions had. The 1899 accord with the Employers' Association both indexed their more favorable position and froze the institutional structure of the union movement, leaving it divided between a small number of centralized industrial unions and the large, heterogeneous, and often obstreperous, general union of unskilled workers. In the years between the accord and the depression (and for many years after) that division repeatedly stymied efforts toward a level of centralization comparable to those found in Norway and Sweden. Danish labor was consequently less centralized in the 1930s and less inclined to and capable of participating in the corporatist bargaining that became characteristic of Norway and Sweden. Denmark, which had a diluted experience of the aliberal transition to mass politics, was now, in effect, to have a diluted version of the Social Democratic corporatist outcome in the 1930s.

An alliance of workers and middle peasants could provide Social Democrats with a secure social base, but ultimately the success of the new order required its acceptance by the middle classes. Rather than the endorsement of middle-class parties, it required the acquiescence of investors, because Social Democrats did not have the means to demand the cooperation of investors. For investors, the Social Democrats' control of the state was a serious setback. Employers could no longer rely on a friendly state to intervene in labor market disputes on their behalf. Moreover, their remained the lingering menace of socialization in at least certain sectors of the economy.

In the near term, acceptance of the new situation came about in part in the same way that workers in less fortunate societies came to acquiesce to fascism: through an understanding that the stabilizing coalition had undercut all other alternatives. As long as peasants remained satisfied with their alliance, there was no plausible strategy for revising the political situation. Traditional notions of popular legitimacy are not helpful in understanding the stabilizing effect of the new coalition. Rather, for investors, as for workers and peasants, the legitimacy at work was of the contingent variety.[14] Workers and peasants supported the new order not because it rested on sacred national myths or inherited traditions, but because it addressed their immediate material needs. For the working-class movement, at least in Norway, it was the new order itself that legitimated old national values and became the incubus of new myths that bound workers to the larger society.[15]

Investors and middle-class voters initially accepted the new order because they had no alternative. Obviously, Social Democrats could not bring to bear the same coercion on investors that fascists could bring to bear on workers (and investors). Investors had correspondingly more leverage. The separation of governmental and economic power created, in effect, a standoff in which the holders of each needed the collaboration of the other.[16] Nonetheless, in Norway, Sweden, and Denmark, business interests soon learned that as long as Social Democrats were able to satisfy their peasant allies, there would be little chance of replacing them. From this, it was concluded that there was no alternative but to work with the coalition.[17] Sweden's Social Democratic finance minister, Ernst Wigforss, succinctly summarized the new reality that social democrats and investors confronted after 1933:

> Expressed without euphemisms this means, on the one hand, that those who have power over larger or smaller sectors of the private economy do not base their actions on the assumption that the current tendencies in government are a transitory phenomenon, that a political change will take place within a future near enough that a discussion based on the possibility of concessions, accommodations and compromise becomes unnecessary.
>
> On the other hand, it also means that the representatives of political power admit the necessity of maintaining favorable conditions for private enterprise in all those areas where they are not prepared without further ado to replace private enterprise with some form of public operations.[18]

A detente with the business community would provide Social Democrats with the fullest amount of control over investment that their still limited political power would allow. The limit of their power was that they could not socialize production on the broad scale. Limited to democratic means, there was always the risk that they could not in any event retain the support of workers during the interval of economic decay that massive socialization would likely entail.[19] There would, moreover, be little point in public ownership if Social Democrats could substitute for it public control. A detente with, rather than a takeover of, the private economy would have other benefits as well: it would allow Social Democrats to shift labor market conflicts and workers' redistributive ambitions to the political arena, where Social Democrats could maximize the use of their principal asset—state power—and thus their control over the labor movement and economy.[20] They would be able to do this, moreover, without making the state an employer and assuming all of the burdens that would entail.

Fascism: The Solution of Germany, Italy, and Spain

Even more than social democracy, fascism represented a radical break with liberalism. Whereas social democracy repudiated the economics of liberalism, fascism repudiated its politics as well. Fascism, as Mussolini declared, proclaimed itself totalitarian both in the comprehensiveness of its ideology and in its mechanisms of social control: "Everything within the state, nothing outside the state, and nothing against the state." The degree to which fascist regimes institutionally approximated pure totalitarianism varied. Germany came closer than Italy; Italy came closer than Spain. But all had in common certain features that set them apart as a class from the traditional dictatorships of Eastern Europe. All three regimes abolished all elected representative institutions. None would accept the existence of competing ideologies or autonomous private associations of interests. Press censorship was unqualified. Indeed, the media became important instruments of social control. Traditional dictatorships almost always preserved some degree of elected rump parliamentarism and through it permitted the articulation of the grievances of the dictatorship's supporters. Traditional dictatorships also permitted restrained dissent in the press, had no comprehensive ideology, failed to exercise monopolistic control of the media, and tolerated autonomous interest associations.

All of the fascist regimes mercilessly suppressed socialist movements. They were not, as traditional dictatorships were, willing to permit domesticated, crippled socialist movements a residual existence. It is typical of the contrast that in the eleven years *after* the Spanish Civil War, the Francoist regime executed, on minimum estimates, 22,000 dissidents.[21] The overwhelming majority of these were from the Left and the working classes. In Hungary, a traditional dictatorship in the years after the Hungarian Civil War permitted the revival of a domesticated socialist movement. Socialists were actually permitted to run for parliament in a few districts and Socialist trade unions were allowed a limited scope.

The fascist regimes not only distinguished themselves in these various ways and by their unrelenting drive to extirpate socialism. They also distinguished themselves by their ambition to reorganize the working classes. Traditional dictatorships revealed no inclination to place comprehensive trade unions and leisure organizations for workers under the strict control of the state and party. These fascist organizations, which certainly detached wages from market mechanisms, had as their purpose the monopolistic penetration of the working and private lives of workers. They were instruments of subordination of workers to the interests of the state, the cardinal one of which was having a disciplined and obedient labor force. Strikes were outlawed, and the conditions of labor, wage rates, and even mobility were determined by state functionaries.[22]

In Germany and Italy, these organizations were also, in limited ways, instruments of inducement. Fascism was not simply an especially vicious version of bourgeois authoritarianism that sought to suppress workers in the interests of capital. Fascist movements had an agenda of their own that focused on national, state, and party power rather than on servicing sectoral, class, or group interests. It was perhaps this ambition to obtain a qualitatively new level of power that led fascists to comprehend that, in highly class-conscious and mobilized societies, it would not do simply to cripple working-class trade unions and parties as more traditional middle-class representatives were sometimes inclined to do in the 1920s and 1930s. With a large part of the working class already politically mobilized, such a solution would be inherently unstable and provide a weaker power base than fascism aspired to.

Fascists, at least in Germany and Italy, seem to have understood that this harnessing of the working class required that workers experience some measure of integration into the new order. This integration had both a psychological and a material dimension. Psychologically, the "basic concept . . . was that of the equality of all 'national comrades' regardless of class."[23] However much of a sham they might have been, "The *Winterhilfe* (Winter Help) and countless other fundraising drives, national labor competitions and model plants, 'Strength through Joy' and nationwide one-pot meals, a people's car for everyone, and finally the classless society of the Hitler Youth and party organizations, of the DAF and the Labor Service—all these manifestations of the 'peoples community' were undeniably effective, even though they were purposeful tools of control."[24] Fascism sought not only organizationally to control workers, but sought to gain their support for the new order by a whole series of programs and policies that aimed at the material and cultural quality of workers' lives, improving health and safety conditions at work, equalizing the work rights and privileges of white- and blue-collar workers, providing increased leisure time and recreational activities, providing propaganda that dignified workers and their contribution and, through all-encompassing organizations tied to the party and state, symbolically legitimizing and equalizing the role of workers in the new social order.[25]

Without doubt, the most important contribution the Nazis made to the material well-being of German workers, unmatched in all other European societies, was to restore full employment by late 1935. "To the many thousands who before 1933 either had become unemployed or had never been employed at all, the loss of trade-union organizations and social freedom was, in the final analysis, less important than the fact that with Hitler came full employment, mobility and opportunities for advancement."[26] That return to full employment, which *preceded* the military buildup, came about through the most radical break with orthodox liberal economics—in both market reorganization and stimulation policies—that Europe has ever witnessed. With extensive public works and government purchases, the Nazis ran large state deficits that infused the economy with new purchasing power.[27] Italian fascism, too, marked a radical break with economic orthodoxy and went well beyond the protectionism and market reorganization of neo-orthodoxy. State intervention and restructuring of markets under so-called parastate organizations reached a level in Italy before 1931 that would not even be approached in liberal societies in the mid-1930s.[28] Italian monetary policy, too, was characterized by a break with orthodoxy in 1934.

In that year, the deflationary policies that had been put in place to support the Lira in 1927 were reversed and the money supply was allowed to grow by 30 percent in a single year. In three years it expanded by 40 percent.[29]

The social welfare accomplishments of Italian fascism, especially in the context of a still comparatively backward society, were likewise not unimpressive. Even as it checked the share of national income going to labor in wages, Italian fascism made marked improvements, sometimes creating programs de novo, in the welfare institutions inherited from the old regime. For the first time, although with some important exceptions, the eight-hour day was established throughout Italian industry. Pensions, paid vacations, maternity insurance and care, and health and disability insurance were much improved. One measure of the regime's success was a 20 percent drop in infant mortality between 1922 and 1936. The rate of death from tuberculosis fell by more than half between 1924 and 1935. Investment in education was dramatically increased, and by 1935 elementary school attendance had risen by 25 percent.[30]

Robert Ley, the leader of the German Labor Front revealed a clear understanding of fascism's prudential interest in working-class integration. As Ley, speaking of those who had belonged to the socialist trade unions of the Republic, observed:

> . . . Nothing is more dangerous to a state than homeless men. In such circumstances, even a bowling club or a skate club assumes a state-maintaining function. A person goes there in the evening and knows that he belongs. . . . It was of tremendous value that the Labor Front put these twelve million people back in their place in the state. They were, to be sure, in some part, oppositional, and in addition filled with distrust and hatred. But if the state had said: No, you don't count; we want nothing to do with you; perhaps one day, your children, but, as for you, you're excluded—believe me, that would have been disastrous.[31]

Students of fascism as diverse as Gordon Craig, Nicos Poulantzas, Karl Dietrich Bracher, Palmiro Togliatti, and Renzo de Felice have agreed that Italian and German fascism, by a judicious mix of coercion, inducement, and propaganda, probably did eventually win the loyalties of a substantial part of the working classes and the acquiescence of the remainder.[32] To go beyond this and contemplate the more controverted question of whether workers would have been better off had the old orders endured is unnecessary for our purposes. Whatever the answer to that question, the essential point is that, by its impulse to build a certain variety of corporatism and social welfarism, fascism revealed the necessity of even an authoritarian regime coming to terms institutionally and ideologically with the high level of class mobilization that characterized these societies. Stable political economies in these societies, whether led by democrats or dictators, could only be corporatist, because only corporatism, whether democratic or authoritarian, offered institutions and ideologies that would ensure labor discipline.

To be sure, the corporatist labor institutions of Franco's Spain existed, especially after the mid-1950s, almost solely on paper. They had no role in workers' lives, and employers found them more of a bureaucratic nuisance than an asset in controlling wage costs.[33] They were intended as instruments of demobilization rather than mobilization. In this, as in other respects, the Francoist state was a pale imitation of the Hitler and Mussolini states. The Falange, the ideological incubator of Spanish Fascism, never gained the leading position of the Nazi party in Germany and the Fascist party in Italy. Rather, it had to compete for influence in the state with traditional bureaucratic, agrarian, and financial interests and even the Catholic Church, which became an integral component of the Francoist social order. No doubt, both Hitler and Mussolini found, once in power, that they, too, had to break and subordinate their own fascist movements and come to terms with, respectively, the army and Catholic and Protestant churches, and the Vatican, monarchy, and army.[34] Nonetheless, the comparative weakness of the Falange stands out. The most accurate summary is that the Francoist regime represented a diluted version of fascism. It had in common with fascism— and was set apart from traditional dictatorships by—a complete destruction of representative institutions, total war on socialism, intolerance of autonomous interest associations, intolerance of competing ideologies, destruction of even a semblance of an autonomous, legal working-class movement, obsessive manipulation of the media and the monopoly of its vision of the social order. It deviated from fascism in the nominal character of its labor corporatism, its satisfaction with labor demobilization, and its indifference to a break with economic orthodoxy.

The more diluted character of Spanish fascism, and especially its labor organizations, can be traced to Franco's having come to power by military conquest rather than by a political movement. The Falange was less well anchored in its society than were the fascist movements in Germany and Italy. It had, moreover, a less valuable function in social control in the wake of Franco's military defeat of his opponents. For Franco, the physical liquidation of his enemies, especially his working-class enemies, occurred primarily through military combat before the Nationalist conquest was complete. Moreover, Franco, once victorious, could rely on his army as an instrument of social control in a way that Hitler and Mussolini never could. Both of them were compelled to concede the autonomy of the army, and neither could assign it the police functions that the Spanish army assumed. For Hitler and Mussolini, gaining political power was just the beginning; the brutal business of physical liquidation still lay ahead of them. Agencies of their fascist movements, for example the *SS*, had a "contribution" to make here that the Falange could not parallel.[35] Because he had physically conquered his opponents on the way to power and could rely extensively on the army once in power, Franco simply had less need for a comprehensive fascist movement and the associated penetrating, subordinating organizations of corporatist labor that figured in German and Italian fascism.

It is true, as well, that Francoist Spain devolved with time into a bureaucratic dictatorship. The Falange became a residual actor after the mid-1950s, steps were taken from 1959 to liberalize the economy, and after 1966 a broad tolerance for ideological dissent developed. The unqualified intolerance of dissident organization, however, was not lifted. Had they lasted, the regimes of Hitler and especially of Mussolini might well have evolved in the same manner. With the elimination of all its opponents, totalitarianism, and especially a reign of terror, becomes a nuisance after a certain point, an obstacle to social and economic efficiency.[36]

Spain in its earlier experience had combined the politics of the more modern West with the social backwardness of the East. By the 1930s it was markedly more advanced socially than Eastern Europe. It was not, however, so modern that its politics could be played out on the mass level that was characteristic of the West. If it was modern enough in the 1930s to become fascist, it was still backward enough to have an officers' corps that could earnestly believe itself the repository of the essential values of Spanish civilization. More to the point, it had an officers' corps that acted on that *mentalité*. To be sure, the German officers' corps fancied itself the embodiment of all that was thought best in traditional German, or at least Prussian, values. But the political dalliances of a Wilhelm Groener or Kurt Schleicher notwithstanding, the German army did not consider that it could bring order to German society by means of a *pronunciamiento*. Spain, which had always combined the burdens of backwardness with the problems of modernity, was little changed in the 1930s in at least this respect, except of course that this time the high level of mobilization meant the *pronunciamiento* provoked a Civil War.

Family Peasantry: A Pivotal Force

While social democracy substituted politics for markets to gain the support of workers, fascism substituted politics for markets to gain their submission. That the social democratic response to the crisis of liberalism in mobilized, class-conscious societies was incalculably more humane is too obvious to belabor here. The point is that both social democracy and fascism recognized, in their ideologies, their respective institutions of labor inclusion and control, and their break with economic orthodoxy, that in the absence of the atomized pluralism of liberal labor, reliance on labor markets to enforce economic and political discipline would result in ungovernable societies and unstable regimes. In this, the institutions and policies of social democracy and fascism responded to the same existential dilemma of interwar aliberal societies, albeit in very different ways. Those different responses reflected the distinctive social coalitions that subtended social democracy and fascism.

The cardinal actors in the mass politics of the interwar years were the urban working classes, the urban middle classes, and the family peasantry. Stabilizing a political economy in the aliberal societies of the West required the inclusion of two of these three actors in an alliance; alone, none of them was so large that it could impose itself, whether by democratic or authoritarian means, on the other two. In light of the inability to make an alliance between the two urban classes and given the extant balances between urban and rural populations in these societies, the alliance had to include the countryside. A social democratic order required a coalition of the urban working classes and the family peasantry. A fascist order required a coalition between the urban middle classes and the family peasantry. The coalition with the countryside had to be with the family peasantry, that large middle strata of agrarian society that owned sufficient land to engage family members full-time and produce for the market, but not so much land that it needed to rely extensively on hired labor. The coalition had to be with the family peasantry because, within the agrarian population, only this sector combined a mass base, a fairly high and stable rate of political participation, a distinct political agenda, *and* the capacity to destabilize the polity until this agenda was realized.

By the 1920s and 1930s, landed elites almost everywhere were a spent political force, one no longer able to control the mass support that was by then the sine qua non of political success. The rural proletariat had its own agenda and in some countries—Italy, Spain, Denmark, Czechoslovakia, and, more marginally, Sweden—the potential to provide a mass base. But it was the interwar equivalent of Marx' "sack of potatoes." It was incapable of leading itself and incapable of creating its own organizations. Whenever it was organized into a durable political force, it was organized by groups that were not actually of it: socialists, reform-minded liberals, and Christian democrats. Because it was incapable of disrupting the political system without external leadership, it could be ignored if the sources of external leadership were eliminated.

The levels of political mobilization among peasants had varied from country to country and region to region before the war. It had been higher in northern Europe than in southern Europe, higher in the north of Italy than in the south, and higher in peripheral Spain than in Castile. By the interwar years peasants across Western Europe had become politically mobilized—had come to see the connection between the political and economic order and their own material well-being. This was a connection they could hardly have failed to see, given the almost total subordination of their activities to state regulations. This peasant awakening completed the mobilization of aliberal societies. These societies were "fully" mobilized at that point—far more, in any event, than their fragile institutions could bear. In this, the war and the agrarian crises that accompanied and followed it were a watershed.

In almost every Western European society, the war provoked a radical increase in state intervention in commodity markets as war-induced scarcities unleashed an explosion of food prices, the closing of some traditional export markets and sources of imports, and a shortage of factors of production, including fertilizer, draft animals, labor, and machinery. Whether the agricultural community was a net exporter, as in Denmark, or a net importer, as in Germany, Norway, Sweden, and Italy, rising prices forced state intervention. One state after another began to fix maximum prices on a lengthening list of agricultural products; these were prices that rarely took adequate account of peasants' increased costs of production. States also established import and export monopolies, introduced rationing schemes, determined what peasants could produce and how much they were expected to deliver, and penalized them for blackmarket sales.[37] In Germany and Italy, the state confiscated draft animals for use at the military front. Even in Denmark, where it had long been oriented toward exports to Britain and Germany, agriculture suffered mightily as a result of the war. During the first several years of the war, rising prices allowed Danish farmers to maintain their share of national income even as production fell by one-third. But that production depended on the importation of machinery and feed grains, and as equipment ran down and grain imports were lost in 1917, stocks were devastated. In just two years the swine inventory was reduced from 2 million to 400,000, and agriculture's share of national income fell from 29 to 21 percent.[38] This agricultural collapse was typical rather than exceptional. In Germany, the swine inventory in 1921 was less than 60 percent of what it had been in 1913; total crop production was about 55 percent lower.[39] In Italy, wheat output fell from 5.6 million tons in 1913 to 3.7 million tons in 1917.[40]

In all of the aliberal societies, many of which already had institutionalized conflicts between the town and countryside, there was an explosive struggle between urban consumers and rural producers in the final two years of the war and the first two years of peace. By the end of the war, high prices and scarcities had created famine conditions in Sweden, Norway, Germany, and Italy. The antagonism between urban consumers and peasants came to overshadow even that between the two urban classes. In Sweden, famine-induced riots were responsible for the fall of the conservative government and the subsequent Social Democratic–Liberal coalition's democratic breakthrough. In general, farmers found themselves in a price squeeze as industrial prices rose more rapidly than regulated commodity prices. In Italy, agricultural prices doubled between 1915 and 1917 as industrial prices nearly trebled in the same period.[41] The inefficiencies of regulatory systems subverted production plans and fostered widespread black markets. It was typical that the lower price the Italian government permitted for grains provoked peasants to feed them to cattle, for which they could receive more favorable prices, thus compounding the grain shortage.[42] When the foundations of the *Burgfrieden* in Germany and similar truces elsewhere began to crack in 1917, it was invariably and above all because of the high cost and scarcity of basic foodstuffs. Bands of urban workers—in Germany they were called *hemsterer*—invaded farmlands near cities, often looting barns and fields. In all of the aliberal societies except Spain, urban manufacturers aligned with workers during the war in demanding state controls on agricultural prices.[43] This realignment was fairly explicit and marked a profound shift in the traditional balance of power. It was a shift that emerged from a growing fear of urban unrest as the war dragged on, and it came at the expense of the traditional deference that had been paid to agricultural over consumer interests. In Italy, the retail price of bread was held to half of its actual cost. The state was able to make good only a fraction of the uncharged cost by payment of a subsidy. As it was, the subsidy became so large—200 million lire a month in 1919—that it provoked a fiscal and financial crisis and killed the opportunity for social reforms in 1919 and 1920.[44]

A widely reprinted newspaper essay probably summarized the sentiments of peasants in Germany and elsewhere after four years of war. Averring that the state had rewarded workers with higher wages and new respect, the author asked rhetorically with what the state rewarded the other essential producer, the peasant.

> [With] a year's prison sentence, and 10,000-mark fine, expropriation and confiscation, checks, threats of punishment, house searches, mandatory levies, controls of acreage planted, harvest checks, livestock checks, mandatory registration, mandatory deliveries, denial of the right to control one's own food supply. . . . Am I a criminal, the peasant asks himself, and if so, what is my crime? . . . We protect the general welfare from the peasant with maximum prices. But who protects the peasant?[45]

It is quite beside the point whether peasants fared better by some objective standard during the war than did other classes for, in the end, that was patently not the way peasants saw it.

Their comparative well-being during the inflations and deflations that followed the war was equally irrelevant, for by their own lights they suffered profoundly. In Germany, the regulated agricultural economy was not entirely dismantled until 1924, when restored output, the stabilization of the mark, and the resumption of imports made it unnecessary. Elsewhere, the deflationary policies that were a prelude to a return to the gold standard encumbered peasants with now falling prices and appreciating debts. In Norway, where the internal value of the krone appreciated by 55 percent, debt as a percentage of assessed farm value rose by 20 percent between 1914 and 1932.[46] It would soon rise further. In Germany, the percentage of farm revenue required to service debt rose from 7.5 percent in 1926 to 14 percent in 1932.[47] The dilemma for farmers was that in the context of falling world prices and saturated domestic markets, increases in production reduced prices and incomes further. The timing of the inflations and deflations varied according to national circumstances, but in no cases did peasants have more than a couple of years of stability before they felt the impact of a new commodity crisis. This crisis, which was only the prelude to the Great Depression, made itself felt across Europe on the mid-1920s and had at its root a global surplus of agricultural commodities, especially grains. The surplus was at least in part a result of the exceptional demand for new production that the war had generated. The putting under plow of new lands in the Americas and Australia, combined with the recovery of European agriculture in the 1920s, brought in train steadily declining world prices. The London price of wheat fell by half between 1927 and 1931. The slump was not limited to grains, but became generalized to almost all agricultural products. The export price of Danish butter, for example, fell by 40 percent between 1927 and 1932 while the price of bacon declined by half.[48] In Scandinavia and Germany, the net rate of return on farm investment effectively fell to zero by 1932.[49] Moreover, agricultural prices fell more rapidly than the price of manufactures, with the net result of a deterioration of the terms of trade between farms and towns and a yawning gap in the incomes of farmers and other groups. Thus, whereas in Norway the value of output per employed person was 70 percent higher in manufacturing than agriculture in 1910, it was 150 percent higher in 1930.[50] In Germany, between 1926 and 1931, the index of agricultural prices fell by one-third while the cost of farm machinery remained unchanged, fertilizer fell by less than 10 percent, and basic consumer goods declined by only about 16 percent.[51] For most commodities, the decline ran unabated until 1933. By that time, peasants in Scandinavia and Germany could look back on two decades of upheaval.

Italian agriculture broke with this trajectory with the consolidation of fascism in the 1920s, having first experienced the upheavals of the war and immediate postwar crises and revolutionary struggles over land reform and agrarian trade unionism that had no parallel in northern Europe. These are struggles to which we shall return. Those sectors of Spanish agriculture that were integrated into the world market, especially wheat and cotton, enjoyed the export boom of the war years and suffered little regulation. The war boom also led to a rapid rise of domestic commodity prices. But for most peasants this was more than offset by a rapid rise in land rents as well as a rise in the cost of manufactured and consumer goods.[52] By this time most Spanish peasants were at least partially engaged in production for the market.[53] When the boom broke in 1920, rents remained inflexibly high, squeezing peasant producers severely. Thus, the index of agricultural commodity prices rose from 100 in 1913 to 201 in 1920; it then fell back to 167 by 1930. Rents per hectare, however, rose from a range of 15 to 35 pesetas in 1913, to 30 to 50 pesetas in 1920, and then to 50 to 100 pesetas in 1930.[54] The rapid rise in rents and a squeeze on real agrarian wages contributed to an upsurge of unrest in 1917. The statistics of the Institute for Social Reform, incomplete as they probably are for these years, indicate that the number of agricultural strikes doubled in each year between 1917 and 1920. The number of agricultural days lost to strikes rose from 43,735 in 1917 to 369,256 in 1920. These "agricultural strikes in 1920 exceeded in number (though probably not in intensity) even the rural walkouts in Italy."[55] In Spain, the mobilizational upheavals in the agricultural community would not reach their peak until the years of the Republic, when the left government stepped up its intervention in the markets and land reform, agrarian trade unions, and rural wage disputes evoked violent passions.[56]

It was against this backdrop of agrarian crisis that the family peasantry became a truly free agent for the first time. In Denmark, it had possessed its own political party, the Agrarian Liberals, even before the war. That party was now even more exclusively based on and oriented toward the agrarian middle classes. In Norway and Sweden, agrarians formed their own political parties in the 1920s. In Bavaria, too, peasants formed their own party. Other Catholic peasants in Bavaria and elsewhere in Germany, lacking a viable alternative to the Catholic Center party, expressed their political independence through the participation of their Peasant Associations in the 1929 Green Front and then even in the Hitler–Hugenberg Harzburg Front. The Green Front was an umbrella organization of peasant and estate owners intended to reassert the unity of agricultural interests.[57] With its dissolution, some Catholic peasant associations joined the Harzburg Front.[58] More important was the ability of Catholic peasants to push the Center to an avowedly authoritarian posture after 1930. As a leading student of the Catholic peasantry, Robert Moeller has persuasively argued that the votes of Catholic peasants for the Center were by no means votes for the Republic and against the Nazis. While confessional sentiments could hold these peasants for the Center, they did so only at the cost of moving the Center to abandon the Republic.[59] In Protestant Germany, peasants manifested their autonomy by abandoning the various party residues of liberalism and the Junkers' party, the German National Peoples party, in favor of the Nazis. In northern Italy, the peasantry assumed a decisive role in the rise of fascism. In Spain, northern peasants would become the rural backbone of the Catholic, conservative CEDA between 1933 and 1936 and then embraced the nationalist cause with the outbreak of the civil war.

In sum, peasants in aliberal societies could no longer be taken for granted politically. They were now politically mobile, ready to shift their allegiance as they calculated and recalculated their interests. By those calculations, traditional liberals were, according to the country in question, quickly found wanting on multiple counts. Liberals' reluctance to stabilize commodity markets at prices peasants found acceptable, their fixation with a return to the gold standard and the consequent deflations, their embrace of urban, secular, sometimes anticlerical, cultures, and the liberal ineffectiveness that derived from the divisions within the urban liberal community all alienated peasants. In Scandinavia and Germany, the 1920s were a decade of liberal failure. In Italy, the peasant experience during the war ensured what had already been made likely by the prewar experience: that peasant mobilization would be *against* liberalism. In Spain, liberals alienated peasants in the final years of the Restoration order by their indifference to rising land rents and in the first few years of the Republic by, above all, their anticlericalism. For all of these reasons, liberal parties failed to make an alliance between their dwindling urban middle-class constituents and the family peasantry. At heart, the failure of liberalism was twofold: liberals, fractionalized and dwindling in the cities, had less and less to offer as a coalition partner, and the liberal fixation with markets made them loath to arrest the collapse of commodity prices.

It is instructive that peasants in France and Switzerland, too, suffered profoundly from the commodity crisis of the late 1920s and 1930s, yet remained allied with the hegemonic liberal right parties and coalitions that dominated interwar politics in those societies.[60] The consolidation of the urban middle classes that was characteristic of interwar liberal politics left them no real alternative. Those hegemonic coalitions of middle-class consolidation, of which agriculture was a part, offered peasants an effective ally— or in any event, the only plausible ally—because they did not suffer the inherited debilities of liberal movements in aliberal societies. Even that fraction of the Swiss peasantry that acted autonomously in supporting the Peasants' party had, in practice, no alternative but to align with the dominant antisocialist coalition of Radical Liberals and Conservative Catholics. For however the Peasant party aligned itself, the dominant coalition would retain a legislative majority. The electoral sociology of the French peasantry is primitive but sufficient to indicate that French peasants were even less inclined than their Swiss brothers to respond to the crises of the twenties and thirties en bloc. Some voted Communist, some Socialist; most voted for Radicals or conservatives and remained wedded to the dominant center–right coalition.[61]

The fractionalization and disintegration of liberalism in Germany, Italy, and Spain have already been examined. The same decline occurred in Scandinavia. In Norway, the Liberal share of the vote fell from 33 percent in 1915 to 16 percent in 1936. In Sweden, it fell from 27 percent in 1914 to 13 percent in 1936; in Denmark, from 29 percent in 1913 to 18 percent in 1935.[62] Moreover, liberal economic policies, rooted in a loyalty to markets, promised peasants little relief. That conclusion was clinched in Germany and Scandinavia by the inadequate relief measures that liberals offered, but were unwilling to go beyond, in response to the commodity crisis of the 1920s.[63] Liberalism's alienation of the peasantry paralleled the alienation of the urban middle classes that followed from the failure to contain organized labor.

Liberalism's bankruptcy was not, however, tantamount to fascism's success. Nowhere—and this is an essential point to keep in mind—did fascism become a significant force until after *both* liberalism and social democracy had failed to accommodate the family peasantry. This means, in the first place, that little can be inferred from the weakness of fascism in Scandinavia in the years before Social Democrats stabilized a new political economy. For in Scandinavia, social democratic parties almost always remained in opposition throughout the 1920s, the years of liberal failure. In Germany, the Nazi party remained a small clique of fanatics with no social base until the failure of both social democrats and liberals to respond adequately to agrarian distress was made unambiguous by the performance of the final social democratic–liberal coalition between 1928 and 1930. To be sure, it was also from that conjuncture that the urban middle classes began to abandon liberal parties in catastrophic numbers. In Italy, Mussolini remained inconsequential in both the 1919 and 1921 elections. It was only with the unqualified failure of liberals, socialists, and the Popolari to make any coalition work and to restore order in the countryside and cities that mass support shifted to the fascists. It was likewise only with the shift of the peasant–middle class coalition that had been formed in the February 1936 election to support the Nationalist rebellion in July 1936 that an identifiably fascist movement can be said to have taken shape in Spain. Fascists were not a significant force at the creation of the Republic. Mass support in the elections of 1931 and 1933 had been overwhelmingly with the established liberal and regional parties and the socialists. The realignment that would provide the mass base for the nationalist cause occurred in 1936, after liberals and socialists had failed—more precisely, *because* liberals and socialists had failed.

Liberalism and social democracy, after all, were political oligopolies in all of these societies. Compared to Nazism and Fascism, these were historic movements, with vested interests attached to them, with long-running loyalties, powerful press organs, and generally well-articulated organizational structures. Initially, fringe movements such as the Nazis and Fascists had none of these assets, and they could hardly hope to displace such well-institutionalized oligopolists unless the oligopolists themselves first failed to make regime stabilizing coalitions.[64]

This was a matter of timing. In Italy, Germany, and Spain liberalism and social democracy (and Christian democracy in Italy) quickly and simultaneously failed in their efforts to make democratic institutions work. In all three countries, as we saw in the previous chapter, liberals alone could not effect a political consolidation of the middle classes of the sorts that occurred in Britain, France, and Switzerland and stabilized interwar democracy in those societies. Nor, as we also saw in the previous chapter, could they and socialists effect a Lib–Lab coalition of the sort that had appeared in liberal societies before 1914. Finally, as we have noted, liberals could not make a coalition with the family peasantry.

In Germany, Spain, and Italy socialists, too, although for reasons distinct from those that account for the failure of liberals, were unable to make a coalition with the family peasantry. In Germany, Spain, and Italy the failure of social democrats to align the urban working classes with the family peasantry was concurrent with the failure of liberalism. In Germany, this occurred in the 1920s, and it is probably accurate to say that the Social Democratic party's last "best" opportunity to align workers with peasants came during 1929 and 1930. After 1930, the SPD's failure to find an effective governing formula was so unmitigated that it began to lose a substantial fraction of even its working-class base.[65] Germany had the best institutionalized party system of the three, so it should come as no surprise that the exodus of mass support from the traditional parties took longer there than in Italy and Spain. To be sure, German Social Democrats were saddled with multiple liabilities by their close association with the Republic they had helped to found. As we shall see, however, their inability to make an effective alliance with the countryside had much more to do with their involvement in agrarian class conflict than it did with the burdens of membership in the initial Weimar coalition per se. The polarization of peasant–worker relations that ensued militated against an alliance that would have embraced measures to address the peasants' grievances as producers.

In Scandinavia, liberalism's failure preceded social democracy's main chance. For in Scandinavia, social democratic parties almost always remained in opposition throughout the years of liberal failure, the 1920s. To be sure, these extra years redounded to the social democrats' benefit. This was perhaps the case above all in Norway, where the Labor party was torn asunder for most of the 1920s and would have been hard pressed to create a stabilizing coalition even if it had had the chance. At the least, the years in opposition provide time for the party to regroup as a credible alternative to liberalism.

It can always be argued as well that those extra years allowed for a recalculation of domestic options as the specter of fascism appeared. It seems problematic that a fear of fascism, either international or domestic, was either necessary or sufficient to account for the farm–labor coalitions that were eventually formed in Scandinavia. In fact, the farm–labor coalition came to power in Denmark on the same day—January 30, 1933—that Hitler came to power in Germany. At that time the long-range Nazi menace was far from obvious. It was a measure of the relative importance of the two events that the leading Danish dailies gave the new Danish coalition predominance over Hitler's.

Felicitous timing appears to be of only secondary importance in accounting for the ultimate success of social democratic parties in Scandinavia. For what was at issue was not simply when socialist parties gained political power, but what they did with it once they had it. Why did social democracy alienate the countryside in Germany, Spain, and Italy but not in Scandinavia? In the end, something much more fundamental than timing was at work in defining the prospects for social democratic success in all of the aliberal societies. That was to be found in the socialists' indifference to or engagement in agrarian class conflict.

Red-Green Alliance and Social Democratic Hegemony

A socialist movement that mobilized a significant fraction of the rural proletariat (agrarian laborers and smallholders dependent on the labor market) contained the seeds of its own failure, for it would become enmeshed in rural class conflict and alienate the family peasantry. A coalition with family peasants required that socialists address conflicts of three kinds: rural class conflict, consumer–producer conflicts, and a miscellany of cultural, clerical–anticlerical, and regional conflicts. Defusing the consumer–producer conflicts was essential to the creation of a worker–peasant coalition, but these conflicts could not be defused if the socialist party found itself in confrontation with family peasants on issues of rural class structure. If the consumer–producer issues could be defused, the less important clerical–anticlerical and regional issues could be also.

Class conflict was central to the political lives of peasants just as it was to the political lives of urban workers and the middle classes. If socialist parties sought to mobilize the rural proletariat, they became enmeshed in this conflict and threatened family peasants in several ways. The greatest threat to them arose from campaigns on behalf of the rural proletariat for land reform. Redistribution was a central issue of rural politics in Spain, Italy, Denmark, and Czechoslovakia. That redistribution would have occurred at the expense of large landowners seems not to have reduced the threat family peasants felt, especially in areas such as northern Italy that had a substantial rural proletariat and little surplus land to redistribute or few large holdings to break up. Pleas from parties born from a collectivist ambition that redistribution would not harm family peasants appeared to them to be incredible. For peasants, the security of the asset around which their entire existence revolved had to be beyond question. Hence, the Spanish Socialists' campaign for land reform in the south of Spain antagonized peasants even in the north.[66]

Socialist mobilization of agrarian workers also threatened the family peasants' productive process. Such peasants, who, by definition, did not rely heavily on hired labor, nonetheless almost always had an employers' perspective. To the extent that peasants did hire a worker or two, year-round or on a seasonal basis, socialist efforts to unionize agrarian workers, establish centralized hiring halls, fix wages, and extend social welfare benefits to agrarian workers all impinged on their costs of production and the freedom to manage their land.

The cumulative effect was to threaten family peasants in a third way. Ultimately their social status was at stake. All of these attempts threatened to disrupt well-established status hierarchies in the countryside and therefore the status of family peasants. In this context, it is easy to understand why socialists' protestations that they were committed to the interests of both agrarian workers and family peasants sounded as implausible to the latter as did reformist liberals' claims that they were committed to the interests of both the middle classes and urban workers. And just as socialist efforts on behalf of urban workers aroused intense resentment among the lower middle classes, even when that sector was not directly and materially threatened by these efforts, socialist efforts on behalf of agrarian workers were bound to generate intense resentment among family peasants. Indeed, whatever the national variation in substantive conflicts, resentment and a sense of neglect were the common feature of all antisocialist peasant movements.

When socialist parties did succeed in making regime-stabilizing coalitions with the peasantry, it was not because they had a superior grasp of the strategic requirements of the moment, but because they did not attempt to organize the rural proletariat. Neither the size of the agricultural population nor the class structure in the countryside had much bearing on this. This can be seen by examining, first, the size of the primary labor force compared to the total labor force and, then, the size of the proletarian labor force compared to the total agrarian labor force. There is no relationship between the size of either of these populations and the coalition and regime outcomes. It is true that some countries in which fascism prevailed, Italy and Spain, had large agrarian proletariats and another in which socialism succeeded, Norway, had a small agrarian proletariat. But others in which social democracy succeeded, Denmark and Czechoslovakia (a country we will consider in greater detail shortly), had large rural proletariats. And still another in which fascism succeeded, Germany, had a comparatively small population of agrarian laborers. Around 1920, the percentages of the labor force that were engaged in agriculture were as follows: Germany, 30.7; Denmark, 37.7; Czechoslovakia, 40.3; Norway, 42.1; Sweden, 43.7; Spain, 56.0; and Italy, 56.2.[67] Thus, of the three least agrarian countries, one became fascist. Of the three most agrarian countries, two also became fascist.

The quality of the data on rural class structures is more problematic, but still adequate to confirm the point that the size of the agrarian proletariat was not determining. Spain and Italy, both of which became fascist, had huge agrarian populations and very large agrarian proletariats, the latter being defined as those landless workers and dwarfholders dependent on the agrarian labor market for the larger part of their income. Edward Malefakis' data indicate that in Spain as a whole, the population thus defined accounted for about 35 to 40 percent of the agrarian work force.[68] For Italy, the figure was probably about the same.[69] Germany had a comparatively small agrarian population and a small agrarian proletariat. In Germany, the agrarian proletariat accounted for about 26 percent of the agrarian labor force.[70] We have fascist outcomes, then, with both large and small agricultural populations and large and small agricultural proletariats. The lack of a pattern continues: Denmark, with a moderately sized agricultural population (37 percent), but a large proletariat (about 43 percent according to census data), produces a democratic outcome.[71] Sweden, with an agricultural population substantially larger than Germany (43 percent versus about 30 percent) and a similarly sized agrarian proletariat (about 26 percent according to census data), produces a democratic outcome.[72] Norway, with a moderately sized agricultural population (42 percent) and a very small proletariat (probably not more than

15 percent), also produces a democratic outcome.[73] Czechoslovakia, with an intermediate-sized agrarian labor force (40 percent) and a rather large agrarian proletariat (about 35 percent, rising to over 60 percent in Slovakia and Ruthenia), also had a democratic outcome.[74]

The outcomes were determined by politics rather than by the size of the agricultural sector or the size of the agrarian proletariat. Socialists succeeded in making a coalition with family peasants wherever the agrarian proletariat had been mobilized by others before socialists had an opportunity to do so. So preempted, the latter could freely negotiate the issues that divided rural producers and urban workers. By contrast, where the rural proletariat was available—as in Spain, Italy, and Germany—it presented socialists with a reservoir of potential support too appealing to ignore. In these cases, the logic of democratic competition and the lure of immediate power undermined the socialists' ability to acquire long-term power because the acquisition of a constituency among the rural proletariat invariably required commitments that alienated family peasants.

The critical distinction between cases of socialist success and failure is to be found in the marginal number of agrarian workers in successful movements. Obviously, no standardized data—voter surveys, for instance—exist to allow easy cross-national comparisons. To estimate the size of the agrarian proletariat as a fraction of the total socialist movement, we have had to resort to a mixture of data on agrarian trade union enrollments, the number of agrarian workers covered by collective agreements, inter-generational voter surveys, and estimates of the maximum possible size of the rural proletariat in the Socialist party's electorate. Taken together, these data are revealing in spite of their lack of strict comparability.

We will begin by looking at the data available for Norway, Sweden, and Denmark, three cases in which socialists were successful in the 1930s in aligning urban workers with family peasants. Norway provides the simplest case. Because of earlier land reforms and the exodus of much of the rural proletariat to North America, the rural social structure had become remarkably egalitarian by the interwar years. As early as 1900, 97 percent of farmers owned their land and employed little or no hired labor.[75] According to an inter-generational survey made by Stein Rokkan, agrarian voters (family peasants, smallholders *and* day laborers) did not account for more than 13 to 15 percent of the total Labor party vote in the 1920s and 1930s.[76] Even if we assume that two-thirds of these voters were at least partly dependent on the agrarian labor market for some income, we find that at most 10 percent of the party's constituency could have consisted of agrarian workers. Within the Norwegian trade union movement, agrarian workers accounted for no more than 5 percent of the membership.[77]

Sweden, with a considerably less equal distribution of land, provides a more demanding test of the hypothesis. In Sweden 26 percent of the agrarian work force—or about 250,000 men and women—consisted of day laborers in the 1920s and early 1930s.[78] Since almost all of these were adult males, we may assume that, including wives and other adult dependents, at least 400,000 potential votes were contained in this labor force. To put this in perspective, consider that the Socialist electorate averaged about 750,000 and the total electorate about 2.2 million, during these years.[79] Yet the Socialist party and the unions almost entirely ignored this potential constituency. As Sven Anders Söderpalm has noted:

> The Swedish agricultural workers' movement was weak and divided for a long time. . . . In the middle of the twenties, not even 5 percent of a total of 250,000 agricultural workers were organized, and only in the large estate areas on Skåne, Ostergötland and the Mälar provinces was there any great support for the movement. The decline in part resulted from the advantage the agricultural crisis gave to employers, but it was also connected to the lack of interest which for a long time had distinguished the labor movement's attitude toward the rural proletarians' efforts.[80]

The Social Democrats did not seriously debate appealing to agrarian workers until 1930; by then, these workers had already been mobilized by the Liberal and Agrarian parties. Liberals and Agrarians, in fact, had succeeded in mobilizing these workers *against* the Social Democrats:

> . . . in the agitation at the grass-roots level, they were strongly susceptible to arguments like "industrial workers are better off than farm workers," "their wages force up prices and place burdens on agriculture," and "the Social Democrats aren't interested in farm workers." In most of the election districts, the majority of farm workers voted for the bourgeois parties.[81]

Although we cannot know the actual amount of support the Social Democratic party received from agrarian laborers and their dependents, we can estimate rather precisely the maximum amount of support it could have received under the most favorable plausible circumstances. Assuming that the rate of participation was slightly less for agrarian workers than for the population as a whole—let us say 50 percent rather than 60 percent—we have an electorate of about 200,000.[82] We know that three parties competed for the votes of this community: the Social Democrats, Liberals, and Agrarians. If we assume that in the early 1930s one half of these votes went to the Social Democrats—an assumption favorable to them—this constituency could not have represented more than 13 or 14 percent of the total Social Democratic vote. With earlier Social Democratic and trade union efforts, however, the participation rate and the Social Democratic share for this group could have been raised, and it might well have accounted for a much more significant 25 percent of the party electorate.

Denmark, with a population of day laborers much larger than those found in Norway and Sweden and comparable to, perhaps even larger than, those found in Spain and Italy, provides an even more demanding test. Of the total agrarian adult labor force of 481,000 in 1934, 210,000, or 43 percent, were hired adult laborers.[83] Because, again, they were overwhelmingly male, we may suppose that, including wives and other adult dependents (parents, grandparents), they represented a voting population of about 400,000. To put this in perspective, we need to note that in 1932 the Social Democratic electorate was just over 660,000 and the total electorate was just over 1.6 million. In principle, this day labor population should have presented the Social Democrats with an extraordinarily tempting target.

In fact, it did not do so because it had already been heavily mobilized by other parties. The first of these was the Liberal party, which maintained an electoral understanding with the Social Democrats until after 1901 that kept the latter from competing in all but a few rural districts. When the Liberals focused almost exclusively on the interests of the agrarian middle class after the change of system in 1901, they provoked the formation of the Radicals. The Radicals came into existence to mobilize agrarian workers against the Liberal party. From 1906 until the introduction of proportional representation in 1918, the Radicals and the Social Democrats had an electoral pact whereby the Social Democrats agreed not to compete against the Radicals in rural Jutland. This allowed the Radicals to run straight fights against Liberal candidates in the districts in which agrarian laborers were significant. In exchange, Radicals agreed not to challenge Social Democrats in a number of urban constituencies. As a result, by the time proportional representation was introduced, the Radicals had captured this constituency.

If we assume that the rate of participation for this potential electorate of 400,000 was slightly less than for the entire population—60 percent against 70 percent in the early 1930s—we have an actual electorate of 240,000.[84] We will assume that the party that had historically organized this population received half of its vote—or 120,000 votes, which in fact approximates what the Radicals received in rural districts in 1935. We will also assume that the remainder was distributed among the Social Democrats and all other parties at a ratio of 4 to 1. Based on the foregoing generous assumptions, 90,000 of these votes went to the Social Democrats.[85] With a total Social Democratic vote of 760,000 in 1935, this represents about 13 percent of the Social Democratic electorate. Had the Social Democrats mobilized this constituency earlier or by themselves after the turn of the century and before the Radicals appeared on the scene, this figure might have been doubled. Finally, we should note that the participation of agrarian workers in Socialist trade unions during these years was virtually nil.[86]

In sum, in Norway and especially Sweden and Denmark, the mobilization of agrarian workers by other parties was decisive. The objection can be made, of course, that the real distinction between these countries and countries that became fascist, especially Italy and Spain, is that in these countries agrarian workers were mobilized by other parties because the transition to mass participation was more gradual. With a more sudden transition, the population would not have been captured, and socialists would have stepped in. In this connection, the case of Czechoslovakia, in which the transition was extremely abrupt, becomes significant.

There are limits to the lessons that can be drawn from Czechoslovak history, and it is for this reason that we have given Czechoslovakia less attention than the other aliberal societies. It had the characteristics of an aliberal society in that within Bohemia and Moravia, as in the larger Habsburg Empire, liberals were prevented by divisions within the middle classes—between Czechs and Germans, between clerical and anticlerical fractions—from establishing their hegemony before 1914. This and the high level of industrialization in Bohemia generated a fairly large and coherent working-class movement, although it, too, was one that remained divided between Germans and Czechs. Just over half of industrial workers were enrolled in trade unions in the 1930s. As elsewhere, 1919 and 1920 were years of upheaval, as formation of the new state and then a radical deflation of the currency were accompanied by a very high level of labor unrest. Labor peace was restored by a remarkable series of legislative measures that included the eight-hour day, the legal enforcement of collective agreements, unemployment benefits, assistance for war widows, orphans, and the infirm, and many other social assistance programs, including in later years, a minimum of one week of paid vacation, twelve weeks of paid maternity leave for women in all types of employment, and a comprehensive system of health and pension insurance.[87] As elsewhere, the liberal political community fractionalized and dwindled in popular support in the 1920s.[88]

During the interwar years, Social Democrats and various regionally defined agrarian and Catholic parties governed together in the directorate known as the *Petka*. Social Democrats participated in this for all but the years between 1925 and 1929. Within this alliance, the Czech and German Social Democratic parties, controlling only about as many legislative seats as their partners, lacked the position of dominance that Scandinavian Social Democrats enjoyed. It cannot be said that in the time available to it Czechoslovakia acquired the corporatist labor institutions of social democratic societies. As in Scandinavia, however, a Red–Green coalition did break decisively with deflationary orthodoxy in a bargain aimed at aiding both peasants and industrial workers in response to the depression. The break with orthodoxy came in 1934, and combined a devaluation of the crown (repeated in 1936) with agricultural relief measures, improved social assistance, import restrictions, and fiscal stimulus. Social Democrats and Agrarians in Czechoslovakia actually did what their Scandinavian counterparts have merely been credited with having done: they used large fiscal deficits to stimulate a recovery. These deficits were fueled by extensive relief measures for peasants and a dramatic increase in public works and social welfare spending. The public debt was used to finance buildings, new railway lines, highways, dams, and electric power facilities. Unemployment compensation for organized workers was subsidized by the state and provided a minimum of two-thirds of a worker's prior earnings.[89] These measures stabilized agricultural incomes and, by import substitution, stimulated demand for industrial products.[90] Starting in 1936, the state assumed a determining role in the labor market, enforcing binding arbitration to prevent wage reductions, severely restricting the right of employers to close plants and lay off workers and, remarkably, compelling employers who did lay off more than 10 percent of their work force to provide three weeks pay and notice. Labor inspectors were given the authority to enforce the operation of factories.[91] By 1937, with remarkable speed, the level of industrial output had nearly returned to its predepression (1929) high and unemployment had been cut to half of its 1933 peak.[92] Unlike the Scandinavian recoveries, this recovery was domestically driven: export volumes remained at just over half of their predepression level even after the overall level of activity had recovered in 1937.[93] Certainly the recovery was assisted from late 1936 by a rapid increase in military spending.

The limit of the Czech case is that we do not know how it would have continued to evolve in the absence of Hitler and Stalin's interventions. In the time that was available to it, Czechoslovakia followed a course that was strikingly similar to that which eventuated in social democratic political economies in Scandinavia: a Red–Green coalition stabilized and preserved what was by any estimates an otherwise vulnerable democratic order. The coalition broke decisively with liberal economic orthodoxy or neo-orthodoxy in response to the depression. Wages and labor market peace became principally subject to political rather than market determination and intimately connected to a larger package of social policy measures.

What we cannot know is whether this pattern would have continued and whether it would have included the leading political role that Scandinavian trade unions were beginning to acquire in the 1930s. Social democratic political economies were built over time; they did not come into existence in full form with the creation of Red–Green coalitions. The panoply of social democratic institutions and policies—comprehensive welfare states, a leading political role for trade unions, social and economic policies that tied incomes to social policies, a commitment to full employment, and labor market peace—were just beginning to take shape in Scandinavia in the 1930s and did not become fully formed until after the Second World War. At the least, Czechoslovakia is suggestive of an intermediate case of a Red–Green alliance capable of stabilizing a democratic order under exceptionally unfavorable conditions and breaking with economic orthodoxy in pursuit of the common interests of workers and peasants. The Czech social democratic parties, given their weaker alliance position, might not have been able to sustain this in the longer run. In the short run, in a world in which working-class leaders were often ignored where democracy endured and imprisoned where it did not, their accomplishments were remarkable.

In a world in which legitimacy was indeed contingent, Czechoslovakia proved to be the paradigmatic case. With Hitler's rise to power in Berlin, the range of alliances open to Sudeten Germans was fundamentally redefined. As German revanchism undermined the Prague government, Slovakian nationalism, too, was revivified. After the election of 1935, at which the German electorate gave its overwhelming support to the Sudeten German party, political leaders in Prague were almost entirely consumed by the German threat and the correlate Sudeten problem. Slovakian nationalism assumed the status of a major nuisance, but by itself lacked the potential to undermine the democratic order.[94]

If the ultimate outcome of a Red–Green alliance in which the working class was the junior partner must remain indeterminate, we can nonetheless make effective use of this case both in confirming the preconditions of democratic stabilization in aliberal societies and in testing a range of hypotheses about the conditions of democratic instability and fascism. The minimum conclusion that is confirmed by Czechoslovakia is that the democratic stabilization of an aliberal society that lacked a hegemonic clerical movement (as in Belgium and the Netherlands) required a coalition of the urban working classes and the family peasantry. We can see as well that this coalition sponsored a break with liberal orthodoxy or neo-orthodoxy in its depression policies. Finally, we can confirm that this coalition was associated with social democratic indifferences to class conflict and income redistribution in the countryside. It is to this last proposition that we now turn.

In Czechoslovakia, the working-class movement was divided ethnically, regionally, and, with the appearance of the Communist party, ideologically. The German Social Democrats, because of their ethnic base, organized almost exclusively among industrial workers. The Czech Social Democrats, limited to Bohemia and Moravia-Silesia, were also exclusively urban. Bohemian and Moravian agrarian workers (there were not many of them) were in fact initially organized by the Social Democratic party during the first few years of the Republic. There were, however, few agricultural workers in these provinces because of a rather egalitarian farm structure. Also, because these were heavily industrialized areas, agricultural workers were in a less dependent position. They routinely moved back and forth between industrial and agricultural employment. In 1921, only 28.4 percent of the labor force of Bohemia was in agriculture. The percentages for the other provinces were Moravia and Silesia, 33.8 percent; Slovakia, 58.7 percent; and Ruthenia, 62.4 percent.[95] The great majority of agrarian workers were thus located in Slovakia and Ruthenia. A conservative estimate would be that, in Slovakia, 40 percent of the agrarian labor force consisted of proletarians; in Ruthenia it was probably close to half. In these provinces there was almost no industry, and large surplus rural populations depended on the agrarian labor market.

The Social Democratic party never had an opportunity to organize these workers. In the schism between social democracy and communism, the Communists captured the party organization in Slovakia and Ruthenia, while Social Democrats prevailed in the industrial areas of Bohemia and Moravia.

The result was that the Social Democratic party became mainly a Bohemian and Moravian party and mainly a party of industrial workers. Thus, in the first post-schism election, in 1925, the Social Democratic party was wiped out in Slovakia and Ruthenia, receiving 4.3 percent and less than 2 percent of the vote, respectively. In contrast, the Communist party received 13 percent of the Slovakian vote; with 30.8 percent of the Ruthenian vote, it became the largest party in Ruthenia.[96]

The Communist party captured the Social Democratic organization in these regions, but it did not succeed in mobilizing agrarian workers.[97] These workers were mainly organized by the regional Catholic Populist parties and the secular Agrarian parties. The Agrarians, who were mainly parties of family peasants, were especially successful in capturing this constituency because of their leading role in the land reform program. They could unite family peasants and day laborers because land reform, which consolidated mainly the position of the former, was aimed specifically at Magyar and German landowners; it consequently exploited ethnic cleavages in the countryside.[98] The net effect of the schism and of the land reform was that the Social Democrats never developed a significant involvement in rural class conflict. The democratic working-class movement (German and Czechoslovak Social Democrats) remained urban and industrial in its orientation, and free to collaborate with the representatives of the family peasantry—the secular Agrarian parties and the Catholic Populist parties.

Czechoslovakia also demonstrates that neither a substantial communist party, a plethora of overlapping cleavages, nor the absence of a united peasant party were sufficient to prevent a democratic coalition. The Czechoslovak Communist party, like its German (and French) counterpart, averaged about 10 percent of the popular vote in the late 1920s and early 1930s. The need to compete with this party for working-class support certainly placed a strain on the Czech Social Democrats and, to the extent that it reduced their popular support, it reduced the strength of their bargaining position, but it did not prevent them from allying with nonsocialist parties. The Czech example also stands as a useful corrective to the proposition drawn from the Spanish, Italian, and German cases: that the absence of united peasant representation and a multiplicity of cleavages in those countries doomed democracy.[99]

It was still possible for socialists to make a coalition with family peasants—to overcome their consumer-producer conflicts—even when socialists were separated from peasants by regionalism and religious cleavages and when peasants were themselves divided by these cleavages. The socialists were divided among themselves by ethnicity and regionalism (autonomist German Social Democrats versus centralizing Bohemian-Moravian Social Democrats versus centralizing Slovakian Social Democrats). The peasant parties were divided from the social democrats by regionalism (centralizing Social Democrats versus autonomist Slovakian Populists) and by religion (secular social democrats versus Catholic Bohemian-Moravian Populists versus Catholic Slovakian Populists). And the peasant parties were themselves divided by religion and regionalism (secular, centralizing Bohemian-Moravian Agrarians versus Catholic, centralizing Bohemian-Moravian Populists versus secular, centralizing Slovakian Agrarians versus Catholic, autonomist Slovakian Populists). These cleavages provoked bitter conflicts—bitter enough to be defining features of the party system, but as long as the coalition served the other interests of the participants in it, they were willing to avoid a showdown on these.

Rural Class Conflicts and Fascist Hegemony

The position of agrarian laborers in the socialist movement looks quite different when we turn our attention to Spain, Italy, and Germany. Although it is difficult to estimate the voting preferences of agrarian workers, data on the composition of socialist trade unions make it clear that these workers exercised enormous leverage in the socialist movements of Italy and Spain; in Germany, their influence was less, but still substantial. In these countries agrarian labor had remained largely unmobilized by other political groups; therefore, it presented socialist parties and trade unions with a vast reservoir of potential support.

In discussing the Italian case, we concentrate on the north and center of Italy, for it was in these regions that rural class conflict pitted socialists against the family peasants. It was also in these regions, rather than the south, that the critical coalition questions, which eventually yielded fascism, were decided.

Class conflict in the Italian countryside pitted day laborers, or *braccianti,* against a mixed group of sharecroppers, tenants, and small and large owners. The two most important points of contention were the local monopoly over hiring, which the sharecroppers, as periodic employers, resented no less than tenants and peasant owners, and the ownership of harvesting equipment, the sharecroppers caring little for the socialist vision of collective ownership.[100]

The socialist cause was pressed in the countryside by the Syndicalists (USI) and Federterra. The latter was the agrarian section of the normally reformist, socialist Confederazione Generale del Lavoro (CGL); Federterra provided 33 percent of the CGL's membership in 1920.[101] Federterra sought to bridge the conflict between laborers and sharecroppers, but its massive postwar mobilization of laborers and its collectivist ambitions made this impossible. As its membership rose from about 93,000 in 1918 to over 300,000 in 1919, Federterra leaders lost control of their members and felt compelled to act more militantly than their past experience would otherwise have recommended.[102]

The strategy of jointly organizing sharecroppers and laborers became untenable, as well, because the end of the war saw a dramatic increase in the size of the middle peasantry as laborers became sharecroppers and land-owners: the percentage of owners rose from 18.3 percent of the males engaged in agriculture in 1911 to 32.4 percent in 1921.[103] The dilemma for Federterra was that, although the absolute membership of laborers was rising, the relative importance of this group in the countryside was declining quickly. Federterra's fear was that its constituency would continue to shift its political loyalties as its class position changed.

As a solution to this, Federterra advocated collective ownership of equipment among sharecroppers. This was an attempt to bind sharecroppers to the Federterra organization, but the effect was not the intended one. Instead, this new emphasis drove sharecroppers into the arms of local Catholic unions, thus transforming Federterra. By 1920, Federterra had become the union of farm labor. The contrast with the Catholic unions (CIL) is striking. Although agrarian laborers represented the great majority of Federterra's membership, they accounted for only 10 percent of the agrarian membership of CIL; the remaining were made up of sharecroppers and small tenants (78.4 percent) and small owners (10 percent).[104]

We can now begin to see how the farm labor constituency bore on the strategy of the Socialist party. Yet attention to Federterra alone provides only a very incomplete picture. The CGL, or at least its urban, industrial wing, had always followed a reformist course, and this did not change substantially after the war. But the CGL was neither the only socialist organizer of day laborers nor the only important union in the socialist movement. In 1907, the syndicalist unions organized about 44 percent of the socialist-oriented labor force.[105] Moreover, the agrarian fraction of their membership was quite high, about 60 percent, with most of this among day laborers, especially the lowest-paid workers of Emilia. By 1920, the three syndicalist unions (USI, UIL, and the independent railwaymen's union) still organized about one-third of the socialist labor force. The agrarian component—still over-whelmingly day laborers—continued to account for about half of the syndicalist membership.[106]

The effect of the syndicalist unions, then, was to still further increase the dependence of the socialist movement on day laborers, for once these workers were politically mobilized by a part of the left, it became imperative that the Socialist party solicit their support. The role of the day laborers, however, did not stop here, because of the special place they occupied in bolstering the position of intransigents (in contrast to accommodationists and revolutionaries) in the Socialist party. The intransigents were dominant in the Socialist party leadership and in the minoritarian syndicalist unions. The accommodationists were dominant in the parliamentary party and the CGL. Since the intransigents in the party leadership could not rely on the support of the CGL, they were inclined to accentuate the claims of the syndicalist unions and the agrarians within them—so much so, it turned out, that even when the fascist threat had convinced the leaders of the CGL of the need for accommodation with the Catholic unions in organizing the sharecroppers and small landowners, the Socialist party leadership resisted.[107]

The lines of class conflict in the Spanish countryside differed from those in Italy. In Spain, class conflict pitted day laborers, tenants, and marginal owners, all of whom depended on the labor market, against middle and large owners; some of the latter were directly involved in cultivation and some were members of the urban middle classes. Two unions had traditionally mobilized farm labor: the anarchists (in the Confederación Nacional del Trabajo, or CNT) and the socialists (in the Unión General de Trabajadores, or UGT). Until Primo de Rivera's dictatorship, the CNT had been by far the more important organizer of agrarian workers. By the 1930s, however, the former was largely a spent force in the countryside, mainly because it had felt the heavy hand of the dictatorship. The UGT, by contrast, had been favored by the dictatorship and, with its well-established presence among industrial workers, was ready to move forcefully into the agricultural areas. The Federación Nacional de Trabajadores de la Tierra (FNTT), the agrarian wing of the UGT, increased its membership from a mere 36,639 in 1930 to 451,337 in 1933, thereby accounting for about 40 percent of the UGT membership.[108] The proportion of the FNTT membership that depended mainly on the labor market for its income was very high, probably in excess of 80 percent.

One indication of this, according to Edward Malefakis, is the close relationship between the socialist vote and the size of the laboring population. Malefakis observed the disparity in the pattern of land tenure between the north (small family owners), the center and litoral (small and intermediate properties), and the southwest (large estates worked by day laborers). He demonstrated that this distribution translated into a steady voting pattern: rightist deputies were elected almost entirely by the small peasant proprietors of Old Castile and Navarre; Socialists were the largest party in southwestern Spain; the political center was elected in the geographic center.[109]

The Socialists left no doubt about the kind of reform they wanted; land had to be redistributed to the poorer rural workers, especially to the landless day laborers. The party bore the primary responsibility for the 1932 legislation that threatened the land titles not only of large landowners in the southwest, but also of small owners who leased out their land in Old Castile and Navarre. Already, in 1931, the Socialists and other San Sebastian parties enacted a series of emergency decrees that forbade expulsion of small tenants, forbade owners from withdrawing their land from cultivation, established rules that favored collectives rather than individuals in the renting of large properties, established an eight-hour day and a de facto wage increase, established what amounted to a closed shop in the labor market, thereby vastly increasing the power of the FNTT, and established arbitration boards that generally reinforced the leading position of the FNTT.

Emboldened or driven by its growing support among the agrarian proletariat, the FNTT was the socialist organization that initiated the turn toward radicalization. This radicalization alienated the Socialists and the UGT from the Catholic family peasants of the north and center. Indeed, this radicalization began with an agricultural issue. In June 1934, the FNTT called a nationwide strike in response to the repeal of the 1931 Municipal Labor Act, the act that had created the arbitration boards on which so much of the FNTT's influence depended. The strike received only lukewarm support from the urban wing of the UGT and eventually failed, causing the loss of tens of thousands of union members. In its aftermath, and especially in the wake of the failed October Revolution, the gulf between the two wings of the socialist movement and between the movement and family peasants became even greater. The polarization came to a head in February 1936, when family peasants in the center and north voted overwhelmingly for the Catholic Confederación Española de Derechos Autonómos (CEDA) and agrarian workers in the center and southwest voted overwhelmingly for the socialists.[110] This electoral outcome mirrored the alignments that formed on behalf of fascism and the Republic a few months later.[111]

Although Germany presents a more complicated picture, the conclusion is the same. Notwithstanding their conventional images as quintessentially urban, the Social Democratic party and the free trade unions (ADGB) were both dependent on the agrarian proletariat. Let us note, to begin with, that in 1928 purely rural districts gave no less than 25 percent of their vote to the socialist parties (SPD and KPD) and 21.5 percent to the SPD alone.[112] These data become more telling when we consider the strength of the ADGB-affiliated agrarian workers' union, the Deutscher Landarbeiterverband (DLV).

Until 1918, Germany's agrarian workers—about 3,000,000 in all—remained politically unorganized. Agrarian trade unions were illegal until the collapse of the empire. This segment of the proletariat must have seemed an especially tempting target for the Social Democrats and the free trade unions. Indeed, in the SPD's vision of the political and economic development of the country, these workers were assigned a vital role. Politically, it was necessary to weaken the position of the Junkers. Land reform was not a plausible solution because in early 1919, when the SPD might have had the political power to introduce it, food shortages militated against further upheavals in the countryside. Moreover, it was unsatisfactory—and this may have been a more decisive factor, given the SPD's complete lack of interest in land reform in 1919—because it conflicted with the party's axiom that "economic development of the country depended on large-scale production in both industry and agriculture."[113] Land reform would have increased the number of allegedly inefficient small farms as well as the size of a middle peasantry that "showed no inclination toward a socialism that considered them fated to lose their holdings."[114] Like their Spanish and Italian counterparts, the German

Social Democrats faced the dilemma of mobilizing agrarian workers while not raising them out of the proletariat.

The German solution was to apply an industrial model to agriculture. Agricultural workers would be collectively organized and share in all of the labor market and social policy rights that applied to industrial workers. This solution addressed all of the concerns of the Social Democrats. Increases in wages and taxes would weaken the Junkers, preserve large units of production, prevent food shortages, and not create more family peasants. At the same time, workers, "at least a considerable number of them, could be won for the Social Democratic party and unionized."[115]

At the end of 1918, there were only 20,000 unionized agricultural workers in all of Germany. By 1920, their number had risen to about 1,000,000. Membership then declined and stabilized at about 200,000 for the remainder of the Republic. This is in contrast to about 9 million industrial workers in ADGB at the peak in 1923, and a stabilized industrial membership of about 4.3 million thereafter. From these figures it appears that socialist unions had only a residual role in the countryside. At the peak of unionization, just over one in ten ADGB members was an agrarian worker. In the last half of the Republic, only about one in twenty-five was.[116]

These figures, however, severely understate the impact of the agrarian unions. This becomes clear when we examine data on the number of industrial and agrarian workers who were covered by collective contracts. The number of industrial workers covered by collective agreements (union members or not) was 13,135,000 in 1924, 12,276,000 in 1929, and 11,950,000 in 1931.[117] The equivalent figures for agrarian workers were 2,371,719 in 1924, 2,749,398 in 1926, and 2,123,110 in 1928.[118] These are extraordinary numbers: the total population of agricultural laborers in Germany was only about 3 million during these years. Thus, two-thirds or more of this population was covered by collective agreements. For Germany as a whole, about 20 percent of the labor force covered by ADGB agreements was in agriculture. We now begin to see the potential importance of this constituency to the SPD and the ADGB. It is likely indeed that a very large part of the 25 percent of the rural kreise vote that went to the SPD and KPD must have come from this constituency.

We can see even more clearly the manner in which this powerful union presence—and the larger political and economic strategy of which it was a part—was bound to antagonize family peasants. For the corollary of that strategy was that the SPD and the ADGB took a strong interest in the living standards of agrarian laborers. Indeed, in the first years of the Republic, the SPD succeeded in winning passage of legislation that extended all of the social policy rights of industrial workers to agrarian workers, guaranteed them the right to unionize, and extended to agriculture the same system of compulsory arbitration that was used in industrial wage disputes. All agrarian workers were covered by compulsory health, pension, unemployment, and disability insurance schemes. The costs of these programs were covered in the same manner as those for industrial workers: by joint employee and employer contributions.[119] German agricultural workers were surely the most comprehensively protected in Europe in the 1920s.

These benefits were being extended to agrarian workers during years in which agricultural income was collapsing. The net share of national income going to agriculture fell from 13.0 percent in 1913 to 7.2 percent in 1929.[120] It is difficult to compare exactly the income of a farm worker with that of a peasant family member working on a family farm. But two studies provide plausible evidence that the income of a peasant was in many cases lower than that of a farm worker. In the first study, Adolf Münzinger, in assuming an interest payment of 5 percent for the invested capital, calculated the income of the Württemberg peasant and members of his family as lower than that of the farm worker.[121] Another study indicates that this was true in other parts of Germany as well.[122]

In this context, the almost hysterical peasant attacks on *Sozialpolitik* and the antipathy of peasants to the SPD become comprehensible. On balance, it appears that the German Social Democrats, too, through their efforts on behalf of the social rights of agrarian workers, legislation that improved the market position of these workers, and the generalization of collective agreements, became entangled in rural class conflict.

It was this entanglement rather than conflicts between urban consumers and rural producers that distinguished socialist movements in Germany, Italy, and Spain from socialist movements in Norway, Sweden, Denmark, and Czechoslovakia. Outside of Spain, competition between the interests of urban consumers and rural producers was a constant, not a variable, during the critical years that preceded the formation of stabilizing coalitions in aliberal societies. In all of these societies, urban socialists continued a longstanding defense of cheap food and maintained their alliance with urban liberals and manufacturers on this issue. Nor does an overlay of other cleavages on the worker–peasant relationship seem to have been determining. In Italy and Spain, often-confessional peasants were certainly put off by the secularism of socialist parties. But the same can be said of Catholic peasants in Czechoslovakia, who were nonetheless able to come to an understanding with secular socialists. The northern Spanish peasants, who rallied to the Catholic CEDA and would later provide Francoism with its social backbone, certainly insisted that the anticlerical provisions of the Republican constitution be rewritten. But the main advocates of that anticlericalism had not been the Socialists, who were only mildly supportive of it, but the Left Republicans. Moreover, in Spain even the interests of urban consumers and rural producers had very little to do with the antagonism between socialists and peasants. Spanish agriculture was not sufficiently wedded to the world market to experience the full force of the international commodity crisis. At every step of the way in the polarization of relations between the peasantry and the Socialists, rural class conflict provided the provocation. In Italy, too, rural class conflict was much more salient than consumer–producer conflict in the polarization of socialists and northern family peasants. In Scandinavia, class relations in the countryside never became a point of contention between socialists and the family peasantry. Instead, the historic antagonism between them turned on the competing interests of producers and consumers and on the labor movements' association with secular, urban cultures.

Scholars have given so much attention to the social bases of the coalitions actually formed by social democrats and fascists that the issue need not detain us for long. The coalitions that came to power in Denmark and Sweden in 1933 and in Norway in 1935 were made between urban labor parties and agrarian parties whose social anchors were in the agrarian middle classes. In Czechoslovakia, the coalition was made with a mixed bag of agrarian and Catholic parties who represented the agrarian middle classes.[123] Whatever the quibbles about precisely who voted for the Nazis in Germany, it is clear that the social core of that support came from the urban middle classes and the Protestant peasantry of the west.[124] The Junker, too, mainly through the agrarian wing of the German National People's party (DNVP), came to support Hitler's coalition. But their contribution to the social base of Nazism was so small that they were a residual element. Moreover, and this is a point we should not forget, the Junkers did not lead the peasantry to Hitler; they followed it. The DNVP did not accept a position of junior ally of the Nazis until the autumn of 1932, well after the Protestant peasantry had shifted its support. If Robert Moeller is correct, peasant support for Hitler was even wider than the conventional historiography has implied. Moeller has argued that Catholic peasants in the Rhineland and Westphalia, although they did not abandon the Center for Hitler, had already forced the Center to abandon the Republic and welcomed Hitler's accession to power.[125]

Mussolini came to power, gaining an effective majority in the Chamber, by extending the support for fascism through a coalition with a hodge-podge of nationalists, Catholics, and right liberals at the time of the March on Rome. Again, the subtending alliance rested on a combination of agrarian and urban middle-class interests and was aimed, above all, at the socialist working class.[126]

Landed elites in southern Italy were even less relevant to the success of Italian fascism than were the Junkers to the success of German Nazism. Italian fascism, which found its social base in the urban and rural middle classes of the north and center, succeeded in spite of, rather than because of, the southern agrarian elites. Fascism was above all a reaction against socialism, and it took root in Italy only in those areas (overwhelmingly in the north and center) which had a strong Socialist party. Because socialism was weak in the south, fascism lacked an enemy there and consequently had little appeal. Only in Apulia, Naples, and the provinces of Syracuse in Sicily was southern socialism a potent force. Only in these areas did fascism gain a mass following before 1923. Elsewhere in the south, political power remained in the hands of local notables whose political orientations were a function of patronage. Before the March on Rome, those notables remained wedded to traditional liberal deputies, ministers, and prefects who could deliver patronage, and fascism consequently hardly benefitted at all from southern support. [127]

In Spain, the right-wing nationalist alliance that coalesced in the voting of 1936 substantially mirrored the regional and class foundations of the civil war parties later in the year. As in Germany and Italy, the social base was rooted in an alliance of urban and rural middle classes against the socialist working classes. The regions with high literacy rates and large populations of Catholic smallholders—Leon, Castile, much of Aragon, Navarre—voted for the Right. The Left had its electoral success among urban workers, dissident regionalists, agrarian workers, especially in the latifundista provinces, and in Galicia. [128]

The precise extent to which the rightist electoral coalition of February 1936 became the Nationalist coalition of the war is a subject on which little adequate research has been possible. The distribution of Nationalist and Republican strength was by no means purely a function of local sentiment, even if the essential conclusion is that those regions and classes that voted for the right in February generally supported Franco's *pronunciamiento* and the Nationalist side in the war. The wartime alliance patterns of the urban working and middle classes are less problematic than the alliance patterns of the peasants. Regarding the latter, the most careful studies have been done by Edward Malefakis, whose conclusions support the proposition that the family peasantry generally sided with the Nationalists. The starting point is the observation, about which there is not much dispute, that the family peasantry of the North, the core of CEDA support, embraced the Nationalist cause. The Nationalist revolt was vigorously supported from the start by the peasants of Old Castile and Navarre. [129] Beyond this, the alliance patterns of family peasants are murkier, and our inferences must rest on the logic of the disdain that family peasants demonstrated for the Republic in the February election and a few simple observations that Malefakis has made about the war itself. He has shown, in the first place, that the war was fought "between a primarily urban Republican zone and a predominantly rural Nationalist zone." Except for the first three months, when the day laborers of Andalusia supported the Republic, and the last two months of the conflict, when the Republicans had been reduced to the quadrant south and east of Madrid, peasants never constituted "even so much as 40 percent of the Republican zone's population." Moreover, a "second observation . . . that can be made with a high degree of certainty is that nowhere did the peasantry display revolutionary spirit and organization to such an extent that the Nationalists were denied effective use of the human and military resources of the regions they conquered." There was neither resistance nor sabotage from peasants in the Nationalist zone. The final point to be stressed is that peasants "supplied [the Nationalist cause] with its primary source of troops." Contrary to the popular misperception, foreigners seldom exceeded 10 percent of the troop strength on either side, and peasants made up a far greater share of the Nationalist force than they did of the Republican force.[130]

The most striking thing about the February coalition in Spain is that it was essentially self-forming. It was the product of neither a fascist party nor a powerful leader. The right alliance in 1936 was a melange of various conservative-to-reactionary urban and rural middle-class parties, cliques, and sentiments. The anchor of the right alliance was provided by the Catholic CEDA, which contained a range of sentiments but was predominantly committed to respect for the legal framework. Neither the party nor its leader Gil Robles can be characterized as fascist.[131] Rather, the formation of the right alliance in the February 1936 election was a station on the way to the alliance that supported the Nationalist rebellion and later the diluted fascist institutions that Franco created to harness and subordinate the working classes and extirpate their socialism.

Epilogue

Given the impuissance of liberal movements, a condition that had its origin in their prewar failure and was mediated through the failure of their interwar alliances and policies, the precondition of fascism was a working-class movement engaged in a defense of the rural proletariat. The coalitions of urban and rural middle classes that took shape in Spain, Italy, and Germany were premised on a common ambition to extirpate the socialist working-class menace. In particular, they were energized by the antisocialism of family peasants. In the end, social science can take us no further; it can never confirm that socialists in Spain, Germany, and Italy would have—or even could have—made alliances with the family peasantry if they had not become ensnared in rural class conflict. No methodology can replicate history, and thus permit such an assertion. Social science can only isolate some of the similarities and differences and help us identify those things that logically could not have accounted for the outcomes. When the similarities and differences are isolated, the engagement of some socialist movements in agrarian class conflict remains.

We are so accustomed to thinking about the antagonism between socialists and peasants in Germany, Italy, and Spain that worker–peasant coalitions in them seem most improbable. We are likewise so accustomed to the stability of Scandinavian democracy that from our distant vantage point it seems most improbable that these societies could have become fascist dictatorships. We would do well to remember the similarities between Scandinavia and Germany, however. In all four countries, urban liberals were in a state of disarray and incapable, by 1933, of providing national leadership either alone or in combination with traditional conservative parties. In Denmark, the vote of the only remaining party of urban liberals, the Radicals, had fallen from 20 percent to 9 percent between 1918 and 1935. The old Liberal party, too, had witnessed an almost total collapse of its urban middle class vote and had become overwhelmingly a party of family peasants. Its vote had fallen from 29 percent to 18 percent. In Norway, the Liberal vote was down to 16 percent, as both farmers and the urban middle classes abandoned it for the Agrarian party, the Christian party, the Conservatives, and various splinter parties. In Sweden, the exodus of the urban middle classes dropped the Liberals to 13 percent of the vote in 1936.[132] In all four countries, urban liberals were unwilling to accommodate the material demands of the peasantry. In all four, the vestigial legitimacy of traditional liberal policies had been lost. In all four, peasants, like workers, were desperately seeking a state that would substitute politics for markets and stabilize incomes.[133] In all four, peasants were violently opposed to trade unions and social welfare measures. As in Germany, Scandinavian Agrarians "stood out as the core of reactionism."[134] What made the antipathy of German peasants toward social democrats even greater than it was in Scandinavia was the fact that German Social Democrats were actively engaged in the redistribution of wealth not simply between the city and the countryside, but within the countryside as well. We would also do well to recall that worker–peasant coalitions seemed most improbable in Scandinavia until they were formed. Their formation truly stunned Norwegian and Swedish liberals, who literally could not conceive of them even as they were being negotiated, and who then confidently predicted their rapid demise.[135]

What is incontrovertible, in retrospect, is that the peasants' demands for relief from the market were not inherently intractable. If they seemed so to German Socialists, it was because they could see no exit from the economic crisis, which provided the SPD with its last, and least likely, opportunity to make a worker–peasant alliance. We might suppose that this was because the ADGB, which was advocating stimulation policies—the so-called WTB plan—could not adduce a politically plausible strategy by which such policies could be implemented.[136] To be sure, historians have rightly adduced the lapidescent Marxism of such men as Rudolph Hilferding to account for the skepticism such policies engendered among German Social Democrats.[137]

It does not seem unreasonable to suppose, however, that the opposition of Hilferding and other doctrinaires would have been much less likely to prevail had it not been perfectly congruent with the Social Democrats' total political inability to pursue an innovative strategy in the first place. With the failure of Lib–Labism and the alienation of the peasantry, the SPD was haplessly reduced to supporting Heinrich Brüning's presidential government and hoping that it could retain control of the Prussian state government until the storm passed.[138] Socialists might have been able to make a plausible case for a strategy of stimulation if they had been able to show that it was politically feasible. And if they had not so completely alienated the peasantry, they might have been able to argue on behalf of an urban–rural alliance that would have made it feasible. The infeasibility of such an alliance had nothing to do with the absence of a peasant party—Hitler demonstrated that much—and everything to do with the extreme antagonism between the peasants and urban socialists. What is ideologically conceivable, after all, is partly a function of what is politically plausible. In the end, peasants' needs were addressed in both Scandinavia and Germany. In the end, the sole question was not whether they would be accommodated nor whether they could be accommodated. It was simply by whom they would be accommodated.

Conclusion:
Class Alliances and Transition
to Mass Politics

A Structuralist Argument

What I have presented in my study is a structuralist argument. Liberal democracy, social democracy, and fascism were alternatives in the sense that they constituted the historically known range of outcomes in interwar Western Europe. They were also alternatives in the sense that they derived from different levels of liberal success and different patterns of labor participation in politics and organization in the labor market before 1914, rested on different interwar class alliances and balances of class power, adopted fundamentally different responses to the economic crises of the twenties and thirties, and, above all, were not moral equivalents.

They were not alternatives in the sense that societies acting collectively, or leaders acting on behalf of societies, could consciously choose among them. One of the cardinal lessons of the story I have told is that leadership and meaningful choice played no role in the outcomes. To be sure, leaders did make choices that had implications for the regime outcomes; leadership choices were the mediating agent between inherited social and political contexts—"structures" in the argot of social science—and the eventual regime outcomes. For better or worse, however, those choices were always consistent with the short-term imperatives of the pursuit of power through the optimization of mass support. To restate what I claimed in the introduction, theories of transition to mass politics must confront the fact that no stable interwar regime was formed that lacked mass support, each regime was based on a distinctive social or class alliance, and each regime had clear material winners and losers. Some social and political contexts encouraged leaders to build alliances across specific social groups; some compelled them to do so; some prohibited them from doing so or made it highly probable that they would fail if they tried. I have found little evidence that similarly situated leaders responded differently, or at least with different levels of success, to similar inherited inducements and constraints. Given the non-replicability of the experiences, that amounts to saying there is no evidence that different leaders, as long as they aspired to lead successful movements, would have made different choices. Mine is, then, an emphatically "structural" argument.

The historical irony, and sometimes tragedy, is that the moral character of the decisions leaders made as they sought power often had little relationship to the regime outcome. For example, in the decades before 1914, the political empowerment of industrial workers was most advanced in those societies—Britain, France, and Switzerland—in which hegemonic liberal movements chose to align with working-class movements. That prewar Lib–Labism, however, institutionalized a pattern of working-class organization that survived World War I and contributed to the political marginalization of workers during the interwar years. In societies in which Lib–Labism had not been a central feature of prewar politics, the historical paradox was of a different sort. In those societies, interwar working-class leaders who embraced democratic competition and committed themselves to social justice for what was before and has been since the forgotten fraction of the working class, the agrarian working class, by their choices made a fascist outcome more likely. Working-class leaders who ignored that part of the working class, paradoxically, made what I deem to be the preferred, most moral, outcome—social democracy—more likely.

Structuralism and Other Arguments Compared

In developing the proposition that the distinction between societies that became social democracies and those that became fascist dictatorships is found in the engagement of the socialist movements of the latter in rural class conflict, we have seen that explanations of interwar politics couched in terms of a multiplicity of overlapping cleavages or the absence of a single coherent peasant party fail to account for the regime outcomes. We should also note, if only in passing, that commonplace explanations of fascism as "caused" by the depression, or by the great inflation in Germany, or by resentment of the Versailles settlement simply do not stand up to comparative analysis.

It is true that industrial production fell further and faster in Germany, vulnerable as it was to the withdrawal of foreign capital, than it did in Scandinavia. The German index of industrial production fell 39 percent between its 1929 peak and its 1932 low. In Norway and Denmark, the index fell only 15 percent; in Sweden it fell just 11 percent. These figures are somewhat deceptive, however; for Scandinavian industry, having experienced less of a boom in the late 1920s, was already operating at a lower level even before the slump. Unemployment, it must be recalled, had been markedly higher in Scandinavia throughout the predepression decade. Moreover, industrial production dropped just as sharply in Czechoslovakia—61 percent between 1929 and 1933—as it did in Germany without provoking a collapse of democracy. When the crash came, unemployment in Norway and Denmark rose, as in Germany, to one-third of the labor force. In Sweden it rose to one-quarter of the labor force. Agriculture in Scandinavia as in Germany, as we have already seen, saw the rate of return on investment collapse to zero in 1932–33. That the depression cannot adequately account for the success of German fascism is made even more apparent by the experiences of Austria, Spain, and Italy. Industrial production in Austria, also heavily dependent on foreign capital, fell just as deeply and rapidly as it did in Germany—by 38 percent between 1929 and 1932. In spite of this, indigenous fascism did not pose the same level of threat that it did in Germany. The local and regional elections held in April 1932 suggest that if a national election had been held, the Socialists, Catholics, and the agrarian Landbund would have together polled about 80 percent of the vote.[1] Moreover, in Spain, where a fascist coalition did form, industrial production fell just 16 percent. And in Italy, where the fascist coalition was formed almost a decade before the depression, industrial production actually *rose* 11 percent between 1919 and 1923.[2]

Similarly, an experience with hyperinflation, alone or in conjunction with the subsequent depression, does not account for much. Both Austria and Poland shared with Germany a radical depreciation and then collapse of the currency in the early 1920s. Moreover, we should keep in mind that most of the societies that escaped a round of hyperinflation did not, in consequence, enjoy stable economies. Rather, they were traumatized by radical deflations pursuant to a return to the gold standard. Finally, resentment of the Versailles settlement, with or without an inflation, with or without a depression, tells us little. Other societies, including Austria and Hungary, shared with Germany the experiences of revanchism, hyperinflation, and depression but did not become fascist. In contrast, Spain, which neither suffered from hyperinflation nor experienced the depression deeply nor had revanchist claims, did become fascist.

The discussion in the previous chapter of the social foundations of regime stabilization has also placed in a new light several other common interpretations of fascism and democratic instability between the wars. Barrington Moore and Alexander Gerschenkron have argued that a fascist outcome was caused by the existence of a landed elite that added the support or acquiescence of a subordinated rural mass to a coalition with the urban middle classes.[3] In this view, what distinguished societies was the presence of a landed elite in control of the rural masses: England and France became liberal democracies because they lacked a politically decisive landed elite; Germany became fascist because it preserved one.

The Moore-Gerschenkron thesis is questionable on several counts. First, as we have observed, there is no cross-national correlation between the rural class structure, in particular the size of the dependent labor force, and the regime outcome. Second, even if a landed elite exercised economic control of a rural mass, that did not necessarily translate into political control. In Spain, southern day laborers voted overwhelmingly for the Socialist party in 1936. Third, rural support for fascism did not require that a landed elite have political control of a rural mass. Indeed, it did not even require the existence of a landed elite: in Germany, Spain, and Italy, rural support for fascism was found mainly in areas—in the Protestant west in Germany; in the north in Spain and Italy—in which the family peasantry rather than landed elites predominated. Finally, the only landed elites in Germany, Spain, and Italy who could actually deliver large numbers of votes were those in southern Italy, and ironically they, who were much more concerned with patronage than with class conflict, remained steadfast supporters of traditional liberal candidates. Fascism did not make inroads among them until after it had come to power and could deliver patronage.

Another type of explanation for the weakness of interwar democracy points to the inability of democrats to overcome social polarization.[4] However, polarization did not so much cause specific outcomes as it reflected an inability to find any stable regime solution. One country that became authoritarian, Spain, was in fact conspicuously depolarized at the beginning of its democratic experiment in 1931.[5] Some countries that became democratic—in particular Norway and Sweden—were, in contrast, if strike activity indicates class polarization, among the most polarized societies in Europe.[6] It is closer to the observed historical sequence to say that where democrats failed, it was not because their societies had become polarized. Rather, the societies had become polarized because democrats had failed.

That so many studies have focused on polarization as the key to explaining the collapse of some interwar democracies can itself be explained by the choice of cases such studies have employed and the comparisons they have made. Almost always, they have contrasted, often implicitly, the breakdown of democracy in Germany or Italy with its interwar continuity in Britain. I hope that by now it is clear that this contrast is patently irrelevant.

This brings us to yet another interpretation of interwar politics, one that accounts for the collapse of democracy according to the radicalism of working-class movements. Yet one of the lessons that emerges from the story we have told is that it mattered little, in the end, whether socialist leaders in aliberal societies were committed to radicalism or reformism.[7] Fascism emerged in a society with a radicalized socialist movement, Italy, and in one with a reformist socialist movement, Germany. The unqualified commitment to the reformist, electoral road to power, which was pursued by the German and, initially, the Spanish socialists, could be as self-defeating as the more radical posture taken by their Italian counterparts. Indeed, the Spanish experience suggests that such a strategy was the cause of party radicalization and societal polarization. The precondition for moderation and democratic stability was that socialists ignore a substantial part of the working class—the agrarian working class—and doing this was often inconsistent with the reformist strategy of electoral competition and gaining power through the ballot box. The historical irony, and tragedy, is that the logic of democratic politics could lead to the destructure of democratic politics. No socialist leaders consciously chose to ignore agrarian workers. Where they did, it was because they had no choice—either as in Norway, because it was a small class, or as in Denmark, Sweden, and Czechoslovakia, because it had already been politically organized. And where socialists had no choice but to ignore the agrarian working class, whether the parties were initially radical after the war, as in Norway, or reformist, as in Denmark and Czechoslovakia, the outcome was a stable democracy. The outcomes were structured.

Drawing Lessons from Europe

The European experience of the transition to mass politics will not be duplicated, indeed will hardly even be approximated, in the contemporary Third World. The international economic order, the balance of military power, new technologies of production, the rapid diffusion of knowledge, and the experiences of Europe itself have created a new context for political mobilization. The very categories of liberal democracy, social democracy, and fascism lose much of their meaning outside of the European experience. Many Third World dictatorships have been based on alliances of the countryside and the urban middle classes. But fascism was a response to liberal and socialist failure, and to conflate Third World dictatorships with fascism merely debases the language and confuses complex etiologies. In drawing inferences from Europe about what might occur in this different environment and in such diverse societies as the Third World, we must be most circumspect.

It seems that there are, nonetheless, certain constants in transitions to mass politics. To begin with, political mobilization poses the same essential conundrum of the conditions that are conducive to stable regimes, especially stable democracies. Moreover, the lines along which mobilization is occurring are at least somewhat similar. Class, religion, language, regionalism, and urban and rural identities seem to be at least as central in contemporary less developed countries as they were in turn-of-the-century Europe. Political mobilization, whatever else may condition it, is likely to continue to occur along these lines. To the extent that these similarities exist, the study of Europe suggests a few observations, if not about the nature of regime outcomes, then at least about the nature of the transition to politically mobilized societies.

One of the central puzzles of studies of the contemporary transition to mass politics in less developed countries is the question of which should come first, participatory rights or modernization? Liberal and conservative politicians and political scientists alike have often suggested that in backward societies, participatory rights in the absence of modernization and industrialization foster inefficiency, demagoguery, corruption, and instability. Marxists have argued that democracy can come only after social equality. These lines of thinking have produced a peculiar convergence of the left and right around the notion that democracy is a goal only for some unspecified future time. This proposition has become so widely accepted on both the left and the right that debate has been largely reduced to the subordinate, implicit, and banal question of whether one prefers dictatorships of the left or right. The assumption among liberals and conservatives is that somehow the pathologies will be attenuated by a certain level of industrialization and that at that time it will be possible to make a comparatively smooth transition to mass politics and democratic participation. The assumption of Marxists must be that left dictators will ameliorate inequalities and then accept democratic competition. Yet there is little empirical evidence to justify either of these assumptions.

The further problem with the liberal assumptions, at least as suggested by the European experience, is that affluence may not ease class accommodation and that, in any event, demands for participatory rights may not wait for affluence. The liberal inference that affluence eases accommodation was certainly not drawn from the experiences of Europe before 1945. By virtually any indicator, the industrial workers of Western Europe were markedly better housed, fed, clothed, and educated in 1914 than they were thirty years earlier. And by virtually any indicator, they were still better off, and much better protected by social policies, by the late 1920s. These increments of affluence did not halt the growth of class conflict. They accompanied it.

The notion that affluence ameliorates class conflict was drawn, rather, from a comparison between the political stability and economic growth the West experienced after 1950 and the political instability and economic turmoil it suffered between the wars. Yet the post-1950 increment of affluence followed the class accommodations of the 1930s and the accommodations that were imposed by the new international and European orders that were built in the late 1940s. It is worth emphasizing that the affluence came after the social pacts; it did not cause them. These social pacts were born in the economic crises of the 1930s and post-World War II reconstruction rather than in the palmier days of the 1950s and 1960s. Rather than supposing that class accommodation followed from economic growth, it is at least as plausible to suppose that the long run of economic growth that the West experienced after 1950 was a consequence of the industrial, agricultural, welfare, and other policies that the earlier social pacts had set in train. Waiting for affluence to cause social peace and political stability may be like waiting for Godot.

For politicians struggling to save fragile democracies or establish them amid economic crises, there may be an important lesson in the fact that in Europe social pacts were usually reached in the midst of economic and political crises. Crises served to break old patterns of thought and behavior, to help politicians and their followers to see new possibilities. They fostered an atmosphere of desperate experimentation that helped leaders to discover policies that joined former antagonists in a partnership. They also created an atmosphere in which it was easier for leaders to sell a realignment to their followers. The inference is that crises are not episodes to be circumvented in anticipation of compromise in more halcyon times. They are rather the main chance for compromise; the balance of probabilities is still less favorable to compromise under conditions of more normal politics.

There is a second lesson that the stabilizing pacts suggest: there will be losers. The pacts implicitly or explicitly always came at someone's expense. In Scandinavia, they came at the expense of the urban middle classes and even more of agrarian workers. In Germany, Italy, and Spain they came at the expense of workers, both urban and rural. Marxists and fascists are seldom troubled by the notion of winners and losers. Liberals often are. Liberals are inclined to try to weld together broad coalitions that combine fractions of all the contending classes. This is a search for a common, centrist ground among the less extreme fractions of competing sectors. It is a search for a ground that probably does not exist. Politics in aliberal Europe in the 1920s was about the failure of the search for moderation through a centrist strategy. The European experience suggests that it is often easier to transform politics by bringing together former antagonists at the expense of a third party than it is to get fractions of all parties to agree to a centrist solution. A centrist solution may obfuscate the question of who loses, but it also obfuscates the question of who wins.

The further problem with a centrist strategy is that political crises in mobilized societies are almost always simultaneously crises of production and distribution. A totalitarian regime of either the left or right will find numerous ways to reconcile the demands of production and distribution. But in a democratic order, surmounting these crises in the end requires a detente between business and labor. That detente is made more likely if its costs can be redistributed. Insofar as it is difficult for firms to simultaneously pay higher taxes, increase investment, and pay the social wage, it is necessary that the state socialize part of the cost of increased production and the social wage through its own policies of taxing the middle classes and spending on production and social programs. Finding such an immediate increment of resources that stimulates production and ameliorates the distributional crises requires losers.

A democratic state, moreover, is seldom in a position to impose such policies—to gain the cooperation of the business community, and the resignation of the tax-paying middle classes—unless it is apparent to the opponents of such policies that the parties to the stabilizing coalition are not going to break the coalition in the near future. The appearance of such a durable coalition appears to require an explicit, overt bargain in which the terms of the settlement, its costs and benefits, are obvious. This is very different from the more normal politics of concessions on the margin, the politics of implicit, incremental, transient, and revocable concessions. Such concessions suggest the impermanence of the alliance and encourage both attacks on it and defections from it. This strategy for a durable coalition is the antithesis of the search for the center ground.

The constrained competition of pre-1914 aliberal societies was in certain ways an effort analogous to the restricted competitiveness of politics in much of the contemporary Third World. Traditional elites and threatened fractions of the urban middle classes sought to protect themselves from the consequences of mobilization. Their aliberal regimes were fundamentally rigged: the working-class opposition could not win, take power, or share power. Those were the essential premises of the regimes; the particular mechanisms that were relied on to enforce those premises were as varied as the societies themselves. Whether those who wielded political power were unambiguously reactionary, as in Germany and Sweden, or sought to accommodate a working-class movement, as did the Giolittian liberals in Italy, made little difference in the end. There was no substitute for empowerment.

When a society enters the phase of mass mobilization—when it reaches the juncture at which millions of ordinary people see the connection between their quotidian well-being, the activities of the state, and their capacity to change the state—a period of restricted competition will do nothing to make social peace more attainable in the future. Barring a ruthlessly totalitarian order, a circumstance admittedly favored by modern technologies, those who mobilize will be all the more alienated and will probably organize themselves much more vigorously in the absence of allies. Self-organization is in fact the quintessence of political mobilization. That organization can take place in alliance with other social sectors, or it can take place against other social sectors. If the latter is the case, when the barriers of limited competition break—because of a war, an international crisis, the withdrawal of the military, or whatever—a period of limited competition, sometimes euphemistically referred to as "tutelary democracy," will compound the problems of stabilization. The lesson of the European experience is that, whatever the problems of widespread participation at an early date, they are fewer than those that will ensue from pent-up demands for participation.

The lesson for astute conservatives is that the transition to mass politics will be smoother if dissidents are allowed to organize as they appear and are coopted by a ruling movement that grants them limited empowerment. At the end of the day, the outcome will be a divided and consequently less effective opposition. The further lesson is that to do otherwise is not to smooth the way for a later expansion of participation, but to make politics more violent and zero-sum when that expansion comes. There is no easy way to manage the transition to mass politics, but attempts to defer it are doomed. And worse still, they will institutionalize in political competition the polarities of the transition. Conservative wisdom seems to be on the side of participatory rights even in advance of the demand for them.

One of the correlates, indeed a central premise, of much development theory is that fragile societies need time to build political institutions—the institutions of the state, the economy, and parties—before mass participation can be effectively managed. The European experience suggests that this vision is flawed. It suggests, in the first place, that the institutions that are built on conditions of restricted participation will be swept away or otherwise fundamentally undermined by the participatory breakthrough. It suggests, further and even more emphatically, that stabilizing democratic institutions are only built *through* mass participation.

In liberal and even more in aliberal societies, the institutions of the modern state, of the economy, and of the party system were the projects of mass movements; they were institutions that reflected the balance of interests those movements contained. In Europe, mass movements *made* modern political economies by establishing their hegemony. Institutionalization did not occur until those movements were unambiguously in power and their hegemony was perforce accepted by their erstwhile opponents. The essence of institutions is, after all, the consensual routinization of a certain distribution of authority, and until that distribution is decided and then accepted in day-to-day mass political and economic behavior, institutions rest only on the democrat's hopes and the dictator's truncheons.

The story of 1919 in aliberal Europe was one of participation breaking through old barriers. At the time, working-class leaders and progressive liberals looked forward optimistically to a new era. The year 1919 did indeed usher in a new era, but not the one they had expected. The democratic breakthroughs were the beginning, not the end, of democracy's hard times. Before 1919, democracy was a mere hypothesis; after 1919, it had to be made to work. That cycle of optimism and disillusionment resonates today, in the late 1980s, in the euphoria and disappointment that routinely follow the installation of democracies in the Third World. For a few months, perhaps a year or two, anything seems possible in a democracy. Then nothing seems possible.

A democratic breakthrough is not tantamount to a stabilizing coalition. A democratic breakthrough in Europe was normally little more than a negative coalition; in the wake of its deconstruction of the old order, there was little to hold it together. Stabilization requires a coalition of construction. In practice, the critical junctures in political mobilization always seems to occur during that developmental epoch in which the balance between the urban classes and between the town and the country is a precarious one. By the nature of the transition, no class or fraction thereof is positioned to exert hegemony without the alliance of another class or substantial fraction thereof. A regime stabilizing coalition must, therefore, be an interclass coalition. This means that political stabilization, especially of the democratic sort, is not possible in the absence of genuine class compromise.

I very much doubt that Europe can teach us much about the alliance possibilities that might subtend such compromises in less developed societies. Class structures are too different. European history does suggest, however, and Third World experiences seem to confirm, that such compromise is least likely to be reached between the urban working and middle classes. The essence of a successful Lib–Lab strategy in managing the transition to mass politics is that it must be effective *before* workers are mobilized as a class. Few less developed societies are likely to benefit from effective Lib–Labism or some equivalent of it.

To the extent that this is the case, the alignment of the countryside becomes the crucial variable, and it is at this juncture that comparisons with Western Europe become most problematic. Most less developed countries lack a politically mobilized agrarian middle class, given that urban mobilization has far outpaced rural mobilization and that patterns of land holding are often so radically unequal that such a class does not exist. An agrarian elite may be able to ensure the apathy of an impoverished agrarian proletariat for a time in an alliance with urban interests. For the longer run, such a sector provides a poor substitute for the stabilizing weight of a politically committed and active agrarian middle class. In crises, the apathetic are likely to rally neither for nor against a regime. They remain indifferent and thereby shift the decisive struggle to the cities.

The absence of a politically active and committed agrarian middle class may, however, be as determining as its alignment. The historical role of that class in interwar Europe was to decide the balance of power between the two urban classes. If such a class does not exist, it may be that *no* stabilizing coalition is possible, that no decisive balance of power can be created because there exists no rural mass whose material interests can be vested in the regime. In its absence, mass political competition may be reduced principally to a struggle between representatives of the two urban classes, with a reforming fraction of the urban middle classes periodically siding with labor when a dictatorship outlives its usefulness, then shifting back to the right when democracy fails. The only stable outcome may then be instability—a cycle of establishment of democracy and its collapse, military intervention, and withdrawal.

Notes

Chapter 1

1. The development of Lib-Labism, the mobilization of labor through an alliance with the liberal establishment, is discussed in Gregory M. Luebbert, "Social Foundations of Political Order in Interwar Europe," *World Politics,* vol. 33, no. 4 (July 1987), pp. 452–53.

Chapter 2

1. Among the standard accounts of the reform period is G. D. H. Cole, *British Working-Class Politics, 1832–1914* (London: George Routledge and Sons, 1941), pp. 25–49.

2. There is little doubt that Conservatives were more responsive to Labor's demands in these years; it is less certain that a majority of voting workers plumbed for the Tories. Cf. Edward H. Hunt, *British Labour History, 1815–1914* (London: Weidenfeld and Nicolson, 1981), p. 237 passim; and Cole, *Politics,* pp. 25–49.

3. Cole, *Politics,* pp. 25–38.

4. James Cornford, "The Transformation of Conservatism in the Late Nineteenth Century," in Peter Stansky, ed., *The Victorian Revolution: Government and Society in Victoria's Britain* (New York: New Viewpoints, 1973) pp. 237–318.

5. On the Tory working class, see Gareth Stedman Jones, *Outcast London: A Study in the Relationship Between Classes in Victorian Society* (Oxford: Clarendon Press, 1971), ch. 19; Gareth Stedman Jones, "Working-Class Culture and Working-Class Politics in London, 1870–1900: Notes on the Remaking of a Working Class," *Journal of Social History,* vol. 7, no. 4 (Summer 1974), pp. 460–508; R. L. Greenall, "Popular Conservatism in Salford, 1868–1886," *Northern History,* vol. 9

(1974), pp. 123–138; Henry M. Pelling, *Popular Politics and Society in Late Victorian Britain* (New York: St. Martin's Press, 1968), ch. 3.

6. In Lancashire's factory towns, it was said, workmen voted "by mills and wards in the spirit in which schoolboys played cricket or football by 'houses' or 'forms.' " The words were those of Frederic Harrison and are cited by P. Joyce, "The Factory Politics of Lancashire in the Later Nineteenth Century," *Historical Journal*, vol. 18, no. 3 (September 1975), p. 526.

7. Cole, *Politics*, pp. 38–49.

8. Friedrich Engels, *Selected Writings*, W. O. Henderson, ed., (Hammondsworth: Penguin, 1967), pp. 96–97.

9. Cole, *Politics*, p. 98.

10. Hunt, *British Labour*, p. 333.

11. Ibid., p. 278.

12. An excellent study of the obstacles activists encountered in inducing workers to think in more class-oriented terms is provided by David Howell, *British Workers and the Independent Labour Party, 1888–1906* (Manchester: Manchester University Press, 1983).

13. Recall Richard Moore on the Durham miners: "The Methodists did not share leisure-time activities with their non-Methodist workmates . . . [they were] divided from their bosses as workers, but united with them as 'respectable men.' " *Pitmen, Preachers and Politics* (Cambridge: Cambridge University Press, 1974), p. 176.

14. Hunt, *British Labour*, p. 333.

15. Ibid., p. 333.

16. On the divisions within the Liberal party during these years, see David Allan Hamer, *Liberal Politics in the Age of Gladstone and Rosebery: A Study in Leadership and Policy* (Oxford: Clarendon Press, 1972).

17. Hamer, *Liberal Politics*, p. 302 passim.

18. On the New Liberalism, see especially, Michael Freeden, *The New Liberalism: An Ideology of Social Reform* (Oxford: Clarendon Press, 1978).

19. Pelling, *Popular Politics and Society*, ch. 1; Bentley B. Gilbert, "The Decay of Nineteenth-Century Provident Institutions and the Coming of Old Age Pensions in Great Britain," *Economic History Review*, vol. 17, no. 3 (April 1965), pp. 551–63; J. R. Hay, *The Origins of the Liberal Welfare Reforms, 1906–1914* (New York: Macmillan, 1975); Pat Thane, "Women and the Poor Law in Victorian and Edwardian England," *History Workshop*, Issue 6 (Autumn 1978), pp. 29–51; Eric C. Midwinter, *Victorian Social Reform* (London: Longmans, 1968), pp. 27–63.

20. On the New Unionism, see Thomas Mann and Benn Tillet, *The 'New' Trades Unionism* (London, 1890); E. J. Hobsbawm, *Labouring Men: Studies in the History of Labour* (London: Weidenfeld and Nicolson, 1964), especially, ch. 9, "British Gas-Workers, 1873–1914," pp. 158–78 and ch. 10, "General Labour Unions in Britain, 1889–1914," pp. 179–203; C. Wrigley, "Liberals and the Desire for Working Class Representatives in Battersea, 1886–1922," in K. D. Brown, ed., *Essays in Anti-Labour History: Response to the Rise of Labour in Britain* (London: Macmillan, 1974), pp. 126–58.

21. Cole, *Politics*, p. 126.

22. "British Socialism is not Utopian. . . . It trusts to no sudden changes, it needs no beginnings afresh, it works under the conditions it has found, its constructive methods are chiefly adaptation and re-arrangement." J. Ramsay MacDonald and

J. Keir Hardy, "The Independent Labour Party's Programme," *The Nineteenth Century*, vol. 45, no. 263 (January 1899), p. 25.

23. Henry M. Pelling, *The Origins of the Labour Party, 1880–1900*, 2nd ed. (Oxford: Clarendon Press, 1965), p. 14.

24. On the SDF, see Henry Collins, "The Marxism of the Social Democratic Federation," in Asa Briggs and John Saville, eds., *Essays in Labour History, 1886–1923*, vol. 2 (London: Macmillan, 1971), pp. 47–69; Paul Richard Thompson, *Socialists, Liberals and Labour: The Struggle for London, 1885–1914* (London: Routledge and Kegan Paul, 1967).

25. Alfred Williams, *Life in a Railway Factory*, reprinted edition with introduction by Leonard Clark (Newton Abbot: David and Charles, 1969), p. 306.

26. Robert Roberts, *The Classic Slum: Salford Life in the First Quarter of the Century* (Manchester: Manchester University Press, 1971), p. 16.

27. James Hinton, *Labour and Socialism: A History of the British Labour Movement, 1867–1974* (Brighton, Sussex: Wheatsheaf Books, 1983), p. 60.

28. Hinton, *Labour and Socialism*, p. 61.

29. On the history of the ILP, see Howell, *Independent Labour Party;* and especially, Hinton, *Labour and Socialism*, pp. 40–63.

30. Cole, *Politics*, pp. 138–53. The idea of independent labor representation was hardly a new one. It had been advanced by the Labor Representation League of 1869 and later the Labor Electoral Association (LEA) and the Social Democratic Federation in the 1880s. The League and the LEA had been infiltrated and coopted by trade unionist Lib–Labs. On the LEA and the LRL, see Cole, *Politics*, pp. 50–75.

31. Cole, *Politics*, p. 110.

32. On the campaign for TUC support for independent representation in the early 1890s, see ibid., pp. 100ff.

33. Ibid., p. 111.

34. Ibid., p. 112.

35. Ibid., pp. 138–67.

36. Hinton, *Labour and Socialism*, pp. 72 passim; Cole, *Politics*, pp. 167–95.

37. Cole, *Politics*, p. 165. On the 1900 election and the LRC, see ibid., pp. 153–66.

38. Hinton, *Labour and Socialism*, pp. 72–73.

39. On the repercussions of the Taff Vale judgment on the trade unions, see G. D. H. Cole, *A Short History of the British Working-Class Movement* (New York: Macmillan, 1927), p. 291; and Hugh Clegg, Alan Fox, and A. F. Thompson, *A History of British Trade Unions Since 1889: Vol. 1, 1889–1910* (Oxford: Clarendon Press, 1964), p. 375.

40. Hinton, *Labour and Socialism*, p. 73.

41. Ibid., pp. 74–75.

42. The pattern of the LRC's success in 1906 is discussed in Cole, *Politics*, p. 182 passim; and Pelling, *Popular Politics and Society*, p. 110. Pelling estimated that without the electoral pact Labour might have won no more than a dozen seats.

43. The results of the first 1910 election are from Cole, *Politics*, pp. 201–02.

44. The results of the second 1910 election are from Cole, *Politics*, p. 203.

45. Ibid., pp. 21–28.

46. Hinton, *Labour and Socialism*, p. 75.

47. Theodore Zeldin, *France, 1848–1945: Politics and Anger* (Oxford: Oxford University Press, 1979), p. 401.

48. Denis William Brogan, *The Development of Modern France, 1870–1939* (London: Hamilton, 1949), p. 427.

49. Zeldin, *Politics and Anger*, p. 301.

50. Ibid., p. 302.

51. Ibid., p. 302.

52. A most useful overview of social reform legislation before 1914 has been written by Judith F. Stone. See her *The Search for Social Peace: Reform Legislation in France, 1890–1914* (Albany: State University of New York, 1985).

53. See, among others, Roger Magraw, *France, 1815–1914: The Bourgeois Century* (New York: Oxford University Press, 1986), pp. 285–313.

54. See ibid., and Cole, *Politics*, pp. 200–10.

55. Hinton, *Labour and Socialism*, pp. 77–81.

56. Zeldin, *Politics and Anger*, p. 323.

57. See the discussion of failed Lib–Labism in Norway and Germany in Chapter 3, and the comparison of inter-class coalitions in France and Germany in this chapter, pp. 36–37. See also the discussion of interclass coalitions in Switzerland in this chapter, pp. 50–52. Switzerland used electoral rules comparable to those found in Norway, Germany, and France. In Switzerland, as in France, interclass coalitions involving socialists and liberals were common.

58. Robert D. Anderson, *France, 1870–1914: Politics and Society* (London: Routledge and Kegan Paul, 1977), p. 134.

59. Anderson, *France*, p. 95.

60. Stone, *Social Peace*, ch. 2; Léo Loubère, "The French Left-Wing Radicals: Their Views on Trade Unionism, 1870–1898," *International Review of Social History*, vol. 7, pt. 2 (1962), pp. 203–30; Léo Loubère, "Left-Wing Radicals, Strikes, and the Military, 1880–1907," *French Historical Studies*, vol. 3, no. 1 (Spring 1963), pp. 93–105; Léo Loubère, "Les Radicaux d'extrême-gauche en France et les rapports entree patrons et ouvriers (1871–1900)," *Revue d'histoire économique et sociale*, vol. 42, no. 1 (1964), pp. 89–103.

61. Léon Bourgeois, *Solidarité*, 7th ed. (Paris: Armand Colin, 1912), p. 136.

62. J. E. S. Hayward, "The Official Social Philosophy of the French Third Republic: Léon Bourgeois and Solidarism," *International Review of Social History*, vol. 6, pt. 1 (1961) pp. 19–48; "Solidarity: The Social History of an Idea in Nineteenth Century France," *International Review of Social History*, vol. 4, pt. 2 (1959), pp. 261–84.

63. Terry Nichols Clark, *Prophets and Patrons: The French University and the Emergence of the Social Sciences* (Cambridge: Harvard University Press, 1973).

64. Stone, *Social Peace*, ch. 2.

65. Ibid., p. 37.

66. For an overview of interventionism, see ibid., pp. 36–54.

67. This theme is developed in Madeleine Rébérioux, "Party Practice and the Jaurésian Vision: the SFIO (1905–1914)," in *Socialism in France: From Jaurés to Mitterand*, Stuart Williams, ed. (London: Frances Pinter, 1983), pp. 15–26.

68. Rébérioux, "Party Practice," p. 23.

69. Ibid.

70. Madeleine Rébérioux, *La Republique Radicale? 1898–1914* (Paris: Editions du Seuil, 1975).

71. Léo A. Loubère, *Radicalism in Mediterranean France: Its Rise and Decline, 1848–1914* (Albany: State University of New York Press, 1974).

72. Lenard R. Berlanstein, *The Working People of Paris, 1871–1914* (Baltimore: Johns Hopkins University Press, 1984).

73. Berlanstein, *Working People,* p. 162.

74. Ibid., pp. 164–65. This rate of success, it might be noted, cannot be explained as a result of antiparty sentiments of syndicalists. In general, the strength of the socialist vote correlated well with the strength of syndicalism in these districts.

75. Stanley Suval, *Electoral Politics in Wilhelmine Germany* (Chapel Hill: University of North Carolina Press, 1985), p. 83.

76. Suval, *Electoral Politics,* p. 89.

77. The share of SPD seats won on the second ballot was 43 (1898), 31 (1903), 33 (1907), and 36 percent (1912). Of the 290 seats the SPD gained in the four elections, 103 were on the second ballot. The source for the performance of the SPD on first and second ballots in every electoral district in which it competed for all elections is Kaiserlichen Statistischen Amt. *Vierteljahrshefte zur Statistik des Deutchen Reichs* (Berlin: Verlag von Buttfammer & Mühlbrecht, 1892–1944), various issues. The share of seats that the French Socialists won on the second ballot was: 63 (1898), 47 (1902), 40 (1906), 61 (1910), 59 percent (1914). The source for 1898 is A. S. Grenier, *Nos Députés: Biographies et Portraits* (Paris: Berger-Levrault, 1899). For other years, *Le Temps* (Paris), postelection issues.

78. On the early history of the union movement and French Socialism, see Georges LeFranc, *Le mouvement syndical sous la Troisième République* (Paris: Payot, 1967); Georges LeFranc, *Le mouvement socialiste sous la Troisième République, 1875–1940* (Paris: Payot, 1963).

79. Based on a labor force of 18.2 million (1911) and a trade union membership of 4 million (1914). See Hunt, *British Labour,* p. 29, for labor force data and pp. 295–96 for trade union membership.

80. Based on a labor force of 20 million (1906) and a 1914 trade union membership of one million. See Zeldin, *Politics and Anger,* p. 210, for labor force; Edward Shorter and Charles Tilly, *Strikes in France, 1830–1968* (London: Cambridge University Press, 1974), p. 372, for union membership.

81. For the Marxist variant of the alienation thesis, see Bernard H. Moss, *The Origins of the French Labor Movement, 1830–1914: The Socialism of Skilled Workers* (Berkeley: University of California Press, 1976). For the liberal variant, see Magraw, *France, 1815–1914,* pp. 285–318.

82. Shorter and Tilly, *Strikes,* p. 20.

83. Of the 4 million British trade unionists in 1913, between 20,000 and 40,000 of them were agricultural workers. See Hunt, *British Labour,* p. 301. In France, there were about 9,300 such workers in the one million strong CGT in 1913. See Theodore Zeldin, *France, 1848–1945: Ambition and Love* (Oxford: Oxford University Press, 1979), p. 252.

84. For Britain, see Hunt, *British Labour,* p. 29; for France, see Georges Dupeux, *La Société française, 1789–1960* (Paris: Librairie A. Colin, 1964), p. 20.

85. Of the 20 million members of the French labor force, 11.6 million people classified themselves as wage earners in the 1906 census. Of this 11.6 million, 2 million were artisans working on their own and another 2 million were classified as *petits patrons,* artisans, and very small merchants who employed no one. See Zeldin, *Ambition and Love,* p. 210.

86. The data on male industrial labor force in France are derived from the figures provided in Zeldin, *Ambition and Love,* p. 210. Of the 11.6 million wage earners in the 1906 census, 4 million were self-employed; another 4 million were females. For Britain, the size of the male industrial proletariat is derived from table 1.9 in Hunt, *British Labour,* p. 29, deducting all figures for females in all categories and for males in categories 1, 9, 10, 12, 14, and 15.

87. The population of male and female trade unionists in Britain is from Hunt, *British Labour,* p. 300. Roger Magraw reports that 10 percent of the membership of the CGT was female in 1913, but does not provide the source for this figure. Magraw, *Bourgeois Century,* p. 291.

88. Shorter and Tilly, *Strikes,* p. 232; Magraw, *Bourgeois Century,* pp. 298 and 233.

89. Peter N. Stearns, *Lives of Labor: Work in Maturing Industrial Society* (New York: Holmes and Meier, 1975), p. 153.

90. Holding skill level constant, the relationship between size and organization would probably reverse itself, since skilled workers were a smaller proportion of the labor force in large firms. In all industrial societies, skilled workers were more likely to organize than unskilled. It was probably the skilled workers in the big factories who were responsible for the high unionization levels of such places in the prewar period. See Shorter and Tilly, *Strikes,* pp. 227–35.

91. Michelle Perrot has suggested that a particular style of authority more characteristic of large plants accounts in part for the greater propensity to organize. See Michelle Perrot, *Les ouvriers en grève, France 1871–1890* (Paris: Mouton, 1974), pp. 971–72 and 984.

92. Peter Flora, Franz Kraus and Winfried Pfenning, *State, Economy and Society in Western Europe, 1815–1975. A Data Handbook: Volume II, The Growth of Industrial Societies and Capitalist Economies* (Chicago: St. James Press, 1987), pp. 260 and 279.

93. Adna Weber, *The Growth of Cities in the Nineteenth Century: A study in Statistics* (New York: Macmillan, 1899), pp. 144–45.

94. Zeldin, *Ambition and Love,* p. 265.

95. Tony Judt, *Marxism and the French Left: Studies on Labor and Politics in France, 1830–1981* (London: Oxford University Press, 1986), pp. 40–41.

96. Eugen Weber, *Peasants into Frenchmen: The Modernization of Rural France, 1870–1914* (Stanford: Stanford University Press, 1976), pp. 213–14.

97. Ibid., p. 282.

98. Ibid.

99. Ibid.

100. Dr. Valatx, *Monographie sur le mouvement de la population dans le departement du Tarn de 1801 a 1911* (Albi, 1917), quoted in Rolande Trempé, *Les Mineurs de Carmaux, 1848–1914,* vol. 1 (Paris: Editions Ouvrières, 1971), pp. 184–85.

101. In a remarkable study, the French sociologist Alain Touraine demonstrated that these differences in attitude continued to appear in workers from agricultural backgrounds even in the 1950s. See Alain Touraine and Orietta Raggazzi, *Ouvriers d'origine agricole* (Paris: Seuil, 1961).

102. The classic study of the impact of peasant values on the French working class is Trempé, *Les Mineurs.*

103. See, among others, Moss, *Origins of the French Labor Movement.*

104. In 1906, there were about 800,000 trade unionists in France; 200,000 of these belonged to the CGT. By 1912, there were about 1 million trade unionists and about 700,000 belonged to the CGT. See Robert Brécy, *Le Mouvement syndical en France 1871–1921, Essai bibliographie* (Paris: Mouton, 1963), p. 9; LeFranc, *Le Mouvement syndical,* pp. 105–06.

105. Felicien Challaye, *Syndicalisme revolutionnaire et syndicalisme reformiste* (Paris: F. Alcan, 1909).

106. For a useful summary of syndicalist ideology, see Frederick F. Ridley, *Revolutionary Syndicalism in France: The Direct Action of Its Time* (Cambridge: Cambridge University Press, 1970).

107. Gabriel Terrail, *Le Syndicalisme contre le socialisme, origine et developpement de la Confederation general du travail* (Paris: Ollendorf, 1907), p. 200.

108. Challaye, *Syndicalisme,* p. 132.

109. Zeldin, *Ambition and Love,* p. 238.

110. Ibid., pp. 256–57.

111. See, among others, Val Lorwin, *The French Labor Movement* (Cambridge: Harvard University Press, 1954).

112. Howell, *British Workers.*

113. Zeldin, *Ambition and Love,* p. 239.

114. Peter Stearns, *Revolutionary Syndicalism and French Labor: A Cause Without Rebels* (New Brunswick, N.J.: Rutgers University Press, 1971), tables 14a and b, p. 131.

115. Stearns, *Revolutionary Syndicalism.*

116. For Tilly and Shorter's discussion of strike waves and their relationship to political conditions, see *Strikes in France,* pp. 104–47. They observe the relationship over the entire span of their study (1848–1968) as well as in select prewar years (1890, 1893, 1899, 1900, 1904, 1906). Focusing on a briefer period and marked upsurges in strike activity within it, I highlight more years, but the point is the same.

117. Shorter and Tilly, *Strikes,* p. 39.

118. Ibid., p. 32.

119. Ibid., p. 33 and passim.

120. Ibid., p. 33.

121. This is based on the male labor force in mining, manufacturing, construction, utilities, and transport enrolled in trade unions. To make it comparable to the French data, it excludes self-employed workers in these sectors and workers in agriculture, commerce, banking, services, and public administration. Data on the Swiss labor force are found in Flora et al., eds., *State, Economy and Society,* vol. 2, p. 600. The 1908 membership of the SGB was 69,250. See Eduard Weckerle, *The Trade Unions in Switzerland,* trans. Pippa Harris (Bern: Swiss Federation of Trade Unions, 1947), p. 65.

122. Schweizerische Statistik, *Die Ergebnisse der eidgenossischen Volkszaehlung vom 1. Dez. 1910,* vol. 3, pt. 1 (Bern: Francke, 1918), p. 518.

123. For the French calculations, see ibid., pp. 59–60.

124. Flora et al., *State, Economy,* vol. 2., p. 276.

125. Weckerle, *Trade Unions,* pp. 6–8; James Murray Luck, *A History of Switzerland* (Palo Alto, Calif.: SPOSS, 1985), pp. 425–38.

126. Marc Vuilleumier, "Mouvement ouvrier et immigration au temps de la

Deuxième Internationale: les travailleurs Italiens en Suisse," *Revue européenne des sciences sociales,* vol. 15, no. 42 (December 1977), pp. 115–27.

127. Weckerle, *Trade Unions,* pp. 64–65.

128. In 1901, the number of factory workers in textiles was 91,000; only 1,700 of them were organized by 1903. Weckerle, *Trade Unions,* pp. 42 and 65.

129. Erich Gruner, *Die Arbeiter in der Schweiz im 19. Jahrhundert* (Bern: Francke Verlag, 1968), pp. 512–13.

130. Hans Rutishauser, "Liberalismus und Sozialpolitk in der Schweiz" (Unpublished Ph.D. Dissertation: Universität Zürich, 1935), pp. 166–69.

131. Marcel Stehli, "Albert Galeer und sein Einfluss auf die Ideengeschichte des schweizerischen Grütlivereins" (Unpublished Ph.D. Dissertation: Universität Zürich, 1948).

132. Gruner, *Arbeiter.*

133. On the importance of referenda in inducing such national organization as there was among Swiss workers, see Weckerle, *Trade Unions,* p. 31.

134. On the decentralization of the SGB, see chs. 5 and 6.

135. On the composition of the Federal Council, see Hans von Greyerz, "Der Bundesstaat seit 1848," in Emil Vogt et al., *Handbuch der Schweizer Geschichte* Band 2 (Zürich: Verlag Berichthaus, 1977), pp. 1023ff and pp. 1091–94.

136. On the Swiss Kulturkampf of 1870–74, see Greyerz, *Der Bundesstaat,* pp. 1066–71.

137. About 38 percent of the Swiss population was Catholic. On the heterogeneity of the Radical community, see Erich Gruner, *Die Parteien in der Schweiz* (Bern: Francke Verlag, 1969), pp. 81–86.

138. On the alliances of the Radicals, see Rutishauser, "Liberalismus," pp. 143–46; Gruner, *Arbeiter,* pp. 689ff.; Greyerz, *Der Bundesstaat,* pp. 1107; Gruner, *Parteien,* pp. 89–91.

139. Gruner, *Arbeiter,* pp. 230–37.

140. Ibid., pp. 252–57.

141. Greyerz, *Der Bundesstaat,* pp. 1071–91.

142. François Masnata, *Le parti socialiste et la tradition démocratique en Suisse* (Paris: A. Colin, 1963).

143. Gruner, *Parteien,* p. 130.

144. Gruner, *Arbeiter,* pp. 692–95.

145. On the Grütliverein, see Gruner, *Parteien,* pp. 129ff; and Greyerz, *Der Bundesstaat,* pp. 1104–06. On the Social Democratic party, see Gruner, *Parteien,* pp. 126–35.

146. Flora, *State, Economy, Society,* vol. 1, p. 147.

147. Erich Gruner, *Die Wahlen in der Schweizerischen Nationalrat, 1848–1919: Vol. 3, Tabellen, Grafiken, Karten* (Bern: Francke, 1978), p. 398.

148. Gruner, *Wahlen,* vol. 3, p. 369, and vol. 1, pt. 2, p. 290.

149. These calculations are based on the data provided by Rutishauser, "Liberalismus and Sozialpolitik in der Schweiz," p. 189 passim; and Gruner, *Wahlen,* vol. 1, pt. 2, pp. 760–68. The socialists sponsored 15 candidates without additional endorsements in runoff elections; 2 of these were successful. They sponsored another 15 with additional endorsements; 11 of these were victorious. Overall, they sponsored 161 candidates without additional endorsements; only 11 of these were elected. They sponsored 47 candidates with additional endorsements; 23 of these were elected.

150. Rutishauer, "Liberalismus," p. 189; Gruner, *Wahlen* vol. 1, pt. 2, pp. 760–68.

Chapter 3

1. Frans van Kalken, *La Belgique contemporaine, 1780–1949,* 2nd ed. (Paris: Colin, 1950).

2. Hans Daalder, "The Netherlands: Opposition in a Segmented Society," in Robert Dahl, ed., *Political Oppositions in Western Democracies* (New Haven: Yale University Press, 1966), p. 202 passim.

3. Douglas Verney, *Parliamentary Reform in Sweden, 1866–1921* (Oxford: Clarendon Press, 1957), p. 89.

4. One influential interpretation is provided by Ralf Dahrendorf in his *Society and Democracy in Germany* (New York: Norton, 1967).

5. Alexander Gerschekron, *Economic Backwardness in Historical Perspective* (Cambridge: Belknap Press, 1962).

6. Division of labor, c. 1900 and as noted.

Country	A	I	S
Western European Societies with Liberal Hegemony			
Britain	8	46	41
France	43	30	28
Switzerland	31	44	25
Western European Societies without Liberal Hegemony			
Belgium	23	37	27
Denmark	45	26	27
Germany	38	37	25 (1895)
Netherlands	31	32	36
Norway	41	27	30
Sweden	50	20	23
Italy	60	24	17
The European Periphery			
Austria	64	20	14
Finland	72	11	9 (1910)
Spain	71	17	12 (1910)
Hungary	68	14	18

Source: Peter Flora, Franz Kraus, and Winfried Pfenning, eds., *State, Economy, and Society in Western Europe 1815–1975: A Data Handbook. Volume II: The Growth of Industrial Societies and Capitalist Economies* (Chicago: St. James Press, 1987), ch. 7. For Spain, Carlo Cipolla, ed., *The Fontana Economic History of Europe* vol. 6, pt. 2 (London: Fontana, 1972), p. 616. For Hungary, Robert A. Kann, *A History of the Habsburg Empire, 1526–1918* (Berkeley: University of California Press, 1974), p. 463.

7. For detailed data, see P. Bairoch, "Niveaux de développement économique de 1810 à 1910." *Annales: Économies, Sociétés, Civilisations,* vol. 20, no. 6 (November–December 1965), pp. 1091–117.

8. Flora, ed., *State and Society*, v. 2., pp. 563–64.

9. See Chapter 2, p. 39 and note 85.

10. Data on Denmark are from Harry Haue et. al., *Det ny Danmark, 1890–1978: Udviklingslinier og tendens* (Copenhagen: Munksgaard, 1979), Table 18, p. 128. Data for France are from Chapter 2, above, p. 39 and note 88.

11. Svend Aage Hansen, *Økonomisk Vaekst i Danmark* (Copenhagen: Akademisk Forlag, 1974), vol. 1, p. 64.

12. Flora et al., eds., *State and Society*, vol. 2, p. 463.

13. Theodore Hamerow, *The Birth of a New Europe: State and Society in the Nineteenth Century* (Chapel Hill: University of North Carolina Press, 1983), p. 39.

14. Hamerow, *New Europe*, pp. 39–40.

15. Svend Aage Hansen and Ingrid Henriksen, *Sociale brydninger, 1914–1939: Dansk social historie, bind 6* (Copenhagen: Gyldendal, 1980), p. 104.

16. Data from Flora, vol. 2, pp. 494 and 512.

17. Hans-Ulrich Wehler, *The German Empire, 1871–1918*, trans. Kim Tranor (Leamington Spa: Berg, 1985), p. 40.

18. Hajo Holborn, *A History of Modern Germany, 1840–1945* (Princeton: Princeton University Press, 1969), p. 373.

19. Hamerow, *New Europe*, p. 41.

20. An excellent comparative discussion of industrialization and social structures in Denmark, Norway, and Sweden, emphasizing the petit bourgeois character of Denmark and Norway and the more concentrated and stratified character of Sweden is provided by Gøsta Esping-Andersen. Esping-Andersen reports (fn. 9, p. 51) that "In 1942, the fifty largest Swedish companies accounted for 16 percent of all employment (compared with only 5 percent in the United States)." See his *Politics Against Markets: The Social Democratic Road to Power* (Princeton: Princeton University Press, 1985), ch. 2.

21. For a nation-by-nation summary of electoral laws, see Peter Flora et al., eds., *State, Economy, and Society in Western Europe, 1815–1975, A Data Handbook. Volume I: The Growth of Mass Democracies and Welfare States* (Chicago: St. James Press, 1983), ch. 3.

22. The comparison with the Prussian Landtag is made by Berndt Schiller, "Years of Crisis, 1906–1914," in Steven Koblik, ed., *Sweden's Development from Poverty to Affluence, 1750–1970* (Minneapolis: University of Minnesota Press, 1975), p. 199.

23. Percentage of male population, 20+ years, enfranchised at election after year.

Country	1870	1880	1890	1900	1910
Belgium	3.7	3.9	3.9	37.7	38.2
Denmark	26.0	27.1	29.4	29.0	30.1
France	43.7	41.6	41.8	43.2	43.4
Germany	33.0	36.2	37.4	38.3	38.7
Netherlands	5.0	5.4	11.5	21.2	25.7
Norway	8.5	9.4	12.6	34.8	58.5
Sweden	9.8	10.7	10.4	12.7	32.5
Switzerland	———	38.7	38.3	37.9	37.0
United Kingdom	14.9	16.4	29.3	28.5	28.8
Italy	3.5	3.8	15.2	12.3	42.0

Source: Flora, ed., *State, Economy and Society*, vol. 1, ch. 3.

24. The term *preindustrial cleavages* and the sociological analysis that led me to think about the fate of liberalism in these terms are found in a classic essay by Seymour Martin Lipset and Stein Rokkan, "Cleavage Structures, Party Systems and Voter Alignments: An Introduction," in Lipset and Rokkan, eds., *Party Systems and Voter Alignments: Cross-National Perspectives* (New York: Free Press, 1967), pp. 1–64.

25. The history of the Liberal Revolution, as it came to be called, is discussed in E. H. Kossman, *The Low Countries, 1780–1940* (New York: Oxford University Press, 1978), pp. 138–60.

26. See Joseph Barthelémy, *L'Organisation du suffrage et l'expérience belge* (Paris: M. Giard and E. Briere, 1912).

27. See Kossman, *Low Countries*, pp. 206–310; Aristide R. Zolberg, "Belgium," in Raymond Grew, ed., *Crises of Political Development in Europe and the United States* (Princeton: Princeton University Press, 1978), pp. 99–138.

28. For example, in the twenty-four circonscriptions in the early 1890s that constituted the province of Liége (which mirrored the country as a whole), eight had a predominantly rural character, nine were predominantly industrial (mainly textiles), and seven were of a mixed character. The eight rural circonscriptions elected eight Catholics, the nine industrial districts elected eight Liberals and one Catholic, and the seven mixed districts elected five Liberals and two Catholics. For a discussion of Liége and the nation as a whole, see Robert Démoulin, "Recherches de Sociologie électorale en régime censitaire," *Révue Française de Science Politique,* vol. 3, no. 4 (October–December 1953), pp. 699–713.

29. See Zolberg, "Belgium," pp. 120–24.

30. Ibid., p. 122. Kossman, *Low Countries*. pp. 310–50.

31. On the Netherlands, see: I. Lipschits, *Ontstaansgeschiedenis van de Nederlandse politieke partijen: Deel I, De protestants-christelijke stroming tot 1940* (Deventer: Kluwer, 1977); Hans Daalder, "Consociationalism, Center and Periphery in the Netherlands," in Per Torsvik, ed., *Mobilization, Center-Periphery Structures and Nation-Building* (Bergen: Universitetsforlaget, 1981).

32. Stein Rokkan, "Norway: Numerical Democracy and Corporate Pluralism," in Robert Dahl, ed., *Political Oppositions in Western Democracy* (New Haven: Yale University Press, 1966), p. 77.

33. Rokkan, "Norway," p. 77.

34. Jens Arup Seip, *Et regime foran undergangen* (Oslo: Tanum, 1945); Alf Kaartvedt, *Kampen mot parlamentarisme, 1880–1884* (Oslo: Universitetsforlaget, 1967).

35. By far the best account of the Venstre's travails is Leiv Mjeldheim, *Folkerørsla som vart parti: Venstre frå 1880 åra til 1905* (Bergen: Universitetsforlaget, 1984). See especially chapters 5 and 6 for the disintegration of the party and Sverdrup's dependence on Conservative votes.

36. Mjeldheim, *Venstre,* pp. 181–204.

37. For a sociogeographical study of linguistic, religious, and cultural politics, see Stein Rokkan, "Geography, Religion and Social Class: Crosscutting Cleavages in Norwegian Politics," in Lipset and Rokkan, eds., *Party Systems*, pp. 367–444.

38. The estimate of 70 percent is from Mjeldheim, *Venstre,* pp. 306–09.

39. In the same elections in the Oslofjord area, the Right received the following percentages of the vote: 62.3, 65.1, 56.8, 56.9 percent. In Trondheim, it received 58.0, 55.7, 48.0, and 51.2 percent. The Liberals did not receive the balance of the

vote: in 1903, the Socialists received 27.7 percent of the Trondheim vote. The pattern of dominance was reversed in Bergen. In these four elections, the Liberals won 68.6, 53.3, 58.8, and 36.8 percent of the vote. In 1903, the Socialists took 22.2 percent of the Bergen vote. For these and other regional data, see Rokkan, "Crosscutting Cleavages in Norwegian Politics," table 10, p. 397 and passim.

40. Rokkan, "Norway," fig. 3.1, p. 85.

41. A general comparative introduction is provided in Esping-Andersen, *Politics Against Markets,* ch. 2.

42. See Franklin D. Scott, *Sweden: The Nation's History* (Minneapolis: University of Minnesota Press, 1977), esp. chs. 8–15.

43. Åke Thulstrup, *Svensk politik, 1905–1939: Från unionsupplösningen till andra världskriget* (Stockholm: Bonnier, 1968), p. 22.

44. The rural share of the Liberal vote is from Schiller, "Years of Crisis, 1906–1914," p. 218.

45. Sten Carlsson and Jerker Rosén, *Svensk historia. 2: Tiden efter 1718,* 4th ed. (Stockholm: Esselte Studium, 1980), p. 454.

46. Knut Bäckström, *Arbetarrörelsen i Sverige: Vol. 2, Den politiska arbetarrörelsens sprängning och ett nytt revolutionärt arbetarpartis uppkomst* (Stockholm: Rabén and Sjögren, 1971), p. 22.

47. Standard accounts of the franchise reform movement can be found in Stig Hadenius et al., *Sverige efter 1900: En modern politisk historia* (Stockholm: Aldus, 1978); Thulstrup, *Svensk politik;* Sven Lundkvist, "Popular Movements and Reforms, 1900–1920," in Koblik, *Sweden's Development,* pp. 180–93; Schiller, "Years of Crisis"; Douglas Verney, "The Foundations of Modern Sweden: The Swift Rise and Fall of Swedish Liberalism," *Political Studies,* vol. 20, no. 1 (March 1972), pp. 42–59; Carlsson, "Rösträttsstreckens tidevarv, 1866–1920," in his *Svensk historia,* pp. 410–97.

48. See, for example, Verney, "The Foundations of Modern Sweden."

49. Carlsson, *Svensk historia,* pp. 460–63.

50. Ibid., pp. 462–63.

51. Ibid., p. 454.

52. Thulstrup, *Svensk politik,* pp. 37–42; Carlsson, *Svensk historia,* p. 461 passim.

53. Between 1911 and 1914, Liberals' share of the Second Chamber electorate declined from 40 to 27 percent. Carlsson, *Svensk historia,* p. 464.

54. Thulstrup, *Svensk politik,* pp. 59–74; Schiller, "Years of Crisis," especially pp. 224–26.

55. See note 6 above.

56. Among the most insightful discussions of political mobilization around this time are to be found in two brief essays by Erik Stig Jørgensen, "Partier og partimodsaetninger 1848–1864," and "Den reviderede grundlovs tilblivelse 1864–1866," in Per Salomonsson, ed., *Den politiske magtkamp, 1866–1901* (Copenhagen: Jørgen Paludans Forlag, 1968), pp. 9–20 and 21–34. The standard accounts of the nineteenth century include Kjeld Mogens Winding, *Danmarks politiske historie* (Copenhagen: Fremad, 1948); Povl Engelstoft and Frantz W. Wendt, *Haandbog i Danmarks politiske historie fra Freden i Kiel til vore dage* (Copenhagen: Gyldendal, 1934); Einar Cohn, *Økonomi og politik i Danmark, 1849–1875* (Copenhagen: Gad, 1967).

57. Jørgensen, "Partier," p. 10.

58. Ibid., pp. 10–13.

59. Ibid., p. 12 passim.

60. Ibid., pp. 12–14.

61. The story of these divisions is well told in Kristian Hvidt, *Venstre og forsvarssagen, 1870–1901* (Århus: Universitets Forlaget, 1960); and especially Troels Fink, *Estruptidens politiske historie, 1875–1894: I. Kampen mellem de to ting. 1875–1885; II. Provisorietiden, 1885–1894* (Odense: Odense Universitetsforlag, 1986).

62. Sometimes referred to as the Grundtvigiearne to indicate the populist–nationalist influence of the philosopher–educator N. F. S. Grundtvig. Per Salomonsson, "Venstregrupperne," in Salomonsson, ed., *Den politiske magtkamp 1866–1901,* p. 41.

63. Fink, *Estruptidens,* vol. 2, pp. 43–61.

64. See especially, Torben Krogh, *Viggo Horup: En illustreret levnedsskildring* (Copenhagen: Gyldendal, 1984), pp. 391–401.

65. See Haue et al., *Det ny Danmark,* p. 49. A comprehensive study of urban voting behavior that points to the hegemony of the Right and the large working-class component of its vote before the success of the Social Democrats is provided by Vagn Dybdahl. See his *Partier og erhverv: studier i partiorganisation og byerhvervenes politiske aktivitet ca.1880–ca.1913,* 2 vols. (Århus: Universitetsforlaget, 1969).

66. Niels Petersen, "Forlig og omgruppering," in Per Salomonsson, ed., *Den politiske magtkamp,* pp. 91–116.

67. Krogh, *Horup.*

68. Erik Rasmussen and Roar Skovmand, *Det Radikale Venstre, 1905–1955* (Copenhagen: Det Danske Forlag, 1955).

69. Concerning the German revolution of 1848 and the agrarian problem, see especially Theodore S. Hamerow, *Restoration, Revolution, Reaction: Economics and Politics in Germany, 1815–1857* (Princeton: Princeton University Press, 1970), pp. 156–72.

70. Hamerow, *Restoration,* p. 180.

71. Ibid., pp. 187–91.

72. On the emergence of the *Fraktionen* in the Frankfurt Parliament and their composition, see Frank Eyck, *The Frankfurt Parliament, 1848–1849* (New York: St. Martin's Press, 1968), pp. 102–57.

73. Ibid., pp. 80–82, 165–66.

74. Ibid., p. 199.

75. Ibid., pp. 322–28.

76. Ibid., pp. 366–69.

77. Ibid., pp. 365–66.

78. Ibid., pp. 363–74.

79. On the petitions to the Frankfurt Assembly and to the state governments, see Hamerow, *Restoration,* pp. 156–60, 180, 187ff.

80. Leonard Krieger, *The German Idea of Freedom: History of a Political Tradition from the Reformation to 1871* (Boston: Beacon Press, 1957), pp. 314ff.

81. Hajo Holborn, *A History of Modern Germany, 1840–1945* (Princeton: Princeton University Press, 1969), p. 20; Theodore S. Hamerow, *The Social Founda-*

tions of German Unification, 1858–1871: Struggles and Accomplishments (Princeton: Princeton University Press, 1972), p. 131.

82. Holborn, *Modern Germany,* p. 132; James J. Sheehan, *German Liberalism in the Nineteenth Century* (Chicago: University of Chicago Press, 1978), p. 81.

83. Hamerow, *Social Foundations,* p. 157.

84. Holborn, *Modern Germany,* pp. 145–46.

85. Holborn, *Modern Germany,* pp. 166–67.

86. "The time of ideals is past. Today politicians must ask not so much as formerly what is desirable but rather what is possible." With those famous words Johannes von Miquel, a prominent leader of the National Liberal party, succinctly frames the new reality for German liberals. Gordon Craig, *Germany, 1866–1945* (New York: Oxford University Press, 1978), p. 255, fn. 8.

87. Craig, *Germany,* pp. 8 and 44.

88. Holborn, *Modern Germany,* p. 192.

89. Sheehan, *German Liberalism,* p. 132.

90. Hamerow, *Social Foundations,* p. 259.

91. In 1871, the Socialist share of the vote was 3.1 percent. In 1881, it had risen to a still modest 6.1 percent. By 1890, it was 19 percent. *Source:* Gerhard A. Ritter, *Wahlgeschichtliches Arbeitsbuch: Materialien zur Statistik des Kaiserreichs* (München: C. H. Beck, 1980), pp. 38–40.

92.

	1871	1874	1877	1878	1881
National Liberals	9	13	11	8	5
Center	2	1	2	1	1
Guelphs	6	4	4	10	10

Source: Ritter, *Wahlgeschichtliches,* p. 76.

93. Craig, *Germany,* p. 19.

94. Ritter, *Wahlgeschichtliches,* p. 89.

95. Ibid., p. 72.

96. Ibid., p. 86.

97. The total share of the seats and votes gained by the Guelphs, Danes, Alsatians *alone* was as follows:

	Seats	Votes
1871	20	6.6%
1874	34	10.4
1877	34	9.7
1878	40	8.7
1881	45	8.8

Source: Ritter, *Wahlgeschichtliches,* pp. 38–39.

98. Ellen Lovell Evans, *The German Center Party, 1870–1933: A Study in Political Catholicism* (Carbondale: Southern Illinois University Press, 1981), p. 12.

99. Evans, *Center Party,* pp. 36–38.

100. Ibid., pp. 36–38.

101. Ritter, *Wahlgeschichtliches*, p. 88.

102. Ibid., p. 81.

103. Ibid., p. 38.

104. Ibid., pp. 99–100.

105. Ibid., p. 81.

106. Ibid., p. 88.

107. Ibid., pp. 99–100.

108. Ibid., p. 121.

109. Ibid., pp. 38–39.

110. P. Ginsborg, "Gramsci and the Era of Bourgeois Revolution in Italy," in John A. Davis, ed., *Gramsci and Italy's Passive Revolution* (London: Groom Helm, 1979), pp. 31–66.

111. Christopher Seton-Watson, *Italy from Liberalism to Fascism, 1870–1925* (London: Methuen, 1967), p. 11.

112. See Franklin Hugh Adler, "Italian Industrialists from Liberalism to Fascism" (Unpublished Ph.D. dissertation: University of Chicago, 1980), pp. 7–10 passim.

113. Quoted from Adler, "Italian Industrialists," p. 13.

114. Seton-Watson, *Italy*, p. 52. Raymond Grew, "Il trasformismo: ultimo stadio del Risorgimento," in Vittorio Frosini, ed., *Il Risorgimento e l'Europa* (Catania: Bonanno, 1969), pp. 151–63.

115. Procacci, quoted in Adler, "Italian Industrialists," p. 15.

116. Raymond Grew, "Italy," in Grew, ed., *Crises of Political Development*, p. 285, fn. 10.

117. Grew, "Italy," p. 298.

118. Adler, "Italian Industrialists," pp. 22–23.

119. On the management of the elections and the role of prefects, see Robert C. Fried, "The Italian Prefects: A Study in Administrative Politics (New Haven: Yale University Press, 1963), pp. 247–49, 255–59.

120. Adler, "Italian Industrialists," p. 36.

121. Ginsborg, "Gramsci."

122. The literature on modernization, and the literature that has been influenced by modernization theory in accounting for the success of liberalism or transitions to democracy (not always distinguished) is, of course, enormous. Among the more influential works are T. H. Marshall, *Citizenship and Social Class and Other Essays* (Cambridge: Cambridge University Press, 1950); Reinhard Bendix, *Nation Building and Citizenship* (Berkeley: University of California Press, 1977); Lucian Pye and Sidney Verba, eds., *Political Culture and Political Development* (Princeton: Princeton University Press, 1965); Dahrendorf, *Society and Democracy in Germany;* Eugen Weber, *Peasants into Frenchmen: The Modernization of Rural France, 1870–1914* (Stanford: Stanford University Press, 1976).

123. See above, p. 59.

124. The latter is done with some effect, for example, in the literature on post-materialism. See Ronald Inglehart, "The Changing Structure of Political Cleavages in Western Society," in Russell Dalton et al., eds., *Electoral Change in Advanced Industrial Democracies* (Princeton: Princeton University Press, 1984), pp. 25–69.

125. In Poland, Serbia, Estonia, Lithuania, and Latvia over 80 percent of the populations were still employed in agriculture in about 1900. Of the three Baltic

states, data are available only for Estonia, but Estonia was generally thought to be the most industrialized of the three. *Sources:* Norman Davies, *God's Playground: A History of Poland, vol. 2, 1795 to the Present* (New York: Columbia University Press, 1982), p. 192; Michael Boro Petrovich, *A History of Modern Serbia, 1804–1918* (New York: Harcourt Brace, 1976), vol. 2, p. 525; Toivo U. Raun, *Estonia and the Estonians* (Stanford: Hoover Institution Press, 1987), pp. 73 and 89.

126. Andrew C. Janos, "The Rise and Fall of Civil Society: The Politics of Backwardness on the European Peripheries, 1780–1945" (Mimeo: University of California, Berkeley, 1987), p. 10.

127. Janos, "Rise and Fall"; and Andrew C. Janos, *The Politics of Backwardness in Hungary, 1825–1945* (Princeton: Princeton University Press, 1982).

128. By 1900, only 41 percent of the labor force in Bohemia remained in agriculture. For Hungary and Austria (postwar territories) the figures were 68 and 64 percent, respectively. For Finland, the figure is 72 percent in 1910. In the same year, 71 percent of the Spanish labor force remained in agriculture. Source for Austria and Finland: Flora, *State, Economy, and Society,* vol. 2, ch. 7. For Bohemia: David F. Good, *The Economic Rise of the Habsburg Empire 1750–1914* (Berkeley: University of California Press, 1984), p. 47. For Hungary: Robert A. Kann, *A History of the Habsburg Empire, 1526–1918* (Berkeley: University of California Press, 1980), p. 463. For Spain: Carlo Cipolla, ed., *The Fontana Economic History of Europe* vol. 6, pt. 2 (London: Fonatana, 1972), p. 616.

129. Fred Riggs, *Administration in Developing Countries: The Theory of Prismatic Society* (Boston: Houghton Mifflin, 1964), pp. 188–93.

130. Janos, "Rise and Fall," pp. 8–9.

131. The distinctive experience of prewar Eastern liberalism is a subject we will take up at greater length in Chapter 7.

132. Among the most insightful analyses of the Restoration order are Juan Linz, "The Party System of Spain: Past and Future," in Lipset and Rokkan, eds., *Party Systems and Voter Alignments,* pp. 197–282, and Luis Sánchez Agesta, *Historia del constitucionalismo español,* 3rd ed. (Madrid: Instituto de Estudios Políticos, 1964), pp. 314ff.

133. On the cacique electoral system, see Raymond Carr, *Spain 1808–1975,* 2nd ed. (Oxford: Oxford University Press, 1982), pp. 366–79.

134. On the repercussions of the 1898 war, see Carr, *Spain,* pp. 379ff.

135. On Basque nationalism, see Stanley G. Payne, *Basque Nationalism* (Reno: University of Nevada Press, 1975); and Rachel Bard, *Navarra, The Durable Kingdom* (Reno: University of Nevada Press, 1982); Joseph Harrison, "Big Business and the Rise of Basque Nationalism," *European Studies Review,* vol. 7, no. 4 (October 1977), pp. 371–91.

136. Joan Connelly Ullman, *The Tragic Week: A Study of Anticlericalism in Spain, 1875–1912* (Cambridge: Harvard University Press, 1968); Joseph Harrison, "Catalan Business and the Loss of Cuba, 1898–1914," *The Economic History Review, Second Series,* vol. 27, no. 3 (August 1974), pp. 431–41; Joseph Harrison, "Big Business and the Failure of Right-Wing Catalan Nationalism, 1901–1923," *The Historical Journal,* vol. 19, no. 4 (December 1976), pp. 901–18.

137. Carr, *Spain,* pp. 473–564; Gerald Brenan, *The Spanish Labyrinth: An Account of the Social and Political Background of the Civil War* (Cambridge: Cambridge University Press, 1960), pp. 17ff.

138. The quotation of Aguilera is from Ullman, *The Tragic Week,* p. 35. Ullman's work is probably the best single-volume study of anticlericalism in this period.

139. In 1901, agriculture employed 59 percent of the Italian labor force versus 71 percent of the Spanish labor force in 1910. Taking the nations as wholes, the illiteracy levels were not much different: 38 percent in Italy in 1910 versus 43 percent in Spain. The Italian figure masks enormous regional differences, however. In southern Italy illiteracy ranged between 65 and 79 percent, by province. In the north it averaged about 25 percent. Sources for industrialization, Flora, *State, Economy, and Society,* vol. 2, ch. 7. For illiteracy, Ullman, *Tragic Week,* p. 2; and Maurice Neufeld, *Italy: School for Awakening Countries: The Italian Labor Movement in its Political, Social, and Economic Setting from 1800 to 1960* (New York: Cornell University Press, 1961), p. 523. Illiteracy rates are for the populations over six years of age.

140. William Salomone, *Italian Democracy in the Making: The Political Scene in the Giolittian Era, 1900–1914* (Philadelphia: University of Pennsylvania Press, 1945).

141. Ullman, *The Tragic Week;* Brenan, *Spanish Labyrinth;* Carr, *Spain,* pp. 473ff.

142. On per capita income, see Smith, *Italy,* p. 232. On illiteracy, see Neufeld, *Italy,* p. 523.

143. The yield of cereals, in quintals per hectare, in the north in 1913 was 19.4, a level virtually identical to that of northeast France (where the yield was 19.9). In southern Italy, the yield was 10.5. Source: Leagues of Nations, *Agricultural Production in Continental Europe during the 1914–18 War and the Reconstruction Period* (Geneva: League of Nations Publications, 1943), pp. 86–91.

144. Seton-Watson, *Italy from Liberalism to Fascism,* pp. 83–84.

145. Denis Mack Smith, *Italy, A Modern History* (Ann Arbor: University of Michigan Press, 1959), p. 236.

146. Smith, *Italy,* pp. 148ff.

147. Carr, *Spain,* p. 435.

148. Brenan, *Spanish Labyrinth,* p. 29.

149. Ullman, *The Tragic Week,* p. 21.

150. Among the most analytically keen accounts of the military's growing involvement in politics in these years, one that focuses on the weakness of civil society rather than the attributes of the military, is provided by Carolyn P. Boyd, *Praetorian Politics in Liberal Spain* (Chapel Hill: University of North Carolina Press, 1979).

151. Boyd, *Praetorian Politics,* pp. 11ff; Joaquín Romero Maura, *The Spanish Army and Catalonia: The "Cu-Cut! Incident" and the Laws of Jurisdictions, 1905–1906* (Beverly Hills, Calif.: Sage Publications, 1976).

152. Brenan, *Spanish Labyrinth,* p. 31.

153. Boyd, *Praetorian Politics,* p. 10.

154. Hans-Günter Zmarzlik, *Bethmann Hollweg als Reichskanzler, 1909–1914: Studien zu Möglichkeiten und Grenzen seiner innenpolitischer Machtstellung* (Düsseldorf: Droste Verlag, 1957), p. 40.

155. Martin Kitchen, *The German Officer Corps, 1890–1914* (New York: Oxford University Press, 1968), ch. 11.

156. See the discussions above, Chapter 2.

Chapter 4

1. The quotation is from Heinrich Volkmann, *Die Arbeiterfrage im preussischen Abgeordnetenhaus, 1848–1869* (Berlin: Duncker and Humbolt, 1968), p. 75.

2. On the influence of French syndicalism in Spain and Italy, see Gerald Brenan, *The Spanish Labyrinth: An Account of the Social and Political Background of the Civil War* (Cambridge: Cambridge University Press, 1960), p. 170; Enzo Santarelli, "Sorel e sorelismo in Italia," *Rivista storica del socialismo,* vol. 3, no. 2 (1960), pp. 289–328; David D. Roberts, *The Syndicalist Tradition and Italian Fascism* (Chapel Hill: The University of North Carolina Press, 1979), pp. 49ff. On Sweden, see Knut Bäckström, *Arbetarrörelsen i Sverige: Vol. 2, Den politiska arbetarrörelsens sprängning och ett nytt revolutionärt arbetarpartis uppkomst* (Stockholm: Rabén and Sjögren, 1971), pp. 160ff.

3. Jorunn Bjørgum, "Fagopposisjonen av 1911." *Tidsskrift for arbeider-bevegelsens historie* (NR.1/1976), pp. 63–131.

4. A brief English-language biography of Tranmael is provided by Walter Galenson, *Labor in Norway* (Cambridge: Harvard University Press, 1949), pp. 20–22. The standard work is Aksel Zachariassen, *Martin Tranmael* (Oslo: Tiden, 1979).

5. Edvard Bull, *Norsk fagbevegelse: Oversikt over fagorganisasjonens utvikling,* 2nd ed. (Oslo: Tiden Norsk Forlag, 1968), p. 91.

6. Bull, *Norsk fagbevegelse,* p. 92.

7. Ibid., p. 91–92.

8. These points are made in a study by Peter Flora and Jens Alber. Flora and Alber measure modernization by a combined index of the percentage of the labor force in the secondary sector and the percentage of the population in cities. The percentage of the popular vote for working-class parties is intended as a proxy measure of political mobilization. See Peter Flora and Jens Alber, "Modernization, Democratization, and the Development of Welfare States in Western Europe," in Peter Flora and Arnold J. Heidenheimer, eds., *The Development of Welfare States in Europe and America* (New Brunswick, N.J.: Transaction Books, 1981), pp. 37–80.

9. This ratio is realized by recomputing the ratios of social insurance realization Flora and Alber provide in Table 2.6 (p. 71) after first reclassifying the countries. The recomputation involves moving legislation for Belgium, Norway, the Netherlands, and Italy to the left column for all periods and moving legislation for Denmark for the period before 1901. The given ratios in the two center columns are then revised and summed up. See their "Modernization, Democratization."

10. Berge Furre, *Norsk historie, 1905–1940* (Oslo: Det Norske Samlaget, 1971), p. 49.

11. On the Bismarckian welfare state, see Gaston V. Rimlinger, *Welfare Policy and Industrialization in Europe, America and Russia* (New York: John Wiley & Sons, 1971), pp. 112ff.

12. Workers were eligible for the pension only after they reached seventy years of age. On this and the other limitations, see Rimlinger, *Welfare Policy,* pp. 121ff.

13. The theme of social and political acceptance as one motor-force of working-class politics is developed in Barrington Moore, Jr., *Injustice: The Social Bases of Obedience and Revolt* (White Plains, N.Y.: M. E. Sharpe, 1978).

14. Guenther Roth, *The Social Democrats in Imperial Germany* (Totowa, N.J.: The Bedminster Press, 1963), p. 40.

15. Jürgen Kocka, "Problems of Working-Class Formation in Germany," in Ira Katznelson and Aristide Zolberg, eds., *Working-Class Formation: Nineteenth Century Patterns in Western Europe and the United States* (Princeton: Princeton University Press, 1986), pp. 331–38.

16. On Marx's reaction to the ADAV and its leader, Ferdinand Lassalle, see George Lichtheim, *Marxism: An Historical and Critical Study* (New York: Columbia University Press, 1982), pp. 90–99.

17. Roger Morgan, *The German Social Democrats and the First International, 1864–1872* (London: Cambridge University Press, 1965), pp. 4–5.

18. John Snell, *The Democratic Movement in Germany, 1789–1914* (Chapel Hill: University of North Carolina Press, 1976), pp. 188–89; Guenther Roth, *The Social Democrats in Imperial Germany,* pp. 28–48.

19. Kocka, "Problems," p. 344.

20. Ibid., pp. 344–45; Morgan, *German Social Democrats,* pp. 6–10.

21. The cleavages within the liberal community and the liberals' fear of a general suffrage are discussed above, in Chapter 3, pp. 87ff.

22. Morgan, *German Social Democrats,* pp. 20–27, 130.

23. Kocka, "Problems," p. 345.

24. Morgan, *German Social Democrats,* pp. 14–15.

25. Concerning the liberal economic reforms at the North German Confederation and the frustrations of workers, see Theodore Hamerow, *The Social Foundations of German Unification, 1858–1871: Struggles and Accomplishments* (Princeton: Princeton University Press, 1972), pp. 337–62.

26. For an account of the Nürnberg Congress, see Morgan, *German Social Democracy,* pp. 140–50.

27. On the Gotha Congress and its program, see Dieter Fricke, *Die Deutsche Arbeiterbewegung, 1869 bis 1914* (Berlin: Das Europäische Buch, 1976), pp. 80–128.

28. Jürgen Kocka, "Die Trennung von bürglicher und proletarischer Demokratie im europäischen Vergleich: Fragestellungen und Ergebnisse," in Kocka, ed., *Europäische Arbeiterbewegungen im 19. Jahrhundert* (Göttingen: Vandenhoeck and Ruprecht, 1983), pp. 5–6.

29. Vernon L. Lidtke, *The Outlawed Party: Social Democracy in Germany, 1878–1890* (Princeton: Princeton University Press, 1966), p. 320.

30. The law was passed by a vote of 221 to 149, with the entire National Liberal fraction and the two conservative parties supporting it. The Center, the Progressives, Social Democrats, and the national minorities voted against it. See James J. Sheehan, *German Liberalism in the Nineteenth Century* (Chicago: University of Chicago Press, 1978), pp. 185–86; Lidtke, *The Outlawed Party,* pp. 70–78.

31. These dates are based on the studies that appear later in this chapter.

32. On the circumstances surrounding the expiration of the law, see Gordon A. Craig, *Germany 1866–1945* (New York: Oxford University Press, 1978), pp. 171ff.

33. Johannes von Miquel, long-time leader of the National Liberals and author of the *Sammlungspolitik,* said of the latter: "The great task of the present is, without prejudice . . . to gather together all the elements that support the state and thereby to prepare for the unavoidable battle against the Social Democratic movement." Craig, *Germany,* p. 255, fn. 8.

34. Limited tactical alliances were made in Berlin in the 1887 elections and,

after the turn of the century, a coalition of Social Democrats and Liberals was formed in the Badenese Landtag. Also, Social Democrats worked with Liberal and other political representatives on numerous town councils and provincial assemblies. See, Lidtke, *The Outlawed Party*, pp. 188–91; Craig, *Germany*, p. 269.

35. On the end of the Bülow Bloc, see Craig, *Germany*, pp. 281–88; Carl Schorske, *German Social Democracy, 1905–1917. The Development of the Great Schism* (Cambridge: Harvard University Press, 1955), pp. 156–58.

36. Schorske, *German Social Democracy*, pp. 152–55.

37. Ibid., pp. 229–35.

38. And as it happened, whether for its own reasons or because of the anticipated voter reaction, the National Liberal leadership did not want the alliance. See Schorske, *German Social Democracy*, pp. 156–58.

39. On the early relationship between workers and the Liberal Party, see Leiv Mjeldheim, *Folkerørlsa som vart parti: Venstre frå 1880 åra til 1905* (Bergen: Universitetsforlaget, 1984), pp. 294 and 320–29 passim.

40. Ibid., p. 295.

41. Ibid., pp. 295–97.

42. Ibid., pp. 320–29.

43. Ibid., pp. 455–56.

44. Ibid., p. 456.

45. Ibid., p. 458.

46. Ibid., pp. 456–57.

47. Ibid., p. 457.

48. Ibid., pp. 457–61.

49. Ibid., pp. 462–67.

50. Ibid., p. 468.

51. Ibid., p. 469.

52. Ibid., pp. 470–72.

53. Ibid., p. 473.

54. Gabriel Øidne, "Venstres valgnederlag i 1903: Politiske strømninger ved århundreskiftet i Norge," *Historisk Tidsskrift* (Oslo), vol. 51, no. 1 (1972), pp. 37–69.

55. Nils Elvander, *Skandinavisk arbetarrörelse* (Stockholm: LiberFörlag, 1980), p. 38.

56. Peter Flora, ed., *State, Economy and Society in Western Europe, 1815–1975, A Data Handbook: Volume I, The Growth of Mass Democracies and Welfare States* (Chicago: St. James Press, 1983), p. 139.

57. Elvander, *Skandinavisk arbettarörelse*, pp. 38ff; Furre, *Norsk historie*, pp. 41–54.

58. Furre, *Norsk historie*, p. 54.

59. Rolf Danielsen, "Samlingpartiet og unionen," *Historisk Tidssskrift* (Oslo), vol. 41, no. 2 (1962), pp. 303–20.

60. Furre, *Norsk historie.*, pp. 41–54.

61. *Social Demokraten* (Stockholm), September 27, 1890; *Arbetet* (Malmö), September 9, 1890.

62. *Social Demokraten* (Stockholm), September 23, 1893.

63. Äke Thulstrup, *Svensk politik. 1905–1939: Från unionsupplösningen till andra världskriget* (Stockholm: Bonnier, 1968), p. 23.

64. *Social Demokraten* (Stockholm) September 12, 1896.

65. Ture Nerman, *Svensk arbetarrörelse under hundra år* (Stockholm: Tidensförlag, 1938), pp. 216–17.

66. Nerman, *Svensk*, p. 217.

67. Gustaf Hilding Nordström, *Sveriges socialdemokratiska arbetareparti under genombrottsåren, 1889–1894* (Stockholm: Kooperativa förbundets bokförlag,. 1938), p. 97.

68. Dankwart A. Rustow, *The Politics of Compromise: A Study of Parties and Cabinet Government in Sweden* (Princeton: Princeton University Press, 1955), p. 55.

69. Rolf Fridholm, "Folkriksdagarna 1893 och 1896," *Statsvetenskaplig tisdkrift för politik-statistik-ekonomi*, vol. 30, no. 5 (December 1927), pp. 411–40.

70. Rustow, *The Politics of Compromise*, p. 56.

71. Hans-Krister Rönnblom, *Frisinnade landsföreningen, 1902–1927* (Stockholm: Saxon and Lindström, 1929), pp. 76ff; Edvard Thermaenius, "Riksdagspartierna" in Karl Hildebrand et al., eds., *Sveriges riksdag*, vol. 17 (Stockholm: Victor Petterson, 1935), pp. 131–56.

72. Nerman, *Svensk*, p. 226.

73. The rate of participation is from Bäckström, *Arbetarrörelsen*, vol. 2, p. 22. For a more general discussion, see Bäckström, *Arbetarrörelsen i Sverige: Vol. 1, Den Svenska arbetarrörelsens uppkomst och förening med socialismen* (Stockholm: Rabén and Sjögren, 1971), 294 passim.

74. Rustow, *The Politics*, pp. 57–58.

75. Rönnblom, *Frisinnade*, pp. 97ff.

76. Data on the size of the Social Democratic vote and the number of constituencies in which the party competed are from Ture Nerman, *Svensk*, p. 281.

77. Estimate of working class vote is from *Social Demokraten* (Stockholm), October 6, 1902. Estimate of total votes cast is from Peter Flora, ed., *State*, vol. 1, pp. 141–42.

78. Nerman, *Svensk*, p. 281.

79. Electoral data are from Nerman, *Svensk*, p. 305.

80. See the discussion above, Chapter 3, pp. 68–73.

81. Knut Wichman, *Gustaf V, Karl Staaff och striden om vårt försvar, 1901–1914* (Stockholm: P. A. Norstedt, 1967).

82. See the discussion above, Chapter 3, pp. 71–72.

83. The general strike is a topic to which we will return subsequently. For a discussion of the Liberal party's response to the strike, see Sven Ulric Palme, *På Karl Staaffs tid* (Stockholm: Aldus/Bonniers, 1964), pp. 150ff.

84. Lindhagen joined the Social Democrats in 1909. On the alienation of the urban radicals he led, see Palme, *Karl Staaffs tid*, pp. 58–66 passim; Thulstrup, *Svensk politik*, pp. 47 and 49.

85. On Norway, see Bull, *Norsk fagbevegelse*. On Sweden: Herbert Tingsten, *Den svenska socialdemokratins idéutveckling* (Stockholm: Tidens Förlag, 1941).

86. From 72 seats in 1891 to 109 in 1906. Sten Carlsson and Jerker Rosén, *Svensk historia: Vol. 2, Tiden efter 1718*, 4th ed. (Stockholm: Esselte Studium, 1980), p. 456.

87. Figures are from Flora, *State, Economy*, vol. 1, pp. 137 and 141.

88. The authority of the national Liberal party in Norway was in its capacity to

grant official recognition to a local liberal association and thereby legitimate both its electoral list in campaigns and its candidates in electoral college jockeying.

89. Extended discussions of the leverage the Folketing could exert can be found in Birgit Nüchel Thomsen, "Konflikt og forhandling, 1870–1890," pp. 73–90, and Niels Petersen, "Forlig og omgruppering," pp. 91–116, in Per Salomonsson, ed., *Den politiske magtkamp, 1866–1901* (Copenhagen: Jørgen Paludans Forlage, 1968); see also Troels Fink, *Estruptidens politiske historie, 1875–1894*, 2 vols. (Odense: Odense Universitetsforlag, 1986).

90. Harry Haue, Jørgen Olsen and Jørn Aarup-Kristensen, *Det ny Danmark, 1890–1978: Udviklingslinier og tendens* (Copenhagen: Munksgaard, 1979), p. 45.

91. Claus Friisberg, *På vej mod et demokrati. Fra junigrundloven 1849 til junigrundloven 1915* (Copenhagen: Fremad, 1975), p. 103.

92. Friisberg, *På vej mod et demokrati*, p. 99.

93. Oluf Bertolt, Ernst Christiansen, and Poul Hansen, *En bygning vi rejser: Den politiske arbejderbevaegelses historie i Danmark*, Vol. 1 (Copenhagen: Forlaget Fremad, 1954), p. 140.

94. Ibid., p. 170.

95. Ibid., p. 216.

96. Ibid., p. 222.

97. Ibid., p. 226.

98. Ibid., p. 268–70; Friisberg, *På vej mod et demokrati*, pp. 198ff; Per Salomonsson, "Socialdemokratiet," in Salomonsson, ed., *Den politiske magtkamp 1866–1901*, pp. 57–63.

99. Bertoldt, *En bygning vi resjer*, pp. 268–70.

100. The count of thirty-nine urban victories is based on the following mandates: 1884, two in Copenhagen; 1887, one in Copenhagen; 1890, two in Copenhagen; 1892, two in Copenhagen; 1895, seven in Copenhagen and one in Århus; 1898, seven in Copenhagen, one each in Århus, Horsens, Ålborg, and Randers; 1901, as in 1898, minus one seat, plus one seat each in northern Århus and Kongens Lyngby and an additional seat in Copenhagen. Based on the classifications in Vagn Dybdahl, *Partier og erhverv: Studier i partiorganisation og byerhvervenes politiske aktivitet. ca 1880–1913*, 2 vols. (Århus: Universitetsforlaget, 1969), and the reported victories in Bertolt, *En bygning vi rejser*, pp. 140, 170, 216, 222, 226, 258, 268–70.

101. Bertoldt, *En bygning*, pp. 216 and 222.

102. The size of the working-class vote for Conservative candidates is based on Vagn Dybdahl's electoral study of twenty-three highly competitive urban districts. See Dybdahl, *Partier*. An English language summary is provided in volume 2, pp. 5–27, especially p. 6, where the data are reported and Dybdahl notes that "within the Conservatives, workers as a total group were the biggest but one."

103. Flora, ed., *State*, vol. 1, p. 107.

104. For data on seat transfers in 1903, see Friisberg, *På vej mod et demokrati*, p. 186.

105. Ibid., pp. 176ff.

106. Ibid., p. 185.

107. Ibid., pp. 202ff; Bertoldt, *En bygning vi rejser*, p. 292 passim.

108. Friisberg, *På vej mod et demokrati*, pp. 74ff; Bertoldt, *En bygning vi rejser*, p. 294 passim.

109. See Chapter 3, pp. 74ff.

110. Fink, *Estruptidens* vol. 2, pp. 260–83.

111. Fourteen of the sixteen seats the Social Democrats won through the 1895 election were in Copenhagen. This was not simply because the party was placing candidates only in Copenhagen during these elections; the majority of its candidacies were in urban areas *other than* the capital. See data and sources in note 100.

112. On the 1903 election, see above, pp. 282–83.

113. See above, p. 282 and note 102.

114. Theo Luykx, *Politieke geschiedenis van België van 1789 tot heden,* 2nd ed. (Brussels: Elsevier, 1969), p. 179, fn. 10.

115. See Chapter 3, pp. 129–31.

116. The events that led to the adoption of franchise reform and the critical role that the strike played in its adoption are discussed in Vicomte Ch. Terlinden, "Histoire politique interne: Formation et évolution des Partis," *Histoire de la Belgique contemporaine, 1830–1914,* vol. 2 (Brussels: Albert Dewit, 1929), pp. 189–200 passim; Henri Pirenne, *Histoire de Belgique: Vol. 7, De la révolution de 1830 a la guerre de 1914* (Brussels: Maurice Lamertin, 1932), pp. 310–20, and É. Vandervelde, L. de Brouckère, L. Vandersmissen, *La Grève générale en Belgique (avril 1913)* (Paris, 1914), pp. 66–68. The estimate of 200,000 workers is from Vandervelde et al., p. 66.

117. The most compelling discussion of the relative benefits parties received from plural voting is to be found in Robert Burns Freeman, "The Origins of the Belgian Party System" (Unpublished Ph.D. dissertation: University of California, Berkeley, 1959), pp. 325–43.

118. For the complete figures, see Luykx, *Politieke geschiedenis,* pp. 562ff.

119. The sense of despair and the almost exclusive concern of Liberals with survival is apparent in a tract written by a contemporary Liberal leader advocating an alliance with the Socialists. See Goblet d'Alviella, *Alliances et coalitions, étude de tactique Libérale* (Brussels: P. Weissenbruch, 1898).

120. Freeman, "Belgian Party System," pp. 255–62.

121. Keith Hill, "Belgium: Political Change in a Segmented Society," in Richard Rose, ed., *Electoral Behavior: A Comparative Handbook* (New York: Free Press, 1974), p. 38.

122. Terlinden, "Histoire politique," pp. 210–12.

123. The emphasis on survival is apparent in the brief on behalf of an alliance written by its leading Liberal champion. See d'Alviella, *Alliances.*

124. The figures are from John Gilissen, *Le régime représentatif en Belgique depuis 1790* (Brussels: La Renaissance du Livre, 1958), pp. 190–91.

125. Frans Van Kalken, *Histoire de Belgique des origines a nos jours* (Brussels: Office de publicité, 1946), p. 494.

126. Of the new seats, five went to Brussels, two to Antwerp, two to Charleroi, and the "remainder to other chief centers of population." *The Times* (London) June 1, 1912, p. 5, and June 2, 1912, p. 5.

127. Van Kalken, *Histoire,* pp. 494ff.

128. *The Times* (London), June 4, 1912, p. 9, June 6, 1912, p. 5; Terlinden, "Histoire politique interne," pp. 225–26.

129. Robert C. K. Ensor, ed., *Modern Socialism* (London and New York: Harper & Brothers, 1904), p. xiv.

130. An analysis of the differential impact of the plural voting arrangements can be found in Freeman, "The Origins," pp. 325–43.

131. Ben Serge Chlepner, *Cent Ans d'histoire sociale en Belgique* (Brussels: Institut de Sociologie Solvay, 1958), pp. 116, 118.

132. "The fundamental explanation of the different impact of the Socialist party . . . is to be found in regional differences in religious practice." Keith Hill, "Belgium," p. 39 and passim.

133. Léon-Eli Troclet, *Les partis politiques en Belgique* (Brussels: L'Eglantine, 1931), pp. 20–21.

134. M. Defourny, "Histoire sociale: Les faits, les idées, la legislation," in *Historie de la Belgique contemporaine, 1830–1914*, vol. 2 (Brussels: Albert Dewit, 1929), p. 326.

135. A summary of the social legislation of the prewar decades and the political battles that surrounded it is available in ch. 4 ("La Législation sociale") of Defourny, "Histoire sociale," pp. 329–64.

136. The dissolution of the Liberals at the time of the franchise debate is discussed in W. J. van Welderen Rengers, *Schets eener parlementaire geschiedenis van Nederland van 1849 tot 1901*, 4th ed., annotation by C. W. de Vries (The Hague: M. Nijhoff, 1949), vol. 2 (1891–1901), pp. 58ff. See also P. Hoekstra, "De laatste tien liberale jaren in het Noorden (1891–1901)" in J. A. van Houtte et al., eds., *Algemene geschiedenis der Nederlanden*, vol. 2 (Antwerp: W. De Haan, 1956), pp. 60–82.

137. For discussion of the debates that took place within the movement about the working class and socialism, see E. H. Kossman, *The Low Countries, 1780–1940* (Oxford: Clarendon Press, 1978), pp. 338–43, 510ff; Hoekstra, "De laatste," p. 138. The figures on party and trade union membership are from Kossman, *Low Countries*, p. 479. A general introduction to the Dutch labor movement is provided in M. Ruppert, *De Nederlands Vakbeweging*, 2 vols. (Haarlem: De Erven F. Bohn, 1953).

139. The reform of 1882 gave the vote to 25.1 percent of males above the voting age. This share rose to 35.2 percent in 1892, before a purging of the electoral registers pressed it back down to 25.2 percent again in 1895. By 1909, the figure had risen back to 32.2 percent. Flora, vol. 2, p. 127.

140. Maurice Neufeld, *Italy: School for Awakening Countries* (Ithaca, N.Y.: Cornell University Press, 1961), pp. 114–15; Daniel L. Horowitz, *The Italian Labor Movement* (Cambridge: Harvard University Press, 1963), pp. 23–30.

141. A survey conducted by the Ministry of Agriculture, Industry and Commerce in 1876 indicated that 2 percent of the total population—or perhaps 6 percent of the labor force—worked in "industrial establishments." Roberto Tremelloni has observed that almost the entire group of workers designated as industrial by the 1876 survey might be more properly assigned to the handicrafts, since even factories at the time still operated along semiartisanal lines. See Neufeld, *Italy*, pp. 140–41.

142. Christopher Seton-Watson, *Italy from Liberalism to Fascism, 1870–1925* (London: Methuen, 1967), p. 73.

143. Neufeld, *Italy*, pp. 368–69; Horowitz, *Italian Labor*, p. 124.

144. The danger of falling into the post hoc, ergo propter hoc sort of fallacy here does not seem to be great. In principle, it is possible that working-class confessionalism after the war reflected not a continuous confessional orientation but a movement from liberalism or socialism *to* confessionalism. Such patterns of political migration, as should be apparent from the other analyses in this chapter, would be

unprecedented in Western Europe. Elsewhere workers routinely moved from liberalism to socialism, and less frequently from confessionalism to socialism. But nowhere did they move from socialism to confessionalism or from liberalism to confessionalism.

145. On the workings of the electoral law, see Gaetano Salvemini, "Introductory Essay," in A. William Salomone, *Italian Democracy in the Making. The Political Scene in the Giolittian Era* (Philadelphia: University of Pennsylvania Press, 1945), p. ix; and Paolo Farneti, *Sistema politico e società civile: Saggi di teoria e ricerca politica* (Turin: Giappichelli, 1971), pp. 167ff.

146. For more than two decades after unification, more than one-third of the electorate habitually abstained. Abstention was highest in the north, where anticlericalism was a more virulent liberal rallying cry. In the south, where the Church had more support and prefects and local magnates could, in any event, be more readily substituted for competing programs and could be counted on to ensure the right outcome, anticlericalism was both less useful and less attractive. Presumably, it was this lesser salience of anticlericalism that accounts for the lower abstention in the south. *Source:* Seton-Watson, *Italy from Liberalism to Fascism*, p. 226, fn. 3.

147. Horowitz, *Italian Labor*, p. 30.

148. Flora et al., *State, Economy, Society*, vol. 2., p. 127.

149. On Crispi's repression of socialism, see Neufeld, *Italy*, pp. 214–17; Seton-Watson, *Italy*, pp. 166–68; H. L. Gualtieri, *The Labor Movement in Italy* (New York: S. F. Vanni, 1946), pp. 183–86.

150. On Crispi's foreign policy and imperialism and its domestic roots, see Seton-Watson, *Italy*, pp. 173–83; Denis Mack Smith, *Italy: A Modern History* (Ann Arbor: University of Michigan Press, 1959), pp. 179–88.

151. On the development of the liberal right's idea of an African colony as a solution to the chronic social and economic problems of the *Mezzogiorno* and Crispi's war, see Seton-Watson, *Italy*, pp. 84–90, 140, and 184.

152. On the history of this authoritarian–imperialist right, see Seton-Watson, *Italy*, pp. 349–65; Salomone, *Italian Democracy*, pp. 86–101.

153. On Di Rudinìs anticlericalism and antisocialism, see Seton-Watson, *Italy*, pp. 188–92.

154. Neufeld, *Italy*, p. 223; Salomone, *Italian Democracy*, p. 44. For a detailed account of the Socialists' alliance with the other members of the Estrema Sinistra and the Constitutional Left, see Michael Spencer Di Scala, "Fillipo Turati and Fractional Strife in the Italian Socialist Party, 1892–1912" (Unpublished Ph.D dissertation: Columbia University, 1969), pp. 71–148.

155. Salomone, *Italian Democracy*, pp. 44–46; Di Scala, "Turati," pp. 149–91.

156. The words are Giolitti's. See Horowitz, *Italian Labor*, p. 49.

157. On the Giolittian system, see Salomone, *Italian Democracy*, especially, pp. 102–114; and Seton-Watson, *Italy*, pp. 246–55.

158. Seton-Waton, *Italy*, p. 247.

159. On Giolitti's labor policy, see Seton-Watson, *Italy*, pp. 231ff; Horowitz, *Italian Labor*, pp. 68ff.

160. Neufeld, *Italy*, p. 243.

161. On the socialist movement during the Giolittian period, see Salomone, *Italian Democracy*, pp. 46–85; Horowitz, *Italian Labor*, pp. 51–58; Neufeld, *Italy*, pp. 228–46; Di Scala, "Turati," pp. 149–352.

162. Neufeld, *Italy*, p. 236.

163. Seldom has Hegel's pessimistic view of the relationship between knowledge and history been more to the point: "To say one more word about preaching what the world ought to be like, philosophy arrives always too late for that. As thought of the world it appears at a time when actuality has completed its developmental process and is finished. What the conception teaches, history also shows as necessary, namely, that only in a maturing actuality the ideal appears and confronts the real. It is then that the ideal rebuilds for itself this same world in the shape of an intellectual realm, comprehending this world in its substance. When philosophy paints its gray in gray, a form of life has become old, and this gray in gray cannot rejuvenate it, only understand it. *The owl of Minerva begins its flight when dusk is falling.*" [emphasis added] Carl J. Friedrich, ed., *The Philosophy of Hegel* (New York: Random House, 1953), p. 227.

164. On social insurance, universal suffrage and the anticipated electoral coalition, see Seton-Watson, *Italy*, pp. 281–83.

165. Franklin Hugh Adler, "Italian Industrialists from Liberalism to Fascism" (Unpublished Ph.D dissertation: University of Chicago, 1980), p. 36; Seton-Watson, *Italy*, p. 367.

166. Salomone, *Italian Democracy*, p. 103.

167. On the Libyan War and the reactions of the Socialists, see Di Scala, "Turati," pp. 301–52.

168. Salomone, *Italian Democracy*, p. 98.

169. Neufeld, *Italy*, p. 240.

170. Raymond Carr, *Spain, 1808–1975*, 2nd ed. (Oxford: Oxford University Press, 1982), p. 451, fn. 1.

171. On Republicanism before 1923, see Carr, *Spain*, pp. 524–64.

172. On the Tragic Week, its origins and aftermath, see Joan Connelly Ullman, *The Tragic Week: A Study of Anticlericalism in Spain 1875–1912* (Cambridge: Harvard University Press, 1968).

173. On the Assembly Movement, see Juan Antonio Lacomba Avellan, *La crisis española de 1917* (Madrid: Editorial Ciencia Nueva, 1970).

174. Seton-Watson, *Italy*, pp. 349–65; Salomone, *Italian Democracy*, pp. 86–101; William Clarence Askew, *Europe and Italy's Acquisition of Libya* (Durham, N.C.: Duke University Press, 1942); R. A. Webster, *Industrial Imperialism in Italy* (Berkeley: University of California Press, 1978).

175. Hans-Ulrich Wehler, *The German Empire, 1871–1918*, trans. by Kim Traynor (Dover, N.H.: Berg Publishers, 1985); Hans-Ulrich Wehler, "Industrial Growth and Early German Imperialism," in Roger Owen and Bob Sutcliffe, eds., *Studies in the Theory of Imperialism* (London: Longman, 1972), pp. 71–92.

176. Geoff Eley, *From Unification to Nazism: Reinterpreting the German Past* (Boston: Allen and Unwin, 1986), especially chs. 5 and 6; Geoff Eley, *Reshaping the German Right: Radical Nationalism and Political Change after Bismarck* (New Haven: Yale University Press, 1980).

177. Seton-Watson, *Italy*, pp. 349–65; Salomone, *Italian Democracy*, pp. 86–101; Askew, *Italy's Acquisition of Libya;* Webster, *Industrial Imperialism;* Carr, *Spain*, pp. 473ff; Carolyn P. Boyd, *Praetorian Politics in Liberal Spain* (Chapel Hill: University of North Carolina Press, 1979).

178. On the function of nationalism in the early Liberal coalition, see Alf Kaartvedt, *Kampen mot parlamentarisme, 1880–1884* (Oslo: Universitetsforlaget, 1967); and Mjeldheim, *Folkerørsla*.

179. On the unfolding of crises within the party and the escalation of nationalist demands, see Mjeldheim, *Folkerørsla.*

180. Danielsen, "Samlingpartiet og unionen," pp. 303–20.

181. Kristian Hvidt, *Venstre og forsvarssagen, 1870–1901* (Århus: Universitetsforlaget, 1960); Fink, *Estruptidens politiske historie.*

182. Berge Furre, *Norsk historie, 1905–1940,* pp. 40ff.

183. Schorske, *German Social Democracy,* pp. 59–63; George Crothers, *The German Elections of 1907* (New York: Columbia University Press, 1941).

184. Salomone, *Italian Democracy,* p. 98; Neufeld, *Italy,* pp. 238–40.

185. Carr, *Spain,* pp. 483ff; Ullman, *Tragic Week,* pp. 9–27, 129ff.

186. Salomone, *Italian Democracy,* p. 104.

187. On Staaff, see Wichman, *Gustav V, Karl Staaff och striden om vårt försvar. 1901–1914;* Palme, *På Karl Staaffs tid.* On Giolitti, see Giampiero Carocci, *Giolitti e l'età giolittiana* (Turin: Einaudi, 1961); Giovanni Spadolini, *Giolitti e i cattolici* (Florence: Le Monnier, 1960).

Chapter 5

1. On the local orientation of labor politics in Britain, see David Howell, *British Workers and the Independent Labour Party, 1888–1906* (Manchester: Manchester University Press, 1983); and James Hinton, *Labour and Socialism: A History of the British Labor Movement, 1867–1974* (Brighton, Sussex; Wheatsheaf Books, 1983), pp. 24ff. On France, see Claude Willard, *Les guesdistes: Le Mouvement socialiste en France, 1893–1905* (Paris: Editions sociales, 1965); and Lenard R. Berlanstein, *The Working People of Paris, 1871–1914* (Baltimore: Johns Hopkins University Press, 1984).

2. Halvard Lange, "Arbeiderpartiet 1905–1914," in Halvdan Koht, ed., *Det norske arbeiderpartis historie, 1887–1937* (Oslo: Det Norske Arbeiderpartis Forlag, 1939), vol. 2, p. 3.

3. This is an implicit theme in both Hinton, *Labour and Socialism,* pp. 60ff, and Howell, *British Workers.*

4. Hinton, *Labor and Socialism,* pp. 74–75.

5. Ibid., pp. 74–75; J. Ramsay MacDonald, *The Socialist Movement* (London: Williams and Norgate, 1911).

6. On these specific instances see, for Germany: Carl Schorske, *German Social Democracy, 1905–1917: The Development of the Great Schism* (Cambridge: Harvard University Press, 1955), pp. 152–58, 229–35. For Denmark: Oluf Bertoldt et al., *En bygning vi rejser: Den politiske arbejderbevegelses historie i Danmark* (Copenhagen: Forlaget Fremad, 1954), vol. 1. See also the citations in notes 90–113, ch. 4. For Belgium: Vicomte Ch. Terlinden, "Histoire politique interne: Formation et évolution des Parties," in *Histoire de la Belgique contemporaine, 1830–1914* (Brussels: Albert Dewit, 1929), vol. 2, pp. 200ff. For Sweden: Hans Krister Rönnblom, *Frisinnade landsföreningen, 1902–1927* (Stockholm: Saxon and Lindström, 1929), pp. 76ff.

7. This is based on the materials used in the accounts of the breakdown of Lib–Labism in Chapter 4.

8. Compare, for example, the lackadaisical attitudes toward organizational work

that are conveyed by the research of G. D. H. Cole, *British Working-Class Politics, 1832–1914* (London: George Routledge and Sons, 1941), pp. 138–200; and Willard, *Le Mouvement socialiste;* and Berlanstein, *Working People of Paris,* with the attention to organization that comes through in the research of Schorske, *German Social Democracy;* Donald J. Blake, "Swedish Trade Unions and the Social Democratic Party: The Formative Years," *Scandinavian Economic History Review,* vol. 8, no. 1 (1960), pp. 19–44; Halvard Lange, "Arbeiderpartiets historie 1887–1937," in Halvdan Koht, ed., *Det norske arbeiderpartis historie, 1887–1937* (Oslo: Det Norske arbeiderpartis Forlag, 1937), vol. 1, pp. 75–244, especially pp. 194ff; Halvard Lange, *Fra sekt til parti: det norske arbeiderpartis organisasjonsmessige og politiske utvikling fra 1891 til 1902* (Oslo: Universitetsforlaget, 1962).

    9. Hjalmar Branting, *Tal och skrifter* (Stockholm: Tiden, 1926–1930), vol. 1, p. 246.

    10. Hinton, *Labor and Socialism,* pp. 71–72.

    11. Hubert Rouger, *La France socialiste* (Paris, 1912), pp. 149–52, cited from Theodore Zeldin, *France, 1848–1945: Politics and Anger* (Oxford: Oxford University Press, 1979), p. 404.

    12. Schorske, *German Social Democracy,* pp. 125–26.

    13. Ibid., pp. 8–16.

    14. See, for examples of early union–party cooperation in establishing locals the histories of the unions, John Lindgren, *Svenska metallindustriarbetareförbundets historia* (Stockholm, 1938), vol. 1, pp. 250–52 passim; Ragnar Casparsson, *Gruvfolk: Svenska Gruvindustriarbetareförbundet under fyra årtionden* (Stockholm, 1935), pp. 88–89 passim; Charles Lindley, *Svenska transportarbetareförbundet: Historia* (Stockholm, 1943), vol. 1, pp. 63ff; Reinhold Olsson and Richard Lindström, *En krönika om sågverksarbetare: Svenska sågverksindustriarbetareförbundets minnesskrift* (Sundsvall, 1953), pp. 197–201; and Tage Lindbom and Evert Kuhm, *Tobaksarbetarnas förbund i Sverge* (Stockholm, 1940), pp. 18–41.

    15. See the records of the relevant conventions: SDAP second convention (1891), *Protokoll,* pp. 4–5, 16–17; third convention (1894), *Protokoll,* pp. 16 and 24; and fourth (1897), *Protokoll,* pp. 10 and 31. See also Torvald Karlbom, *Svenska grov- och fabriksarbetareförbundets historia,* vol. 1 (Stockholm, 1941), pp. 127–29, 136, 150–51, 333–34.

    16. See Chapter 4, pp. 121–25.

    17. See Bertoldt, *En bygning vi rejser,* vol. 1, and especially the richly detailed study by Jens Frese, "Den tvaerfaglige centralisationsbevaegelse i Danmark for 1900, med saerligt henblik på De samvirkende Fagforeninger 1886 og De Samvirkende Fagforbund 1898" (Historie hovedfag, Specialeopgave, 1969). This unpublished manuscript is available from the Arbejderbevaegelsens Bibliotek og Arkiv, Copenhagen.

    18. On the PSI-CGL relationship, see Daniel Horowitz, *The Italian Labor Movement* (Cambridge: Harvard University Press, 1963), pp. 64–94; Spencer Michael di Scala, "Filippo Turati and Factional Strife in the Italian Socialist Party" (Unpublished Ph.D Dissertation: Columbia University, 1969), pp. 224–36.

    19. See, especially, Theodore Zeldin, *France, 1848–1945: Ambition and Love* (Oxford: Oxford University Press, 1979), p. 237 passim.

    20. See Chapter 2, pp. 20–23.

    21. See Chapter 2, pp. 23–24.

22. Zeldin, *Politics and Anger*, pp. 361–424; Dick Geary, *European Labour Protest, 1848–1939* (London: Methuen, 1984), pp. 116–17; Robert D. Anderson, *France, 1870–1914: Politics and Society* (London: Routledge and Kegan Paul, 1977), pp. 120ff.

23. Walter Galenson, *Labor In Norway* (Cambridge: Harvard University Press, 1949), pp. 20ff; Lange, "Arbeiderpartiet, 1905–1914," pp. 1–93, especially pp. 72ff.

24. Stanley G. Payne, *The Spanish Revolution: A Study of the Social and Political Tensions that Culminated in the Civil War in Spain* (New York: Norton, 1970), pp. 1–62.

25. Knut Bäckström, *Arbetarrörelsen i Sverige: Vol. 2, Den politiska arbetarrörelsens sprängning och ett nytt revolutionärt arbetarpartis uppkomst* (Stockholm: Rabén and Sjögren, 1971).

26. Spencer di Scala, *The Dilemma of Italian Socialism* (Amherst: University of Massachusetts Press, 1980).

27. Schorske, *German Social Democracy.*

28. D. A. Smart, ed., *Pannekoek and Gorter's Marxism* (London: Pluto Press, 1978).

29. Galenson, *Labor in Norway*, p. 23.

30. Stanley Hoffmann, "Paradoxes of the French Political Community," in Hoffmann, ed., *In Search of France: The Economy, Society and Political System in the Twentieth Century* (New York: Harper & Row, 1963), pp. 1–118, especially pp. 11ff.

31. On the evidence on rates of membership turnover in French and German unions and on per capita trade union dues, see Peter Stearns, *Revolutionary Syndicalism and French Labor: A Cause Without Rebels* (New Brunswick, N.J.: Rutgers University Press, 1971), p. 24.

32. These figures are the ratio of the male labor force in the secondary and tertiary sectors to the combined total number of party-affiliated daily/weekly newspaper copies printed per issue in 1914. The secondary and tertiary sectors are used to control for the level of industrialization. Males were used because in most societies they alone were enfranchised before the war and because they were the principal targets of party organizers. The labor force data on which the ratios were computed are from B. R. Mitchell, *European Historical Statistics, 1750–1970* (New York: Columbia University Press, 1975), pp. 153–65. The press figures used are as follows: For Britain, 50,000, which was the press run of the *Daily Herald*, strictly speaking not a party-affiliated paper. (Hinton, *Labor and Socialism,* p. 95.) For France, 148,000, which reflects a printing of 88,000 copies of Jean Jaurès' *Humanité,* the newspaper of the SFIO *and* a printing of 60,000 for Gustave Hervés unaffiliated and insurgent *Guerre Sociale* (Roger Magraw, *France, 1815–1914: The Bourgeois Century* [New York: Oxford University Press, 1986], pp. 313–314). For Norway, 80,000, based on 29 daily newspapers with this combined press run (Edvard Bull, *Norsk fagbevegelse: Oversikt over Fagorganisasjonens utvikling,* 2nd ed. [Oslo: Tiden Norsk Forlag, 1968] p. 61). For Sweden, 160,000, the figure provided by Stig Hadenius, Jan-Olof Seveborg, and Lennart Weibull, *Socialdemokratisk press och prespolitik, 1899–1909* (Stockholm: Tidens Förlag, 1968), p. 56 passim. For Denmark, 120,000, based on Bertoldt et al., *En bygning vi rejser,* vol. 1, p. 326. For Belgium, 200,000. This figure, the only one available, is for 1923, and it undoubted-

ly overstates the size of the prewar press (Emile Vandervelde, *Le Parti Ouvrier Belgie, 1885–1925* [Brussels: L'Elgantine, 1925] p. 415). For the Netherlands 30,000 (Harmen de Vos, *Geschiedenis van het socialisme in Nederland in het kader van zijn tijd* [Baarn: Het Wereldvenster, 1976], vol. 1, p. 109). For Germany, 1,500,000 (Schorske, *German Social Democracy*, p. 269). For Italy, 75,000, the 1914 press run of *Avanti!* (Valerio Castronovo, *La Stampa Italiana dall'Unità al Fascismo* [Bari: Editori Laterza, 1970] p. 202). For Switzerland, 60,000, a figure that is inferred from the only available reliable figures of 49,000 in 1900 and 127,000 in 1930. More reliable, and revealing, for Switzerland is the fact that less than 10 percent of the total circulation of prewar newspapers with party orientations was supportive of the Social Democrats. No Socialist party newspaper per se existed in Switzerland. Rather, cantonal parties published their own papers. The figure of 60,000 refers to these. See Erich Gruner, *Die Parteien in der Schweiz* (Bern: Francke, 1969), pp. 218–26; Karl Weber, *The Swiss Press: An Outline* (Bern: Herbert Lang, 1948); Malcolm Davis and Walter Mallory, eds., *A Political Handbook of the World: Parliaments, Parties and Presses* (New York: Harvard University Press, 1928), pp. 184–85.

33. Hunt, *British Labor*, p. 332.

34. The figure for Norway is for the 1915 election, and is from Einhart Lorenz, *Arbeiderbevegelsens historie, En innføring: Norsk socialisme i internasjonalt perspecktiv. 1. del, 1789–1930* (Oslow: Pax Forlag, 1972), p. 85. All other figures are from Flora, ed., *State, Economy, Society*, vol. 1, pp. 103–51. The Italian figure combines the support for the Socialists, Reformist Socialists, and Independent Socialists.

35. The rank order is based on the data in B. R. Mitchell, *European Historical Statistics*.

36. See Chapter 2, pp. 35–36 and 52.

37. See Chapter 2, p. 52.

38. On Germany, see Chapter 2, pp. 36–37.

39. Olle Johansson, "Socialdemokratins väljare 1911 och 1914: En kvantitativ analys av regional och social gruppering och struktur," *Historisk tidskrift* (Stockholm) vol. 86, no. 3 (1967), pp. 297–357.

40. Hunt, *British Labor*, p. 333.

41. Flora, *State, Economy and Society*, vol. 1, p. 147.

42. See Chapter 2, p. 39.

43. See Chapter 2, p. 48.

44. All estimates of CGL membership as a fraction of the prewar industrial labor force are suspect because of the unreliability of figures for male industrial workers. If we rely on the 1911 census report, there were about 2.3 million male industrial workers in Italy defined as the male workers in Flora's categories 2, 3, 4, 5, and 7 (*State, Economy, Society*, vol. 2). Given the figure of a *paid* membership (nominal membership was about double the paid) of about 200,000 industrial workers in the CGL, this yields a membership of about 8 percent of male industrial workers in CGL federations. (The figure on CGL membership is from U.S. Department of State, *Report on the Labor Situation of Italy* [Washington, D.C., 1919] p. 11.) The census data whence Flora's figures derive are most problematic, however. According to the more jaundiced 1918 report of the American Embassy in Rome, the male industrial labor force in 1914 amounted to only 1.2 million workers. Taking this figure, CGL

membership would have included 16 percent of the male industrial labor force. (*Report on the Labor Situation of Italy*, p. 27.)

45. The size of the male industrial labor force enrolled in trade unions and in unions affiliated with a national socialist confederation has been computed by taking the number of male workers so enrolled as a fraction of the male industrial labor force figures provided in Flora, ed., *State, Economy, Society*, vol. 2, pp. 443ff. The industrial labor force is defined as the work force in mining, manufacturing, construction, utilities, and transport. These correspond to Flora's sectors 2, 3, 4, 5, and 7. This omits workers in agriculture, including forestry and fishing, retail trade, banking, services, and public administration. We have used the last figures Flora provides for the prewar period, typically 1911. Male trade union enrollment is for 1914 and has been calculated by deducting, as with Britain and France in Chapter 2, 10 percent of membership for females. This appears to correspond to the size of female membership that was common throughout prewar Europe. The data have been reduced to males because, in the industrial sectors in question, the fraction of females employed was miniscule (see Flora's data) and because males were the main target of trade union and socialist organizers before 1914. They were the core of the industrial proletariat. The sources of trade union membership data are E. H. Kossman, *The Low Countries, 1780–1940* (Oxford: Oxford University Press, 1978), p. 479 (Belgium and the Netherlands); Geary, *European Labor Protest*, p. 98 (Germany); Lorenz, *Arbeiderbevegelsens historie*, p. 93 (Norway); Seppo Hentilä, *Den svenska arbetarklassen och reformismens genombrott inom SAP före 1914: Arbetarklassens ställning, strategi och ideologi* (Helsinki: Suomen Historiallinen Seura, 1979), p. 151 (Sweden); Nils Elvander, *Skandinavisk arbetarrörelse* (Stockholm: LiberFürlag, 1980), p. 40 (Denmark, Norway, Sweden); Stanley G. Payne, *The Spanish Revolution*, p. 65; Colin M. Winston, *Workers and the Right in Spain, 1900–1936* (Princeton: Princeton University Press, 1985), pp. 51, 98–99 (Spain). Data for the Spanish industrial labor force is from B. R. Mitchell, *European Historical Statistics*, p. 161.

46. On the postwar feebleness of the CGT and TUC, see Chapter 6.

47. Edward Shorter and Charles Tilly, *Strikes in France, 1830–1968* (London: Cambridge University Press, 1974), p. 170.

48. Eduard Weckerle, *The Trade Unions in Switzerland* (Bern: Swiss Federation of Trade Unions, 1947), p. 30.

49. Zeldin, *Ambition and Love*, p. 239.

50. On the latter point, see Chapter 2, p. 43.

51. Weckerle, *Trade Unions in Switzerland*, pp. 21–31.

52. Barrington Moore, Jr., *Injustice: The Social Bases of Obedience and Revolt* (White Plains, N.Y.: M. E. Sharpe, 1978), p. 182.

53. The balance belonged to the syndicalist CNT (15,000) or Catholic (5,000) and autonomous unions (85,000). Payne, *Spanish Revolution*, p. 65; Winston, *Workers*, pp. 51, 98–99.

54. Juan Gómez Casas, *Historia del anarcosindicalismo español*, 4th ed. (Madrid: ZYX, 1978), pp. 77–110, esp. 105ff; Manuel Tuñon de Lara, *El movimiento obrero en la historia de España* (Madrid: Taurus, 1972), pp. 537ff.

55. Stanley G. Payne, *Spanish Revolution*, p. 65; Tuñon de Lara, *El movimiento*, p. 649.

56. Tuñon de Lara, *El movimiento*, pp. 320–25, 505, 574ff.

57. Gómez Casas, *Historia*, pp. 77–110; José Luis Guinea, *Los movimientos*

obreros y sindicales en España de 1833 a 1978 (Madrid: Iberico Europea, 1978), pp. 19ff.

58. Tuñon de Lara, *El movimiento,* pp. 457ff.

59. Board of Trade, *Seventeenth Abstract of Labour Statistics of the United Kingdom* (London: Government Stationary Office, 1915), pp. 204–08.

60. On the weakness of the CGT and of the national federations and the decision to strike, see Shorter and Tilly, *Strikes in France,* pp. 165ff; Stearns, *Revolutionary Syndicalism,* pp. 9–73.

61. Average union size is from Stearns, *Revolutionary Syndicalism,* p. 23.

62. Dieter Fricke, *Die deutsche Arbeiterbewegung, 1869 bis 1914: Ein handbuch über ihre Organisation und Tätigkeit im Klassenkampf* (Berlin: Das Europäische Buch, 1976), pp. 696–99.

63. Fricke, *Die deutsche Arbeiterbewegung,* table 102, p. 672.

64. U.S. Department of State, *Report on the Labor Situation of Sweden* (Washington, D.C., 1919), pp. 12–13.

65. U.S. Department of State, *Report on the Labor Situation of Denmark* (Washington, D.C., 1919), pp. 2–4.

66. U.S. Department of State, *Report on the Labor Situation of Norway* (Washington, D.C., 1919), p. 9.

67. Vandervelde, *Le Parti Ouvrier Belge,* p. 285.

68. Ibid., p. 281. The five largest federations were in the building trades (137,500), metal industries (138,042), mining (103,273), textile production (68,191), and state employment (85,000). The total membership of the national confederation was 698,084.

69. At its peak in September 1920, the CGL included 1.9 million workers, 890,000 of which were in agriculture. The four largest industrial federations were in the building trades (200,000), metallurgy (160,000), textiles (155,000), and the gas works (68,000). Luigi Einaudi, *La condotta economica e gli effetti sociali della guerra italiana* (Bari: Laterza and Figli, 1933), p. 322.

70. Tuñon de Lara, *El movimiento,* pp. 648–49.

71. Hinton, *Labor and Socialism,* p. 70.

72. G. D. H. Cole, *A Short History of the British Working-Class Movement* (New York: Macmillan, 1927), vol. 3, pp. 70ff, 125ff; Walter Citrine, *Fackföreningsrörelsen i Storbritannien,* skriftserie 14 (Stockholm: Landsorganisationen, 1927); John Aspley and Eugene Whitmore, eds., *The Handbook of Industrial Relations* (London: Dartnell Corporation, 1944), pp. 12–15.

73. Shorter and Tilly, *Strikes in France,* pp. 164–65.

74. See Chapter 6, pp. 211ff.

75. Adolf Braun, Herman Müller and Richard Seidel, *Die Gewerkschaften, ihre Entwicklung und ihre Kämpfe: Vol. 2, Die Gewerkschaften nach dem Kriege* (Berlin: Buchhandlung Vorwärts, 1925), pp. 88ff.; Ludwig Heyde, ed., *Internationales Handwörterbuch des Gewerkschaftenswesens,* 2 vols. (Berlin: Werk und Wirtschaft Verlagaktionengeselschaft, 1931–1932).

76. Galenson, *Labor in Norway,* pp. 13–20.

77. On the growth of the LO's authority in the years before the strike and its conduct during the strike, see Jörgen Westerståhl, *Svensk fackföreningsrörelse: Organisationsproblem, verksamhetsformer, förhållande till staten* (Stockholm: Tidens Förlag, 1946), pp. 59–83, especially pp. 63ff.

78. On the strike–lockout, see Westerståhl, *Svensk fackföreningsrörelse*, pp. 77ff; Bäckström, *Arbetarrörelsen i Sverige*, vol. 2, pp. 94ff.

79. Walter Galenson, *The Danish System of Labor Relations: A Study in Industrial Peace* (Cambridge: Harvard University Press, 1952), p. 98 passim.

80. Daniel L. Horowitz, *The Italian Labor Movement* (Cambridge: Harvard University Press, 1963), pp. 70–94 passim; Maurice Neufeld, *Italy: School for Awakening Countries* (Itaca, N.Y.: Cornell University Press, 1961), pp. 316–70; Kirkland Kenneth Judson, "The Italian Chambers of Labor, 1890–1914: The Formation of Working-Class Consciousness" (Unpublished Ph.D. Dissertation: University of Michigan, 1976).

81. Galenson, *The Danish System*, pp. 24ff.

82. Westerståhl, *Svensk fackföreningsrörelse*, pp. 59–83.

83. Localists also were more likely to advocate the continued subordination of trade unions to the Social Democratic party; centralists wanted an autonomous, politically neutral union movement. See Schorske, *German Social Democracy*, pp. 8ff.

84. On the early opposition to a powerful General Commission and resistance to the formation of Zentralverbände, see John A. Moses, *Trade Unionism in Germany from Bismarck to Hitler, 1869–1933* (Totawa, N.J.: Barnes and Noble, 1982), vol. 1, pp. 113ff, especially pp. 117–20.

85. On the establishment of the Zentralverbände, see Fricke, *Deutsche Arbeiterbewegung*, table 101, pp. 668–69, where the number of associations in each craft is provided; table 102, where the changing number of Zentralverbände is shown; and for a discussion of the cartel agreements and the creation of the Zentralverbände, pp. 690ff.

86. Galenson, *Labor in Norway*, pp. 9ff.

87. Erik Hansen, "Workers and Socialists: Relations Between the Dutch Trade-Union Movement and Social Democracy, 1894–1914," *European Studies Review*, vol. 7, no. 2 (April 1977), pp. 214ff.

88. Ger Harmsen and Bob Reinalda, *Voor de bevrijding van de arbeid: Beknopte geschiedenis van de nerderlandse vakbeweging* (Nijmegen: Socialistiese Uitgeverij, 1975), pp. 88ff; Ernest Hueting, Frits de Jong Edz., and Robert Neij, *Naar groter eenheid: De geschiedenis van het Nederlands Verbond van Vakverenigingen, 1906–1981* (Amsterdam: Van Gennep, 1983), pp. 33–63; J. M. Welcker, *Heren en arbeiders in de vroege Nederlandse arbeidersbeweging, 1870–1914* (Amsterdam: Van Gennep, 1978), pp. 557ff.

89. By 1914, there were about eight workers in NVV unions for every one in an NAS union. See Hueting, *Naar groter eenheid*, p. 62.

90. Corneille Mertens, *The Trade Union Movement in Belgium* (Amsterdam: International Federation of Trade Unions, 1925), p. 13.

91. Ibid., p. 16.

92. Ibid., p. 31.

93. Moses, *Trade Unionism*, vol. 1, p. 113.

94. Galenson, *Labor in Norway*, p. 15.

95. Gunnar Ousland, *Fagorganisasjonen i norge* (Oslo, 1927), p. 157, cited from Galenson, *Labor in Norway*, pp. 15–16.

96. On the Swedish strike–lockout, see Westerståhl, *Svensk fackföreningsrörelse*, pp. 77ff; Bäckström, *Arbetarrörelsen*, vol. 2, pp. 94ff. On the

Danish strike–lockout, see Sophus Agerholm and Anders Vigen, *Arbejdsgiver-foreningen gennem 25 år, 1896–1921* (Copenhagen: Trykt and Langkjaers, 1921), p. 63; H. L. Bisgaard, "Den Store Lockout," *Nationaløkonomisk Tidsskrift*, vol. 37 (1899), p. 497; Georg Nørregård, *Arbejdsforhold inden for Dansk Industri og håndvaerk, 1857–1899* (Copenhagen: Gyldendal, 1943), pp. 514ff.

97. Agerholm and Vigen, *Arbejdsgiverforeningen*, p. 63; Bisgaard, "Den Store Lockout," p. 497.

98. Adequate data are available for only these countries. The ratios were computed using the average annual number of workers directly effected by strikes and lockouts, excluding those effected indirectly and by mixed strikes–lockouts, for the twelve years between 1903 and 1914. The data are found in Flora, *State, Economy and Society*, vol. 2, pp. 679ff.

99. On the organization of German employers and the tactics they employed against the trade unions, see Karl Erich Born, *Wirtschafts- und Sozialgeschichte des deutschen Kaisserreichs* (Stuttgart: Franz Steiner Verlag, 1985), pp. 93, 98–100 passim; Jürgen Kuczynski, *Die Geschichte der Lage der Arbeiter unter dem Kapitalismus: Vol. 3, Part 1, Darstellung der Lage der Arbeiter in Deutschland von 1871 bis 1900* (Berlin: Tribune, 1962), pp. 43ff.

100. Webster, *Industrial Imperialism in Italy*, pp. 167–90. See also Franklin Hugh Adler, "Italian Industrialists from Liberalism to Fascism" (Unpublished Ph.D. Dissertation: University of Chicago, 1980), ch. 1, pp. 48–106.

101. Neufeld, *Italy*, pp. 341 and 377; Seton-Watson, *Italy*, p. 298.

102. Westerståhl, *Svensk fackföreningsrörelse*, p. 58.

103. Peter Stearns, "Against the Strike Threat: Employer Policy Toward Labor Agitation in France, 1900–1914," *Journal of Modern History*, vol. 40, no. 4 (December 1968), pp. 474–500, especially pp. 488–89.

104. Charles Maier, *Recasting Bourgeois Europe: Stabilization in France, Germany and Italy in the Decade After World War I* (Princeton: Princeton University Press, 1975), pp. 75–76.

105. Henry Ehrmann, *Organized Business in France* (Princeton: Princeton University Press, 1957), pp. 3–57.

106. This commonly advanced interpretation has been developed for the postwar context by a comparison of Britain and Sweden by Geoffrey K. Ingham, *Strikes and Industrial Conflict: Britain and Scandinavia* (London: Macmillan, 1974).

107. Data on the distribution of industrial employees by size of firm are not available for Norway for the years before World War II. It is suggestive that, in 1958, 73 percent of industrial employees in Norway were in firms of fewer than ten employees. For Denmark, the figure for the same year was 52 percent. My use of Norway as an example of a society whose industrial structure was characterized by petit bourgeois production is based on the work of Gosta Esping-Andersen, *Politics Against Markets: The Social Democratic Road to Power* (Princeton: Princeton University Press, 1985), p. 54 passim.

108. On Sweden, see Esping-Andersen, *Politics Against Markets*, ch. 2. On Germany, see Chapter 3, pp. 63ff.

109. On this point, see Geary, *European Labor Protest*, pp. 74ff; Dick Geary, "The German Labor Movement, 1848–1918," *European Studies Review*, vol. 6, no. 3 (1976), p. 310; Dieter Fricke, *Zur organisation und Tätigkeit der deutschen Arbeiterbewegung, 1890–1914: Dokumente und Materialien* (Leipzig: Verlag En-

zyklopadie, 1962), pp. 73ff and 210ff; Harry J. Marks, "The Sources of Reformism in the Social Democratic Party of Germany, 1890–1914," *Journal of Modern History*, vol. 11, no. 3 (September 1939), pp. 353ff.

110. Moore, *Injustice*, p. 183.

111. Geary, *European Labor Protest*, pp. 40–47, 74–80, 95–104.

112. On the New Unions, see Hinton, *Labor and Socialism*, pp. 40ff.

113. Bäckström, *Arbettarrörelsen i Sverige*, vol. 2, pp. 29ff.

114. Lange, "Arbeiderpartiet 1905–1914," pp. 93ff. As it was, the war would soon provide one more reason for such legislation, and it would be enacted the following year.

115. A. J. C. Rüter, *De spoorwegstakingen van 1903: Een spiegel der arbeidersbeweging in Nederland* (Leiden: E. J. Brill, 1935), pp. 222ff.

116. W. H. Vermeulen, "1901–1914," in W. J. Van Welderen baron Rengers, ed., *Schets eener parlementaire geschiedenis van Nederland*, vol. 3 (The Hague: Martinus Nijhoff, 1949), pp. 100–16.

117. Moore, *Injustice*, p. 183.

118. Ibid., p. 183 passim.

119. Raymond Carr, *Spain, 1808–1975*, 2nd ed. (Oxford: Oxford University Press, 1982), p. 359.

120. Webster, *Industrial Imperialism in Italy*, pp. 167–90; Adler, "Italian Industrialists," pp. 48–106.

121. Westerståhl, *Svensk fackföreningsrörelse*, pp. 77ff; Bäckström, *Arbetarrörelsen*, vol. 2, pp. 94ff.

122. Geary, *European Labor Protest*, pp. 107ff.

123. Bull, *Norsk fagbevegelse*, p. 57.

124. The words are from a speech Legien delivered to the SPD at the Gotha Conference of 1896. *Protokolle über die Verhandlungen der Sozialdemokratischen Partei Deutschlands, Abgehalten zu Gotha, 11–16 October 1896*, p. 157.

Chapter 6

1. James Joll, *Europe Since 1870: An International History* (London: Weidenfeld, 1973), p. 256.

2. On the discrediting of liberalism, see especially Karl Polanyi, *The Great Transformation* (Boston: Beacon Press, 1957; and Michael Freeden, *Liberalism Divided: A Study in British Political Thought, 1914–1939* (London: Oxford University Press, 1986).

3. Robert Keith Middlemas, *Politics in Industrial Society: The Experience of the British System Since 1911* (London: André Deutsch, 1979), p. 133.

4. Cited in ibid., p. 144.

5. Cited in ibid., p. 145.

6. The Communist share of the popular vote, which stagnated at about 10 percent throughout the 1920s, rose from 8.3 to 15.3 percent between 1932 and 1936, that is, during the years in which it nominally abandoned its Stalinism and endorsed the Republican institutions. Peter Flora, *State, Economy and Society in Western Europe, 1815–1975. A Data Handbook: Volume I. The Growth of Mass Democracies* (Chicago: St. James Press, 1983), p. 115.

7. For Britain:

	Disputes	Nos. Involved	Days Lost
1915	672	448,000	2,953,000
1916	532	276,000	2,446,000
1917	730	872,000	5,647,000
1918	1165	1,116,000	5,875,000

For France:

	Disputes	Nos. Involved	Days Lost
1915	98	9,344	44,344
1916	315	41,409	235,907
1917	696	293,810	1,481,621
1918	499	176,187	979,632

Sources: (Britain) Keith Middlemas, *Politics in Industrial Society,* p. 105. (France) Marjorie R. Clark, *A History of the French Labor Movement, 1910–1928* (Berkeley: University of California Press, 1930), p. 53.

8. David Thomson, *Democracy in France Since 1870,* 4th. ed. (London: Oxford University Press, 1964), p. 45.

9. Among the discussions of the British response to labor that I have found most insightful are Middlemas, *Politics in Industrial Society,* and Alan Fox, *History and Heritage: The Social Origins of the British Industrial Relations System* (London: Allen and Unwin, 1985).

10. Middlemas, *Politics in Industrial Society,* p. 154.

11. Ibid., pp. 163 and 202.

12. Joel Colton, *Léon Blum: Humanist in Politics* (Durham, N.C.: Duke University Press, 1987), p. 170.

13. Val Lorwin, *The French Labor Movement* (Cambridge: Harvard University Press, 1954), p. 55; David Saposs, *The Labor Movement in Post-War France* (New York: Columbia University Press, 1931), pp. 136–37.

14. John Lovell and B. C. Roberts, *A Short History of the TUC* (London: Macmillan, 1968), p. 101.

15. Hugh A. Clegg, *A History of British Trade Unions Since 1889: Volume II, 1911–1933* (Oxford: Clarendon Press, 1985), p. 306.

16. Lovell and Roberts, *The TUC,* p. 100.

17. Clegg, *British Trade Unions,* p. 308.

18. Lovell and Roberts, *The TUC,* p. 100 and passim.

19. Ibid., p. 59.

20. From 1914 to 1919, the money wage index rose more slowly than the cost of living index. Only in 1919–20, did it rise more quickly; in 1921, the cost of living index (CLI) fell more quickly than money wages. After 1921, however, the money wage index (MWI) fell more quickly than the cost of living index. Thus, workers lost purchasing power between 1914 and 1919, gained it between 1919 and 1921, and lost it thereafter.

	1914	1916	1917	1918	1919	1920	1921	1922	1923
CLI	63.6	91.3	114	130	141	171	127	115	113
MWI	52	61	72	93	121	162	130	101	100

(1930 = 100) *Source:* Middlemas, *Politics in Industrial Society*, p. 124.

21. Middlemas, *Politics in Industrial Society*, p. 134.

22. Ibid.

23. James Hinton, *Labour and Socialism: A History of the British Labor Movement, 1867–1974* (Brighton: Wheatsheaf Books, 1983), p. 110.

24. Cited in Middlemas, *Politics in Industrial Society*, p. 150.

25. Hinton, *Labour and Socialism*, p. 112.

26. Middlemas, *Politics in Industrial Society*, p. 151.

27. Lovell and Roberts, *The TUC*, p. 64.

28. Hinton, *Labour and Socialism*, p. 115.

29. The 1924 General Council report to the TUC makes it evident that on this final score, not much had changed three years later: "It is regretted that the General Council is not kept adequately informed of negotiations which are being conducted between unions and employers' associations. . . . The Council is sometimes entirely dependent on press reports, and disputes of first class importance may be developing, a strike or lock-out may take place, without the Council having first hand knowledge." (*Source:* Lovell and Roberts, *The TUC*, p. 81.)

30. Keith Middlemas aptly summarizes the polarization the confrontation induced: "It was obvious that the coal owners would seek to force wages down, and that, to defend themselves against a policy of wage-cutting, other unions were virtually bound to support the miners; also that, to ensure a general saving in the price of basic energy and hence of industrial costs, the NCEO [National Congress of Employer Organizations] were bound to stand by the Coal Owners' Association." (Middlemas, *Politics in Industrial Society*, p. 197).

31. Lovell and Roberts, *The TUC*, pp. 82–86.

32. For background on the 1926 strike, see the essays in Jeffrey Skelley, ed., *The General Strike 1926* (London: Lawrence and Wishart, 1976); Alan Bullock, *The Life and Times of Ernest Bevin* (London: Heinemann, 1960), pp. 279–371; Wilfred H. Crook, *The General Strike: A Study of Labor's Tragic Weapon in Theory and Practice* (Chapel Hill: University of North Carolina Press, 1931).

33. For background on the Samuel Report and Steel-Maitland's views, see Middlemas, *Politics in Industrial Society*, pp. 190–200.

34. Background on the wartime collaboration can be found in Richard Kuisel, *Capitalism and the State in Modern France, Renovation and Economic Management in the Twentieth Century* (London: Cambridge University Press, 1981), pp. 31–59.

35. For the text of the Minimum Program, see Léon Jouhaux, *Le Syndicalisme et la CGT* (Paris: Bibliotheque d'evolution sociale, 1920), pp. 205–13.

36. On the CGT's structure, see Eduard Shorter and Charles Tilly, *Strikes in France, 1830–1968* (London: Cambridge University Press, 1974), pp. 168–72; Theodore Zeldin, *France, 1848–1945: Ambition and Love* (Oxford: Oxford University Press, 1979), pp. 230–60; Bernard Georges and Denise Tintant, *Léon Jouhaux: cinquante ans de syndicalisme* (Paris: Presses Universitaires de France, 1962), pp. 336–41.

37. Kuisel, *Capitalism and the State*, pp. 31–59; Georges and Tintant, *Léon Jouhaux*, pp. 336ff.

38. Georges and Tintant, *Léon Jouhaux*, pp. 336–41.

39. Maurice Labi, *La grande division des travailleurs: prémière scission de la CGT (1914–1921)* (Paris: Les Editions Ouvrières, 1964), pp. 118ff.

40. David J. Saposs, *The Labor Movement in Postwar France* (New York: Columbia University Press 1931), pp. 191–92.

41. On the strike, see Nicholas Papayanis, "Masses révolutionnaires et directions réformistes: les tensions au cours des grèves des métallurgistes français en 1919," *Le mouvement social*, no. 93 (October–December 1975), pp. 51–73; Bertrand Abhervé, "Les origines la grève des méttallurgistes parisiens, juin 1919," *Le mouvement social*, no. 93 (October–December 1975), pp. 75–85.

42. Annie Kriegel, "Histoire du mouvement ouvrier français, 1914–1920" (Unpublished Ph.D. Dissertation: University of Paris, 1964), p. 404.

43. Kriegel, "Histoire du mouvement," pp. 479–80.

44. Clark, *History*, p. 88.

45. Ibid., pp. 88ff.

46. See, for example, the arguments of Abhervé, "La grève des métallurgistes," and Papayanis, "Masses révolutionnaires."

47. It then sank to 70,000 in the second half of 1920. For the figures, see Labi, *La grande division*, pp. 248–49.

48. Kriegel, "Histoire du mouvement," pp. 275–76.

49. Ibid., p. 401.

50. In many unions, membership and then leadership shifted sharply, if not always decisively, to the left in the three years following the armistice. See Labi, *La grande division*, pp. 271, 292, 312–13.

51. Kriegel, "Histoire du mouvement," p. 401 passim.

52. Jean-Paul Brunet, *Saint-Denis, la ville rouge: Socialisme et communisme en banlieue ouvriere, 1890–1939* (Paris: Hachette, 1980), ch. 10.

53. Kriegel, "Histoire du mouvement," p. 312.

54. The restraining effects of leadership independent of ideology are apparent in Brunet, *Saint-Denis*, ch. 10.

55. Laurent Batsch and Michel Bouvet, *CGT autour de la scission de 1921* (Paris: Editions La Breche, 1983), p. 98.

56. Brunet, *Saint-Denis*, p. 220.

57. Kriegel, "Histoire du mouvement," p. 424.

58. Georges and Tintant, *Léon Jouhaux*, pp. 382ff.

59. Kriegel, "Histoire du mouvement," pp. 485–86.

60. Ibid., p. 492.

61. Ibid., chs. 5 and 6.

62. Clark, *History*, p. 96.

63. Ibid., p. 97.

64. Charles S. Maier, *Recasting Bourgeois Europe: Stabilization in France, Germany and Italy in the Decade After World War I* (Princeton: Princeton University Press, 1975), pp. 79f.

65. Ibid., p. 80 passim.

66. This strategy is discussed by Georges LeFranc, who was the leader of the teachers' union. See his *Le mouvement syndical sous la Troisième République* (Paris: Payot, 1967), pp. 283ff.

67. Theodore Zeldin, *France, 1848–1945: Ambition and Love* (Oxford: Oxford University Press, 1979), p. 276.

68. Zeldin, *Ambition and Love*, p. 277.

69. Clark, *History*, pp. 99–114.

70. The literature on the Popular Front is vast. In addition to the titles cited below, see Louis Bodin and Jean Touchard, *Front populaire 1936* (Paris: A. Colin, 1961); Nathaniel Greene, *Crisis and Decline: The French Socialist Party in the Popular Front Era* (Ithaca: Cornell University Press, 1969); Georges LeFranc, *Histoire du front populaire, 1934–1938* (Paris: Payot, 1965); Daniel Guérin, *Front populaire, révolution manquée*, rev. ed. (Paris: Maspero, 1970).

71. Arthur Mitzman, "The French Working Class and the Blum Government (1936–37)," *International Review of Social History*, vol. 9, part 3 (1964), p. 366.

72. Colton, *Léon Blum*, p. 136.

73. Ibid., p. 137.

74. See Alexander Werth, *Which Way France?* (London: Harper & Brothers, 1937), pp. 72–92.

75. Henry Ehrmann says that "the CPGF flatly turned down requests by the government to facilitate the working of the new legislation through a new and more elaborate understanding with labor." Henry Walter Ehrmann, *Organized Business in France* (Princeton: Princeton University Press, 1957), p. 37.

76. Mitzman, "French Working Class," pp. 374–78.

77. Joel Colton, *Compulsory Labor Arbitration in France, 1936–1939* (New York: King's Crown Press, 1951), pp. 36–38.

78. Arthur Mitzman has discussed at length the alienation of workers from the government and emphasized that this was the result of the government's policies rather than the machinations of the Communist Party. Mitzman argues that the upsurge of strikes in the autumn of 1936 and subsequently was not caused by communists in the CGT, but rather that the party was eventually compelled against its strategy to embrace these strikes because it was itself losing its working class base. "French Working Class," p. 383 passim.

79. Ehrmann, *Organized Business in France*, pp. 115–20.

80. Michel Collinet, *L'Ouvrier français: II. Esprit du syndicalisme* (Paris: Editions ouvrières, 1951), p. 127.

81. Collinet, *Esprit du syndicalisme*, p. 125. Ehrmann, using an official union estimate, says that there were still about 2 million members at the outbreak of the war. The actual figure was probably closer to Collinet's. In either case, membership had collapsed.

82. On the nine-point program, see Hans von Greyerz, "Der Bundesstaat seit 1848," in Emil Vogt et al., *Handbuch der Schwizer Geschichte*, Band 2 (Zürich: Verlag Berichthaus, 1979), p. 1138.

83. Greyerz, "Der Bundesstaat," pp. 1133–40; Christopher Hughes, *Switzerland* (New York: Praeger, 1975), pp. 111–15; Erich Gruner, *Die Parteien in der Schweiz* (Bern: Francke Verlag, 1969), pp. 137–41; Ulrich Imhof et al., *Geschichte der Schweiz und der Schweizer*, Band 3 (Basel: Helburg and Lichtenhahn Verlag, 1983), pp. 135–40.

84. On the introduction of proportional representation and its impact, see Greyerz, "Der Bundesstaat," pp. 1140–42; George Arthur Codding, Jr., *The Federal Government of Switzerland* (Boston: Houghton Mifflin Co., 1961), pp. 75–78.

85. For the SGB membership, see Eduard Weckerle, *The Trade Unions in*

Switzerland (Bern: Swiss Federation of Trade Unions, 1947), p. 65. Data on the male industrial labor force are from B. R. Mitchell, *European Historical Statistics, 1750–1970* (New York: Columbia University Press, 1975), p. 162. On the coverage of collective contracts, see Lukas Burckhardt, "Industry-Labor Relations: Industrial Peace," in J. Murray Luck, ed., *Modern Switzerland* (Palo Alto, Calif.: SPOSS, 1978), p. 196.

86. Weckerle, *Trade Unions in Switzerland*, pp. 27–33; Burckhardt, "Industry-Labor Relations," p. 196.

87. Weckerle, *Trade Unions in Switzerland*, pp. 61–33.

88. Ibid., pp. 42 and 64.

89. Ibid.

90. Ibid., pp. 42 and 64ff.

91. Luck, *A History*, p. 543.

92. On the composition of the Federal Council, see Christopher Hughes, *The Parliament of Switzerland* (London: Cassell and Co., 1962), pp. 74–78.

93. On the antisocialist animus that drove the coalition, see Greyerz, "Der Bundesstaat," pp. 1167–68.

94. Ibid., pp. 1164ff and 1178.

95. Gruner, *Der Parteien in der Schweiz*, pp. 143ff; Greyerz, "Der Bundesstaat," pp. 1178–80.

96. Ulrich Imhof et al., *Geschichte der Schweiz*, Band 3, pp. 165ff; Greyerz, "Der Bundesstaat," pp. 1166 and 1199ff.

97. The level of strike activity in Switzerland and elsewhere in Europe in the 1920s is discussed in Chapter 7, pp. 256–57.

98. We will compare the course of real wages in Switzerland with real wages elsewhere in Europe in Chapter 7. For the moment let me note only that Switzerland managed to combine in the 1920s the lowest unemployment rate with the second worst improvement in real wages in Europe. Unemployment was nil; real wages remained stagnant. See Chapter 7, pp. 255–56.

99. Gruner, *Parteien*, p. 178.

100. On the negotiation of the accord and the circumstances that led to it, see Hughes, *Switzerland*, pp. 115–17; Luck, *History of Switzerland*, pp. 563–64; Burckhardt, "Industry-Labor Relations," pp. 173–98.

101. Burckhardt, "Industry-Labor Relations," pp. 194–95.

102. Ibid., pp. 175–77.

103. Ibid., p. 178; Luck, *History of Switzerland*, pp. 544–46.

104. On the evolution of the trade unions into employers' junior partner in the operation of industry, see Peter J. Katzenstein, *Small States in World Markets: Industrial Policy in Europe* (Ithaca: Cornell University Press, 1985), pp. 80ff.

105. The following table provides the average percentage of the noncommunist, socialist/labor vote by decade and country.

	1920s	1930s
France (PSF only)	20	20
France (PSF + PCF)	28	32
Britain	33	34
Switzerland	25	27
Netherlands	22	22

(continued)

	1920s	1930s
Belgium	37	33
Denmark	35	44
Germany (SPD only)	25	21
Germany (SPD + ISDP + KPD)	37	34
Norway (Labor only)	26	37
Norway (Lab + SDWP)	32	—
Sweden	36	44
Italy (socialist only)	32 (1919)	25 (1921)

Source: Flora, ed., *State, Economy,* vol. 1, pp. 89ff.

106. Hinton, *Labour and Socialism,* p. 132.

107. Colton, *Léon Blum,* p. 276.

108. Ibid., p. 278.

109. Hinton, *Labour and Socialism,* pp. 144–48.

110. "Had Lloyd George enjoyed the confidence and support of the fifty-eight Liberals in the Commons, he might have used the situation to the party's and the country's advantage. But at least one-third of the Parliamentary Liberal Party were distrustful of him. . . . From early 1930 Lloyd George and MacDonald were in informal coalition—many found this offensive. In October 1930, the Liberal whip resigned and Sir John suggested that every Liberal M.P. should vote independently of any official party policy. Simon and several others virtually withdrew from party councils." Alfred F. Havighurst, *Twentieth Century Britain,* 2nd ed. (New York: Harper & Row, 1966), p. 220.

111. See Peter Gourevitch, *Politics in Hard Times: Comparative Responses to International Economic Crises* (Ithaca, N.Y.: Cornell University Press, 1986), p. 136 and passim. This is one of the few points on which I have found myself in disagreement with the argument Gourevitch has made in his exceedingly important study of responses to international economic crises. Gourevitch also places more weight than I do on the depression itself and the responses to it as causes of the regime continuities and shifts of the interwar years. I have placed a great deal more emphasis on the prewar legacies of mass mobilization discussed in previous chapter in differentiating the range of outcomes possible in each society, *given the occurrence of the war.* In the argument I am developing, economic crises and crises more generally are endemic to politics. They have, as Gourevitch's own work makes clear, a certain cyclical regularity. The question is thus why some political and economic orders have been able to endure them with few institutional adjustments, others are capable of responding in innovative ways, and others must respond in ways that deform civilized life for generations to come.

In the main, although I am more interested in this chapter and in Chapters 7 and 8 with *institutional* continuities and shifts, while Gourevitch accents *policy* continuities and shifts, our arguments are parallel and complementary rather than in conflict. We both argue for the importance of coalitional possibilities in limiting policy possibilities. In addition, in the present chapter and especially in Chapters 7 and 8, I argue that the prewar patterns of economic and political organization in the labor market limited the coalitional possibilities, which in turn limited the interwar state and market institutions and the policy possibilities available to societies.

112. On the economic policies of Blum's government, see Jean Bouvier, "Un débat toujours ouvert: La politique économique du Front Populaire," *Le mouvement*

social, no. 54 (January–March 1966), pp. 175–81; M. Kalecki, "The Lesson of the Blum Experiment," *Economic Journal*, vol. 48, no. 189 (March 1938), pp. 26–41; Robert Marjolin, "Reflections on the Blum Experiment," *Economica*, vol. 5 (New Series), no. 18 (May 1938), pp. 177–91; Alfred Sauvy, *Histoire économique de la France entre les deux guerres: Vol. 2, 1931–39* (Paris: Fayard, 1967).

113. Colton, *Léon Blum*, p. 186.

114. Ibid., p. 193.

115. On British and French neo-orthodoxy, see Gourevitch, *Politics in Hard Times*. On Swiss economic policies in response to the depression and the rejection by referendum of the Swiss Social Democrats' plans for stimulation of the economy, see Francoise Loertscher-Rouge, "La politique de la FOHM dans l'horlogerie lors de la crise des années trente," *Revue Européenne des Sciences Sociales*, vol. 15, no. 42 (1977), pp. 143–99. See also Hans Von Greyerz, "Der Bundesstaat seit 1848," in Emil Vogt et al., *Handbuch der Schweizer Geschichte*, Band 2 (Zürich: Verlag Berichthaus, 1979), pp. 1191–98.

Chapter 7

1. On the Radical–Social Democratic coalition and politics during the war, see Oluf Bertolt, Ernst Christiansen, and Poul Hansen, *En Bygning vi rejser: Den politiske arbejderbevaegelses historie i Danmark* (Copenhagen: Forlaget Fremad, 1954), vol. 1, pp. 359ff.

2. On the level of strike activity, see Peter Flora, Franz Kraus, and Winfried Pfenning, eds., *State, Economy and Society in Western Europe, 1815–1975, A Data Handbook. Volume II: The Growth of Industrial Societies and Capitalist Economies* (Chicago: St. James Press, 1987), pp. 682ff.

3. On the crisis and its various interpretations, see Tage Kårsted, *Påskeskrisen, 1920* (Århus: Universitetsforlaget i Århus, 1973).

4. On the social bases of the parties, see Chapter 3, pp. 73–80, and Chapter 4, pp. 133–39. See also Palle Svensson, "Support for the Danish Social Democratic Party, 1924–1939—Growth and Response," *Scandinavian Political Studies*, vol. 9 (1974), pp. 127–46.

5. Barrington Moore, Jr., *Injustice: The Social Bases of Obedience and Revolt* (White Plains, N.Y.: M. E. Sharpe, 1978), pp. 376ff.

6. The story of the dissolution of this coalition had been brilliantly told by Charles Maier in, *Recasting Bourgeois Europe: Stabilization in France, Germany and Italy in the Decade After World War I* (Princeton: Princeton University Press, 1975), pp. 53–88, 233–305, 355–87.

7. M. Rainer Lepsius, "From Fragmented Party Democracy to Government by Emergency Decree and National Socialist Takeover: Germany," in Juan J. Linz and Alfred Stepan, eds., *The Breakdown of Democratic Regimes: Europe* (Baltimore: Johns Hopkins University Press, 1978), pp. 34–79.

8. Lepsius, "Germany," pp. 34–79; Maier, *Recasting Bourgeois Europe*.

9. Lepsius, "Germany," p. 44.

10. Stolper's words originally appeared in *Der deutsche Volkswirt*, vol. 13 (December 1929), p. 333, and are cited in Lepsius, "Germany," p. 44.

11. Carl-Göran Andrae, "The Swedish Labor Movement and the 1917–1918 Revolution," in Steven Koblik, ed., *Sweden's Development from Poverty to Affluence, 1750–1970*, trans. Joanne Johnson (Minneapolis: University of Minnesota Press, 1975), p. 234.

12. Andrae, "1917–1918 Revolution," p. 233.

13. Ibid., pp. 232–54.

14. Koblik, "Introduction to Chapter 10," in Koblik, ed., *Sweden's Development*, p. 255.

15. Andrae, "1917–1918 Revolution," p. 250.

16. It was, in fact, ultimately over questions of Leninist organization that the party broke with the Third International: it refused to end collective affiliation through the trade unions; it refused to recreate itself as a secretive and centralized band of cadres. On the Norwegian Labor party and trade unions during these years, see Berge Furre, *Norsk historie, 1905–1940* (Oslo: Det Norske Samlaget, 1971), pp. 105ff.; Knut Langfeldt, *Moskva-tesene i norsk politik* (Oslo: Universitetsforlaget, 1961); Håkon Meyer, "Arbeiderpartiet, 1914–1923," in Halvdan Koht, ed., *Det norske arbeiderpartis historie, 1887–1937*, vol. 2 (Oslo: Det Norske Arbeiderpartis Forlag, 1939), pp. 179ff.; Hans Frederik Dahl, *Norge mellom krigene: Det norske samfunnet i krise og konflikt, 1918–1940* (Oslo: Pax Forlag, 1971).

17. See Chapter 4, p. 124.

18. The franchise extension came about principally by a lowering of the age requirement from twenty-five to twenty-three years; paupers were also given the right to vote. The rate of participation among adults over twenty years of age rose from 80.4 percent in 1918 to 86.9 percent in 1921. Women (thought to be more conservative than men) had been given a qualified right to vote in 1909 (as a counterweight to the Labor party, in fact) and an equal right to vote in 1915. Peter Flora et al., eds., *State, Economy, and Society in Western Europe, 1815–1975, A Data Handbook. Volume 1: The Growth of Mass Democracies and Welfare States* (Chicago: St. James Press, 1983), p. 137.

19. See especially Furre, *Norske historie*, pp. 124–76; and Hans Fredrik Dahl, *Fra klassekamp til nasjonal samling; Arbeiderpartiet og det nasjonale spørsmål i 30-årene* (Oslo: Pax Forlag, 1969).

20. Furre, *Norske historie*, pp. 124–76.

21. Ibid., p. 132.

22. On the continued fragmentation of the middle classes in the interwar period, see Stein Rokkan, "Geography, Religion and Social Class: Cross-Cutting Cleavages in Norwegian Politics," in Stein Rokkan and Seymour Martin Lipset, eds., *Party Systems and Voter Alignment: Cross-national Perspectives* (New York: Free Press, 1967), pp. 367–444.

23. Furre, *Norske historie*, p. 172 passim.

24. On the elections of 1919 and 1921 and the Italian case more generally, see Paolo Farneti, "Social Conflict, Parliamentary Fragmentation, Institutional Shift, and the Rise of Fascism: Italy," in Linz and Stepan, eds., *Breakdown*, pp. 3–33.

25. The fragmentation of the secular middle classes is a central focus of most accounts of the period. See, especially, Nino Valeri, *Da Giolitti a Mussolini: Momenti della crisi del liberalismo* (Florence: Parenti, 1956); Roberto Vivarelli, *Il dopoguerra in Italia e l'avvento del fascismo, 1918–1922: vol. 1, Dalla fine della guerra all'impresa di Fiume* (Naples: Istituto Italiano per gli Studi Storici, 1967).

26. Christopher Seton-Watson, *Italy from Liberalism to Fascism, 1870–1925* (London: Methuen, 1967), p. 548.

27. Seton-Watson, *Italy*, pp. 547–53, 561–70.

28. Ibid., pp. 585–612.

29. Pietro Nenni, *Storia di quattro anni, 1919–1922*, 2nd ed. (Rome: Einaudi, 1946), p. 29.

30. Angelo Tasca, *Nascita e avvento del fascismo: L'Italia dal 1918 al 1922* (Florence: La Nuova Italia, 1950), p. 116; Luigi Salvatorelli and G. Mira, *Storia del fascismo* (Rome: Edizioni di Novissima, 1952), p. 70.

31. Seton-Watson, *Italy*, p. 561, especially fn. 2.

32. Stefano Jacini, *Storia del Partito Popolare Italiano* (Milan: Garzanti, 1951), pp. 130–31; E. P. Howard, *Il Partito Popolare Italiano* (Florence: La Nuova Italia, 1957), pp. 148–50.

33. Stanley G. Payne, *The Spanish Revolution: A Study of the Social and Political Tensions That Culminated in the Civil War in Spain* (New York: Norton, 1970), p. 23.

34. Gerald Brenan, *The Spanish Labyrinth. An Account of the Social and Political Background of the Civil War* (Cambridge: Cambridge University Press, 1960), p. 64.

35. Ibid., pp. 64–66.

36. Ibid., p. 74, fn. 2.

37. Payne, *Spanish Revolution*, p. 83 passim; Raymond Carr, *Spain, 1808–1975*, 2nd ed. (Oxford: Oxford University Press, 1982), pp. 564–603.

38. Payne, *Spanish Revolution*, p. 83.

39. Anthony D. McIvor, "Spanish Labor Policy During the Dictablanda of Primo De Rivera" (Unpublished Ph.D. Dissertation: Department of History, University of California, San Diego, 1982); Carr, *Spain, 1808–1975*, pp. 564–603.

40. Payne, *Spanish Revolution*, p. 78.

41. McIvor, "Spanish Labor Policy"; Carr, *Spain*, pp. 570–73.

42. By June 1932, UGT membership incorporated 31 percent of industrial workers in Spain. In Italy, the same figure for the socialist union CGL was 35 percent in 1920. The UGT figure is based on the data from Brenan, *Labyrinth*, pp. 273 and 295; and B. R. Mitchell, *European Historical Statistics, 1750–1970* (New York: Columbia University Press, 1975), p. 161. The CGL figure is calculated from the data by Maurice Neufeld, *Italy: School for Awakening Countries: The Italian Labor Movement in Its Political, Social, and Economic Setting from 1800 to 1960* (New York: Cornell University Press, 1961), p. 368; A. James Gregor, *Italian Fascism and Developmental Dictatorship* (Princeton: Princeton University Press, 1979), p. 183; and Flora et al., *State, Economy, and Society*, vol. 2, p. 555.

43. McIvor, "Spanish Labor Policy, pp. 1–25; Carr, *Spain*, pp. 574–81.

44. Brenan, *Labyrinth*, p. 79.

45. McIvor, "Spanish Labor Policy," p. 14.

46. On the lack of polarization, see Juan Linz, "From Great Hopes to Civil War: The Breakdown of Democracy in Spain," in Linz and Stepan, *Breakdown*, pp. 143–44.

47. Carr, *Spain*, pp. 591–603.

48. The literature on the Republican years is enormous but often remains flawed by partisanship. Among the best works, either for their insights or their empirical

richness, are Gabriel Jackson, *The Spanish Republic and the Civil War, 1931–1939* (Princeton: Princeton University Press, 1965); Juan Linz, "From Great Hopes to Civil War"; Juan Linz, "The Party System of Spain: Past and Future," in Lipset and Rokkan, eds., *Party Systems and Voter Alignments*, pp. 197–282; Ricardo de la Cierva, *Historia de la Guerra Civil Española, Antecedents: Monoarquí y Repuública, 1898–1936* (Madrid: San Martín, 1969); Manuel Tuñon de Lara, *La II República*, 2 vols. (Madrid: Siglo XXI de España Editores, 1976); Edward Malefakis, *Agrarian Reform and Peasant Revolution in Spain: Origins of the Civil War* (New Haven: Yale University Press, 1970); Payne, *The Spanish Revolution*.

49. Payne, *The Spanish Revolution*, p. 103.

50. See especially Jackson, *Spanish Republic*, pp. 56–78, 98–121.

51. Jackson, *Spanish Republic*, p. 141.

52. See, especially, Jackson, *Spanish Republic*, pp. 121ff.

53. For an analysis of the elections held during the Republic, see Jackson, *Spanish Republic*, pp. 518ff.

54. Eric Hansen, "Depression Decade Crisis: Social Democracy and Planisme in Belgium and the Netherlands, 1929–1939," *Journal of Contemporary History*, vol. 16, no. 2 (April 1981), pp. 300–01.

55. On coalitions and the balances of party power between the wars, see Jan Dhondt, "De evolutie van de partijen tussen de twee wereldoorlogen," *Res Publica*, vol. 4 (1962), pp. 370–80; Hans Daalder, "Parties and Politics in the Netherlands," *Political Studies*, vol. 3, no. 1 (February 1955), pp. 1–16.

56. On British neo-orthodoxy, see Peter Gourevitch, *Politics in Hard Times: Comparative Responses to International Economic Crises* (Ithaca, N.Y.: Cornell University Press, 1986), pp. 135–40; on Switzerland, see Françoise Loertscher-Rouge, "La politique de la FOHM dans l'horlogerie lors de la crise des années trente (1930–1937)," *Revue Européenne des Sciences Sociales*, vol. 15, no. 42 (1977), pp. 143–99.

57. For an excellent discussion of the Dutch and Belgian responses to the depression and the political debate that ensued, see Hansen, "Depression Decade Crisis."

58. Hansen, "Depression Decade Crisis," p. 315.

59. The fraction of the labor force (now male and female) enrolled in a union affiliated with the national socialist confederation in the late 1920s was as follows: Switzerland, 20 percent; Netherlands, 27 percent; France, 33 percent (CGT and CGTU); Belgium, 37 percent; Britain, 40 percent; Germany, 44 percent; Norway, 47 percent; Sweden, 83 percent; Denmark, 92 percent. These figures refer to all confederation members as a fraction of the industrial labor force. The latter excludes workers in services, government offices, and agriculture. Since some trade unionists were actually employed in these excluded sectors, the figures overstate to some degree the fraction of the industrial workforce actually enrolled. In France, half of the CGT membership consisted of government employees in the late 1920s. Elsewhere, government employees more typically accounted for about 10 percent of trade unionists. Agricultural workers have been deleted from the trade union memberships. *Sources:* Flora, Kraus, and Pfenning, *State, Economy, Society*, vol. 2, pp. 441ff; Theodore Zeldin, *France, 1848–1945: Ambition and Love*, (Oxford: Oxford University Press, 1979), pp. 277–79; A. H. Halsey, ed., *Trends in British Society Since 1900: A Guide to the Changing Social Structure of Britain* (London: Macmillan, 1972), p. 125; J. Dhondt, E. Evalenko, and R. Resjohazy, "L'influence de la crise de 1929 sur les

mouvements ouvriers en Belgique," in Internationaal Instituut Voor Sociale Geschiedenis Amsterdam, ed., *Mouvements ouvriers et dépression économique de 1929 à 1939* (Assen: Van Gorcum, 1966), pp. 81–82; Walter Galenson, *The Danish System of Labor Relations: A Study in Industrial Peace* (Cambridge: Harvard University Press, 1952), p. 283; Karl Zwing, *Geschichte der Deutschen Freien Gewerkschaften: Ein Kurzgefasster Abriss* (Jena: Volkesbuchhandlung, 1928); Gregor, *Italian Fascism and Developmental Dictatorship*, p. 183; Ger Harmsen and Bob Reinalda, *Voor de bevrijding van de arbeid: Beknopte geschiedenis van de nederlandse vakbeweging* (Nijmegen: Socialistiese Uitgeverij, 1975), p. 430.

60. Derek H. Aldcroft, *From Versailles to Wall Street, 1919–1929* (Berkeley: University of California Press, 1977), p. 201.

61. Data on real wages are presented on pp. 255–56.

62. The declines in 1920–21 were 27 percent for income, 25 percent for industrial production, and 24 percent for export volumes. E. Lundberg, "Business Cycle Experiences in Sweden, with Special Reference to Economic Policy Issues," in Erik Lundberg, ed., *The Business Cycle in the Post-War World* (London: Macmillan, 1955), p. 56.

63. Richard Allen Lester, "The Gold-Parity Depression in Norway and Denmark, 1925–1928, and Devaluation in Finland, 1925," Chapter 9 in R. A. Lester, *Monetary Experiments: Early American and Recent Scandinavian* (Princeton: Princeton University Press, 1939), pp. 221–22.

64. Aldcroft, *Versailles to Wall Street*, p. 150.

65. Ibid., pp. 145–48.

66. Raymond Carr collected the following data on Spanish wages and prices. Industrial wages: 1914, 100; 1920, 186. General wages: 1914, 100; 1920, 156. Prices: 1913, 100; 1915, 111; 1917, 149; 1920, 188; 1921, 182; 1922, 162. Carr, *Spain*, pp. 498–99, fn. 3. See also the indices of wages of skilled and unskilled workers in Barcelona in the electrical, textile, and metallurgy industries in the same footnote. For a detailed discussion of Spanish wages and prices, Manuel Tuñon de Lara, *El movimiento obrero en la historia de España* (Madrid: Taurus, 1972), pp. 550–72, 675–81, 755–67.

67. Tuñon de Lara, *Movimiento obrero*, pp. 755–74; McIvor, "Spanish Labor Policy," p. 14 passim.

68. Manuel Fuentes Irurozqui, *Síntesis de la economía española* (Madrid: Diana, 1946).

69. The available figures are 3.1 (1921), 3.6 (1922), 1.7 (1923), 3.4 (1926), 2.7 (1927), 2.1 (1928), 1.8 (1929). The rates for 1921, 1922, and 1923 refer to the percentage of the unemployed among the economically active population and are from James Murray Luck, *A History of Switzerland* (Palo Alto, Calif.: SPOSS, 1985), p. 553. The figures from 1926 on refer to annualized monthly averages of unemployed insured workers and are from Mitchell, *European Historical Statistics*, p. 168.

70. The figures are Sauvy's estimates for the entire labor force. Alfred Sauvy, *Histoire économique de la France entre les deux guerres: Vol. 1, 1918–1931* (Paris: Fayard, 1965), p. 459.

71. Walter Galenson and Arnold Zellner, "International Comparisons of Unemployment Rates," in National Bureau of Economic Research, ed., *The Measurement and Behavior of Unemployment* (Princeton: Princeton University Press, 1957), p. 523.

72. Galenson and Zellner, "International Comparisons," p. 523.

73. For Britain the annual rates were 14.8, 15.2, 11.3, 10.9, 11.2, 12.7, 10.6, 11.2, and 11.0. Before 1923 they refer to trade unionists; after 1923, registered unemployed. *Source:* Mitchell, *European Historical Statistics,* p. 168.

74. For the Netherlands, the annual rates were 3.3, 4.5, 4.8, 4.0, 3.7, 3.3, 3.4, 2.7, and 3.0. For Belgium, the rates were 11.5, 4.2, 1.3, 1.6, 2.4, 2.0, 2.5, 1.7, and 1.9. The Dutch rate refers to the unemployed as a percentage of the total employed labor force. The Belgian rate refers to insured workers. *Sources:* Central Bureau voor de Statistiek, *Zestig jaren statistiek in tijdreeksen. 1899–1959* (Zeist: W. de Haan, 1959), p. 44, col. 15. Mitchell, *European Historical Statistics,* pp. 166ff.

75. For Germany, the rates were 2.8, 1.5, 9.6, 13.5, 6.7, 18.0, 8.8, 8.4, and 13.1. For Sweden: 26.6, 22.9, 12.5, 10.1, 11.0, 12.2, 12.0, 10.6, and 11.2. For Norway: 17.6, 17.1, 10.6, 8.5, 13.2, 24.3, 25.4, 19.1, and 15.4. For Denmark: 19.7, 19.3, 12.7, 10.7, 14.7, 20.7, 22.5, 18.5, and 15.5. All of these rates refer to registered unemployed trade unionists. If anything, then, they tend to understate the total volume of unemployment in these societies. In contrast, the figures for Britain, France, and Switzerland are either estimates for the entire labor force (and additionally certain industries in the case of France) or registered unemployed among the entire labor force. They are probably closer to reality, therefore. The source for the data on Germany, Sweden, Norway, and Denmark is Mitchell, *European Historical Statistics,* pp. 166ff.

76. This decline is based on an increase in the cost of living index of 89 percent and of the money wage index of 67 percent. Mitchell, *European Historical Statistics,* pp. 186 and 745.

77. See the cost of living and money wage indices in ibid., pp. 187 and 746.

78. Ibid.

79. Ibid., pp. 186 and 745.

80. Ibid., pp. 187 and 746.

81. See the index of real wages in Cesare Vannutelli, "Occupazione e salari dal 1861 al 1961," in Amintore Fanfani, ed., *L'economia italiana dal 1861 al 1961: Studi nel 1' centenario dell'unita d'Italia.* Economia e storia, Ser. 6 (Milan: Giuffrè, 1961), pp. 570–71.

82. Gerhard Bry, *Wages in Germany, 1871–1945* (Princeton: Princeton University Press, 1960), p. 473.

83. K. G. Hildebrand, "Labour and Capital in the Scandinavian Countries in the Nineteenth and Twentieth Centuries," Peter Mathias and M. M. Postan, eds., *The Cambridge Economic History of Europe. Volume VII, The Industrial Economies: Capital, Labour and Enterprise. Part I, Britain, France, Germany and Scandinavia* (London: Cambridge University Press, 1978), p. 616.

84. The gains in real wages are based on the indices of real average hourly earnings of male workers in Walter Galenson, *The Danish System of Labor Relations: A Study in Industrial Peace* (Cambridge: Harvard University Press, 1952), pp. 279ff.

85. Paul Jostock, "The Long-Term Growth of National Income in Germany," in Simon Kuznets, eds., *Review of Income and Wealth,* Series 5 (London: Bowes and Bowes, 1955), p. 109.

86. The profit figures cover extractive industry, manufacturing, construction, public utilities, transport, and distribution. Peter E. Hart, *Studies in Profit, Business Saving and Investment in the United Kingdom, 1920–1962,* vol. 1 (London: Allen and Unwin, 1965). For data on wages, in addition to the sources cited previously, see

Derek H. Aldcroft, *The Inter-War Economy: Britain, 1919–1939* (London: Batsford, 1970), p. 352.

87. Flora et al., *State, Economy and Society*, vol. 2, p. 636.

88. Aldcroft, *Versailles to Wall Street*, p. 207.

89. Ibid., p. 206.

90. See the figures for industrial production, constant price net domestic product, and population change in Mitchell, *European Historical Statistics*, pp. 19ff, 356ff, 782ff.

91. The percentage rate of change in net domestic product per worker in non-agricultural activity for 1921–29 to 1931–39 was just 6.7 percent, whereas real average hourly wages in industry rose by just under 80 percent for the interwar period. See Hildebrand, "Labour and Capital," p. 616 and table IV, "Average Working Hours and Net Domestic Product Per Worker Adjusted for Changes in Working Hours," in Kjeld Bjerke, "The National Product of Denmark, 1870–1952," in Kuznets, *Income and Wealth*, p. 128.

92. These problems are discussed in Flora et al., *State, Economy and Society*, vol. 2, pp. 679–80.

93. Volume of strike activity = number of strikes × the number of strikers × the duration of the strikes. For the details, see Douglas Hibbs, Jr., "On the Political Economy of Long-Run Trends in Strike Activity," *British Journal of Political Science*, vol. 8, part 2 (April 1978), pp. 153–75. Intuitively this measure of volume seems a more satisfactory measure of strike activity than the simple number of man-days lost per 1,000 workers because it taps more fully the disruptive impact of strikes. Moreover, it provides a more powerful discriminant of strike activity among nations; the range of variation of man-days lost per 1,000 workers is surprisingly narrow. It is for this reason that I have relied primarily on Hibbs' data rather than Korpi and Shalev's. The number of man-days lost is, however, sufficient to locate the outliers Germany and Switzerland among the most and least strikeprone societies, respectively. For Germany, the arithmetic mean of man-days lost annually per 1,000 workers for 1919 through 1932 is 775; for Britain and Norway for 1919 through 1938, it is 396 and 384, respectively; for Switzerland, 1919 through 1938, it is 42. Walter Korpi and Michael Shalev, "Strikes, Power and Politics in Western Nations," *Political Power and Social Theory*, vol. 1 (1980), pp. 301–34; Hibbs, "Long-Run Trends," pp. 153–75.

94. The most useful display of these comparatively compressed trends is provided by Hibbs' graphing of strike volume in his "Long-Run Trends," fig. 2, pp. 158ff. The trends for Germany and Switzerland are found in Korpi and Shalev, fig. 1, p. 312, where they can be compared with the other nations in the Korpi-Shalev study. The logged scale that Korpi and Shalev have employed tends to flatten out variations across time and make comparatively short (ten year or less) trends difficult to discern. Their data can be supplemented by the unlogged annual data on strikers per 1,000 nonagricultural workers and more revealing logged displays of this found in Flora et al., *State, Economy and Society*, vol. 2, pp. 689ff.

95. The most effective comparison of Britain and Denmark can be made with the logged trend lines and the unlogged data in Flora et al., *State, Economy, Society*, vol. 2, pp. 682, 687, 701, and 753.

96. The figures are for about 1930. See Wilbert E. Moore, *Economic Demography of Southern and Eastern Europe* (Geneva: League of Nations, 1945), pp. 26 and 35.

97. Moore, *Economic Demography*, p. 125.

98. *Concise Statistical Yearbook of Poland* (Warsaw: Central Statistical Office, 1931), p. 29, table 4.

99. Jan Marczewski, *Planification et croissance économique des démocraties populaires*, vol. 1 (Paris: Presses Universitaires de France, 1956), p. 58; Royal Institute of International Affairs, *The Problem of International Investment* (London: Oxford University Press, 1937), p. 246.

100. For other countries, the figures would be Bulgaria, 53 percent; Estonia, 0.4 percent; Greece, 50 percent; Lithuania, 27 percent; Poland, 51 percent; Rumania, 51 percent; Yugoslavia, 61 percent. See Moore, *Economic Demography*, p. 63.

101. Based on Jozo Tomasevich, *Peasants, Politics and Economic Change in Yugoslavia* (Palo Alto, Calif.: Stanford University Press, 1955), pp. 312–14.

102. Hugh Seton-Watson, *Eastern Europe Between the Wars, 1918–1941* (London: Cambridge University Press, 1945), pp. 146–47.

103. Georg von Rauch, *The Baltic States, the Years of Independence: Estonia, Latvia, Lithuania, 1917–1940*, trans. Gerald Onn (Berkeley: University of California Press, 1974), p. 82.

104. Von Rauch, *Baltic States*, p. 84.

105. *Rocznik statystyki Rzeczypospolitej Polskiej*, vol. 4, 1925–26 (Warsaw: Druk L. Boguslawskiego, 1927), p. 26, table 5.

106. F. Beranek, "Das Judentum in Polen," in Werner Markert, ed., *Osteuropa Handbuch: Vol. 2, Polen* (Cologne: Böhlau, 1959), p. 120.

107. *Breviarul statistic al Romaniei* (Bucharest: Institul Central de Statistica, 1939), pp. 53–60.

108. Based on Werner Markert, ed., *Osteuropa Handbuch: Vol. 1, Jugoslawien* (Cologne: Böhlau, 1954), p. 16.

109. Randolph L. Braham, ed., *Hungarian Jewish Studies* (New York: World Federation of Hungarian Jews, 1966), vol. 1, p. 144, vol. 2 (1969), pp. 79, 146–48.

110. Antony Polonsky, *The Little Dictators: The History of Eastern Europe Since 1918* (London: Routledge and Kegan Paul, 1975), pp. 108–09.

111. See Von Rauch, *The Baltic States*, pp. 154–65.

112. On interwar Finland, see Risto Alapuro and Erik Allardt, "The Lapua Movement: The Threat of Rightist Takeover in Finland, 1930–1932," in Linz and Stepan, eds., *The Breakdown*, pp. 122–41; Krister Wahlbäck, *Från Mannerheim til Kekkonen: Huvudlinjer i finländsk politik, 1917–1967* (Stockholm: Bonniers, 1967); Jorma Kalela, "Right-Wing Radicalism in Finland During the Interwar Period," *Scandinavian Journal of History*, vol. 1, no. 2 (1976), pp. 105–24.

113. Hugh Seton-Watson, *Eastern Europe Between the Wars, 1918–1941* (London: Cambridge University Press, 1945), p. 204 passim.

114. Antony Polonsky, *Politics in Independent Poland, 1921–1939* (Oxford: Oxford University Press, 1972).

115. Andrew C. Janos, *The Politics of Backwardness in Hungary, 1825–1945* (Princeton: Princeton University Press, 1982), pp. 201–38.

116. István Deák, "Hungary," in Hans Rogger and Eugen Weber, eds., *The European Right: A Historical Profile* (Berkeley: University of California Press, 1965), p. 375.

117. Deák, "Hungary," pp. 364–408; Janos, *Politics of Backwardness*, pp. 190ff.

118. On the Austrian labor movement and for an account of interwar politics

highly sympathetic to the Socialists, see Charles A. Gulick, *Austria: From Habsburg to Hitler*, 2 vols. (Berkeley: University of California Press, 1948).

119. On the decline of Austro-German liberalism, see especially Robert A. Kann, *The Multinational Empire: Nationalism and National Reform in the Habsburg Monarchy* (New York: Columbia University Press, 1950), vol. 1, pp. 89–168.

120. William A. Jenks, *Austria Under the Iron Ring, 1879–1913* (Charlottesville: University of Virginia Press, 1965).

121. The words were those of Julian Dunajewski, the Minister of Finance and a Pole; quoted in Carlile A. Macartney, *The Habsburg Empire, 1790–1918* (London: Weidenfeld and Nicolson, 1969), p. 659.

122. Robert A. Kann, *A History of the Habsburg Empire, 1526–1918* (Berkeley: University of California Press, 1980), pp. 438ff.

123. In 1910, 62 percent of the Bohemian population was Czech; 37 percent was German. Seventy-one percent of the Moravian population was Czech; 22 percent was German. In 1918, about two-thirds of the total industrial plant of the old Habsburg territories was located in Bohemia and Moravia. Kann, *History*, p. 439.

124. Ibid., p. 97.

125. On the Heimwehr, see Clifton Earl Edmondson, *The Heimwehr and Austrian Politics, 1918–1936* (Athens: University of Georgia Press, 1978); Ludwig Jedlicka, "The Austrian Heimwehr," *Journal of Contemporary History*, vol. 1, no. 1 (1966), pp. 127–44.

126. Walter B. Simon, "Democracy in the Shadow of Imposed Sovereignty: The First Republic of Austria," in Linz and Stepan, eds., *Breakdown*, pp. 80–121. Gerhard Jagschitz, "Bundeskanzler Dollfuss und der Juli 1934," in *Österreich 1927 bis 1938*, ed. the Wissenschaftliche Kommission (München: Oldenbourg, 1973), pp. 150ff.

127. Polonsky, *Dictators*, p. 72.

128. Irmgard Bärnthaler, *Die Vaterländische Front: Geschichte und Organisation* (Vienna: Europa Verlag, 1971); Bruce F. Pauley, *Hitler and the Forgotten Nazis: A History of Austrian National Socialism* (Chapel Hill: University of North Carolina Press, 1981), especially pp. 155–72.

129. Pauley, *Forgotten Nazis*, pp. 172–93.

130. Gulick, *Austria*, vol. 2, pp. 1793–96, 1816–21; Jürgen Gehl, *Austria, Germany and the Anschluss, 1931–1938* (Oxford: Oxford University Press, 1963), p. 184 passim.

131. Pauley, *Forgotten Nazis*, pp. 193–216.

Chapter 8

1. For comparative overviews of the formation of these alliances, see the special issues of *Tidsskrift for arbeiderbevegelsens historie* (Oslo); "1930—åra—Reformismens gjennembrudd," vol. 3, no. 1 (1978), pp. 3–178; and "Arbeiderpartiet og bøndene, 1930–1939," vol. 3, no. 2 (1978), pp. 1–424.

2. The main points of the Kanslergade Agreement are from, Harry Haue, Jørgen Olsen, and Jørn Aarup-Kristensen, *Det ny Danmark, 1890–1978: Udviklingslinier og tendens* (Copenhagen: Munksgaard, 1979), p. 166.

3. The Kanslergade Agreement and the subsequent legislation and agreements that elaborated it are discussed in Svend Aage Hansen, *Økonomisk vaekst i Danmark*, Bind II: 1914–1970 (Copenhagen: Akademisk Forlag, 1974), pp. 31ff; Karin Hansen and Lars Torpe, Socialdemokratiet og krisen i 30'erne (Århus: Mod Tryk, 1977), pp. 138ff.

4. Sven Anders Söderpalm, "The Crisis Agreement and the Social Democratic Road to Power," in Steven Koblik, ed., *Sweden's Development from Poverty to Affluence, 1750–1970*, trans. Joanne Johnson (Minneapolis: University of Minnesota Press, 1975), p. 273.

5. Söderpalm, "Crisis Agreement," p. 270.

6. Fritz Hodne, *The Norwegian Economy, 1920–1980* (London: Croom Helm, 1983), p. 96.

7. The net effect of fiscal policies has been a point of some contention. Fritz Hodne has referred to the "myth" of stimulation policies. See Hodne, *Norwegian Economy*, pp. 93ff; and Ted Hanisch, *Hele folket i arbeid* (Oslo: Pax, 1977). See also Bo Gustafsson, "A Perennial of Doctrinal History: Keynes and the 'Stockholm School'," *Economy and History*, vol. 16 (1973), pp. 114–28; Donald Winch, "The Keynesian Revolution in Sweden," *Journal of Political Economy*, vol. 74, no. 2 (April 1966), pp. 168–76; Carl. G. Uhr, "The Emergence of the 'New Economics' in Sweden: A Review of a Study by Otto Steiger," *History of Political Economy*, vol. 5, no. 1 (Spring 1973), pp. 243–60.

8. Hodne, *Norwegian Economy*, p. 95.

9. Sven A. Nilsson, Karl-Gustaf Hildebrand, and Bo Öhngren, eds., *Kriser och krispolitik i Norden under mellankrigstiden: Nordiska historikermötet i Uppsala 1974. Mötesrapport* (Uppsala: Almqvist and Wiksell, 1974), tables 1.9 and 1.10, pp. 306–07.

10. Data on volume of money in circulation is from B. R. Mitchell, *European Historical Statistics, 1750–1970* (New York: Columbia University Press, 1975), pp. 677ff.

11. On the expectations generated, their possible role in recovery, and the political benefits that fell to the Social Democrats, see the citations in notes 1 and 7.

12. See Nils Elvander, "Staten och organisationerne på arbetsmarknaden i de nordiska länderna: En komparativ översikt," in L. Brantgärde, ed., *Konfliktlösning på arbetsmarknaden* (Lund: Gleerups, 1974), pp. 88ff; Jorunn Bjørgum, Christer Bogefeldt, and Jorma Kalela, "Krisen og arbeiderbevegelsen," in Nilsson et al., eds., *Kriser och krispolitik*, pp. 267ff; Berge Furre, *Norsk historie, 1905–1940* (Oslo: Det Norske Samlaget, 1971), pp. 195–244, 251–68, 282–86; Hansen and Torpe, *Socialdemokratiet*.

13. On the economic theories of Swedish and Norwegian Social Democrats, see the citations in note 7 and Furre, *Norsk historie*, pp. 230ff; Herbert Tingsten, *Den svenska Socialdemokratiens idéutveckling* (Stockholm: Tidens Förlag, 1941), pp. 268ff. See Hans Christian Johansen, *The Danish Economy in the Twentieth Century* (London: Croom Helm, 1987), pp. 44ff.

14. On contingent legitimacy, see Adam Przesworski's important essay, "Material Bases of Consent: Economics and Politics in a Hegemonic System," *Political Power and Social Theory*, vol. 1 (1980), pp. 21–66.

15. See the especially revealing work of Hans Fredrik Dahl, *Fra klassekamp til nasjonal samling: Arbeiderpartiet og det nasjonale spørsmål i 30-årene* (Oslo: Pax Forlag, 1969).

16. This idea is developed by Walter Korpi, in *The Democratic Class Struggle* (London: Routledge and Kegan Paul, 1983), pp. 47–60.

17. The historiography of the Norwegian and Danish business communities is particularly inadequate on these matters. Peter Gourevitch has argued that in Sweden Social Democratic hegemony was first acquiesced to by smaller, domestically oriented businesses and then by larger export-oriented firms. Peter Gourevitch, *Politics in Hard Times: Comparative Responses to International Economic Crises* (Ithaca, N.Y.: Cornell University Press, 1986), p. 133. Also see Sven Anders Söderpalm, *Direktörsklubben: Stor industrin i svensk politik under 1930- och 40-talen* (Stockholm: Rában and Sjögren, 1976).

18. The quotation appears in Korpi, *Democratic Class Struggle*, p. 48.

19. This is discussed in Adam Przeworski, "Social Democracy as a Historical Phenomenon," *New Left Review,* no. 122 (July–August 1980), pp. 27–58.

20. Andrew Martin has made a parallel argument about the impact of Social Democratic power on the Swedish trade unions. On the Swedish trade unions' strategic reorientation from "labor market confrontation" to the "political alternative" in the wake of the Social Democrats' coming to power, see his "Trade Unions in Sweden: Strategic Responses to Change and Crisis," in Peter Gourevitch et al., *Unions and Economic Crisis: Britain, West Germany and Sweden* (London: George Allen and Unwin, 1984), pp. 195–99.

21. Raymond Carr, *Spain 1808–1975,* 2nd ed. (Oxford: Oxford University Press, 1982), p. 719.

22. On the labor policies of Francoist Spain, see Jon Amsden, *Collective Bargaining and Class Conflict in Spain* (London: Weidenfeld and Nicolson, 1972). On Italy and Germany, see Alberto Aquarone, *L'organizzazione dello stato totalitario* (Turin: Einaudi, 1965); G. Lowell Field, *The Syndical and Corporative Institutions of Italian Fascism* (New York: Columbia University Press, 1938); A. James Gregor, *Italian Fascism and Developmental Dictatorship* (Princeton: Princeton University Press, 1979); J. Noakes and G. Pridham, eds., *Nazism, 1919–1945: A Documentary Reader: Vol. 2, State, Economy and Society, 1933–1939,* Exeter Studies in History, no. 8 (Exeter: University of Exeter, 1984), pp. 327–75.

23. Karl Dietrich Bracher, *The German Dictatorship: The Origins, Structure, and Effects of National Socialism* (New York: Praeger, 1970), p. 338.

24. Bracher, *German Dictatorship,* p. 338.

25. On the social policies pursued by the Fascists and Nazis, see Gregor, *Italian Fascism and Developmental Dictatorship,* pp. 172–300; Richard Grunberger, *The 12-Year Reich: A Social History of Nazi Germany, 1933–1945* (New York: Holt, Rinehart and Winston, 1971); David Schoenbaum, *Hitler's Social Revolution: Class and Status in Nazi Germany, 1933–1939* (Garden City, N.Y.: Doubleday, 1966).

26. Bracher, *German Dictatorship,* p. 339.

27. Gourevitch, *Hard Times,* p. 147 and passim; Alan Milward, "Fascism and the Economy," in Walter Laqueur, ed., *Fascism: A Reader's Guide* (Berkeley: University of California Press, 1976), pp. 379–412.

28. On the reorganization of the Italian economy, see Gregor, *Italian Fascism,* pp. 127–62.

29. Figures on the growth of the money supply are from Mitchell, *European Historical Statistics,* p. 677.

30. William Welk wrote that "it must be recognized that under Fascism social

welfare has been in the forefront of public attention and that institutions of considerable benefit to the mass of the Italian people have been perfected or created de novo." William Welk, *Fascist Economic Policy: An Analysis of Italy's Economic Experiment* (Cambridge: Harvard University Press, 1938), p. 105. See also Claudio Schwarzenberg, *Breve storia dei sistemi previdenziali in Italia* (Turin: ERI, 1971), pp. 178ff.; Herman Finer, *Mussolini's Italy* (London: Frank Cass, 1964), pp. 470ff.

31. Cited in Timothy Mason, *Arbeiterklasse und Volksgemeinschaft: Dokumente und Materialien zur deutschen Arbeiterpolitik, 1936–1939* (Opladen: Westdeutscher Verlag, 1975), p. 36.

32. See Gordon Craig, *Germany, 1866–1945* (New York: Oxford University Press, 1978), pp. 618–27; Bracher, *German Dictatorship,* pp. 338–39; Nicos Poulantzas, *Fascism and Dictatorship* (London: Verso, 1979), pp. 165–68, 188–222; Renzo De Felice, *Mussolini il duce: Gli anni del consenso, 1929–1936* (Turin: Einaudi, 1974), pp. 193ff and passim, and Palmiro Togliatti, *Lezioni sul fascismo,* 3rd ed. (Rome: Riuniti, 1970), p. 56.

33. Juan Linz, "A Century of Politics and Interests in Spain," in Suzanne D. Berger, ed., *Organizing Interests in Western Europe* (Cambridge: Cambridge University Press, 1981), pp. 388f; Juan Linz, "From Falange to Movimiento-Organizacion: The Spanish Single Party and the Franco Regime, 1936–1968," in Samuel P. Huntington and Clement H. Moore, eds., *Authoritarian Politics in Modern Society* (New York: Basic Books, 1970), p. 149.

34. On Mussolini's need to discipline the PNF and come to terms with the Vatican, army, and monarchy, see Adrian Lyttelton, *The Seizure of Power: Fascism in Italy, 1919–1929,* 2nd ed. (Princeton: Princeton University Press, 1987). On Hitler's need to break the autonomous ambitions of the Nazi party and accommodate the churches and army, see Martin Broszat, *The Hitler State: The Foundations and Development of the Internal Structure of the Third Reich* (London: Longman, 1981), especially pp. 193ff.

35. See the section on the rise of the SS state in Bracher, *German Dictatorship,* pp. 350ff.

36. See Geoffrey Hosking, *The First Socialist Society: A History of the Soviet Union from Within* (Cambridge: Harvard University Press, 1985), pp. 326ff.

37. On the regulation of the wartime agricultural economy, see for Germany, Robert G. Moeller, *German Peasants and Agrarian Politics, 1914–1924: The Rhineland and Westphalia* (Chapel Hill: University of North Carolina Press, 1986); for Norway, Fritz Hodne, *Norges økonomiske historie, 1815–1970* (Oslo: J. W. Cappelens Forlag, 1981), pp. 442ff; For Denmark, Einar Cohn, *Danmark under den store krig: En økonomisk oversigt* (Copenhagen: Gad, 1982); and Svend Aage Hansen and Ingrid Henriksen, *Sociale brydninger, 1914–1939: Dansk social historie, bind 6* (Copenhagen: Gyldendal, 1980), pp. 17ff.; for Sweden, Olle Gellerman, *Staten och jordbruket, 1867–1918,* Skrifter utgivna av Statsvetenskapliga föreningen i Uppsala, vol. 39 (Stockholm: Almqvist and Wiksell, 1958); Sten Carlsson and Jerker Rosén, *Svensk historia.2: Tiden efter 1718,* 4th ed. (Stockholm: Esselte Studium, 1980), pp. 442ff; for Italy, Luigi Einaudi, *La condotta economica e gli effetti sociali della guerra italiana* (Bari: Laterza and Figli, 1933), pp. 82–84; and especially Arrigo Serpieri, *La guerra e le classi rurali italiane* (Bari: Laterza and Figli, 1930), pp. 61–69, 94–107.

38. Harry Haue et al., *Det ny Danmark,* pp. 89–90.

39. Alexander Gerschenkron, *Bread and Democracy in Germany* (Berkeley: University of California Press, 1943), p. 96.

40. Shepard B. Clough, *The Economic History of Modern Italy* (New York: Columbia University Press, 1964), p. 188.

41. Clough, *Economic History*, p. 189.

42. Ibid., pp. 188–89.

43. The Spanish middle classes, even if they could not find common ground with workers in opposition to rising prices, were by no means mute in their opposition to the price increases. Middle-class demonstrations against food prices became rather common after 1917. See Jorge Montojo Sureda, *La política española sobre trigos y harinas: Años 1900–1945* (Madrid: Afrodisio Agudo, 1945), pp. 17–28, 113.

44. On the bread subsidy see, Clough, *Economic History*, pp. 203–04, and Charles Maier, *Recasting Bourgeois Europe: Stabilization in France, Germany and Italy in the Decade After World War I* (Princeton: Princeton University Press, 1975), pp. 173, 180, 190, 325, 328, 427.

45. Quoted in Moeller, *German Peasants*, p. 68.

46. Hodne, *Norwegian Economy*, p. 53.

47. Robert Lorenz, *The Essential Features of Germany's Agricultural Policy from 1870 to 1937* (New York: Columbia University Press, 1941), pp. 75 and 91; Walter G. Hoffmann, *Das Wachstum der deutschen Wirtschaft seit der Mitte des 19. Jahrhunderts* (Berlin: Springer Verlag, 1965), p. 237.

48. Michael Tracy, *Agriculture in Western Europe* (New York: Praeger, 1964), p. 119; Erik Helmer Pedersen, Per Thullberg, and Stein Tveite, "Nordens jordbruk under världskrisen, 1929–1933," Sven Nilsson et al., eds., *Kriser och krispolitik*, p. 163.

49. For the years 1925–26 through 1931–32 the net rate of return was as follows. For Denmark: 1.2, 1.1, 1.5, 4.9, 4.3, 0.5, −0.4 percent. For Norway: 1.1, 0.0, 1.7, 1.7, 2.0, 1.4, 0.4 percent. For Sweden: 2.5, 2.1, 1.9, 2.1, 2.4, 1.3, −0.2 percent. For Germany, for the years 1927–28 through 1932–33, the rate of return was 1.3, 2.1, 1.9, 1.7, 1.2, and 0.89 percent. *Sources:* Pedersen et al., "Nordens jordbruk," p. 180; and *Statistisches Jahrbuch für das Deutsche Reich*, vol. 57 (Berlin: Verlag für Sozialpolitik, Wirtschaft und Statistik, 1938), p. 567.

50. Hodne, *Norwegian Economy*, p. 56.

51. Max Sering, ed., *Die Deutsche Landwirstschaft unter volks- und weltwirtschaftslichen Geschichtspunkten*, Berichte über Landwirtschaft, Sonderheft no. 50 (Berlin: Paul Parey, 1932), tables, 22, 23, and 31.

52. Antonio Vázquez Humasqué, "El problema agrario español," *El Trimestre Economico*, vol. 7, no. 3 (October–December 1940), pp. 470–75.

53. On the extent of peasant involvement in the market, we can do no better than accept the judgment of Edward Malefakis. Referring to those who worked miniscule plots in the south, among the sectors of Spanish agriculture least likely to be engaged in the market, Malefakis has written: "To what extent were these owners, tenants and sharecroppers subsistence farmers and to what extent did they take part in the market economy? I have not been able to devise any satisfactory method of answering these questions. The poorest among them obviously used their lands exclusively to grow food for their own consumption and relied upon occasional wage labor, either in agriculture or other activities, for their cash requirements. A majority, however, probably sold varying proportions of their produce. . . . Moreover, since even the

subsistence farmers owned some capital, in the form of animals and tools, and exercised a few managerial functions, at least to the extent of deciding how much seed to save and whether or when to perform agricultural tasks, I have adopted the term 'impoverished entrepreneurs'. " Edward Malefakis, *Agrarian Reform and Peasant Revolution in Spain: Origins of the Civil War* (New Haven: Yale University Press, 1970), p. 112.

54. Instituto de Reforma Agraria, *Agrarian Reform in Spain: An Historical Study by the Spanish Institute for Agrarian Reform* (London: United Editorial, 1938), p. 26.

55. Malefakis, *Agrarian Reform,* p. 147.

56. These are matters to which we shall return. Malefakis, *Agrarian Reform,* provides a brilliant account of conflicts in agriculture during the Republican years.

57. On the formation of the Green Front and the Center's attitude toward it, see Erwin Topf, *Die Grüne Front: Der Kampf um den Deutschen Acker* (Berlin: Rowohlt, 1933), pp. 46–50, 114–15; Dieter Gessner, *Agrarverbände in der Weimarer Republik* (Düsseldorf: Droste Verlag, 1976); Klaus Müller, "Agrarische Interessenverbände in der Weimarer Republik," *Rheinische Vierteljahrsblätter,* vol. 38 (1974), pp. 386–405.

58. On the support of some Catholic peasant organizations for the Harzburg Front, see Müller, "Agrarische Interessenverbände," pp. 402–05.

59. Moeller, *German Peasants,* see especially pp. 139–55.

60. Britain, with its miniscule agricultural sector, hardly counts here.

61. François Goguel, *La politique des partis sous la IIIe République* (Paris: Seuil, 1946); Michel Auge-Laribe, *La politique agricole de la France de 1880 a 1940* (Paris: Presses Universitaires de la France, 1950); Charles K. Warner, *Winegrowers of France and the Government since 1875* (New York: Columbia University Press, 1960).

62. Peter Flora, ed., *State, Economy and Society in Western Europe, 1815–1975. A Data Handbook: Volume I, The Growth of Mass Democracies and Welfare States* (Chicago: St. James Press, 1983), pp. 107ff.

63. See the citations in note 1 and David Abraham, *The Collapse of the Weimar Republic: Political Economy and Crisis* (Princeton: Princeton University Press, 1981), pp. 180ff.

64. In a similar vein Juan Linz has discussed the initial difficulty of the fascist political movement as a "latecomer on the political scene" in finding political space of its own. See his, "Some Notes Toward a Comparative Study of Fascism in Sociological-Historical Perspective," in Laqueur, ed., *Fascism,* pp. 4ff.

65. The inference that the SPD's losses came from among workers is a crude one: the SPD share of Reichstag seats fell from 31 percent in 1928 to 25 percent in 1930 to 22 percent in 1932. The Communist share rose from 11 to 13 to 15 percent in the same elections.

66. Edward Malefakis, "Peasants, Politics and Civil War in Spain, 1931–1939," in Robert Bezucha, ed., *Modern European Social History* (Lexington, Mass.: D. C. Heath, 1972), p. 219 and passim.

67. Mitchell, *European Historical Statistics,* pp. 151–66.

68. Malefakis, "Peasants, Politics," p. 196 passim.

69. J. C. Adams, "Italy," in Walter Galenson, ed., *Comparative Labor Movements* (New York: Russell and Russell, 1968), pp. 413–14.

70. Frieda Wunderlich, *Farm Labor in Germany, 1810–1945* (Princeton: Princeton University Press, 1961), p. 15.

71. Source for size of the Danish agrarian population that depended on the agricultural labor market for the larger share of its income is *Danmarks Statistik, Statistiske Meddelelser: Landbrugets Arbejdeskraft, 1904 og 1935*, ser. 4, vol. 102, no. 3 (Copenhagen: Statistical Department, 1937), p. 15.

72. Source for size of Swedish agrarian population that depended on the agricultural labor market for the larger share of its income is *Statistisk Årsbok för Sverige*, 1932 (Stockholm: Statistiska Centralbyrån, 1932), pp. 24–25.

73. Kåre Lunden, "The Growth of Co-operatives Among the Norwegian Dairy Farmers During the Period 1856–1905," *Cahiers Internationaux D'Histoire Economique Et Sociale*, vol. 6 (Geneva: Librairie Droz, 1973), p. 342.

74. Source for estimate of Czechoslovakian proletariat: State Statistical Office, *Manuel statistique, 1931*, vol. 3 (Prague: Statistical Bureau of the Czechoslovak Republic, 1931), p. 300.

75. Lunden, "Growth of Co-operatives," p. 342.

76. Stein Rokkan, "Geography, Religion and Social Class: Crosscutting Cleavages in Norwegian Politics," in Stein Rokkan and Seymour Martin Lipset, *Party Systems and Voter Alignments: Cross-National Perspectives* (New York: Free Press, 1967), table 26, p. 429.

77. Two sources indicate that within the LO agricultural and forestry workers together constituted only 10 percent of the membership in 1931, and that forestry workers were a majority of these. See Hans Fredrik Dahl, *Norge mellom krigene: Det norske samfunnet i krise og konflikt, 1918–1940* (Oslo: Pax Forlag, 1971), p. 91; and Furre, *Norsk historie*, p. 200.

78. *Statistisk Arsbok för Sverige* pp. 24–25.

79. Election data for Sweden from Stig Hadenius et al., *Sverige efter 1900: En modern politisk historia* (Stockholm: Aldus, 1978), table I.C, pp. 306–07.

80. Söderplam, "Crisis Agreement," pp. 263–64.

81. Ibid., p. 264.

82. Data on share of the valid vote cast as a percentage of the population over twenty years of age are from Flora, ed., *State, Economy and Society*, vol. 1, pp. 141–44.

83. Size of the dependent labor force is from *Danmarks Statistisk*, p. 15.

84. The participation rate is the share of the valid vote cast as a percentage of the population over twenty years of age and is from Flora, ed., *State, Economy, Society*, vol. 1, pp. 105–06.

85. Election data for Denmark are from Flora, ed., *State, Economy, Society*, vol. 1, pp. 105–06.

86. Even in 1948, after the Social Democrats had been in power for a decade and a half, agricultural workers constituted less than 6 percent of the LO membership. Walter Galenson, *The Danish System of Labor Relations* (Cambridge: Harvard University Press, 1952), p. 30.

87. Frantisek Nemec, *From Social Welfare to Social Justice* (London: Lincolns-Prager, 1943); Brackett Lewis, "Social Reform and Social Legislation," in Robert J. Kerner, ed., *Czechoslovakia: Twenty Years of Independence* (Berkeley: University of California Press, 1940), pp. 251–71.

88. In Bohemia and Moravia-Silesia, the urban middle classes divided their

support among the Protestant Czech Nationalist party (sometimes referred to as National Socialist party, but not to be confused with the Nazis), the Catholic Populist party, the National Democrats, and the Tradesmen's party. Over the years the first two parties held their own while the latter two dwindled to insignificance. This pattern was replicated in the German community and in Slovakia, although the divisions were compounded because there Protestant parties favored a centralization of power in Prague; Catholic parties favored a decentralization.

89. Lewis, "Social Reform and Social Legislation," p. 260.

90. On economic policies after 1933, see Lewis, "Social Reform and Social Legislation," pp. 251–71; Zora P. Pryor, "Czechoslovak Economic Development in the Interwar Period," in Victor Mamatey and Radomír Luža, eds., *A History of the Czechoslovak Republic, 1918–1948* (Princeton: Princeton University Press, 1973), pp. 203–04.

91. Nemec, *Social Welfare,* p. 15 passim; Lewis, "Social Reform," pp. 252–71; Esther Bloss, *Labor Legislation in Czechoslovakia, with Special Reference to the Standards of the International Labor Organization* (New York: Columbia University Press, 1938).

92. The index of industrial production (1929 = 100) rose from 60 in 1933 to 95 in 1937. Pryor, "Czechoslovak Economic Development," p. 189. On unemployment, see Lewis, "Social Reform," pp. 252–71.

93. Data on volume of exports are contained in Státní úřad statisticky Republiky československé, *Zprávy,* vol. 19 (1938), nos. 97–100. See also Zora Procházka, "Foreign Trade and Economic Development of Czechoslovakia, 1919–1937" (Unpublished Ph.D. Dissertation: Radcliffe College, 1960).

94. On the unfolding of the Sudeten crisis, see Jörg Hoensch, *Geschichte der Tschechoslowakischen Republik, 1918–1978* (Stuttgart: W. Kohlhammer, 1978), pp. 57–89; and Joseph S. Roucek, "Czechoslovakia and Her Minorities," in Kerner, ed., *Czechoslovakia,* pp. 181–83. On the diplomatic crisis, see S. Harrison Thomson, *Czechoslovakia in European History* (Hamden: Archon Books, 1965), pp. 370–408; and Piotr S. Wandycz, "Foreign Policy of Edvard Benes, 1918–1938," in Mamatey and Luža, eds., *History of the Czechoslovak Republic,* pp. 228ff.

95. Václav L. Beneš, "Czechoslovak Democracy and Its Problems, 1918–1920," in ibid., table 2, p. 41.

96. Victor S. Mamatey, "The Development of Czechoslovak Democracy, 1920–1938," in ibid., p. 129.

97. The rural Communist vote came mainly from ethnic minorities. See Richard V. Burks, *The Dynamics of Communism in Eastern Europe* (Westport, Ct.: Greenwood Press, 1976) p. 42 and passim.

98. Czech land reform is discussed in Harry Klepetar, *Seit 1918 . . . Eine Geschichte der Tschechoslowakischen Republik* (Moravska Ostrava: Verlag Julius Kittls, 1937).

99. On the first point, see Gøsta Esping-Andersen, *Politics Against Markets: The Social Democratic Road to Power* (Princeton: Princeton University Press, 1985), pp. 41ff.

100. Christopher Seton-Watson, *Italy from Liberalism to Fascism, 1870–1925* (London: Methuen, 1967), pp. 303–04.

101. Daniel L. Horowitz, *The Italian Labor Movement* (Cambridge: Harvard University Press, 1963), p. 124.

102. Maurice Neufeld, *Italy: School for Awakening Countries: The Italian Labor Movement in Its Political, Social and Economic Setting from 1800 to 1960* (Ithaca, N.Y.: Cornell University School for Industrial and Labor Relations, 1961), p. 367.

103. Maier, *Recasting Bourgeois Europe*, p. 311.

104. Horowitz, *Italian Labor*, p. 124.

105. See Neufeld, *Italy*, p. 347; also Michael F. Hembree, "The Politics of Intransigence: Costantino Lazzari and the Italian Socialist Left, 1882–1919" (Unpublished Ph.D. Dissertation: Florida State University, 1981), p. 232.

106. The size of the agrarian membership is an estimate. It is based on the assumption that the agrarian membership of the USI was equal to the membership taken away from the CGL: 80,000. For the data, see Horowitz, *Italian Labor*, p. 75.

107. Seton-Watson, *Italy*, p. 599.

108. Malefakis, *Agrarian Reform*, p. 292.

109. Malefakis, "Peasants, Politics," p. 206.

110. Ibid., p. 214.

111. Ibid., p. 219.

112. Derek Urwin and Frank Aarebrot, "Socio-geographic Correlates of Left Voting in Weimar Germany, 1924–1932," Per Torsvik ed. *Mobilization, Center-Periphery Structures and Nation-Building* (Oslo: Universitetforlaget, 1981), pp. 259–60.

113. Wunderlich, *Farm Labor*, p. 35.

114. Ibid., p. 35.

115. Ibid., pp. 35–36.

116. Data on union membership are from Gerhard Bry, *Wages in Germany, 1871–1945* (Princeton: Princeton University Press, 1960), p. 32.

117. Bry, *Wages*, p. 42.

118. Wunderlich, *Farm Labor*, p. 84, fn. 14.

119. Ibid., pp. 126–59.

120. Data on agriculture's share of national income from Paul Jostock, "The Long-Term Growth of National Income in Germany," in Simon Kuznets, ed., *Review of Income and Wealth*, Series 5 (London: Bowes and Bowes, 1955), p. 109.

121. Adolf Münzinger, *Der Arbeitsertrag der bäuerlichen Familienwirtschaft: Eine bäuerliche Betriebserhebung in Württemberg* (Berlin, 1929), vol. 2, p. 873.

122. Constantin von Dietze, "Die Lage der deutschen Landwirtschaft," *Jahrbücher für Nationalökonomie und Statistik* (Jena, 1929), no. 130, p. 3; no. 75, pp. 659–60.

123. Beneš, "Czechoslovak Democracy"; Mamatey, "Development of Czechoslovak Democracy."

124. Thomas Childers, *The Nazi Voter: The Social Foundations of Fascism in Germany, 1919–1933* (Chapel Hill: University of North Carolina, 1983); Richard F. Hamilton, *Who Voted for Hitler?* (Princeton: Princeton University Press, 1982).

125. Moeller, *German Peasants*, pp. 139–59.

126. Lyttelton, *Seizure of Power*, pp. 43–77.

127. Ibid., pp. 188ff.

128. Malefakis, "Peasants, Politics"; Carlos M. Rama, *Ideologia, regiones y clases sociales en la España contemporánea* (Montevidep: Ediciones Nuestro Tiem-

po, 1958); Stanley Payne, *The Spanish Revolution: A Study of the Social and Political Tensions That Culminated in the Civil War in Spain* (New York: Norton, 1970), pp. 157–85; Gabriel Jackson, *Spanish Republic and the Civil War 1931–1939* (Princeton: Princeton University Press, 1965), pp. 184–96.

129. See Malefakis, "Peasants, Politics," especially p. 225.

130. Ibid., pp. 218–21.

131. The attitudes of Gil Robles and the CEDA toward the Republic have long been a source of debate among historians. For a balanced assessment, see Malefakis, *Agrarian Reform*, pp. 330–32 passim, 340–41, 344, 353, 358, n. 42, 366.

132. Figures on the share of the vote are from Flora, *State, Economy, Society*, vol. 1, pp. 107ff. For a discussion of the social composition of the Scandinavian parties and the departure of the middle classes from liberal parties, see Sten Berglund and Ulf Lindström, *The Scandinavian Party System(s): A Comparative Study* (Lund: Studentlitteratur, 1978); Hans Frederik Dahl et al., "Krisen og det politiske liv," in Nilsson et al., *Kriser och krispolitik*, pp. 71–104; Stein Rokkan, "Norway: Numerical Democracy and Corporate Pluralism," and Nils Stjernquist, "Sweden: Stability or Deadlock?" in Robert Dahl, ed., *Political Oppositions in Western Democracies* (New Haven: Yale University Press, 1966), pp. 70–115 and 116–46.

133. On the condition of agriculture and urban liberal attitudes toward it in Scandinavia, see Dahl et al., "Krisen og det politiske liv," and Pedersen, "Nordens jordbruk," in Nilsson et al., eds., *Kriser och Krispolitik;* Jorunn Bjørgum, *Venstre og krise forliket: Landbrukspolitikk og parlamentarisk spill, 1934–1935* (Oslo: Universitetsforlaget, 1978); Fridlev Skrubbeltrang, "Danske landboforhold," in K. Hansen, ed., *Det danske landbrugs historie: vol. 5, 1934–1945* (Copenhagen), pp. 559–75; Vagn Dybdahl et al., *Krise i Danmark* (Copenhagen: Gyldendal, 1975), pp. 74–122.

134. The words are those of Söderpalm on the Swedish Agrarians, but apply equally well to Norway and Denmark. "Crisis Agreement," p. 263.

135. Bjørgum, *Venstre og krise forliket;* Söderpalm, "Crisis Agreement."

136. The Woytinsky–Tarnow–Baade Plan was a proposal developed in the ADGB in 1931 and 1932 to create jobs through the public sector through countercyclical spending, public works, state regulation of capitalism, and so forth. On the origins and content of the plan, see Michael Schneider, *Das Arbeitsbeschaffungsprogramm des ADGB* (Bonn-Bad Godesberg: Verlag neue Gesellschaft, 1975), pp. 61–89.

137. Hans-Ulrich Wehler, "Der Aufstieg des Organisierten Kapitalismus and Interventionsstaates in Deutschland," in Heinrich A. Winkler, ed., *Organisierter Kapitalismus: Voraussetzungen und Anfänge* (Göttingen: Vandenhoeck and Ruprecht, 1974), pp. 36–57; Robert Gates, "Von der Sozialpolitik zur Wirtschaftspolitik?: Das Dilemma der deutschen Sozialdemokratie in der Krise 1929–1933," in Hans Mommsen, Dietmar Petzina, and Bernd Weisbrod, eds., *Industrielles System und politische Entwicklung in der Weimarer Republik* (Düsseldorf: Droste Verlag, 1974), pp. 206–25; Robert Gates, "The Economic Policies of the German Free Trade Unions and the German Social Democratic Party, 1930–1933" (Unpublished Ph.D. Dissertation: University of Oregon, 1970), pp. 182–263.

138. Richard Breitman, *German Socialism and Weimar Democracy* (Chapel Hill: University of North Carolina Press, 1981), pp. 161–89.

Chapter 9

1. Walter B. Simon, "Motivations of a Totalitarian Mass Vote," *British Journal of Sociology,* vol. 10, no. 4 (December 1959), pp. 338–45.

2. All data on industrial production and unemployment are from B. R. Mitchell, *European Historical Statistics, 1750–1970* (New York: Columbia University Press, 1975), pp. 166ff and 355ff.

3. Alexander Gerschenkron, *Bread and Democracy in Germany* (Berkeley: University of California Press, 1943); Barrington Moore, Jr., *Social Origins of Dictatorship and Democracy: Lord and Peasant in the Making of the Modern World* (Boston: Beacon Press, 1966).

4. This is a central theme of the essays in Juan Linz and Alfred Stepan, eds., *The Breakdown of Democratic Regimes: Europe* (Baltimore: Johns Hopkins University Press, 1978).

5. This is a point emphasized by Linz in his essay, "From Great Hopes to Civil War: The Breakdown of Democracy in Spain," in Linz and Stepan, eds. *Breakdown: Europe,* pp. 142–215.

6. Norway and Sweden had the highest rates of strike activity in Europe in the 1920s. See the preceding discussion in Chapter 7.

7. Among the most important efforts to account for the origins of radicalism and reformism in labor movements is Seymour Martin Lipset's essay, "Radicalism or Reformism: The Sources of Working-Class Politics," *American Political Science Review,* vol. 77, no. 1 (March 1983), pp. 1–18. See especially pp. 14–16, wherein Lipset contends that radicalism and reformism were one of several important variables in accounting for regime outcomes between the wars.

Bibliography

Abherve, Bertrand, "Les origines la grève des métallurgistes parisiens, juin 1919," *Le mouvement social,* no. 93 (October–December 1975) pp. 75–85.

Abraham, David, *The Collapse of the Weimar Republic: Political Economy and Crisis* (Princeton: Princeton University Press, 1981).

Adams, J. C., "Italy," in Walter Galenson, ed., *Comparative Labor Movements* (New York: Russell and Russell, 1968) pp. 410–79.

Adler, Franklin Hugh, "Italian Industrialists from Liberalism to Fascism" (Unpublished Ph.D. Dissertation: University of Chicago, 1980).

Agerholm, Sophus and Vigen, Anders, *Arbejdsgiverforeningen gennem 25 år, 1896–1921* (Copenhagen: Trykt and Langkjaers, 1921).

Alapuro, Risto and Allardt, Erik, "The Lapua Movement: The Threat of Rightist Takeover in Finland, 1930–1932," in Juan J. Linz and Alfred Stepan, eds., *The Breakdown of Democratic Regimes: Europe* (Baltimore: Johns Hopkins University Press, 1978) pp. 122–41.

Aldcroft, Derek H., *From Versailles to Wall Street, 1919–1929* (Berkeley: University of California Press, 1977).

Aldcroft, Derek H., *The Inter-War Economy: Britain, 1919–1939* (London: Batsford, 1970).

Amsden, Jon, *Collective Bargaining and Class Conflict in Spain* (London: Weidenfeld and Nicolson, 1972).

Anderson, Robert D., *France, 1870–1914: Politics and Society* (London: Routledge and Kegan Paul, 1977).

Andrae, Carl-Göran, "The Swedish Labor Movement and the 1917–1918 Revolution," in Steven Koblik, ed., *Sweden's Development from Poverty to Affluence, 1750–1970,* trans. Joanne Johnson (Minneapolis: University of Minnesota Press, 1975) pp. 232–53.

Aquarone, Alberto, *L'organizzazione dello stato totalitario* (Turin: Einaudi, 1965).

Arbetet (Malmö) September 9, 1890.

Askew, William Clarence, *Europe and Italy's Acquisition of Libya* (Durham, North Carolina: Duke University Press, 1942).

Aspley, John and Whitmore, Eugene, eds., *The Handbook of Industrial Relations* (London: Dartnell Corporation, 1944).

Auge-Laribe, Michel, *La politique agricole de la France de 1880 a 1940* (Paris: Presses Universitaires de la France, 1950).

Bäckström, Knut, *Arbetarrörelsen i Sverige: Vol. 1, Den Svenska arbetarrörelsens uppkomst och förening med socialismen* (Stockholm: Rabén and Sjögren, 1971).

Bäckström, Knut, *Arbetarrörelsen i Sverige: Volume 2, Den politiska arbetarrörelsens sprängning och ett nytt revolutionärt arbetarpartis uppkomst* (Stockholm: Rabén and Sjögren, 1971).

Bairoch, P., "Niveaux de développement économique de 1810 à 1910." *Annales: Économies, Sociétés, Civilisations,* vol. 20, no. 6 (November–December 1965) pp. 1091–117.

Bard, Rachel, *Navarra, the Durable Kingdom* (Reno: University of Nevada Press, 1982).

Bärnthaler, Irmgard, *Die Vaterländische Front: Geschichte und Organisation* (Vienna: Europa Verlag, 1971).

Barthelémy, Joseph, *L'Organisation du suffrage et l'expérience belge* (Paris: M. Giard and E. Briere, 1912).

Batsch, Laurent and Bouvet, Michel, *CGT autour de la scission de 1921* (Paris: Editions La Breche, 1983).

Bendix, Reinhard, *Nation Building and Citizenship* (Berkeley: University of California Press, 1977).

Beneš, Václav L., "Czechoslovak Democracy and Its Problems, 1918–1920," in Victor Mamatey and Radomír Luža, eds., *A History of the Czechoslovak Republic, 1918–1948* (Princeton: Princeton University Press, 1973) pp. 39–98.

Berglund, Sten, and Lindström, Ulf, *The Scandinavian Party System(s): A Comparative Study* (Lund: Studentlitteratur, 1978).

Berlanstein, Lenard R., *The Working People of Paris, 1871–1914* (Baltimore: Johns Hopkins University Press, 1984).

Bertolt, Oluf, Christiansen, Ernst, and Hansen, Poul, *En bygning vi rejser: Den politiske arbejderbevaegelses historie i Danmark,* 3 vols. (Copenhagen: Forlaget Fremad, 1954–55).

Bezucha, Robert, ed., *Modern European Social History* (Lexington, Mass.: D. C. Heath, 1972).

Bisgaard, H. L., "Den Store Lockout," *Nationaløkonomisk Tidsskrift,* vol. 37 (1899) pp. 479–521.

Bjørgum, Jorunn, "Fagopposisjonen av 1911." *Tidsskrift for arbeiderbevegelsens historie* (NR.1/1976) pp. 63–131.

Bjørgum, Jorunn, *Venstre og krise forliket: Landbrukspolitikk og parlamentarisk spill, 1934–1935* (Oslo: Universitetsforlaget, 1978).

Bjørgum, Jorunn, Bogefeldt, Christer, and Kalela, Jorma, "Krisen og arbeiderbevegelsen," in Sven A. Nilsson, Karl-Gustaf Hildebrand and Bo Öhngren, eds., *Kriser och krispolitik i Norden under mellankrigstiden: Nordiska histo-*

rikermötet i Uppsala 1974. Mötesrapport (Uppsala: Almqvist and Wiksell, 1974) pp. 247–93.

Blake, Donald J. "Swedish Trade Unions and the Social Democratic Party: The Formative Years," *Scandinavian Economic History Review,* vol. 8, no. 1 (1960) pp. 19–44.

Bloss, Esther, *Labor Legislation in Czechoslovakia, with Special Reference to the Standards of the International Labor Organization* (New York: Columbia University Press, 1938).

Board of Trade, *Seventeenth Abstract of Labour Statistics of the United Kingdom* (London: Government Stationery Office, 1915).

Bodin, Louis, and Touchard, Jean, *Front populaire 1936* (Paris: A. Colin, 1961).

Born, Karl Erich, *Wirtschafts- und Sozialgeschichte des deutschen Kaisserreichs* (Stuttgart: Franz Steiner Verlag, 1985).

Bourgeois, Léon, *Solidarité,* 7th ed. (Paris: A. Colin, 1912).

Bouvier, Jean, "Un débat toujours ouvert: La politique économique du Front Populaire," *Le mouvement social,* no. 54 (January–March 1966) pp. 175–81.

Boyd, Carolyn P., *Praetorian Politics in Liberal Spain* (Chapel Hill: University of North Carolina Press, 1979).

Bracher, Karl Dietrich, *The German Dictatorship: The Origins, Structure, and Effects of National Socialism* (New York: Praeger, 1970).

Braham, Randolph L., ed., *Hungarian Jewish Studies* (New York: World Federation of Hungarian Jews, 1966).

Brantgärde, L., ed., *Konfliktlösning på arbetsmarknaden* (Lund: Gleerups, 1974).

Branting, Hjalmar, *Tal och skrifter* (Stockholm: Tiden, 1926–30) vol. 1.

Braun, Adolf, Müller, Herman, and Seidel, Richard, *Die Gewerkschaften, ihre Entwicklung und ihre Kämpfe: Vol. 2, Die Gewerkschaften nach dem Kriege* (Berlin: Buchhandlung Vorwärts, 1925).

Brécy, Robert, *Le Mouvement syndical en France 1871–1921: Essai bibliographie* (Paris: Mouton, 1963).

Breitman, Richard, *German Socialism and Weimar Democracy* (Chapel Hill: University of North Carolina Press, 1981).

Brenan, Gerald, *The Spanish Labyrinth: An Account of the Social and Political Background of the Civil War* (Cambridge: Cambridge University Press, 1960).

Breviarul statistic al Romaniei (Bucharest: Institul Central de Statistica, 1939).

Brogan, Denis William, *The Development of Modern France, 1870–1939* (London: Hamilton, 1949).

Broszat, Martin, *The Hitler State: The Foundations and Development of the Internal Structure of the Third Reich* (London: Longman, 1981).

Brunet, Jean-Paul, *Saint-Denis, la ville rouge: Socialisme et communisme en banlieue ouvrière, 1890–1939* (Paris: Hachette, 1980).

Bry, Gerhard, *Wages in Germany, 1871–1945* (Princeton: Princeton University Press, 1960).

Bull, Edvard, *Norsk fagbevegelse: Oversikt over Fagorganisasjonens utvikling,* 2nd ed. (Oslo: Tiden Norsk Forlag, 1968).

Bullock, Alan, *The Life and Times of Ernest Bevin* (London: Heinemann, 1960).

Burckhardt, Lukas, "Industry-Labor Relations: Industrial Peace," in J. Murray Luck, ed., *Modern Switzerland* (Palo Alto, Calif.: SPOSS, 1978) pp. 173–98.

Burks, Richard V., *The Dynamics of Communism in Eastern Europe* (Westport, Ct.: Greenwood Press, 1976).

Carlsson, Sten, and Rosén, Jerker, *Svensk historia. 2: Tiden efter 1718*, 4th ed. (Stockholm: Esselte Studium, 1980).

Carocci, Giampiero, *Giolitti e l'età giolittiana* (Turin: Einaudi, 1961).

Carr, Raymond, *Spain 1808–1975*, 2nd ed. (Oxford: Oxford University Press, 1982).

Casparsson, Ragnar, *Gruvfolk: Svenska Gruvindustriarbetareförbundet under fyra årtionden* (Stockholm, 1935).

Castles, Francis, *The Social Democratic Image of Society* (London: Routledge & Kegan Paul, 1978).

Castronovo, Valerio, *La Stampa Italiana dall'Unità al Fascismo* (Bari: Editori Laterza, 1970).

Central Bureau voor de Statistiek (Belgium), *Zestig jaren statistiek in tijdreeksen, 1899–1959* (Zeist: W. de Haan, 1959).

Challaye, Felicien, *Syndicalisme revolutionnaire et syndicalisme reformiste* (Paris: F. Alcan, 1909).

Childers, Thomas, *The Nazi Voter: The Social Foundations of Fascism in Germany, 1919–1933* (Chapel Hill: University of North Carolina, 1983).

Chlepner, Ben Serge, *Cent Ans d'histoire sociale en Belgique* (Brussels: Institut de Sociologie Solvay, 1958).

Cipolla, Carlo, ed., *The Fontana Economic History of Europe* vol. 6, pt. 2 (London: Fontana, 1976).

Citrine, Walter, *Fackföreningsrörelsen i Storbritannien*, skriftserie 14 (Stockholm: Landsorganisationen, 1927).

Clark, Marjorie R., *A History of the French Labor Movement, 1910–1928* (Berkeley: University of California Press, 1930).

Clark, Terry Nichols, *Prophets and Patrons: The French University and the Emergence of the Social Sciences* (Cambridge: Harvard University Press, 1973).

Clegg, Hugh A., *A History of British Trade Unions Since 1889: Vol. 2, 1911–1933* (Oxford: Clarendon Press, 1985).

Clegg, Hugh A., Fox, Alan, and Thompson, A. F., *A History of British Trade Unions Since 1889: Vol. 1, 1889–1910* (Oxford: Clarendon Press, 1964).

Clough, Shepard B., *The Economic History of Modern Italy* (New York: Columbia University Press, 1964).

Codding, Jr., George Arthur, *The Federal Government of Switzerland* (Boston: Houghton Mifflin Co., 1961).

Cohn, Einar, *Økonomi og politik i Danmark, 1849–1875* (Copenhagen: Gad, 1967).

Cohn, Einar, *Danmark under den store krig: En økonomisk oversigt* (Copenhagen: Gad, 1982).

Cole, G. D. H., *A Short History of the British Working-Class Movement* (New York: Macmillan, 1927).

Cole, G. D. H., *British Working-Class Politics, 1832–1914* (London: George Routledge and Sons, 1941.)

Collinet, Michel, *L'Ouvrier français: II. Esprit du syndicalisme* (Paris: Editions ouvrières, 1951).

Collins, Henry, "The Marxism of the Social Democratic Federation," in Asa Briggs and John Saville, eds., *Essays in Labour History, 1886–1923*, vol. 2 (London: Macmillan, 1971) pp. 47–69.

Colton, Joel, *Compulsory Labor Arbitration in France, 1936–1939* (New York: King's Crown Press, 1951).

Colton, Joel, *Léon Blum: Humanist in Politics* (Durham: Duke University Press, 1987).

Concise Statistical Yearbook of Poland (Warsaw: Central Statistical Office, 1931).

Cornford, James, "The Transformation of Conservatism in the Late Nineteenth Century," in Peter Stansky, ed., *The Victorian Revolution: Government and Society in Victoria's Britain* (New York: New Viewpoints, 1973) pp. 287–318.

Craig, Gordon, *Germany, 1866–1945* (New York: Oxford University Press, 1978).

Crook, Wilfred H., *The General Strike: A Study of Labor's Tragic Weapon in Theory and Practice* (Chapel Hill: University of North Carolina Press, 1931).

Crothers, George, *The German Elections of 1907* (New York: Columbia University Press, 1941).

Daalder, Hans, "Consociationalism, Center and Periphery in the Netherlands," in Per Torsvik, ed., *Mobilization, Center-Periphery Structures and Nation-Building* (Bergen: Universitetsforlaget, 1981).

Daalder, Hans, "Parties and Politics in the Netherlands," *Political Studies,* vol. 3, no. 1 (February 1955) pp. 1–16.

Daalder, Hans, "The Netherlands: Opposition in a Segmented Society," in Robert Dahl, ed., *Political Oppositions in Western Democracies* (New Haven: Yale University Press, 1966) pp. 188–236.

Dahl, Hans Fredrik, *Fra klassekamp til nasjonal samling: Arbeiderpartiet og det nasjonale spørsmål i 30-årene* (Oslo: Pax Forlag, 1969).

Dahl, Hans Fredrik, *Norge mellom krigene: Det norske samfunnet i krise og konflikt, 1918–1940* (Oslo: Pax Forlag, 1971).

Dahl, Hans Frederik et al., "Krisen og det politiske liv," in Sven A. Nilsson, Karl-Gustaf Hildebrand, and Bo Öhngren, eds., *Kriser och krispolitik i Norden under mellankrigstiden: Nordiska historikermötet i Uppsala 1974. Mötesrapport* (Uppsala: Almqvist and Wiksell, 1974) pp. 71–104.

Dahrendorf, Ralf, *Society and Democracy in Germany* (New York: Norton, 1967).

D'Alviella, Goblet, *Alliances et coalitions, étude de tactique Libérale* (Brussels: P. Weissenbruch, 1898).

Danielsen, Rolf, "Samlingpartiet og unionen," *Historisk Tidsskrift* (Oslo), vol. 41, no. 2 (1962) pp. 303–20.

Danmarks Statistik, Statistiske Meddelelser: Landbrugets Arbejdeskraft, 1904 og 1935, ser. 4, vol. 102, no. 3 (Copenhagen: Statistical Department, 1937).

Davies, Norman, *God's Playground: A History of Poland, vol. 2, 1795 to the Present* (New York: Columbia University Press, 1982).

Davis, Malcolm, and Mallory, Walter, eds., *A Political Handbook of the World: Parliaments, Parties and Presses* (New York: Harvard University Press, 1928).

De Felice, Renzo, *Mussolini il duce: Gli anni del consenso, 1929–1936* (Turin: Einaudi, 1974).

De La Cierva, Ricardo, *Historia de la Guerra Civil Española, Antecedents: Monoarquí y República, 1898–1936* (Madrid: San Martín, 1969).

De Lara, Manuel Tuñon, *El movimiento obrero en la historia de España* (Madrid: Taurus, 1972).

De Lara, Manuel Tuñon, *La II República*, 2 vols. (Madrid: Siglo XXI de España Editores, 1976).

De Vos, Harmen, *Geschiedenis van het socialisme in Nederland in het kader van zijn tijd* (Baarn: Het Wereldvenster, 1976).

Deák, István, "Hungary," in Hans Rogger and Eugen Weber, eds., *The European Right: A Historical Profile* (Berkeley: University of California Press, 1965) pp. 364–407.

Démoulin, Robert, "Recherches de Sociologie électorale en régime censitaire," *Révue Française de Science Politique*, vol. 3, no. 4 (October–December 1953) pp. 699–713.

Defourny, M., "Histoire sociale: Les faits, les idées, la législation," in *Histoire de la Belgique contemporaine, 1830–1914*, vol. 2 (Brussels: Albert Dewit, 1929) pp. 241–371.

Dhondt, Jan, "De evolutie van de partijen tussen de twee wereldoorlogen," *Res Publica*, vol. 4 (1962) pp. 370–80.

Dhondt, J., Evalenko, E., and Resjohazy, R., "L'influence de la crise de 1929 sur les mouvements ouvriers en Belgique," in Internationaal Instituut Voor Sociale Geschiedenis Amsterdam, ed., *Mouvements ouvriers et dépression économique de 1929 à 1939* (Assen: Van Gorcum, 1966) pp. 76–102.

Di Scala, Spencer Michael, "Filippo Turati and Factional Strife in the Italian Socialist Party" (Unpublished Ph.D. dissertation: Columbia University, 1969).

Di Scala, Spencer Michael, *The Dilemma of Italian Socialism* (Amherst: University of Massachusetts Press, 1980).

Dupeux, Georges, *La Société française, 1789–1960* (Paris: A. Colin, 1964).

Dybdahl, Vagn, *Partier og erhverv: studier i partiorganisation og byerhvervenes politiske aktivitet ca.1880–ca.1913*, 2 vols. (Århus: Universitetsforlaget, 1969).

Dybdahl, Vagn et al., *Krise i Danmark* (Copenhagen: Gyldendal, 1975).

Edmondson, Clifton Earl, *The Heimwehr and Austrian Politics, 1918–1936* (Athens: University of Georgia Press, 1978).

Ehrmann, Henry, *Organized Business in France* (Princeton: Princeton University Press, 1957).

Einaudi, Luigi, *La condotta economica e gli effetti sociali della guerra italiana* (Bari: Laterza and Figli, 1933).

Eley, Geoff, *From Unification to Nazism: Reinterpreting the German Past* (Boston: Allen and Unwin, 1986).

Eley, Geoff, *Reshaping the German Right: Radical Nationalism and Political Change after Bismarck* (New Haven: Yale University Press, 1980.)

Elvander, Nils, *Skandinavisk arbetarrörelse* (Stockholm: LiberFörlag, 1980).

Engels, Friedrich, *Selected Writings*, W. O. Henderson, ed., (Hammondsworth: Penguin, 1967).

Engelstoft, Povl, and Wendt, Frantz W., *Haandbog i Danmarks politiske historie fra Freden i Kiel til vore dage* (Copenhagen: Gyldendal, 1934).

Ensor, Robert C. K., ed., *Modern Socialism* (London and New York: Harper & Brothers, 1904).

Esping-Andersen, Gøsta, *Politics Against Markets: The Social Democratic Road to Power* (Princeton: Princeton University Press, 1985).

Evans, Ellen Lovell, *The German Center Party, 1870–1933: A Study in Political Catholicism* (Carbondale: Southern Illinois University Press, 1981).

Eyck, Frank, *The Frankfurt Parliament, 1848–1849* (New York: St. Martin's Press, 1968).

Fanfani, Amintore, ed. *L'economia italiana dal 1861 al 1961: Studi nel l'centenario dell'unita d'Italia* (Milan: Giuffrè, 1961).

Farneti, Paolo, *Sistema politico e società civile: Saggi di teoria e ricerca politica* (Turin: Giappichelli, 1971).

Farneti, Paolo, "Social Conflict, Parliamentary Fragmentation, Institutional Shift, and the Rise of Fascism: Italy," in Juan J. Linz and Alfred Stepan, eds., *The Breakdown of Democratic Regimes: Europe* (Baltimore: Johns Hopkins University Press, 1978) pp. 3–33.

Field, G. Lowell, *The Syndical and Corporative Institutions of Italian Fascism* (New York: Columbia University Press, 1938).

Finer, Herman, *Mussolini's Italy* (London: Frank Cass, 1964).

Fink, Troels, *Estruptidens politiske historie, 1875–1894: I. Kampen mellem de to ting, 1875–1885; II. Provisorietiden, 1885–1894* (Odense: Odense Universitetsvorlag, 1986).

Flora, Peter et al., eds., *State, Economy, and Society in Western Europe, 1815–1975, A Data Handbook. Volume I: The Growth of Mass Democracies and Welfare States* (Chicago: St. James Press, 1983).

Flora, Peter, and Alber, Jens, "Modernization, Democratization, and the Development of Welfare States in Western Europe," in Peter Flora and Arnold J. Heidenheimer, eds., *The Development of Welfare States in Europe and America* (New Brunswick, N.J.: Transaction Books, 1981) pp. 37–80.

Flora, Peter, Kraus, Franz, and Pfenning, Winfried, eds., *State, Economy, and Society in Western Europe 1815–1975: A Data Handbook. Volume II: The Growth of Industrial Societies and Capitalist Economies* (Chicago: St. James Press, 1987).

Fox, Alan, *History and Heritage: The Social Origins of the British Industrial Relations System* (London: Allen and Unwin, 1985.)

Freeden, Michael, *The New Liberalism: An Ideology of Social Reform* (Oxford: Clarendon Press, 1978).

Freeden, Michael, *Liberalism Divided: A Study in British Political Thought, 1914–1939* (London: Oxford University Press, 1986).

Freeman, Robert Burns, "The Origins of the Belgian Party System" (Unpublished Ph.D. dissertation: University of California, Berkeley, 1959).

Frese, Jens, "Den tvaerfaglige centralisationsbevaegelse i Danmark for 1900, med saerligt henblik på De samvirkende Fagforeninger 1886 og De samvirkende Fagforbund 1898" (Mimeograph: Arbejderbevaegelsens Bibliotek og Arkiv, Copenhaven, 1969).

Fricke, Dieter, *Die deutsche Arbeiterbewegung. 1869 bis 1914: Ein handbuch über ihre Organisation und Tätigkeit im Klassenkampf* (Berlin: Das Europäische Buch, 1976).

Fricke, Dieter, *Zur organisation und Tätigkeit der deutschen Arbeiterbewegung, 1890–1914: Dokumente und Materialien* (Leipzig: Verlag Enzyklopadie, 1962).

Fridholm, Rolf, "Folkriksdagarna 1893 och 1896," *Statsvetenskaplig tisdkrift för politik-statistik-ekonomi*, vol. 30, no. 5 (December 1927) pp. 411–40.

Fried, Robert C., *The Italian Prefects: A Study in Administrative Politics* (New Haven: Yale University Press, 1963).

Friedrich, Carl J., ed., *The Philosophy of Hegel* (New York: Random House, 1953).

Friisberg, Claus, *På vej mod et demokrati: Fra junigrundloven 1849 til junigrundloven 1915* (Copenhagen: Fremad, 1975).

Frosini, Vittorio, ed., *Il Risorgimento e l'Europa* (Catania: Bonanno, 1969).

Furre, Berge, *Norsk historie, 1905–1940* (Oslo: Det Norske Samlaget, 1971).

Galenson, Walter, *The Danish System of Labor Relations: A Study in Industrial Peace* (Cambridge: Harvard University Press, 1952).

Galenson, Walter, *Labor in Norway* (Cambridge: Harvard University Press, 1949).

Galenson, Walter, and Zellner, Arnold, "International Comparisons of Unemployment Rates," in National Bureau of Economic Research, ed., *The Measurement and Behavior of Unemployment* (Princeton: Princeton University Press, 1957) pp. 439–581.

Gates, Robert, "The Economic Policies of the German Free Trade Unions and the German Social Democratic Party, 1930–1933" (Unpublished Ph.D. dissertation: University of Oregon, 1970).

Gates, Robert, "Von der Sozialpolitik zur Wirtschaftspolitik?: Das Dilemma der deutschen Sozialdemokratie in der Krise 1929–1933," in Hans Mommsen, Dietmar Petzina, and Bernd Weisbrod, eds., *Industrielles System und politische Entwicklung in der Weimarer Republik* (Düsseldorf: Droste Verlag, 1974) pp. 206–25.

Geary, Dick, *European Labour Protest, 1848–1939* (London: Methuen, 1984).

Geary, Dick, "The German Labor Movement, 1848–1918" *European Studies Review*, vol. 6, no. 3 (1976) pp. 297–330.

Gehl, Jürgen, *Austria, Germany and the Anschluss, 1931–1938* (Oxford: Oxford University Press, 1963.)

Georges, Bernard, and Tintant, Denise, *Léon Jouhaux: cinquante ans de syndicalisme* (Paris: Presses Universitaires de France, 1962).

Gellerman, Olle, *Staten och jordbrucket, 1867–1918*, Skrifter utgivna av Statsvetenskapliga föreningen i Uppsala, vol. 39 (Stockholm: Almqvist and Wiksell, 1958).

Gerschenkron, Alexander, *Bread and Democracy in Germany* (Berkeley: University of California Press, 1943).

Gerscherkron, Alexander, *Economic Backwardness in Historical Perspective* (Cambridge: Belknap Press, 1962).

Gessner, Dieter, *Agrarverbände in der Weimarer Republik* (Düsseldorf: Droste Verlag, 1976).

Gilbert, Bentley B. "The Decay of Nineteenth-Century Provident Institutions and the Coming of Old Age Pension in Great Britain," *Economic History Review*, vol. 17, no. 3 (April 1965) pp. 551–63.

Gilissen, John, *Le régime représentatif en Belgique depuis 1790* (Brussels: La Renaissance du Livre, 1958).

Ginsborg, P., "Gramsci and the Era of Bourgeois Revolution in Italy," in John A. Davis, ed., *Gramsci and Italy's Passive Revolution* (London: Groom Helm, 1979) pp. 31–66.

Goguel, François, *La politique des partis ous la IIIe République* (Paris: Seuil, 1946).

Gómez Casas, Juan, *Historia del anarcosindicalismo español* 4th ed. (Madrid: ZYX, 1978).

Good, David F., *The Economic Rise of the Habsburg Empire 1750–1914* (Berkeley: University of California Press, 1984).

Gourevitch, Peter, *Politics in Hard Times: Comparative Responses to International Economic Crises* (Ithaca, N.Y.: Cornell University Press, 1986).

Gourevitch, Peter et al., *Unions and Economic Crisis: Britain, West Germany and Sweden* (London: George Allen and Unwin, 1984).

Greenall, R. L., "Popular Conservatism in Salford, 1868–1886," *Northern History*, vol. 9 (1974) pp. 123–38.

Greene, Nathaniel, *Crisis and Decline: The French Socialist Party in the Popular Front Era* (Ithaca, N.Y.: Cornell University Press, 1969).

Gregor, A. James, *Italian Fascism and Developmental Dictatorship* (Princeton: Princeton University Press, 1979).

Grenier, A. S., *Nos Députés: Biographies et Portraits* (Paris: Berger-Levrault, 1899).

Grew, Raymond, "Il trasformismo: ultimo stadio del Risorgimento," in Vittorio Frosini, ed., *Il Risorgimento e l'Europa* (Catania: Bonanno, 1969) pp. 151–63.

Grew, Raymond, "Italy," in Raymond Grew, ed., *Crises of Political Development in Europe and the United States* (Princeton: Princeton University Press, 1978) pp. 271–311.

Grunberger, Richard, *The 12-Year Reich: A Social History of Nazi Germany, 1933–1945* (New York: Holt, Rinehart and Winston, 1971).

Gruner, Erich, *Die Arbeiter in der Schweiz im 19. Jahrhundert* (Bern: Francke Verlag, 1968).

Gruner, Erich, *Die Parteien in der Schweiz* (Bern: Francke Verlag, 1969).

Gruner, Erich, *Die Wahlen in der Schweizerischen Nationalrat, 1848–1919*, 3 vols. (Bern: Francke, 1978).

Gualtieri, H. L., *The Labor Movement in Italy* (New York: S. F. Vanni, 1946).

Guérin, Daniel, *Front populaire, révolution manquée*, rev. ed. (Paris: Maspero, 1970).

Gulick, Charles A., *Austria: From Habsburg to Hitler*, 2 vols. (Berkeley: University of California Press, 1948).

Gustafsson, Bo, "A Perennial of Doctrinal History: Keynes and the 'Stockholm School'," *Economy and History*, vol. 16 (1973) pp. 114–28.

Hadenius, Stig et al., *Sverige efter 1900: En modern politisk historia* (Stockholm: Aldus, 1978).

Hadenius, Stig, Seveborg, Jan-Olof, and Weibull, Lennart, *Socialdemokratisk press och presspolitik, 1899–1909* (Stockholm: Tidens Förlag, 1968).

Halsey, A. H., ed., *Trends in British Society Since 1900: A Guide to the Changing Social Structure of Britain* (London: Macmillan, 1972).

Hamer, David Allan, *Liberal Politics in the Age of Gladstone and Rosebery: A Study in Leadership and Policy* (Oxford: Clarendon Press, 1972).

Hamerow, Theodore, *The Birth of a New Europe: State and Society in the Nineteenth Century* (Chapel Hill: University of North Carolina Press, 1983).

Hamerow, Theodore S., *Restoration, Revolution, Reaction: Economics and Politics in Germany, 1815–1857* (Princeton: Princeton University Press, 1970).

Hamerow, Theodore S., *The Social Foundations of German Unification, 1858–1871: Struggles and Accomplishments* (Princeton: Princeton University Press, 1972).

Hamilton, Richard F., *Who Voted for Hitler?* (Princeton: Princeton University Press, 1982).

Hanisch, Ted, *Hele folket i arbeid* (Oslo: Pax, 1977).

Hansen, Erik, "Depression Decade Crisis: Social Democracy and Planisme in Belgium and the Netherlands, 1929–1939," *Journal of Contemporary History*, vol. 16, no. 2 (April 1981) pp. 293–322.

Hansen, Erik, "Workers and Socialists: Relations Between the Dutch Trade-Union Movement and Social Democracy, 1894–1914," *European Studies Review*, vol. 7, no. 2 (April 1977) pp. 199–226.

Hansen, Karin and Torpe, Lars, *Socialdemokratiet og krisen i 30'erne* (Århus: Mod Tryk, 1977).

Hansen, Svend Aage, *Økonomisk Vaekst i Danmark*, 2 vols. (Copenhagen: Akademisk Forlag, 1974).

Hansen, Svend Aage, and Henriksen, Ingrid, *Sociale brydninger, 1914–1939: Dansk social historie, bind 6* Copenhagen: Gyldendal, 1980).

Harmsen, Ger, and Reinalda, Bob, *Voor de bevrijding van de arbeid: Beknopte geschiedenis van de nerderlandse vakbeweging* (Nijmegen: Socialistiese Uitgeverij, 1975).

Harrison, Joseph, "Big Business and the Failure of Right-Wing Catalan Nationalism, 1901–1923," *The Historical Journal*, vol. 19, no. 4 (December 1976) pp. 901–18.

Harrison, Joseph, "Big Business and the Rise of Basque Nationalism," *European Studies Review*, vol. 7, no. 4 (October 1977) pp. 371–91.

Harrison, Joseph, "Catalan Business and the Loss of Cuba, 1898–1914," *The Economic History of Review, Second Series* vol. 27, no. 3 (August 1974) pp. 431–41.

Hart, Peter E., *Studies in Profit, Business Saving and Investment in the United Kingdom, 1920–1962* (London: Allen and Unwin, 1965).

Haue, Harry, Olsen, Jørgen, and Aarup-Kristensen, Jørn, *Det ny Danmark, 1890–1978: Udviklingslinier og tendens* (Copenhagen: Munksgaard, 1979).

Havighurst, Alfred F., *Twentieth Century Britain*, 2nd ed. (New York: Harper & Row, 1966).

Hay, J. R., *The Origins of the Liberal Welfare Reforms, 1906–1914* (New York: Macmillan, 1975).

Hayward, J. E. S., "The Official Social Philosophy of the French Third Republic: Léon Bourgeois and Solidarism." *International Review of Social History*, vol. 6, pt. 1 (1961) pp. 19–48.

Hayward, J. E. S., "Solidarity: The Social History of an Idea in Nineteenth Century France," *International Review of Social History*, vol. 4, pt. 2 (1959) pp. 261–84.

Hembree, Michael F., "The Politics of Intransigence: Costantino Lazzari and the Italian Socialist Left, 1882–1919" (Unpublished Ph.D. dissertation: Florida State University, 1981).

Hentilä, Seepo, *Den svenska arbetarklassen och reformismens genombrott inom SAP före 1914: Arbetarklassens ställning, strategi och ideologi* (Helsinki: Suomen Historiallinen Seura, 1979).

Heyde, Ludwig, ed., *Internationales Handwörterbuch des Gewerkschaftenswesens*, 2 vols. (Berlin: Werk und Wirtschaft Verlagaktionengeselschaft, 1931–1932).

Hibbs, Jr., Douglas, "On the Political Economy of Long-Run Trends in Strike

Activity," *British Journal of Political Science*, vol. 8, pt. 2 (April 1978) pp. 153–75.

Hildebrand, K. G., "Labour and Capital in the Scandinavian Countries in the Nineteenth and Twentieth Centuries," Peter Mathias and M. M. Postan, eds., *The Cambridge Economic History of Europe. Volume VII, The Industrial Economies: Capital, Labour and Enterprise. Part I, Britain, France, Germany and Scandinavia* (London: Cambridge University Press, 1978) pp. 590–628.

Hill, Keith, "Belgium: Political Change in a Segmented Society," in Richard Rose, ed., *Electoral Behavior: A Comparative Handbook* (New York: Free Press, 1974) pp. 29–107.

Hinton, James, *Labour and Socialism: A History of the British Labour Movement, 1867–1974* (Brighton, Sussex: Wheatsheaf Books, 1983).

Hobsbawm, E. J., *Labouring Men: Studies in the History of Labour* (London: Weidenfeld and Nicolson, 1964).

Hodne, Fritz, *Norges økonomiske historie, 1815–1970* (Oslo: J. W. Cappelens Forlag, 1981).

Hodne, Fritz, *The Norwegian Economy, 1920–1980* (London: Croom Helm, 1983).

Hoekstra, P., "De laatste tien liberale jaren in het Noorden (1891–1901)" in J. A. van Houtte et al., eds., *Algemene geschiedenis der Nederlanden* (Antwerp: W. De Haan, 1956) vol. 2, pp. 60–82.

Hoensch, Jörg, *Geschichte der Tschechoslowakischen Republik, 1918–1978* (Stuttgart: W. Kohlhammer, 1978).

Hoffmann, Stanley, "Paradoxes of the French Political Community," in Stanley Hoffmann, ed., *In Search of France: The Economy, Society and Political System in the Twentieth Century* (New York: Harper & Row, 1963) pp. 1–118.

Hoffmann, Walter G., *Das Wachstum der deutschen Wirtschaft seit der Mitte des 19. Jahrhunderts* (Berlin: Springer Verlag, 1965).

Holborn, Hajo, *A History of Modern Germany, 1840–1945* (Princeton: Princeton University Press, 1969).

Horowitz, Daniel L., *The Italian Labor Movement* (Cambridge: Harvard University Press, 1963).

Hosking, Geoffrey, *The First Socialist Society: A History of the Soviet Union from Within* (Cambridge: Harvard University Press, 1985).

Howard, E. P., *Il Partito Popolare Italiano* (Florence: La Nuova Italia, 1957).

Howell, David, *British Workers and the Independent Labour Party, 1888–1906* (Manchester: Manchester University Press, 1983).

Hueting, Ernest, De Jong Edz., Frits, and Neij, Robert, *Naar groter eenheid: De geschiedenis van het Nederlands Verbond van Vakverenigingen, 1906–1981* (Amsterdam: Van Gennep, 1983).

Hughes, Christopher, *Switzerland* (New York: Praeger, 1975).

Hughes, Christopher, *The Parliament of Switzerland* (London: Cassell and Co., 1962).

Hunt, Edward H., *British Labour History, 1815–1914* (London: Weidenfeld and Nicolson, 1981).

Hvidt, Kristian, *Venstre og forsvarssagen, 1870–1901* (Århus: Universitets Forlaget, 1960).

Imhof, Ulrich et al., *Geschichte der Schweiz und der Schweizer* (Basel: Helburg and Lichtenhahn Verlag, 1983).

Ingham, Geoffrey K., *Strikes and Industrial Conflict: Britain and Scandinavia* (London: Macmillan, 1974).

Inglehart, Ronald, "The Changing Structure of Political Cleavages in Western Society," in Russell Dalton et al., eds., *Electoral Change in Advanced Industrial Democracies* (Princeton: Princeton University Press, 1984) pp. 25–69.

Instituto de Reforma Agraria, *Agrarian Reform in Spain: An Historical Study by the Spanish Institute for Agrarian Reform* (London: United Editorial, 1938).

Irurozqui, Manuel Fuentes, *Sintesis de la economía española* (Madrid: Diana, 1946).

Jacini, Stefano, *Storia del Partito Popolare Italiano* (Milan: Garzanti, 1951).

Jackson, Gabriel, *The Spanish Republic and the Civil War, 1931–1939* (Princeton: Princeton University Press, 1965).

Jagschitz, Gerhard, "Bundeskanzler Dollfuss und der Juli 1934," in *Österreich 1927 bis 1938*, ed. the Wissenschaftliche Kommission (München: Oldenbourg, 1973), pp. 150–60.

Janos, Andrew C., "The Rise and Fall of Civil Society: The Politics of Backwardness on the European Peripheries, 1780–1945" (Mimeograph: University of California, Berkeley, 1987).

Janos, Andrew C., *The Politics of Backwardness in Hungary, 1825–1945* (Princeton: Princeton University Press, 1982).

Jedlicka, Ludwig, "The Austrian Heimwehr," *Journal of Contemporary History,* vol. 1, no. 1 (1966) pp. 127–44.

Jenks, William A., *Austria Under the Iron Ring, 1879–1913* (Charlottesville: University of Virginia Press, 1965).

Johansen, Hans Christian, *The Danish Economy in the Twentieth Century* (London: Croom Helm, 1987).

Johansson, Olle, "Socialdemokratins väljare 1911 och 1914: En kvantitativ analys av regional och social gruppering och struktur," *Historisk tidskrift* (Stockholm) vol. 86, no. 3 (1967) pp. 297–356.

Joll, James, *Europe Since 1870: An International History* (London: Weidenfeld, 1973).

Jones, Gareth Stedman, *Outcast London: A Study in the Relationship Between Classes in Victorian Society* (Oxford: Clarendon Press, 1971).

Jones, Gareth Stedman, "Working-Class Culture and Working-Class Politics in London, 1870–1900: Notes on the Remaking of a Working Class," *Journal of Social History,* vol. 7, no. 4 (Summer 1974) pp. 460–508.

Jørgensen, Erik Stig, "Partier og partimodsaetninger 1848–1864," in Per Salomonsson, ed., *Den politiske magtkamp, 1866–1901* (Copenhagen: Jørgen Paludans Forlag, 1968) pp. 9–20.

Jørgensen, Erik Stig, "Den reviderede grundlovs tilblivelse 1864–1866," in Per Salomonsson, ed., *Den politiske magtkamp, 1866–1901* (Copenhagen: Jørgen Paludans Forlag, 1968) pp. 21–34.

Jouhaux, Léon, *Le Syndicalisme et la CGT* (Paris: Bibliotheque d'evolution socialie, 1920).

Joyce, P., "The Factory Politics of Lancashire in the Later Nineteenth Century," *Historical Journal,* vol. 18, no. 3 (September 1975) pp. 525–53.

Judson, Kirkland Kenneth, "The Italian Chambers of Labor, 1890–1914: The Formation of Working-Class Consciousness" (Unpublished Ph.D. dissertation: University of Michigan, 1976).

Judt, Tony, *Marxism and the French Left: Studies on Labor and Politics in France, 1830–1981* (London: Oxford University Press, 1986).

Kaartvedt, Alf, *Kampen mot parlamentarisme, 1880–1884* (Oslo: Universitetsforlaget, 1967).

Kaiserlichen Statistischen Amt, *Vierteljahrshefte zur Statistik des Deutschen Reichs* (Berlin: Verlag von Buttfammer & Mühlbrecht, various 1892–1944).

Kalecki, M., "The Lesson of the Blum Experiment," *Economic Journal*, vol. 48, no. 189 (March 1938) pp. 26–41.

Kalela, Jorma, "Right-Wing Radicalism in Finland During the Interwar Period," *Scandinavian Journal of History*, vol. 1, no. 2 (1976) pp. 105–24.

Kann, Robert A., *The Multinational Empire: Nationalism and National Reform in the Habsburg Monarchy* (New York: Columbia University Press, 1950).

Kann, Robert A., *A History of the Habsburg Empire, 1526–1918* (Berkeley: University of California Press, 1980).

Karlbom, Torvald, *Svenska grov- och fabriksarbetareförbundets historia* (Stockholm, 1941).

Kårsted, Tage, *Påskeskrisen, 1920* (Århus: Universitetsforlaget i Århus, 1973).

Katzenstein, Peter J., *Small States in World Markets: Industrial Policy in Europe* (Ithaca, N.Y.: Cornell University Press, 1985).

Kerner, Robert J., ed., *Czechoslovakia: Twenty Years of Independence* (Berkeley: University of California Press, 1940).

Kitchen, Martin, *The German Officer Corps, 1890–1914* (New York: Oxford University Press, 1968).

Klepetař, Harry, *Seit 1918 . . . Eine Geschichte der Tschechoslowakischen Republik* (Moravska Ostrava: Verlag Julius Kittls, 1937).

Koblik, Steven, ed., *Sweden's Development from Poverty to Affluence, 1750–1970* (Minneapolis: University of Minnesota Press, 1975).

Kocka, Jürgen, ed., *Europäische Arbeiterbewegungen im 19. Jahrhundert* (Göttingen: Vandenhoeck and Ruprecht, 1983).

Kocka, Jürgen, "Problems of Working-Class Formation in Germany," in Ira Katznelson and Aristide Zolberg, eds., *Working-Class Formation: Nineteenth Century Patterns in Western Europe and the United States* (Princeton: Princeton University Press, 1986) pp. 279–351.

Kocka, Jürgen, "Die Trennung von bürglicher und proletarischer Demokratie im europäischen Vergleich: Fragestellungen und Ergebnisse," in Jürgen Kocka, ed., *Europäische Arbeiterbewegungen im 19. Jahrhundert* (Göttingen: Vandenhoeck and Ruprecht, 1983) pp. 5–20.

Koht, Halvdan, ed., *Det norske arbeiderpartis historie. 1887–1937*, 2 Vols. (Oslo: Det Norske Arbeiderpartis Forlag, 1939).

Korpi, Walter, *The Democratic Class Struggle* (London: Routledge and Kegan Paul, 1983).

Korpi, Walter, and Shalev, Michael, "Strikes, Power and Politics in Western Nations," *Political Power and Social Theory*, vol. 1 (1980) pp. 301–34.

Kossman, E. H., *The Low Countries, 1780–1940* (New York: Oxford University Press, 1978).

Kriegel, Annie, "Histoire du mouvement ouvrier français, 1914–1920" (Unpublished Ph.D. Dissertation: University of Paris, 1964).

Krieger, Leonard, *The German Idea of Freedom: History of a Political Tradition from the Reformation to 1871* (Boston: Beacon Press, 1957).

Krogh, Torben, *Viggo Horup: En illustreret levnedsskildring* (Copenhagen: Gyldendal, 1984).

Kuczysnki, Jürgen, *Die Geschichte der Lage der Arbeiter unter dem Kapitalismus: Vol. 3, Part 1, Darstellung der Lage der Arbeiter in Deutschland von 1871 bis 1900* (Berlin: Tribune, 1962).

Kuisel, Richard, *Capitalism and the State in Modern France, Renovation and Economic Management in the Twentieth Century* (London: Cambridge University Press, 1981).

Kuznets, Simon, ed., *Review of Income and Wealth*, Series 5 (London: Bowes and Bowes, 1955).

Labi, Maurice, *La grande division des travailleurs: prémière scission de la CGT (1914–1921)* (Paris: Les Editions Ouvrières, 1964).

Lacomba Avellan, Juan Antonio, *La crisis española de 1917* (Madrid: Editorial Ciencia Nueva, 1970).

Lange, Halvard, "Arbeiderpartiet 1905–1914," in Halvdan Koht, ed., *Det norske arbeiderpartis historie, 1887–1937* (Oslo: Det Norske Arbeiderpartis Forlag, 1939) vol. 2, pp. 1–111.

Lange, Halvard, "Arbeiderpartiets historie 1887–1937," in Halvdan Koht, ed., *Det norske arbeiderpartis historie. 1887–1937* (Oslo: Det Norske Arbeiderpartis Forlag, 1937) vol. 1, pp. 75–244.

Lange, Halvard, *Fra sekt til parti: det norske arbeiderpartis organisasjonsmessige og politiske utvikling fra 1891 til 1902* (Oslo: Universitetsforlaget, 1962).

Langfeldt, Knut, *Moskva-tesene i norsk politik* (Oslo: Universitetsforlaget, 1961).

Laqueur, Walter, ed., *Fascism: A Reader's Guide* (Berkeley: University of California Press, 1976).

League of Nations, *Agricultural Production in Continental Europe During the 1914–18 War and the Reconstruction Period* (Geneva: League of Nations Publications, 1943).

LeFranc, Georges, *Histoire du front populaire, 1934–1938,* (Paris: Payot, 1965).

LeFranc, Georges, *Le mouvement syndical sous la Troisième République* (Paris: Payot, 1967).

LeFranc, Georges, *Le mouvement socialiste sous la Troisième République, 1875–1940* (Paris: Payot, 1963).

Lepsius, M. Rainer, "From Fragmented Party Democracy to Government by Emergency Decree and National Socialist Takeover: Germany," in Juan J. Linz and Alfred Stepan, *The Breakdown of Democratic Regimes: Europe* (Baltimore: Johns Hopkins University Press, 1978) pp. 34–79.

Lester, Richard Allen, *Monetary Experiments: Early American and Recent Scandinavian* (Princeton: Princeton University Press, 1939).

Le Temps (Paris), various issues, 1902–1914.

Lewis, Brackett, "Social Reform and Social Legislation," in Robert J. Kerner, ed., *Czechoslovakia: Twenty Years of Independence* (Berkeley: University of California Press, 1940) pp. 251–71.

Lichtheim, George, *Marxism: An Historical and Critical Study* (New York: Columbia University Press, 1982).

Lidtke, Vernon L., *The Outlawed Party: Social Democracy in Germany, 1878–1890* (Princeton: Princeton University Press, 1966).

Lindbom, Tage, and Evert Kuhm, Tage, *Tobaksarbetarnas förbund i Sverge* (Stockholm, 1940).

Lindgren, John, *Svenska metallindustriarbetareförbundets historia* (Stockholm, 1938).

Lindley, Charles, *Svenska transportarbetareförbundet: Historia* (Stockholm, 1943).

Linz, Juan, "A Century of Politics and Interests in Spain," in Suzanne D. Berger, ed., *Organizing Interests in Western Europe* (Cambridge: Cambridge University Press, 1981) pp. 365–415.

Linz, Juan, "The Party System of Spain: Past and Future," in Seymour Martin Lipset and Stein Rokkan, eds., *Party Systems and Voter Alignments: Cross-National Perspectives* (New York: Free Press, 1967) pp. 197–282.

Linz, Juan, "From Falange to Movimiento-Organizacion: The Spanish Single Party and the Franco Regime, 1936–1968," in Samuel P. Huntington and Clement H. Moore, eds., *Authoritarian Politics in Modern Society* (New York: Basic Books, 1970) pp. 128–201.

Linz, Juan, "From Great Hopes to Civil War: The Breakdown of Democracy in Spain," in Juan J. Linz and Alfred Stepan, ed., *The Breakdown of Democratic Regimes: Europe* (Baltimore: Johns Hopkins University Press, 1978) pp. 142–215.

Linz, Juan, "Some Notes Toward a Comparative Study of Fascism in Sociological-Historical Perspective," in Walter Laqueur, ed., *Fascism: A Reader's Guide* (Berkeley: University of California Press, 1976) pp. 3–121.

Linz, Juan J., and Stepan, Alfred, ed., *The Breakdown of Democratic Regimes: Europe* (Baltimore: Johns Hopkins University Press, 1978).

Lipschits, I., *Ontstaansgeschiedenis van de Nederlandse politieke partijen: Deel I. De protestants-christelijke stroming tot 1940* (Deventer: Kluwer, 1977).

Lipset, Seymour Martin, "Radicalism or Reformism: The Sources of Working-Class Politics," *American Political Science Review*, vol. 77, no. 1 (March 1983) pp. 1–18.

Lipset, Seymour Martin, and Rokkan, Stein, "Cleavage Structures, Party Systems and Voter Alignments: An Introduction," in Lipset and Rokkan, eds., *Party Systems and Voter Alignments: Cross-National Perspectives* (New York: Free Press, 1967) pp. 1–64.

Loertscher-Rouge, Françoise, "La politique de la FOHM dans l'horlogerie lors de la crise des années trente (1930–1937)" *Revue Européenne des Sciences Sociales*, vol. 15, no. 42 (1977) pp. 143–99.

Lorenz, Einhart, *Arbeiderbevegelsens historie, En innføring: Norsk socialisme i internasjonalt perspecktiv, 1. del. 1789–1930* (Oslo: Pax Forlag, 1972).

Lorenz, Robert, *The Essential Features of Germany's Agricultural Policy from 1870 to 1937* (New York: Columbia University Press, 1941).

Lorwin, Val, *The French Labor Movement* (Cambridge: Harvard University Press, 1954).

Loubère, Léo A., *Radicalism in Mediterranean France, Its Rise and Decline, 1848–1914* (Albany: State University of New York Press, 1974).

Loubère, Léo, "Left-Wing Radicals, Strikes, and the Military, 1880–1907," *French Historical Studies*, vol. 3, no. 1 (Spring 1963) pp. 93–105.

Loubère, Léo, "Les Radicaux d'extrême-gauche en France et les rapports entre patrons et ouvriers (1871–1900)," *Revue d'histoire économique et sociale*, vol. 42, no. 1 (1964) pp. 89–103.

Loubère, Léo, "The French Left-Wing Radicals: Their Views on Trade Unionism, 1870–1898," *International Review of Social History*, vol. 7, pt. 2 (1962) pp. 203–30.

Lovell, John, and Roberts, B. C., *A Short History of the TUC* (London: Macmillan, 1968).

Luck, James Murray, *A History of Switzerland* (Palo Alto, Calif.: SPOSS, 1985).

Luis Guinea, José, *Los movimientos obreros y sindicales en España de 1833 a 1978* (Madrid: Iberico Europea, 1978).

Lundberg, E., "Business Cycle Experiences in Sweden, with Special Reference to Economic Policy Issues," in Erik Lundberg, ed., *The Business Cycle in the Post-War World* (London: Macmillan, 1955) pp. 55–77.

Lunden, Kåre, "The Growth of Co-operatives Among the Norwegian Dairyfarmers During the Period 1856–1905," *Cahier Internationaux D'Histoire Economique et Sociale*, vol. 6 (Geneva: Librairie Droz, 1973) pp. 335–62.

Lundkvist, Sven, "Popular Movements and Reforms, 1900–1920," in Steve Koblik, ed., *Sweden's Development from Poverty to Affluence, 1750–1970* (Minneapolis: University of Minnesota Press, 1975) pp. 180–93.

Luykx, Theo, *Politieke geschiedenis van België van 1789 tot heden*, 2nd ed. (Brussels: Elsevier, 1969).

Lyttelton, Adrian, *The Seizure of Power: Fascism in Italy, 1919–1929* 2nd ed. (Princeton: Princeton University Press, 1987).

Macartney, Carlile A., *The Habsburg Empire, 1790–1918* (London: Weidenfeld and Nicolson, 1969).

MacDonald, J. Ramsay, *The Socialist Movement* (London: Williams and Norgate, 1911).

MacDonald, J. Ramsay, and Hardy, J. Keir, "The Independent Labor Party's Programme," *The Nineteenth Century*, vol. 45, no. 263 (January 1899) pp. 20–38.

Magraw, Roger, *France, 1815–1914: The Bourgeois Century* (New York: Oxford University Press, 1986).

Maier, Charles, *Recasting Bourgeois Europe: Stabilization in France, Germany and Italy in the Decade after World War I* (Princeton: Princeton University Press, 1975).

Malefakis, Edward, *Agrarian Reform and Peasant Revolution in Spain: Origins of the Civil War* (New Haven: Yale University Press, 1970).

Malefakis, Edward, "Peasants, Politics and Civil War in Spain, 1931–1939," in Robert Bezucha, ed., *Modern European Social History* (Lexington, Mass.: D. C. Heath, 1972) pp. 192–227.

Mamatey, Victor S., "The Development of Czechoslovak Democracy, 1920–1938," in Victor Mamatey and Radomír Luža, eds., *A History of the Czechoslovak Republic, 1918–1948* (Princeton: Princeton University Press, 1973) pp. 99–166.

Mamatey, Victor, and Luža, Radomír, eds., *A History of the Czechoslovak Republic, 1918–1948* (Princeton: Princeton University Press, 1973).

Mann, Thomas, and Tillet, Benn, *The "New" Trades Unionism* (London, 1890).

Marczewski, Jan, *Planification et croissance économique des démocraties populaires* (Paris: Presses Universitaires de France, 1956).

Marjolin, Robert, "Reflections on the Blum Experiment," *Economica* (New Series), vol. 5, no. 18 (May 1938) pp. 177–91.

Markert, Werner, ed., *Osteuropa Handbuch: Vol. 1, Jugoslawien* (Cologne: Böhlau, 1954).

Markert, Werner, ed., *Osteuropa Handbuch: Vol. 2, Polen* (Cologne: Böhlau, 1959).

Marks, Harry J., "The Sources of Reformism in the Social Democratic Party of Germany, 1890–1914," *Journal of Modern History*, vol. 11, no. 3 (September 1939) pp. 334–56.

Marshall, T. H., *Citizenship and Social Class and Other Essays* (Cambridge: Cambridge University Press, 1950).

Martin, Andrew, "Trade Unions in Sweden: Strategic Responses to Change and Crisis," in Peter Gourevitch et al., *Unions and Economic Crisis: Britain, West Germany and Sweden* (London: George Allen and Unwin, 1984) pp. 190–359.

Masnata, François, *Le parti socialiste et la tradition démocratique en Suisse* (Paris: A. Colin, 1963).

Mason, Timothy, *Arbeiterklasse und Volksgemeinschaft: Dokumente und Materialien zur deutschen Arbeiterpolitik, 1936–1939* (Opladen: Westdeutscher Verlag, 1975).

McIvor, Anthony D., "Spanish Labor Policy During the Dictablanda of Primo De Rivera" (Unpublished Ph.D. dissertation: Department of History, University of California, San Diego, 1982).

Mertens, Corneille, *The Trade Union Movement in Belgium* (Amsterdam: International Federation of Trade Unions, 1925).

Meyer, Håkon, "Arbeiderpartiet, 1914–1923," in Halvdan Koht, ed., *Det norske arbeiderpartis historie, 1887–1937*, vol. 2 (Oslo: Det Norske Arbeiderpartis Forlag, 1939) pp. 113–370.

Middlemas, Robert Keith, *Politics in Industrial Society: The Experience of the British System Since 1911* (London: André Deutsch, 1979).

Midwinter, Eric C., *Victorian Social Reform* (London: Longmans, 1968).

Milward, Alan, "Fascism and the Economy," in Walter Laqueur, ed., *Fascism: A Reader's Guide* (Berkeley: University of California Press, 1976) pp. 379–412.

Mitchell, B. R., *European Historical Statistics, 1750–1970* (New York: Columbia University Press, 1975).

Mitzman, Arthur, "The French Working Class and the Blum Government (1936–37)," *International Review of Social History*, vol. 9, pt. 3 (1964) pp. 363–90.

Mjeldheim, Leiv, *Folkerørsla som vart parti: Venstre frå 1880 åra til 1905* (Bergen: Universitetsforlaget, 1984).

Moeller, Robert G., *German Peasants and Agrarian Politics, 1914–1924: The Rhineland and Westphalia* (Chapel Hill: University of North Carolina Press, 1986).

Mommsen, Hans, Petzina, Dietmar, and Weisbrod, Bernd, eds., *Industrielles System und politische Entwicklung in der Weimarer Republik* (Düsseldorf: Droste Verlag, 1974).

Montojo Sureda, Jorge, *La política española sobre trigos y harinas: Años 1900–1945* (Madrid: Afrodisio Aguado, 1945).

Moore, Barrington, Jr., *Social Origins of Dictatorship and Democracy: Lord and Peasant in the Making of the Modern World* (Boston: Beacon Press, 1966).

Moore, Barrington, Jr., *Injustice: The Social Bases of Obedience and Revolt* (White Plains, N.Y.: M. E. Sharpe, 1978).

Moore, Richard, *Pitmen, Preachers and Politics* (Cambridge: Cambridge University Press, 1974).

Moore, Wilbert E., *Economic Demography of Southern and Eastern Europe* (Geneva: League of Nations, 1945).

Morgan, Roger, *The German Social Democrats and the First International, 1864–1872* (London: Cambridge University Press, 1965).

Moses, John A., *Trade Unionism in Germany from Bismarck to Hitler, 1869–1933* (Totawa, N.J.: Barnes and Noble, 1982).

Moss, Bernard H., *The Origins of the French Labor Movement, 1830–1914: The Socialism of Skilled Workers* (Berkeley: University of California Press, 1976).

Müller, Klaus, "Agrarische Interessenverbände in der Weimarer Republik," *Rheinische Vierteljahrsblätter*, vol. 38 (1974) pp. 386–405.

Münzinger, Adolf, *Der Arbeitsertrag der bäuerlichen Familienwirtschaft: Eine bäuerliche Betriebserhebung in Württemberg* (Berlin, 1929).

Nemec, Frantisek, *From Social Welfare to Social Justice* (London: Lincolns-Prager, 1943).

Nenni, Pietro, *Storia di quattro anni, 1919–1922*, 2nd ed. (Rome: Einaudi, 1946).

Nerman, Ture, *Svensk arbetarrörelse under hundra år* (Stockholm: Tidensförlag, 1938).

Neufeld, Maurice, *Italy: School for Awakening Countries: The Italian Labor Movement in Its Political, Social, and Economic Setting from 1800 to 1960* (New York: Cornell University Press, 1961).

Nilsson, Sven A., Hildebrand, Karl-Gustaf, and Öhngren, Bo, eds., *Kriser och krispolitik i Norden under mellankrigstiden: Nordiska historikermötet i Uppsala 1974. Mötesrapport* (Uppsala: Almqvist and Wiksell, 1974).

Noakes, J., and Pridham, G., eds., *Nazism, 1919–1945: A Documentary Reader: Vol. 2, State, Economy and Society, 1933–1939*, Exeter Studies in History, no. 8 (Exeter: University of Exeter, 1984).

Nordström, Gustaf Hilding, *Sveriges socialdemokratiska arbetareparti under genombrottsåren, 1889–1894* (Stockholm: Kooperativa förbundets bokförlag, 1938).

Nørregård, Georg, *Arbejdsforhold inden for Dansk industri og håndvaerk, 1857–1899* (Copenhagen: Gyldendal, 1943).

Øidne, Gabriel, "Venstres valgnederlag i 1903: Politiske strømninger ved århundreskiftet i Norge," *Historisk Tidsskrift* (Oslo), vol. 51, no. 1 (1972) pp. 37–69.

Olsson, Reinhold, and Lindström, Richard, *En krönika om sågverksarbetare: Svenska sågverksindustriarbetareförbundets minnesskrift* (Sundsvall, 1953).

Owen, Roger, and Sutcliffe, Bob, eds., *Studies in the Theory of Imperialism* (London: Longman, 1972).

Palme, Sven Ulric, *På Karl Staaffs tid* (Stockholm: Aldus/Bonniers, 1964).

Papayanis, Nicholas, "Masses révolutionnaires et directions réformistes: Les tensions au cours des grèves des métallurgistes français en 1919," *Le mouvement social*, no. 93 (October–December 1975) pp. 51–73.

Pauley, Bruce F., *Hitler and the Forgotten Nazis: A History of Austrian National Socialism* (Chapel Hill: University of North Carolina Press, 1981).

Payne, Stanley G., *The Spanish Revolution: A Study of the Social and Political Tensions That Culminated in the Civil War in Spain* (New York: Norton, 1970).

Payne, Stanley G., *Basque Nationalism* (Reno: University of Nevada Press, 1975).

Pedersen, Erik Helmer, Thullberg, Per, and Tveite, Stein, "Nordens jordbruk under världskrisen, 1929–1933," in Sven A. Nilsson, Karl-Gustaf Hildebrand, and Bo Öhngren, eds., *Kriser och krispolitik i Norden under mellankrigstiden: Nordiska historikermötet i Uppsala 1974. Mötesrapport* (Uppsala: Almqvist and Wiksell, 1974) pp. 155–206.

Pelling, Henry M., *The Origins of the Labour Party, 1880–1900*, 2nd ed. (Oxford: Clarendon Press, 1965).

Pelling, Henry M., *Popular Politics and Society in Late Victorian Britain* (New York: St. Martin's Press, 1968).

Perrot, Michelle, *Les ouvriers en grève, France 1871–1890* (Paris: Mouton, 1974).

Petersen, Niels, "Forlig og omgruppering," in Per Salomonsson, ed., *Den politiske magtkamp, 1866–1901* (Copenhagen: Jørgen Paludans Forlag, 1968) pp. 91–116.

Petrovich, Michael Boro, *A History of Modern Serbia, 1804–1918* (New York: Harcourt Brace, 1976).

Pirenne, Henri, *Histoire de Belgique: Vol. 7, De la révolution de 1830 à la guerre de 1914* (Brussels: Maurice Lamertin, 1932).

Polanyi, Karl, *The Great Transformation* (Boston: Beacon Press, 1957).

Polonsky, Antony, *The Little Dictators: The History of Eastern Europe Since 1918* (London: Routledge and Kegan Paul, 1975).

Polonsky, Antony, *Politics in Independent Poland, 1921–1939* (Oxford: Oxford University Press, 1972).

Poulantzas, Nicos, *Fascism and Dictatorship* (London: Verso, 1979).

Procházka, Zora, "Foreign Trade and Economic Development of Czechoslovakia, 1919–1937" (Unpublished Ph.D. Dissertation: Radcliffe College, 1960).

Protokoll (SDAP fourth convention; 1897).

Protokoll (SDAP second convention; 1891).

Protokoll (SDAP third convention; 1894).

Pryor, Zora P., "Czecholsovak Economic Development in the Interwar Period," in Victor Mamatey and Radomír Luža, eds., *A History of the Czechoslovak Republic, 1918–1948* (Princeton: Princeton University Press, 1973) pp. 188–215.

Przeworski, Adam, "Material Bases of Consent: Economics and Politics in a Hegemonic System," *Political Power and Social Theory*, vol. 1 (1980) pp. 21–66.

Przeworski, Adam, "Social Democracy as a Historical Phenomenon," *New Left Review*, no. 122 (July–August 1980) pp. 27–58.

Pye, Lucian, and Verba, Sidney, eds., *Political Culture and Political Development* (Princeton: Princeton University Press, 1965).

Rama, Carlos M., *Ideologia, regiones y clases sociales en la España contemporánea* (Montevidep: Ediciones Nuestro Tiempo, 1958).

Rasmussen, Erik, and Skovmand, Roar, *Det Radikale Venstre. 1905–1955* (Copenhagen: Det Danske Forlag, 1955).

Raun, Toivo U., *Estonia and the Estonians* (Stanford: Hoover Institution Press, 1987).

Rébérioux, Madeleine, "Party Practice and the Jaurésian Vision: The SFIO (1905–1914)" in Stuart Williams, ed., *Socialism in France: From Jaurés to Mitterand* (London: Frances Pinter, 1983) pp. 15–26.

Rébérioux, Madeleine, *La Republique Radicale? 1898–1914* (Paris: Editions du Seuil, 1975).

Ridley, Frederick F., *Revolutionary Syndicalism in France: The Direct Action of Its Time* (Cambridge: Cambridge University Press, 1970).

Riggs, Fred, *Administration in Developing Countries: The Theory of Prismatic Society* (Boston: Houghton Mifflin, 1964).

Rimlinger, Gaston V., *Welfare Policy and Industrialization in Europe, America and Russia* (New York: John Wiley & Sons, 1971).

Ritter, Gerhard A., *Wahlgeschichtliches Arbeitsbuch: Materialien zur Statistik des Kaiserreichs* (München: C. H. Beck, 1980).

Roberts, David D., *The Syndicalist Tradition and Italian Fascism* (Chapel Hill: University of North Carolina Press, 1979).

Roberts, Robert, *The Classic Slum: Salford Life in the First Quarter of the Century* (Manchester: Manchester University Press, 1971).

Rocznik statystyki Rzeczypospolitej Polskiej, vol. 4, 1925–26 (Warsaw: Druk L. Boguslawskiego, 1927).

Rokkan, Stein, "Geography, Religion and Social Class: Crosscutting Cleavages in Norwegian Politics," in Seymour Martin Lipset and Stein Rokkan, eds., *Party Systems and Voter Alignments: Cross-National Perspectives* (New York: Free Press, 1967) pp. 367–444.

Rokkan, Stein, "Norway: Numerical Democracy and Corporate Pluralism," in Robert Dahl, ed., *Political Oppositions in Western Democracy* (New Haven: Yale University Press, 1966) pp. 70–115.

Romero Maura, Joaquin, *The Spanish Army and Catalonia: The "Cu-Cut! Incident" and the Laws of Jurisdictions, 1905–1906* (Beverly Hills, Calif.: Sage Publications, 1976).

Rönnblom, Hans-Krister, *Frisinnade landsföreningen. 1902–1927* (Stockholm: Saxon and Lindström, 1929).

Roth, Guenther, *The Social Democrats in Imperial Germany* (Totowa, N.J.: The Bedminster Press, 1963).

Roucek, Joseph S., "Czechoslovakia and Her Minorities," in Robert J. Kerner, ed., *Czechoslovakia: Twenty Years of Independence* (Berkeley: University of California Press, 1940) pp. 171–92.

Royal Institute of International Affairs, *The Problem of International Investment* (London: Oxford University Press, 1937).

Ruppert, M., *De Nederlands Vakbeweging*, 2 vols. (Haarlem: De Erven F. Bohn, 1953).

Rustow, Dankwart A., *The Politics of Compromise: A Study of Parties and Cabinet Government in Sweden* (Princeton: Princeton University Press, 1955).

Rüter, A. J. C., *De spoorwegstakingen van 1903: Een spiegel der arbeidersbeweging in Nederland* (Leiden: E. J. Brill, 1935).

Rutishauser, Hans, "Liberalismus und Sozialpolitk in der Schweiz," (Unpublished Ph.D. Dissertation: Universität Zürich, 1935).

Salomone, William, *Italian Democracy in the Making: The Political Scene in the Giolittian Era, 1900–1914* (Philadelphia: University of Pennsylvania Press, 1945).

Salomonsson, Per, "Venstregrupperne," in Per Salomonsson, ed., *Den politiske magtkamp 1866–1901* (Copenhagen: Jørgen Paludans Forlag, 1968) pp. 35–56.

Salomonsson, Per, "Socialdemokratiet," in Per Salomonsson, ed., *Den politiske magtkamp 1866–1901* (Copenhagen: Jørgen Paludans Forlag, 1968) pp. 57–63.

Salomonsson, Per, ed., *Den politiske magtkamp, 1866–1901* (Copenhagen: Jørgen Paludans Forlag, 1968).

Salvatorelli, Luigi, and Mira, G., *Storia del fascismo* (Rome: Edizioni di Novissima, 1952).

Salvemini, Gaetano, "Introductory Essay," in A. William Salomone, *Italian Democracy in the Making. The Political Scene in the Giolittian Era* (Philadelphia: University of Philadelphia Press, 1945) p. ix.

Sánchez Agesta, Luis, *Historia del constitucionalismo español*, 3rd ed. (Madrid: Instituto de Estudios Políticos, 1974).

Santarelli, Enzo, "Sorel e sorelismo in Italia," *Rivista storica del socialismo* vol. 3, no. 2 (1960) pp. 289–328.

Saposs, David J., *The Labor Movement in Postwar France* (New York: Columbia University Press 1931).

Sauvy, Alfred, *Histoire économique de la France entre les deux guerres: Vol. 1: 1918–1931* (Paris: Fayard, 1965).

Sauvy, Alfred, *Histoire économique de la France entre les deux guerres: Vol. 2: 1931–1939* (Paris: Fayard, 1967).

Schiller, Berndt, "Years of Crisis, 1906–1914," in Steven Koblik, ed., *Sweden's Development from Poverty to Affluence, 1750–1970* (Minneapolis: University of Minnesota Press, 1975) pp. 197–228.

Schneider, Michael, *Das Arbeitsbeschaffungsprogramm des ADGB* (Bonn-Bad Godesberg: Verlag neue Gesellschaft, 1975).

Schoenbaum, David, *Hitler's Social Revolution: Class and Status in Nazi Germany, 1933–1939* (Garden City, N.Y.: Doubleday, 1966).

Schorske, Carl, *German Social Democracy, 1905–1917: The Development of the Great Schism* (Cambridge: Harvard University Press, 1955).

Schwarzenberg, Claudio, *Breve storia dei sistemi previdenziali in Italia* (Turin: ERI, 1971).

Schweizerische Statistik, *Die Ergebnisse der eidgenossischen Volkszaehlung vom 1. Dez. 1910*, vol. 3, pt. 1 (Bern: Francke, 1918).

Scott, Franklin D., *Sweden: The Nation's History* (Minneapolis: University of Minnesota Press, 1977).

Seip, Jens Arup, *Et regime foran undergangen* (Oslo: Tanum, 1945).

Sering, Max, ed., *Die Deutsche Landwirstschaft unter volks- und weltwirtschaftslichen Geschichtspunkten*, Berichte über Landwirtschaft, Sonderheft no. 50 (Berlin: Paul Parey, 1932).

Serpieri, Arrigo, *La guerra e le classi rurali italiane* (Bari: Laterza and Figli, 1930).

Seton-Waton, Christopher, *Italy From Liberalism to Fascism, 1870–1925* (London: Methuen, 1967).

Seton-Watson, Hugh, *Eastern Europe Between the Wars, 1918–1941* (London: Cambridge University Press, 1945).

Sheehan, James J., *German Liberalism in the Nineteenth Century* (Chicago: University of Chicago Press, 1978).

Shorter, Edward, and Tilly, Charles, *Strikes in France: 1830–1968* (London: Cambridge University Press, 1974).

Simon, Walter B., "Democracy in the Shadow of Imposed Sovereignty: The First Republic of Austria," in Juan J. Linz and Alfred Stepan, *The Breakdown of Democratic Regimes: Europe* (Baltimore: Johns Hopkins University Press, 1978) pp. 80–121.

Simon, Walter B., "Motivation of a Totalitarian Mass Vote," *British Journal of Sociology*, vol. 10, no. 4 (December 1959) pp. 338–45.

Skelley, Jeffrey, ed., *The General Strike 1926* (London: Lawrence and Wishart, 1976).

Skrubbeltrang, Fridlev, "Danske landboforhold," in K. Hansen, ed., *Det danske landbrugs historie: vol. 5, 1934–1945* (Copenhagen) pp. 559–75.

Smart, D. A., ed., *Pannekoek and Gorter's Marxism* (London: Pluto Press, 1978).

Smith, Denis Mack, *Italy, A Modern History* (Ann Arbor: University of Michigan Press, 1959).

Snell, John, *The Democratic Movement in Germany, 1789–1914* (Chapel Hill: University of North Carolina Press, 1976).

Social Demokraten (Stockholm) September 27, 1890, September 12, 1896, and October 6, 1902.

Söderpalm, Sven Anders, *Direktörsklubben: Stor industrin i svensk politik under 1930- och 40-talen* (Stockholm: Rában and Sjögren, 1976).

Söderpalm, Sven Anders, "The Crisis Agreement and the Social Democratic Road to Power," in Steven Koblik, ed., *Sweden's Development from Poverty to Affluence, 1750–1970*, trans. Joanne Johnson (Minneapolis: University of Minnesota Press, 1975) pp. 258–78.

Spadolini, Giovanni, *Giolitti e i cattolici* (Florence: Le Monnier, 1960).

Stansky, Peter, ed., *The Victorian Revolution: Government and Society in Victoria's Britain* (New York: New Viewpoints, 1973).

State Statistical Office (Czechoslovakia), *Manuel statistique, 1931*, vol. 3 (Prague: Statistical Bureau of the Czechoslovak Republic, 1931).

Statistisches Jahrbuch für das Deutsche Reich, vol. 57 (Berlin: Verlag für Sozialpolitik, Wirtschaft und Statistik, 1938).

Statistisk Årsbok för Sverige, 1932 (Stockholm: Statistiska Centralbyrån, 1932).

Státní úřad statisticky Republiky československé, *Zprávy*, vol. 19 (1938), nos. 97–100.

Stearns, Peter N., *Lives of Labor: Work in Maturing Industrial Society* (New York: Holmes and Meier, 1975).

Stearns, Peter N., *Revolutionary Syndicalism and French Labor: A Cause Without Rebels* (New Brunswick, N.J.: Rutgers University Press, 1971).

Stearns, Peter, "Against the Strike Threat: Employer Policy Toward Labor Agitation in France, 1900–1914," *Journal of Modern History*, vol. 40, no. 4 (December 1968) pp. 474–500.

Stehli, Marcel, "Albert Galeer und sein Einfluss auf die Ideengeschichte des schweizerischen Grütlivereins," (Unpublished Ph.D. Dissertation: Universität Zürich, 1948).

Stjernquist, Nils, "Sweden: Stability or Deadlock?" in Robert Dahl, ed., *Political Opposition in Western Democracies* (New Haven: Yale University Press, 1966) pp. 116–46.

Stone, Judith F., *The Search for Social Peace: Reform Legislation in France, 1890–1914* (Albany: State University of New York: 1985).

Suval, Stanley, *Electoral Politics in Wilhelmine Germany* (Chapel Hill: University of North Carolina Press, 1985).

Svensson, Palle, "Support for the Danish Social Democratic Party, 1924–1939— Growth and Response," *Scandinavian Political Studies,* vol. 9 (1974) pp. 127–46.

Tasca, Angelo, *Nascita e avvento del fascismo: L'Italia dal 1918 al 1922* (Florence: La Nuova Italia, 1950).

Terlinden, Vicomte Ch., "Histoire politique interne: Formation et évolution des partis," in *Histoire de la Belgique contemporaine, 1830–1914,* vol. 2 (Brussels: Albert Dewit, 1929) pp. 5–239.

Terrail, Gabriel, *Le Syndicalisme contre le socialisme, origine et developpement de la Confederation general du travail* (Paris: Ollendorf, 1907).

Thane, Pat, "Women and the Poor Law in Victorian and Edwardian England," *History Workshop,* Issue 6 (Autumn 1978) pp. 29–51.

Thermaenius, Edvard, "Riksdagspartierna" in Hildebrand et al., eds., *Sveriges riksdag,* vol. 17 (Stockholm: Victor Petterson, 1935).

The Times (London), various issues.

Thomsen, Birgit Nüchel, "Konflikt og forhandling, 1870–1890," in Per Salomonsson, ed., *Den politiske magtkamp, 1866–1901* (Copenhagen: Jørgen Paludans Forlag, 1968) pp. 73–90.

Thompson, Paul Richard, *Socialists, Liberals and Labour: The Struggle for London, 1885–1914* (London: Routledge and Kegan Paul, 1967).

Thomson, David, *Democracy in France Since 1870,* 4th ed. (London: Oxford University Press, 1964).

Thomson, S. Harrison, *Czechoslovakia in European History* (Hamden: Archon Books, 1965).

Thulstrup, Äke, *Svensk politik, 1905–1939: Från unionsupplösningen till andra världskriget* (Stockholm: Bonnier, 1968).

Tidsskrift for arbeiderbevegelsens historie (Oslo) various issues.

Tingsten, Herbert, *Den svenska Socialdemokratiens idéutveckling* (Stockholm: Tidens Förlag, 1941).

Tingsten, Herbert, *Den svenska socialdemokratins ideutveckling* (Stockholm: Bonnier, 1967).

Togliatti, Palmiro, *Lezioni sul fascismo,* 3rd ed. (Rome: Riuniti, 1970).

Tomasevich, Jozo, *Peasants, Politics and Economic Change in Yugoslavia* (Palo Alto, Calif.: Stanford University Press, 1955).

Topf, Erwin, *Die Grüne Front: Der Kampf um den Deutschen Acker* (Berlin: Rowohlt, 1933).

Touchard, Jean, *Front populaire 1936* (Paris: A. Colin, 1961).

Touraine, Alain, and Raggazzi, Orietta, *Ouvriers d'origine agricole* (Paris: Seuil, 1961).

Tracy, Michael, *Agriculture in Western Europe* (New York: Praeger, 1964).

Trempé, Rolande, *Les Mineurs de Carmaux, 1848–1914 vol. 1* (Paris: Editions Ouvrières, 1971).

Troclet, Léon-Eli, *Les partis politiques en Belgique* (Brussels: L'Eglantine, 1931).

Uhr, Carl. G., "The Emergence of the 'New Economics' in Sweden: A Review of a Study by Otto Steiger," *History of Political Economy,* vol. 5, no. 1 (Spring 1973) pp. 243–60.

Ullman, Joan Connelly, *The Tragic Week: A Study of Anticlericalism in Spain, 1875–1912* (Cambridge: Harvard University Press, 1968).

U.S. Department of State, *Report on the Labor Situation of Italy* (Washington, D.C., 1919).

U.S. Department of State, *Report on the Labor Situation of Sweden* (Washington, D.C., 1919).

U.S. Department of State, *Report on the Labor Situation of Denmark* (Washington, D.C., 1919).

U.S. Department of State, *Report on the Labor Situation of Norway* (Washington, D.C., 1919).

Urwin, Derek, and Aarebrot, Frank, "Socio-geographic correlates of Left Voting in Weimar Germany, 1924–1932," in Per Torsvik, ed. *Mobilization, Center-Periphery Structures and Nation-Building* (Oslo: Universitetforlaget, 1981).

Valeri, Nino, *Da Giolitti a Mussolini: Momenti della crisi del liberalismo* (Florence: Parenti, 1956).

Van Kalken, Frans, *La Belgique contemporaine, 1780–1949,* 2nd ed. (Paris: A. Colin, 1950).

Van Kalken, Frans, *Histoire de Belgique des origines a nos jours* (Brussels: Office de publicité, 1946).

Van Welderen Rengers, W. J., *Schets eener parlementaire geschiedenis van Nederland,* 4th ed., annotation by C. W. de Vries (The Hague: M. Nijhoff, 1949).

Vandervelde, É., De Brouckère, L., Vandersmissen, L., *La Grève générale en Belgique (avril 1913)* (Paris, 1914).

Vandervelde, Emile, *Le Parti Ouvrier Belge, 1885–1925* (Brussels: L'Eglantine, 1925).

Vannutelli, Cesare, "Occupazione e salari dal 1861 al 1961," in Amintore Fanfani, ed., *L'economia italiana dal 1861 al 1961: Studi nel l' centenario dell'unita d'Italia,* Economia e storia, Ser. 6 (Milan: Giuffrè, 1961) pp. 560–96.

Vázquez Humasqué, Antonio, "El problema agrario español," *El Trimestre Economico,* vol. 7, no. 3 (October–December 1940) pp. 463–93.

Vermeulen, W. H., "1904–1914," in W. J. Van Welderen baron Rengens, ed. *Schets eener parlementaire geschiedenis van Nederland,* Vol. 3 (The Hague: Martinus Nijhoff, 1949) pp. 100–16.

Verney, Douglas, "The Foundations of Modern Sweden: The Swift Rise and Fall of Swedish Liberalism," *Political Studies,* vol. 20, no. 1 (March 1972) pp. 42–59.

Verney, Douglas, *Parliamentary Reform in Sweden, 1866–1921* (Oxford: Clarendon Press, 1957).

Vivarelli, Roberto, *Il dopoguèrra in Italia e l' avvento del fascismo, 1918–1922:*

Vol. 1, Dalla fine della guerra all'impresa di Fiume (Naples: Istituto Italiano per gli Studi Storici, 1967).

Vogt, Emil et al., *Handbuch der Schweizer Geschichte* (Zurich: Verlag Berichthaus, 1977).

Volkmann, Henrich, *Die Arbeiterfrage im preussischen Abgeordnetenhaus, 1848–1869* (Berlin: Duncker and Humbolt, 1968).

Von Greyerz, Hans, "Der Bundesstaat seit 1848," in Emil Vogt et al., *Handbuch der Schwiezer Geschichte,* Band 2 (Zurich: Verlag Berichthaus, 1979) pp. 1019–254.

Von Rauch, Georg, *The Baltic States, The Years of Independence: Estonia: Latvia, Lithuania, 1917–1940,* trans. Gerald Onn (Berkeley: University of California Press, 1974).

Vuilleumier, Marc, "Mouvement ouvrier et immigration au temps de la Deuxième Internationale: les travailleurs Italiens en Suisse," *Revue européenne des sciences sociales,* vol. 15, no. 42 (December 1977) pp. 115–27.

Wahlbäck, Krister, *Från Mannerheim til Kekkonen: Huvudlinjer i finländsk politik, 1917–1967* (Stockholm: Bonniers, 1967).

Wandycz, Piotr S., "Foreign Policy of Edvard Benes, 1918–1938," in Victor Mamatey and Radomír Luža, eds., *A History of the Czechoslovak Republic, 1918–1948* (Princeton: Princeton University Press, 1973) pp. 216–38.

Warner, Charles K., *Winegrowers of France and the Government since 1875* (New York: Columbia University Press, 1960).

Weber, Adna, *The Growth of Cities in the Nineteenth Century: A Study in Statistics* (New York: Macmillan, 1899).

Weber, Eugen, *Peasants into Frenchmen: The Modernization of Rural France, 1870–1914* (Stanford: Stanford University Press, 1976).

Weber, Karl, *The Swiss Press: An Outline* (Bern: Herbert Lang, 1948).

Webster, R. A., *Industrial Imperialism in Italy* (Berkeley: University of California Press, 1978).

Weckerle, Eduard, *The Trade Unions in Switzerland,* trans. Pippa Harris (Bern: Swiss Federation of Trade Unions, 1947).

Wehler, Hans-Ulrich, "Der Aufstieg des Organisierten Kapitalismus und Interventionsstaates in Deutschland," in Heinrich A. Winkler, ed., *Organisierter Kapitalismus: Voraussetzungen und Anfänge* (Göttingen: Vandenhoeck and Ruprecht, 1974) pp. 36–57.

Wehler, Hans-Ulrich, *The German Empire, 1871–1918* trans. Kim Traynor (Dover, N.H.: Berg Publishers, 1985).

Wehler, Hans-Ulrich, "Industrial Growth and Early German Imperialism," in Roger Owen and Bob Sutcliffe, eds., *Studies in the Theory of Imperialism* (London: Longman, 1972) pp. 71–92.

Welcker, J. M., *Heren en arbeiders in de vroege Nederlandse arbeidersbeweging, 1870–1914* (Amsterdam: Van Gennep, 1978).

Welk, William, *Fascist Economic Policy: An Analysis of Italy's Economic Experiment* (Cambridge: Harvard University Press, 1938).

Werth, Alexander, *Which Way France?* (London: Harper & Brothers, 1937).

Westerståhl, Jörgen, *Svensk fackföreningsrörelse: Organisationsproblem, verksamhetsformer, förhållande till staten* (Stockholm: Tidens Förlag, 1946).

Wichman, Knut, *Gustaf V, Karl Staaff och striden om vårt försvar, 1901–1914* (Stockholm: P. A. Norstedt, 1967).

Willard, Claude, *Les guesdistes: Le Mouvement socialiste en France 1893–1905* (Paris: Editions sociales, 1965).

Williams, Alfred, *Life in a Railway Factory*, reprinted ed., with introduction by Leonard Clark (Newton Abbot: David and Charles, 1969).

Winch, Donald, "The Keynesian Revolution in Sweden," *Journal of Political Economy*, vol. 74, no. 2 (April 1966) pp. 168–76.

Winding, Kjeld Mogens, *Danmarks politiske historie* (Copenhagen: Fremad, 1948).

Winkler, Heinrich A. ed., *Organisierter Kapitalismus: Voraussetzungen und Anfänge* (Göttingen: Vandenhoeck and Ruprecht, 1974).

Winston, Colin M., *Workers and the Right in Spain, 1900–1936* (Princeton: Princeton University Press, 1985).

Wrigley, C., "Liberals and the Desire for Working Class Representatives in Battersea, 1886–1922," in K. D. Brown, ed., *Essays in Anti-Labour History: Response to the Rise of Labour in Britain* (London: Macmillan, 1974) pp. 126–58.

Wunderlich, Frieda, *Farm Labor in Germany, 1810–1945* (Princeton: Princeton University Press, 1961).

Zachariassen, Aksel, *Martin Tranmael* (Oslo: Tiden, 1979).

Zeldin, Theodore, *France, 1848–1945: Ambition and Love* (Oxford: Oxford University Press, 1979).

Zeldin, Theodore, *France, 1848–1945: Politics and Anger* (Oxford: Oxford University Press, 1979).

Zmarzlik, Hans-Günter, *Bethmann Hollweg als Reichskanzler, 1909–1914: Studien zu Möglichkeiten und Grenzen seiner innenpolitischer Machtstellung* (Düsseldorf: Droste Verlag, 1957).

Zolberg, Aristide R., "Belgium," in Raymond Grew, ed., *Crises of Political Development in Europe and the United States* (Princeton: Princeton University Press, 1978) pp. 99–138.

Zwing, Karl, *Geschichte der Deutschen Freien Gewerkschaften: Ein Kurzgefasster Abriss* (Jena: Volkesbuchhandlung, 1928).

Index